Franciscan Virtue

Studies in the History of Christian Traditions

VOLUME 161

The titles published in this series are listed at brill.nl/shct

Franciscan Virtue

Spiritual Growth and the Virtues in Franciscan Literature and Instruction of the Thirteenth Century

By

Krijn Pansters

BRILL

LEIDEN · BOSTON
2012

Cover illustration: Francis giving his mantle to a poor man. Giotto, San Francesco, Assisi. © S. Diller/ www.assisi.de 2011.

This book is printed on acid-free paper.

Library of Congress Cataloging-in-Publication Data

Pansters, Krijn, 1975-
  Franciscan virtue : spiritual growth and the virtues in Franciscan literature and instruction of the thirteenth century / by Krijn Pansters.
    p. cm. -- (Studies in the history of Christian traditions, ISSN 1573-5664 ; v. 161)
  Includes bibliographical references (p.   ) and index.
  ISBN 978-90-04-22156-7 (hardback : alk. paper) 1. Franciscans--History. 2. Spiritual formation.
3. Virtue. 4. Church history--Middle Ages, 600-1500. I. Title.

  BX3606.3.P36 2012
  241'.40882713--dc23

                                                                                              2011046096

This publication has been typeset in the multilingual "Brill" typeface. With over 5,100 characters covering Latin, IPA, Greek, and Cyrillic, this typeface is especially suitable for use in the humanities. For more information, please see www.brill.nl/brill-typeface.

ISSN 1573-5664
ISBN 978 90 04 22156 7 (hardback)
ISBN 978 90 04 22340 0 (e-book)

MIX
Paper from
responsible sources
FSC® C004472
www.fsc.org

PRINTED BY DRUKKERIJ WILCO B.V. - AMERSFOORT, THE NETHERLANDS

For Melanie

CONTENTS

LIST OF ILLUSTRATIONS

ACKNOWLEDGEMENTS

Of the many virtues that Francis of Assisi, Bonaventure of Bagnoregio, and David of Augsburg recommend in their fascinating corpus of works, many have received much less attention in this book than they actually deserve. Although they are far too religious in nature to be mentioned only for the current purpose of acknowledgement, I would like to name three of these virtues, specifically, in order to make up for this negligence at least a little bit. First of all, *justice* ("giving to each one his due") should be done to my colleagues at the Franciscan Study Centre of Tilburg University in Utrecht (Hubert Bisschops, Jan van den Eijnden, Gerard Pieter Freeman, Jan Sloot, and Willem Marie Speelman) for their ongoing help and support in the process of writing this book. Without them, it would not have been such a pleasant experience. Secondly, I would like to express *gratitude* ("bringing close to the giver") towards the many from whom I received kind attention and encouragement throughout my recent years of research: Guerric Aerden, Arnoud-Jan Bijsterveld, Hein Blommestijn, Dick de Boer, Cornelius Bohl, Ramses van Bragt, Charles Caspers, Albrecht Diem, Rob Dückers, Hildo van Engen, Tom Gaens, Jean-François Godet-Calogeras, Jan Hoeberichts, James Hogg, Michael Hohlstein, Jan Klok, Bart Koet, Erik Kwakkel, Matthieu van der Meer, Gert Melville, Scott Montgomery, Richard Newhauser, Meta Niederkorn, Peter Nissen, Peter Raedts, Bert Roest, Richard Unger, Arjo Vanderjagt, John Van Engen, Rik Verbeek, Kees Waaijman, and Rolf de Weijert, and many others. Thirdly, *reverence* ("admiring God's immensity and beholding one's own smallness") is given to the spirituality and strength of the great Franciscan tradition without which this book, in several ways, would not have been written. Furthermore, of the virtues that I *have* dealt with in this book, I would like to repeat here, especially, those of truth, joy, and peace: the *truth* that real virtue is often most lacking in the one that is assumed to be most virtuous, in this case, the researcher of virtues; the *joy* of working together, in this case, with Arjan van Dijk and Ivo Romein of BRILL, and the series editor, Robert Bast; and the *peace* that lies in the realization of a long-term project, in this case, *Franciscan Virtue. Spiritual Growth and the Virtues in Franciscan Literature and Instruction of the Thirteenth Century.*

LIST OF ABBREVIATIONS

Works of Francis of Assisi

Adm	*Admonitiones*
Cant Sol	*Canticum fratris solis/ Laudes creaturarum*
Laud Dei	*Chartula fr. Leoni data- Laudes Dei altissimi*
Ben Leo	*Chartula fr. Leoni data- Benedictio fratri Leoni data*
Ep Ant	*Epistola ad sanctum Antonium*
Ep Cler 1	*Epistola ad clericos (recensio prior)*
Ep Cler 2	*Epistola ad clericos (recensio posterior)*
Ep Cust 1	*Epistola ad custodes 1*
Ep Cust 2	*Epistola ad custodes 2*
Ep Fid 1	*Epistola ad fideles (recensio prior)*
Ep Fid 2	*Epistola ad fideles (recensio posterior)*
Ep Leo	*Epistola ad fratrem Leonem*
Ep Min	*Epistola ad ministrum*
Ep Ord	*Epistola toti ordini missa*
Ep Pop	*Epistola ad populorum rectores*
Ex Laud	*Exhortatio ad laudem Dei*
Ex Pat	*Expositio in Pater Noster*
Form Viv	*Forma vivendi S. Clarae*
Laud Hor	*Laudes ad omnes horas dicendae*
Of Pas	*Officium passionis Domini*
Or Cruc	*Oratio ante crucifixum dicta*
RB	*Regula bullata*
RnB	*Regula non bullata*
Reg Er	*Regula pro eremitoriis data*
Sal Mar	*Salutatio beatae Mariae virginis*
Sal Virt	*Salutatio virtutum*
Test	*Testamentum*
Laet	*De vera et perfecta laetitia*

Works of Bonaventure

Trip Via	*De triplici via*
Sol	*Soliloquium de quatuor mentalibus exercitiis*
Lign Vit	*Lignum vitae*

Quin Fest	*De quinque festivitatibus pueri Iesu*
Praep Mis	*Tractatus de praeparatione ad missam*
Perf	*De perfectione vitae ad sorores*
Reg An	*De regimine animae*
Sex Alis	*De sex alis seraphim*
Of Pas	*Officium de passione Domini*
Vit Myst	*Vitis mystica/ Tractatus de passione Domini*
Ap Paup	*Apologia pauperum*
Ep Quaest	*Epistola de tribus quaestionibus*
Det Quaest	*Determinationes quaestionum circa Regulam FF. Min.*
Quare	*Quare fratres minores praedicent et confessiones audiant*
Ep San	*Epistola de sandaliis apostolorum*
Ex Reg	*Expositio super Regulam fratrum minorum*
Serm Reg	*Sermo super Regulam fratrum minorum*
Con Narb	*Constitutiones generales Narbonenses*
Ep Off	*Epistolae officiales*
Reg Nov	*Regula novitiorum*
Ep Mem	*Epistola continens XXV memorialia*
Ep Im	*Epistola de imitatione Christi*
Leg Fran	*Legenda S. Francisci*
Leg Min	*Legenda minor S. Francisci*
Brevi	*Breviloquium*
Itin	*Itinerarium mentis in Deum*
Sent	*Commentaria in quatuor Libros Sententiarum*
Serm	*Sermones de Sanctis*

Work of David of Augsburg

Prof	*De exterioris et interioris hominis compositione*

CHAPTER ONE

VIRTUE

"Beware of and abstain from every evil and persevere in good till the end."[1]

"By virtue we mean a movement of the will acting in accord with a legitimate judgement formed by the intellect. Broadly speaking, such judgements will concern themselves in determining what is good and what is evil, and in fixing the varying degrees of both."[2]

1. BACKGROUND

The virtues are back. Following important critiques of contemporary ethics such as A. MacIntyre's *After Virtue*, modern-day moral philosophy has more or less distanced itself from a long-established perspective of emotivism, non-necessity, and liberal individualism.[3] A new generation of moral philosophers now pleads for a return to the rationale underlying classical ethical traditions that are virtue-based, teleological, and built around the norms and values operative in social structures and practices.[4] Accordingly, a revival of the Aristotelian and Thomistic traditions with their teaching on virtues as (socially embedded) individual qualities has taken place.[5] New interpretations of age-old definitions and schemes of virtue have appeared in modern ethics and present morality, and this

---

[1] Francis of Assisi, *RnB* 21,9. *Cavete et abstinete ab omni malo et perseverate usque in finem in bono* (Armstrong, *Francis of Assisi*, 78).

[2] David of Augsburg, *Prof* 3,27. *Virtus est ordinatus secundum veritatis iudicium mentis affectus. Sed iudicium veritatis circa quatuor generaliter versatur: circa bonum et malum, et magis bonum et magis malum* (*David ab Augusta*, 215; Devas, *Spiritual Life* 2, 54–55).

[3] MacIntyre, *After Virtue*.

[4] See for instance: Crisp & Slote, *Virtue Ethics*; Dent, *The Moral*; Gardiner, *Virtue Ethics*; Gill, *Virtue*; Van Hooft, *Understanding*; Welchman, *The Practice*.

[5] Critics of this fairly recent development in moral philosophy argue that traditional virtue ethics is itself always historically and socially determined and that it is, therefore, highly problematic to use its definitions "a-historically" and "idealtypically," as if virtues were "anthropological constants" (see for instance: Houdijk, "Deugd de deugd?").

return to virtue has also had effects on other fields of science and society.[6]

2. Material Object – Franciscan Virtue

In this book, I return to the Franciscan virtues. By studying – from a much-needed new perspective[7] – a selection of thirteenth-century writings by three major Franciscan authors, I try to answer the following questions: How do Francis of Assisi and his followers define, describe, and prescribe the essential virtues of evangelical life? How do people, in their eyes, acquire, keep, or lose these virtues? How do the practice, development, and application of these virtues shape "perfect" individuals as well as the "good" of the community? I am concerned here with the *Gehalt und Gestalt*[8] of late medieval Franciscan "virtue ethics" and the historical importance of the Franciscan conception of the virtuous "habit."[9] It is not my chief aim to concentrate on the spiritual "fruits" that may be reaped from a profound study of the earliest Franciscan sources, even though its authors consider virtue to be primarily a gift from God (or his property), and its realization, therefore, also the fruit of spiritual merit.[10]

Virtues are a key element in the medieval Franciscan writings. They are most important building blocks of a life according to "the teaching and footprints of our Lord Jesus Christ,"[11] representing steps on the way to the "treasure in heaven"[12] and "eternal life."[13] The importance of the virtues is already expressed in the opening sentence of Francis's *Earlier Rule*: "The rule and life of these brothers is this, namely: "to live in obedience, in

---

[6] See for instance: Drewermann, *Ein Mensch*; Hauerwas & Pinches, *Christians*; Mieth, *Die neuen Tugenden*; Murphy, *Virtues*; Peterson & Seligman, *Character*; Schuster, *Moralisches*; Streithofen, *Macht*.

[7] See below, 1.5–1.8.

[8] Cf. Walzel, *Gehalt und Gestalt*.

[9] Cf. *Sal Virt* 5. *Nullus homo est penitus in toto mundo, qui unam ex vobis possit habere, nisi prius moriatur* (Armstrong, *Francis of Assisi*, 164); *Prof* 2,5. *...ita virtus per corporalia exercitia addiscitur et in habitum vertitur* (David ab Augusta 87; Devas, *Spiritual Life* 1, 83). Servants of God "possess" (*habere*) certain "fundamental characteristics" (Armstrong, *Francis of Assisi*, 137). See below, 1.9–1.10, and 3.2. I use the word "habit" here and elsewhere not as "habit" but as *habitus*; not as a "gradually increasing tendency of behavior" ("Gewohnheit") or "routine in everyday-life" ("habits"), but as "actions performed by routine" and "with the soul" ("mit ganzer Seele")" (Nickl, *Ordnung*, 2; Stoellger, "Ordnung").

[10] See below, 1.7–1.8, and 3.4.

[11] *RnB* 1,1. *...et Domini nostri Jesu Christi doctrinam et vestigia sequi...* (Armstrong, *Francis of Assisi*, 63–64).

[12] *RnB* 1,2. *...et habebis thesaurum in caelo...* (Armstrong, *Francis of Assisi*, 64).

[13] *RnB* 1,5. *...et vitam aeternam possidebit* (Armstrong, *Francis of Assisi*, 64).

Figure 1. Francis giving his mantle to a poor man. Giotto, San Francesco, Assisi. © S. Diller/www.assisi.de 2011.

chastity, and without anything of their own.""[14] Although many more virtues are mentioned in the following chapters of the *Earlier Rule*, these three virtues (*obedientia, castitas, sine proprio/paupertas*) reflect the kind of spiritual program that Francis designed and wished to convey: spiritual perfection[15] is reached by living a virtuous life. The other writings of Francis and his two intellectual followers dealt with here are likewise characterized by a recurrent precept of virtue (*virtus*) and a strong incentive to virtuous zeal (*studium*),[16] confirming that virtues play a central role in Franciscan spiritual and moral thought.

3. SELECTION – AUTHORS AND SOURCES

This investigation starts with the writings of Francis of Assisi (ca 1181–1226), "founder" of the Franciscan Order and spiritual father of Franciscan life and thought. His oeuvre consists of 28 writings (*opuscula*), which will all be discussed here, and some *opuscula dictata*.[17] Francis is a spiritual author who deals with spiritual concerns such as the purity of religious practice, the eradication of vice, the possession of virtue, and the aim at heavenly things. He is not a theologian but, rather, a man of experience and practice, intelligently determined to preach the Gospel by his words and deeds and promote the good in others for the sake of God. In all of his writings, written between 1206 and 1226, Francis displays a firm commitment to the message of Christ and the life of the apostles, the realization of Truth, and the attainment of eternal salvation. His deeply religious writings, in turn, form the coherent basis for the spiritual and moral thought, or "moral spirituality,"[18] of later Franciscan generations.

---

[14] *RnB* 1,1. *Regula et vita istorum fratrum haec est, scilicet vivere in obedientia, in castitate et sine proprio...* (Armstrong, *Francis of Assisi*, 63). As will be explained below, *sine proprio* becomes the virtue of poverty (*paupertas*).

[15] *RnB* 1,2. *Si vis perfectus esse...* (Armstrong, *Francis of Assisi*, 64). See 3.6.

[16] E.g., *Prof* 3,29. *Quintum est studium familiare ad expugnanda vel mortificanda vitia et virtutes usitandas* (David ab Augusta, 219; Devas, *Spiritual Life* 2, 58). See 3.4.

[17] Menestò & Brufani, *Fontes*; Esser & Grau, *Die Opuscula*. See also Appendix 1, which is based on Menestò & Brufani. I have counted the different versions of the *Epistola ad clericos, Epistola ad custodes, Epistola ad fideles,* and *Regula* as separate works. Only one of the *opuscula dictata,* namely, *De vera et perfecta laetitia,* will be dealt with here. On Francis and his writings, see for instance: Armstrong, *Francis of Assisi*; Bisschops, *Franciscus*; Feld, *Franziskus*; Van den Goorbergh & Zweerman, *Was getekend*; House, *Francis*; Lehmann, *Franz von Assisi*; Manselli, *San Francesco*; Maranesi, *Facere misericordiam*; Matanic, *Francesco d'Assisi*; Mockler, *Francis*; Moorman, *Saint Francis*; Morant, *Unser Weg*; Nolthenius, *Een man*; Robson, *St. Francis*; Rotzetter, *Franz von Assisi*; Sabatier, *Vie*.

[18] See below, 1.8.

Figure 2. Bonaventure. Victor Crivelli, Musée Jacquemart-André, Paris.

Apart from Francis, two other early Franciscan authors will be treated here: Bonaventure (ca. 1217–1274), the foremost theologian and most prominent minister general of the Franciscan Order, and David of Augsburg (ca. 1200–1272), the influential Franciscan writer and novice-master in Augsburg. The larger part of Bonaventure's oeuvre consists of Bible commentaries and philosophical and theological treatises, some including treatments of theological and philosophical virtues such as the cardinal virtues of prudence, justice, temperance, and fortitude.[19] But for the current purpose (see below), I have selected from his *opera omnia* the so-called "mystical" (i.e., "spiritual, edifying") writings and the writings "concerning the Franciscan Order." These are, in the order of the Quaracchi edition,[20] the following: *De triplici via; Soliloquium de quatuor mentalibus exercitiis; Lignum vitae; De quinque festivitatibus pueri Iesu; Tractatus de praeparatione ad missam; De perfectione vitae ad sorores; De regimine animae; De sex alis seraphim; Officium de passione Domini; Vitis mystica* (spiritual works); *Apologia pauperum; Epistola de tribus quaestionibus; Determinationes quaestionum circa Regulam fratrum minorum; Quare fratres minores praedicent et confessiones audiant; Epistola de sandaliis apostolorum; Expositio super Regulam fratrum minorum; Sermo super Regulam fratrum minorum; Constitutiones generales Narbonenses; Epistolae officiales; Regula novitiorum; Epistola continens XXV memorialia; Epistola de imitatione Christi; Legenda Sancti Francisci;* and *Legenda minor Sancti Francisci* (works concerning the Franciscan Order).

These spiritual writings (pastoral treatises, edifying works) and writings concerning the Franciscan Order (apologies, letters, sermons, and legends) display more than the other (exegetical, philosophical, theological) works a concern with the *practical* sides of Christian religion and religious living, and the *spiritual* fate of the readers.[21] Thoroughly "Franciscan" in his approach, Bonaventure, as a learned man, uses his philosophical knowledge for his practically oriented works, keeping the original themes and approaches of Francis alive but pouring them

[19] E.g., *Brevi* 5,4 (*Doctoris* 5, 256–257; De Vinck, *The Works* 2, 193–196); *Serm* 4,14 (*Doctoris* 9, 590).
[20] *Doctoris* 8. On Bonaventure and his writings, see for instance: Bougerol, *Introduction*; Cullen, *Bonaventure*; Delio, *Simply Bonaventure*; Gilson, *La philosophie*; Hayes, "Bonaventure"; *S. Bonaventura*.
[21] Cf. Hayes, *The Hidden*, 8: "We might legitimately divide Bonaventure's works into academic and practical writings not because the practical and speculative are separated from each other but because these two dimensions appear with a difference of emphasis."

into certain intellectual, academically acquired, educational frames and formats. The fact that there are many parallels to the spiritual contents of Francis's writings (precisely in these works more than in his exegetical and philosophical works) but also many differences with regard to the intellectual level and approach (as is the case in his exegetical and philosophical works), prompts the question to what extent conceptions of virtue vary between the two authors, and how definitions of virtue and contents of virtues change in the decennia after Francis.

The third author is David of Augsburg, whose *opus magnus* entitled *De exterioris et interioris hominis compositione secundum triplicem statum incipientium, proficientium et perfectorum libri tres* will be considered here.[22] It is a manual for spiritual life, composed in three books according to the triad *incipientes, proficientes, perfecti*. The first book (*ad novitios*, "for beginners") is a rule of life for novices. The second book (*ad proficientes*, "for the advanced") deals with inner reform and the battle against the seven capital sins. The third book (*de septem processibus religiosorum*, for all stages of religious life) contains an exhortation to ascend to perfection in seven steps (*processus*). The sixth of these seven steps is the development of the virtues, but progress in the virtues (*profectus virtutum*) is, in fact, the underlying, connecting theme of all three books of the *Profectus religiosorum*.[23] Relating to the whole process (*processus*) from beginning (*incipere*) to end (*perfectio*), the life of virtue is situated in the dynamics of spiritual development as a continuous discovery and interiorization of the Good (*in bonis*) that is God.[24]

There are several reasons to include the *Profectus religiosorum* in the present study. One is the fact that it is one of the most successful works of the later Middle Ages, at least in terms of circulation of manuscripts.[25] Another is that David is still a relatively unknown and underrated author

---

[22] *Prof* 1–3. The short title of this work, *Profectus religiosorum*, is derived from the beginning of the third book: *Profectus religiosi septem processibus distinguitur*. The first book has also been handed down separately under the title *Speculum monachorum*. On David and his writings, see: Bohl, *Geistlicher*; Müller, *Gesellschaft*; Rüegg, *David*; Ruh, "David".

[23] The concept of *profectus virtutum* is based on Ps 83,8 (84,7): "They go from virtue to virtue."

[24] Pansters, "*Profectus virtutum*. The Roots".

[25] There are more than 380 preserved manuscripts. On the reception of this work, see: Pezzini, "La tradizione"; Smits, "David van Augsburg"; Stooker & Verbeij, "'Uut Profectus"; Viller, "Le *Speculum*".

in present research, whose works prove, among other things, that early
Franciscans were quick to adopt key monastic elements into their mendicant theology.[26] David's vernacular works such as his *Die sieben Vorregeln
der Tugend* and *Die sieben Staffeln des Gebetes* are not given consideration
here, mainly because they are, to a large extent, taken from his Latin work.
Thus, the only vernacular work to be considered for the current purpose
remains Francis's *Canticum fratris solis* (*Il cantico del sole*), which was
originally sung and written in Umbrian.

Due to practical reasons, many other important works such as those of
Clare of Assisi (1194–1253), or relevant pre-Bonaventurian "Franciscan
School" treatises such as the fundamental *Summa theologica* (started)
by Alexander of Hales (ca. 1183–1245), and the *Summa de virtutibus*
(probably) of William of Meliton (-1257), have to be left out of account.
My trajectory (Francis, Bonaventure, David) may be a very represen-
tative one, but I am in no way claiming that these authors sufficiently
constitute together "the" early Franciscan outlook concerning the essential virtues for the pursuit of the evangelical life, especially since the
Franciscan Order saw an enormous and very heterogeneous scholarly
and religious output during the thirteenth century. The study of the
virtues in other early Franciscan works (for example, by Peter John Olivi,
Guibert of Tournai, Bernard of Besse, Anthony of Padua, Servasanto da
Faenza, Berthold of Regensburg, to name a few), however, must be left
to others. The idea behind my specific selection of early Franciscan
authors and works is that there is a fundamental similarity as regards
their theory and application of virtue (in the framework of a recurrent
precept of virtue and a strong incentive to virtuous zeal), but that there
is also a transition from a primary and what may be called "immediate"
spirituality (Francis)[27] to, on the one hand, an academically and socially

---

[26] Cf. Müller, *Gesellschaft*, 224: "In diesem Zusammenhang ist anzumerken, will man
den hier behandelten Quellen ‚spezifisch Franziskanisches' entnehmen, daß dies nicht in
den Tugendkatalogen oder mystisch-aszetischen Metaphern zu finden ist. Beides ist
ordensübergreifend, unabhängig von männlichem und weiblichem Schreiben, schließlich
zum Teil – übersetzungsbedingt – interkulturell in traktathaften religiösen Texten zu finden. Allein in den Praktiken, hier also der Tugend*übung*, und in gewissen Grundannahmen
bezüglich der Gotteserkenntnis finden sich spezifische Eigenarten franziskanischer
Auffassungen (der zweiten Generation) wieder. Auch diese beruhen natürlich in starkem
Maße auf monastischen Traditionen etwa der Benediktiner, Zisterzienser und Viktoriner."
See below, 1.9–1.10.

[27] Lambert, *Franciscan*, 35: "His thought was always immediate, personal, and concrete.
Ideas appeared to him as images."

informed, philosophically and politically colored, but pastorally and
practically inclined Franciscan theology (Bonaventure), and, on the
other hand, a more monastic and less "Franciscan" but equally pastoral
and practical form of spiritual discourse (David).[28] The fact that David of
Augsburg *"n'a plus grand chose de franciscain,"*[29] thereby forms an extra
challenge to the investigation of the concept of virtue and the conception
of virtues in thirteenth-century Franciscan spirituality.

4. Selection – Virtues

Not all the virtues mentioned by Francis, Bonaventure, and David can be
studied here.[30] As there is no "definite" scheme of Franciscan virtues in the
sense of Aristotle's moral virtues or, a more recent example, Bertocci and
Millard's cardinal virtue-traits,[31] a selection has been made based on the
following criteria. First of all, there are a few instances where Francis
deals with the virtues quite extensively. One of these is *Admonition* 27,[32]
where we read the following:

> Where there is **charity** and **wisdom**, there is neither fear nor
> ignorance.
> Where there is **patience** and **humility**, there is neither anger nor
> disturbance.
> Where there is **poverty** with **joy**, there is neither greed nor avarice.
> Where there is **rest** and meditation, there is neither anxiety nor
> restlessness.

---

[28] Although David of Augsburg seems to have had some influence on Bonaventure (Phillips, "The Way", 39–40), I maintain the order Francis-Bonaventure-David
to avoid the suggestion that the influence of Francis's thought on Bonaventure is indirect
(via David or otherwise; cf. Daniel, "St. Bonaventure"); and that the influence
of Francis on David's *Profectus religiosorum* is significant, which it is not (Bohl,
Geistlicher, 148), notwithstanding David's commentary on Francis's Rule (Flood, "Die
Regelerklärung"). A (substantial) influence of Bonaventure on David's work, on the other
hand, has neither been established.

[29] Desbonnets, *De l'intuition*, 67. Cf. Bohl, *Geistlicher*, 143–148; Einhorn, "Der Begriff",
363–367.

[30] On the present problem of the definition of "virtue," see below, 1.5. On the definition
of virtue by the authors, see below, 1.10.

[31] Aristotle: Courage, temperance, liberality, magnanimity, pride, sincerity, distributive
justice, corrective justice, equity. Cf. Bertocci & Millard, "Traits". Bertocci & Millard: hon-
esty, courage, gratitude, temperance, humility, meekness, justice, repentance, kindness,
forgiveness (Bertocci & Millard, "A Scheme").

[32] Armstrong, *Francis of Assisi*, 136–137.

Where there is **fear** of the Lord to guard an entrance, there the enemy cannot have a place to enter.
Where there is a heart full of **mercy** and **discernment**, there is neither
excess nor hardness of heart.[33]

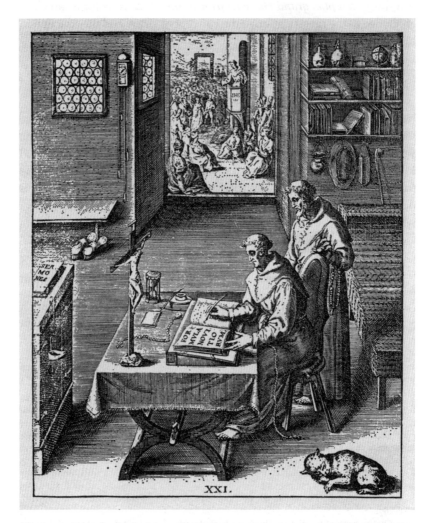

Figure 3. David of Augsburg. In: Dominicus Custos, *Sancti Augustani. Die
Augspurgischen Heilligen* (Augsburg 1601).

---

[33] *Ubi **caritas** est et **sapientia**, ibi nec **timor** nec ignorantia. Ubi est **patientia** et **humilitas**,
ibi nec ira nec perturbatio. Ubi est **paupertas** cum **laetitia**, ibi nec cupiditas*

Caritas, sapientia, patientia, humilitas, paupertas, laetitia, quies, timor Domini, misericordia, and *discretio*: these are essential virtues according to Francis.

The second place where Francis gives an "enumerative description" of the virtues is the *Salutation of the Virtues*:[34]

> Hail, Queen **Wisdom**!
> May the Lord protect You,
> with Your Sister, holy **pure Simplicity**!
> Lady holy **Poverty**,
> may the Lord protect You,
> with Your Sister, holy **Humility**!
> Lady holy **Charity**,
> may the Lord protect You,
> with Your Sister, holy **Obedience**.
> Most holy Virtues,
> may the Lord protect all of You
> from Whom You come and proceed.
>
> There is surely no one in the whole world
> who can possess any one of You
> without dying first.
> Whoever possesses one
> and does not offend the others
> possesses all.
> Whoever offends one
> does not possess any
> and offends all.
> And each one confounds vice and sin.
> Holy **Wisdom** confounds
> Satan and all his cunning.
> Pure holy **Simplicity** confounds
> all the wisdom of this world
> and the wisdom of the body.
> Holy **Poverty** confounds
> the desire for riches,
> greed,
> and the cares of this world.
> Holy **Humility** confounds
> pride,

---

*nec avaritia. Ubi est **quies** et meditatio, ibi neque sollicitudo neque vagatio. Ubi est **timor** Domini ad atrium suum custodiendum* (cfr. Luke 11,21), *ibi inimicus non potest habere locum ad ingrediendum. Ubi est **misericordia** et **discretio**, ibi nec superfluitas nec induratio* (Armstrong, *Francis of Assisi*, 136–137).

[34] Armstrong, *Francis of Assisi*, 164–165.

all people who are in the world
and all that is in the world.
Holy **Charity** confounds
every diabolical and carnal temptation
and every carnal fear.
Holy **Obedience** confounds
every corporal and carnal wish,
binds its mortified body
to **obedience** of the Spirit
and **obedience** to one's brother,
so that it is
subject and submissive
to everyone in the world,
not only to people
but to every beast and wild animal as well
that they may do whatever they want with it
insofar as it has been given to them
from above by the Lord.[35]

Sapientia, puritas, simplicitas, paupertas, humilitas, caritas, and *obedientia*: here, again, Francis presents a number of traditional virtues as essential virtues for his brothers.

To decide which virtues should be studied further, I have made an inventory based on a count of the virtues mentioned in Francis's writings.[36] Next, I have collated this *quantitative* list of virtues with four

---

[35] *Ave, regina **sapientia**, Dominus te salvet cum tua sorore sancta **pura simplicitate**. Domina sancta **paupertas**, Dominus te salvet cum tua sorore sancta **humilitate**. Domina sancta **caritas**, Dominus te salvet cum tua sorore sancta **obedientia**. Sanctissimae **virtutes**, omnes vos salvet Dominus, a quo venitis et proceditis. Nullus homo est penitus in toto mundo, qui unam ex vobis possit habere, nisi prius moriatur. Qui unam habet et alias non offendit, omnes habet. Et qui unam offendit, nullam habet et omnes offendit* (cfr. Jac 2,10). *Et unaquaque confundit vitia et peccata. Sancta **sapientia** confundit satan et omnes malitias eius. Pura sancta **simplicitas** confundit omnem **sapientiam** huius mundi* (cfr. 1 Cor 2,6) *et **sapientiam** corporis. Sancta **paupertas** confundit cupiditatem et avaritiam et curas huius saeculi. Sancta **humilitas** confundit superbiam et omnes homines, qui sunt in mundo, similiter et omnia, quae in mundo sunt. Sancta **caritas** confundit omnes diabolicas et carnales tentationes et omnes carnales timores* (cfr. 1 Joa 4,18). *Sancta **obedientia** confundit omnes corporales et carnales voluntates et habet mortificatum corpus suum ad **obedientiam** spiritus et ad **obedientiam** fratris sui et est subditus et suppositus omnibus hominibus, qui sunt in mundo et non tantum solis hominibus, sed etiam omnibus bestiis et feris, ut possint facere de eo, quicquid voluerint, quantum fuerit eis datum desuper a Domino* (cfr. Joa 19,11) (Armstrong, *Francis of Assisi*, 164–165).
[36] See below: Table 1.1–1.3. See Appendix 1 for all the virtues mentioned in Francis's writings (with virtues in **bold**). I have included in the count all grammatical forms (noun, adjective, verb, adverb) of a virtue, e.g., *veritas* and *vera*, but excluded all alternative words with the same meaning or alternative phrasings implying the same meaning, e.g., *nihil sibi appropriare* (for *paupertas*).

noticeable lists of virtues in four places in the other sources, selected here
purely for illustrative purposes, namely, Bonaventure's *Perfection of Life*
and *Letter on the Imitation of Christ*, and David's *Profectus religiosorum*
books 1 and 3, respectively. The first list of virtues can be found in the
"Table of Contents" of Bonaventure's *Perfection of Life*:

I.   On true self-knowledge.
II.   On **true humility**.
III.   On perfect **poverty**.
IV.   On **silence** and **quiet**.
V.   On assiduity in prayer.
VI.   On remembering the passion of Christ.
VII.   On perfect **love** for God.
VIII.   On final **perseverance**.[37]

The main virtues of the perfect life are *ipsius cognitio, humilitas, paupertas, silentio, studium orationis, passionis memoria*, and *caritas*. Second,
in his *Letter on the Imitation of Christ*, Bonaventure lists the main virtues that one needs to have in order to follow Christ and walk in his
footsteps:

(...) we will find that Christ first walked the path of profound **humility**.
Second, the path of extreme **poverty**.
Third, the path of perfect **charity**.
Fourth, the path of immense **patience**.
Fifth, the path of admirable **obedience**.
We need to walk this path if we want to follow Christ and find Him.[38]

The main virtues here are *humilitas, paupertas, caritas, patientia*, and
obedientia. Third, in the first book of his *Profectus religiosorum*, David
of Augsburg describes certain virtues as being especially suitable for
novices. Special virtues recommended in these chapters are: *bonitas,
pax, quies, caritas, obedientia, humilitas, paupertas, diligentia, puritas,
sapientia, timor, verecundia, misericordia, benignitas, discretio, patientia,
castitas, devotio*, and *iustitia*.[39] Fourth, in the sixth part of the third book of

---

[37] *Et primo agitur de vera sui ipsius cognitione. Secundo, de* **vera humilitate**. *Tertio, de*
perfecta paupertate. *Quarto, de* **silentio** *et* **taciturnitate**. *Quinto, de* **studio** *orationis. Sexto, de*
passionis Christi memoria. Septimo, de perfecta Dei **caritate**. *Octavo, de finali* **perseverantia**
(*Doctoris* 8, 108; De Vinck, *The Works* 1, 211).

[38] *Ep Im* 3. *...inveniemus, quod ipse primo ambulavit per viam profundae* **humilitatis**.
Secundo, per viam extremae **paupertatis**. *Tertio, per viam perfectae* **caritatis**. *Quarto, per*
viam immensae **patientiae**. *Quinto, per viam admirabilis* **obedientiae**. *Per istam viam oportet*
nos ambulare, si volumus Christum sequi et invenire (*Doctoris* 8, 499–500).

[39] *David ab Augusta*, 3–62; Devas, *Spiritual Life* 1, 1–49.

the *Profectus religiosorum*, David presents six main virtues for the religious:

31: **Charity**, and its divisions.
37: **Humility**, and its divisions.
39: **Patience**, and its divisions.
42: **Obedience**, and its divisions.
44: On **poverty**, and its divisions.
46: On **temperance** and its divisions.
50: On **chastity**: its value and how to win it.[40]

These four lists, roughly corresponding to the list of Francis's favourite virtues, indicate which virtues can be taken to be main Franciscan virtues.

The result of this inventory and collation is an overview of the most important virtues, on the basis of which a list can be drawn up of the main Franciscan virtues to be studied further in this book. I am confining myself to the first *eight* of them:

Table 1.1 Franciscan virtues

Virtue	Francis Opusc.	Francis Adm 27	Francis Sal Vir	Bonav. Perf	Bonav. Epist	David Prof 1	David Prof 3,6
Caritas/amor/ dilectio	106	x	x	x	x	x	x
Obedientia	59		x		x	x	x
Bonitas	57					x	
Veritas	48			x			
Fides[41]	47						
Humilitas	40	x	x	x	x	x	x
Laetitia[42]	38	x					
Paupertas	33	x	x	x	x	x	x

---

[40] *Prof* 3,31–50. *XXXI. De **caritate** et eius distinctione. XXXVII. De **humilitate** et eius triplici distinctione. XXXIX. De virtute **patientiae** eiusque distinctionibus. XLII. De **obedientia** eiusque distinctionibus. XLIV. De virtute **paupertatis** eiusque distinctionibus. XLVI. De **sobrietate** eiusque distinctionibus. L. De **castitate** eiusque utilitatibus et acquisitione* (David ab Augusta, 223–289; Devas, *Spiritual Life* 2, 62–122).

[41] /fiducia/confidentia.

[42] /gaudium/iucunditas/hilaritas.

These eight virtues, some of which are also known as "fruits of the Holy Spirit,"[43] will be analyzed in the next chapters.

In the next scheme, I list the remaining virtues under discussion in the above-mentioned key chapters of Francis, Bonaventure, and David. Here, a quantitative list of virtues in the *opuscula* is, again, "backed up" by a qualitative overview:

Table 1.2 Franciscan virtues, continued

Virtue	Francis Opusc.	Francis Adm 27	Francis Sal Vir	Bonav. Perf	Bonav. Epist	David Prof 1	David Prof 3,6
Studium[44]	29			x		x	
Misericordia[45]	27	x				x	
Puritas/ munditia	24		x			x	
Sapientia	24	x	x			x	
Timor	17	x				x	
Iustitia	14					x	
Simplicitas	13		x				
Verecundia	12					x	
Benignitas	11					x	
Perseverantia	10			x			
Patientia	8	x			x	x	x
Discretio	7	x				x	
Castitas/ continentia	6					x	x
Quies/requies/ quietas	6	x				x	
Devotio	5					x	
Silentium/ taciturnitas	3			x			
Sobrietas	0						x

---

[43] Gal 5,22–23: love, joy, peace, patience, kindness, goodness, faithfulness, gentleness, self-control. Cf. Engemann, *Entflammt*, 105–107. See also 3.1.

[44] /diligentia/zelus.

[45] /miseratio/compassio.

These Franciscan virtues are beyond the scope of this book, but will hopefully be the object of much further research.[46]

Finally, two other "virtues" have to be mentioned here:

Table 1.3 Franciscan virtues, extra

Virtue	Francis *Opusc.*	Francis *Adm 27*	Francis *Sal Vir*	Bonav. *Perf*	Bonav. *Epist*	David *Prof 1*	David *Prof 3,6*
Poenitentia	26						
Pax/"pacificus"	18				x		

For the following reasons, these two virtues will be added to the first eight
selected for further research. Penance (*poenitentia*) is a crucial Franciscan
concept, which not only provides the name for the "Order of the Brothers
of Penance," but also constitutes its spiritual program of evangelical life,
called "doing penance" by Francis.[47] Peace (*pax*) is another crucial
Franciscan concept: it lends its name to the Franciscan ideal of the "good"
of the community as well as society's *bonum commune*, and it is still actu-
alized daily in the Franciscan greeting, *Pax et bonum*.[48] Both penance and
peace are Franciscan "virtues" but also more than "virtues," more than a
concretized form of "Franciscan asceticism" or a symbol of the common
good (*bonum*): they stand for the identity and the integrity of the
Franciscan fraternity.

5. PROBLEMS OF RESEARCH – CONTENTS

The three virtues (*obedientia, castitas, sine proprio/paupertas*) mentioned by Francis as keystones of "the rule and life of these brothers," con-
front us with some of the main problems of this investigation. The first
problem concerns the *definition* of the virtues. Is "without anything" (*sine*

---

[46] See also 3.7.

[47] *Test* 1,3. *Dominus ita dedit mihi fratri Francisco incipere faciendi poenitentiam* (Armstrong, *Francis of Assisi*, 124).

[48] Francis greeted those he met on the road with this greeting (*The Legend of the Three Companions* 26: "Therefore, in all his preaching, he greeted the people at the beginning of his sermon with a proclamation of peace. It is certainly astonishing, if not miraculous, that this greeting of peace was used before his conversion by a precursor who frequently went through Assisi greeting the people with "Peace and good! Peace and good!" " (Armstrong, *Francis of Assisi* 2, 84)).

proprio) really a virtue, for example? And, if so, is it really the same virtue as poverty (*paupertas*)? The problem here is that many definitions and descriptions of virtues are interchangeable, a fact that the medieval authors are perfectly aware of: "Verbal definition will emphasize the distinction between patience on the one hand, and fortitude, constancy, magnanimity, longanimity, meekness and gentleness, yet how often they are used to signify what is really the same thing, and to define and describe each other."[49] The second problem that this triad of basic Franciscan virtues illustrates concerns the general *significance* of virtues mentioned at a certain place, in a certain context. The "crucial" virtue of chastity (*castitas*), for example, turns out to be a rather marginal virtue in a quantitative respect, measured by the frequency of its use in the *Earlier Rule* as well as in the whole of Francis's writings (cf. Table 1.2).

So how important are the virtues, and are they virtues? What is the medieval interpretation of the concepts in question, and how should we interpret them?[50] The problem of *interpretation* is shown first and foremost in the – often turbid – medieval use of the concept of "virtue" itself. Two complicating, and paradoxical, factors can be discerned here. First, the term *virtus* has a wide range of meanings which lends it a certain multicoloredness, especially in spiritual, non-scholastic discourse.[51] The same goes for specific virtues like *caritas* and *poenitentia*, equally burdened with a diversity of meanings. Second, the meaning of *virtus/virtutes* is often *not* specified, which lends it a certain indefinability. Much the same can be found for related concepts such as "progress in the virtues" (*profectus virtutum*), which is often more casually brought up than

---

[49] *Prof* 3,39. *Et quamvis aliqua differentia esse videatur inter patientiam et fortitudinem et constantiam et magnanimitatem et longanimitatem et mititatem et mansuetudinem, sicut etiam ex earum definitionibus colligitur, tamen saepe unum pro altero positum invenitur, et mutuo se inter se definiunt et describunt* (David ab Augusta, 253; Devas, *Spiritual Life* 2, 90).

[50] After the so-called "linguistic turn" in historical writing, the problem of the interpretation of historical facts and concepts (such as "virtue" and "peace") is no longer (primarily) a matter of the sources, but of the quality of the questions asked and criteria devised by the researcher of the sources. As G. Eley and P.Q. Hirst put it: "Facts are not given, it is only relative to a question that we can begin to assess the value of those materials which are to constitute evidence for the answer to it.... In fact, the "real" past is beyond retrieval. Instead, the historian both evaluates documentary residues by the technical procedures of the profession and assigns them relevance via the construction of a significant problem" (Eley, "Is All", 46).

[51] Meanings range from the specific angelic host (called "Virtues") to a man's physical strength, and from God's power to moral excellence inhabited ("*habitus*") in the human soul. See below, 1.9.

conceptually worked out, and is usually being dealt with more implicitly
than explicitly.[52] It is worth noting that traditional theological distinctions are often ignored or simply irrelevant, for example, in much of
Francis's use of the biblical "virtues" (*virtutes*)/"fruits of the Holy Spirit"
(*fructus*) love, goodness, faith, joy, and peace. Another complicating
factor for the correct interpretation of concepts and schemes of virtues
may be added here: the – typically medieval – "mechanical" use of words
and concepts.[53] Especially outside learned circles and universities – and
thus on lower levels of theological and spiritual teaching – we find that
intellectual concepts are often transmitted in a fairly static and stereo-
typical way, whether they are non-descriptive or not.[54] The gap between
medieval and modern mind and mentality thus reveals itself in the
fact that medieval conceptualization generally lacks much variety and
originality.

Next, there is the problem of *ambiguity*. Quite a few virtues are virtues
in one place and vices in another, and vice versa. For example, fear (*timor*)
out of ignorance is pointless but fear (*timor*) of God is indispensable.[55]
Francis condemns the wisdom (*sapientia*) and prudence (*prudentia*) of
the world while praising wisdom (*sapientia*) and prudence (*prudence*)
from the spiritual variety.[56] The difference here of course lies in the (good
or bad) end to which the "virtue" is determined. A virtue can also be a
virtue in one case and its opposite in another, or a virtue in one case while

[52] Pansters, "*Profectus virtutum*. From Psalm".

[53] Pansters, *De kardinale*, 211–216.

[54] This is what D. Bell already found for the medieval use of the Platonic trilogy (*rationabilitas, irascibilitas* and *concupiscibilitas*, the three powers of the soul) in Christian theology: "The very fact that it *was* stereotyped indicates a formal rather than an enthusiastic
acceptance of the idea. In the ethical and social and political thought of Plato himself the
tripartition unquestionably fulfilled a vitally important role, but we cannot say the same
for the part it plays in the long series of his devoted followers" (Bell, "The tripartite soul",
52).

[55] E.g., *Adm* 27,1. *Ubi caritas est et sapientia, ibi nec timor nec ignorantia* (Armstrong,
Francis of Assisi, 136); *Adm* 27,5. *Ubi est timor Domini ad atrium suum custodiendum* (cfr.
Luke 11,21), *ibi inimicus non potest habere locum ad ingrediendum* (Armstrong, *Francis of
Assisi*, 137).

[56] *RnB* 17,10. *Et custodiamus nos a sapientia huius mundi et a prudentia carnis*
(Rom 8,6)... (Armstrong, *Francis of Assisi*, 75); *Adm* 21,1. *Beatus servus, qui quando loquitur,
sub specie mercedis omnia sua non manifestat et non est velox ad loquendum* (cfr. Prov
29,20), *sed sapienter providet, quae debet loqui et respondere* (Armstrong, *Francis of Assisi*,
135); *Adm* 23,3. *Fidelis et prudens servus est* (cfr. Matt 24,45), *qui in omnibus suis offensis non
tardat interius punire per contritionem et exterius per confessionem et operis satisfactionem*
(Armstrong, *Francis of Assisi*, 136).

its opposite is a virtue in another. For example, Francis firmly (*firmus*) wishes to obey the general minister,[57] but considers himself simple and infirm (*infirmus*).[58] And, as some virtues might be seen as vices, some vices might be used metaphorically as virtues, for example, satiety (*saturitas*) and ebriety (*ebrietas*) as the hunger and thirst for love of God (Bonaventure).[59]

Finally, we must concern ourselves with the problem of the *intellectual origin* of the virtues involved. Classical philosophy and Christian theology provide many schemes and distinctions of virtues, and "moral," "theological," "natural," and "supernatural" are only some of them.[60] This brings up the question how much "academic" theory or how many "theological" schemes of virtue may be found in our authors' spiritual and "applied" moral writings. It is highly uncertain, for example, if Francis was aware of the leading definitions of *virtus* in the early scholastic tradition, such as *habitus electivus in medietate exsistens*[61] or any other predecessor of Aquinas's *habitus perficiens hominem ad bene operandum.*[62] But do the learned Bonaventure and the educated David themselves use these definitions, or do they come up with new ones for the purpose of spiritual clarification? And, if so, are new definitions specifically Franciscan in nature? For example, what is traditional and what is new in Bonaventure's words: *ut exerceantur [incipientes] in operibus virtutum, quia non sufficit scire bonum, nisi etiam opere exerceatur?*[63] Does David have both the definition by Thomas Aquinas and the actual Franciscan observances in mind when he tells us that *sicut artifex per instrumentum artis suae operatur, ita virtus per corporalia exercitia addiscitur et in habitum vertitur?*[64]

---

[57] *Test* 27. *Et firmiter volo obedire ministro generali huius fraternitatis et alio guardiano, quem sibi placuerit mihi dare* (Armstrong, *Francis of Assisi*, 126).

[58] *Test* 29. *Et quamvis sim simplex et infirmus, tamen semper volo habere clericum, qui mihi faciat officium, sicut in regula continetur* (Armstrong, *Francis of Assisi*, 126).

[59] *Trip Via* 2,4,10. *Quartus gradus est ebrietas, quae oritur ex saturitate. Ebrietas autem in hoc consistit, quod quis tanto amore diligat Deum, ut iam non solum fastidiat solatium, sed etiam delectetur et quaerat tormentum pro solatio...* (*Doctoris* 8, 10; De Vinck, *The Works* 1, 78).

[60] See below, 1.9.

[61] According to Aristotle, *Ethica Nicomachea* 2,6 (*Aristotle*, 94–95).

[62] Thomas Aquinas, *Summa theologiae* 1a2ae,58,3 (Busa, *S. Thomae Aquinatis*, 428).

[63] "Beginners must be trained in the practice of virtue, for it is not enough to have the knowledge of good: such knowledge must also be put into action"; *Sex* 1,2 (*Doctoris* 8, 132; De Vinck, *The Works*, 136).

[64] "As the artist works with instruments suited to his purpose, so in spiritual matters sanctity [virtue] is learnt and developed into a habit by the use of bodily, i.e., exterior observances"; *Prof* 2,5 (*David ab Augusta* 87; Devas, *Spiritual Life* 1, 83).

In order to explain the contents and meaning of the main Franciscan virtues, these and similar questions must also be dealt with.

6. Problems of Research – Canon

There is no recent systematic study of Franciscan virtue, but there are some older Italian studies dealing with this subject quite extensively, for example: L. Bracaloni, "Le virtù religiose fondamentali secondo la spiritualità francescana" (1933); A. Ghinato, "La vita virtuosa" in his *Profilo spirituale di san Francesco. Tratto dai suoi scritti e dalle primitive biografie* (1961); L. Iriarte, *Vocazione francescana. Sintesi degli ideali di san Francesco e di santa Chiara* (1987²); and A. Matanic, "Virtù e devozioni francescane" in his *Francesco d'Assisi. Fattori causali della sua spiritualità* (1984).[65] These studies show that "virtues" are "ideals" central to the "spiritual profile" of Francis and thus of "causal" significance and "fundamental" importance to Franciscan thought. The authors (except for Matanic) also list and briefly explain the "most important" Franciscan virtues such as obedience, poverty, and chastity (Bracaloni); piety, humility, obedience, patience, and charity (Ghinato); and penance, charity, chastity, poverty, humility, simplicity, obedience, and courtesy (Iriarte).

Some groundbreaking German post-war studies pursue the matter incidentally, such as K. Esser & E. Grau, *Antwort der Liebe* (1958/1960; in particular, penance, poverty, chastity, obedience); M. Geulen, *Die Armut des heiligen Franz von Assisi im Lichte der Wertethik* (1947/2005; in particular, poverty, humility, freedom, peace, joy); and P. Morant, *Unser Weg zu Gott. Das Vollkommenheitsstreben im Geiste des hl. Franziskus* (1965; in particular, penance, obedience, simplicity, poverty, humility, chastity, charity). Some recent German and Dutch studies follow in their footsteps, for instance: H. Bisschops, *Franciscus van Assisi. Mysticus en mystagoog* (2008; in particular, obedience, chastity, poverty, humility, obedience); H. Feld, *Franziskus von Assisi und seine Bewegung* (1994; in particular, poverty, simplicity, humility, peace, chastity); E. van den Goorbergh & T. Zweerman, *Was getekend: Franciscus van Assisi. Aspecten van zijn schrijverschap en brandpunten van zijn spiritualiteit* (1998/2002; in particular,

---

[65] It is one of the aims of this study to make a broad inventory of (Franciscan) literature regarding the virtues (see footnotes in 1.9, 1.10 and 2.1–2.10). In the present *status quaestionis*, I will confine myself to the studies dealing with the spirituality and thought of Francis.

penance, faith, patience, wisdom, obedience, humility, mercy, diffidence);
H. van Munster, *De mystiek van Franciscus. De macht van barmhartigheid*
(2002/2003; in particular, mercy, humility, charity, patience, justice, joy,
peace); and F. Peters, *Aus Liebe zur Liebe. Der Glaubensweg des Menschen
als Nachfolge Christi in der Spiritualität des hl. Franziskus von Assisi*
(1995; humility, charity, poverty, patience, obedience). There are also
studies treating individual Franciscan works or chapters on virtues, particularly the *Salutation of the Virtues* and *Admonition 27*.[66] Of the recent
works of this category, however, only J. Hoeberichts's, *Paradise Restored.
The Social Ethics of Francis of Assisi. A Commentary on Francis' "Salutation
of the Virtues"* (2004) develops what might be called a new, although
unconvincing, Franciscan "theory of virtue." Other studies dealing with
Franciscan virtue focus on a (small) selection of virtues, or on one particular virtue.[67]

Some of the above-mentioned studies have appeared to be so fundamental and influential to the study of Franciscan spirituality and virtues that, together, they make up what might be called a "canon" of
Franciscan virtue literature. To this belong the works of K. Esser, E. Grau,
N. Nguyen-Van-Khanh, A. Rotzetter, L. Veuthey, and S. Verhey, among
others. Especially the work of K. Esser is of immense importance to the
modern study of Franciscan spirituality.[68] However indispensable and
deeply instructive as these studies may be (my frequent use of them
hopefully testifies to my respect for them), they generally do not escape
the severe problem that burdens the larger part of the older franciscanological literature: a strong ideological, viz., Christian/Franciscan,
agenda. A good example is K. Esser & E. Grau, whose introductory commentary on the beginning of the 23rd chapter of Francis's *Earlier Rule*[69]
reads:

---

[66] See Appendix 2 for a bibliographical overview.

[67] See Appendix 2.

[68] To Esser's essential contributions to modern franciscanology belong his spiritual
commentaries (e.g., *Antwort der Liebe* (1958)) and the fruits of his historical and textual
research (e.g., *Anfänge und ursprüngliche Zielsetzungen des Ordens der Minderbrüder*
(1966); *Die endgültige Regel der Minderen Brüder im Lichte der neuesten Forschung* (1965)),
displaying his consequent systematic analysis of the sources and his innovative reading of
their spiritual contents.

[69] "All-powerful, most holy, Almighty and supreme God, Holy and just Father,
Lord King of heaven and earth, we thank You for Yourself, for through Your holy
will and through your only Son, with the Holy Spirit, You have created everything spiritual
and corporal and, after making us in Your own image and likeness, You placed us in paradise" etc. (Armstrong, *Francis of Assisi*, 81–82).

> Nicht zufällig [*sic*] beginnt Franziskus seine zusammenfassende Darlegung des „Lebens in Buße" in diesem Kapitel seiner Regel mit diesem großen Dankgebet; denn der Ausgangspunkt unseres [*sic*] Bußlebens ist nichts anderes [*sic*] als der überströmende, Himmel und Erde umspannende Dank für die Großtaten des göttlichen Erbarmens, die uns der Vatergott in seiner wahren und heiligen Liebe durch seinen Sohn, unseren Herrn Jesus Christus, geschenkt hat. Es ist heute [*sic*] sicherlich von großer Wichtigkeit, diesen Ausgangspunkt franziskanischen Ordenslebens [*sic*] wieder ganz klar herauszustellen [*sic*].[70]

Another example is the assertion (in one and the same paragraph!) of E. Rohr in his *Der Herr und Franziskus*, that "wer Franziskus kennenlernen will, sich von aller eigenen Voreingenommenheit freimachen können [muß] und auch von der so mancher seiner Lebensbeschreiber, die fortweben an den duftenden Legenden, die seine wahre Gestalt [*sic*] verschleiern," but that "es ist, als ob Gott sich aufs neue offenbart [*sic*] in diesem demütigen mittelalterlichen Menschen und ihn benützt, um uns den Weg zum Gottesreich zu zeigen [*sic*]."[71] A final example is P. Morant, who wishes his book *Unser Weg zu Gott* to be understood "als Nachvollzug von Franziszi Begegnung und Vereinigung mit dem dreipersönlichen Gott."[72]

Such spiritual a priori assumptions (or "Nachfolge") can be said to pervade many of the franciscanological post-war studies, and a lot of contemporary ones, groundbreaking as they may be in historical, philological, or theological respect.[73] This is by no means surprising considering the fact that most of the earlier franciscanologists were Franciscans. But it forms a challenge to the modern (Franciscan) historian and theologian, making a critical distance to the canon of Franciscan literature, as well as a constant re-reading of the sources, exceedingly necessary. Fortunately, there are several exceptions to the rule of interfering religious bias and sacrosanct belief: critical historical works having the advantage of (a certain degree of) historical detachment such as M.D. Lambert, *Franciscan Poverty*, albeit that the author feels himself at a disadvantage "writing for

---

[70] Esser & Grau, *Antwort*, 18.

[71] Dukker, *Umkehr*, 9.

[72] Morant, *Unser Weg*, 12.

[73] A related problem is the political bias of some of the more recent studies (e.g., Hoeberichts, *Paradise*, 267: "Basic to the Franciscan alternative are the six virtues of *The Salutation of the Virtues* which form a complete antithesis to the "values" of neo-liberal globalism"); another is the distortion or misuse (for commercial or new-age related purposes) of the spiritual concept of "mysticism" in recent Franciscan literature (e.g., Van Munster, *De mystiek van Franciscus*).

those who have taken it as their regular way of life" while "having no expe-rience of it" himself.[74] I would certainly agree with that feeling. An exam-ple of a theological work lacking the Franciscan subjectivity surplus of older publications is J. Garrido OFM, *Die Lebensregel des Franz von Assisi* (translated from Spanish by A. Rotzetter), showing that a strong religious commitment is no obstacle to valid theological argumentation (although the author's enmity towards Franciscan contemplativity remains ques-tionable). Other studies that are not on the above-mentioned list but served here as an example of quality research are K.B. Osborne (ed.), *The History of Franciscan Theology* (2007[2]), and B. Roest, *Franciscan Literature of Religious Instruction before the Council of Trent* (2004). The present study aims to follow these works in their historical soundness and/or the-ological balance, acknowledging, as a matter of course, the impossibility of absolute objectivity, and the great virtue lying in the works of the founding franciscanologists.

7. Method

It is my aim to present a minimal description by maximal use of the sources. In answering the main research questions (What do Francis of Assisi, Bonaventure, and David of Augsburg say about virtues? What is their concept of virtue? What constitutes for them a virtuous person or a virtuous community? etc.), I will let the writings speak as much as possible and myself (and others) theologize as little as possible. My main object is the authors' consideration and conceptualization of the virtues against the background of "what it was that moved Francis"[75] *cum suis*; my object is not Francis or the other authors themselves, nor the words of his biographers such as Thomas Celano and the *Three Companions* (the so-called "Franciscan sources"),[76] nor, in the formal sense of perspective, the theological relevance of their message for today's Church. Unfortunately, in the older literature these four dimensions usu-ally combine into one research object, even when it is the author's aim to keep theological interpretations of previous generations at a distance.[77]

---

[74] Lambert, *Franciscan*, xvii.
[75] Dalarun, *The Misadventure*, 46.
[76] Menestò & Brufani, *Fontes*, 257–2219; Armstrong, *Francis of Assisi* 1–3. Cf. Dalarun, *The Misadventure*, 43, 51.
[77] E.g., Morant, *Unser Weg*, 9: "Da stellt sich die für jeden Interessierten dringende Frage: Was war eigentlich die geschichtliche Sendung des hl. Franziskus? Ist sein Ideal

The downside of my *ad fontes*, "fresh perspective," "inventory" approach is that the writings are not studied in a chronological order, that possible shifts in meaning and function of virtues in relation to biographical or institutional changes can therefore not be traced effectively, and that definitions and schemes of virtues are inevitably pulled out of their wider theological context. The answer to this is that the authors' images of virtue remain fairly consistent. Furthermore, my approach has the advantage of avoiding the hagiographical distortion from the "Franciscan sources" as well as the moralizing tone of much Franciscan literature. Thus, only after a fundamental analysis of the virtuous contents of the individual writings within the context of the corpus of selected writings am I able to plot, or start to develop, a "theory of thirteenth-century Franciscan virtue."

8. FORMAL OBJECT – HISTORY, MORALITY, SPIRITUALITY

The virtues as described and elaborated in late medieval normative (spiritual, pastoral, institutional) Franciscan texts are the starting point of my investigation. They will be regarded from the viewpoint of late medieval Franciscan history, morality, and spirituality, which are therefore my formal objects. In combining and prioritizing these three research perspectives, my analysis of the early Franciscan writings takes the form of an intellectual history, viz., of moral spirituality. My analysis is, first of all, an intellectual *history*: moral and spiritual ideas (in written form) are produced in a certain historical context and function within a certain culture; and concepts and schemes of *virtues*, in particular, are essential elements in the developing culture of early Franciscanism, defining the social and spiritual spearheads of the arising fraternity, directing the emerging process of the Franciscan Order, and shaping early Franciscan thought.[78] Next, it is a history of Franciscan *spirituality*. Spirituality may be defined

---

unabdinglich, überzeitlich, evangelisch? Für seine Söhne, Töchter und Geistesverwanten noch heute verpflichtend und vollziehbar? Diese Fragen, die schon seit Jahrzehnten in der Luft liegen, riefen immer wieder einer neuen franziskanischen Aszetik. Eine zufriedenstellende Antwort kann nur erfolgen, wenn Franziskus aus seinen Schriften und den ältesten Geschichtsquellen selbst befragt und von späterer Interpretation und Nachfolge weitgehend abgesehen wird."

[78] These developments, which form the historical context of my research, will nevertheless need much further investigation in the light of my research results. See 3.7.

as the "divine-human relational process,"[79] and this is indeed the intellectual backbone and guiding principle of all early Franciscan consideration and conceptualization, notably that of virtue and virtues. Finally, it is a history regarding the *moral* dimension of Franciscan spirituality. As spirituality defines the relationship with God (in the perspective of the afterlife), morality defines the relationship with others here and now, with oneself as with another, and with God as with the Other. Virtues play a central role in this (hence, "virtue ethics"), as they determine how one behaves or should behave toward God, toward others, and toward oneself.

Morality is not used here normatively "to refer to a code of conduct that, given specified conditions, would be put forward by all rational persons," but, as my historical approach implies, morality is used descriptively "to refer to a code of conduct put forward by a society or some other group, such as a religion, or accepted by an individual for her own behavior."[80] This definition naturally applies to Francis and his brothers and sisters, in whose spiritual worldview and moral mindset virtues are the building blocks of the code. The many implications of the existence of a Franciscan code of conduct, such as the institution of rules of life and a system of pastoral care, or the application of models of behavior and correctional measures, are furthermore contained in the concept of morality.

In order to illustrate the deep connection between spirituality and morality in Franciscan thought (or theology), and to avoid the definitional weaknesses of parataxis ("spirituality and moral theology" etc.), I propose the formal category of "moral spirituality." Franciscan moral spirituality is concerned with the Franciscan code of conduct, or precept of virtuous living, that is formulated according to religious parameters and spiritual notions.[81] It stands for the fact that both in theory and in practice, religious zeal is the moving force behind Franciscan

---

[79] Waaijman, *Spirituality*, 6, 312.

[80] "The Definition" (1 August 2010).

[81] For example, one of the basic ideas of Franciscan spirituality is that Christ is the "Master and Lord of Virtues" (*Ap Paup* 7,39; *Doctoris* 8, 285; De Vinck, *The Works* 4, 162); according to Ps 23,10 (24,10) (*quis est iste rex gloriae Dominus virtutum ipse est rex gloriae diapsalma*) and Francis's *Praises of God* (Armstrong, *Francis of Assisi*, 109). Another example is the fact that there are many relations between biblical schemes such as the beatitudes (Matt 5,3–10) and works of mercy (Matt 25,31–46), and Franciscan virtues.

virtue.[82] Within my (historical, moral, spiritual) approach of late medieval Franciscan virtue, certain issues will be the points of focus: the configuration of virtues, their conceptualization, the systematization of virtue thought, and the elaboration of spiritual contents of virtue in relation to certain theological key themes (viz., vice, precept, will, zeal, and fruit). While virtue (*virtus/virtutes*) is my material object or subject matter, these issues are formal objectives, helping to direct the attention toward it. Three further themes will then complete my investigation, mainly in the form of suggestions for further research: the influential concept of progress in the virtues (*profectus virtutum*), the crucial Christian idea of perfection (*perfectio*) in the Franciscan tradition, and the wider intellectual, operational context (viz., further history, broader morality, deeper spirituality) and fruits, or "virtue," of Franciscan virtue. All of these will return in Chapter Three.

9. Medieval Virtue

Definitions of virtue

The modern return to virtue[83] is a return to the "history of conceptions of the virtues in which Aristotle provides a central point of focus, but which yield the resources of a whole tradition of acting, thinking and discourse of which Aristotle's is only a part."[84] It is the revitalized classical tradition that once more provides extremely useful definitions of virtue and schemes of behavior.[85] For Aristotle, virtue

> is a settled disposition of the mind determining the choice of actions and emotions, consisting essentially in the observance of the mean relative to us, this being determined by principle, that is, as the prudent man would determine it. And it is a mean state between two vices, one of excess and one of defect. Furthermore, it is a mean state in that whereas the vices either fall short of or exceed what is right in feelings and in actions, virtue ascertains and adopts the mean.[86]

---

[82] See the end of this Chapter for some introductory examples (*ex toto corde, ex tota anima et mente, ex tota virtute; cum summa diligentia; debito studio virtutum*).

[83] See above, 1.1.

[84] MacIntyre, *After Virtue*, 119.

[85] On the classical definition of virtue, see for instance: Cessario, *The Moral*; Van Omme, *"Virtus"*; Van Tongeren, *Deugdelijk leven*; "Virtus"; "Virtus, virtutis".

[86] Aristotle, *Ethica Nicomachea* 2,6,15–16 (*Aristotle*, 94–95). In the Latin reception of Aristotle's *Ethica*, virtue, therefore, is a *habitus voluntarius in medietate exsistens* (cf. *Aristoteles latinus*, 14).

Further, this definition applies to the particular moral virtues of courage (ἀνδρεία, *fortitudo*), temperance (σωφροσύνη, *castitas/temperantia*), liberality (ἐλευθερία, *liberalitas*), magnificence (μεγαλοπρέπεια, *magnificentia*), greatness of soul (μεγαλοψυχία, *magnanimitas*), gentleness ("πραότης," *mansuetudo/humilitas*), truthfulness (ἀλήθεια, *veritas*), wittiness (εὐτραπελία, *eutrapelia*), friendliness (φιλία, *amicitia*), modesty (αἴδως, *verecundia*), righteous indignation (νέμεσις, *nemesis*), and justice (δικαιοσύνη, *iustitia*).[87] Other famous classical definitions of virtue are, for example, those by Cicero (*virtus est animi habitus naturae modo atque rationi consentaneus*)[88] and Boethius (*...an habitus mentis bene constitutae sit virtutis diffinitio*).[89]

Medieval moral philosophy and theology forms the solid bridge between classical virtue thought and modern virtue ethics; it is a substantial part of MacIntyre's "whole tradition of acting, thinking and discourse."[90] Medieval moral thought focuses on the virtues as key elements of good character and behavior (medieval virtues are "action dispositions") and as essential building blocks for a just society (medieval definitions are "social order based").[91] Among the most influential definitions are those by Peter Lombard (*virtus est... bona qualitas mentis, qua recte vivitur, et qua nullus male utitur, quam Deus solus in homine operatur*)[92] and Thomas Aquinas (*virtus humana est quidam habitus perficiens hominem ad bene operandum*).[93]

Modern ethical concepts of virtue generally follow these classical and medieval examples. Many modern examples show that lists of virtues and descriptions of virtuous behavior from past traditions, such as those of Aristotle and Thomas, form the basis of new virtue-based

---

[87] Aristotle, *Ethica Nicomachea* 2, 7, 2–16 (*Aristotle*, 98–107).

[88] Cicero, *De inventione* 159. "Virtue may be defined as a habit of mind in harmony with reason and the order of nature" (*Cicero, De inventione*, 326–327).

[89] Boethius, *De differentiis topicis* 2. "(...) whether habit of a well-ordered mind is the definition of virtue" (*PL* 64, 1188D; Stump, *Boethius's*, 51).

[90] See for instance: Bautz, *Virtutes*; Bejczy, *Virtue Ethics*; Borok, *Der Tugendbegriff*; Gründel, "Tugend"; Lottin, *Psychologie*; Newhauser, *The Treatise*; Partoens, *Virtutis imago*; Pieper, "Tugend"; "Tugend"; "Tugenden".

[91] Cf. D'Andrea, *Tradition*, 267–268.

[92] Peter Lombard, *Sententiarum* 2,27,1. "Virtue is (...) a good quality of the mind, by which we live uprightly, and which no one uses badly, which God alone works in man" (*Magistri*, 480). This definition is adopted and adjusted by Thomas Aquinas (*Summa theologiae* 1a2ae,55,4).

[93] Thomas Aquinas, *Summa theologiae* 1a2ae,58,3. "Human virtue is a habit perfecting man so that he may act well" (Busa, *S. Thomae Aquinatis*, 428; Hughes, *St. Thomas Aquinas*, 71).

theories of morality.[94] One such example is, of course, the theory of MacIntyre, who defines virtue as "an acquired human quality the possession and exercise of which tends to enable us to achieve those goods which are internal to practices and the lack of which effectively prevents us from achieving any such goods."[95] Another recent theory is that of A. Preußner, who defines virtue as "the ability to cope with every situation in the course of action."[96] A final example is R.M. Adams, who develops a theory of virtue around the concept of "excellence in being for the good."[97]

Medieval virtue

What does "virtue" stand for in the Middle Ages? J.F. Niermeyer lists the following meanings of *virtus* in medieval Latin: the power to perform miracles; a miracle; a relic; a church considered as property; a strength (force, vigour); violence (force); authority (power); an area under sway of an authority; competence (right, power); validity (legality); and the armed forces.[98] What concerns us here is virtue in the meaning of "strength," in a twofold sense: virtue as the power of God; and virtue as *vis ad bene vivendum necessaria*.[99] In the first sense, God is the source and giver of all strength in the world, as is reported in the first book of *Paralipomenon* (*Chronicles*) of the Latin Vulgate:

> Wealth and honor come from you;
> you are the ruler of all things.

---

[94] Cf. D'Andrea, *Tradition*, 267.

[95] MacIntyre, *After Virtue*, 191. Cf. "The virtues therefore are to be understood as those dispositions which will not only sustain practices and enable us to achieve the goods internal to practices, but which will also sustain us in the relevant kind of quest for the good, by enabling us to overcome harms, dangers, temptations and distractions which we encounter, and which will furnish us with increasing self-knowledge and increasing knowledge of the good" (MacIntyre, *After Virtue*, 219).

[96] Preußner, *Die Komplexität*, 137: "Tugend ist eine Fähigkeit, jeder Situation im Handlungsverlauf gewachsen zu sein, d.h. mit der Situativität als solcher fertig zu werden. Das Vermögen, einer Situation gewachsen zu sein, verdankt sich der dauernden Bereitschaft, neue Regeln zu suchen, nach denen sich das Handeln richten kann. Die Bereitschaft, neue Regeln zu suchen, ist eine sich beständig auslassende Kraft, die von den Handlungsbedingtheiten sowohl Hemmung als auch Verstärkung erfährt."

[97] Adams, *A Theory*.

[98] "Virtus", 1111–1112. Cf. "Virtus, virtutis", 5358–5361: power (*vis*; *potentia*); effect (*effectus*); miracle (*miraculum*); virtue (*vis ad bene vivendum necessaria*).

[99] "Virtus, virtutis", 5361. Cf. Welzen, "Weest"; Zagzebski, "The Virtues".

> In your hands are strength (*virtus*) and power (*potentia*)
> to exalt and give strength to all.[100]

Derived from this meaning (the *virtus* of God) are further biblical meanings such as the virtues as the heavenly stars,[101] the virtues as heavenly
powers and angelic hosts,[102] the power of nature,[103] and the healing and
saving power of Jesus Christ.[104]

In the second sense, virtue is the strength of God in man.[105] It is a characteristic of faith (e.g., "Love the Lord your God with all your heart and
with all your soul and with all your mind and with all your strength"[106]),
a physical strength,[107] and a good character quality (e.g., "Finally, brothers, whatever is true, whatever is noble, whatever is right, whatever is
pure, whatever is lovely, whatever is admirable—if anything is excellent
(*virtus*) or praiseworthy—think about such things"[108]). Philosophically
speaking, in the words of Thomas Aquinas, this quality of character is not
a "quality" but a "habit" (*habitus*):

> It would seem that the definition of virtue usually given, namely, *Virtue
> is a good quality of mind by which one lives righteously, of which no one
> can make bad use, which God works in us without us*, is not suitable. Virtue
> is indeed man's goodness, since it makes the one having it (*habentem*) good.
> Goodness, however, does not seem to be a good thing, as neither is white-
> ness a white thing. It is, therefore, unsuitable to describe virtue as a good
> quality.[109]

> Virtue denotes a determinate perfection of a power. The perfection
> of anything, however, is considered especially in its relation to its end. Yet
> the end of a power is its act. A power is said to be perfect, therefore, in so
> far as it is determined to its act. Now there are some powers which
> according to their very natures are set towards their acts, such as inborn
> active powers. These in themselves are accordingly called virtues. The

---

[100] 1 Chron 29,12. Other examples are Ps 20,14 (21,13); Ps 45,2 (46,1); Ps 67,36 (68,35); Ps 77,4 (78,4); Ps 146,5 (147,5); Luke 1,35; Rom 1,16; Rom 1,20; 1 Cor 1,18; 1 Pet 2,9.

[101] Ps 32,6 (33,6).

[102] E.g., Ps 102,21 (103,21); Dan 3,61; Matt 24,29; Mark 13,25; Luke 21,26.

[103] Wis 7,17; Wis 7,20.

[104] E.g., Matt 11,20–23; Mark 6,2; Luke 5,17; 2 Cor 12,9; Gal 3,5.

[105] E.g., Matt 7,22; Matt 14,2; Mark 6,14; Acts 8,10; 1 Cor 12,28–30.

[106] Mark 12,30. Other examples are Ps 137,3 (138,3); Lam 1,14; Rom 15,13; 1 Cor 2,5; 1 Pet 1,5.

[107] Ps 70,9 (71,9); Wis 18,22; Eccl 46,9; Isa 37,3.

[108] Phil 4,8. Other examples are Ps 17,33 (18,32); Eccl 6,2; Bar 3,14; 2 Cor 6,7; 2 Pet 1,5.

[109] Thomas Aquinas, *Summa theologiae* 1a2ae,55,4 (Busa, *S. Thomae Aquinatis*, 424; Hughes, *St. Thomas Aquinas*, 11–13).

rational powers, proper to a man, however, are not determined to one act, but rather in themselves are (*se habent*) poised before many. It is through habits (*habitus*) that they are set towards acts; this we have shown above [1a2ae,49,4]. Human virtues, therefore, are habits (*habitus*).[110]

The Christian definition of virtue as a habit stems from Boethius (ca. 480–525) and is already current in the early phase of the high scholastic period, for example, in the writings of William of Auvergne (1180–1249).[111] This is the time of Francis of Assisi (ca. 1181–1226) and early Franciscan scholars like Alexander of Hales (ca. 1185–1245), who speaks of a *habitus animi*[112] and a *habitus voluntarius*,[113] and the "Franciscan" teacher Robert Grosseteste (ca. 1175–1253), who sees the *habitus* of virtue established by good behavior.[114]

Place of the virtues within late medieval theology

The late twelfth and early thirteenth century is also the time of the radical rationalization and systematization of theology and the rise of the theological *summa*. In moral theology a system of distinctions and categories of virtues develops, already half a century before Thomas Aquinas's *Summa theologiae* (begun in the late 1260's) virtually canonizes the theological distinction between virtues, gifts, beatitudes, and fruits, and the logical classification of intellectual and moral virtues, cardinal and theological virtues, and natural and supernatural virtues.[115] There are now various virtues, according to their origin, function, and object, within logical arrangements. These arrangements of the virtues can themselves be part of larger dogmatic arrangements in which central theological

---

[110] Thomas Aquinas, *Summa theologiae* 1a2ae,55,1 (Busa, *S. Thomae Aquinatis*, 423; Hughes, *St. Thomas Aquinas*, 5). Cf. Thomas Aquinas, *Summa theologiae* 1a2ae,49,4. "A disposition, as was said above, is a good state or a bad state of adaptation to the nature, operation, or goals of its possessor" (Busa, *S. Thomae Aquinatis*, 417; Kenny, *St. Thomas Aquinas*, 21).

[111] Borok, *Der Tugendbegriff*, 31.

[112] *Doctoris irrefragabilis*, 197; *Magisti Alexandri* 3, 395 (Dist. 33); *Magistri Alexandri de Hales Quaestiones* 2, 1118 (Quaest. 57) (according to Cicero).

[113] *Magistri Alexandri de Hales Quaestiones* 1, 557 (Quaest. 32) (according to Aristotle).

[114] ...*habitus autem virtutis acquisitus ex frequenti bene agere est firma et stabilis et difficile mobilis* (McEvoy, *Robert Grosseteste*, 178).

[115] Borok, *Der Tugendbegriff*, 119–153. We now tacitly shift from "virtue" to "virtues"; cf. Thomas Aquinas: "Virtue denotes a determinate perfection of *a power* (...) Now there are some *powers* which according to their very natures are set towards their acts, such as inborn active powers" (Thomas Aquinas, *Summa theologiae* 1a2ae,55,1).

schemes appear, such as the ten commandments, the seven vices, the seven gifts, the eight beatitudes, the seven works of mercy, the three evangelical counsels, the twelve fruits, the four affects, the four last things, and the seven sacraments.[116]

Related to these dogmatic schemes are other canonical schemes of a theological or spiritual nature, such as the three "lower" (Platonic) powers of the soul (*rationabilitas, irascibilitas, concupiscibilitas*), the three "higher" (Augustinian) powers of the soul (*ratio, memoria, voluntas*), and the *exercitiones* (*lectio, meditatio, oratio, contemplatio*) by Guigo the Carthusian.[117] The medieval authors do not always make a clear (modern) distinction between "virtues," "practices," "gifts," "works," "exercises," and the like, or they simply call "non-virtue" schemes and "non-virtue" elements "virtues." One example of many is the remark in Bonaventure's spiritual treatise *De perfectione* that "silence" (*silentium*) is a virtue;[118] another example is the combined list of self-knowledge (*sui ipsius cognitio*), humility (*humilitas*), poverty (*paupertas*), taciturnity (*taciturnitas*), prayer (*oratio*), memory of the passion (*passionis memoria*), charity (*caritas*), and perseverance (*perseverantia*) that structures this work.[119]

Classification of the virtues

The mutual relation (*connexio*) of the Christian virtues, and specifically that between originally classical and biblical ones, has always been one of the major concerns of Christian moral thinkers. Ambrose, for example, tried to identify the four (classical) cardinal virtues (*prudentia, iustitia, temperantia, fortitudo*) with the eight (biblical) beatitudes; Augustine described these four virtues as various manifestations of the one (biblical) virtue of charity; and Alcuin explicitly connected these four virtues with the three (biblical) theological virtues of faith, hope, and charity.[120] However, separate statements by early Christian and early medieval authors should not be overestimated by regarding them as a sign of an ever advancing amalgam connecting philosophical and theological

---

[116] Cf. Troelstra, *Stof*; Borok, *Der Tugendbegriff*, 140–153.
[117] None of these schemes can be found in the writings of Francis. He is much more concerned with the basic habit of the good Christian than he is with theological schemes or individual "works" and "exercises" (Esser & Grau, *Antwort*, 255).
[118] *Perf* 4,1 (*Doctoris* 8, 297).
[119] *Doctoris* 8, 270–335.
[120] Mähl, *Quadriga*, 14, 18, 42.

schemes, in the sense of scholastic moral thought.[121] The systematic teachings by Thomas Aquinas on the cardinal and theological virtues, on the
other hand, do not at all change the uncomfortable position that the four
cardinal virtues take up in monastic and spiritual theology and, more generally, in the context of the *practice* of Christian virtuous life. In other
words, the cardinal virtues in general remained a dogmatic problem for
medieval morality outside of the universities.[122]

Taking into account this more or less schizophrenic (academic vs.
applied moral thought) aspect of medieval virtue discourse, it should
further be examined how the virtues are defined, arranged, and posi-
tioned in high scholastic thought, and how traditional schemes are integrated into a larger whole. Thomas Aquinas, whose influential systematic
views build on a much longer development in moral thought,[123] makes
the following distinction of questions in the part of his *Summa theologiae* that deals with virtue:[124] the nature of virtue; the seat of virtue; intellectual virtues; the difference between moral and intellectual virtues;
the relationship of moral virtues to passion; the difference of moral virtues among themselves; the cardinal virtues; the theological virtues;
the cause of the virtues; the mean of virtue; reciprocity among the virtues;
comparison of virtues; and the duration of virtues after this life. Three
main distinctions within "the division of virtue into the various genera
of virtue"[125] made in these questions concern us here: moral and intellectual virtues; cardinal and theological virtues; natural and supernatural
virtues.

First, virtue (in the sense of Aquinas's "habit perfecting man so that he
may act well") can be called either "intellectual" or "moral":

> Now in man there are but two principles of human actions, namely,
> the intellect or reason and the appetite: for these are the twin sources of

---

[121] Mähl, *Quadriga*, 42.

[122] Pansters, *De kardinale*, 19.

[123] Cf. Lottin, *Psychologie*, 99–194. The question remains how much Francis was
acquainted with the scholastic views of his time, and how much high scholastic thought
regarding the virtues (e.g., of Thomas Aquinas and Bonaventure) had already crystallized
in his time. The works of early Franciscan scholars like Alexander of Hales and John of la
Rochelle, however, indicate early developments and substantial continuities in the thirteenth century.

[124] Thomas Aquinas, *Summa theologiae* 1a2ae,55–67 (Busa, *S. Thomae Aquinatis*, 423–
440; Hughes, *St. Thomas Aquinas*).

[125] Thomas Aquinas, *Summa theologiae* 1a2ae,61,1 (Busa, *S. Thomae Aquinatis*, 431;
Hughes, *St. Thomas Aquinas*, 119).

human motion, as stated in [Aristotle's] *De Anima*. Consequently, every human virtue is necessarily perfective of one of these principles. Accordingly, if it perfects man's speculative or practical intellect in order that his activity may be good, it will be an intellectual virtue (*virtus intellectualis*); whereas if it perfects his appetite, it will be a moral virtue (*virtus moralis*). It follows, therefore, that every human virtue is either intellectual or moral.[126]

Second, there are "cardinal" virtues and "theological" virtues. The theological virtues of faith (*fides*), hope (*spes*), and charity (*caritas*)[127] differ from the cardinal virtues of prudence (*prudentia*), justice (*iustitia*), temperance (*temperantia*), and fortitude (*fortitudo*),[128] and from all other moral virtues such as magnanimity (*magnanimitas*), humility (*humilitas*), and patience (*patientia*), in that they are divine and not human virtues. They are called "theological"

> because God is their object, inasmuch as they direct us rightly to him, and because they are infused in us by God alone; and because they are made known to us by divine Revelation contained in Sacred Scripture.[129]

The cardinal virtues, on the other hand, are the principal among the moral (human) virtues:

> Of all the moral virtues prudence is the principal simply speaking. The other three are principal in their own class of activity (...) All the other virtues, which follow a certain precedence, can be put under the above four headings [virtues], both as to their seat and as to their formal principles.[130]

---

[126] Thomas Aquinas, *Summa theologiae* 1a2ae,58,3 (Busa, *S. Thomae Aquinatis*, 428; Hughes, *St. Thomas Aquinas*, 71). An important Franciscan parallel can be found in the *Tractatus de divisione multiplici potentiarum animae* by John of la Rochelle: *Virtutes enim intellectuales sunt, quibus regitur contemplativa vita, que secundum Aristotelem consistunt in cognitione summi boni et discretione eiusdem; virtutes consuetudinales sunt, quibus regitur vita activa, que secundum Aristotelem ex frequenti bene agere relinquuntur (Jean de la Rochelle,* 157).

[127] 1 Cor 13,13. On the theological virtues, see for instance: Aubert, "Vertus"; Bars, *Trois vertus-clefs*; Engemann, *Das neue Lied*; Pieper, *Lieben*; Robinson, *These Three*; Schuster, *Moralisches*, 183–230; Söding, *Die Trias*; Walter, *Glaube*.

[128] Plato, *Politeia*, 427a e.v. (*Platonis opera*, 427–434). On the cardinal virtues in the Middle Ages, see for instance: Houser, *The Cardinal*; Mähl, *Quadriga*; Pansters, *De kardinale*; Pieper, *Das Viergespann*.

[129] Thomas Aquinas, *Summa theologiae* 1a2ae,62,1 (Busa, *S. Thomae Aquinatis*, 433; Hughes, *St. Thomas Aquinas*, 137–139).

[130] Thomas Aquinas, *Summa theologiae* 1a2ae,61,2 (Busa, *S. Thomae Aquinatis*, 432; Hughes, *St. Thomas Aquinas*, 121).

This distinction between cardinal/moral and theological virtues frequently occurs in early Franciscan works, such as those by Alexander of Hales, William of Meliton, and Servasanto da Faenza.[131]

Third, virtues are "natural" or "supernatural." The moral virtues are "inborn active powers set towards their acts," but they can also be infused, "effected in us directly by God."[132] Inborn (natural) virtues set a man towards certain natural ends, while infused (supernatural) ones set him towards his supernatural end:

> The power of those inborn principles does not go beyond the measure of nature. Consequently, in order to be set towards his supernatural end, a man needs to be endowed with additional springs of activity.[133]

The Franciscan variations on this theme are endless.[134] Aquinas, furthermore, states that apart from the infused moral virtues that shape us to our supernatural end (God), certain other virtues "that come from another as a gift perfect a person for right action."[135] These virtues are

---

[131] E.g., *Dicendum quod morales dici debent, quoniam istae virtutes habent suos actus transeuntes in iis quae sunt ad finem et non immediate in finem. Sed actus virtutum theologicarum transeunt immediate in finem, Deum* (*Magistri Alexandri* 3, 387–388, 401 (Dist. 33)); *Quemadmodum enim in virtutibus quae sunt in finem, ut fides, spes, caritas... non autem sic est in virtutibus quae sunt eorum quae sunt ad finem, ut in iustitia et fortitudine...* (*Doctoris irrefragabilis*, 7); *Sunt enim quaedam virtutes quae immediate referuntur ad Deum, sicut virtutes theologicae; quaedam quae mediate, sicut virtutes cardinales* (*Magistri Alexandri de Hales Quaestiones* 2, 1137 (Quaest. 58)); *Duplex, sive quasi duplex, scilicet subiectum sive materiam et finem, sicut est de virtutibus theologicis. Unicum, sicut est de quibusdam cardinalibus...* (*Guillelmi de Militona* 2, 807); *Mentes autem purgari non possunt nisi optimis moribus, mores vero bonos anime humane non induunt, nisi sacris virtutibus, theologicis quidem et cardinalibus, pro fine summum bonum habentibus* (Oliger, "Servasanto", 173 (Prologo)).

[132] Thomas Aquinas, *Summa theologiae* 1a2ae,63,3 (Busa, *S. Thomae Aquinatis*, 434; Hughes, *St. Thomas Aquinas*, 159).

[133] Thomas Aquinas, *Summa theologiae* 1a2ae,63,3 (Busa, *S. Thomae Aquinatis*, 434; Hughes, *St. Thomas Aquinas*, 161).

[134] E.g., *Item, quidquid habuerunt in sui primaria conditione, fuit eis naturale; ergo, si creati essent in gratuitis, virtutes gratuitae essent eis naturales* (*Magistri Alexandri* 2, 35 (Dist. 3)); *Sic gratia adveniens in animam, in qua sunt seminaria habituum virtutum, facit ipsam germinare, ita quod, ipsa habita, habentur per consequens et virtutes, et continue facit illa germina crescere, quousque perducat usque ad perfectionem* (*Sent* 3,23,2 (*Doctoris* 3, 500)); *...in virtutibus infusis non habet locum haec distinctio potentiarum. Non enim facilitas ibi praecedit perfectionem, quia ex habitu infuso est perfectio et facilitas ad operandum. Unde perfectio ibi natura praecedit facilitatem ad opus: prius enim inest habitus quam reddit potentiam facilem ad eliciendum actum virtutis. In virtutibus acquisitis locum habet, ut patet in exemplis propositis* (*Guillelmi de Militona* 1, 372); *Primo itaque de bonis hiis maximis locuturus, principium sumam a gratia, que omnium virtutum generalis est forma, generaliter totam perficiens animam* (Oliger, "Servasanto", 174 (Prologo)).

[135] Thomas Aquinas, *Summa theologiae* 1a2ae,68,1 (Busa, *S. Thomae Aquinatis*, 441; O'Connor, *St. Thomas Aquinas*, 5).

infused into us by God, and can therefore be called gifts (*dona*) of the Spirit. Although, on the other hand, certain gifts can be called virtues, "there is something in them that transcends the common meaning of virtue, in that they are divine virtues and perfect man in so far as he is moved by God."[136] The theological virtues, to conclude, are supernatural virtues *tout court*.

The monastic virtues

It remains to be clarified how the various (other than theological) *biblical* and *monastic* virtues relate to these scholastic schemes and, conversely, how these scholastic schemes fit into the teachings of late medieval monastic and spiritual theology.[137] First of all, many biblical "virtues" constitute the already mentioned theological schemes of beatitudes, works of mercy, fruits, theological virtues, and the like. Secondly, in theory, all "moral" virtues can be situated under the cardinal virtues.[138] Thirdly, the scholastics connect certain philosophical schemes, such as the three "lower" powers of the soul, with various "affective" virtues that have great significance for the practice of Christian life. For example, William of Auvergne, in his *De virtutibus*, associates the concupiscible power (*vis concupiscibilis*) with the four "affects" of love (*amor*), hate (*odium*), sorrow (*dolor*) and joy (*gaudium*), while he connects the irascible power (*vis irascibilis*) to the "affective" virtues of righteous anger (*ira obediens*), concession (*tractabilitas*), endurance (*duritia*), humanity (*humanitas*), strenuosity (*strenuitas*), equanimity (*aequanimitas*), truthfulness (*verecundia*), opportunity (*opportunitas*), righteous desire (*iuste*

---

[136] Thomas Aquinas, *Summa theologiae* 1a2ae,68,2 (Busa, *S. Thomae Aquinatis*, 441; O'Connor, *St. Thomas Aquinas*, 11). The question of how virtues and gifts exactly relate to each other is too complex for the scope of this book and will not be investigated further here. Although most of the scholastic argumentation around this subject is post-Francis, see for instance: Engemann, *Das neue Lied*, 125–126.

[137] Cf. Mähl, *Quadriga*, 163: "So gibt es Gruppen spezifisch mönchischer Tugenden, wie sie etwa in der Benediktiner-Regel oder in den Werken Cassians gefordert werden. Gewiß konnte derjenige, der das Schema der vier Grundtugenden einmal anerkannt hatte, theoretisch auch alle diese Tugenden darunter subsumieren, aber es ist nur natürlich, daß man Werte wie Demut, Geduld, Gehorsam, Enthaltsamkeit, Bescheidenheit usw., zu denen Mönche und Kleriker von Jugend auf erzogen wurden, als ein eigenständiges sittliches Ordnungsgefüge betrachtete, welches in der Praxis die Kardinaltugenden in den Hintergrund drängte." Important virtues in the works of Cassian and the rule of Benedict are, for example, obedience, humility, charity, abstinence, and poverty.

[138] Thomas Aquinas, *Summa theologiae* 1a2ae,61,2 (Busa, *S. Thomae Aquinatis*, 432; Hughes, *St. Thomas Aquinas*, 121).

velle), humility (*humilitas*), dignity (*dignitas*), persistence (*consistentia*), excellence (*praecellentia*), right measure (*mensura vera*), tenacity (*pertinacia*), patience (*patientia*), hope (*spes*), constancy (*constantia*), piety (*religiositas*), companionship (*sodalitas*), and friendly service (*officium verae amicitiae*).[139]

The "philosophical" virtues, by contrast, can also be integrated into monastic schemes. In the *Profectus religiosorum* by David of Augsburg, for example, the four cardinal virtues and three theological virtues are parts of the monastic (Augustinian) scheme of the "various names of charity":

> Charity, then, directed towards God is *love of God*; towards our neighbour, is *love of others*. Where it moves us to compassionate suffering, it is *mercy*; to rejoice in another's welfare, *noble-mindedness*. In helping us to bear our own trials well, it is *patience*; in inspiring us with kindness towards enemies, *benignity*. Holding us back from self-assertion, it is *humility*; prompting us to be compliant with authority, *obedience*; restraining us from material superfluities, *sobriety*; urging us to renunciation of wealth, *poverty of spirit*. As *generosity*, it inclines us to give liberally to the poor; as *longanimity*, it rouses us against the tedium of delay; as *prudence*, it knows how to differentiate wisely between the degrees of good and evil. Giving to each one his due, it is *justice*; restraining us from soft surrender to pleasure, it is *temperance*; encouraging us in face of difficulties, it is *fortitude*; vitalizing our beliefs, it is *faith*; confirming our confidence, it is *hope*.[140]

Finally, many medieval monastic and spiritual authors do not adopt philosophical schemes of virtues and do not even seem to be affected by

---

[139] Borok, *Der Tugendbegriff*, 143–145.

[140] *Prof* 3,32: *Ita caritas est una virtus in se omnem habens virtutem, sed propter diversos effectus eius ex diversis extrinsecis occasionibus vel causis illatis, quibus se vel contra malum opponit, vel ad bonum extendit, diversa officia vel nomina sortitur. Virtus enim, sicut definit Augustinus, 'est amor ordinatus', videlicet, ut amet solum quod debet et sicut debet et quantum debet. Quantum vero amas aliquid, tantum odis et fugis eius contrarium, ubi potes. Caritas igitur, cum se extendit ad diligendum Deum,* dilectio Dei *dicitur; cum ad proximum,* dicitur dilectio proximi; *cum eius miseriae compatitur,* misericordia *appellatur; cum eius bono congaudet,* congratulatio *vocatur; cum aequanimiter adversa tolerat,* patientia *dicitur; cum benefacit se odientibus,* benignitas *nuncupatur; cum non extollitur inaniter supra se,* humilitas *est; cum obtemperat superioribus, ut iustum est,* obedientia *est; cum exsecratur turpia,* castitas *est; cum resecat superflua corporalis necessitatis,* sobrietas *est; cum divitias abiicit,* paupertas spiritus *est; cum ad pauperes eas liberaliter effundit,* largitas *est; cum taedio exspectationis promissorum non frangitur,* longanimitas *est; cum inter bonum et melius et inter malum et peius discernit,* prudentia *est; cum ius suum cuique tribuit,* iustitia *est; cum delectationibus non emollitur,* temperantia *est; cum duris non terretur,* fortitudo *est; cum credit credenda,* fides *est; cum sperat speranda,* spes est (*David ab Augusta*, 226–227; Devas, *Spiritual Life* 2, 65–66).

scholastic moral thought. One of the best examples is Francis of Assisi, who prescribes and recommends many virtues, none of which can be considered "natural," "intellectual," or "moral" virtues in a scholastic sense. In fact, all virtues in his writings (the most important of which are charity, obedience, goodness, truth, faith, humility, joy, poverty, penance, and peace) are simply "spiritual" virtues;[141] they spring from the zeal (or "attention of love") for God which is a gift (*donum*) one receives through the Spirit from God.[142] But from here it is not far to Bonaventure's academically informed and monastically inspired conviction that "no matter how well-ordered the steps of our interior life may be, nothing will happen if the divine aid does not accompany us."[143]

10. FRANCISCAN VIRTUE

Francis

Francis gives no definitions of virtue, but he uses the word *virtus* in several circumstances.[144] First, God is our Power (*virtus*) and

[141] Cf. *Sal Mar* 6. *...et vos omnes sanctae virtutes, quae per gratiam et illuminationem Spiritus sancti infundimini in corda fidelium...* (Armstrong, *Francis of Assisi*, 163). See also 3.2.

[142] Cf. Beemer, "Over de deugden", 200; Morant, *Unser Weg*, 20–21; Rohr, *Der Herr*, 83–86: "In Ihm findet er seine „Aszetik". So viel uns die Menschen auch über Tugend und Tugendübung zu sagen wissen, ihm liegt mehr daran, vom Herrn selbst zu lernen, *wie* wir das Arm-Sein, die Demut, den Gehorsam u.a.m. verstehen und üben sollen. So tief er auch von seiner Kleinheit und Unwürdigkeit durchdrungen ist, so will er doch nicht zu lange dabei verweilen, um nicht sich selbst mehr Aufmerksamkeit zuzuwenden als dem Herrn, der ihm soviel Liebe und Vertrauen geschenkt hat (...) So entspringen die sogenannten franziskanischen Tugenden – Armut, Demut, Gehorsam, Dankbarkeit, heilige Freudigkeit und reine Einfalt – in Wahrheit nicht einem aszetisch-moralischen Eifer, sondern der reinen Aufmerksamkeit der Liebe zum Herrn. Franziskus dachte aber sicher nicht daran, dadurch etwas Besonderes zu leisten, um persönlich zur Vollkommenheit zu gelangen; er wollte nur das erfüllen, was ein noch weithin unerfülltes Anliegen des Herrn war."

[143] *Itin* 1,1: *Quantumcumque enim gradus interiores disponantur, nihil fit, nisi divinum auxilium comitetur* (*Doctoris* 5, 296–297; Hayes, *Works*, 45). Cf. Veuthey, *Itinerarium*, 20.

[144] Cf. Freeman, "Franciscus' vrede", 38: "Franciscus heeft 'vrede' of 'de vrede in het hart' nooit gedefinieerd. Definities horen niet bij zijn wijze van denken of spreken. Zij palen een begrip af, waar Franciscus door middel van zijn woorden juist werelden wil openen." On Francis and virtue(s), see for instance: Bisschops, *Franciscus*, 220–221; Bracaloni, "Le virtù"; Ghinato, *Profilo*, 157–159; Gobry, *St. François*, 77; Goorbergh & Zweerman, *Was getekend*, 100–101, 112, 162–170, 200–208, 226–234; Hoeberichts, *Paradise*, 37–46, 144–150, 153–170; Karris, *The Admonitions*, 237–252; Matanic, *Francesco d'Assisi*, 55–60; Matanic, "Virtù"; Matanic, *Virtù*; Van Leeuwen & Verheij, *Woorden*, 138–139; Van Munster, *De mystiek*, 48–56, 146–150; Zweerman, *Om de eer*, 132–134.

38 CHAPTER ONE

Strength,[145] so that virtue is God (revealing Himself in us and effica-
ciously working through us).[146] Second, the power (*virtus*) of God is
operative through Christ in the sacraments[147] and in prayer.[148] Third,
there is a species of angels called "virtues."[149] Fourth, virtue is the inner
faculty (power) with which man loves God: "All those who love the Lord
with their whole heart, with their whole soul and mind, with their
whole strength (*virtus*)."[150] Fifth, the holy "virtues" (*virtutes*) in Francis's
Salutation of the Virtues and *Salutation of the Blessed Virgin Mary* can

---

[145] *Ep Fid* 2,62. *...quia ipse est virtus et fortitudo nostra....* (Armstrong, *Francis of Assisi*,
49). Cf. *Laud Dei* 4–6. *Tu es amor, caritas; tu es sapientia, tu es humilitas, tu es patientia* (Ps
70,5), *tu es pulchritudo, tu es mansuetudo, tu es securitas, tu es quietas, tu es gaudium, tu es
spes nostra et laetitia, tu es iustitia, tu es temperantia, tu es omnia divitia nostra ad sufficientiam. Tu es pulchritudo, tu es mansuetudo; tu es protector* (Ps 30,5), *tu es custos et defensor
noster; tu es fortitudo* (cfr. Ps 42,2), *tu es refrigerium. Tu es spes nostra, tu es fides nostra, tu
es caritas nostra, tu es tota dulcedo nostra, tu es vita aeterna nostra: Magnus et admirabilis
Dominus, Deus omnipotens, misericors Salvator* (Armstrong, *Francis of Assisi*, 109); *Of Pas*
2,9,11–12. *Ecce dabit voci suae vocem virtutis, date gloriam Deo super Israel magnificentia
eius et virtus eius in nubibus* (Ps 67,34b-35) *Mirabilis Deus in sanctis suis Deus Israel ipse
dabit virtutem et fortitudinem plebi suae, benedictus Deus* (Ps 67,36) (Armstrong, *Francis of
Assisi*, 149); *Of Pas* 3,10,2. *Dicite Deo, quam terribilia sunt opera tua, Domine in multitudine
virtutis tuae mentientur tibi inimici tui* (Ps 65,3) (Armstrong, *Francis of Assisi*, 151); *Laud Hor*
3. *Dignus est agnus qui occisus est, accipere virtutem et divinitatem et sapientiam et fortitudinem et honorem et gloriam et benedictionem* (Apoc 5,12) (Armstrong, *Francis of Assisi*,
161). Here, the Lamb Who was slain, Christ the Son of God, is "worthy to receive power and
divinity, wisdom and strength, honor and glory and blessing." Elsewhere, in the hour of his
death, Christ's "strength has been dried up like baked clay" (*Of Pas* 1,6,8. *Aruit tamquam
testa virtus mea et lingua mea adhaesit faucibus meis* (Ps 21,16a-b) (Armstrong, *Francis of
Assisi*, 146)).
[146] Van Leeuwen & Verheij, *Woorden*, 139.
[147] *Ep Ord* 37. *Multa enim sanctificantur per verba Dei* (cfr. 1 Tim 4,5), *et in
virtute verborum Christi altaris conficitur sacramentum* (Armstrong, *Francis of
Assisi*, 119).
[148] *Ex Pat* 7. *Et dimitte nobis debita nostra: per tuam misericordiam ineffabilem, per passionis dilecti Filii tui virtutem et per beatissimae Virginis et omnium electorum tuorum merita
et intercessionem* (Armstrong, *Francis of Assisi*, 159).
[149] *Of Pas* 1,1 (Ant 3) *...ora pro nobis cum S. Michaele archangelo et omnibus virtutibus
caelorum et omnibus sanctis apud tuum sanctissimum dilectum Filium, Dominum et magistrum* (Armstrong, *Francis of Assisi*, 141); *RnB* 23,6. *...et omnes choros beatorum seraphim,
cherubim, thronorum, dominationum, principatuum, potestatum* (cfr. Col 1,15), *virtutum,
angelorum, archangelorum...* (Armstrong, *Francis of Assisi*, 83); *Test* 40. *Et quicumque haec
observaverit, in caelo repleatur benedictione altissimi Patris et in terra repleatur benedictione dilecti Filii sui cum sanctissimo Spiritu Paraclito et omnibus virtutibus caelorum et
omnibus sanctis* (Armstrong, *Francis of Assisi*, 127).
[150] *Ep Fid* 1,1,1. *Omnes qui Dominum diligunt ex toto corde, ex tota anima et mente, ex tota
virtute* (cfr. Mark 12,30)... (Armstrong, *Francis of Assisi*, 41); *RnB* 23,8. *Omnes diligamus ex
toto corde, ex tota anima, ex tota mente, ex tota virtute* (cfr. Mark 12,30)... (Armstrong,
Francis of Assisi, 84).

be considered to be "possessions" of the one who is predisposed to good behavior or "fundamental characteristics" of the religious person, elsewhere in Christian theology defined as "good qualities of the mind" (Lombard) or "habits perfecting man" (Aquinas). Last, "true virtue" (*vera virtus*) is the inner strength or substance (*in hoc est*) of virtuous behavior that leads to salvation, viz., being joyful in patience and unmoved by rejection.[151] The brothers are called the heirs of the Kingdom of Heaven: in their most exalted poverty they are "poor in temporal things but exalted in virtue (*virtutibus sublimavit*)."[152] Here, too, virtue is the way to salvation.

Although Francis does not move on a philosophical level or expand on any philosophical concepts, he tells us that "whoever possesses one [of the virtues] and does not offend the others possesses all."[153] With this statement on the *connexio* of the virtues he joins prevailing theological thought and shows himself to be fairly acquainted with current philosophical views on the nature and the function of the virtues.[154] Two more indications for this are his reference to the "divine infusion" of the virtues (in accordance with the scholastic *virtutes infusae* and/or *dona*) and his opposition of the virtues and the vices (in accordance with the scholastic scheme of *vitia contraria virtutibus*). Francis says that the virtues proceed from the Lord and "are poured into the hearts of the faithful through the grace and enlightenment of the Holy Spirit."[155] Virtue therefore "responds to God's virtuous presence in the life of every Christian."[156] Furthermore, "each one [of the virtues] confounds vice and sin."[157] It is no surprise that

[151] *Laet* 15. *Dico tibi quod si patientiam habuero et non fuero motus, quod in hoc est vera laetitia et vera virtus et salus animae* (Armstrong, *Francis of Assisi*, 167).

[152] *RB* 6,4. *Haec est illa celsitudo altissimae paupertatis, quae vos, carissimos fratres meos, heredes et reges regni caelorum instituit, pauperes rebus fecit, virtutibus sublimavit* (cfr. Jac 2,5) (Armstrong, *Francis of Assisi*, 103).

[153] *Sal Virt* 6. *Qui unam habet et alias non offendit, omnes habet* (Armstrong, *Francis of Assisi*, 164).

[154] Cf. Matanic, "Virtù", 1981.

[155] *Sal Virt* 4. *Sanctissimae virtutes, omnes vos salvet Dominus, a quo venitis et proceditis* (Armstrong, *Francis of Assisi*, 164); *Sal Mar* 6. *...et vos omnes sanctae virtutes, quae per gratiam et illuminationem Spiritus sancti infundimini in corda fidelium, ut de infidelibus fideles Deo faciatis* (Armstrong, *Francis of Assisi*, 164).

[156] Armstrong, *Francis of Assisi*, 163. Cf. Beemer, "Over de deugden", 200; Bisschops, *Franciscus*, 220; Goorbergh & Zweerman, *Was getekend*, 207; Rohr, *Der Herr*, 83–86; Veuthey, *Kleine reisgids*, 35.

[157] *Sal Virt* 8. *Et unaquaque confundit vitia et peccata* (Armstrong, *Francis of Assisi*, 164). Cf. *Adm* 27,1–6. *Ubi caritas est et sapientia, ibi nec timor nec ignorantia. Ubi est patientia et humilitas, ibi nec ira nec perturbatio. Ubi est paupertas cum laetitia, ibi nec cupiditas nec*

in Francis's *Rule* (1223) as in the many edifying works that come into use after the Fourth Lateran Council of 1215, the virtues and their opposing vices (*vitia*) are recommended sermon material.[158]

Bonaventure

Unlike brother Francis, theologian and minister Bonaventure gives several definitions of virtue.[159] Only in his *theological* works can larger expositions on grace and virtue be found;[160] but even in his spiritual works and his works concerning the Franciscan Order he defines "virtue" in some places before expounding on "the virtues" and their specific contents. Every virtue is a "right reason," according to Augustine,[161] and perfect virtue is "reason attaining its final end, which is followed by beatific life."[162] Pure virtues (humility, chastity, charity, mercy, and the like) proceed from the eternal law, in the absence of which no man may be saved at any time.[163] The law, indeed, establishes a "program for worship and salvation," aimed at God-conformity through the adoption of virtue and the abandonment of vice:

> It is plainly established by the inviolable law of the supreme Legislator that worship must be rendered the supreme Majesty to the exclusion of any cult of idols: that the created intellect must serve the supreme Truth to the exclusion of any assent to falsehood; that man must strive mightily toward salvation, not yielding to the flesh in its pleasures; finally, that he

---

avaritia. Ubi est quies et meditatio, ibi neque sollicitudo neque vagatio. Ubi est timor Domini ad atrium suum custodiendum (cfr. Luke 11,21), *ibi inimicus non potest habere locum ad ingrediendum. Ubi est misericordia et discretio, ibi nec superfluitas nec induratio* (Armstrong, *Francis of Assisi*, 136–137); Goorbergh & Zweerman, *Was getekend*, 106–110.

[158] *RB* 9,4. *...annuntiando eis vitia et virtutes, poenam et gloriam cum brevitate sermonis...* (Armstrong, *Francis of Assisi*, 105). Cf. Pansters, *De kardinale*, 77–89.

[159] On Bonaventure and virtue(s), see for instance: Borak, "Le beatitudini"; Bougerol, *Lexique*, 134–136; Cullen, *Bonaventure*, 91–104; Cuttini, *Ritorno*, 121–148; Delhaye, "Les conditions"; Elsässer, *Christus*; Emery Jr., "Reading"; Hochschild, "Porphyry"; Israël, *Die Tugendlehre*; Schlosser, *Cognitio*, 130–165; Speer, *Triplex*, 162–172; Synan, "Cardinal".

[160] E.g., *Brev* 5,4 (*Doctoris* 5, 256–257; De Vinck, *The Works* 2, 193–196).

[161] *Ap Paup* 2,3. *Denique, cum virtus omnis, ut ait Augustinus, sit ratio recta...* (*Doctoris* 8, 240; De Vinck, *The Works* 4, 21).

[162] *Ap Paup* 3,2. *Vere, perfecta virtus est ratio perveniens usque ad finem, quem beata vita consequitur* (*Doctoris* 8, 245; De Vinck, *The Works* 4, 38).

[163] *Sex Alis* 2,7. *Horum quaedam procedunt a lege aeterna, ut purae virtutes: humilitas, castitas, caritas, misericordia et similes, sine quibus nullus quocumque tempore poterit salvari...* (*Doctoris* 8, 134; De Vinck, *The Works* 3, 144).

must consent to the righteousness of God-conforming virtue, shunning the depravity of deforming vice."[164]

Within this program, virtue has a double function: to elevate the mind to God by personal devotion, and to regulate relationships with others by way of peace.[165] Not every virtue is perfect and not everyone who possesses the virtues is perfect,[166] but "that perfection is higher from the viewpoint of perfect virtue in which the root of love is stronger, the quality of the deed more elevated, and the fruit of fraternal edification more plentiful."[167] All of us should therefore take great care to grieve over sins committed and to "proceed from virtue to virtue" (*Psalm* 83,3) so as to finally reach the promised land.[168]

David

In the sixth *processus* of the third book, David deals with "the development of pure virtues."[169] The general definition of virtue is: "a movement of the will acting in accord with a legitimate judgement."[170] There are

---

[164] *Ap Paup*, Prol,1. *Summi legislatoris inviolabili constat definitione sancitum, sic maiestati aeternae cultum debitum esse reddendum, quod idolorum cultura vitetur; sic redigendum intellectum creatum in summae veritatis obsequium, quod nullus falsitati praebeatur assensus; sic vacandum sanctificationi spirituum, quod ferietur a servitute carnalium voluptatum; sic denique virtutum deiformium approbandam esse rectitudinem, quod deformantium vitiorum pravitas reprobetur* (Doctoris 8, 233; De Vinck, *The Works* 4, 1). Cf. *Ex Reg* 1,3. *Licet enim virtutum actus sint in praecepto...* (Doctoris 8, 394).

[165] *Serm Reg* 7–9. *Sed duplex est virtus, scilicet ordinans in Deum per mentis elevationem, ordinans in proximum per pacificam conversationem. Ordinans in Deum est devotio... Item, virtus ordinans in proximum est pax* (Doctoris 8, 439–440).

[166] *Ap Paup* 4,17. *Ex quo etiam sequitur, quod omnis virtus sit perfecta, et quod omnis virtutem habens perfectus sit... Quae omnia tanquam falsa et inconvenientia sunt in praecedentibus multipliciter improbata* (Doctoris 8, 256; De Vinck, *The Works* 4, 74).

[167] *Ap Paup* 3,19. *...primo secundum exercitium perfectae virtutis illa perfectio est eminentior, in qua radix caritatis est pinguior et sublimitas operationis excelsior et fraternae aedificationis fructus uberior* (Doctoris 8, 249; De Vinck, *The Works* 4, 52).

[168] *Trip Via* 1,4. *Debet enim unusquisque cum summa diligentia deflere mala commissa, repellere diabolica tentamenta, proficere de una virtute in aliam, ut sic possit pervenire ad terram promissam* (Doctoris 8, 4; De Vinck, *The Works* 1, 65). Cf. *Perf* 1,2. *Debes enim cum summa diligentia deflere mala commissa, repellere diabolica tentamenta et proficere de una virtute in aliam, ut possis pervenire ad terram promissam* (Doctoris 8, 108; De Vinck, *The Works* 1, 212–213); *Perf* 7,1. *...ut quasi gradatim ascendere possis et de virtute in virtutem proficere* (Doctoris 8, 124; De Vinck, *The Works* 1, 248).

[169] *Prof* 3,27–51 (David ab Augusta, 214–294; Devas, *Spiritual Life* 2, 54–127). Cf. Pansters, *De kardinale*, 229–231; Pansters, "*Profectus virtutum*. The Roots"; Bohl, *Geistlicher*; Einhorn, "Der Begriff", 345–348.

[170] *Prof* 3,27. *Virtus est ordinatus secundum veritatis iudicium mentis affectus* (David ab Augusta, 215; Devas, *Spiritual Life* 2, 54). This definition is based on the definition by

seven movements of the mind (will)[171] and various classifications of
the virtues: theological and cardinal virtues; civic virtues, cleansing virtues, virtues characteristic of the soul in the state of purgation, and exemplary virtues.[172] There are six "outward coverings" that adorn and shield
virtue:[173] religious habit, ceremonial observances, good manners, works of
penance, banishing vice and practicing virtue (*studium familiare ad
expugnanda vel mortificanda vitia et virtutes usitandas*), and affective virtue. The virtues combat the seven capital vices, and each virtue has three
different stages: beginning, progress, and perfection.[174] In order to progress in each and every virtue and "reach a higher degree of sanctity,"[175]
one may ask oneself: "What is the use of professing a higher standard and
of indicating outwardly, by my habit, my choice thereof, if, in fact, my zeal
for holiness (*studio virtutum*) and alertness in well-doing hardly differ
from that of the uninterested who yet hope to save their souls?"[176]

After the general remarks on "virtue" and "virtues," David goes on to
describe the virtues individually. The most important one is charity[177]
because this virtue contains all other virtues.[178] It has three successive
degrees: beginning, progress, and perfection.[179] It is necessary to proceed

---

William of St. Thierry: *Virtus est ad iudicium rationis usus liberae voluntatis* (*Guillelmi a
Sancto Theodorico* 3, 275). Cf. *Prof* 3,32. *Virtus enim, sicut definit Augustinus, est amor ordinatus...* (*David ab Augusta*, 226; Devas, *Spiritual Life* 2, 65). As mentioned before (1.2, 1.5),
David also defines virtue as a *habitus* (*Prof* 2,5; *David ab Augusta* 87; Devas, *Spiritual Life* 1,
83).

[171] *Prof* 3,28. *Septem autem sunt affectiones mentis communiter: spes et timor, gaudium et
moeror, amor et odium et pudor* (*David ab Augusta*, 215–216; Devas, *Spiritual Life* 2, 55).

[172] *Prof* 3,28. *Multae sunt aliae virtutum artificiales divisiones, secundum quod aliae
dicuntur theologicae, ut fides, spes, caritas; aliae cardinales, ut prudentia, iustitia, fortitudo,
temperantia; item, aliae politicae, aliae purgatoriae, aliae animi purgati, aliae exemplares...*
(*David ab Augusta*, 217; Devas, *Spiritual Life* 2, 56).

[173] *Prof* 3,29 (*David ab Augusta*, 218–221; Devas, *Spiritual Life* 2, 57–60).

[174] *Prof* 3,30 (*David ab Augusta*, 221–223; Devas, *Spiritual Life* 2, 61–62).

[175] *Prof* 3,30. ...*quantum in singulis virtutibus profecerint... Profectus ad Religiosos magis
congrue pertinent, qui meliores esse studere debent...* (*David ab Augusta*, 221–222; Devas,
Spiritual Life 2, 61–62).

[176] *Prof* 3,30. *Quid prodest altiora profiteri et exterius in habitu perfectiora praetendere, si
in studio virtutum et exercitio operis non distamus ab infimis, qui in spe sunt salvationis?*
(*David ab Augusta*, 222; Devas, *Spiritual Life* 2, 62). Cf. *Prof* 2,48. ...*et ad examinationem
propriarum virtutum, quia in adversitate plenius videmus, quantum profecerimus in eis...*
(*David ab Augusta*, 146; Devas, *Spiritual Life* 1, 137).

[177] *Prof* 3,31–36 (*David ab Augusta*, 223–243; Devas, *Spiritual Life* 2, 62–80).

[178] *Prof* 3,32. ....*ita caritas est una virtus in se omnem habens virtutem...* (*David ab Augusta*,
226; Devas, *Spiritual Life* 2, 65). Cf. Bohl, *Geistlicher*, 435–437. See also 2.1.

[179] *Prof* 3,33. *Unaquaeque enim virtus, teste beato Gregorio, habet initium suum et profectum et perfectionem... Caritas Dei, mater et nutrix omnium virtutum, tres habet gradus: infimum, medium et summum...* (*David ab Augusta*, 227–228; Devas, *Spiritual Life* 2, 66).

from virtue to virtue (*de virtute in virtutem eundo proficere*) in the hierarchy of virtues (*virtutum hierarchia*)[180] to be able to ascend to the highest
virtue, the love of God.[181] After charity, David discusses the characteristics
and degrees of the other six key virtues (humility, patience, obedience,
poverty, sobriety, and chastity),[182] the fact that a virtue lies between two
extremes (vices),[183] and the fact that certain vices pose as virtues.[184]

Much more than Francis, and even Bonaventure in his spiritual writings, David focuses on the "monastic," "ascetic," or "didactic-methodic"[185]
aspects of the practice of devotion and the pursuit of virtue (*studium virtutis*; *virtutum assuefactio*; *virtutum conatus*; *virtutes cordi inserere*; *opera
virtutum*; *virtutibus insistere*; *augmentum virtutis*; *vias virtutum*).[186] This
pursuit consists primarily of the rooting out of vices and the fostering of
virtues (*exercitium virtutis*) and the gradual acquisition of the interior
love of God.[187] Certain schemes, degrees, and functions of virtues thereby
constitute the means for and way to spiritual progress (*profectus
virtutis*).[188]

Some quotations

To conclude this chapter with a foretaste of things to come, I would like to
quote some key passages that are programmatic for the Franciscan "project" of virtuous living:

---

[180] *Prof* 3,33. ...*cur non etiam spirituales virtutum hierarchiae eundem ordinem in terris
imitentur... Laboremus tantum hic fideliter de virtute in virtutem eundo proficere...* (*David ab
Augusta*, 228; Devas, *Spiritual Life* 2, 66–67).

[181] *Prof* 3,33 (*David ab Augusta*, 227–228; Devas, *Spiritual Life* 2, 66–67). Cf. *Prof* 3,37. ...
*quanto quisque magis fuerit ordinatus in virtutibus, tanto magis erit capax supernae beati-
tudinis* (*David ab Augusta*, 243; Devas, *Spiritual Life* 2, 80); *Prof* 3,38. *Qui ergo cito desiderat
virtutis culmen attingere... magnis virtutibus attollendo* (*David ab Augusta*, 249; Devas,
Spiritual Life 2, 86); *Prof* 3,44. ...*quia retardant hominem a profectu virtutum* (*David ab
Augusta*, 270; Devas, *Spiritual Life* 2, 105); *Prof* 3,46. *Tota autem intentio debet esse circa
optimum occupata, circa profectum animae in Dei notitia et amore...* (*David ab Augusta*, 277;
Devas, *Spiritual Life* 2, 111); *Prof* 3,46. *Item, ad multarum virtutum habilitationem...* (*David
ab Augusta*, 279; Devas, *Spiritual Life* 2, 113).

[182] *Prof* 3,37–47, 50–51 (*David ab Augusta*, 243–282, 286–294; Devas, *Spiritual Life* 2,
80–116, 120–127).

[183] *Prof* 3,48 (*David ab Augusta*, 282–284; Devas, *Spiritual Life* 2, 116–117).

[184] *Prof* 3,49 (*David ab Augusta*, 284–286; Devas, *Spiritual Life* 2, 118–120).

[185] Bohl, *Geistlicher*, 301.

[186] E.g., *Prof* 1,18. *De Deo libenter loquere et libentius audi quod incitat cor ad studium virtutis et affectum devotionis* (*David ab Augusta*, 23; Devas, *Spiritual Life* 1, 20–21).

[187] *Prof* 2, Epist. *Studium verae Religionis circa duo maxime versatur, circa exercitium
virtutis et affectum internae devotionis* (*David ab Augusta*, 59; Devas, *Spiritual Life* 1, 53).

[188] E.g., *Prof* 1,40. ...*ut proprium statum ordinent ad profectum virtutis* (*David ab Augusta*,
55; Devas, *Spiritual Life* 1, 47).

"All those who love the Lord with their whole heart, with their whole soul and mind, with their whole strength (*virtus*) and love their neighbours as themselves, who hate their bodies with their vices and sins, who receive the Body and Blood of our Lord Jesus Christ, and who produce worthy fruits of penance. O how happy and blessed are these men and women while they do such things and persevere in doing them, because the Spirit of the Lord will rest upon them and make Its home and dwelling place among them, and they are children of the heavenly Father Whose works they do, and they are spouses, brothers, and mothers of our Lord Jesus Christ."[189]

"Observe to what extent you are, or may have been, negligent in doing penance, in resisting evil, or in making spiritual progress. You must earnestly deplore your sins, reject all diabolical temptations, and proceed from one virtue (*virtus*) to another until you reach the promised land."[190]

"So is a man, and especially a religious, foolish who abandons the right-ordered quest of virtue (*virtutes*), wherein such great merit is to be won, such perfection of holy wisdom, such joyous security, and busies himself instead with other matters less useful and more harassing, till he becomes as one troubled about many things: and all the while the one sole Good is there, highest of all, enriching all, needed by all, waiting to be sought for."[191]

---

[189] Francis, *Ep Fid* 1,1,1–7. *Omnes qui Dominum diligunt ex toto corde, ex tota anima et mente, ex tota virtute* (cfr. Mark 12,30) *et diligunt proximos suos sicut se ipsos* (cfr. Matt 22,39), *et odio habent corpora eorum cum vitiis et peccatis, et recipiunt corpus et sanguinem Domini nostri Jesu Christi, et faciunt fructus dignos poenitentiae: O quam beati et benedicti sunt illi et illae, dum talia faciunt et in talibus perseverant, quia requiescet super eos spiritus Domini* (cfr. Isa 11,2) *et faciet apud eos habitaculum et mansionem* (cfr. Joa 14,23), *et sunt filii patris caelestis* (cfr. Matt 5,45), *cuius opera faciunt et sunt sponsi, fratres et matres Domini nostri Jesu Christi* (cfr. Matt 12,50) (Armstrong, *Francis of Assisi*, 41–42).

[190] Bonaventure, *Perf* 1,2. *Item debes recogitare, quam negligens sis vel fueris ad poenitendum, quam negligens ad resistendum et quam negligens ad proficiendum. Debes enim cum summa diligentia deflere mala commissa, repellere diabolica tentamenta et proficere de una virtute in aliam* [cfr. Ps. 83,8], *ut possis pervenire ad terram promissam* (*Doctoris* 8, 108; De Vinck, *The Works* 1, 212–213).

[191] David, *Prof* 2,5. *Ita est de homine, maxime Religioso, magna imprudentia, si, relicto debito studio virtutum, in quo est maximum meritum, maxima perfectio sanctitatis et sapientiae, maxima etiam delectatio et securitas, occupat se circa alia minus utilia et curiosa et turbatur circa plurima* [cfr. Luke 10,41], *quando unum solum summum bonum est petendum et requirendum, quod valet ad omnia* (*David ab Augusta*, 87; Devas, *Spiritual Life* 1, 82–83).

CHAPTER TWO

VIRTUES

The main Franciscan virtues are charity (*caritas*), obedience (*obedientia*), goodness (*bonitas*), truth (*veritas*), faith (*fides*), humility (*humilitas*), joy (*gaudium*), poverty (*paupertas*), penance (*poenitentia*), and peace (*pax*).[1] This chapter deals with their meaning in the works of Francis, Bonaventure, and David of Augsburg.

1. CHARITY

Origin

Charity (*caritas, amor, dilectio*) is the main Christian virtue.[2] Conceived in the Bible as the love of God for man, the love of man for God, or the love of man for his fellow man, it has developed into a comprehensive doctrine concerned with nature, motives, and practices. Its biblical origin lies in the Mosaic laws: "Love the Lord your God with all your heart and with all your soul and with all your strength,"[3] which was repeated by Jesus to his disciples,[4] and: "Do not seek revenge or bear a grudge against one of your people, but love your neighbour as yourself."[5] The Gospel abounds in references to charity, such as, "My command is this: Love each other as I have loved you,"[6] or, "Love your neighbour as yourself."[7] In the Pauline

---

[1] See 1.4.

[2] "Liebt der Mensch Gott, den Inbegriff alles Guten und Großen, so bemüht er sich, sich von den Fesseln irdischer Freude zu lösen, wächst über seine naturhafte Schwäche hinaus und wird von der Gnade Gottes eingezogen und innerlich umgewandelt; er wird Gott ähnlich und damit sittlich vollkommen. Von der Art der Liebe und vom Grad der Liebe hängt die ganze sittliche Größe des Menschen ab" (Morant, *Unser Weg*, 262). Cf. Allen, "The Standard"; Brümmer, *The Model*; "Charité"; Chydenius, *The Symbolism*; Dominian, *The Capacity*; *Deus*; Ford, *Love*; Glazier, *Gospel Love*; Graham, *The Idea*; Hallett, *Christian*; Hödl & Dinzelbacher, "Liebe"; Jackson, *The Priority*; Kuhn, *"Liebe"*; MacNamara, "The Truth"; Newlands, *Theology*; Post, *A Theory*; Singer, *The Nature*; Vanstone, *Love's Endeavour*; Welte, *Dialektik*.

[3] Deut 6,5.

[4] Matt 22,37; Mark 12,30; Luke 10,27.

[5] Lev 19,18.

[6] John 15,12.

[7] Matt 22,39. Cf. Varghese, *The Imagery*, 14; Deden, *De bijbel*; Furnish, *The Love Command*; Hardick, "„Schenke mir""; Kieffer, *Le primat*; Kiilunen, *Das Doppelgebot*;

corpus it can be found as part of a number of catalogues of virtues (including such virtues as faith, justice, purity, and patience) forming a program of Christian virtuous living.[8] Charity is also the first of the three theological virtues[9] and a co-virtue of faith and purity;[10] faith, righteousness, and peace;[11] and faith, patience, and endurance.[12] Following the example of Jesus, Paul puts charity at the centre of his thought.[13] He declares it to be the primary fruit of the Holy Spirit: "But the fruit of the Spirit is love, joy, peace, patience, kindness, goodness, faithfulness, gentleness, and self-control."[14] Charity is everything: patient, kind, just, joyful, truthful, faithful, hopeful, everlasting, perfect.[15] In practice, it requires a sincere heart directed at the good[16] because the one who loves God is known by Him,[17] and the one who loves his neighbour nourishes godliness.[18]

Francis

God and man

In the Christian tradition charity is perfection; it is virtue *par excellence*.[19] Naturally, Francis places himself in this tradition when he defines God as Charity,[20] and at the same time recommends charity towards God and towards others.[21] God, who is Charity (*tu es amor,*

Perkins, *Love Commands*; Popkes, *Die Theologie*; Ward, *The Rule*; Warnach, *Agape*; Warnach, "Liebe"; Wiener, *Récherches*.

[8] Eph 4,2–3; 2 Cor 6,6; Gal 5,22–23; 1 Tim 6,11. Cf. Wibbing, *Die Tugend- und Lasterkataloge*, 77–127; Quinten, *Die Liebe*.

[9] 1 Cor 13,13; 1 Thess 1,3; 1 Thess 5,8; Phil 1,5; Gal 5,5. Cf. Bars, *Trois vertus-clefs*; Ratzinger, *Auf Christus*; Robinson, *These Three*; Schuster, *Moralisches*, 183–230; Söding, *Die Trias*; Walter, *Glaube*.

[10] 1 Tim 4,12.

[11] 2 Tim 2,22.

[12] 2 Tim 3,10.

[13] Romaniuk, *L'amour*; Söding, *Die Trias*.

[14] Gal 5,22–23.

[15] 1 Cor 13.

[16] Rom 12,9.

[17] 1 Cor 8,3.

[18] 2 Pet 1,7; Rom 14,15; 1 Thess 4,9; 1 Thess 5,15.

[19] Cf. "Charité", 557–558; Canning, *The Unity*.

[20] Cf. 1 John 4,8; e.g., Ambrosius, *Expositio Psalmi*, Serm. 5.

[21] On Francis and charity, see for instance: Bisschops, *Franciscus*, 378–392; Engemann, *Das neue Lied*; Gerken, "Die theologische", 6–14; Ghinato, *Profilo*, 165–166; Gobry, *St. François*, 60–63; Haskamp, ",,Du bist""; Hoeberichts, *Paradise*, 108–121, 214–225; Iriarte, *Vocazione*, 85–86; Koper, *Das Weltverständnis*, 103–105, Lang, *Ins Freie*, 50–56; Lehmann,

caritas),[22] loves man (*caritas Dei* as *genetivus subjectivus*) and should be loved by man (*caritas Dei* as *genetivus objectivus*): the idea of *caritas Dei* (love of God) can be interpreted in both ways, dependent on the context in which it appears.[23] God imparts charity[24] and this charity should not only be returned by man,[25] but also passed on to

---

Franz von Assisi, 179–184; Linden, *Vater*, 117–125, 207–216; Morant, *Unser Weg*, 262–288; Peters, *Aus Liebe*; Rohr, *Der Herr*, 83–91, 102–115, 222–233; Rotzetter, „„Aus Liebe"'; Rotzetter, *Franz von Assisi*, 137–138; Verhey, *Der Mensch*, 122–126.

[22] *Laud Dei* 4–6; *Ep Fid* 1,2,19. *Omnes illos quibus litterae istae pervenerint, rogamus in caritate quae Deus est* (cfr. 1 Joa 4,16)...; *Ep Fid* 2,87. *Ego frater Franciscus, minor servus vester, rogo et obsecro vos in caritate, quae Deus est* (cfr. 1 Joa 4,16)...; *RnB* 17,5. *Unde deprecor in caritate, quae Deus est* (cfr. 1 Joa 4,16)...; *RnB* 22,26. *Sed in sancta caritate, quae Deus est* (cfr. 1 Joa 4,16)...; *Exp Pat* 2. *...inflammans ad amorem, quia tu, Domine, amor es.*

[23] "Dans saint Paul, caritas Dei ou Christi signifie toujours l'amour de Dieu ou du Christ pour nous et non pas notre amour pour Dieu ou pour le Christ, tandis qua dans saint Jean ces expressions ont les deux sens, que le seul contexte distingue" ("Charité", 512). Cf. Hemmerle, *Theologie*, 31: "(...) so erscheint es als die Explikation der *Liebe*, die Gott in sich selbst und über sich hinaus ist und die ihrerseits Liebe wirkt und zur Liebe ruft. Doch die Dynamik der sich verschenkenden, mitteilenden und in der Antwort einholenden Liebe ist wiederum keine andere als die der Nachfolge."

[24] *RnB* 17,16. *Et semper super omnia desiderat divinum timorem et divinam sapientiam et divinum amorem Patris et Filii et Spiritus Sancti*; *RnB* 22,53. *Non pro eis rogo tantum, sed pro eis, qui credituri sunt propter verbum eorum in me* (cfr. Joa 17,17–20) *ut sint consummati in unum, et cognoscat mundus, quia tu me misisti et dilexisti eos, sicut me dilexisti* (Joa 17,23); *RnB* 23,3. *Et gratias agimus tibi, quia sicut per Filium tuum nos creasti, sic per sanctam dilectionem tuam, qua dilexisti nos* (cfr. Joa 17,26)...; *RnB* 23,6. *... propter tuum amorem humiliter deprecamur...*

[25] *Adm* 20,1–2. *Beatus ille religiosus, qui non habet iucunditatem et laetitiam nisi in sanctissimis eloquiis et operibus Domini et cum his producit homines ad amorem Dei cum gaudio et laetitia* (cfr. Ps 50,10); *Ep Fid* 1,1,10; *Ep Fid* 2,52. *Matres, quando portamus eum in corde et corpore nostro* (cfr. 1 Cor 6,20) *per divinum amorem et puram et sinceram conscientiam...*; *Ep Fid* 1,1,13; *Ep Fid* 2,56. *O quam sanctum et quam dilectum, beneplacitum, humilem, pacificum, dulcem, amabilem et super omnia desiderabilem habere talem fratrem et talem filium: Dominum nostrum Jesum Christum, qui posuit animam pro ovibus suis* (cfr. Joa 10,15) *et oravit patri dicens...*; *Ep Fid* 1,2,19. *Omnes illos quibus litterae istae pervenerint, rogamus in caritate quae Deus est* (cfr. 1 Joa 4,16), *ut ista supradicta odorifera verba Domini nostri Jesu Christi cum divino amore benigne recipiant*; *Ep Fid* 2,1. *...frater Franciscus, eorum servus et subditus, obsequium cum reverentia, pacem veram de caelo et sinceram in Domino caritatem*; *Ep Fid* 2,87. *...quod haec verba et alia Domini nostri Jesu Christi cum humilitate et caritate debeatis recipere et operari et observare*; *Ep Ord* 24. *Et sicut super omnes propter hoc ministerium honoravit vos Dominus Deus, ita et vos super omnes ipsum diligite, reveremini et honorate*; *Of Pas* 2,8,5. *...Magnificetur Dominus: qui diligunt salutare tuum*; *Of Pas* 4,14,9. *...et qui diligunt nomen eius habitabunt in ea* (Ps 68,37); *RnB* 22,26. *Sed in sancta caritate, quae Deus est* (cfr. 1 Joa 4,16), *rogo omnes fratres tam ministros quam alios, ut omni impedimento remoto et omni cura et sollicitudine postposita, quocumque modo melius possunt, servire, amare, honorare et adorare Dominum Deum mundo corde et pura mente faciant, quod ipse super omnia quaerit...*; *RnB* 22,54. *Et notum faciam eis nomen tuum, ut dilectio, qua dilexisti me, sit in ipsis et ego in ipsis* (cfr. Joa 17,26); *Reg Er* 5. *Et, quando placuerit, possint petere ab eis eleemosynam sicut parvuli pauperes propter amorem Domini Dei.*

fellow man.[26] Vertical charity (loving God) must also reveal itself in hori-
zontal charity (loving others).[27] This dynamic is the heart of living according to the Gospel: "Der Liebe, die sich uns in Wort und Tat geoffenbart
hat, zu antworten im Loben und Danken und seine Liebe zu erwidern,
indem wir ihn und den Nächsten lieben, das ist der Kern des Lebens nach
dem Evangelium."[28] Francis explains how we should love in his commentary on the *Pater Noster*:

> *Your will be done on earth as in heaven*: That we may love You with our whole
> heart by always thinking of You, with our whole soul by always desiring You,
> with our whole mind by always directing all our intentions to You, and by
> seeking Your glory in everything, with all our whole strength by exerting all
> our energies and affections of body and soul in the service of Your love and
> of nothing else; and we may love our neighbor as ourselves by drawing them
> all to Your love with our whole strength, by rejoicing in the good of others as
> in our own, by suffering with others at their misfortunes, and by giving
> offense to no one. *Give us this day*: in remembrance, understanding, and
> reverence of that love which [our Lord Jesus Christ] had for us and of those
> things that He said and did and suffered for us.[29]

---

[26] *Adm* 9,2–3. *Ille enim veraciter diligit inimicum suum, qui non dolet de iniuria, quam
sibi facit, sed de peccato animae suae uritur propter amorem Dei; Adm* 15,2. *...propter
amorem Domini nostri Jesu Christi in animo et corpore pacem servant; Cant Sol* 10. *Laudato
si, mi signore, per quelli ke perdonano per lo tuo amore, et sostengo infirmitate et tribulatione; Ep Fid* 1,1,1. *Omnes qui Dominum diligunt ex toto corde, ex tota anima et mente, ex tota
virtute* (cfr. Mark 12,30) *et diligunt proximos suos sicut se ipsos* (cfr. Matt 22,39)...; *Ep Fid*
2,18–19. *Sed, o quam beati et benedicti sunt illi, qui Deum diligunt et faciunt, sicut dicit ipse
Dominus in evangelio: Diliges Dominum Deum tuum ex toto corde et ex tota mente, et proximum tuum sicut te ipsum* (Matt 22,37.39). *Diligamus igitur Deum et adoremus eum puro
corde et pura mente...; Ep Min* 2–11. *Dico tibi, sicut possum, de facto animae tuae, quod ea
quae te impediunt amare Dominum Deum, et quicumque tibi impedimentum fecerit sive fratres sive alii, etiam si te verberarent, omnia debes habere pro gratia. Et ita velis et non aliud.
Et hoc sit tibi per veram obedientiam Domini Dei et meam, quia firmiter scio, quod ista est
vera obedientia. Et dilige eos qui ista faciunt tibi. Et non velis aliud de eis, nisi quantum
Dominus dederit tibi. Et in hoc dilige eos; et non velis quod sint meliores christiani. Et istud sit
tibi plus quam eremitorium. Et in hoc volo cognoscere, si tu diligis Dominum et me servum
suum et tuum, si feceris istud, scilicet quod non sit aliquis frater in mundo, qui peccaverit,
quantumcumque potuerit peccare, quod, postquam viderit oculos tuos, numquam recedat
sine misericordia tua, si quaerit misericordiam. Et si non quaereret misericordiam, tu
quaeras ab eo, si vult misericordiam. Et si millies postea coram oculis tuis peccaret, dilige
eum plus quam me ad hoc, ut trahas eum ad Dominum; et semper miserearis talibus; Exp Pat*
8. *Sicut et nos dimittimus debitoribus nostris: et quod non plene dimittimus, tu, Domine, fac
nos plene dimittere, ut inimicos propter te veraciter diligamus et pro eis apud te devote intercedamus...; Laet* 12. *Et ego iterum sto ad ostium et dico: Amore Dei recolligatis me ista nocte.*

[27] Rotzetter, "„Aus Liebe"", 163.

[28] Lehmann, *Franz von Assisi*, 180.

[29] *Ex Pat* 5–6. *Fiat voluntas tua sicut in caelo et in terra: ut amemus te ex toto corde* (cfr.
Luke 10,27) *te semper cogitando, ex tota anima te semper desiderando, ex tota mente omnes
intentiones nostras ad te dirigendo, honorem tuum in omnibus quaerendo et ex omnibus*

God's charity was revealed to the utmost degree in his compassion (*misericordia*) with us, viz., the suffering of Jesus Christ. So should our charity be compassionate charity to the fullest extent.[30] All charity, including active or "humanitarian" *caritas* (charitable deeds), is charity *propter Deum.*[31]

Man

Loving God is part of a complex of spiritual components of which faith, hope, and charity (the theological virtues) are of central importance:

> Wherever we are, in every place, at every hour, at every time of the day, every day and continually, let all of us truly and humbly believe, hold in our heart and love, honor, adore, serve, praise and bless, glorify and exalt, magnify and give thanks to the Most High and Supreme Eternal God, Trinity and Unity, Father, Son and holy Spirit, Creator of all, Savior of all who believe and hope in Him and love him, Who, without beginning and end, is unchangeable, invisible, indescribable, ineffable, incomprehensible, unfathomable, blessed, praiseworthy, glorious, exalted, sublime, most high, gentle, lovable, delightful, and totally desirable above all else for ever. Amen.[32]

---

viribus nostris omnes vires nostras et sensus animae et corporis in obsequium tui amoris et non in alio expendendo; et proximos nostros amemus sicut et nosmetipsos omnes ad amorem tuum pro viribus trahendo, de bonis aliorum sicut de nostris gaudendo et in malis compatiendo et nemini ullam offensionem dando (cfr. 2 Cor 6,3). *Panem nostrum quotidianum: dilectum Filium tuum, Dominum nostrum Jesum Christum, da nobis hodie: in memoriam et intelligentiam et reverentiam amoris, quem ad nos habuit, et eorum, quae pro nobis dixit, fecit et sustulit* (Armstrong, *Francis of Assisi*, 158–159). Cf. *RnB* 23,8. *Omnes diligamus ex toto corde, ex tota anima, ex tota mente, ex tota virtute* (cfr. Mark 12,30) *et fortitudine, ex toto intellectu* (cfr. Mark 12,33), *ex omnibus viribus* (cfr. Luke 10,27), *toto nisu, toto affectu, totis visceribus, totis desideriis et voluntatibus Dominum Deum* (Mark 12,30par.)....

[30] As opposed to erotic love. Cf. Lang, *Ins Freie*, 55–56: "Im Unterschied zu der Gestalt der Liebe, wie sie im platonischen Eros vor den Menschen tritt, ist die barmherzige Liebe *die eigentlich göttliche Gestalt der Liebe*. Während nämlich die Eros-Liebe das Große und das Schöne anstrebt, um daran Anteil zu erlangen, ist die barmherzige Liebe nicht darauf aus, etwas zu haben, sondern etwas zu schenken. Letztlich sich selbst. (...) Eros holt in sich hinein, barmherzige Liebe tritt aus sich heraus, verläßt sich, neigt sich vor dem Darniederliegenden, ist ek-statische Liebe, Entäußerung. Insofern ist diese Gestalt der Liebe eigentlich nur von Gott selbst aus zu Leben." There is a strong parallel here with the connection between divine and human humility; see below, 2.6.

[31] Haskamp, „"Du bist""", 73; Koper, *Das Weltverständnis*, 105; Lang, *Ins Freie*, 53.

[32] *RnB* 23,11. ...*ubique nos omnes omni loco, omni hora et omni tempore, quotidie et continue credamus veraciter et humiliter et in corde teneamus et amemus, honoremus, adoremus, serviamus, laudemus et benedicamus, glorificemus et superexaltemus, magnificemus et gratias agamus altissimo et summo Deo aeterno, trinitati et unitati, Patri et Filio et Spiritui Sancto, creatori omnium et salvatori omnium in se credentium et sperantium et diligentium eum, qui sine initio et sine fine immutabilis, invisibilis, inenarrabilis, ineffabilis, incomprehensibilis, investigabilis* (cfr. Rom 11,33), *benedictus, laudabilis, gloriosus, superexaltatus* (cfr. Dan 3,52), *sublimis, excelsus, suavis, amabilis, delectabilis et totus super omnia*

Charity is a possession of the soul that acknowledges the supremacy of
God (faith), totally desires her Savior (hope), and constantly honors the
"lovable" One. Faith, hope, and charity are thus the true constructive
powers of Christian life and the virtues that lead the praying soul to communion with Christ.[33]

Fellow men

To love one's neighbour means to love others, even enemies,[34] as oneself.[35]
Anger, on the other hand, obstructs charity.[36] The brothers always have to
love the *Rule* given by Francis[37] and, as this *Rule* confirms most explicitly,
each other.[38] Loving each other involves many other virtues. When the

---

desiderabilis in saecula. Amen (Armstrong, *Francis of Assisi*, 85–86). Cf. *Or Cruc. Summe,
gloriose Deus, illumina tenebras cordis mei et da mihi fidem rectam, spem certam et caritatem perfectam, sensum et cognitionem, Domine, ut faciam tuum sanctum et verax
mandatum.*

[33] Engemann, *Das neue Lied.*

[34] *Adm* 9,1–4. *Dicit Dominus: Diligite inimicos vestros [benefacite his qui oderunt vos,
et orate pro persequentibus et calumniantibus vos]* (Matt 5,44). *Ille enim veraciter diligit
inimicum suum, qui non dolet de iniuria, quam sibi facit, sed de peccato animae suae uritur
propter amorem Dei. Et ostendat ei ex operibus dilectionem; Adm* 14,4. *Hi non sunt pauperes
spiritu; quia qui vere pauper est spiritu, se ipsum odit et eos diligit qui eum percutiunt in
maxilla* (cfr. Matt 5,39); *Ep Fid* 2,38. *Debemus diligere inimicos nostros et benefacere his,
qui nos odio habent* (cfr. Matt 5,44; Luke 6,27); *RB* 10,10. *...et diligere eos qui nos persequuntur et reprehendunt et arguunt, quia dicit Dominus: Diligite inimicos vestros et orate pro
persequentibus et calumniantibus vos* (cfr. Matt 5,44); *RnB* 16,11. *Et pro eius amore debent se
exponere inimicis tam visibilibus quam invisibilibus...; RnB* 22,1. *Attendamus, omnes fratres,
quod dicit Dominus: Diligite inimicos vestros et benefacite his qui oderunt vos* (cfr. Matt
5,44par.)...; *RnB* 22,4. *...quos multum diligere debemus, quia ex hoc quod nobis inferunt,
habemus vitam aeternam; Of Pas* 1,1,3. *Et posuerunt adversum me mala pro vobis et odium
pro dilectione mea* (cfr. Ps 108,5). *Pro eo, ut me diligerent, detrahebant mihi ego autem orabam* (Ps 108,4).

[35] *Ep Fid* 2,26–27. *Et diligamus proximos sicut nos ipsos* (cfr. Matt 22,39). *Et si quis non
vult eos amare sicut se ipsum, saltim non inferat eis mala, sed faciat bona.*

[36] *Adm* 11,2. *Et quocumque modo aliqua persona peccaret, et propter hoc servus Dei non
ex caritate turbaretur et irasceretur, thesaurizat sibi culpam* (cfr. Rom 2,5); *RB* 7,3. *Et cavere
debent, ne irascantur et conturbentur propter peccatum alicuius, quia ira et conturbatio in se
et in aliis impediunt caritatem.*

[37] *RnB* 24,3. *...et deprecor omnes cum osculo pedum, ut multum diligant, custodiant et
reponant.*

[38] *RB* 6,8. *Et secure manifestet unus alteri necessitatem suam, quia, si mater nutrit et
diligit filium suum* (cfr. 1 Thess 2,7) *carnalem, quanto diligentius debet quis diligere et nutrire
fratrem suum spiritualem?; RnB* 9,11. *Et quilibet diligat et nutriat fratrem suum, sicut mater
diligit et nutrit filium suum* (cfr. 1 Thess 2,7), *in quibus ei Deus gratiam largietur; RnB* 11,5–6.
*Et diligant se ad invicem, sicut dicit Dominus: Hoc est praeceptum meum ut diligatis
invicem sicut dilexi vos* (Joa 15,12). *Et ostendant ex operibus* (cfr. Jac 2,18) *dilectionem, quam
habent ad invicem, sicut dicit apostolus: Non diligamus verbo neque lingua, sed opere*

brothers really follow Francis's wishes, they always love each other and observe holy poverty.[39] While charity incites a brother, furthermore, to proper obedience,[40] ministers especially ought to be an example of charity, humility, and benignity.[41] Charity is accompanied by wisdom and humility, encourages almsgiving, and dispels sin.[42] It is aimed at the light instead of darkness,[43] at sincerity instead of pleasing others,[44] and at the soul instead of the body.[45] In short, it is aimed at charity itself.[46]

---

et veritate (1 Joa 3,18); *Adm* 24–25. *Beatus servus, qui tantum diligeret fratrem suum, quando est infirmus, quod non potest ei satisfacere, quantum quando est sanus, qui potest ei satisfacere. Beatus servus, qui tantum diligeret et timeret fratrem suum, cum esset longe ab ipso, sicuti quando esset cum eo, et non diceret aliquid post ipsum, quod cum caritate non posset dicere coram ipso; Ep Ord* 2. *Reverendis et multum diligendis fratribus universis...; Ep Ord* 12. *Deprecor itaque omnes vos fratres cum osculo pedum et ea caritate, qua possum....*

[39] *Testamentum Senis factum* 3–4. *...ut in signum memoriae meae benedictionis et mei testamenti semper diligant se ad invicem, semper diligant et observent dominam nostram sanctam paupertatem.*

[40] *RnB* 5,14. *...immo magis per caritatem spiritus voluntarie serviant et obediant invicem* (cfr. Gal 5,13); *Test* 8. *Et ipsos et omnes alios volo timere, amare et honorare, sicut meos dominos; Adm* 3,6. *Nam haec est caritativa obedientia* (cfr. 1 Pet 1,22), *quia Deo et proximo satisfacit; Sal Virt* 3. *Domina sancta caritas, Dominus te salvet cum tua sorore sancta obedientia.* Cf. Haskamp, „„Du bist"", 77–80; Rotzetter, „„Aus Liebe"", 162.

[41] *RB* 10,1. *Fratres, qui sunt ministri et servi aliorum fratrum, visitent et moneant fratres suos et humiliter et caritative corrigant eos, non praecipientes eis aliquid, quod sit contra animam suam et regulam nostram; RB* 10,5. *Ministri vero caritative et benigne eos recipiant et tantam familiaritatem habeant circa ipsos, ut dicere possint eis et facere sicut domini servis suis....*

[42] *Adm* 27,1. *Ubi caritas est et sapientia, ibi nec timor nec ignorantia; Ep Fid* 2,30. *Habeamus itaque caritatem et humilitatem; et faciamus eleemosynas, quia ipsa lavat animas a sordibus peccatorum* (cfr. Tob 4,11; 12,9); *RnB* 9,9. *Et fratres, qui eam acquirendo laborant, magnam mercedem habebunt et faciunt lucrari et acquirere tribuentes; quia omnia quae relinquent homines in mundo peribunt, sed de caritate et de eleemosynis, quas fecerunt, habebunt praemium a Domino; Sal Virt* 13. *Sancta caritas confundit omnes diabolicas et carnales tentationes et omnes carnales timores* (cfr. 1 Joa 4,18).

[43] I.e., (not) observing the commandments. *Ep Fid* 2,16. *Qui nolunt gustare, quam suavis sit Dominus* (cfr. Ps 33,9) *et diligunt tenebras magis quam lucem* (Joa 3,19) *nolentes adimplere mandata Dei, maledicti sunt....*

[44] *Ep Fid* 14. *Rogo etiam in Domino omnes fratres meos sacerdotes, qui sunt et erunt et esse cupiunt sacerdotes Altissimi, quod quandocumque missam celebrare voluerint, puri pure faciant cum reverentia verum sacrificium sanctissimi corporis et sanguinis Domini nostri Jesu Christi sancta intentione et munda non pro ulla terrena re neque timore vel amore alicuius hominis, quasi placentes hominibus* (cfr. Eph 6,6; Col 3,22).

[45] *RnB* 10,4. *...quia plus diligit corpus quam animam; RnB* 22,5. *Et odio habeamus corpus nostrum cum vitiis et peccatis suis; quia carnaliter vivendo vult diabolus a nobis auferre amorem Jesu Christi et vitam aeternam et se ipsum cum omnibus perdere in infernum.*

[46] Cf. *Ep Ord* 31. *Si vero plures in loco fuerint sacerdotes, sit per amorem caritatis alter contentus auditu celebrationis alterius sacerdotis....* Cf. Rotzetter, „„Aus Liebe"".

Bonaventure

The form of perfection

In Francis's writings, charity is the atmosphere of his prayer, the seal of his spirituality, the first law of his fraternity, and the fundamental message that his brothers have to preach.[47] In Bonaventure's spiritual writings, charity has a slightly different, and particularly more theological, function.[48] In his line of approach it is, first, a gift of the Holy Spirit without which "perfection of merit cannot be obtained," and, second, the form of the virtues *(forma virtutum)*, which "alone leads man to perfection."[49] Because charity is the root, form, purpose, fulfilment, and bond of perfection[50] – but some forms of charity are still imperfect[51] – no one should deem himself perfect before reaching the state and the level of perfect love.[52]

In the third chapter of his *Defense of the Mendicants*, in which Bonaventure deals with the "conditions of evangelical perfection and its sublime state and many levels," the role of charity is further explained.

---

[47] Iriarte, *Vocazione*, 86.

[48] Cf. Iriarte, *Vocazione*, 86. On Bonaventure and charity, see for instance: Alszeghy, *Grundformen*; Châtillon, "Le primat"; Delhaye, "La charité"; Ennis, "The Place"; Ennis, "The Primacy"; Fehlner, *The Role*, 111–144, 160–176; "Frères", 1330–1331; Guardini, *Systembildende*, 57–60; Hayes, *The Hidden*, 37–38; Hellmann, *Ordo*; Hoefs, *Erfahrung*, 62–81; Kaup, *Die theologische*; Prentice, *The Psychology*; Schlosser, *Cognitio*; Speer, *Triplex*, 143, 163–172; Strack, *Christusleid*, 39–51, 114–120.

[49] *Ap Paup* 3,22. *...perfectio vero meriti obtineri non possit sine caritate, quae est donum Spiritus sancti...* (*Doctoris* 8, 250; De Vinck, *The Works* 4, 55); *Perf* 7,1. *Nunc septimo loco restat dicendum de forma virtutum, scilicet caritate, quae sola ducit hominem ad perfectionem* (*Doctoris* 8, 124; De Vinck, *The Works* 1, 248). Cf. *Trip Via* Prol,1. *...perfectio ad caritatem* (*Doctoris* 8, 3; De Vinck, *The Works* 1, 63). It should be noted that love is not possible without good deeds ("merit"): *...si autem operari renuit, amor non est* (*Doctoris* 8, 250; De Vinck, *The Works* 4, 53).

[50] *Ap Paup* 3,2. *Sciendum est igitur, quod radix, forma, finis, complementum et vinculum perfectionis caritas est...* (*Doctoris* 8, 244; De Vinck, *The Works* 4, 37). Cf. *Ap Paup* 3,19. *...in qua radix caritatis est pinguior... Quamquam enim totius huius perfectionis origo sit caritas...* (*Doctoris* 8, 249; De Vinck, *The Works* 4, 52); *Ap Paup* 7,1. *In caritate radicati et fundati...* (*Doctoris* 8, 272; De Vinck, *The Works* 4, 125); *Ap Paup* 1,8. *Perfectum autem secundum se est actus difficilis a caritatis sublimitate procedens...* (*Doctoris* 8, 238; De Vinck, *The Works* 4, 14).

[51] *Ap Paup* 2,3. *Cum ergo aliqua caritas sit imperfecta...* (*Doctoris* 8, 240; De Vinck, *The Works* 4, 21). There are also false forms of charity, e.g., *...qui amaritudines mundi diligunt...* (*Sol* 2,2,8; *Doctoris* 8, 47; De Vinck, *The Works* 3, 83).

[52] *Trip Via* 2,3,8. *Et hic est status et gradus perfectae caritatis, ante cuius assecutionem nemo debet se aestimare perfectum* (*Doctoris* 8, 9; De Vinck, *The Works* 1, 76). Cf. *Ap Paup* 6,2. *...utrumque tamen perfectum in Christo, quia ex perfectissima caritate processit* (*Doctoris* 8, 267; De Vinck, *The Works* 4, 108).

Theologically speaking, charity functions on three different levels of perfection, and has a corresponding threefold act:

> Now, this love may exist in a threefold state. The first and lower consists in the observance of the commandments of the Law; the second and intermediate, in the fulfillment of the spiritual counsels; the third and supreme in the enjoyment of eternal delights [through mystical contemplation].
> Thus there is a threefold gradation of perfection, as the Scriptures show.[53]

> But these two, indeed, the counsels as well as the commands, tend toward the fulfillment and observance of that love which the Apostle describes to Timothy: Now the end of the commandment is charity, from a pure heart, and a good conscience and an unfeigned faith. This betokens in reality a threefold act of love: avoiding evil, pursuing good, and bearing with adversity. For as regards the avoidance of evil, charity is said to be from a pure heart; as regards the pursuit of good, from a good conscience; and as regards the bearing of adversity, from a faith unfeigned.[54]

To reach perfect love one starts with the observance of the commandments, the avoidance of evil (as "indicated by the Holy Scriptures"), and purity of heart; one develops it further with the fulfilment of the evangelical counsels, the pursuit of good (this "more eagerly than is required by precept"), and a good conscience; one accomplishes it in the enjoyment of mystical delights, the bearing of adversity (this "more perfectly than is required by precept"), and sincere faith.[55] The following scriptural passages may further illustrate these three levels of perfection and love: "If anyone would come after me, he must deny himself and take up his cross

---

[53] *Ap Paup* 3,2. *Ipsa vero caritas triplicem habet statum: unum quidem infimum, in observantia mandatorum legalium; secundum vero medium, qui constat in adimpletione spiritualium consiliorum; tertium autem supremum, in perfruitione sempiternalium iucunditatum. Ideo triplex est perfectionis differentia in Scriptura sacra descripta...* (*Doctoris* 8, 244; De Vinck, *The Works* 4, 37).

[54] *Ap Paup* 3,3. *Omnia vero, tam praecepta quam consilia, referuntur ad caritatis illius impletionem et observantiam, quam sic describit Apostolus ad Timotheum: Caritas est finis praecepti de corde puro, conscientia bona et fide non ficta, insinuans triplicem actum caritatis, videlicet declinare mala, prosequi bona et patienter ferre adversa. Nam propter declinationem malorum dicitur de corde puro; propter prosecutionem bonorum, de conscientia bona; propter tolerantiam adversorum, de fide non ficta...* (*Doctoris* 8, 245; De Vinck, *The Works* 4, 38–39).

[55] Cf. *Ap Paup* 3,6. *Consistit autem supererogativa condescensio caritatis ad proximum in hoc... Per hunc etiam modum supererogativa sursumactio mentis in Deum in hoc attenditur, ut secundum legem mentalis munditiae ac pacis per amorem ecstaticum in divinos splendores et ardores sacrum mens devota sentiat et patiatur excessum...* (*Doctoris* 8, 246; De Vinck, *The Works* 4, 40–41); *Ap Paup* 3,7. *...verum etiam, ut ex fervore divini amoris magno desiderio illa praeoptet et cum gaudio magno sustineat...* (*Doctoris* 8, 246; De Vinck, *The Works* 4, 41).

and follow me"; "Love your enemies and pray for those who persecute you"; and "Perseverance must finish its work so that you may be mature and complete, not lacking anything."[56]

Origin and effects

Charity and all the other pure virtues (humility, chastity, mercy, and the like) proceed from the eternal law, in the absence of which no man may be saved at any time.[57] At the same time, "charity is brevity," containing the whole law in itself;[58] divine law is made up entirely of charity.[59] Because its foundation is the eternal Good, charity cannot be defeated.[60] It has many good qualities and it is the source of many good things:

> (...) love is longsuffering in adversity, restrained in prosperity, powerful against passion, joyful in good works, secure in temptation, generously hospitable, happy among true brothers, patient among the false, undisturbed by abuse, doing good while bearing evil, remaining peaceful in the midst of anger and innocent among deceitful men, weeping over sin, and living by truth.
>
> O faithful love, the source of strong character, pure affection, penetrating thought, holy desire, noble work, rich virtue, lofty merit, great reward and honor![61]

With his ode to charity, which quotes Augustine, Bonaventure shows himself to be deeply convinced of the miraculous and powerful effects of

---

[56] *Ap Paup* 3,5–7. *Qui vult venire post me adneget semetipsum* [cfr. Matt 16,24].... *Diligite inimicos vestros, benefacite his qui oderunt vos* [cfr. Matt 5,44].... *Patientia opus perfectum habet, ut sitis perfecti et integri, in nullo deficientes* [cfr. Jac 1,4] (*Doctoris* 8, 245–246; De Vinck, *The Works* 4, 40–41).

[57] *Sex Alis* 2,7. *Horum quaedam procedunt a lege aeterna, ut purae virtutes: humilitas, castitas, caritas, misericordia et similes, sine quibus nullus quocumque tempore poterit salvari...* (*Doctoris* 8, 134; De Vinck, *The Works* 3, 144).

[58] *Ex Reg* 9,12. *...brevitas est caritas, quae Legem continet in se totam* (*Doctoris* 8, 430).

[59] *Ap Paup* 10,14. *...servata divina lege, quae tota completur in caritate* (*Doctoris* 8, 309; De Vinck, *The Works* 4, 233).

[60] *Ex Reg* 6,26. *...tum quia caritas fundamentum habet sui bonum infinitum, propter quod nihil finitum praevalet contra eam* (*Doctoris* 8, 425). Cf. *Ap Paup* 1,7. *Tertium autem est bonum secundum se, quod nullo modo potest male fieri, sicut est opus virtutis ex caritatis radice procedens* (*Doctoris* 8, 238; De Vinck, *The Works* 4, 13).

[61] *Sol* 1,4,45. *...in adversitatibus tolerat, in prosperitatibus temperat, in duris passionibus est fortis, in bonis operibus hilaris, in tentatione tutissima, in hospitalitate liberalissima, inter veros fratres laetissima, inter falsos patientissima, inter opprobria secura, inter odia benefica, inter iras placida, inter insidias innocens, in iniquitate gemens, in veritate respirans. O felix amor, ex quo oritur strenuitas morum, puritas affectuum, subtilitas intellectuum, sanctitas desideriorum, claritas operum, fecunditas virtutum, dignitas meritorum, sublimitas praemiorum et honorum* (*Doctoris* 8, 43; De Vinck, *The Works* 3, 73). Cf. *Trip Via* 2,4,11. *Studendum est igitur ad proficiendum in caritate, cum profectus eius inducat perfectionem omnium bonorum...* (*Doctoris* 8, 11; De Vinck, *The Works* 1, 78–79).

the "fecundity (*fecunditas*) of all virtues," "queen (*principata*) of all virtues," and "essence (*forma*) and life (*vita*) and virtue (*virtus*) of all virtues," charity.[62] In its absence all virtues are worthless and in its presence all virtues are implied, says the Gloss on the words of the apostle Paul.[63] Charity alone "closes hell, opens heaven, restores the hope of salvation, and makes a soul agreeable to God."[64]

Charity is twofold, according to the "double commandment": love God above all else and love the neighbour for the sake of God.[65] The love of God has six degrees: sensitivity, avidity, satiety, ebriety, security, and tranquillity.[66] Only when these are realized, can one also reach perfect love of others.[67] Morally speaking, the love for God inflames us with zeal for justice, while the love for others moves us to kindness.[68] We should, therefore, strive for it more than for anything else.[69] Spiritually speaking, the love of God brings hunger for divine sweetness.[70] Thus, continuous and intense prayer (i.e., deploring one's misery, imploring God's mercy, rendering worship) is a necessity.[71] Mystically speaking, perfect charity and

---

[62] *Sol* 1,4,45. *Caritas enim omnium virtutum obtinet principatum* (*Doctoris* 8, 43–44; De Vinck, *The Works* 3, 73); *Perf* 7,1. *Nunc septimo loco restat dicendum de forma virtutum, scilicet caritate... Caritas est vita virtutum... Tantae virtutis caritas est, quod ipsa sola inter virtutes virtus nominata est...* (*Doctoris* 8, 124; De Vinck, *The Works* 1, 248). Cf. *Trip Via* Prol,1. *...et secundum quod circa haec versatur, suscipit meriti incrementum* (*Doctoris* 8, 3; De Vinck, *The Works* 1, 63).

[63] *Perf* 7,1. *Attende, quanta sit caritas, quae si desit, frustra habentur cetera; si autem adsit, habentur omnia...* (*Doctoris* 8, 124; De Vinck, *The Works* 1, 248).

[64] *Perf* 7,1. *Tantae siquidem virtutis est caritas, quod ipsa sola claudit infernum, sola aperit caelum, sola spem salutis tribuit, sola Deo amabilem reddit* (*Doctoris* 8, 124; De Vinck, *The Works* 1, 248).

[65] *Perf* 7,1. *...et non cuilibet caritati, sed ei solum, qua Deus diligitur super omnia et proximus propter Deum* (*Doctoris* 8, 124; De Vinck, *The Works* 1, 248). Cf. *Ap Paup* 1,8. *...ut est motus fervidae et ecstaticae dilectionis in Deum, vel purae et plenae dilectionis ad inimicum* (*Doctoris* 8, 238; De Vinck, *The Works* 4, 14).

[66] *Trip Via* 2,4,9–11 (*Doctoris* 8, 10–11; De Vinck, *The Works* 1, 77–79).

[67] *Trip Via* 2,3,8. *Ad hanc perfectam dilectionem proximi non pervenitur, nisi prius perveniatur ad perfectam dilectionem Dei, propter quem diligitur proximus, qui non est amabilis nisi propter Deum* (*Doctoris* 8, 10; De Vinck, *The Works* 1, 76–77).

[68] *Sex Alis* 3,1. *... sicut eum caritas Dei ad zelum iustitiae inflammat, ita fraterna dilectio ad pietatem informet* (*Doctoris* 8, 136; De Vinck, *The Works* 3, 151); *Sex Alis* 2,5. *Zelus enim iustitiae quasi coccus bis tinctus duplici caritatis colore rutilat, amoris Dei et proximi* (*Doctoris* 8, 133; De Vinck, *The Works* 3, 143).

[69] *Perf* 7,1. *...prae cunctis virtutibus caritati est insistendum...* (*Doctoris* 8, 124; De Vinck, *The Works* 1, 248); *Trip Via* 2,4,11. *Studendum est igitur ad proficiendum in caritate...* (*Doctoris* 8, 11; De Vinck, *The Works* 1, 78–79).

[70] *Trip Via* 2,4,9. *...quando meditationes circa amorem Dei suavitatem pariunt in corde... quando scilicet anima assuefieri coeperit circa illam suavitatem, nascitur in ea tanta esuries...* (*Doctoris* 8, 10; De Vinck, *The Works* 1, 77).

[71] *Trip Via* 2,4,12. *Qui autem sic excitaverit se continue et intente, proficiet in caritate...* (*Doctoris* 8, 11; De Vinck, *The Works* 1, 79).

the love of the Holy Spirit are attained gradually by alert watchfulness, comforting trust, inflaming desire, uplifting rapture, joyful peace, trans-porting happiness, and perfecting intimacy.[72] Through these seven steps lovers of Christ "fly to this garden of love" and "rise to the paradise of love," the heights of the heart, on the wings of faith and hope.[73]

David

Context

Charity is the most important virtue in the *Profectus religiosorum*. It is a constant theme in the first and second book, and a central theme in the third. There, David deals with the seven stages (*processus*) of religious life: fervor, austerity, consolation, temptation, self-mastery (remedies), holi-ness (virtues), and wisdom. In the fifth stage, the remedies dealt with in the second book return in the form of discipline, exercise, and virtue against the vices. More important here is the sixth stage, the development of the virtues, which is conceived as a remedy of vice in itself. David pre-sents seven key virtues of spiritual progress: charity, humility, patience, obedience, poverty, sobriety, and chastity. Of these virtues, all of which are dealt with profoundly and extensively, charity is the director, the "charioteer."

---

[72] *Trip Via* 3,4,6. *Gradus veniendi ad dulcorem caritatis per susceptionem Spiritus sancti sunt isti septem, scilicet vigilantia sollicitans, confidentia confortans, concupiscen-tia inflammans, excedentia elevans, complacentia quietans, laetitia delectans, adhaeren-tia conglutinans; in quibus hoc ordine progredi debes, qui vis ad perfectionem caritatis pertingere et ad amorem Spiritus sancti* (*Doctoris* 8, 14; De Vinck, *The Works* 1, 86). Cf. *Trip Via* 3,5,8. *...adhaerentia te conglutinet propter amoris eius fortitudinem...* (*Doctoris* 8, 15; De Vinck, *The Works* 1, 88); *Trip Via* 2,4,11. *...quia impossibile est ad istam tranquillitatem pertingere nisi per caritatem* (*Doctoris* 8, 11; De Vinck, *The Works* 1, 78); *Trip Via* 3,1,1. *Necesse est ergo, ut qui vult ad illam beatitudinem per merita pervenire, istorum trium similitudinem, secundum quod possibile est, in via sibi comparet, ut scilicet habeat soporem pacis, splendorem veritatis, dulcorem caritatis* (*Doctoris* 8, 12; De Vinck, *The Works* 1, 80).

[73] *Vit Myst* 24,1. *Confortare nunc igitur, anima mea, et elevare, misera et infirma, et alis fidei et spei ad hunc hortum caritatis enitere... ad paradisum caritatis ascende, ascende, inquam, ad cor altum, quia ecce, quem quaeris exaltatus est* (*Doctoris* 8, 187; De Vinck, *The Works* 1, 202). Cf. *Vit Myst* 24,3. *Tandem accedendum est ad cor illud humillimum altissimi Iesu, per ianuam videlicet lateris lanceati; ibi procul dubio thesaurus ineffabilis desiderabilis caritatis latet...* (*Doctoris* 8, 188; De Vinck, *The Works* 1, 204). Here, in the context of the love of Christ, charity is also one of the three theological virtues (faith, hope, charity). Cf. *Ap Paup* 7,1. *Hoc quidem in nostro intellectu collocatur per fidem, quam idem Apostolus ad Hebraeos dicit rerum sperandarum esse substantiam, in affectu vero per caritatem...* (*Doctoris* 8, 272; De Vinck, *The Works* 4, 125).

Charity and the other virtues

Charity leads the train of virtues that function together as the most effective remedy of vice and the substratum of spiritual progress. On account of its diversity of action, this virtue is even said to be the mother and wet-nurse of all other virtues[74] and "to be carrying" them (*in se omnem habens virtutem*), containing them as a variety of functions and a variety of names. Virtue in Augustinian terms being "well-ordered love" (*amor ordinatus*), charity is virtue in the following "order":

> Charity, then, directed towards God is *love of God*; towards our neighbour, is *love of others*. Where it moves us to compassionate suffering, it is *mercy*; to rejoice in another's welfare, *noble-mindedness*. In helping us to bear our own trials well, it is *patience*; in inspiring us with kindness towards enemies, *benignity*. Holding us back from self-assertion, it is *humility*; prompting us to be compliant with authority, *obedience*; restraining us from material super-fluities, *sobriety*; urging us to renunciation of wealth, *poverty of spirit*. As *generosity*, it inclines us to give liberally to the poor; as *longanimity*, it rouses us against the tedium of delay; as *prudence*, it knows how to differentiate wisely between the degrees of good and evil. Giving to each one his due, it is *justice*; restraining us from soft surrender to pleasure, it is *temperance*; encouraging us in face of difficulties, it is *fortitude*; vitalizing our beliefs, it is *faith*; confirming our confidence, it is *hope*.[75]

---

[74] *Prof* 3,33. *Caritas Dei, mater et nutrix omnium virtutum* (*David ab Augusta*, 228; Devas, *Spiritual Life* 2, 66). Cf. "Frères", 1330.

[75] *Prof* 3,32. *Ita caritas est una virtus in se omnem habens virtutem, sed propter diversos effectus eius ex diversis extrinsecis occasionibus vel causis illatis, quibus se vel contra malum opponit, vel ad bonum extendit, diversa officia vel nomina sortitur. Virtus enim, sicut definit Augustinus, 'est amor ordinatus', videlicet, ut amet solum quod debet et sicut debet et quantum debet. Quantum vero amas aliquid, tantum odis et fugis eius contrarium, ubi potes. Caritas igitur, cum se extendit ad diligendum Deum,* dilectio Dei *dicitur; cum ad proximum,* dicitur dilectio proximi; *cum eius miseriae compatitur,* misericordia *appellatur; cum eius bono congaudet,* congratulatio *vocatur; cum aequanimiter adversa tolerat,* patientia *dicitur; cum benefacit se odientibus,* benignitas *nuncupatur; cum non extollitur inaniter supra se,* humilitas *est; cum obtemperat superioribus, ut iustum est,* obedientia *est; cum exsecratur turpia,* castitas *est; cum resecat superflua corporalis necessitatis,* sobrietas *est; cum divitias abiicit,* paupertas spiritus *est; cum ad pauperes eas liberaliter effundit,* largitas *est; cum taedio exspectationis promissorum non frangitur,* longanimitas *est; cum inter bonum et melius et inter malum et peius discernit,* prudentia *est; cum ius suum cuique tribuit,* iustitia *est; cum delectationibus non emollitur,* temperantia *est; cum duris non terretur,* fortitudo *est; cum credit credenda,* fides *est; cum sperat speranda,* spes est (*David ab Augusta*, 226–227; Devas, *Spiritual Life* 2, 65–66). Cf. *Prof* 3,37. *Vera beatitudo consistit in cognitione summae veritatis, in dilectione vel delectatione summae bonitatis...* (*David ab Augusta*, 243; Devas, *Spiritual Life* 2, 80); *Prof* 3,38. *Hic est humilis, non cogente necessitate, sed veritatis caritate* (*David ab Augusta*, 251; Devas, *Spiritual Life* 2, 87); *Prof* 3,39. *Ex caritate et humilitate nascitur virtus patientiae* (*David ab Augusta*, 251; Devas, *Spiritual Life* 2, 87); *Prof* 3,42. *Et quia obedientia ex caritate et humilitate et patientia nascitur...* (*David ab Augusta*, 261; Devas, *Spiritual Life* 2,

Here, charity takes the form of many virtues, such as the four cardinal virtues (prudence, justice, temperance, fortitude),[76] and *is* the other theological virtues (faith, hope). Elsewhere in the *Profectus religiosorum*, charity is one *of* the three theological virtues: in the third stage ("consolation") of the third book, where the three theological virtues of faith, hope, and charity are "strengthened and enkindled" by genuine spiritual consolations;[77] in the sixth stage ("virtue") of this book, where the theological virtues *precede* the four cardinal virtues;[78] and in the seventh stage ("wisdom") of this book, where an increase in faith, hope, and charity is received through prayer.[79]

Together with the moon of faith and the stars of virtue (the other virtues), the sun of charity brings light, warmth, coherence, vigor, and merit into the lives of the faithful.[80] Charity is one of the seven "movements of the will," with hope, fear, joy, sorrow, hatred, and remorse;[81] it is one of the seven "kinds of devotion" or "human affections directed towards God," with fear, sorrow, desire, compassion, joy, and rapture of admiration;[82] and it is one of the "affections" that have to be ordered "into virtues" under

---

97); *Est enim triplex obedientia: necessitatis, cupiditatis, caritatis* (*David ab Augusta*, 263; Devas, *Spiritual Life* 2, 98); Bohl, *Geistlicher*, 435–437.

[76] Pansters, *De kardinale*, 180–183.

[77] *Prof* 3,2. *Item, ad confortationem fidei, ad robur spei, ad caritatis accensionem* (*David ab Augusta*, 166; Devas, *Spiritual Life* 2, 8).

[78] *Prof* 3,28. *Multae sunt aliae virtutum artificiales divisiones, secundum quod aliae dicuntur theologicae, ut fides, spes, caritas; aliae cardinales, ut prudentia, iustitia, fortitudo, temperantia...* (*David ab Augusta*, 217; Devas, *Spiritual Life* 2, 56).

[79] *Prof* 3,57. *Vult enim Deus non tam orari, ut donet quod et ante dare disposuit, sed vult, ut plus orando mereamur per fidem, qua credimus orandum quem non videmus; per spem, qua obtinere confidimus petita; per caritatem, qua exauditorem amplius amemus...* (*David ab Augusta*, 323; Devas, *Spiritual Life* 2, 156).

[80] *Prof* 3,56. *...quia per solem caritatis et lunam fidei et stellas aliarum virtutum corda fidelium illuminantur et vitam et ordinem et meritorum vigorem quasi per lucem et calorem siderum consequuntur* (*David ab Augusta*, 318; Devas, *Spiritual Life* 2, 151).

[81] *Prof* 3,28. *Septem autem sunt affectiones mentis communiter: spes et timor, gaudium et moeror, amor et odium et pudor* (*David ab Augusta*, 215–216; Devas, *Spiritual Life* 2, 55). These affections are derived from the Aristotelian passions appetite, anger, fear, confidence, envy, joy, friendly feeling, hatred, longing, emulation, pity, and in general the feelings that are accompanied by pleasure or pain (Aristotle, *Ethica Nicomachea* 2,5; Aristotle, 86–87).

[82] *Prof* 3,65. *Aut enim surgit devotio ex timore, aut ex dolore, aut ex desiderio, aut ex amore, aut ex compassione, aut ex gaudio, aut ex admirationis stupore* (*David ab Augusta*, 352; Devas, *Spiritual Life* 2, 183); *Prof* 3,65. *Aliquando commixtum ex diversarum affectionum motibus devotio conflatur, ut timor cum dolore, amor cum gaudio et admiratione, compassio cum desiderii ardore iungatur* (*David ab Augusta*, 354; Devas, *Spiritual Life* 2, 186). Cf. *Prof* 3,64. *Nec mirum, si hoc possunt affectiones divinae efficere, quarum virtus fortior est, cum etiam humanae affectiones hoc interdum valeant, ut subitus terror et subita et immoderata laetitia et subitus dolor et odium immensum et intemperatus amor* (*David ab Augusta*, 349; Devas, *Spiritual Life* 2, 181).

the calm guidance of right reason, with fear, hate, sorrow, and joy.[83] Elsewhere, the "devout affections that adorn human will" consist of fervor of faith, steadfastness of hope, sweetness of charity, alacrity in well doing, confidence about the forgiveness of past sin, and devotion to the person of Christ.[84] In the heart of God's servant, divine love, holy fear, the fervor of a good will, humility, alertness (piety) and joy born of hope, and devotion reign.[85]

Next, charity is one of the virtues in which a good religious should exercise himself constantly: humility, charity, obedience, meekness, and care in giving good example.[86] It is one of the virtues by which religious are bound to good actions, the virtues "that should be manifest to men": faith, charity, justice, truth, chastity, obedience, and contempt for worldly interests.[87] These virtues should be loved, like vices should be hated.[88] Charity is, furthermore, one of the "remedial" and "real" virtues that are acquired by "the third and best kind of religious," the Caathites (as opposed to the Gersonites and the Merarites), virtues that are possessed by the holy. Together with the other remedial virtues of humility, self-control (benignity), zeal, generosity, temperance (sobriety), and chastity, "real" charity combats the capital vices and "sets up the inward sanctuary of the soul."[89] Elsewhere, the virtues of humility, love of one's neighbour,

---

[83] *Prof*, Epist 2. *...et omnes affectus in virtutes ordinare, ut non amet nisi amanda, et prout sunt amanda, nec timeat nisi timenda, odiat odienda, doleat dolenda, gaudeat de gaudendis, et sic in omnibus rationis ductu quasi naturali motu tranquille feratur...* (*David ab Augusta*, 61–62; Devas, *Spiritual Life* 1, 54–55).

[84] *Prof* 3,2. *Ornatus voluntatis sunt sanctae affectiones et devotio ad Deum, fervor fidei, fiducia spei, dulcedo caritatis et bonae voluntatis alacritas, spes de remissione peccatorum, devotio circa Christi humanitatem et passionem nec non circa eius divinitatem... quae afficiunt hominem ad Deum et ad amorem virtutum et ad odium vitiorum et dilectionem proximorum et ad studia bonorum operum...* (*David ab Augusta*, 165; Devas, *Spiritual Life* 2, 7).

[85] *Prof* 3,59. *Affectus enim amoris Dei et sancti timoris cum fervore bonae voluntatis, in spiritu humilitatis et motu pietatis et gaudio spei nunquam debet in corde servi Dei exstingui. Ista namque sunt in quibus virtus devotionis maxime consistit* (*David ab Augusta*, 329; Devas, *Spiritual Life* 2, 161–162).

[86] *Prof*, Epist 2. *Tertius, opera exercitare virtutum, ut obsequia humilitatis, servitia caritatis, assiduitas obediendi, mansuete loquendi, variis exercitiis bonum exemplum dandi...* (*David ab Augusta*, 60; Devas, *Spiritual Life* 1, 54).

[87] *Prof* 2,12. *Bona nostra, ad quae tenemur ex praecepto Dei vel Ecclesiae, vel ad quae ex manifesto voto adstringimur, debemus hominibus ostendere, ut fidem, caritatem, iustitiam, veritatem, castitatem, obedientiam et contemptum mundanorum* (*David ab Augusta*, 97; Devas, *Spiritual Life* 1, 93).

[88] *Prof* 3,2. *...quae afficiunt hominem ad Deum et ad amorem virtutum et ad odium vitiorum et dilectionem proximorum et ad studia bonorum operum...* (*David ab Augusta*, 165; Devas, *Spiritual Life* 2, 7).

[89] *Prof* 2,3. *Hi sunt qui student interiorem hominem suum, in quo Christus inhabitat per fidem, componere et ad veras virtutes se exercere et vitia carnis et spiritus exstirpare, iram,*

meekness, love of God, contempt of riches, sobriety, and chastity make up the order of virtues (*ordo virtutum*) opposing the seven vices,[90] but this kind of variation fits in with a general inconsistency in the tradition of defining the "remedial virtues."[91]

The virtue

Caritas, dilectio, and *amor* all mean the same thing.[92] David alternates smoothly between the three terms. He defines charity as "the strong and well-ordered will to serve God, to please God, and to rejoice in the possession of God."[93] Charity first of all consists in *will*, determining what is good; in *action*, furthering what is good and removing evil; and in *affection*, joy in the very labor itself by way of recompense and alleviation.[94] Then, charity has three degrees, three "grades of excellence," marked by three stages, i.e., beginning, progress, and perfection.[95] Fear of God's punishments marks the love of beginners; desire for benefits from God, the love of those who progress; a deep affection of pure love, the love of the perfect.[96] Next, charity is "ordered virtue" with a variety of functions and names, as explained above. After that, charity is "first charity": the resolute good and

---

invidiam, avaritiam, accidiam, superbiam, gulam, luxuriam, viriliter expugnare et his contrarias virtutes cordi inserere: humilitatem, caritatem, mansuetudinem, devotionem, largitatem, sobrietatem et castitatem. Istae enim virtutes sunt verum sanctuarium, et qui habet eas sanctus est (David ab Augusta, 81; Devas, *Spiritual Life* 1, 76).

[90] *Prof* 3,30. *Huic per contrarium opponitur ordo virtutum, scilicet humilitas contra superbiam, dilectio proximi contra invidiam, mititas contra iram, caritas Dei contra accidiam, contemptus divitiarum contra avaritiam, sobrietas contra gulam, castitas contra luxuriam (David ab Augusta,* 222; Devas, *Spiritual Life* 2, 61). Cf. *Prof* 3,39. *...sicut caritas Dei opponitur accidiae, et caritas proximi invidiae...* (*David ab Augusta,* 253; Devas, *Spiritual Life* 2, 89).

[91] Pansters, *De kardinale,* 19.

[92] *Prof* 3,31. *Caritas, dilectio Dei et amor idem sunt (David ab Augusta,* 223; Devas, *Spiritual Life* 2, 62).

[93] *Prof* 3,31. *Caritas est ordinata et magna voluntas serviendi Deo, placendi Deo, fruendi Deo (David ab Augusta,* 223; Devas, *Spiritual Life* 2, 62).

[94] *Prof* 3,31. *Dilectio nostra in tribus consistit: in voluntate, in opere, in affectu (David ab Augusta,* 224; Devas, *Spiritual Life* 2, 62–63). Cf. *Prof* 3,2. *...voluntas accenditur ad amorem boni...* (*David ab Augusta,* 164; Devas, *Spiritual Life* 2, 6).

[95] *Prof* 3,33. *...et quibus profectuum gradibus distinguantur. Unaquaeque enim virtus, teste beato Gregorio, habet initium suum et profectum et perfectionem...* (*David ab Augusta,* 227; Devas, *Spiritual Life* 2, 66).

[96] *Prof* 3,42. *Obedientia caritatis est, quando ex caritate Dei vel propter Deum et propter divinam remunerationem obeditur, large sumto nomine caritatis, quo tam timor poenae quam desiderium praemii quam affectus amoris Dei includitur, quorum primum est incipientium, secundum proficientium, tertium perfectorum (David ab Augusta,* 263; Devas, *Spiritual Life* 2, 99).

the fervor of the early days when coming to the monastery.[97] Finally, man has been given the faculty of love in order to love God above all things, and himself and his neighbour for God's sake.[98] Love is, therefore, rightly directed toward God and toward one's neighbour, the first being nourished and developed by the second,[99] the second being born of the first.[100]

Love of God

God is Love (1 John 4,8).[101] He is the loving and generous Giver of noble and precious gifts.[102] Even our suffering is a mark of his love, as though He would share something of his own burden.[103] God seeks special friends (*quos specialius diligunt*) to help Him with what He carries.[104] Our suffering

---

[97] *Prof* 2,1: *Habeo adversum te, quod caritatem primam reliquisti, quapropter poeniten-tiam age et prima opera fac. Caritatem primam reliquunt* [cfr. Apoc 2,4]... (*David ab Augusta*, 66; Devas, *Spiritual Life* 1, 61).

[98] *Prof* 2,25. *Affectus dilectionis etiam datus fuit homini, ut diligeret Deum super omnia et se et proximum propter Deum et secundum Deum...* (*David ab Augusta*, 110; Devas, *Spiritual Life* 1, 105). Cf. *Prof* 3,70. *Aliquos trahit amor Dei... Aliquos caritas et compassio proximo-rum...* (*David ab Augusta*, 377–378; Devas, *Spiritual Life* 2, 211).

[99] *Prof* 2,49. *...cum ex dilectione proximi nutriatur et augeatur amor Dei...* (*David ab Augusta*, 148; Devas, *Spiritual Life* 1, 140). Cf. *Prof*, Epist 2. *...pro amore Dei et proximi salute...* (*David ab Augusta*, 61; Devas, *Spiritual Life* 1, 55); *Prof* 3,2. *...quae afficiunt hominem ad Deum et ad amorem virtutum et ad odium vitiorum et dilectionem proximorum et ad studia bonorum operum...* (*David ab Augusta*, 165; Devas, *Spiritual Life* 2, 7).

[100] *Prof* 3,34. *Dilectio proximi ex dilectione Dei nascitur...* (*David ab Augusta*, 232; Devas, *Spiritual Life* 2, 70).

[101] *Prof* 2,36. *...quia singulariter caritati, quae Deus est...* (*David ab Augusta*, 125; Devas, *Spiritual Life* 1, 120); *Prof* 3,31. *Deus caritas est* (*David ab Augusta*, 224; Devas, *Spiritual Life* 2, 63); *Prof* 3,64. *Deus caritas est, quid mirum, si fervor divinae caritatis cordi infusus totum hominem commovet...* (*David ab Augusta*, 349; Devas, *Spiritual Life* 2, 181). The Holy Spirit is the Love of Father and Son: *...quia Spiritus sanctus amor est et benevolentia et iucunditas Patris et Filii* (*Prof* 3,67; *David ab Augusta*, 364; Devas, *Spiritual Life* 2, 196).

[102] *Prof* 3,11. *Beneficia Dei nobilia et pretiosa sunt ex dignitate dantis, ex affectu liberalitatis et caritatis...* (*David ab Augusta*, 183; Devas, *Spiritual Life* 2, 24). Cf. *Prof* 3,55. *Tanto etiam affectu et benevolentia dat beneficia sua homini, quod, si etiam modica daret, gratanter essent recipienda; caritas enim eius supereminet omni scientiae* [cfr. Eph 3,19]... (*David ab Augusta*, 309; Devas, *Spiritual Life* 2, 141); *Prof* 3,55. *...et pro dilectione et beneficiis reddimus ei contumelias et contemptum...* (*David ab Augusta*, 310; Devas, *Spiritual Life* 2, 142).

[103] *Prof* 3,40. *Signum etiam dilectionis specialis videtur, cui Dominus dat adversa perpeti, ut quasi impartiri ei dignetur partem oneris sui portandi...* (*David ab Augusta*, 256; Devas, *Spiritual Life* 2, 92).

[104] *Prof* 3,40. *Solent enim socii in via, cum lassantur, rogare eos, quibus plus confidunt et quos specialius diligunt, ut partem oneris sui pro se ad horam ferant... Sic et Dominus, qui nobiscum est omnibus diebus, in via hac, qua ambulamus, lassatus usque ad mortem labore passionis, quaerit, quis nostrum velit ei compati et onus tribulationum suarum, quod adhuc in corpore suo mystico, quod est Ecclesia, sustinet, secum portare* (*David ab Augusta*, 256; Devas, *Spiritual Life* 2, 92).

enables us to make some sort of return to Our Lord, who showed his love for us when he "did not spare his own Son, but gave him up for us all."[105] God is a loving Father whom we can trust.[106] Man should strive most earnestly (e.g., by not wanting a "special" love of God)[107] *to be loved* by Him.[108] Then his soul will become like a spouse of Christ, yearning for the love of her sole Beloved.[109]

For three reasons, therefore, should we *love* Him above all things: because He is good; because He first loved us; and because of what He has done for us to prove his love for us.[110] The way to love God is with our whole being, mind, and strength, "so that at least in that exiguous measure of which alone we are capable we may make some loyal return of love to Him of whose greatness there is no end."[111] The whole intent of a man should therefore be turned towards increasing the knowledge and love of God.[112]

---

[105] *Prof* 3,38. *Pater caelestis, qui etiam pro dilectione, qua dilexit nos, proprio Filio suo non pepercit, sed pro nobis omnibus tradidit illum* [cfr. Rom 8,32]... (*David ab Augusta*, 249; Devas, *Spiritual Life* 2, 85). Cf. *Prof* 3,40. ...*quod sic occasionem habent et opportunitatem aliquo modo retribuendi Domino pro illa magna caritate, qua pro nobis animam posuit*... (*David ab Augusta*, 256; Devas, *Spiritual Life* 2, 92). The Sacrament, therefore, is the proof of his love of men: *Prof* 1,10. ...*et quod est admodum praecipuum indicium divinae dignationis et dilectionis ad hominem... Et ideo reliquit nobis in hoc memoriale totius dilectionis suae*... (*David ab Augusta*, 14–15; Devas, *Spiritual Life* 1, 13).

[106] *Prof* 3,58. *Aliquando, quasi filius confidens de dilectione paterna*... (*David ab Augusta*, 327; Devas, *Spiritual Life* 2, 160).

[107] *Prof* 3,60. ...*quasi pro tua sanctitate te Deus exaudierit et pro tui dilectione fecerit quod rogasti*... (*David ab Augusta*, 334; Devas, *Spiritual Life* 2, 165).

[108] *Prof* 1,41. *Committe te Deo, et ab illo diligi te stude fideliter*... (*David ab Augusta*, 56–57; Devas, *Spiritual Life* 1, 49).

[109] *Prof* 3,54. *Aliquando anima quasi sponsa Dei in ipso unico dilecto suo quiescere desiderans et eius frui solum amplexibus ardenter sitiens, pro cuius amore omnia ei inferiora viluerunt*... (*David ab Augusta*, 304; Devas, *Spiritual Life* 2, 137). Cf. *Prof* 3,63. *Amantissimus Domini habitabit confidenter in eo*... (*David ab Augusta*, 343; Devas, *Spiritual Life* 2, 175).

[110] *Prof* 3,31. *Diligere Deum super omnia debemus propter tria: quia bonus est in se... Item, quia ipse prior dilexit nos* [cfr. 1 John 4,10] *et plus diligit nos quam nos ipsi nos... Tertio, propter dilectionis eius multiplicem effectum*... (*David ab Augusta*, 223–224; Devas, *Spiritual Life* 2, 63). Cf. *Prof* 1,1. *Ecce, quantum nos tenemur servire Deo prae ceteris creaturis et diligere super omnia eum, qui nos prae omnibus creaturis amavit* (*David ab Augusta*, 4; Devas, *Spiritual Life* 1, 4–5); *Prof* 3,37. ...*sed pure pro sua bonitate dilexit nos*... (*David ab Augusta*, 247; Devas, *Spiritual Life* 2, 84).

[111] *Prof* 3,31. ...*et ideo iustum est, nos eum vicissim diligere ex omni, quod sumus et scimus et possumus, ut saltem cum exigua mensura nostrae possibilitatis fideliter remetiamur ei diligendo, cuius magnitudinis non est finis* (*David ab Augusta*, 224; Devas, *Spiritual Life* 2, 63).

[112] *Prof* 3,46. *Tota autem intentio debet esse circa optimum occupata, circa profectum animae in Dei notitia et amore et in his, quae ad hunc profectum promovent et conducunt*... (*David ab Augusta*, 277; Devas, *Spiritual Life* 2, 111). Cf. *Prof* 3,33. ...*quia amore langueo* [Song 2,5]... (*David ab Augusta*, 232; Devas, *Spiritual Life* 2, 70); *Prof* 3,52. ...*quae illuminet ad Dei notitiam, accendat ad eius amorem*... (*David ab Augusta*, 295; Devas, *Spiritual Life* 2, 129);

The love of God has three degrees: lowest, middle, and highest.[113] The first stage in the love of God is to value and use the gifts imparted to us, to shun evil, and to give the love of God priority over every other. The second stage is not only to keep the commandments but to be actively devoted to all that pertains to God's service (i.e., by following the evangelical counsels of obedience, poverty, and chastity) and to promote similar desires and zeal in others. The third stage is that of "a love for God so intense and so deeply rooted in the soul as almost to render life itself irksome," a love in which deep patience and ardent joy thrive even in the event of suffering and persecution.[114]

Loving God, the supreme Good, provides the best remedy for anger and a strong resistance to evil.[115] When we bring God, the Provider, more closely in our hearts each time we long for worldly things, we become poor in spirit and grow in spiritual love; we acquire *spiritual* wealth.[116] Spiritual love and spiritual wealth can be experienced each time we become entranced in the spirit: no longer conscious of self, fully dedicated to God in prayer, and clinging to Him by love.[117]

Prof 3,54. ...*quo te perfectius agnoscere et amare et revereri possimus*... (*David ab Augusta*, 306; Devas, *Spiritual Life* 2, 139); *Prof* 3,60. ...*et ex his crescas in amore Dei...ut, cum rogatus exaudierit, magis ametur a nobis*... (*David ab Augusta*, 334; Devas, *Spiritual Life* 2, 166).

[113] *Prof* 3,33. *Caritas Dei, mater et nutrix omnium virtutum, tres habet gradus*... (*David ab Augusta*, 228; Devas, *Spiritual Life* 2, 66).

[114] *Prof* 3,33. *Caritatis Dei primus gradus est sic diligere concessa et eis uti, ut tamen illicita devitet et amori Dei nullius rei amorem praeponat*... *Secundus gradus potest esse, cum homo voluntate pleniori et affectu ferventiori non solum communia contentus est praecepta servare, sine quibus non est salus, sed etiam ad omnia, quae Dei sunt, studiosus est et voluntarius, tam faciendo in se quam in aliis promovendo et desiderando*... *Tertius gradus est tanto affectu aestuare ad Deum, quod sine ipso quasi vivere non possit*... (*David ab Augusta*, 229–230; Devas, *Spiritual Life* 2, 67–69). Cf. *Prof* 3,33 ...*quia amore langueo, desidero dissolvi et esse cum Sponso*... (*David ab Augusta*, 232; Devas, *Spiritual Life* 2, 70).

[115] *Prof* 2,40. ...*et maxime amor ipsius boni. Tam potens est quisque malo resistere, quantum amor boni in cordis eius affectu convaluerit* (*David ab Augusta*, 131; Devas, *Spiritual Life* 1, 124).

[116] *Prof* 3,23. ...*et quidquid penuriae patimur, loco illius Deum in corde ponamus, qui omnia implet; et: Beati pauperes spiritu, id est voluntate, amore spiritualis profectus* (*David ab Augusta*, 211; Devas, *Spiritual Life* 2, 50). Cf. *Prof* 3,28. *Summum autem bonum, quod est Deus, summe amandum est*... (*David ab Augusta*, 216; Devas, *Spiritual Life* 2, 56); *Prof* 3,44. *Quidam sunt pauperes spiritu et non rebus, ut qui libenter essent inopes rebus, sed non permittuntur, qui divitias non pro ipsarum amore possident, sed pro amore Dei, ut cultum Dei per eas amplificent et defendant, vel pro amore proximi in Dei, ut proximis inde subveniant*... (*David ab Augusta*, 268–269; Devas, *Spiritual Life* 2, 103); *Prof* 3,44. ...*quanto etiam in divitiis ab eius amore non sunt separati* (*David ab Augusta*, 269; Devas, *Spiritual Life* 2, 104); *Prof* 3,44. ...*quia earum amor retrahit ab amore Dei et caelestis patriae*... (*David ab Augusta*, 270; Devas, *Spiritual Life* 2, 105).

[117] *Prof* 3,54. *Aliquando quasi inebriatus spiritu et immemor suimet, homo Deo deditus et ei per amorem inhaerens*... (*David ab Augusta*, 305; Devas, *Spiritual Life* 2, 138).

Man's love of God is rooted in and arises from God's love of man:

> Devotion will arise from love as the soul recalls how sweetly love has
> dealt with her (...) or again, as she contemplates the ineffable goodness
> of God in Himself, great beyond all measuring, infinite like His omnipres-
> ence, eternal, and so, without measure or term, to be, by her, loved in return.
> It is pre-eminently through this affection of the love of God that the Spirit
> himself giveth testimony to our spirit that we are the sons of God; and
> of it, we read these great words: If any man love God the same is known by
> him; and again, I love them that love me. To be known by God, to be loved
> by God, means to be looked upon by God with approbation; and it is pre-
> cisely the love of God that imparts value to what we do; and the more the
> activities of the will are steeped in it, the more will God relish them. Only
> from the root of the love of God can any good work or devout affection
> arise.[118]

No creature can love God to the same degree which it is loved by
Him.[119] But divine love, whose power is like a flame enlightening and
enkindling,[120] will transform human love in such a way that all the powers
and affections of the faithful soul, including love itself, are purified and
permeated:

Cf. *Prof* 3,56. *...qui super omnia vult, hominem in se quiescere et sibi per amorem tenaciter
inhaerere* (David ab Augusta, 319; Devas, *Spiritual Life* 2, 152); *Prof* 3,59. *Valde autem Deus
delectatur in hoc, ut frequenter oretur propter multiplicem orantis profectum, qui est, ut Deo
indesinenter inhaereat... ut abundantiori affectu devotionis in amorem Dei excrescat* (David
ab Augusta, 328; Devas, *Spiritual Life* 2, 160); *Prof* 3,62. *Omnis igitur orationis fructus et finis
est Deo adhaerere et unus cum eo spiritus* [cfr. 1 Cor 6,17] *fieri per liquefactionem purissimi
amoris...* (David ab Augusta, 338; Devas, *Spiritual Life* 2, 169–170); *Prof* 3,63. *Amor enim Dei
cum pura intelligentia conditus inebriat mentem et abstractam ab exterioribus sursum ele-
vat et sua virtute Deo conglutinat et coniungit, et quanto amor vehementior et intelligentia
lucidior, tanto validius mentem in se rapit...* (David ab Augusta, 344–345; Devas, *Spiritual
Life* 2, 177).

[118] *Prof* 3,65. *Ex amore divino, cum recolit, quam benigne secum egerit... vel cum ipsius Dei
ineffabilem intuetur benignitatem, quae tanta est, sicut eius immensitas et aeternitas, quae
nec mensuram habent nec finem; et ideo sine mensura diligendus est et sine fine. Amore Dei
nihil potest esse delectabilius, nil honorabilius, nil utilius. Per hanc affectionem dilectionis Dei
singulariter Spiritus sanctus testimonium reddit spiritui nostro, quod sumus filii Dei* [cfr.
Rom 8,16]. *De hac specialiter dicitur: Qui diligit Deum, hic cognitus est ab eo etc.* [cfr. 1 Cor
8,3]; *et: Ego diligentes me diligo* [cfr. Prov 8,17]; *cognosci a Deo et diligi est ab eo approbari.
Amor Dei est omnium affectionum bonarum condimentum, et tanto plus sapiunt Deo ceterae
virtutum affectiones, quanto plus de hoc habuerint condimento, nec potest esse virtus vel
devotio, quae ex amoris Dei radice non pullulat* (David ab Augusta, 353; Devas, *Spiritual Life*
2, 185). Cf. *Prof* 3,59. *...quae licet ex verae caritatis radice non profluat...* (David ab Augusta,
330; Devas, *Spiritual Life* 2, 162).

[119] *Prof* 3,63. *Nulla creatura potest amare Deum, sicut amata est ab ipso...* (David ab
Augusta, 342; Devas, *Spiritual Life* 2, 175).

[120] *Prof* 3,64. *...quia virtus amoris divini sicut ignis illuminat et inflammat* (David
ab Augusta, 350; Devas, *Spiritual Life* 2, 182).

As the tide of divine love rises so is every power and holy affection of the soul purified till love permeates them through and through. Fear and grief, hope and shame, all yield before her, and love alone remains mistress of all, delighting in and clinging to God who alone can satisfy the yearnings of the soul, and who alone can ultimately so transfigure her that she will know even as she is known and love even as she is loved (...).[121]

Then, when all the affective powers of the soul are fastened on the supremely Good and supremely True, which is God, love will bear fruit and nothing will hold it back from its perfection.[122]

Love of one's neighbour

To rightly love one's neighbour is to love him as oneself.[123] It is loving for the sake of God, loving "in God," and loving in accordance with God's will:

---

[121] *Prof* 3,63. *Quanto ergo caritas magis augetur, tanto et aliae virtutes et virtuosae affectiones amplius purificantur, quousque omnes in eam solam transformentur, ut iam non sit timor, non dolor, spes vel pudor, sed tantum suo gaudio fruens amor, et illi bono tenaciter inhaerens, quod solum sufficit animae desiderium adimplere et ipsum amorem eius in se potenter transformare, ut iam agnoscat, sicut et cognita est, et amet, sicut amata est...* (David ab Augusta, 342; Devas, *Spiritual Life* 2, 174–175); *Prof* 3,64. *...ad amandum amantem se Deum et liquescens ad recipiendum divinae virtutis impressiones... Anima mea liquefacta est ex amore divini amoris* (David ab Augusta, 351; Devas, *Spiritual Life* 2, 183); *Prof* 3,67. *... quanto ergo magis cordis affectus exhilaratur et devotior efficitur in se, cum cogitat et optat quod desiderat non ex levitate vel vanitate, sed ex maturitate et caritate...* (David ab Augusta, 363–364; Devas, *Spiritual Life* 2, 196).

[122] *Prof* 3,63. *Et sic quod in solo intellectu fuit scientia, accedente sapore affectus, dicitur sapientia, id est sapida scientia: scientia ex cognitione veri, sapientia ex adiuncto amore boni. Licet enim omnes animae affectiones suos habeant proprios sapores, id est motus sibi convenientes; amor tamen quasi principalis suo motu omnes alios informat, maxime cum ipse ad summum, verum bonum debito modo fuerit conversus, qui natus est nihil solidius amare quam summum bonum* (David ab Augusta, 341; Devas, *Spiritual Life* 2, 173–174). Cf. *Prof* 2,4. *...ut ei imprimatur et conformetur per cognitionem intellectus, per affectum amoris et fruitionis iucunditatem* (David ab Augusta, 84; Devas, *Spiritual Life* 1, 80); *Prof* 2,8. *Perfectio voluntatis est unum cum Deo spiritum esse per amorem...* (David ab Augusta, 90; Devas, *Spiritual Life* 1, 86); *Prof* 3,63. *...et tunc reliquae affectiones debitos motus suos exercent iuxta ipsius amoris mensuram. Quantum enim amas quodcumque bonum, tantum gaudes de eius adeptione, vel spe, dum cupis id adipisci; tantum times vel odis hoc, quod posset id, quod amas, auferre; tantum doles de non habito et tantum pudet de contrario, si quod diligis sit honestum... etiam dum adhuc spei locus est, nondum potest esse perfectus, dum non habet quod amat in fruitione, sed tantum in exspectatione, et quanto exspectatio incertior, tanto et amor tepidior...* (David ab Augusta, 341–342; Devas, *Spiritual Life* 2, 174); *Prof* 3,63. *...fructuosa caritas et meritoria sublimium praemiorum* (David ab Augusta, 344; Devas, *Spiritual Life* 2, 176); *Prof* 3,63. *...et omnes affectus, in amoris gaudio uniti, in sola Conditoris fruitione suaviter quiescant... et voluntas perfecte afficitur ad amandum summam bonitatem...* (David ab Augusta, 346; Devas, *Spiritual Life* 2, 178); *Prof* 3,37. *Sicut ergo caritas ordinat nos ad bonitatem...* (David ab Augusta, 243; Devas, *Spiritual Life* 2, 80).

[123] *Prof* 2,36. *Hoc est contra caritatem proximi, quem tenemur diligere sicut nosmetipsos...* (David ab Augusta, 124; Devas, *Spiritual Life* 1, 119). Cf. *Prof* 3,36. *Diliges proximum tuum sicut te ipsum* [cfr. Matt 19,19]... (David ab Augusta, 240; Devas, *Spiritual Life* 2, 77).

The love of one's neighbour is born of the love of God. Our neighbour is to be loved for God's sake, in God and in accordance with God's will. *For God's sake*, such being His wish: And this commandment we have from God, writes St. John (1 4,21), that he who loveth God love also his brother. Secondly, *In God*, i.e. the love we have for our neighbour should be the same love which we have for God, though not of the same degree; it, too, should be a supernatural love. Lastly, *In accordance with God's will*, i.e. we should love our neighbour for the same end which God has in loving us, viz. growth in holiness and final salvation.[124]

Love of one's neighbour is seeing and loving God in a person (*pro amore proximi in Deo*).[125] It is the kind of love that is true, pure, and well-ordered:

> *True*, because absolutely sincere, in deed and in truth, not merely, as St. John warns us, in word or in tongue (1 3,18). *Pure*, i.e. free from carnal taint, neither motived by personal gain, nor determined by such pleasure it may chance to win us. Not that there is necessarily anything wrong in either purpose, but simply that love of that kind, unless the motives are in some way spiritualized, is devoid of merit. Lastly, *right-ordered*, i.e. mainly concerned not with vice or material well-being or earthly prosperity, but with the issues involved in eternal salvation.[126]

True neighbourly love, therefore, is not carnal love (prompted by pleasure), avaricious love (motivated by gain), natural love (based on "animal" attraction), or social love (aimed only at those we know and live with), but spiritual love: flowing from the Holy Spirit and infused into us from God.[127]

---

[124] *Prof* 3,34. *Dilectio proximi ex dilectione Dei nascitur, quia propter Deum et in Deo et secundum Deum est proximus diligendus: propter Deum, quia ipse mandavit; Ioannes: Hoc mandatum habemus a Deo, ut qui diligit Deum diligat et fratrem suum; in Deo, id est ea affectione diligere proximum, qua Deum, licet non tanta; in Deo, id est in spiritu Dei; secundum Deum, id est ea forma, vel ad hoc diligere debemus proximum, ad quod nos diligit Deus, id est ad salutem animae et profectum in spiritu* (David ab Augusta, 232; Devas, *Spiritual Life* 2, 70). The religious has abandoned the wordly love of friends and of oneself for God's sake: *Prof* 1,29. *...nec pro amore amicorum vel proprii corporis dubitavit se tradere carceri poenitentiae propter Deum...* (David ab Augusta, 39; Devas, *Spiritual Life* 1, 34).
[125] *Prof* 3,44. *...vel pro amore proximi in Deo, ut proximis inde subveniant...* (David ab Augusta, 268; Devas, *Spiritual Life* 2, 103).
[126] *Prof* 3,34. *...vere, ut non ficte, sicut illi, qui verbo tantum et lingua diligunt, non opere et veritate; pure, ut non ex carnali affectione, non pro utilitate propria, non ex casuali et saeculari societate tantum, quae, etsi non sint semper mala, tamen non sunt meritoria, nisi ex spirituali dilectione accipiant condimentum; ordinate, ut non ad vitia et commoda carnis et temporalem prosperitatem, sed ad aeternam salutem* (David ab Augusta, 232–233; Devas, *Spiritual Life* 2, 71). Cf. *Prof* 3,38. *...quia veritatem amat...* (David ab Augusta, 248; Devas, *Spiritual Life* 2, 85).
[127] *Prof* 3,34. *Unde notandum, quod est dilectio carnalis et est dilectio cupiditatis et dilectio naturalis et est dilectio socialis et est dilectio spiritualis* (David ab Augusta, 233; Devas, *Spiritual*

Illegitimate love

Spiritual love can be a guise for carnal love but in reality they are opposites:[128] spiritual love relishes in spiritual conversation, while carnal love is busy with useless talk; spiritual love dictates equal reserve, while carnal love is unseemly in gesture and manner; spiritual love is free of turmoil, while carnal love is disquiet and worrying; spiritual love aims at universality, while carnal love is jealous; spiritual love is reasonable and tolerant, while carnal love has a tendency to violent anger; spiritual love is supported by prayer and generosity, while carnal love treasures trifling relics as tokens of undying friendship; and, finally, spiritual love hates vice, while carnal love disregards sin.[129] It is a fact, however, that carnal love is sinful as it pursues vices, worldly pleasures, and women. It delights in the fictitious aid of the senses,[130] the temptations of the flesh,[131] the gratification of worldly things,[132] honor, wealth, and pleasure,[133] and women's private attention.[134] Therefore, carnal love's only remedy can be

---

Life 2, 71). *Prof* 3,34. *Spiritualis dilectio a Spiritu sancto denominata, a quo fluit, qui amor Patris et Filii dicitur, est illa, quae mandatur nobis a Domino...* (David ab Augusta, 234; Devas, *Spiritual Life* 2, 72). Cf. *Prof* 3,50. *...nec affectus dilectionis ad coniugem et filios ligat...* (David ab Augusta, 287; Devas, *Spiritual Life* 2, 121); *Prof* 3,64. *Ebrietas spiritus potest dici quaelibet magna amoris et gaudii devotio...* (David ab Augusta, 348; Devas, *Spiritual Life* 2, 180).

[128] *Prof* 2,49. *...se sub specie spiritualis amoris carnali dilectione et delectatione deludi...* (David ab Augusta, 148; Devas, *Spiritual Life* 1, 140). Cf. *Prof* 1,33. *...quod ad omnia, quae ad corporis curam vel commodum spectant, studiosissimus es, quae vero ad spiritualem profectum vel fraternae caritatis exhibitionem vel ad praelati obedientiam vel ad carnis castigationem spectant, desidiosus es...* (David ab Augusta, 45; Devas, *Spiritual Life* 1, 39).

[129] *Prof* 3,35 (David ab Augusta, 236–239; Devas, *Spiritual Life* 2, 74–77).

[130] *Prof* 2,49. *...nec corporalibus amplexibus indiget...* (David ab Augusta, 148; Devas, *Spiritual Life* 1, 140).

[131] *Prof* 3,13. *Tentationibus, in quibus delectatio consisit, maxime teneri et infirmi superantur, in quibus amor mundi nondum exstinctus est, et ideo citius reaccenditur ex concupiscentiis mundi...* (David ab Augusta, 187; Devas, *Spiritual Life* 2, 27).

[132] *Prof* 2,10. *Quia enim homo amore visibilium ab invisibilium amore cecidit...* (David ab Augusta, 93–94; Devas, *Spiritual Life* 1, 89); *Prof* 3,44. *...qui divitias non pro ipsarum amore possident...* (David ab Augusta, 268; Devas, *Spiritual Life* 2, 103).

[133] *Prof* 2,15. *Omnia vero vitia et peccata ex uno fonte oriuntur, id est superbia, et ex duobus rivulis derivantur: malo amore et malo timore... Ista sunt quasi materia et occasio homini ad tentationem, quae mundus proponit nobis: honores, divitias et voluptates* (David ab Augusta, 101; Devas, *Spiritual Life* 1, 96).

[134] *Prof* 1,24. *...magnam generat inquietudinem cordis talis privata affectio, dum semper illi cupis ostendere dilectionem...* (David ab Augusta, 33; Devas, *Spiritual Life* 1, 28). Cf. *Prof* 1,41. *Item, a feminis velle diligi etiam...* (David ab Augusta, 56; Devas, *Spiritual Life* 1, 49); *Prof* 2,50. *...donec per longam familiaritatem et incautam securitatem affectus amborum ita conflati et conglutinati fuerint in amore...* (David ab Augusta, 152; Devas, *Spiritual Life* 1, 144); *Prof* 3,13. *...de mutuo ipsorum amore et fide, et amorosi aspectus et munuscula pro memorialibus caritatis* (David ab Augusta, 188; Devas, *Spiritual Life* 2, 29).

spiritual love;[135] only the love of God and the yearning for heaven can draw one away from the love of the world and the wrong sense (*indiscrete*) of neighbourly love.[136]

Spiritual neighbourly love

A sinful man loves himself[137] and wants to be loved,[138] but he can be loved by none and is incapable of love.[139] His avaricious, suspicious, envious, indulgent, and frivolous way of loving can only be overcome by "a seriousness of the right kind": spiritual neighbourly love.[140] Spiritual neighbourly love is true, pure, and well-ordered love that (according to its three degrees of beginning, progression, and perfection) neither in act nor desire hurts anyone but wishes well to all; delights in the good fortune of the other and sympathizes with his sorrows; and sincerely loves enemies.[141] Thus, when necessary, the spiritual lover of man gives priority to good works or daily communal work over personal prayer, even when this in itself is the most useful spiritual exercise and the one that most closely unites man to God.[142]

---

[135] *Prof* 2,49. ...*et e converso spiritualis amor carnalem reprimit et expellit* (*David ab Augusta*, 148; Devas, *Spiritual Life* 1, 140).

[136] Cf. *Prof* 3,44. ...*quia earum amor retrahit ab amore Dei et caelestis patriae...* (*David ab Augusta*, 270; Devas, *Spiritual Life* 2, 105); *Prof* 3,36. *Nam si ista, quae mundi sunt, diligerent et de amissis valde dolerent, non esset caritas Dei Patris in eis* [cfr. 1 John 2,15] (*David ab Augusta*, 242; Devas, *Spiritual Life* 2, 79); *Prof* 3,48. *Caritas proximi, si indiscrete tenetur, facit proximo favere vel cooperari in detrimentum salutis propriae et illius...* (*David ab Augusta*, 283; Devas, *Spiritual Life* 2, 117).

[137] *Prof* 3,38. ...*et se privato amore non diligit contra veritatem...* (*David ab Augusta*, 248; Devas, *Spiritual Life* 2, 85). Cf. *Prof* 2,2. ...*quos aut vano amore sui, aut malo timore retinet in peccato* (*David ab Augusta*, 74; Devas, *Spiritual Life* 1, 69); *Prof* 2,16. *Superbia est amor propriae excellentiae...* (*David ab Augusta*, 103; Devas, *Spiritual Life* 1, 98); *Prof* 2,29. ...*et studet amore propriae gloriae...* (*David ab Augusta*, 115; Devas, *Spiritual Life* 1, 110).

[138] *Prof* 1,41. *Non multum affectes diligi...* (*David ab Augusta*, 56; Devas, *Spiritual Life* 1, 49).

[139] *Prof* 3,23. ...*et ideo nullum potest vere diligere, cum a nullo se vere diligi suspicetur* (*timor enim suspiciosus non est in perfecta dilectione*)... (*David ab Augusta*, 209; Devas, *Spiritual Life* 2, 49).

[140] *Prof* 3,25. *Serium bonum intus amorem ad proximum habet... Dissolutio est devotioni sicut aqua igni, et qui ducit in consuetudinem vix dissuescet, maxime ioculari* (*David ab Augusta*, 213; Devas, *Spiritual Life* 2, 52). Cf. *Prof* 3,30. ...*dilectio proximi contra invidiam...* (*David ab Augusta*, 222; Devas, *Spiritual Life* 2, 61); *Prof* 3,39. ...*et caritas proximi invidiae...* (*David ab Augusta*, 253; Devas, *Spiritual Life* 2, 89).

[141] *Prof* 3,36 (*David ab Augusta*, 240–243; Devas, *Spiritual Life* 2, 77–80).

[142] *Prof* 3,52. *Quod autem horum utilius sit simpliciter, sciendum, quod illud, quod magis unit hominem cum Deo, cum tota beatitudo hominis sit in Deum transformari. Alia tamen quoad quid quandoque utiliora sunt, ut cum propter obedientiam vel caritatem proximi*

2. Obedience

Origin

When God gave the people of Israel his commandments, he made his promise of land and election conditional, i.e., dependent on their obedience (*obedientia*): "Hear now, O Israel, the decrees and laws I am about to teach you. Follow them so that you may live and may go in and take possession of the land that the Lord, the God of your fathers, is giving you";[143] "If you fully obey the Lord your God and carefully follow all his commands I give you today, the Lord your God will set you high above all the nations on earth,"[144] etc. In the Bible, especially in the Old Testament, obedience is primarily connected to God's law and commandments. But, in the New Testament, there is a shift towards obeying Jesus Christ,[145] towards "obedience that accompanies your confession of the gospel of Christ,"[146] and towards "obedience that comes with faith,"[147] obedience beyond the law.[148] Furthermore, while Jesus was obedient to the Father in his suffering,[149]

---

oratio intermittitur, et operibus pietatis insistitur... (*David ab Augusta*, 296; Devas, *Spiritual Life* 2, 130). Cf. *Prof* 1,31. *...bona actio, maxime condita pinguedine caritatis et obedientiae vel alterius virtutis...* (*David ab Augusta*, 42; Devas, *Spiritual Life* 1, 36); *Prof* 1,10. *In hoc enim ministerio multiplex fructus est: primo, boni operis exercitium est; secundo, opus caritatis est et promovens proximum in bono...* (*David ab Augusta*, 14; Devas, *Spiritual Life* 1, 13). *Prof* 1,37. *...facere quod est faciendum, vel obedientia iubente vel caritate instigante* (*David ab Augusta*, 50; Devas, *Spiritual Life* 1, 43); *Prof* 3,20. *...sit promptus ad quaeque spiritualia exercitia, quae vel obedientia iusserit, vel caritas fraterna requirit...* (*David ab Augusta*, 205; Devas, *Spiritual Life* 2, 45).

[143] *Deut* 4,1. On Christianity and obedience, see for instance: Von Balthasar, "Gehorsam"; "Christelijke gehoorzaamheid"; Eilers, "Der biblische"; Fischediek, *Der Gehorsamsverständnis*; Greshake, *Gottes Willen*; Hertling, "Die professio"; Hillmann, "Perfectio"; Lamparter, *Der Aufruf*; Leclercq, "Gehorsam"; März, *Hören*; "Obéissance"; *l'Obéissance*; Stöger & Scholz, "Gehorsam"; Stolzenburg, *Gehoorzaamheid*.

[144] Deut 28,1.

[145] E.g., 1 Pet 1,2.

[146] 2 Cor 9,13; Rom 16,19.

[147] Rom 1,5. Cf. Garlington, *Faith*, 108–109, commenting on Rom 5: "Paul, however, does not contemplate the obedience of Christ as an end in itself, because it is *through* the one man that obedience has been disseminated *to* all. At heart, human obedience is the acceptance of one's identity as the image of God and the consequent obligation of creaturely service. The obedience of the Christian is thus the antipode of his former disobedience, his rejection of Creator/creature distinction. In short, the believer has been delivered from the slavery of his former existence (...) and enabled to persevere in the faith-commitment incumbent originally on the first Adam."

[148] Cf. Eilers, "Der biblische"; Kittredge, *Community*; Miller, *The Obedience*; "Obéissance"; Stöger & Scholz, "Gehorsam".

[149] Rom 5,19; Heb 5,8.

Paul asks of his addressees full obedience to Christ[150] and full obedience to himself.[151]

Francis

Fraternity

As is the case for the people of Israel and in the early Christian community, obedience is a very important virtue in the fraternity of Francis.[152] In fact, the fraternity itself is the "obedience" to which brothers can be admitted when they promise to follow the rule and live according to the Gospel.[153] In this way, the brothers' loyalty and behavior determine whether they wander "*extra obedientiam*" or remain "*in obedientia*":

> Let whoever wishes to be the greater among them be their minister and servant. Let whoever is the greater among them become the least. Let no brother do or say anything evil to another, on the contrary, through the charity of the Spirit, let them serve and obey one another voluntarily. This is the true and holy obedience of our Lord Jesus Christ. As often as they have turned away from the commands of the Lord and "wandered outside obedience," let all the brothers know, as the Prophet says, they are cursed outside obedience as long as they knowingly remain in such a sin. When they have persevered in the Lord's commands – as they have promised by the Holy Gospel and their life, let them know they have remained in true obedience and are blessed by the Lord.[154]

---

[150] 2 Cor 10,5.

[151] 2 Cor 10,6; Phil 1,21.

[152] See for instance: Bracaloni, "Le virtù", 147–159; Corselis, "Les ordres"; Desbonnets, *De l'intuition*, 59–67; Dukker, *Umkehr*, 125–130; Esser, "Gehorsam"; Esser & Grau, *Antwort*, 191–218; Garrido, *Die Lebensregel*, 256–268; Ghinato, *Profilo*, 163–164; Grau, "Der heilige Franziskus", 56–58; Hoeberichts, *Paradise*, 121–144, 225–229, 231–254; Iriarte, *Vocazione*, 178–195; Van Leeuwen, "Gehoorzaamheid"; Linden, *Vater*, 227–236; Longpré, *François*, 104–107; Longpré, "Saint François", 1291–1292; Miccoli, *Le testament*, 51–69; Micó, "Obedience"; Morant, *Unser Weg*, 71–79; Van Munster, *De mystiek*, 137–138; Peters, *Aus Liebe*, 89–90; Reijsbergen, "Bevrijdende"; Rohr, *Der Herr*, 135–148, 173–178; Rotzetter, *Franz von Assisi*, 70–80; Senftle, *Menschenbildung*; Sevenhoven, "How Obedience"; Synowczyk, "l'Obbedienza"; Verhey, *Der Mensch*, 126–133; Verhey, "Gehoorzaamheid"; Verhey, *Naar het land*, 162–167.

[153] RB 2,11; RnB 2,9. *Finito vero anno probationis, recipiantur ad obedientiam promittentes vitam istam semper et regulam observare*; RnB 12,4. *Et nulla penitus mulier ab aliquo fratre recipiatur ad obedientiam, sed dato sibi consilio spirituali, ubi voluerit agat poenitentiam*; Adm 3,9. *Nam qui prius persecutionem sustinet, quam velit a suis fratribus separari, vere permanet in perfecta obedientia, quia ponit animam suam* (cfr. Joa 15,13) *pro fratribus suis*; RB 2,14; RnB 2,13. *Et illi qui iam promiserunt obedientiam habeant unam tunicam cum caputio et aliam sine caputio qui voluerint habere.*

[154] RnB 5,11–17. *...et quicumque voluerit inter eos maior fieri, sit eorum minister* (cfr. Matt 20,26b) *et servus; ...et qui maior est inter eos fiat sicut minor* (cfr. Luke 22,26). *Nec aliquis*

Obedience here refers to a metaphorical but determined space in which the commandments and counsels of the Lord are observed,[155] and in which brothers serve and obey each other.[156] Consequently, formulations such as *"ex obedientia"*[157] or *"per obedientiam"*[158] point to a general meaning of the word that implicitly joins obedience to the Lord[159] or to the Spirit[160]

---

frater malum faciat vel malum dicat alteri; immo magis per caritatem spiritus voluntarie serviant et obediant invicem (cfr. Gal 5,13). *Et haec est vera et sancta obedientia Domini nostri Jesu Christi. Et omnes fratres, quoties declinaverint a mandatis Domini et extra obedientiam evagaverint, sicut dicit propheta* (Ps 118,21), *sciant se esse maledictos extra obedientiam quousque steterint in tali peccato scienter. Et quando perseveraverint in mandatis Domini, quae promiserunt per sanctum evangelium et vitam ipsorum, sciant se in vera obedientia stare, et benedicti sint a Domino* (Armstrong, *Francis of Assisi*, 67–68).

[155] *Ep Fid* 2,39. *Debemus observare praecepta et consilia Domini nostri Jesu Christi.* Cf. Freeman, *Franciscus*, 44: "Franciscus en zijn tijdgenoten vatten de gehoorzaamheid op als een ruimte waarbinnen de mens zijn bestemming vindt;" Esser, "Gehorsam", 3–4: "Wie das Monasterium der Lebensraum des alten Mönchtums war, so ist die *obedientia* der Lebensraum des franziskanischen Menschen, in dem er lebt und sich bewegt;" Verhey, "Gehoorzaamheid", 197, 200–201: "gehoorzaamheid als levensruimte, als binding aan de levenswijze van een gemeenschap."

[156] *Ep Fid* 2,41–42. *Et nullus homo teneatur ex obedientia obedire alicui in eo, ubi committitur delictum vel peccatum. Cui autem obedientia commissa est et qui habetur maior, sit sicut minor* (Luke 22,26) *et aliorum fratrum servus.*

[157] *Ep Fid* 2,41–42.

[158] *Ep Cust* 1,10. *Et ista sint eis per veram et sanctam obedientiam; Ep Min* 14. *Si quis fratrum instigante inimico mortaliter peccaverit, per obedientiam teneatur recurrere ad guardianum suum; Ep Min* 16. *Similiter per obedientiam teneantur eum mittere custodi suo cum socio; RB* 12,3. *Ad haec per obedientiam iniungo ministris...; RnB* 24,4. *Et ex parte Dei omnipotentis et domini papae et per obedientiam ego frater Franciscus firmiter praecipio et iniungo...; Test* 25. *Praecipio firmiter per obedientiam fratribus universis...; Test* 31. ...*omnes fratres, ubicumque sunt, per obedientiam teneantur...; Test* 32. *Et custos firmiter teneatur per obedientiam ipsum fortiter custodire...; Test* 33. *Et minister firmiter teneatur per obedientiam mittendi ipsum per tales fratres...; Test* 35. *Et generalis minister et omnes alii ministri et custodes per obedientiam teneantur...; Test* 38. *Et omnibus fratribus meis clericis et laicis praecipio firmiter per obedientiam....*

[159] *Ep Fid* 2,40. *Debemus etiam nosmetipsos abnegare* (cfr. Matt 16,24) *et ponere corpora nostra sub iugo servitutis et sanctae obedientiae, sicut unusquisque promisit Domino; Ep Ord* 6. *Inclinate aurem* (Isa 55,3) *cordis vestri et obedite voci Filii Dei; Ep Ord* 10. *In disciplina et obedientia sancta perseverate* (Hebr 12,7) *et quae promisistis ei bono et firmo proposito adimplete; Ep Ord* 2. ...*et omnibus fratribus simplicibus et obedientibus....* Francis also refers to the obedience of the Son to his Father (*Ep Ord* 46. ...*quoniam Dominus noster Jesus Christus dedit vitam suam, ne perderet sanctissimi Patris obedientiam* (cfr. Phil 2,8)) and uses some biblical connotations: *Adm* 2,2. *De omni ligno paradisi poterat comedere, quia, dum non venit contra obedientiam, non peccavit; Adm* 5,2. *Et omnes creaturae, quae sub caelo sunt, secundum se serviunt, cognoscunt et obediunt Creatori suo melius quam tu.*

[160] *Sal Virt* 14–15. *Sancta obedientia confundit omnes corporales et carnales voluntates et habet mortificatum corpus suum ad obedientiam spiritus et ad obedientiam fratris sui....* Cf. Desbonnets, *De l'intuition*, 61: "Il s'agit toujours d'obéir à l'esprit, mais le médiateur privilégié de cette obéissance, ce sont les frères, c'est la fraternité."

with obedience to others, including Francis himself[161] and other (ecclesi-
astical) superiors.[162]

Man and fellow men

Obedience is also a moral virtue,[163] especially linked to charity (*Adm* 3,6;
Sal Virt 3),[164] and one of the three evangelical counsels, the others of which
are poverty and chastity.[165] Although these counsels (*obedientia, paupertas, castitas*) after Francis took the shape of the well-known monastic
vows,[166] monastic obedience as such is not directly based on any text of

---

[161] *RB* 1,3; *RnB* Prol,4. *Et alii fratres teneantur fratri Francisco et eius successoribus obedire.* Obedience to God and obedience to Francis coincide: *Ep Min* 4. *Et hoc sit tibi per
veram obedientiam Domini Dei et meam, quia firmiter scio, quod ista est vera obedientia; Ep
Leo* 3. *...faciatis cum beneditione* [!] *Domini Dei et mea obedientia.*

[162] *Adm* 3,3–4. *Ille homo relinquit omnia, quae possidet, et perdit corpus suum, qui se
ipsum totum praebet ad obedientiam in manibus sui praelati. Et quidquid facit et dicit, quod
ipse sciat, quod non sit contra voluntatem eius, dum bonum sit quod facit, vera obedientia est;
RB* 1,2. *Frater Franciscus promittit obedientiam et reverentiam domino papae Honorio ac
successoribus eius canonice intrantibus et Ecclesiae Romanae; RB* 8,1. *Universi fratres unum
de fratribus istius religionis teneantur semper habere generalem ministrum et servum totius
fraternitatis et ei teneantur firmiter obedire; RnB* Prol,3. *Franciscus et quicumque erit caput
istius religionis promittat obedientiam domino Innocentio papae et reverentiam et suis successoribus; RnB* 4,3. *Et omnes alii fratres mei benedicti diligenter obediant eis in his quae
spectant ad salutem animae et non sunt contraria vitae nostrae; Reg Er* 8. *...et per obedientiam sui ministri custodiant filios suos ab omni persona, ut nemo possit loqui cum eis; Test*
27–28. *Et firmiter volo obedire ministro generali huius fraternitatis et alio guardiano, quem
sibi placuerit mihi dare. Et ita volo esse captus in manibus suis, ut non possim ire vel facere
ultra obedientiam et voluntatem suam, quia dominus meus est; Test* 30. *Et omnes alii fratres
teneantur ita obedire guardianis suis et facere officium secundum regulam.*

[163] Cf. Bisschops, *Franciscus*, 169–170: "Een deugd met een drieledige functie:" individual, relational, cosmic.

[164] Cf. 1 Pet 1,22; Armstrong, ""If My Words", 80: "Obedience as a virtue of love" and
"understood as *ob-audire* (to listen to another), as opposed to *obedire* (to incline one's
will)"; Desbonnets, *De l'intuition*, 61: "Notons que, pour François, l'humilité fait route avec
la pauvreté et que l'obéissance, elle, se joint à la charité." In the *Regula Benedicti* (5,1) obedience is the first degree of humility.

[165] *RB* 1,1; *RnB* 1,1. *Regula et Vita Minorum Fratrum haec est, scilicet Domini nostri Jesu
Christi sanctum Evangelium observare vivendo in obedientia, sine proprio et in castitate.* In
Christian theology, a distinction is made between precepts and counsels: "The vocation of
the rich man (Matt 19) and St. Paul's advice on virgins suggested to the Church Fathers the
distinction between precept and counsel in the path of spiritual progress. One, an act of
authority, obliged all Christians; the other, a friendly proposition, oriented freedom without imposing it. From then on, two counsels appeared clearly: poverty and chastity"
(Vicaire, "Evangelical", 509).

[166] "St. Francis's two Rules (1221, 1223) defined the life of the friars by the triad *"paupertas, castitas, obedientia."* This very soon became general during the 13th c. as a summary of
the evangelical counsels and the specific characteristics of the religious life. Among theologians and canonists, it ended in the theory of the three evangelical vows of religion.
From 1257 to 1269, in his three polemical works, St. Thomas Aquinas used the new triad

the New Testament (nowhere is it stated that the members of a community should "voluntarily" obey a superior), nor can it be based without any problem on the example of Jesus Christ (monastic obedience is more an intermediary obedience than an immediate obedience to the will of God).[167] For Francis, obedience is real (*Adm* 3,4; *Ep Min* 4; *Ep Cust* 1,10; *RnB* 5,15) and holy (*Ep Fid* 2,40; *Ep Ord* 10; *Ep Cust* 1,10; *RnB* 5,15; *Sal Virt* 14) when the self is denied, God is loved and served, brothers are forgiven and served, and superiors obeyed. While obeying superiors does justice to God and fellow man,[168] this obedience goes hand in hand with obedience to the Lord, to conscience,[169] and to the *Rule*: "Therefore, I strictly command them to obey their ministers in everything they have promised the Lord to observe and which is not against their soul or our Rule."[170]

For God

Francis pays more attention to obedience than to poverty,[171] the alleged Franciscan virtue *par excellence*. Obedience is, in fact, a constituent of poverty, the highest form of *expropriatio*, the expropriation of the self.[172] In obedience, man is "bound to freedom": becoming more and more freed from the self, he makes himself totally available for God, lays his will in the will of the Father,[173] and is "released to the freedom of God": "Aber

---

against the opponents of the mendicants" (Vicaire, "Evangelical", 509). Cf. Hertling, "Die professio"; Hödl, "Evangelische"; Leclercq, "Gehorsam".

[167] Hillmann, "Perfectio", 163–164.

[168] *Adm* 3,5–6. *Et si quando subditus videat meliora et utiliora animae suae quam ea, quae sibi praelatus praecipiat, sua voluntarie Deo sacrificet; quae autem sunt praelati, opere studeat adimplere. Nam haec est caritativa obedientia* (cfr. 1 Pet 1,22), *quia Deo et proximo satisfacit.*

[169] When going against one's own conscience, obedience to superiors is not obligatory: *Si vero praelatus aliquid contra animam suam praecipiat, licet ei non obediat, tamen ipsum non dimittat* (*Adm* 3,7); *Si quis autem ministrorum alicui fratrum aliquid contra vitam nostram praeciperet vel contra animam suam, non teneatur ei obedire; quia illa obedientia non est, in qua delictum vel peccatum committitur* (*RnB* 5,2).

[170] *RB* 10,3. *Unde firmiter praecipio eis, ut obediant suis ministris in omnibus quae promiserunt Domino observare et non sunt contraria animae et regulae nostrae* (Armstrong, *Francis of Assisi*, 105).

[171] See below, 2.8.

[172] Esser, "Gehorsam", 17.

[173] Cf. *Ep Fid* 2,10. *Posuit tamen voluntatem suam in voluntate Patris dicens: Pater, fiat voluntas tua* (Matt 26,42); *RB* 10,2. *...quod propter Deum abnegaverunt proprias voluntates; RnB* 22,9. *...nihil aliud habemus facere, nisi sequi voluntatem Domini et placere sibi ipsi;* and in the will of his superiors: *Adm* 3,4. *Et quidquid facit et dicit, quod ipse sciat, quod non sit contra voluntatem eius, dum bonum sit quod facit, vera obedientia est; Test* 7. *...nolo praedicare ultra voluntatem ipsorum; Test* 28. *Et ita volo esse captus in manibus suis, ut non possim ire vel facere ultra obedientiam et voluntatem suam, quia dominus meus est.*

christlicher Gehorsam, wofern er unter evangelischem Leitbild steht, ist
Bindung zur Freiheit, weil er den Menschen von sich selbst löst und
frei macht für den Herrn, indem er ungehindert Gottes Wort hört und
befolgt (...)."[174] Brothers who have become so free from themselves that
they do not want anything for themselves will demand and display
obedience in the right way, namely *propter Deum*, so that the will of God
be done.[175]

Bonaventure

Sacrifice

According to Bonaventure, obedience is the greatest sacrifice one can
make because in being obedient one gives up his own will.[176] This is a
major difficulty for man (for "virtue is concerned with the more diffi-
cult"[177]), which necessarily increases merit.[178] Christ, our Vine, provides
the perfect example. He was tied, as "the vine is tied to keep the branches
off the ground and thus prevent the loss or spoiling of the fruit," by the
Virgin's womb, by the manger, by the ropes with which He was tied at the
time of his arrest, and by the first bond (*vinculum*) of all, obedience:

---

[174] Esser, "Gehorsam", 18. Cf. Verhey, *Der Mensch*, 130–131: "Die eigentliche, tiefste
Bedeutung des Gehorsams ist, daß der Mensch seine gottfeindliche Ichhaftigkeit und
Eigenwilligkeit überwindet und daß Gott über ihn Herr wird (...) Der wahre Gehorsam,
wie Franziskus ihn auffaßt, ist immer ein liebender Gehorsam, der sich, besonders in
seiner vollkommenen Realisierung, vollzieht in der Hingabe der totalen Selbstverleugnung.
In diesem Gehorsam wird Gott wirklich Herr über den Menschen. Die Gemeinschafts-
funktion des Gehorsams ist nicht an erster Stelle die Ordnung der Verhältnisse innerhalb
der Gemeinschaft, sondern vielmehr die Verwirklichung der Herrschaft Gottes unter
den Menschen, sofern Gott seinen Willen durch menschliche Autorität deutlich macht.
Die Gemeinschaft der Menschen ist der Raum, in dem der Mensch Gottes Willen erfüllt.
Eine besondere Form dieser Gehorsamsgemeinschaft ist der Orden der Minderbrüder, zu
dem Gott einzelne beruft, um in dienender Liebe und Selbsthingabe den Gehorsam
Christi an den Vater und zum Heil der Menschen nachzuahmen und beispielhaft
darzustellen."

[175] Cf. *Ep Fid* 1,1,9; *Ep Fid* 2,52. *Fratres ei sumus, quando facimus voluntatem patris qui in
caelis est* (Matt 12,50); *Ex Pat* 5. *Fiat voluntas tua sicut in caelo et in terra.*...

[176] *Ep Im* 13. *Sacrificium obedientiae est maius sacrificium omnium aliorum, quia dat propriam voluntatem ad sacrificium* (*Doctoris* 8, 502); *Ex Reg* 1,5. ...*altissimum ergo est sacrificium eam totaliter Domino consecrare...* (*Doctoris* 8, 394). On Bonaventure and obedience,
see for instance: Hayes, "Spirituality", 37; Hellmann, *Ordo*, 148–150; Marcucci, "La virtù";
Strack, *Christusleid*, 51–54, 120–125.

[177] *Ap Paup* 3,15. ...*quia circa magis difficile virtus consistit...* (*Doctoris* 8, 248; De Vinck,
The Works 4, 48).

[178] *Ap Paup* 3,15. ...*et omnino se alienae propter Deum voluntati subiicere. Et haec absque
dubio meritum auget...* (*Doctoris* 8, 248; De Vinck, *The Works* 4, 49).

He obeyed the Father to death, even to death on a cross. He obeyed both His mother and Joseph, according to the words: And He (...) came to Nazareth, and was subject to them. He also obeyed the judges of the world by paying the didrachma.[179]

Christ obeyed wholly to God and to man.[180] It is precisely this double function of obedience (to obey God and to obey man because of God) that makes it such an eminent virtue.[181] The deeds and words of Christ show that there is no surer way to salvation than by subjecting oneself to God and to men[182] and by denying oneself through humble obedience:

That is why the Truth himself told his followers: If anyone wants to come after me to eternal life, let him deny himself through humble obedience, take up his cross by mortifying his flesh, and follow me through total surrender.[183]

In Christ we find that obedience, with poverty and patience, is the companion of humility: without "humiliating oneself" and "bowing to others' commands" one cannot be truly humble.[184] "The obedient man shall speak of victory," the book of Proverbs rightly testifies.[185]

---

[179] *Vit Myst* 4,1. *Primum igitur vinculum, ut puto, obedientia fuit. Obedivit enim Patri usque ad mortem, mortem autem crucis* [cfr. Phil 2,8]. *Obedivit et Matri et Ioseph secundum illud: Venit Nazareth cum illis et erat subditis eis* [cfr. Luke 2,51]. *Obedivit etiam terrenis iudicibus solvens didrachma... Ligantur vites, ne, si iaceant in terra, aut minuatur aut corrumpatur fructus earum* (*Doctoris* 8, 165; De Vinck, *The Works* 1, 157).

[180] Cf. *Ex Reg* 1,5. *...altissimum ergo est sacrificium eam totaliter Domino consecrare, non tantum ipsi Deo obediendo, sed etiam homini propter Deum...* (*Doctoris* 8, 394).

[181] *Ex Reg* 4,1. *Alio modo obedientia dicit statum eminentem huius virtutis, quando aliquis non tantum obedit Deo, verum etiam homini propter Deum...* (*Doctoris* 8, 394). Cf. *Reg Nov* 14,2. *Item, toto tempore vitae tuae studeas omnibus secundum Deum subiacere et semper humiliter obedire, non solum praelatis, sed etiam subditis...* (*Doctoris* 8, 488; Monti, *Works* 5, 171).

[182] *Ap Paup* 2,13. *...Deo et hominibus se ipsum subiicere...* (*Doctoris* 8, 243; De Vinck, *The Works* 4, 31).

[183] *Reg Nov* 14,1. *Quoniam ad viam salutis nihil est tutius quam per humilem obedientiam adnegare se ipsum, idcirco sequentibus se Veritas dicit: Qui vult venire post me, scilicet ad vitam aeternam, abneget semetipsum, per obedientiae subiectionem, et tollat crucem suam, per carnis macerationem, et sequatur me* [cfr. Matt 16,24], *per finalem consummationem* (*Doctoris* 8, 488; Monti, *Works* 5, 171). Cf. *Ep Im* 12. *...et quia fuit multum obediens, ideo fuit multum exaltatus. Qui ergo vult exaltari studeat pure et perfecte obedire* (*Doctoris* 8, 502).

[184] *Lign Vit* 2,8. *Quoniam autem humilitatem perfectam trium specialiter adornari decet comitatu virtutum, scilicet paupertatis in fugiendo divitias ut fomenta superbiae, patientiae vero in aequanimi perpessione contemptus, obedientiae quoque in alienis parendo mandatis...* (*Doctoris* 8, 72; De Vinck, *The Works* 1, 108–109). Cf. *Reg Nov* 14,2. *Item, toto tempore vitae tuae studeas omnibus secundum Deum subiacere et semper humiliter obedire...* (*Doctoris* 8, 488; Monti, *Works* 5, 171).

[185] *Reg Nov* 14,1. *Vir obediens loquetur victorias* [cfr. Prov 21,28] (*Doctoris* 8, 488; Monti, *Works* 5, 171).

The virtue of obedience
Obedience has three degrees: it is absolute (in Christ, who gave his whole
life for the glory of his Creator); it is accommodating (in secular clerics,
who subject to the Church); and it is monastic (in monks, who promise
obedience to the place of the monastery and to the rule).[186] Obedience is
one of the three "monastic vows" (evangelical counsels), as recommended
in the *Rule* of Francis.[187] The religious vow makes the virtue of poverty in
it greater, the virtue of chastity more becoming, and the virtue of obedience more universal.[188] The perfectly obedient man

> does not know what it is to delay; he abhors procrastination, but has his
> eyes always ready for seeing, his ears for hearing, his tongue for speaking,
> his hands for doing, his feet for walking: in short he keeps himself always on
> the alert in order to carry out promptly and fully the will of the one who
> gave the order.[189]

To further illustrate the necessity of obedience for a person desiring
"to serve God perfectly" and "follow the Lord and Saviour,"[190] I quote
here the complete twentieth point (i.e., spiritual ability to remember) in
Bonaventure's *Letter Containing Twenty-five Points to Remember*:

> Show honor and reverence to all men, out of both duty and devotion.
> Endeavor always to keep intact the rule of holy obedience, as you would the
> apple of your eye, not only in matters of certain or possible importance, but

---

[186] *Ex Reg* 1,6. *Obedientia tamen, secundum quod dicit statum eminentem virtutis obedientiae, plures habet gradus. Quidam enim in omnibus obediunt absolute, ut dictum est;
quidam vero in omnibus accommode... quia clerici saeculares in sacri ordinis susceptione
renuntiant propriis voluntatibus, et ex tunc penitus debent subiici ecclesiasticae potestati...
Amplius, sublimior est obedientia monachorum... Monachorum autem obedientia duobus
constringitur: primo, quia obedientiam vovent, salva stabilitate ad locum; secundo, quia
ad nihil obedire tenentur, quod Regulam suam transcendere demonstratur* (Doctoris 8,
394–395).

[187] *Ex Reg* 1,4. *Vivendo in obedientia, sine proprio et in castitate* (Doctoris 8, 394); *Ap Paup*
3,10. *...vivendo in obedientia, sine proprio et in castitate* (Doctoris 8, 247; De Vinck, *The Works*
4, 43).

[188] *Ap Paup* 3,20. *Similiter quantum ad votum Religionis illius est professio perfectior, in
qua vovetur et paupertas altior et obedientia universalior et forma castitatis honestior*
(Doctoris 8, 250; De Vinck, *The Works* 4, 53); *Ap Paup* 8,16. *...et sicut perfectio castitatis et
obedientiae potest esse maior et minor, sic et paupertatis...* (Doctoris 8, 291; De Vinck, *The
Works* 4, 181).

[189] *Reg Nov* 14,3. *Verus obediens nescit moram, mandatum non procrastinat, sed statim
parat oculos visui, aures auditui, linguam voci, manus operi, pedes itineri et totum se interius
recolligit, ut imperantis exterius perficiat voluntatem* (Doctoris 8, 488; Monti, *Works* 5, 172–
173). Here, Bonaventure quotes Bernard of Clairvaux.

[190] *Ep Mem* Prol,1. *...perfecte Deo servire possit... si sequi volumus Dominum Salvatorem...*
(Doctoris 8, 491; De Vinck, *The Works* 3, 249).

even in the slightest details. Obey not only prelates and all those above you, but also all those below you, submitting yourself to everyone in a spirit of self-denial for the sake of Christ. In all things good and indifferent, always try to follow the wish of others. Never be a burden to anyone, but, loving all in the charity of Christ, make yourself agreeable to all men in general. Avoid particular kindness, friendship, and familiarity. Try your very best never in any way or for any reason, through word, deed, or gesture, directly or indirectly to be the cause or occasion of bitterness, hatred, complaining, injustice, disturbance, grumbling, slander, scandal, flattery, or any such thing.[191]

Saint Francis, "who wanted to obey (*subesse*) rather than command (*praeesse*)," is reported to have told his brothers that a corpse may best illustrate this habit of true obedience.[192]

David

The primacy of obedience
According to the first chapters of the *Profectus religiosorum*, religious life starts with the obligation to serve and love God (chapter 1), and the commitment of oneself to a superior who may lead one in the ways of God (chapter 2).[193] From obedience follows peace with one's superiors (chapter 3) and discipline in the many daily works and exercises (chapters 4–25).[194] In David's order of beginner's virtues, therefore, obedience,

---

[191] *Ep Mem* 20. *Vigesimum, ut honorem et reverentiam omnibus exhibeas tam debitam quam devotam, sanctissimae obedientiae normam non solum in magnis et dubiis, verum etiam in minimis quasi pupillam oculi studeas semper servare illaesam, obediens quidem non solum maioribus et praelatis, verum etiam minoribus omnibus, te subiiciens quibuscumque, abnegando te ipsum pro Christo. In bonis et indifferentibus semper alterius studeas facere voluntatem, in nullo praebens te alicui onerosum, sed potius in caritate Christi diligens universos, te ipsum omnibus communiter gratum reddens. Affabilitates, amicitias et familiaritates fugias singulares; summopere caveas, ne unquam verbo, facto vel gestu alicuius rancoris, odii, clamoris, iniuriae, turbationis, murmurationis, detractionis, scandali, vel adulationis et quorumcumque similium aliqua ratione vel modo, per te vel per alium, causa vel occasio fias* (Doctoris 8, 495; De Vinck, *The Works* 3, 257–258). Cf. *Reg An* 9. *Exerce te quoque ad iustitiam... Ad iustitiam ordinatam per obedientiam ad superiores, per sociabilitatem ad pares, per castigationem ad inferiores* (Doctoris 8,130; De Vinck, *The Works* 3, 245).
[192] *Leg Franc* 6,4. *...non tam praeesse voluit quam subesse... Cum vero vice quadam quaereretur ab eo, quis esset vere obediens iudicandus, corporis mortui similitudinem pro exemplo proposuit* (Doctoris 8, 520; Cousins, *Bonaventure*, 231–232).
[193] *Prof* 1,1–2. *Ecce, quantum nos tenemur servire Deo prae ceteris creaturis et diligere super omnia eum, qui nos prae omnibus creaturis amavit... ideo commisisti te superiori tuo, ut ipse te regat, et dedisti ei manum tuam in professione, ut ipse te ducat in via Dei* (David ab Augusta, 4; Devas, *Spiritual Life* 1, 4–5).
[194] Obedience and discipline complement each other: *In cella libenter esto et aliquid semper age in ea quod aedificet te, vel quod a maiori tibi iniungitur. Nam tam voluntarius*

backed up by peace with one's superior, is practically the first virtue to be acquired. Obedience, in other words, is the beginning of all good in religious life.[195] Novices should first of all be obedient: move as their guide tells them, refrain from what he forbids, give up their own notions, submit their own will to the judgment of their superior, neither act nor speak in any way which they think the master would not approve, act in such wise that he may feel under no constraint in his dealings with them, and never indulge in criticism, murmur, ill-will towards or contempt for them.[196] In all of this, the superior is God's vicar, who should be obeyed as the Lord and not as a mere man.[197]

Obedience and the other virtues

Obedience is one of the three monastic vows (based on the evangelical counsels), together with chastity and poverty.[198] With these begins the life "in the Order of obedience and stability."[199] Obedience belongs to the virtues of Christ, who became obedient unto death, even to the death on the Cross (Phil 2,8).[200] Religious should imitate Him on their own path of "service, contumeliousness and contempt": humility, patience, poverty, and

---

debes esse ad obedientiam, quod, si in omni hora tibi praeciperetur, quid facere deberes, libenter acciperes (Prof 1,12; David ab Augusta, 16; Devas, Spiritual Life 1, 14).

[195] *Prof 1,3. His de obedientia praemissis, quae est initium boni in Religione... (David ab Augusta, 7; Devas, Spiritual Life 1, 6).*

[196] *Prof 1,2. ...sed quo ductor tuus te ire iubet, solum ire debes, et quod ipse prohibet, hoc debes cavere... et proprias adinventiones relinquere... Ita et tu nihil facias vel dicas, quod magistrum tuum nolle praesumis... Idcirco talem te exhibeas ei, ut libere iubeat, te facere vel omittere quidquid videtur ei expedire... (David ab Augusta, 4–5; Devas, Spiritual Life 1, 5); Prof 1,26. Esto praelatis humiliter obediens nec rancores contra eos teneas nec spernas eos nec iudices nec murmures de eis (David ab Augusta, 35; Devas, Spiritual Life 1, 30); Prof 3,42. Obedientia est propriae voluntatis subiectio arbitrio superioris ad licita et honesta (David ab Augusta, 261; Devas, Spiritual Life 2, 97). Cf. Prof 1,22. ...ad egrediendum, nisi quando vel obedientiae cogit mandatum...nisi obedientia vel utilitas animae aliud requirat (David ab Augusta, 29; Devas, Spiritual Life 1, 25–26).*

[197] *Prof 1,2. ...et ideo debemus eis sicut Domino obedire, et non quasi hominibus [cfr. Eph 6,7]... (David ab Augusta, 5; Devas, Spiritual Life 1, 5). Cf. Prof 3,42. ...vel creaturae rationali vice Dei, Angelo vel homini, in his, quae Deus requirit a nobis, et quae ad Deum conducunt (David ab Augusta, 261; Devas, Spiritual Life 2, 97).*

[198] *Prof 3,16. ...voti proprii sponsionem discretam, ut est votum continentiae, obedientiae et abdicationis proprietatis... (David ab Augusta, 193; Devas, Spiritual Life 2, 34). Cf. Prof 2,30. ...ut qui obligant se voto ad obedientiam, castitatem, paupertatem et similia... (David ab Augusta, 117; Devas, Spiritual Life 1, 111).*

[199] *Prof 2, Praef. ...promittit obedientiam et stabilitatem in Ordine per verba (David ab Augusta, 65; Devas, Spiritual Life 1, 69–60).*

[200] *Prof 3,43. ...sicut Christus factus est pro nobis obediens usque ad mortem, mortem autem crucis (David ab Augusta, 267; Devas, Spiritual Life 2, 102).*

obedience.[201] Accordingly, it is one of the virtues in which a good religious should exercise himself constantly: humility, charity, obedience, meekness, and care in giving good example.[202] It is one of the virtues by which religious are bound to good actions: faith, charity, justice, truth, chastity, obedience, and contempt for worldly interests.[203] Furthermore, it is one of the seven key virtues of spiritual progress in David's sixth stage of religious life, the development of the virtues of charity, humility, patience, obedience, poverty, sobriety, and chastity. Thus, obedience is founded on charity, humility, and patience.[204] It is one of the eighteen sub-virtues of charity, which, among other things, prompts us to be compliant with authority.[205] Finally, it is charity's sister in all matters daily and charitable.[206]

Distinctions, degrees, and examples

The principle of obedience rests on a triple foundation. First, God has arranged a hierarchy wherein the lower being is subject to the higher, and the higher exercises sway over the lower. Second, not all men are taught of God (John 6,45) and, consequently, it is expedient to choose and follow some leader experienced in spiritual matters, "lest in ignorance we stray

---

[201] *Prof* 2,28. *Pudet nos imitari Dominum in humilitate, patientia, paupertate, religione, obedientia et despectione et contumeliis et confusione...* (*David ab Augusta*, 113; Devas, *Spiritual Life* 1, 107). Cf. *Prof* 3,59. *Item, sublimia virtutum exercitia pauca videmus, ut eximiae obedientiae, perfectae patientiae et humilitatis praecipuae et paupertatis extremae* (*David ab Augusta*, 331; Devas, *Spiritual Life* 2, 163).

[202] *Prof,* Epist 2. *Tertius, opera exercitare virtutum, ut obsequia humilitatis, servitia caritatis, assiduitas obediendi, mansuete loquendi, variis exercitiis bonum exemplum dandi...* (*David ab Augusta*, 60; Devas, *Spiritual Life* 1, 54).

[203] *Prof* 2,12. *Bona nostra, ad quae tenemur ex praecepto Dei vel Ecclesiae, vel ad quae ex manifesto voto adstringimur, debemus hominibus ostendere, ut fidem, caritatem, iustitiam, veritatem, castitatem, obedientiam et contemptum mundanorum* (*David ab Augusta*, 97; Devas, *Spiritual Life* 1, 93).

[204] *Prof* 3,42. *Et quia obedientia ex caritate et humilitate et patientia nascitur...* (*David ab Augusta*, 261; Devas, *Spiritual Life* 2, 97).

[205] *Prof* 3,32. *...cum obtemperat superioribus, ut iustum est, obedientia est...* (*David ab Augusta*, 226; Devas, *Spiritual Life* 2, 65).

[206] *Prof* 1,37. *...facere quod est faciendum, vel obedientia iubente vel caritate instigante* (*David ab Augusta*, 50; Devas, *Spiritual Life* 1, 43). Cf. *Prof* 1,31. *...bona actio, maxime condita pinguedine caritatis et obedientiae vel alterius virtutis...* (*David ab Augusta*, 42; Devas, *Spiritual Life* 1, 36); *Prof* 1,33. *...quae vero ad spiritualem profectum vel fraternae caritatis exhibitionem vel ad praelati obedientiam vel ad carnis castigationem spectant...* (*David ab Augusta*, 45; Devas, *Spiritual Life* 1, 39); *Prof* 3,20. *...sit promptus ad quaeque spiritualia exercitia, quae vel obedientia iusserit, vel caritas fraterna requirit...* (*David ab Augusta*, 205; Devas, *Spiritual Life* 2, 45); *Prof* 3,52. *...ut cum propter obedientiam vel caritatem proximi oratio intermittitur, et operibus pietatis insistitur...* (*David ab Augusta*, 296; Devas, *Spiritual Life* 2, 130).

from the path that leads to the glory of heaven." Third, man originally refused to obey God, and must now obey man for God's sake and win back from God by humility the grace lost by pride.[207]

There are other distinctions: obedience is general, more general, or most general; special, more special, or most special;[208] of the first, second, and third objective (*ad illa, in quibus obediendum est*) degree; and of the first, second, and third subjective (*ad mentem vel affectum obedientis*) degree. The three *objective* degrees are obedience to the commandments of God and the Church, obedience to the counsels of perfection, and obedience in all matters that are good and possible.[209] The three *subjective* degrees are those which are motivated by, respectively, fear of punishment (a mark of beginners), desire for benefits (a mark of those who progress), and the love of God (a mark of the perfect). Thus, obedience is of three kinds, corresponding to compulsion, avarice, or love at work.[210]

Finally, the good religious can find some perfect examples of obedience based on ardent love, promptitude, and constancy:

It is obedience of this kind that we read of in the life of our holy father St. Francis. His first companions would promptly fulfil not merely the express commands of their holy father, but equally what, from any sign, they conjectured to be his will; a practice they learnt from the holy father

[207] *Prof* 3,42. *Ratio obedientiae triplex est: una, quod omnis creatura ita ordinata est a Deo… ut inferiora superioribus subdita sint, et superiora inferioribus praesint et ea regant… Secunda ratio est, quod, cum nondum sit omnibus datum esse docibiles Dei, ne ignari errent a via Dei, qua necesse est, eos pervenire ad gloriam caelestem, expedit, ut sequantur ducatum doctorum suorum… Tertia ratio est, ut homo, qui subesse Deo noluit peccando et ita superbiendo gratiam Dei perdidit, satisfaciat ei, subiiciendo se homini propter Deum, et ita per humilitatis meritum gratiam Dei recuperet, quam amisit* (David ab Augusta, 262–263; Devas, *Spiritual Life* 2, 97–98). Cf. *Prof* 3,48. *Obedientia indiscreta sic fugit propriae voluntatis vitium, ut obediat superiori etiam ad peccatum, cum tamen obedire Deo magis oporteat prohibenti omne peccatum quam cuivis homini praecipienti peccatum* (David ab Augusta, 283–284; Devas, *Spiritual Life* 2, 117).

[208] *Prof* 3,42. *Item, alia est distinctio obedientiae: quia alia est generalis, alia generalior, alia generalissima; item, alia specialis, alia specialior, alia specialissima* (David ab Augusta, 263; Devas, *Spiritual Life* 2, 99).

[209] *Prof* 3,43. *Profectus vel gradus obedientiae, quantum ad illa, in quibus obediendum est, colligi possunt ex praedictis, id est obedire ad praecepta communia, obedire ad aliqua etiam consilia, obedire ad omnia bona et possibilia* (David ab Augusta, 265; Devas, *Spiritual Life* 2, 100).

[210] *Prof* 3,42. *Est enim triplex obedientia: necessitatis, cupiditatis, caritatis… Obedientia caritatis est, quando ex caritate Dei vel propter Deum et propter divinam remunerationem obeditur, large sumto nomine caritatis, quo tam timor poenae quam desiderium praemii quam affectus amoris Dei includitur, quorum primum est incipientium, secundum proficientium, tertium perfectorum* (David ab Augusta, 263; Devas, *Spiritual Life* 2, 98–99). Cf. *Prof* 3,43 (David ab Augusta, 265–268; Devas, *Spiritual Life* 2, 100–103).

himself. Such, too, was the obedience of Abraham in leaving his own country and going to dwell as a stranger in a foreign land; and again in his readiness to sacrifice his only son Isaac. Such was the obedience of the prophets and apostles and other saints who, for Christ's sake, exposed themselves to every kind of labour and danger, to exile, poverty, persecution and death. It was to such especially Our Lord referred when He said: If any man will come after me, let him deny himself. He denies himself who renounces his own independence, and, for the love of Christ, wholly subjects himself to the will of another. So did Christ come, not to do His own will, but the will of His Father.[211]

3. GOODNESS

Origin

Goodness (*bonitas*) is a primary virtue in the Bible.[212] It is one of the main attributes of God, the very content of his name, as is shown in his promise to his people: "I will cause all my goodness (*omne bonum*) to pass in front of you, and I will proclaim my name, the Lord, in your presence."[213] As a result of this divine goodness, it is also the first property (the beginning) of his creation, as is evident from the story of the Creation: "And God saw

---

[211] *Prof* 3,43. *Et licet servorum Dei obedientia quantum ad affectum ex maiori fervore prodeat; tamen quoad actum ille perfectus videretur, qui ita promptus et constans esset ad omnia iussa implenda, sicut in servis saecularibus invenitur; sicut de sanctissimo Patre nostro Francisco legimus et primis eius sociis, qui non solum ea, quae beatus Pater eis verbo expressit, prompte adimplebant, sed etiam si aliquo indicio beneplacitum eius poterant coniicere, studiosissime perfecerunt, sicut ab ipso didicerant sancto Patre. Hac virtute Abraham obedivit exire de terra sua et peregrinus esse in aliena, sed et unicum filium Isaac voluit immolare. Hac Prophetae et Apostoli et alii Sancti exposuerunt se omnibus laboribus, periculis, exsiliis, penuriis et persecutionibus et morti pro Christo, de quibus Dominus specialiter dicit: Si quis vult post me venire, abneget semetipsum. Semetipsum abnegat qui sui iuris esse recusat et totum se alterius arbitrio subiicit propter Christum, sicut Christus non venit facere voluntatem suam, sed Patris* (David ab Augusta, 267–268; Devas, *Spiritual Life* 2, 102–103). Cf. *Prof* 2,2. *...ut ostenderetur magna devotio obedientiae Abraham et fidei ad Deum...* (David ab Augusta, 75; Devas, *Spiritual Life* 1, 70); *Prof* 2,1. *...sed totum mactetur et immoletur Domino obedientiae ferro per sacerdotis ministerium...* (David ab Augusta, 67; Devas, *Spiritual Life* 1, 62).

[212] On Christianity and goodness, see for instance: Bertocci, *The Goodness*; "Bonté"; "Gut"; "Gut, das Gute, das Gut"; Hollencamp, «*Nemo bonus*; Long, *The Goodness*; MacDonald, *Being*; Mörschel, "Gut"; Strack, "Das bonum"; Wenham, *The Goodness*.

[213] Exod 33,19. Where the people in the Old Testament acknowledge God's goodness, the Vulgate uses words like *dulcedo* and *suavitas* for His goodness, e.g., Ps 30,20 (31,19) ("How great is your goodness (*multitudo dulcedinis*), which you have stored up for those who fear you, which you bestow in the sight of men on those who take refuge in you"), and Ps 144,7 (145,7) ("They will celebrate your abundant goodness (*abundantiae suavitatis*) and joyfully sing of your righteousness").

that it was good."[214] After the fall of man, however, the goodness of creation is no longer evident, and man has to be called back and restored
to his original state, viz., goodness. But even more than in the Jewish
tradition, where goodness remains first and foremost the attribute of God,
in the Christian tradition the concept of goodness gets a strong moral
connotation: as God is entirely good, so should we be entirely good.[215]
Goodness here means virtuous perfection.[216] To enter the life of the One
who is good we should follow the commandments[217] and add goodness
(*virtus*) to our faith.[218] Goodness now becomes one of the Christian virtue
catalogues' main virtues, for example, as one of the fruits of the Light (with
justice and truth) and one of the fruits of the Holy Spirit (with love, joy,
peace, patience, kindness, faithfulness, gentleness, and self-control).[219] The
Christian concept or virtue of *bonitas* implies that only when it is understood that all goodness "is from above, coming down from the Father,"[220]
can the human task of realizing goodness in this world fully succeed.[221]

Francis of Assisi

God is good

The central, most important themes in the life and thought of Francis are
the Bible, Christ the Son of God, his humanity, and God the Most High,

---

[214] Cf. Gen 1,10; Rice, *God*; "Gut", 1115: "...durch die biblische Überzeugung von der
grundsätzlichen Güte der Schöpfung und aller Geschöpfe, wie sie [diese inhaltliche
Bestimmung des Guten] auch die Möglichkeit bot, den göttlichen Urheber als das allen
Gütern ihr Gutsein gewährende höchste Gut zu deuten."

[215] Matt 5,48. Naturally, "doing good" in the eyes of the Lord is also an important theme
in the Old Testament, especially in the Psalms (e.g., "Turn from evil and do good" (Ps 33,15
(34,14)); "Trust in the Lord and do good" (Ps 36,3 (37,3))). In accordance with the distinction between the goodness of God and goodness as a human quality or virtue to be pur-
sued, Augustine distinguishes between the good as a perfect quality of being/God (*bonum
qua ens*), an object of human pursuit (*bonum qua appetibile*), and a human quality of being
(*bonum hominis*) (Brechtken, *Augustinus*, 58–77). Cf. Welzen, "Weest".

[216] "Bonté", 1860.

[217] Matt 19,17.

[218] 2 Pet 1,5.

[219] Gal 5,22–23; Eph 5,9; Col 3,12 (*benignitas*); 2 Cor 6,6 (*suavitas*); 2 Pet 1,5 (*virtus*). Cf.
Wibbing, *Die Tugend- und Lasterkataloge*, 77–127.

[220] Jac 1,17.

[221] Cf. Esser & Grau, *Antwort*, 155; "Gut", 1115: "...als im eigenen realen Handeln
gestaltbares Streben nach Gütern darzustellen, die zu einem guten Leben im Sinne eines
endgültig, d.h. vor Gott gelingenden Lebens gehören." This is opposed to the many
modern secular (analytical-ethical, autonomous, philosophical) theories of goodness, e.g.,
Blanshard, *Reason*; Johnson, *Rightness*; Murdoch, *The Sovereignty*; Pybus, *Human*;
Sparshott, *An Enquiry*; Von Wright, *The Varieties*.

All-efficacious, and All-good.[222] Whereas Christ for him is the Good Shepherd who bore the suffering of the cross to save his sheep,[223] the Lord God, without whom there is no good and to whom all good belongs, is "good, all good, supreme good, full of goodness, totally good, true good, and the only One who is good."[224] From Him comes all good, and to Him all good should be referred (*reddamus*):

> All-powerful, most holy, most high, supreme God: all good, supreme good, totally good, You Who alone are good, may we give You all praise, all glory, all thanks, all honor, all blessing, and all good.
> So be it! So be it! Amen.[225]

To "refer" (i.e., to attribute, trace back, or give back something to whom it belongs) here is a laudatory acknowledgement of God as the origin of all good; it is, therefore, an act of praise, gratitude, and justice.[226]

---

[222] Dettlof, "Franziskanertheologie", 388–391. On Francis and goodness, see for instance: Esser & Grau, *Antwort*, 277; Iriarte, *Vocazione*, 82–84; Rotzetter, *Franz von Assisi*, 138; Tils, *Der heilige*, 79.

[223] *Adm* 6,1. *Attendamus, omnes fratres, bonum pastorem, qui pro ovibus suis salvandis crucis sustinuit passionem; RnB 22,32. Ego sum pastor bonus, qui pasco oves meas et pro ovibus meis pono animam meam.* Likewise, there is "every good" in Mary: *...in qua fuit et est omnis plenitudo gratiae et omne bonum* (*Sal Mar* 3).

[224] *Adm* 7,4. *...sed verbo et exemplo reddunt ea altissimo Domino Deo cuius est omne bonum; Cant Sol 1. Altissimu onnipotente bon signore...; Laud Dei 3. Tu es trinus et unus Dominus Deus deorum* (cfr. Ps 135,2); *tu es bonum, omne bonum, summum bonum, Dominus Deus vivus et verus* (cfr. 1 Thess 1,9); *Ep Fid 2,62. ...quia ipse est virtus et fortitudo nostra, qui est solus bonus, solus altissimus, solus omnipotens, admirabilis, gloriosus et solus sanctus, laudabilis et benedictus per infinita saecula saeculorum; Ex Laud 10. Laudate Dominum, quoniam bonus est* (Ps 146,1)*...; Ex Pat 2. ...quia tu, Domine, summum bonum es, aeternum, a quo omne bonum, sine quo nullum bonum; RnB 23,9. ...solus verus Deus, qui est plenum bonum, omne bonum, totum bonum, verum et summum bonum, qui solus est bonus* (cfr. Luke 18,19)....

[225] *Laud Hor* 11. *Omnipotens sanctissime, altissime et summe Deus, omne bonum, summum bonum, totum bonum, qui solus es bonus* (cfr. Luke 18,19), *tibi reddamus omnem laudem, omnem gloriam, omnem gratiam, omnem honorem, omnem benedictionem et omnia bona. Fiat. Fiat. Amen* (Armstrong, *Francis of Assisi*, 162). Cf. *Ex Pat* 2. *...quia tu, Domine, summum bonum es, aeternum, a quo omne bonum, sine quo nullum bonum; Of Pas 4,13,6. ... cantabo Domino, qui bona tribuit mihi...; RnB 23,8. ...qui nobis miserabilibus et miseris, putridis et foetidis, ingratis et malis omnia bona fecit et facit; Adm 18,2. Beatus servus, qui omnia bona reddit Domino Deo...; Of Pas 1, Or. Benedicamus Domino Deo vivo et vero: laudem, gloriam, honorem, benedictionem et omnia bona referamus ei semper; RnB 17,17–18. Et omnia bona Domino Deo altissimo et summo reddamus et omnia bona ipsius esse cognoscamus et de omnibus ei gratias referamus, a quo bona cuncta procedunt. Et ipse altissimus et summus, solus verus Deus habeat et ei reddantur et ipse recipiat omnes honores et reverentias, omnes laudes et benedictiones, omnes gratias et gloriam, cuius est omne bonum, qui solus est bonus* (cfr. Luke 18,19).

[226] Van den Goorbergh & Zweerman, *Was Getekend*, 52–54, 78–80; Zweerman, ""Danken"", 121–128.

Man should be good

To "refer all good to the Lord" means to recognize God as the giver of all good, but also to reciprocate the reverence and honor that He has rendered to man by "returning the favour" and being good and doing good oneself. "Doing good," in laudation of the Lord, is one of Francis's important brotherly commands. First of all, well-doers confound evildoers: "When we see or hear evil spoken or done or God blasphemed, let us speak well and do well (*bene faciamus*) and praise God Who is blessed forever."[227] Thus, doing good works (*bona opera*) combats evil (i.e., the devil) and sin:

> Let all the brothers always strive to exert themselves in doing good works, for it is written: "Always do something good that the devil may find you occupied." And again: "Idleness is an enemy of the soul." Servants of God, therefore, must always apply themselves to prayer or some good work.[228]

Furthermore, while confounding sins like idleness, envy, and blasphemy,[229] doing good works confounds the evil of self-will: going against obedience, making your will your own (*appropriare*), exalting yourself over the good things the Lord says or does in you, and not revealing them in good behavior (exalting Him by your deeds), holding them in your heart, and storing them up in heaven.[230] When we are of good will (opposing self-will) and

---

[227] *RnB* 17,19. *Et quando nos videmus vel audimus malum dicere vel facere vel blasphemare Deum, nos bene dicamus et bene faciamus et laudemus Deum* (cfr. Rom 12,21), *qui est benedictus in saecula* (Rom 1,25). Cf. *Adm* 8,2. *Non est qui faciat bonum, non est usque ad unum* (Rom 3,12); *Ep Fid* 2,27. *Et si quis non vult eos amare sicut se ipsum, saltim non inferat eis mala, sed faciat bona; Of Pas* 1,5,14. *Retribuebant mihi mala pro bonis* (Ps 34,12a) *et detrahebant mihi quoniam sequebar bonitatem* (Ps 37,21); *Ex Pat* 5. ...*de bonis aliorum sicut de nostris gaudendo et in malis compatiendo et nemini ullam offensionem dando* (cfr. 2 Cor 6,3).

[228] *RnB* 7,10–12. *Omnes fratres studeant bonis operibus insudare, quia scriptum est: Semper facito aliquid boni, ut te diabolus inveniat occupatum. Et iterum: Otiositas inimica est animae. Ideo servi Dei semper orationi vel alicui bonae operationi insistere debent* (Armstrong, *Francis of Assisi*, 69).

[229] Cf. *Adm* 8,3. *Quicumque ergo invidet fratri suo de bono, quod Dominus dicit et facit in ipso, pertinet ad peccatum blasphemiae, quia ipsi Altissimo invidet* (cfr. Matt 20,15), *qui dicit et facit omne bonum; RnB* 22,6. ...*quia nos per culpam nostram sumus foetidi, miseri et bono contrarii, ad mala autem prompti et voluntarii...; Sal Virt* 8. *Et unaquaque confundit vitia et peccata.*

[230] *Adm* 2,1–3. *Dixit Dominus ad Adam: De omni ligno comede, de ligno autem scientiae boni et mali non comedas* (cfr. Gen 2,16.17). *De omni ligno paradisi poterat comedere, quia, dum non venit contra obedientiam, non peccavit. Ille enim comedit de ligno scientiae boni, qui sibi suam voluntatem appropriat et se exaltat de bonis quae Dominus dicit et operatur in ipso...; Adm* 3,4. *Et quidquid facit et dicit, quod ipse sciat, quod non sit contra voluntatem eius,*

good heart (retaining the good in us),[231] goodness will confound evil, produce ever more good, and become a virtue supportive of other virtues
like obedience (in which self-will is annulled), humility (in which self-
exaltation is discarded), and perseverance (in which the promise to God
is kept).[232] The human virtue of goodness, then, is so powerful that it realizes in this world the *bonum*, i.e., the Good Lord Himself. But it can only
do so because God, the source of all goodness,[233] restores good in man "by
saying and doing good things in him."

Bonaventure

Divine and human, perfect and imperfect
Bonaventure distinguishes three categories of appropriated divine attributes.[234] The first of these consists of unity (*unitas*; attributed to the Father),
truth (*veritas*; attributed to the Son), and goodness (*bonitas*; attributed to
the Holy Spirit). As a consequence, supreme love and supreme sweetness

---

*dum bonum sit quod facit, vera obedientia est; Adm 12,2–3. ...cum Dominus operaretur per
ipsum aliquod bonum, si caro eius non inde se exaltaret, quia semper est contraria
omni bono, sed si magis ante oculos se haberet viliorem et omnibus aliis hominibus minorem
se existimaret; Adm 17,1. Beatus ille servus* (Matt 24,46), *qui non magis se exaltat de bono,
quod Dominus dicit et operatur per ipsum, quam quod dicit et operatur per alium; RnB
17,6. ...non gloriari nec in se gaudere nec interius se exaltare de bonis verbis et operibus,
immo de nullo bono, quod Deus facit vel dicit et operatur in eis aliquando et per ipsos...;
Adm 21,2. Vae illi religioso, qui bona, quae Dominus sibi ostendit, non retinet in corde suo*
(cfr. Luke 2,19.51) *et aliis non ostendit per operationem, sed sub specie mercedis magis hominibus verbis cupit ostendere; Ep Ord 8. Confitemini ei quoniam bonus* (Ps 135,1) *et exaltate
eum in operibus vestris* (Tob 13,6); *Adm 28,1. Beatus servus, qui thesaurizat in caelo* (cfr. Matt
6,20) *bona, quae Dominus sibi ostendit et sub specie mercedis non cupit manifestare
hominibus....*
   [231] Cf. *Of Pas* 5,15,8. *Gloria in altissimis Domino Deo et in terra pax hominibus bonae voluntatis* (cfr. Luke 2,14); *RB 2,6. Quod si facere non potuerint, sufficit eis bona voluntas; RnB
22,17. Quod autem in terram bonam* (Luke 8,15) *seminatum est* (Matt 13,23), *hi sunt, qui in
corde bono et optimo audientes verbum* (Luke 8,15) *intellegunt et* (cfr. Matt 13,23) *retinent et
fructum afferunt in patientia* (Luke 8,15).
   [232] Cf. *Ep Ord* 10. *In disciplina et obedientia sancta perseverate* (Hebr 12,7) *et quae promisistis ei bono et firmo proposito adimplete; RnB 21,9. Cavete et abstinete ab omni malo et
perseverate usque in finem in bono.*
   [233] Cf. Iriarte, *Vocazione*, 82.
   [234] *Trip Via* 3,7,12. *Prima appropriata sunt unitas, veritas, bonitas. Attribuitur unitas
Patri, quia origo; veritas Filio, quia imago; bonitas Spiritui sancto, quia connexio (Doctoris* 8,
17; De Vinck, *The Works* 1, 92). The other two corresponding categories consist of power
(*potestas*), wisdom (*sapientia*), and will (*voluntas*); and loftiness (*altitudo*), beauty (*pulcritudo*), and sweetness (*dulcedo*). Consequently, the Spirit is sweet (*dulcedo*) because of His
goodness (*bonitas*) and His will (*voluntas*). On Bonaventure and goodness, see for instance:
Speer, *Triplex*, 95, 202–207.

are found wherever supreme goodness is united to the divine will.[235] God is the origin and end of all good.[236] For mankind there lies great consolation in the fact that God's goodness is infinite, and even extended unto the wicked and unworthy.[237] He is a Good so great as to exceed every possible request, desire, or surmise.[238] His generosity cannot deplete his infinite perfection, his goodness.[239] He deems us worthy of his good so great if we love and desire Him above all else, and for his own sake; therefore, He should be loved with perfect love.[240] Moreover, man is perfectly just (justified) when he, accordingly, "assents to all truth, supports all goodness, and opposes to all evil by thought and word and deed."[241] He is good insofar as he participates in the supreme Good (*summum bonum*) itself,[242] since human goodness, unlike divine goodness, may still be destroyed at any time by some defective circumstance or improper intention.[243]

---

[235] *Trip Via* 3,7,12. *Ubi est summa bonitas iuncta cum voluntate, ibi est summa caritas et summa dulcedo* (*Doctoris* 8, 17; De Vinck, *The Works* 1, 92).

[236] *Trip Via* 1,2,14. *...qui est fons et finis omnium bonorum...* (*Doctoris* 8, 7; De Vinck, *The Works* 1, 70). Cf. *Lign Vit* 12,48. *...qui est fons et origo bonorum...* (*Doctoris* 8, 85; De Vinck, *The Works* 1, 143).

[237] *Praep Mis* 2,5. *Si vero consolationem sentis aliquam, non tibi tribuas, sed suae bonitati immensae, quae etiam ad malos extenditur et indignos consolatur...* (*Doctoris* 8, 106; De Vinck, *The Works* 3, 238).

[238] *Trip Via* 1,2,14. *...qui est tantum bonum, quod excedit omnem petitionem, omne desiderium, omnem aestimationem...* (*Doctoris* 8, 7; De Vinck, *The Works* 1, 70).

[239] *Sol* 2,3,19. *Si enim sua liberalitas suam infinitam bonitatem diminueret...* (*Doctoris* 8, 52; De Vinck, *The Works* 3, 93).

[240] *Trip Via* 1,2,14. *...et nos tanto bono dignos reputat, si diligimus et appetimus ipsum super omnia et propter se...* (*Doctoris* 8, 7; De Vinck, *The Works* 1, 70); *Sol* 4,5,27. *...quanto, putas, desiderio aestuare debes ad aeternam bonitatem perfecte diligendam et summam maiestatem aeternaliter possidendam?* (*Doctoris* 8, 66; De Vinck, *The Works* 3, 127–128).

[241] *Reg An* 9. *Ad iustitiam perfectam, ut omni veritati assentias, bonitati faveas, malitiae adverseris tam mente quam verbo quam opere...* (*Doctoris* 8, 130; De Vinck, *The Works* 3, 245). Cf. *Sex Alis* 2,1. *Tantum enim quisque bonus aestimandus est, quanto plus et purius odit malum...* (*Doctoris* 8, 133; De Vinck, *The Works* 3, 141).

[242] *Ap Paup* 2,12. *Et quemadmodum ab illo uno aeterno exemplari indiviso tam diversae manant creaturarum naturae et naturarum perfectiones secundum variam ipsius summi boni participationem...* (*Doctoris* 8, 243; De Vinck, *The Works* 4, 30).

[243] *Ap Paup* 1,7. *Et haec duo bona depravari possunt per alicuius circumstantiae defectum, et maxime propter inordinationem intentionis...* (*Doctoris* 8, 237; De Vinck, *The Works* 4, 13). Cf. *Sex Alis* 6,2. *Nam nec bonum simpliciter bonum est, nisi bene fiat, id est, sicut decet* (*Doctoris* 8, 142; De Vinck, *The Works* 3, 172); *Ap Paup* 6,1. *...quod tam ieiunare quam comedere fieri potest non solum perfecte et imperfecte, verum etiam bene et male, sancte et impie, secundum rationem diversorum finium et circumstantiarum* (*Doctoris* 8, 266; De Vinck, *The Works* 4, 107–108).

David

Good things and the good

The adjective "good" appears on almost every second page of David's *Profectus religiosorum*: there are good people, inside (*boni, boni homines, boni servi Dei*) as well as outside (*boni saecularii*) the monastery; there are good works, good manners, good ways, good thoughts, good actions, good occupations (*in bonis studiis occupare*), good undertakings, good examples, good angels, and good meals; there is seriousness of the right kind (*serium bonum*), good measure, and good wine; there are religious customs and practices such as mortification that under certain circumstances are good; and there are faculties of the mind such as the will and conscience that should be good. David uses the *substantive* "good" for good fortune (*bonum*) or good things (*bona*) and goods in general, and for our good deeds (*bona nostra*) and qualities (*bona nostra*) such as the mind's faculties (*bona mentis nostrae*). There are natural qualities (*bona naturae*) such as nobility of birth, good looks, physical health, and mental ability; gifts of fortune (*bona fortunae*) such as dignities and honours; and gifts of grace (*bona gratiae*) such as habits of virtue, knowledge, and good works like preaching or fasting.[244] The good is, finally, not only personal or actual, but also communal (e.g., *bonum commune*) or heavenly (e.g., *bonum aeternum*).

God's goodness and our goodness

All things are good and true (*bonum et verum*)[245] insofar as they are opposed to the bad (*malum*) and the false (*falsum*),[246] and insofar as they correspond to "the Good," which is God:

---

[244] *Prof* 2,12. *Bona gratiae sunt virtutes, scientia et opera de genere bonorum, ut praedicare, ieiunare et similia. Bona naturae sunt quae natura contulit, ut nobilitas, pulchritudo, fortitudo, ingenium et similia. Bona fortunae sunt divitiae, dignitates, honores et similia...* (*David ab Augusta*, 96; Devas, *Spiritual Life* 1, 92). Cf. *Prof* 1,39. *...ut non sit tibi exsecrabile bonum, quod est ex natura in praesenti, vel ex gratia forsitan in futuro* (*David ab Augusta*, 52; Devas, *Spiritual Life* 1, 45).

[245] E.g., *Prof* 1,18. *Cito cede, quia, si bonum est et verum, quod alter proponit, tuum non est resistere propter aliquam ostentationem...* (*David ab Augusta*, 24; Devas, *Spiritual Life* 1, 21).

[246] E.g., *Prof* 1,13. *...ut scias discernere verum a falso, bonum a malo, vitium a virtute et remedia vitiorum ac tentationum* (*David ab Augusta*, 17; Devas, *Spiritual Life* 1, 17); *Prof* 2,6. *Ratio recipit saepius falsum pro vero; voluntas eligit deterius pro bono* (*David ab Augusta*, 88; Devas, *Spiritual Life* 1, 84); *Prof* 2,16. *Ignorantia excaecat, ne verum agnoscamus et erremus in iudicio boni et mali* (*David ab Augusta*, 102; Devas, *Spiritual Life* 1, 97); *Prof* 3,12. ...

For three reasons should we love God above all things. Firstly, because He is good; and not merely that, but because He is goodness itself and the source of whatever goodness may be found outside of Him, and because His goodness is such that nothing more good exists or can be conceived of. If whatever is good is to be loved in proportion to its goodness, He who is the supreme and infinite good should be loved – were it possible – to an infinite degree as His dignity deserves.[247]

God is good (the good),[248] all good,[249] true good (good and true),[250] and the highest Good (*summum bonum*).[251] Supreme goodness (*summa bonitas*), together with truth and joy,[252] is what He is and what He has.[253] This goodness can be fancied and confided in;[254] it should be praised and

---

rationabilitas caecatur, ut bonum malum iudicet et malum bonum... (*David ab Augusta*, 185; Devas, *Spiritual Life* 2, 25).

[247] *Prof* 3,31. *Diligere Deum super omnia debemus propter tria: quia bonus est in se, nec tantummodo bonus, sed etiam ipsa bonitas est, quo nihil melius cogitari vel esse potest et quo omne, quod aliquo modo bonum est, bonum est. Si enim omne, quod bonum est, diligendum est in quantum bonum, ille, qui summe bonus est et infinitum bonum est, summe, et si possibile esset, in infinitum diligendus est iuxta meritum dignitatis eius* (*David ab Augusta*, 223; Devas, *Spiritual Life* 2, 63). The other reasons for loving God are that He first loved us, and that his love has led Him to do great things for us. See above, 2.1.

[248] E.g., *Prof* 3,32. *Deus est unum simplex et perfectissimum bonum, in quo est omne bonum perfecte, et cui nullum bonum deest* (*David ab Augusta*, 226; Devas, *Spiritual Life* 2, 65).

[249] E.g., *Prof* 2,5. *...et in quo nullus defectus est omnis boni* (*David ab Augusta*, 85; Devas, *Spiritual Life* 1, 81).

[250] E.g., *Prof* 3,37. *Sicut ergo caritas ordinat nos ad bonitatem, ita humilitas habet nos ordinare ad veritatem* (*David ab Augusta*, 243; Devas, *Spiritual Life* 2, 80). See below, 2.4.

[251] E.g., *Prof* 3,28. *Summum autem bonum, quod est Deus* (*David ab Augusta*, 216; Devas, *Spiritual Life* 2, 56).

[252] *Prof* 3,37. *Vera beatitudo consistit in cognitione summae veritatis, in dilectione vel delectatione summae bonitatis, in fruitione aeternae iucunditatis* (*David ab Augusta*, 243; Devas, *Spiritual Life* 2, 80). Elsewhere, God has goodness, wisdom, and power: *Prof* 3,2. *...et in operibus Dei admirari potentiam, sapientiam et bonitatem ipsius* (*David ab Augusta*, 165; Devas, *Spiritual Life* 2, 6); *Prof* 3,56. *Laudatio Dei dignissimus est affectus et nascitur ex consideratione divinae bonitatis et ex admiratione profunditatis sapientiae Dei et ex stupore altitudinis divinae potentiae et immensitate maiestatis...* (*David ab Augusta*, 311; Devas, *Spiritual Life* 2, 143–144).

[253] *Prof* 3,63. *...et voluntas perfecte afficitur ad amandum summam bonitatem...* (*David ab Augusta*, 346; Devas, *Spiritual Life* 2, 178); *Prof* 2,42. *...contra cuius bonitatem peccata omnium nostrum sunt sicut gutta ad mare* (*David ab Augusta*, 135; Devas, *Spiritual Life* 1, 128); *Prof* 3,3. *Unde dilexit nos et elegit nos, non propter nos, sed propter se ipsum ex sola bonitate sua...* (*David ab Augusta*, 170; Devas, *Spiritual Life* 2, 12); *Prof* 3,60. *...sed cogita, quod pro sua bonitate id facere per se disposuerit, vel aliorum bonorum preces potius attenderit...* (*David ab Augusta*, 334; Devas, *Spiritual Life* 2, 164); *Prof* 3,64. *...ex intuitu beneficiorum Dei et futurae gloriae et bonitatis divinae...* (*David ab Augusta*, 351; Devas, *Spiritual Life* 2, 182–183).

[254] *Prof* 2,26. *Spes data est homini, qui confidat de bonitate Dei... Tantum confidunt quidam de bonitate Dei...* (*David ab Augusta*, 111–112; Devas, *Spiritual Life* 1, 106). Cf. *Prof*

thanked.[255] Imitation of God's goodness is imperative.[256] The good news is that people who fear God will be disposed towards inner goodness.[257] When they do things for the sake of the good,[258] and love the good for the sake of God,[259] their souls, by their own will, can touch the goodness of God and also reach the highest Good.[260]

4. TRUTH

Origin

The question of whether God exists is a philosophical and modern one: it investigates the truth (*veritas*) of God's existence. In Christian theology, however, the question about the truth of God (who does exist) concerns such things as the extent to which He can be known, the ways to know Him, and the meaning of God in our lives. Christians regard "truth" *a priori* as one of the essential names of God, as eternal and present in their lives.[261] For them, God is the Truth and the Life Himself; He is living and true (*vivus et verus*); He (Jesus) is the Way and the Truth and the

---

3,57. *Pater vester dabit Spiritum bonum petentibus se* [cfr. Luke 11,13] (*David ab Augusta*, 322; Devas, *Spiritual Life* 2, 155).

[255] *Prof* 3,56. *Laudatio Dei dignissimus est affectus et nascitur ex consideratione divinae bonitatis...* (*David ab Augusta*, 311; Devas, *Spiritual Life* 2, 143–144); *Prof* 3,56. *Laudatur etiam bonitas Dei...* (*David ab Augusta*, 315–316; Devas, *Spiritual Life* 2, 149); *Prof* 3,56. *Ibi pura et plena laus resonat de omni corde suo laudantium Deum pro tam supermagnifica bonitate eius...* (*David ab Augusta*, 317; Devas, *Spiritual Life* 2, 150); *Prof* 3,55. *Gratias Deo agimus, cum de bono, quod nobis ab ipso profluit, eius bonitatem commendamus* (*David ab Augusta*, 308; Devas, *Spiritual Life* 2, 140).

[256] *Prof* 2,1. *Noli imitari malum, sed bonum* [cfr. 3 John 11] (*David ab Augusta*, 69; Devas, *Spiritual Life* 1, 64); *Prof* 2,10. ...*sed ex imitatione bonitatis...* (*David ab Augusta*, 94; Devas, *Spiritual Life* 1, 90).

[257] *Prof* 1,15. *Sicut enim timor Dei hominem componit et ordinat intrinsecus ad bonitatem...* (*David ab Augusta*, 20; Devas, *Spiritual Life* 1, 18).

[258] *Prof* 1,3. ...*quod pro bono faciunt* (*David ab Augusta*, 6; Devas, *Spiritual Life* 1, 6); *Prof* 1,10. ...*secundo, opus caritatis est et promovens proximum in bono...* (*David ab Augusta*, 14; Devas, *Spiritual Life* 1, 13); *Prof* 3,70. ...*aut pro bonis, quae cupimus, adipiscendis* (*David ab Augusta*, 378; Devas, *Spiritual Life* 2, 212).

[259] *Prof* 1,14. *Qui autem magis veretur hominum aspectus quam Dei et Angelorum et propriae conscientiae non est castus amator boni, quia non declinat malum ex amore veri boni...* (*David ab Augusta*, 19; Devas, *Spiritual Life* 1, 17).

[260] *Prof* 2,5. ...*per voluntatem potens est capere bonitatem Dei* (*David ab Augusta*, 85; Devas, *Spiritual Life* 1, 81); *Prof* 2,5. *Cum ergo summa dignitas animae sit, quod est capax summi boni, et summa utilitas eius sit Deum in se habere et cum ipso omne bonum* (*David ab Augusta*, 85; Devas, *Spiritual Life* 1, 81).

[261] Cf. White, *Truth*, 215.

Life.[262] The divine attribute of truth makes God the One who people can rely on: "Into your hands I commit my spirit; redeem me, O Lord, the God of truth";[263] "I have chosen the way of truth; I have set my heart on your laws."[264] In this way in the Bible, and notably in the Psalms, the truth of God is delineated as reliability, as certainty for the people who are loyal to Him.[265]

As a derivate of its theological function, i.e., divine truth as reliable guidance from above or religious truth as "being truthful" towards God by "worshiping in spirit and in truth,"[266] Christian truth also has a *social* function, constituting harmony and conformity between men. In the Old Testament, "to tell the truth," and truthfulness, is a well-known imperative.[267] The New Testament equally shows that God's truth is a transcendental and total truth as opposed to only being revealed in human reality,[268] granting people surety as well as social accord.[269] The corresponding human attitude is one of being the servant of God, who speaks truthfully, "loves with actions and in truth," and "lives as a child of light," which means to live in all goodness, righteousness, and truth.[270]

---

[262] John 14,6; 1 Thess 1,9; John 14,6. On Christianity and truth, see for instance: Böhm, "Wahrheit"; Krings & Gnilka, "Wahrheit"; Laudien, "Wahrheit, ewige"; Lüdke, "Christus"; Newbigin, *Truth*; O'Neill, *Biblical Truth*; Smith, *The Analogy*; Smith, *The Truth*; Splett, "Wahrheit Gottes"; Trappe, "Wahrheit"; Vennix, *Wat is waarheid ?*; "Verité"; Von Balthasar, *Theologik*; Vorgrimler, "Wahrheit"; Vroom, "Waarheid"; "Wahrheit"; White, *Truth*; Zimmermann, "Wahrheit".

[263] Ps 30,6 (31,5).

[264] Ps 118,30 (119,30). Cf. Ps 24,5 (25,5); Ps 25,3 (26,3); Ps 39,11–12 (40,10–11); Ps 42,3 (43,3); Ps 44,4 (54,4); Ps 85,11 (86,11); Ps 95,13 (96,13); Ps 144,18 (145,18).

[265] Cf. Alencherry, *The Truth*; 178–179; Krings & Gnilka, "Wahrheit", 795.

[266] John 4,23–24. Cf. Ibuki, *Die Wahrheit*, 311–335.

[267] E.g., Gen 42,16; 2 Chr 18,15; Ps 14,3 (15,2).

[268] Cf. John 16,13: "The Spirit of truth will guide into all truth;" Krings & Gnilka, "Wahrheit", 786–787, 798: "Der Mensch ist in der Lage, die Wahrheit zu verstehen, aber die Begründung hierfür liegt letztlich in der Wahrheit selbst. Die göttliche Offenbarung ist für Johannes notwendig die Wahrheit, denn sonst gäbe es überhaupt keine Offenbarung. Damit nimmt der johanneische Wahrheitsbegriff sowohl atl.-hebräische als auch griechische Elemente in sich auf, insofern er das absolut Zuverlässige und Gültige und gleichzeitig das Wirkliche und Erkennbare meint" (798).

[269] The three main meanings of "truth" in the New Testament can be summarized as truthfulness (sincerity), the truth of the Gospel itself, and the fullness of revelation in Christ (Alencherry, *The Truth*, 181–184). On "truth" in the New Testament, see further: Böhm, "Das Wahrheitsverständnis"; Böhm, "Wahrheit", 57–58; Ebeling, *Die Wahrheit*; Ibuki, *Die Wahrheit*; Kaiser, *In der Wahrheit*; Krings & Gnilka, "Wahrheit"; Lambrecht, *The Truth*; Tantiono, *Speaking*; "Verité", 416–427; Vroom, "Waarheid", 174–177; "Wahrheit", 933–935; Young & Ford, *Meaning*.

[270] 2 Cor 6,4; 2 Cor 6,7; 1 John 3,18; Eph 5,8–9. Cf. Tantiono, *Speaking*.

Francis

God is truth

Christian truth is a transcendental and total truth, and Francis is one of its main promoters. For him, God is Truth.[271] He is the Almighty and Most High, the only true God (*solus verus Deus*), who alone is good.[272] He alone is good, merciful, gentle, delightful, sweet, holy, just, true (*verus*), holy, upright, kind, innocent, and clean.[273] Being totally good and supremely good, God is living and true (*vivus et verus*).[274] He is true and supreme, eternal and living.[275]

The way to God the Father is through his Son, his true Word, who is the Way, the Truth (*veritas*), and the Life Himself.[276] Christ is the true Son of God (*verum Filium Dei*),[277] true God and true man (*ipsum verum Deum et verum hominem*).[278] As He revealed Himself to the holy apostles in true flesh, so He reveals Himself to us now in sacred bread and wine as the

---

[271] *RnB* 22,49–52. *Mirifica eos in veritate. Sermo tuus veritas est... Et pro eis sanctifico meipsum, ut sint ipsi sanctificati in veritate; Of Pas 3,11. ...et usque ad nubes veritas tua* (Ps 56,11). It is interesting to notice that all "truth"-claims (so abundant in the *Regula non bullata*) have totally disappeared from the *Regula bullata*.

[272] *RnB* 17,18. *Et ipse altissimus et summus, solus verus Deus... qui solus est bonus* (cfr. Luke 18,19); *RnB* 23,9. *Nihil ergo aliquid aliud desideremus, nihil aliud velimus, nihil aliud placeat et delectet nos nisi Creator et Redemptor et Salvator noster, solus verus Deus, qui est plenum bonum, omne bonum, totum bonum, verum et summum bonum, qui solus est bonus* (cfr. Luke 18,19)....

[273] *RnB* 23,9. *...qui solus est bonus* (cfr. Luke 18,19), *pius, mitis, suavis et dulcis, qui solus est sanctus, iustus, verus, sanctus et rectus, qui solus est benignus, innocens, mundus....*

[274] *Laud Dei* 3. *Tu es trinus et unus Dominus Deus deorum* (cfr. Ps 135,2); *tu es bonum, omne bonum, summum bonum, Dominus Deus vivus et verus* (cfr. 1 Thess 1,9); *Adm* 16,2. *Vere mundo corde sunt qui terrena despiciunt, caelestia quaerunt et semper adorare et videre Dominum Deum vivum et verum mundo corde et animo non desistunt; Ep Cust* 1,7. *...et, quando a sacerdote sacrificatur super altare et in aliqua parte portatur, omnes gentes flexis genibus reddant laudes, gloriam et honorem Domino Deo vivo et vero; Of Pas* 1, Or. *Benedicamus Domino Deo vivo et vero...; Of Pas* 15,1. *...iubilate Domino Deo vivo et vero in voce exsultationis* (cfr. Ps 46,2b).

[275] *RnB* 23,6. *...pro his tibi gratias referant summo vero Deo, aeterno et vivo....*

[276] *Adm* 1,1. *Ego sum via, veritas et vita; nemo venit ad Patrem nisi per me; RnB* 22,40. *Ego sum via, veritas et vita* (Joa 14,6); *RnB* 22,50. *Sermo tuus veritas est....*

[277] *Adm* 1,8. *Unde omnes qui viderunt Dominum Jesum secundum humanitatem et non viderunt et crediderunt secundum spiritum et divinitatem, ipsum esse verum Filium Dei, damnati sunt; Adm* 1,15. *Ut quid non cognoscitis veritatem et creditis in Filium Dei* (cfr. Joa 9,35)?

[278] *RnB* 23,3. *Et gratias agimus tibi, quia sicut per Filium tuum nos creasti, sic per sanctam dilectionem tuam, qua dilexisti nos* (cfr. Joa 17,26), *ipsum verum Deum et verum hominem ex gloriosa semper Virgine beatissima sancta Maria nasci fecisti et per crucem et sanguinem et mortem ipsius nos captivos redimi voluisti.*

true Sacrifice.[279] His Body and Blood are indeed living and true.[280] He is the true Light[281] and the true Wisdom of the Father, who has sent his mercy and truth from heaven.[282]

Faith is truth, and truly virtuous

Man must believe in Christ, the true Word and true Wisdom of the Father. Through the Son, who sanctified Himself, the deceitful will be condemned in truth and the faithful will be sanctified in truth (*sanctificati in veritate*).[283] While the deceitful "trample on the Son of God," the faithful love and truly and humbly believe in (*credamus veraciter et humiliter*) the Most High and Supreme Eternal God, Trinity and Unity, Father, Son and Holy Spirit, Creator of all, Savior of all.[284] Truly adoring God the Father is to adore Him in the Spirit of truth.[285]

The truly faithful man perseveres in the true faith (*in vera fide*) and in penance.[286] He perseveres in his commands and therefore "remains in true obedience."[287] For Francis, the "true and holy obedience" (*vera et*

---

[279] *Adm* 1,19. *Et sicut sanctis apostolis in vera carne, ita et modo se nobis ostendit in sacro pane; Ep Fid* 2,4. *...ex cuius utero veram recepit carnem humanitatis et fragilitatis nostrae; Ep Ord* 14. *...puri pure faciant cum reverentia verum sacrificium sanctissimi corporis et sanguinis Domini nostri Jesu Christi....*

[280] *Adm* 1,21. *...sic et nos videntes panem et vinum oculis corporeis videamus et credamus firmiter, eius sanctissimum corpus et sanguinem vivum esse et verum; Adm* 1,9. *...et non vident et credunt secundum spiritum et divinitatem, quod sit veraciter sanctissimum corpus et sanguis Domini nostri Jesu Christi, damnati sunt....*

[281] *Ep Fid* 1,2,7; *Ep Fid* 2,66. *...quia verum lumen non vident Dominum nostrum Jesum Christum.*

[282] *Ep Fid* 1,2,8–9; *Ep Fid* 2,67. *Sapientiam non habent spiritualem, quia non habent Filium Dei, qui est vera sapientia Patris, de quibus dicitur: Sapientia eorum deglutita est* (Ps 106,27)...; *Of Pas* 3,5. *Misit Deus misericordiam suam et veritatem suam....*

[283] *Ep Ord* 18–20. *Quanto maiora et deteriora meretur pati supplicia, qui Filium Dei conculcaverit... Et sacerdotes, qui nolunt hoc ponere super cor in veritate condemnat dicens: Maledicam benedictionibus vestris* (Mal 2,2); *RnB* 22,52. *Et pro eis sanctifico meipsum, ut sint ipsi sanctificati in veritate.*

[284] *RnB* 23,11. *...ubique nos omnes omni loco, omni hora et omni tempore, quotidie et continue credamus veraciter et humiliter et in corde teneamus et amemus, honoremus, adoremus, serviamus, laudemus et benedicamus, glorificemus et superexaltemus, magnificemus et gratias agamus altissimo et summo Deo aeterno, trinitati et unitati, Patri et Filio et Spiritui Sancto, creatori omnium et salvatori omnium....*

[285] *Ep Fid* 2,19–20. *Veri adoratores adorabunt Patrem in spiritu et veritate* (Joa 4,23). *Omnes enim, qui adorant eum, in spiritu veritatis oportet eum adorare* (cfr. Joa 4,24); *RnB* 22,31. *Spiritus est Deus et eos qui adorant eum, in spiritu et veritate oportet eum adorare* (cfr. Joa 4,23–24).

[286] *RnB* 23,7. *...ut omnes in vera fide et poenitentia perseveremus, quia aliter nullus salvari potest.*

[287] *RnB* 5,17. *Et quando perseveraverint in mandatis Domini, quae promiserunt per sanctum evangelium et vitam ipsorum, sciant se in vera obedientia stare, et benedicti sint a Domino.*

sancta obedientia) is the fraternity's metaphorical space in which the brothers, through the charity of the Spirit, truly and voluntarily serve and obey one another.[288] True obedience is whatever one does and says, which he knows is not contrary to his brother's will, provided that what he does is good.[289] It is one's resigned acceptance of all that impedes him from loving God and whoever has become an impediment, whether brothers or others, even if they lay hands on him.[290] The truly faithful man therefore possesses other true virtues such as true peace of the spirit (*veram pacem spiritus*),[291] true love, and true joy. In his *Letter to the Faithful* (*Second Version*), Francis sends esteem and reverence, true peace (*veram pacem*) from heaven and sincere love in the Lord to all Christian religious people.[292] Sincere love in the Lord for him is to love not in word or speech, but in deed and truth.[293] As true obedience, it is loving one's enemy because of one's love of God.[294] In the same vein, it is the virtue of patience that makes up a true believer's true joy (*vera laetitia*) and true virtue (*vera virtus*).[295]

---

[288] *RnB* 5,14–15. ...*immo magis per caritatem spiritus voluntarie serviant et obediant invicem* (cfr. Gal 5,13). *Et haec est vera et sancta obedientia Domini nostri Jesu Christi; Ep Cust* 1,10. *Et ista sint eis per veram et sanctam obedientiam.* For obedience as the metaphorical space of the fraternity, see above, 2.2.

[289] *Adm* 3,4. *Et quidquid facit et dicit, quod ipse sciat, quod non sit contra voluntatem eius, dum bonum sit quod facit, vera obedientia est.*

[290] *Ep Min* 2–4. *Dico tibi, sicut possum, de facto animae tuae, quod ea quae te impediunt amare Dominum Deum, et quicumque tibi impedimentum fecerit sive fratres sive alii, etiam si te verberarent, omnia debes habere pro gratia. Et ita velis et non aliud. Et hoc sit tibi per veram obedientiam Domini Dei et meam, quia firmiter scio, quod ista est vera obedientia.*

[291] *RnB* 17,15. *Et studet ad humilitatem et patientiam et puram et simplicem et veram pacem spiritus.*

[292] *Ep Fid* 2,1. *Universis christianis religiosis, clericis et laicis, masculis et feminis, omnibus qui habitant in universo mundo, frater Franciscus, eorum servus et subditus, obsequium cum reverentia, pacem veram de caelo et sinceram in Domino caritatem.*

[293] *RnB* 11,6. *Et ostendant ex operibus* (cfr. Jac 2,18) *dilectionem, quam habent ad invicem, sicut dicit apostolus: Non diligamus verbo neque lingua, sed opere et veritate* (1 Joa 3,18).

[294] *Adm* 9,2–3. *Ille enim veraciter diligit inimicum suum, qui non dolet de iniuria, quam sibi facit, sed de peccato animae suae uritur propter amorem Dei; Ex Pat* 8. ...*et quod non plene dimittimus, tu, Domine, fac nos plene dimittere, ut inimicos propter te veraciter diligamus et pro eis apud te devote intercedamus, nulli malum pro malo reddentes* (cfr. 1 Thess 5,15) *et in omnibus in te prodesse studeamus.*

[295] *Laet* 3–7. *Scribe - inquit - quae est vera laetitia. Venit nuntius et dicit quod omnes magistri de Parisius venerunt ad Ordinem, scribe, non vera laetitia. Item quod omnes praelati ultramontani, archiepiscopi et episcopi; item quod rex Franciae et rex Angliae: scribe, non vera laetitia. Item, quod fratres mei iverunt ad infideles et converterunt eos omnes ad fidem; item, quod tantam gratiam habeo a Deo quod sano infirmos et facio multa miracula: dico tibi quod in his omnibus non vera laetitia. Sed quae est vera laetitia?; Laet* 15. *Dico tibi quod si patientiam habuero et non fuero motus, quod in hoc est vera laetitia et vera virtus et salus animae.*

Bonaventure

Reaching the truth

Bonaventure distinguishes between three categories of appropriated divine attributes.[296] The first of these consists of unity (*unitas*; attributed to the Father), truth (*veritas*; attributed to the Son), and goodness (*bonitas*; attributed to the Holy Spirit). Truth here implies "the unity of all ideas with their object," for example, in the Gospel.[297] But the truth is threefold, corresponding to the nine angelic hierarchies, to be reached on three different levels (*hierarchia*).[298] These levels together constitute a complete program for truthful religious living, for discovering "the fountain of life":

> Note that on the first level, truth is to be invoked by sighs and prayer, which pertains to the Angels; it is to be received by study and reading, which pertains to the Archangels; it is to be communicated by example and preaching, which pertains to the Principalities. On the second level, truth is to be sought by recourse and dedication to it, which pertains to the Powers; it is to be grasped by activity and endeavor, which pertains to the Virtues; it is to be assimilated by self-contempt and mortification, which pertains to the Dominations. On the third level, truth is to be adored by sacrifice and praise, which pertains to the Thrones; it is to be admired in ecstasy and contemplation, which pertains to the Cherubim; it is to be embraced with caresses and love, which pertains to the Seraphim. Note these things carefully, for they hold the fountain of life.[299]

---

[296] *Trip Via* 3,7,12. *Prima appropriata sunt unitas, veritas, bonitas. Attribuitur unitas Patri, quia origo; veritas Filio, quia imago; bonitas Spiritui sancto, quia connexio* (*Doctoris* 8, 17; De Vinck, *The Works* 1, 92). The other two corresponding categories consist of power (*potestas*), wisdom (*sapientia*), and will (*voluntas*); and loftiness (*altitudo*), beauty (*pulcritudo*), and sweetness (*dulcedo*). Consequently, the Son is beautiful (*pulcritudo*) because of his truth (*veritas*) and his wisdom (*sapientia*). On Bonaventure and truth, see for instance: Schlosser, "Wahrheitsverständnis"; Speer, *Triplex*; "Verité", 438–440.

[297] *Trip Via* 3,7,12. *...veritas autem aequalitatem includit...* (*Doctoris* 8, 17; De Vinck, *The Works* 1, 92); *Ep San* 12. *...et evangelicae veritatis regulam et lux clarissimam expositione tua mystica non obscures* (*Doctoris* 8, 389); *Ap Paup* Prol,3. *...quatenus triangulari huiusmodi armatura evangelici milites, velut veritatis scuto circumdati...* (*Doctoris* 8, 234; De Vinck, *The Works* 4, 3). Cf. *Ap Paup* 6,16. *...cuiusmodi est veritas divinae legis...* (*Doctoris* 8, 271; De Vinck, *The Works* 4, 121).

[298] The truth is threefold (*triplex veritas*): *veritas rerum* (*naturalis*); *veritas morum* (*moralis*); *veritas vocum* (*rationalis*) (Speer, *Triplex*).

[299] *Trip Via* 3,7,14. *Nota, quod in prima hierarchia Veritas est advocanda per gemitum et orationem, et hoc est Angelorum; audienda per studium et lectionem, et hoc Archangelorum; annuntianda per exemplum et praedicationem, et hoc Principatuum. In secunda hierarchia Veritas est adeunda per refugium et commissionem, et hoc Potestatum; apprehendenda per zelum et aemulationem, et hoc Virtutum; associanda per sui contemptum et mortificationem, et hoc Dominationum. In tertia hierarchia Veritas est adoranda per sacrificium et*

In addition, the full reward of spiritual life and wisdom consists in supreme peace, truth, and goodness or love, corresponding with the highest heavenly hierarchies of Thrones, Cherubim, and Seraphim.[300] With these three sanctifying virtues (peace, truth, love) another trio corresponds: purification, illumination, and perfection. These are the three stages (or "threefold hierarchical action") of religious life.[301]

Intellectually, spiritually, morally
Man is essentially made to desire, seek, and love the truths of faith and morals.[302] Indeed, the truth has an intellectual and a spiritual as well as a moral connotation. Intellectually, man "must serve the supreme Truth to the exclusion of any assent to falsehood."[303] Spiritually, there are "seven steps by which the splendor of truth is attained through the imitation of Christ": assent of reason; movement of compassion; gaze of admiration; outgoing of devotion; clothing in likeness; acceptance of the cross; contemplation of truth.[304] Morally, man "must strive mightily toward salvation" by overcoming desires, by fasting, by suffering pain, and doing good works (virtuous acts).[305] Loving the truth makes these things easy

---

laudationem, et hoc Thronorum; admiranda per excessum et contemplationem, et hoc Cherubim; amplectenda per osculum et dilectionem, et hoc Seraphim. Nota diligenter praedicta, quoniam in illis fons vitae (Doctoris 8, 18; De Vinck, *The Works* 1, 93–94). Bonaventure ends his famous treatise on *The Triple Way* with these words.

[300] *Trip Via* 3,1,1. *In gloria autem triplex est dos, in qua consistit perfectio praemii, scilicet summae pacis aeternalis tentio, summae veritatis manifesta visio, summae bonitatis vel caritatis plena fruitio. Et secundum hoc distinguitur triplex ordo in suprema hierarchia caelesti, scilicet Thronorum, Cherubim et Seraphim* (Doctoris 8, 11–12; De Vinck, *The Works* 1, 80).

[301] *Trip Via* Prol,1. *Purgatio autem ad pacem ducit, illuminatio ad veritatem, perfectio ad caritatem...* (Doctoris 8, 3; De Vinck, *The Works* 1, 63).

[302] *Ap Paup* Prol,1. *...Propterea, sicut veritatem fidei et morum amore iubemur praecipuo desiderare ac quaerere...* (Doctoris 8, 233; De Vinck, *The Works* 4, 1). Cf. *Det Quaest* 20. *...una, cum non omnes agnoscant aequaliter veritatem in omnibus...* (Doctoris 8, 351).

[303] *Ap Paup* Prol,1. *...sic redigendum intellectum creatum in summae veritatis obsequium, quod nullus falsitati praebeatur assensus...* (Doctoris 8, 233; De Vinck, *The Works* 4, 1). Cf. *Ap Paup* 9,10. *Et quoniam qui a recta veritatis via discedit per devia vagatur errorum...* (Doctoris 8, 297; De Vinck, *The Works* 4, 196).

[304] *Trip Via* 3,3,3. *Gradus perveniendi ad splendorem veritatis, ad quem pervenitur per imitationem Christi, sunt hi septem, scilicet assensus rationis, affectus compassionis, aspectus admirationis, excessus devotionis, amictus assimilationis, amplexus crucis, intuitus veritatis; in quibus hoc ordine progrediendum est* (Doctoris 8, 12; De Vinck, *The Works* 1, 82). Cf. *Trip Via* 3,3,5. *Unde ipsa crux est clavis, porta, via et splendor veritatis...* (Doctoris 8, 14; De Vinck, *The Works* 1, 86).

[305] *Ap Paup* Prol,1. *...sic vacandum sanctificationi spirituum, quod ferietur a servitute carnalium voluptatum...* (Doctoris 8, 233; De Vinck, *The Works* 4, 1); *Ap Paup* 6,16. *Per ieiunium etiam impetratur perfecta intelligentia veritatis, primo quidem in operandis...* (Doctoris 8, 270; De Vinck, *The Works* 4, 121).

for him[306] because the virtue of truth (*veritatis virtus*) always conquers and grows in strength.[307]

David

The True and the Good

David frequently combines truth/the true (*veritas/verum*) and goodness/ the good (*bonitas/bonum*) in order to show that things can be "true and good," as opposed to "false and bad,"[308] and to show that God is "Truth and Goodness," "the True and the Good," "the true Good."[309] Truth is one of the primary names of God: God is "supreme Goodness, supreme Truth, and

---

[306] *Sol* 2,3,16. ...*quia quos amor veritatis afficit bonorum operum exercitatio et malorum perpessio nunquam frangit* (*Doctoris* 8, 50; De Vinck, *The Works* 3, 89–90).

[307] *Ap Paup* 5,29. *Tandem quia veritas semper vincit et invalescit...* (*Doctoris* 8, 265; De Vinck, *The Works* 4, 104); *Ap Paup* 5,30. ...*quam de ipsius impugnantis ore eiusdem invincibilis veritatis virtus extorsit?* (*Doctoris* 8, 266; De Vinck, *The Works* 4, 105).

[308] *Prof* 1,13. ...*ut scias discernere verum a falso, bonum a malo, vitium a virtute et remedia vitiorum ac tentationum* (*David ab Augusta*, 17; Devas, *Spiritual Life* 1, 17); *Prof* 1,18. *Cito cede, quia, si bonum est et verum, quod alter proponit, tuum non est resistere propter aliquam ostentationem... si autem non esset bonum, melius est corrigere eum pacifice advertendo et humiliter ei veritatem demonstrando quam acriter astruendo* (*David ab Augusta*, 24; Devas, *Spiritual Life* 1, 21); *Prof* 2,6. *Ratio recipit saepius falsum pro vero; voluntas eligit deterius pro bono* (*David ab Augusta*, 88; Devas, *Spiritual Life* 1, 84); *Prof* 3,12. ...*quo verum a falso discernere debui... et sub specie veri a falsitate deluditur* (*David ab Augusta*, 185; Devas, *Spiritual Life* 2, 26). Cf. *Prof* 1,37. ...*quia iudicium humanum caecum est frequentius et ignorat veritatem et fallitur saepissime...* (*David ab Augusta*, 49; Devas, *Spiritual Life* 1, 43); *Prof* 2,16. *Ignorantia excaecat, ne verum agnoscamus et erremus in iudicio boni et mali* (*David ab Augusta*, 102; Devas, *Spiritual Life* 1, 97); *Prof* 3,63. ...*et pro spiritu veritatis sequatur spiritum erroris...* (*David ab Augusta*, 340; Devas, *Spiritual Life* 2, 173); *Prof* 3,66. *Item, quod quandoque verae sunt, et per eas erudiuntur aliqui ad veritatem, et quandoque deceptoriae, et aliqui eis deluduntur* (*David ab Augusta*, 357; Devas, *Spiritual Life* 2, 189).

[309] *Prof* 2,26. *Tantum confidunt quidam de bonitate Dei, quod etiam salvet eos in peccatis contra iustitiam et veritatem suam...* (*David ab Augusta*, 112; Devas, *Spiritual Life* 1, 106); *Prof* 3,37. *Sicut ergo caritas ordinat nos ad bonitatem, ita humilitas habet nos ordinare ad veritatem* (*David ab Augusta*, 243; Devas, *Spiritual Life* 2, 80); *Prof* 3,62. ...*ubi omnes vires animae et potentiae a suis dispersionibus simul collectae et in unum verum et simplicissimum et summum bonum fixae...* (*David ab Augusta*, 338; Devas, *Spiritual Life* 2, 170); *Prof* 1,14. *Qui autem magis veretur hominum aspectus quam Dei et Angelorum et propriae conscientiae non est castus amator boni, quia non declinat malum ex amore veri boni...* (*David ab Augusta*, 19; Devas, *Spiritual Life* 1, 17); *Prof* 3,2. ...*memoria tranquillatur ad fruendum et inhaerendum vero bono* (*David ab Augusta*, 164; Devas, *Spiritual Life* 2, 6); *Prof* 3,12. ...*dereliquit me virtus mea, qua debui vero bono tenaciter inhaerere* (*David ab Augusta*, 185; Devas, *Spiritual Life* 2, 26); *Prof* 3,63. ...*scientia ex cognitione veri, sapientia ex adiuncto amore boni... amor tamen quasi principalis suo motu omnes alios informat, maxime cum ipse ad summum, verum bonum debito modo fuerit conversus...* (*David ab Augusta*, 341; Devas, *Spiritual Life* 2, 173–174). See above, 2.3.

eternal Joy."[310] He is the highest Truth[311] and Christ is truly his Son.[312] God is true and righteous, and his truth can be trusted.[313] He is truly merciful and full of kindness towards us.[314] His Spirit, the Spirit of Truth, guides into all truth,[315] and his Word, the Bible, is the word of Truth for those who cannot find truth for themselves.[316]

Divine and human truth

As truth is an emanating divine virtue, it can also be found in man.[317] First, God's law, the law of truth, is written in the hearts of men.[318] Second, as truth is the will of God actually loved and observed by man and replicated by his own will,[319] it is the substrate of all human virtue: "By virtue we mean a movement of the will acting in accord with a judgement of truth [a legitimate judgement] formed by the intellect."[320] Third, although truth

---

[310] *Prof* 3,37. *Vera beatitudo consistit in cognitione summae veritatis, in dilectione vel delectatione summae bonitatis, in fruitione aeternae iucunditatis* (David ab Augusta, 243; Devas, *Spiritual Life* 2, 80).

[311] *Prof* 3,54. *...ut illi summae Veritati placeamus... et quia magis esset ad placitum ibi summae Veritatis...* (David ab Augusta, 304; Devas, *Spiritual Life* 2, 136–137); *Prof* 3,63. *...qui est summa veritas...* (David ab Augusta, 346; Devas, *Spiritual Life* 2, 178).

[312] *Prof* 3,69. *...eum esse verum Dei Filium...* (David ab Augusta, 370; Devas, *Spiritual Life* 2, 203). Cf. *Prof* 3,69. *...donec per multa argumenta de veritate eius certificati sunt... donec pluribus indiciis experiantur veritatem et utilitatem suae visitationis...* (David ab Augusta, 371; Devas, *Spiritual Life* 2, 203).

[313] *Prof* 2,26. *...quod etiam salvet eos in peccatis contra iustitiam et veritatem suam...* (David ab Augusta, 112; Devas, *Spiritual Life* 1, 106); *Prof* 3,3. *Mandasti iustitiam testimonia tua et veritatem tuam nimis...sed recurre ad illa vera testimonia et consolare in ipsis, scilicet, ut confidas veritati Dei...* [cfr. Ps 118,138] (David ab Augusta, 169; Devas, *Spiritual Life* 2, 11).

[314] *Prof* 3,58. *...qui mitis et benignus est et in veritate pius et misericors...* (David ab Augusta, 325; Devas, *Spiritual Life* 2, 158).

[315] *Prof* 2,5. *Spiritus veritatis docebit vos omnem veritatem* [cfr. John 16,13] (David ab Augusta, 86; Devas, *Spiritual Life* 1, 82).

[316] *Prof* 2,7. *Nam, quia ratio nostra lippa facta est, et intellectus obscuratus per peccatum, quod non possumus veritatem per nos invenire; Deus condescendit nobis, ne in errore essemus, deditque nobis notitiam veritatis in Scripturis, quibus voluit nos credere, ubi omnia, quae ad salutem nobis sunt necessaria, sufficienter et veraciter invenimus...* (David ab Augusta, 89; Devas, *Spiritual Life* 1, 84–85). Cf. *Prof* 3,44. *...et iuxta ipsius Veritatis testimonium...* (David ab Augusta, 270; Devas, *Spiritual Life* 2, 105); *Prof* 3,70. *...manifeste apparente illius sententiae veritate...* (David ab Augusta, 375; Devas, *Spiritual Life* 2, 208).

[317] Cf. *Prof* 3,54. *...et veritas in nobis non est* (David ab Augusta, 305; Devas, *Spiritual Life* 2, 137).

[318] *Prof* 3,27. *Et quia lex veritatis scripta est in corde hominis per iudicium rationis* [cfr. Rom 2,15]... (David ab Augusta, 215; Devas, *Spiritual Life* 2, 55).

[319] Cf. *Prof* 3,38. *...quia veritatem amat et se privato amore non diligit contra veritatem...* (David ab Augusta, 248; Devas, *Spiritual Life* 2, 85).

[320] *Prof* 3,27. *Virtus est ordinatus secundum veritatis iudicium mentis affectus* (David ab Augusta, 215; Devas, *Spiritual Life* 2, 54). Cf. *Prof* 3,28. *Cum ergo istae affectiones ordinatae*

is not in the self-deceived,[321] and although man cannot attach absolute
assurance (*secundum veritatem*) to suggestions received as to his own
spiritual state,[322] he can always know the truth about himself: that he is
worthless and despicable.[323] The truly humble man loves this truth and
does not prefer to love himself in opposition to it,[324] because his humility
is based on the love of truth.[325] He knows the truth about where he stands
from experience[326] and shows it in his deeds.[327] Truth, therefore, is one of
the virtues (faith, charity, justice, truth, chastity, obedience, and contempt for worldly interests) that manifestly holds a spiritual man to good
actions, and that should be manifest to men.[328]

---

sunt ad quod debent et secundum quod debent iuxta rationis et veritatis iudicium; tunc homo
est virtuosus... (David ab Augusta, 216; Devas, Spiritual Life 2, 55); Prof 3,67. ...quid secundum veritatis iudicium sit melius, vel non melius; sicut docet omnes iustos declinare a malo et
facere bonum... (David ab Augusta, 362; Devas, Spiritual Life 2, 194).

[321] Prof 3,38. ...semet ipsum redarguat et castiget quasi deceptum, et in quo veritas non sit
[cfr. John 8,44] (David ab Augusta, 248; Devas, Spiritual Life 2, 84).

[322] Prof 3,69. ...si non possumus secundum veritatem cuique consulere, quid sentire in
huiusmodi debeat et facere... (David ab Augusta, 369; Devas, Spiritual Life 2, 201). Cf. Prof
3,69. ...aut maiorem esse gratiam sibi datam, quam tamen sit in veritate... (David ab Augusta,
371; Devas, Spiritual Life 2, 204); Prof 3,69. ...praesente gratia, gaudent de consolatione et
securi sunt de veritate; absente ea, utriusque muneris solatio carent... (David ab Augusta, 371;
Devas, Spiritual Life 2, 203).

[323] Prof 1,37. ...sicut sum despicabilis in veritate... (David ab Augusta, 51; Devas, Spiritual
Life 1, 44); Prof 3,24. Verum enim est, nos esse viles et inopes, et quantum ex hac aestimatione
deviamus, tantum erramus in veritate (David ab Augusta, 212; Devas, Spiritual Life 2, 51);
Prof 3,37. Sicut ergo caritas ordinat nos ad bonitatem, ita humilitas habet nos ordinare ad
veritatem... Humilitas est virtus, qua homo verissima cognitione sui sibimet ipsi vilescit
(David ab Augusta, 243; Devas, Spiritual Life 2, 80).

[324] Prof 3,38. ...quia veritatem amat et se privato amore non diligit contra
veritatem... (David ab Augusta, 248; Devas, Spiritual Life 2, 85). Cf. Prof 2,29. ...cum aut
homo plus placet sibi, quam debeat, et maiorem se existimat, quam sit in veritate... Haec est
inanis gloria, quia vacua veritate et utilitate salutis (David ab Augusta, 115; Devas, Spiritual
Life 1, 110).

[325] Prof 3,38. ....item, si pauper se pauperem reputat et ab aliis vult pauper agnosci, veritati
consentit in istis, sed non est admirationi talis humilitas; si vero dives se pauperibus confor-
mat, et altus nihil altum sapit, et gloriosus nihil sibi de gloria attribuit, sed totum refundit ei,
a quo habet, unde gloriosus videtur; hic est humilis, non cogente necessitate, sed veritatis
caritate (David ab Augusta, 250–251; Devas, Spiritual Life 2, 87).

[326] Prof 3,65. ...tamen ex ipso saporis gustu naturales veritatis differentias cognoscere
magis valeant... (David ab Augusta, 355; Devas, Spiritual Life 2, 187).

[327] Prof 3,16. Indecens est quod non bonam speciem praetendit et colorem illiciti habet,
etiamsi non expressam veritatem, ut omne scandalum et quod alicuius vitii et peccati notam
habere videtur... (David ab Augusta, 193; Devas, Spiritual Life 2, 34).

[328] Prof 2,12. Bona nostra, ad quae tenemur ex praecepto Dei vel Ecclesiae, vel ad quae ex
manifesto voto adstringimur, debemus hominibus ostendere, ut fidem, caritatem, iustitiam,
veritatem, castitatem, obedientiam et contemptum mundanorum (David ab Augusta, 97;
Devas, Spiritual Life 1, 93).

Fourth, the search after truth and devotion to prayer are like brothers.[329] Devotion and adoration are true when one seeks the good pleasure of his loving Father,[330] and adores Him in spirit and in truth.[331] Every true thought or word one may form about God constitutes true praise and ardent love.[332] Fifth, although the figures perceived in corporeal and in imaginative visions are not real in fact (Jesus, for example, did not appear in reality in visions to saints and holy persons), the truth from the point of view of the spiritual message can be perceived in them.[333] Finally, man sees Truth as it really is in the highest form of contemplation.[334]

5. FAITH

Origin

In the Nicene-Constantinopolitan Creed of the year 381 we find a formulation of the basic doctrine of Christian faith:

> We believe in one God, the Father, the Almighty, maker of heaven and earth, of all that is, seen and unseen. We believe in one Lord, Jesus Christ, the only Son of God, eternally begotten of the Father, God from God, Light from Light, true God from true God, begotten, not made, of one Being with

---

[329] *Prof*, Epist 2. *Duo autem filii Rachel sunt profunda veritatis inquisitio et devotae orationis in Deum pura intentio* (David ab Augusta, 61; Devas, *Spiritual Life* 1, 55).

[330] *Prof* 3,54. *Vere filialis et fidelis affectus est nulla, quae sua sunt, quaerere... sed solummodo placitum pii Patris* (David ab Augusta, 304; Devas, *Spiritual Life* 2, 136). Cf. *Prof* 3,54. ... *ut illi summae Veritati placeamus... et quia magis esset ad placitum ibi summae Veritatis...* (David ab Augusta, 304; Devas, *Spiritual Life* 2, 136–137).

[331] *Prof* 3,57. *Veri adoratores adorabunt Patrem in spiritu et veritate. Spiritus est Deus, et qui adorant eum in spiritu et veritate oportet adorare* [cfr. John 4,23] (David ab Augusta, 320; Devas, *Spiritual Life* 2, 152).

[332] *Prof* 3,56. *Omnia, quae de Deo secundum veritatem cogitari vel dici possunt vel sentiri, non nisi laus ipsius sunt... et quanto perfectius cognoscitur, tanto verius laudatur et ardentius amatur* (David ab Augusta, 311; Devas, *Spiritual Life* 2, 144).

[333] *Prof* 3,66. *Ipsae enim imaginariarum vel corporalium visionum figurae, etiam cum verae sunt secundum spiritualem significantiam, non sunt verae secundum rei existentiam... et tamen sic saepe refertur aliquibus Sanctis et devotis apparuisse in visione.... non quod ita secundum veritatem fuerit...* (David ab Augusta, 359; Devas, *Spiritual Life* 2, 191). Cf. *Prof* 3,68. *Quae cum verae sunt et a Deo... in quibus maior vis est et certior veritas et fructuosior profectus et purior perfectio...* (David ab Augusta, 365–366; Devas, *Spiritual Life* 2, 197–198).

[334] *Prof* 3,66. *Alia visio est intellectualis, qua illuminatus mentis oculus luce veritatis pure ipsam veritatem in se contemplatur, vel intelligit in visione imaginaria veritatem, quae in illa significatur...* (David ab Augusta, 358; Devas, *Spiritual Life* 2, 190). Cf. *Prof* 3,67. ...*sicut et Prophetas et Sanctos docuit, quibus non solum vera ostendit, sed etiam per veritatis testimonium, quia vera essent, interius demonstravit* (David ab Augusta, 364; Devas, *Spiritual Life* 2, 196–197).

the Father; through him all things were made. For us and for our salvation
he came down from heaven, was incarnate of the Holy Spirit and the Virgin
Mary and became a human being. For our sake he was crucified under
Pontius Pilate; he suffered death and was buried. On the third day he rose
again in accordance with the Scriptures; he ascended into heaven and is
seated at the right hand of the Father. He will come again in glory to judge
the living and the dead, and his kingdom will have no end. We believe in the
Holy Spirit, the Lord, the giver of life, who proceeds from the Father [and
the Son], who with the Father and the Son is worshipped and glorified, who
has spoken through the prophets. We believe in one holy catholic and apostolic Church. We acknowledge one baptism for the forgiveness of sins. We
look for the resurrection of the dead, and the life of the world to come.
Amen.[335]

Christian faith (*fides*) amounts to believing in the existence of God
the Creator, Jesus Christ who is his Son, the Holy Spirit who is the giver of
life, the one catholic Church, one baptism, forgiveness of sins, the resurrection of the dead, and heaven. These are, in short, the essentials of
Christianity.[336]

Christian faith has many dimensions: epistemological, psychological, spiritual, ethical, political, etc.[337] Theologically speaking, it is concerned with God's reality, his otherness, and his self-revelation and
incarnation (the cognitive component of faith); with his attributes

---

[335] *Credo in unum Deum, Patrem omnipotentem, factorem caeli et terrae, visibilium
omnium et invisibilium. Et in unum Iesum Christum, Filium Dei unigenitum, et ex Patre
natum ante omnia saecula, Deum de Deo, lumen de lumine, Deum verum de Deo vero, geni-
tum, non factum, consubstantialem Patri: Per quem omnia facta sunt; qui propter nos
homines et propter nostram salutem descendit de caelis, et incarnatus est de Spiritu Sancto
ex Maria virgine, et homo factus est, crucifixus etiam pro nobis sub Pontio Pilato; passus et
sepultus est, et resurrexit tertia die secundum Scripturas, et ascendit in caelum, sedet ad
dexteram Patris, et iterum venturus est cum gloria, iudicare vivos et mortuos; cuius regni non
erit finis. Et in Spiritum Sanctum, Dominum et vivificantem, qui ex Patre Filioque procedit,
qui cum Patre et Filio simul adoratur et conglorificatur, qui locutus est per prophetas. Et
unam sanctam catholicam et apostolicam Ecclesiam. Confiteor unum baptisma in remissionem peccatorum. Et exspecto resurrectionem mortuorum, et vitam venturi saeculi. Amen*
(recensio latina) (Denzinger & Hünermann, *Kompendium*, 83–85; Hebblethwaite, *The
Essence*, 1–2).
[336] Based on the Creed are various lists of "Articles of faith" (e.g., Griffith Thomas,
The Principles; Pelikan, *Credo*; Wingren, *Credo*). On Christianity and faith, see for
instance: Berkhof, "Christian Faith"; Coventry, *Christian Truth*; Dillenberger, "Faith";
Dulles, *The Assurance*; Ernst, "Glaube"; "Foi"; Gilman, *Faith*; Kemp, "The Virtue";
Newbigin, *Proper Confidence*; Reynolds, *The Phenomenon*; Schmaus, *Der Glaube*; Seckler,
"Glaube".
[337] Cf. Bishop, *Believing* (epistemology of faith); Fowler, *Stages*; Jones, *Psychology* (psychology of faith); Schillebeeckx, *On Christian Faith* (spiritual, ethical, and political dimensions of faith); Springsted, *The Act* (phenomenology of faith).

(Father, Almighty, Creator, Omnipotent, Omniscient, Eternal, Love, and the like) and his will; and with the hiddenness and experience of God (the evaluative-affectional component).[338] Evaluative-affectionally, faith may present itself as a virtue: "the believer's welcoming the content of the cognitive component of his faith" in his behavior and actions.[339] Faith is, indeed, the first of the three theological virtues.[340]

The Bible contains the dogmatic essence of Christian faith. Faith in the Old Testament is a (collective) *Gesamthaltung* implying membership of the community that is founded on the Jahwe-bond, following the historical models of faith, and determining all individual relationships with God.[341] Faith and existence are identical.[342] In the New Testament, as in the Old Testament, faith is grounded on the historical revelation of God to his people and its response to it.[343] With the Birth of Christ, faith more specifically relates to believing in eschatology, miracles, baptism, Scripture, laws and prophets, the words of Jesus, and divine providence: "But seek first his kingdom and his righteousness, and all these things will be given to you as well."[344] Paul's thought centres on the Birth of Christ and the necessity of individual conversion as an act of faith and a way to salvation. In the reality of faith, that justice or righteousness that emanates from God is given and known.[345] Paul defines faith according to its object,[346] its doctrine,[347] its unity,[348] and its normativity.[349] Furthermore,

---

[338] Here, I follow Hebblethwaite, *The Essence*, 33–54, and Bishop, *Believing*, 104–105: faith has a cognitive component, which amounts to the propositions held and taken to be true by the believer, and an evaluative-affectional component, which amounts to the believer's welcoming the content of the cognitive component of his faith. Positivily formulated, Christian faith is "a living confidence and trust in God in the experience of knowing God's gracious presence as manifest in Christ" (Dillenberger, "Faith", 182).

[339] Cf. Van den Beld, "Is geloof".

[340] 1 Cor 13,13; 1 Thess 1,3; 1 Thess 5,8; Phil 1,5; Gal 5,5. Cf. Bars, *Trois vertus-clefs*; Engemann, *Das neue Lied*; Pieper, *Lieben*; Ratzinger, *Auf Christus*; Robinson, *These Three*; Schuster, *Moralisches*, 183–230; Söding, *Die Trias*; Walter, *Glaube*.

[341] Seckler, "Glaube", 528–529.

[342] Isa 7,9. In the New Testament, accordingly, it is especially in (and throughout) John that "faith in Jesus encompasses all of religious life" (Springsted, *The Act*, 94–100).

[343] Seckler, "Glaube", 529. Cf. Von Balthasar, *Herrlichkeit*; Blank & Hasenhüttl, *Glaube*; Garlington, *Faith*; Springsted, *The Act*, 69–104; Ulrichs, *Christusglaube*; Wallis, *The Faith*.

[344] Matt 6,33; Seckler, "Glaube", 529–530.

[345] Dillenberger, "Faith", 184; Seckler, "Glaube", 531.

[346] Rom 3,27; Rom 10,8; Gal 1,23; Acts 6,7. Faith is "being sure of what we hope for and certain of what we do not see" (Heb 11,1).

[347] 1 Tim 4,6; Tit 1,13.

[348] Eph 4,5; Tit 1,4.

[349] Rom 3,27; Seckler, "Glaube", 530.

faith is one of his virtue catalogues' main virtues,[350] and one of the Pauline spiritual charisms.[351]

Francis

Faith in the Lord

Francis is a strong believer of faith in the Lord Jesus Christ and the Word of God.[352] Non-believers (*infideles*) may come to believe (*credant*) in the Father, the Son and the Holy Spirit, be baptized, and become Christians when they hear the Word of God.[353] Those who hear the word and do not understand it, on the other hand, may be led astray by the devil, who takes the word from their hearts so that they cannot believe and be saved.[354] And those who believe only for a time and fall away in times of trial, need to remind themselves that "we have nothing else to do but to follow the will of the Lord and to please Him."[355] In Francis's eyes, true faith needs effort, understanding, concentration, and steadfastness. Faithful souls, who are spouses joined by the Holy Spirit to the Lord Jesus Christ,[356] see and believe that the bread and wine are truly the Body and Blood of Christ,[357] and truly believe that He is the Son of the Holy Father, the true

---

[350] Gal 5,22; 1 Tim 4,12; 1 Tim 6,11; 2 Tim 2,22; 2 Tim 3,10; 2 Pet 1,5–7. Cf. Wibbing, *Die Tugend- und Lasterkataloge*, 77–127.

[351] 1 Cor 12,9.

[352] On Francis and faith, see for instance: Doyle & McElrath, "St. Francis"; Engemann, *Das neue Lied*; Garrido, *Die Lebensregel*, 108–110; Van den Goorbergh & Zweerman, *Was getekend*, 23–30; Koper, *Das Weltverständnis*, 83–93; Lehmann, *Tiefe*, 45–47; Strack, "„Gib mir""; Rohr, *Der Herr*, 107–108.

[353] *RnB* 16,7. *Alius modus est, quod, cum viderint placere Domino, annuntient verbum Dei, ut credant Deum omnipotentem, Patrem et Filium et Spiritum Sanctum, creatorem omnium, redemptorem et salvatorem Filium, et ut baptizentur et efficiantur christiani; Laet. Item, quod fratres mei iverunt ad infideles et converterunt eos omnes ad fidem.*

[354] *RnB* 22,13. *...et confestim* (Mark 4,15) *venit diabolus* (Luke 8,12) *et rapit* (Matt 13,19), *quod seminatum est in cordibus eorum* (Mark 4,15) *et tollit verbum de cordibus eorum, ne credentes salvi fiant* (Luke 8,12).

[355] *RnB* 22,15. *...quia ad tempus credunt et in tempore tentationis recedunt* (Luke 8,13); *RnB* 22,9. *Nunc autem, postquam dimisimus mundum, nihil aliud habemus facere, nisi sequi voluntatem Domini et placere sibi ipsi* (Armstrong, *Francis of Assisi*, 79).

[356] *Ep Fid* 1,1,8. *Sponsi sumus, quando Spiritu Sancto coniungitur fidelis anima Domino nostro Jesu Christo.*

[357] *Adm* 1,9. *...ita et modo omnes qui vident sacramentum, quod sanctificatur per verba Domini super altare per manum sacerdotis in forma panis et vini, et non vident et credunt secundum spiritum et divinitatem, quod sit veraciter sanctissimum corpus et sanguis Domini nostri Jesu Christi, damnati sunt...; Adm* 1,12. *Unde spiritus Domini, qui habitat in fidelibus suis, ille est qui recipit sanctissimum corpus et sanguinem Domini; Adm* 1,20–21. *Et sicut ipsi*

Son of God.[358] They do not fear but act with confidence (*fiducialiter*) because He is the Savior who will always be with his faithful.[359]

Faith in the Church and observance of the precepts
Francis demonstrated his own unlimited faith in the Lord when he "left the world" and put his life completely in God's hands.[360] Now all members "of the Catholic faith" (*de fide catholica*), i.e., the holy Catholic and Apostolic Church, all those who truly believe in the Lord Jesus Christ, are asked and begged by Francis and his brothers to also "persevere in the true faith and in penance, for otherwise no one will be saved."[361] This universal appeal is an echo of the penitential appeal made within the fraternity of *fratres minores*, those who have not "strayed in word or in deed from Catholic faith and life" or who have amended their ways in order not to do so anymore.[362] These men truly believe, faithfully profess, and steadfastly observe all things concerning the Catholic faith and the sacraments

---

intuitu carnis suae tantum eius carnem videbant, sed ipsum Deum esse credebant oculis spiritualibus contemplantes, sic et nos videntes panem et vinum oculis corporeis videamus et credamus firmiter, eius sanctissimum corpus et sanguinem vivum esse et verum.

[358] *Ep Fid* 1,1,15; *Ep Fid* 2,51. *Et verba, quae mihi dedisti, dedi eis, et ipsi acceperunt et crediderunt vere, quia a te exivi et cognoverunt, quia tu me misisti* (Joa 17,8); *Ep Fid* 1,1,18; *Ep Fid* 2,58. *Non pro eis rogo tantum, sed pro eis qui credituri sunt per verbum illorum in me* (Joa 17,20)...; *Adm* 1,8. *Unde omnes qui viderunt Dominum Jesum secundum humanitatem et non viderunt et crediderunt secundum spiritum et divinitatem, ipsum esse verum Filium Dei, damnati sunt; Adm* 1,15. *Ut quid non cognoscitis veritatem et creditis in Filium Dei* (cfr. Joa 9,35)?; *RnB* 22,42. *...et ipsi acceperunt et cognoverunt, quia a te exivi et crediderunt quia tu me misisti; RnB* 22,53. *Non pro eis rogo tantum, sed pro eis, qui credituri sunt propter verbum eorum in me* (cfr. Joa 17,17–20), *ut sint consummati in unum, et cognoscat mundus, quia tu me misisti et dilexisti eos, sicut me dilexisti* (Joa 17,23).

[359] *Of Pas* 4,14,2. *Tu es Deus salvator meus, fiducialiter agam et non timebo* (cfr. Isa 12,2a-b); *Adm* 1,22. *Et tali modo semper est Dominus cum fidelibus suis, sicut ipse dicit: Ecce ego vobiscum sum usque ad consummationem saeculi* (cfr. Matt 28,20).

[360] *Test* 3. *...et postea parum steti et exivi de saeculo.* Cf. Van den Goorbergh & Zweerman, *Was getekend,* 23.

[361] *RB* 2,2. *Ministri vero diligenter examinent eos de fide catholica et ecclesiasticis sacramentis; RnB* 23,7. *Et Domino Deo universos intra sanctam ecclesiam catholicam et apostolicam servire volentes et omnes sequentes ordines, sacerdotes, diaconos, subdiaconos, acolythos, exorcistas, lectores, ostiarios et omnes clericos, universos religiosos et religiosas, omnes conversos et parvulos, pauperes et egenos, reges et principes, laboratores et agricolas, servos et dominos, omnes virgines et continentes et maritatas, laicos, masculos et feminas, omnes infantes, adolescentes, iuvenes et senes, sanos et infirmos, omnes pusillos et magnos, et omnes populos, gentes, tribus et linguas* (cfr. Apoc 7,9), *omnes nationes et omnes homines ubicumque terrarum, qui sunt et erunt, humiliter rogamus et supplicamus nos omnes fratres minores, servi inutiles* (Luke 17,10), *ut omnes in vera fide et poenitentia perseveremus, quia aliter nullus salvari potest* (Armstrong, *Francis of Assisi,* 84).

[362] *RnB* 19,2. *Si quis vero erraverit a fide et vita catholica in dicto vel in facto et non se emendaverit, a nostra fraternitate penitus expellatur* (Armstrong, *Francis of Assisi,* 77).

of the Church.[363] Always submissive and subject at the feet of the Holy
Church and steadfast in the Catholic Faith, they observe poverty, humility, and the Holy Gospel of the Lord Jesus Christ as they have firmly promised.[364] They follow the true example of Francis, whom the Lord gave to
begin doing penance and faith (*fides*) in churches and in catholic priests,[365]
for they have faith in the clergy and live uprightly according to the rite of
the Roman Church.[366] Because of this the brothers, who live their faith
from day to day, work faithfully (*fideliter*) and devotedly,[367] and go seeking
alms with confidence (*confidenter*),[368] humbly and faithfully fulfil the
penance imposed on them by Catholic priests,[369] and faithfully and pru-
dently punish themselves for all their offenses.[370]

Creed and virtues
Like many of his contemporaries, Francis knew the Nicene Creed well.[371]
Basing himself on certain propositions of the Creed, he recommends an

---

[363] *RB* 2,2–3. *Ministri vero diligenter examinent eos de fide catholica et ecclesiasticis sacramentis. Et si haec omnia credant et velint ea fideliter confiteri et usque in finem firmiter
observare...*
[364] *RB* 12,4. ...*ut semper subditi et subiecti pedibus eiusdem sanctae Ecclesiae stabiles in
fide* (cfr. Col 1,23) *catholica paupertatem et humilitatem et sanctum evangelium Domini nostri Jesu Christi, quod firmiter promisimus, observemus.*
[365] *Test* 1. *Dominus ita dedit mihi fratri Francisco incipere faciendi poenitentiam...;
Test* 4–6. *Et Dominus dedit mihi talem fidem in ecclesiis, ut ita simpliciter orarem et
dicerem: Adoramus te, Domine Jesu Christe, et ad omnes ecclesias tuas, quae sunt in toto
mundo, et benedicimus tibi, quia per sanctam crucem tuam redimisti mundum. Postea
Dominus dedit mihi et dat tantam fidem in sacerdotibus, qui vivunt secundum formam sanctae Ecclesiae Romanae propter ordinem ipsorum, quod si facerent mihi persecutionem, volo
recurrere ad ipsos.*
[366] *Adm* 26,1. *Beatus servus, qui portat fidem in clericis, qui vivunt recte secundum formam Ecclesiae Romanae.*
[367] *RB* 5,1. *Fratres illi, quibus gratiam dedit Dominus laborandi, laborent fideliter et
devote....*
[368] *RB* 6,2. *Et tanquam peregrini et advenae* (cfr. 1 Pet 2,11) *in hoc saeculo in paupertate et
humilitate Domino famulantes vadant pro eleemosyna confidenter....*
[369] *RnB* 20,2. ...*si poenitentiam sibi iniunctam procuraverint humiliter et fideliter
observare.*
[370] *Adm* 23,3. *Fidelis et prudens servus est* (cfr. Matt 24,45), *qui in omnibus suis offensis
non tardat interius punire....*
[371] *RnB* 3,10. *Laici dicant Credo in Deum et viginti quattuor Pater noster cum Gloria Patri
pro matutino; pro laudibus vero quinque; pro prima Credo in Deum et septem Pater noster
cum Gloria Patri; pro tertia, sexta et nona et unaquaque hora septem; pro vesperis duodecim;
pro completorio Credo in Deum et septem Pater noster cum Gloria Patri; pro mortuis septem
Pater noster cum Requiem aeternam; et pro defectu et negligentia fratrum tria Pater noster
omni die.*

unremittant belief (*quotidie et continue credamus*) in God as Unity and Trinity, in all aspects of his divine reality:

> Wherever we are, in every place, at every hour, at every time of the day, every day and continually, let all of us truly and humbly believe, hold in our heart and love, honor, adore, serve, praise and bless, glorify and exalt, magnify and give thanks to the Most High and Supreme Eternal God, Trinity and Unity, Father, Son and holy Spirit, Creator of all, Savior of all who believe and hope in Him and love him, Who, without beginning and end, is unchangeable, invisible, indescribable, ineffable, incomprehensible, unfathomable, blessed, praiseworthy, glorious, exalted, sublime, most high, gentle, lovable, delightful, and totally desirable above all else for ever. Amen.[372]

Here, in his Creed, Francis not only follows the traditional Nicene scheme, but also integrates Paul's threefold scheme of what came to be known as the theological virtues, thus connecting faith (*fides*, here *credere*) to hope (*spes*/*sperare*) and charity (*caritas*, here *diligere*). In correspondence with Francis's statement elsewhere that God *is* "our faith, our hope and our charity,"[373] these three function here as principal attributes of God, emanating from Him as supernatural virtues and flowing into the hearts of true believers.[374] The moral implication here, which sets these three apart from the other divine attributes such as his eternity and his unchangeability, is that believing in God without hope and charity is not "true and humble" (*veraciter et humiliter*) faith but "undesirable" belief;[375] faith, in other words, needs truth and humility as much as it needs hope and charity.

---

[372] *RnB* 23,11. *...ubique nos omnes omni loco, omni hora et omni tempore, quotidie et continue credamus veraciter et humiliter et in corde teneamus et amemus, honoremus, adoremus, serviamus, laudemus et benedicamus, glorificemus et superexaltemus, magnificemus et gratias agamus altissimo et summo Deo aeterno, trinitati et unitati, Patri et Filio et Spiritui Sancto, creatori omnium et salvatori omnium in se credentium et sperantium et diligentium eum, qui sine initio et sine fine immutabilis, invisibilis, inenarrabilis, ineffabilis, incomprehensibilis, investigabilis* (cfr. Rom 11,33), *benedictus, laudabilis, gloriosus, superexaltatus* (cfr. Dan 3,52), *sublimis, excelsus, suavis, amabilis, delectabilis et totus super omnia desiderabilis in saecula. Amen* (Armstrong, *Francis of Assisi*, 85–86). Cf. *Or Cruc. Summe, gloriose Deus, illumina tenebras cordis mei et da mihi fidem rectam, spem certam et caritatem perfectam, sensum et cognitionem, Domine, ut faciam tuum sanctum et verax mandatum.*
[373] *Laud Dei* 6. *Tu es spes nostra, tu es fides nostra, tu es caritas nostra, tu es tota dulcedo nostra, tu es vita aeterna nostra....*
[374] *Sal Mar* 5–6. *Ave vestimentum eius; ave ancilla eius; ave mater eius et vos omnes sanctae virtutes, quae per gratiam et illuminationem Spiritus sancti infundimini in corda fidelium, ut de infidelibus fideles Deo faciatis.*
[375] Cf. Söding, *Die Trias*, 169–170.

Bonaventure

Christ, Savior, Fundament, and Root of faith
The foundation and root of the Christian religion, the Catholic Faith (*fides catholica*), is Jesus Christ.[376] The foundation of Christ is laid in our intellect by faith (*fides*), defined by Paul as "the substance of things to be hoped for." It is laid in our affections by charity, as it "is rooted and grounded in love."[377] Faith substantiates hope and works through charity.[378] The edifice of the human soul is built with the stones of the articles of faith and grounded on the theological virtues of faith, hope, and charity, a fundamental triad on the basis of which the truths of faith and morals can be desired and loved.[379] Many most wonderful signs from God have prompted men's minds to conceive faith.[380] Faith leads from the visible to the invisible; it means to believe in what one cannot see.[381] One must most of all

---

[376] On Bonaventure and faith, see for instance: Bissen, "Les conditions", 396–397; Bougerol, "La perfection", 399–400; Carr, "Poverty", 419–421; Ennis, "The Primacy", 449–452; Guardini, *Systembildende*, 57–60; Hülsbusch, *Elemente*, 196–202; Van Leeuwen, "Het geloof"; Sakaguchi, *Der Begriff*, 93–115; Schlosser, *Cognitio*, 140–147, 249–251; Sequeira, "The Act"; Sequeira, "The Concept"; Strack, *Christusleid*, 88–92.

[377] *Ex Reg* 2,4. *Ad fidem catholicam pertinent omnia, quae ipsi fidei obsequuntur* (*Doctoris* 8, 398); *Ap Paup* 7,1. *Christianae religionis fundamentum esse Christum Iesum... Hoc quidem in nostro intellectu collocatur per fidem, quam idem Apostolus ad Hebraeos dicit rerum sperandarum esse substantiam* [cfr. Heb 11,1], *in affectu vero per caritatem; de qua idem ad Ephesios scribit: In caritate radicati et fundati* [cfr. Eph 3,17]... (*Doctoris* 8, 272; De Vinck, *The Works* 4, 125). Cf. *Trip Via* 2,2,3. *...cum fiducia spei, quam habemus a Christo...* (*Doctoris* 8, 8; De Vinck, *The Works* 1, 74); *Trip Via* 2,5,12. *...cum fiducia spei per Christum crucifixum...* (*Doctoris* 8, 11; De Vinck, *The Works* 1, 79); *Sex Alis* 7,2. *Scientiam fidei dulcem reddit... Spem in fiduciam erigit...* (*Doctoris* 8, 148; De Vinck, *The Works* 3, 187–188). Faith exceeds knowledge: *Quod quidem vitare non potest, nisi rationi fidem... praeferat...* (*Lign Vit* Prol,5; *Doctoris* 8, 69; De Vinck, *The Works* 1, 100). Cf. *Praep Mis* 1,3. *...et captiva mentem tuam sub iugo fidei...* (*Doctoris* 8, 100; De Vinck, *The Works* 3, 221); *Trip Via* 3,6,9. *...per captivationem iudiciorum, fide formata* (*Doctoris* 8, 16; De Vinck, *The Works* 1, 89).

[378] *Ap Paup* 7,1. *Ut igitur haec duo iungantur in unum, christianae religionis fundamentum et radix est fides, quae per caritatem operatur* [cfr. Gal 5,6]... (*Doctoris* 8, 272; De Vinck, *The Works* 4, 125).

[379] *Ap Paup* 12,3. *Quod enim sunt lapides in aedificio sunt articuli fidei in animo...* (*Doctoris* 8, 317; De Vinck, *The Works* 4, 257); *Ap Paup* Prol,1. *...sicut veritatem fidei et morum amore iubemur praecipuo desiderare ac quaerere...* (*Doctoris* 8, 233; De Vinck, *The Works* 4, 1). Cf. *Ap Paup* 1,6. *...eligere disposuimus exemplo David quinque limpidissimos lapides de torrente redundantis sapientiae catholicorum doctorum, quibus si pia fide veritati assentiri voluerit...* (*Doctoris* 8, 236; De Vinck, *The Works* 4, 10).

[380] *Lign Vit* 1,2. *...ut per multa millia temporum et annorum magnis et miris multiplicatis oraculis et intelligentias nostras ad fidem erigeret...* (*Doctoris* 8, 71; De Vinck, *The Works* 1, 105).

[381] *Serm Reg* 5. *...quia fides dirigit ad invisibilia; secundum Augustinum, fides est credere quod non vides* (*Doctoris* 8, 439). Philosophical enquiry is necessary to be able to

and most firmly believe in the truth and the essence of the Sacrament, i.e., that "when Christ spoke, the material and visible bread lent its shape, that is, the accidental visible species, to the forthcoming heavenly Bread of Life."[382] Without constant faith in this teaching and similar teachings of the Catholic Faith, no one can be saved.[383]

David

Catholic faith

Francis of Assisi wanted his brothers to "truly believe, faithfully profess, and steadfastly observe all things concerning the Catholic faith and the sacraments of the Church."[384] David asks the same of his novices when he says that "the foundation on which all renovation of the understanding must rest is a firm belief in the truths of the Catholic faith."[385] No matter what happens, they must hold on to their initial faith,[386] ask wisdom of

---

understand the truths one believes in: *Quodsi verba philosophorum aliquando plus valent ad intelligentiam veritatis... maxime cum multae sint quaestiones fidei, quae sine his non possunt terminari* (Ep Quaest 12; *Doctoris* 8, 335).

[382] *Praep Mis* 1,1. *Attende igitur ista quatuor singula per se et primo vide, quam fidem habere debes circa veritatem vel essentiam huius Sacramenti. Credere enim firmiter debes et nullatenus dubitare, secundum quod docet et praedicat catholica fides, quod in hora expressionis verborum Christi panis materialis atque visibilis advenienti vivifico et caelesti pani, velut vero Creatori honorem deferens, locum suum, scilicet visibilem speciem accidentium, pro ministerio et sacramentali servitio relinquit...* (*Doctoris* 8, 99; De Vinck, *The Works* 3, 219). Cf. *Ap Paup* 1,1. *...malum esse constat nullatenus tolerandum in fide vel moribus eius definitioni dogmatizare contrarium...* (*Doctoris* 8, 235; De Vinck, *The Works* 4, 6).

[383] *Praep Mis* 1,3,8. *Ideo inter vos multi imbecilles, scilicet per fidei inconstantiam...* (*Doctoris* 8, 102; De Vinck, *The Works* 3, 225); *Ap Paup* 3,3. *...propter tolerantiam adversorum, de fide non ficta...* (*Doctoris* 8, 245; De Vinck, *The Works* 4, 39); *Praep Mis* 1,1. *...secundum quod docet et praedicat catholica fides...* (*Doctoris* 8, 99; De Vinck, *The Works* 3, 219); *Det Quaest* 1,3. *Veritas enim fidei et vitae sanctitas non aliunde quam ex Scripturarum fonte hauritur; sine quibus impossibile est, quemquam salvari* (*Doctoris* 8, 339).

[384] *RB* 2,2–3. *Ministri vero diligenter examinent eos de fide catholica et ecclesiasticis sacramentis. Et si haec omnia credant et velint ea fideliter confiteri et usque in finem firmiter observare...*

[385] *Prof* 2,7. *Initium ergo reformationis rationis est fidem catholicam firmiter credere* (*David ab Augusta*, 89; Devas, *Spiritual Life* 1, 84). Cf. *Prof* 2,7. *...sed regulis fidei sensum nostrum humiliter subiiciamus... Profectus rationis est ex illuminatione divina rationes fidei aliquatenus intelligere, quia, etsi fides supra rationem sit, ita quod eam per se non valet comprehendere, illuminata tamen divinitus ratio videt, nihil rationabilius esse, quam fides est christiana...* (*David ab Augusta*, 89; Devas, *Spiritual Life* 1, 85). To these truths belong the continued passion of Christ and such evils as the subversion of justice and the persecution of faith (*Prof* 3,25; *David ab Augusta*, 212–213; Devas, *Spiritual Life* 2, 52).

[386] *Prof* 3,3. *...credentes, Deum a se esse aversum, vel etiam in fide titubare incipiunt, an vera sint quae de Deo senserunt...* (*David ab Augusta*, 168–169; Devas, *Spiritual Life* 2, 10).

God in faith,[387] and rely more on the truths of faith and Holy Scripture (by learning from the teachings of faith[388]) than on their personal experience alone, which is supernaturally without merit.[389] When they bend before the will of God, who "will call the infidel by faith to the recognition of Truth and the faithful by love to the graces of holiness,"[390] their faith will grow stronger and their steps unfaltering in the path of his commandments.[391] True believers do not only not relinquish faith (*fidem veram*) when the devil tries to undermine it by instilling thoughts of blasphemy and other kindred suggestions;[392] they are also ready to suffer contempt, ridicule, and persecution "in the cause of faith and of justice [holy living]."[393] They accept that "God is faithful and will not allow anyone to be tempted above that which he is able,"[394] and they endure in the spirit of humility and patience so that their faith and love of God grow stronger.[395]

Cf. *Prof* 3,69. *...saepe vacillabant in fide Christi* (David ab Augusta, 370; Devas, *Spiritual Life* 2, 203).

[387] *Prof* 3,57. *Si quis vestrum indiget sapientia, postulet in fide nihil haesitans...* (David ab Augusta, 322; Devas, *Spiritual Life* 2, 155).

[388] *Prof* 3,56. *...per doctrinam fidei intelligimus...* (David ab Augusta, 311; Devas, *Spiritual Life* 2, 144).

[389] Cf. *Prof* 3,3. *Vult autem Dominus erudire nos per subtractionem consolationis inniti veritati Scripturae et fidei potius quam nostrae qualicumque experientiae, quia fides non haberet meritum, si in sola experientia consisteret...* (David ab Augusta, 169; Devas, *Spiritual Life* 2, 11). Cf. *Prof* 3,4. *Fides ibi probatur, si credat, vera esse quae iam desiit per gustum dulcedinis experiri* (David ab Augusta, 172; Devas, *Spiritual Life* 2, 14).

[390] *Prof* 3,54. *...infideles ad cognitionis suae lumen vocando per fidem et fideles ad sanctificationis suae gratiam convertendo per amorem...* (David ab Augusta, 306; Devas, *Spiritual Life* 2, 138).

[391] *Prof* 2,2. *..et iussionibus eius devote obtemperandum est, ut et fortes simus in fide et a mandatis eius nunquam declinemus* (David ab Augusta, 76; Devas, *Spiritual Life* 1, 71).

[392] *Prof* 2,2. *...cum aut fidem veram conatur nobis auferre et spiritu blasphemiae subvertere, et huiusmodi cogitationibus nos infestat...* (David ab Augusta, 74; Devas, *Spiritual Life* 1, 69). Cf. *Prof* 2,2. *Tentationes vero contra fidem et de spiritu blasphemiae et similes nec fugere possumus nec repugnando vincere...* (David ab Augusta, 75; Devas, *Spiritual Life* 1, 71). There are four kinds of temptation: against Faith; to despair; to blaspheme God; and to take one's own life (*Prof* 3,9; David ab Augusta, 180; Devas, *Spiritual Life* 2, 21).

[393] *Prof* 1,29. *Cum vero pro iustitia sicut et pro fide debeamus pati non solum irrisiones et despectiones, sed etiam persecutiones quaslibet et mortem (sicut passi sunt Sancti ante nos et patientur post nos in diebus novissimis), potius quam fidem deserere vel iustitiam vitae peccando relinquere...* (David ab Augusta, 39; Devas, *Spiritual Life* 1, 34–35). Cf. *...et fidei conculcatione...* (David ab Augusta, 213; Devas, *Spiritual Life* 2, 52);

[394] *Prof* 3,3. *Fidelis autem Deus, qui non patietur, vos tentari supra id, quod potestis...* (David ab Augusta, 168; Devas, *Spiritual Life* 2, 10).

[395] *Prof* 2,2. *Divinae vero castigationes humiliter et patienter tolerandae sunt, et iussionibus eius devote obtemperandum est, ut et fortes simus in fide et a mandatis eius nunquam*

Confidence

A man who is "instructed by temptation" and being tested, should have unfaltering faith (*fidei certitudo*) and be filled with trust in God (*fiducia ad Deum*).[396] As the example of Abraham shows, obedient devotion is proof of unswerving confidence (*fides*) in God.[397] Another example of absolute confidence is Moses, who asked God to "either forgive them or blot me out of the book you have written."[398] Temptations are really overcome in the security born of great confidence: although I am helpless and frail, God will lovingly come to help me.[399] He

> permits a man to be tried by temptation and difficulty precisely that he may learn to pray, that he may turn to Our Lord, that he may have experience of His help, that, filled with consolation at finding himself the object of such tenderness, he may grow in the ardour of his love, and that thus there may be a real advance in virtues [holiness] and in confidence (*fiducia*).[400]

Furthermore:

> A revelation may be imparted by the Holy Spirit in an indirect way when he allows a man, who is praying very earnestly by God's grace, for some particular cause, to understand from the very ardour of his devotion and sense of assurance (*fiducia*) that all is well and that his prayer will be answered.[401]

---

declinemus (*David ab Augusta*, 76; Devas, *Spiritual Life* 1, 71); *Prof* 3,14. *Sic etiam in tentationibus contra fidem vel de blasphemia Spiritus meretur fidelis bellator quandoque in fide clarius illuminari et in amore Dei ardentius inflammari...* (*David ab Augusta*, 191; Devas, *Spiritual Life* 2, 31–32). Cf. *Prof* 3,4. *...nisi fidei et spei firmitate se muniat et patientia et humilitate se defendat...* (*David ab Augusta*, 172; Devas, *Spiritual Life* 2, 14).

[396] *Prof* 3,3. *Eruditur etiam, quod non tantum innitatur experientiis consolationum, quantum in fiducia ad Deum vel fidei certitudine...* (*David ab Augusta*, 168; Devas, *Spiritual Life* 2, 10).

[397] *Prof* 2,2. *...ut ostenderetur magna devotio obedientiae Abraham et fidei ad Deum...* (*David ab Augusta*, 75; Devas, *Spiritual Life* 1, 70).

[398] *Prof* 3,58. *...aut dimitte eis hanc noxam, aut, si non dimittis, dele me de libro tuo, quem scripsisti. Magna fiducia hominis Dei ad Deum! Non rogat, se deleri de libro Dei, sed ea fiducia, qua praesumit, se non delendum de libro vitae, ea petit, peccatum illud remitti, non dubitans, se exaudiendum...* (*David ab Augusta*, 328; Devas, *Spiritual Life* 2, 160).

[399] *Prof* 3,10. *Ascendunt usque ad caelos, per fiduciae securitatem... aspiciendo ad divinae pietatis auxilium... intuendo propriae fragilitatis defectum* (*David ab Augusta*, 182; Devas, *Spiritual Life* 2, 23).

[400] *Prof* 3,14. *Ad hoc enim Deus permittit, hominem tentari et tribulari, ut excitetur ad orationis studium et confugiat ad Dominum et experiatur eius auxilium et ad eius exauditionis solatium amplius in eius amorem exardescat, et sic tam in merito virtutum quam in fiducia dignationis eius excrescat* (*David ab Augusta*, 190–191; Devas, *Spiritual Life* 2, 31).

[401] *Prof* 3,67. *Est et alius modus revelationis per Spiritum sanctum, cum homo ex Dei inspiratione orat Deum pro aliqua speciali causa propria vel aliena et per affectum devotionis et fiduciam exauditionis intelligit se exauditum in hac petitione* (*David ab Augusta*, 362; Devas, *Spiritual Life* 2, 194). Cf. *Prof* 3,67. *...et cum iam fuerit in affectu devotionis et fiducia divinae*

Confidence comes with the right kind of prayer.[402] In prayer, the Lord is like a close friend whom we turn to with respect (*fiducia*) and reverence.[403] Good works, too, undertaken in obedience and out of charity, fill the soul with joy and great trust in God (*fiduciam spei in Deum*).[404]

Faith, virtues, and works

For those "who endeavour to build up in the soul an inward sanctuary wherein Christ may dwell through faith,"[405] faith is an inner virtue. The faithful religious, who is "espoused by faith and chastity to Christ,"[406] sets himself to the rooting out of vice and the acquisition of real virtues. He manifests virtues like faith, charity, justice, truth, chastity, obedience, and contempt for worldly interests,[407] and interiorizes humility, charity, self-control (benignity), zeal, generosity, temperance (sobriety), and chastity.[408]

---

propitiationis, antequam istud optaret, accedente modo optatae rei desiderio, fit affectus ferventior et fiducia ad Deum ex fervore constantior... (*David ab Augusta*, 363; Devas, *Spiritual Life* 2, 195).

[402] *Prof* 3,58. *Quandoque namque, cum petitio nostra uno modo formata haesitationem facit, quasi non debeat admitti, si aliter formetur, fiduciam exauditionis reportat* (*David ab Augusta*, 326; Devas, *Spiritual Life* 2, 159). Cf. *Prof* 3,61. *...ut in orationis actu et pietatis affectu merearis et in exauditionis fiducia consoleris...* (*David ab Augusta*, 334; Devas, *Spiritual Life* 2, 165–166); *Prof* 3,62. *...quod orantem magis secundum Deum delectat et quod devotionis spiritum promptius excitat et mentis fiduciam erigit in Deum* (*David ab Augusta*, 338; Devas, *Spiritual Life* 2, 169).

[403] *Prof* 3,58. *Aliquando assumit formam familiaris amici et domestici et cum reverentia et fiducia rogat et quasi a latere consulit Domino...* (*David ab Augusta*, 327; Devas, *Spiritual Life* 2, 159). Of course, trust is also an interhuman virtue: *...quod maiorem habeant de eorum dilectione fiduciam* (*Prof* 3,40; *David ab Augusta*, 256; Devas, *Spiritual Life* 2, 92).

[404] *Prof* 1,31. *...bona actio, maxime condita pinguedine caritatis et obedientiae vel alterius virtutis, laetificat conscientiam et dat fiduciam spei in Deum...* (*David ab Augusta*, 42; Devas, *Spiritual Life* 1, 36). Cf. *Prof*, Epist 2. *...quia orationis devotio cetera virtutum opera facit sapida, sine qua forent arida et minorem fiduciam praestantia apud Deum* (*David ab Augusta*, 62; Devas, *Spiritual Life* 1, 56).

[405] *Prof* 2,3. *Hi sunt qui student interiorem hominem suum, in quo Christus inhabitat per fidem* [cfr. Eph 3,17], *componere et ad veras virtutes se exercere et vitia carnis et spiritus exstirpare... Istae enim virtutes sunt verum sanctuarium, et qui habet eas sanctus est* (*David ab Augusta*, 81; Devas, *Spiritual Life* 1, 76).

[406] *Prof* 2,50. *Sic et anima Religiosi, quae est Christo desponsata per fidem et votum castitatis* (*David ab Augusta*, 159; Devas, *Spiritual Life* 1, 150).

[407] *Prof* 2,12. *Bona nostra, ad quae tenemur ex praecepto Dei vel Ecclesiae, vel ad quae ex manifesto voto adstringimur, debemus hominibus ostendere, ut fidem, caritatem, iustitiam, veritatem, castitatem, obedientiam et contemptum mundanorum* (*David ab Augusta*, 97; Devas, *Spiritual Life* 1, 93).

[408] *Prof* 2,3. *...et his contrarias virtutes cordi inserere: humilitatem, caritatem, mansuetudinem, devotionem, largitatem, sobrietatem et castitatem* (*David ab Augusta*, 81; Devas, *Spiritual Life* 1, 76).

He is "patient under contumelious and contemptuous treatment, chaste, frugal, poor by choice, humble, generous, devoted to prayer, wise in counsel, and constant in faith (*fide constans*)."[409] He adorns his will by fervor of faith, steadfastness of hope, sweetness of charity, alacrity in well doing, confidence about the forgiveness of past sin, and devotion to the person of Christ.[410] His faith, hope, and charity increase with each prayer.[411] He conditions his prayer on the effort to vanquish sin, on fervent and persevering faith and trust (*fervor et instantia et fidei confidentia*), and on humility, among other things.[412] The faithful religious is a virtuous religious, and his works are an expression of interior habit. Nevertheless, as "we walk by faith and not by sight," "the full beauty of virtue is itself hidden from us, and we ourselves must necessarily veil it by the outward works wherewith we clothe it."[413]

---

[409] *Prof* 3,40. *...plures videmus castos, abstinentes, pauperes, se ipsos humiliantes, eleemosynas facientes vel orationibus instantes, bona docentes, fide constantes; sed paucos admodum in contumeliis et detractionibus et despectionibus humiliter patientes* (David ab Augusta, 255; Devas, *Spiritual Life* 2, 91).

[410] *Prof* 3,2. *Ornatus voluntatis sunt sanctae affectiones et devotio ad Deum, fervor fidei, fiducia spei, dulcedo caritatis et bonae voluntatis alacritas, spes de remissione peccatorum, devotio circa Christi humanitatem et passionem nec non circa eius divinitatem... quae afficiunt hominem ad Deum et ad amorem virtutum et ad odium vitiorum et dilectionem proximorum et ad studia bonorum operum...* (David ab Augusta, 165; Devas, *Spiritual Life* 2, 7).

[411] *Prof* 3,57. *Vult enim Deus non tam orari, ut donet quod et ante dare disposuit, sed vult, ut plus orando mereamur per fidem, qua credimus orandum quem non videmus; per spem, qua obtinere confidimus petita; per caritatem, qua exauditorem amplius amemus...* (David ab Augusta, 323; Devas, *Spiritual Life* 2, 156). Cf. *Prof* 3,2. *Item, ad confortationem fidei, ad robur spei, ad caritatis accensionem* (David ab Augusta, 166; Devas, *Spiritual Life* 2, 8); *Prof* 3,3. *...quia fides non haberet meritum, si in sola experientia consisteret, et spes, quae iam tenetur experientia, spes non esset* (David ab Augusta, 169; Devas, *Spiritual Life* 2, 11); *Prof* 3,4. *...nisi fidei et spei firmitate se muniat...* (David ab Augusta, 172; Devas, *Spiritual Life* 2, 14); *Prof* 3,28. *Multae sunt aliae virtutum artificiales divisiones, secundum quod aliae dicuntur theologicae, ut fides, spes, caritas...* (David ab Augusta, 217; Devas, *Spiritual Life* 2, 56); *Prof* 3,32. *...cum credit credenda, fides est...* (David ab Augusta, 227; Devas, *Spiritual Life* 2, 66); *Prof* 3,56. *...quia per solem caritatis et lunam fidei et stellas aliarum virtutum corda fidelium illuminantur...* (David ab Augusta, 318; Devas, *Spiritual Life* 2, 151).

[412] *Prof* 3,61. *...quae valeant ad exauditionem orationis, scilicet culpae remotio, fervor et instantia et fidei confidentia, humilitas et aliorum suffragia et acceptae gratiae cum gratiarum actione studiosa conservatio...* (David ab Augusta, 337; Devas, *Spiritual Life* 2, 168).

[413] *Prof* 2,3. *Velata tamen portabant ea, quia, dum hic per fidem ambulamus et non per speciem* [cfr. 2 Cor 5,7], *nondum videmus virtutum decorem pure, sicut est, et in exteriorum operum exercitiis necesse est nos ea involvere tam pro nostro exercitio quam pro exemplo aliorum, qui mentem nostram non vident nisi per vestigia exteriorum operum et morum* (David ab Augusta, 82; Devas, *Spiritual Life* 1, 78).

6. HUMILITY

Origin

Humility (*humilitas*) is a basic Christian virtue and one of the key virtues in the history of Christian theology.[414] In the course of this history it has had many theological and psychological implications, and to this day it evokes many negative as well as positive associations.[415] With *humus* meaning "ground," it forms the basic demeanor (*habitus*) of the good Christian, paving the way for perfect charity, the highest virtue according to Augustine.[416] Humility is a biblical virtue *pur sang*. It is an important virtue in the Old Testament as well as in the New Testament.[417] Like charity and goodness, in the New Testament it can be found as part of a number of catalogues of virtues forming a program of Christian virtuous living.[418] Paul urges his readers to live a life worthy of the calling they have received, with the following words: "Be completely humble and gentle; be patient, bearing with one another in love. Make every effort to keep the unity of the Spirit through the bond of peace."[419] The foundation of humility is Christ Himself. Christ humbled Himself when He took the nature of a servant: "And being found in appearance as a man, he humbled himself and became obedient to death – even death on a cross!"[420] Accordingly, as Christ has humbled Himself for us, we have to humble ourselves.[421] For as Christ, the Gentle and Humble in heart,[422] has been exalted by God the Father,[423] so will the humble be exalted.[424]

---

[414] See for instance: Auer, "Demut"; "Humilité"; Casey, *A Guide*; Lawson, *Be Yourself*; Macquarrie, *The Humility*; Murray, *Humility*; Nouwen, *The Selfless*; Pansters, "Deemoed"; Rondholz, *Die Demut*; Schaffner, *Christliche*; Schaffner, "Demut"; Varillon, *L'humilité*; Zemmrich, *Demut*.

[415] "The term *humility* has negative associations. One might think of a humble person as weak and passive, with eyes downcast and lacking self-respect and confidence. Others might associate humility with humiliation, prompting images of shame, embarrassment, or disgust with the self. However, humility need not imply such negative views of the self. In fact, some humble individuals can have quite positive opinions of themselves if they base their sense of worth on their intrinsic value, their good qualities, a sense of compassion toward the self, their connections with other people, or their alignment with a higher power" (Peterson & Seligman, "Humility", 463).

[416] E.g., *De civitate Dei* 15,22.

[417] Wengst, *Demut*.

[418] Wibbing, *Die Tugend- und Lasterkataloge*, 77–127.

[419] Eph 4,2–3. Other examples of these catalogues are: 2 Cor 6,6; Gal 5,22–23; 1 Tim 6,11.

[420] Phil 2,8.

[421] Matt 18,4; John 3,30.

[422] Matt 11,29.

[423] Phil 2,9.

[424] Matt 23,12; Luke 1,52; Luke 14,11; Luke 18,14; Jac 1,9; Jac 4,10; 1 Pet 5,5–6.

Francis

God and man

For Francis, the virtue of humility has several meanings: eucharistic (*Adm* 1; *Ep Cust* 1, *Ep Ord*), evangelical (*RnB, RB*), theocentric (*Laud Dei*), trinitarian (*Ep Fid*), and moral (*Sal Virt*).[425] In his eyes, all virtues originate in God. His being comprises all the virtues: He *is* Love, He *is* Wisdom, He *is* Humility (*tu es humilitas*), and He *is* all the other virtues.[426] A sublime witness to God's virtuousness is his own creation, e.g., the element of water which is praised for its usefulness, humility, preciousness and chastity.[427] Following the movement described by Paul,[428] Francis finds God to be most sublime in his humility and most humble in his sublimity. For our salvation (viz., exaltation) He has taken the nature of the servant and is hiding Himself under an ordinary piece of bread:

> O wonderful loftiness and stupendous dignity!
> O sublime humility!
> O humble sublimity!
> The Lord of the universe,
> God and the Son of God,
> so humbles Himself
> that for our salvation
> He hides Himself
> under an ordinary piece of bread![429]

---

[425] Freyer, *Der demütige*, 205. On Francis and humility, see for instance: Armstrong, *St. Francis of Assisi*, 166–172; Bisschops, *Franciscus*, 329–338; Esser & Grau, *Antwort*, 311–328; Feld, *Franziskus*, 204–208; Gerken, "Die theologische", 21–23; Geulen, *Die Armut*, 96–103; Ghinato, *Profilo*, 161–162; Gobry, *St. François*, 64–68; Haskamp, ",,Du bist"'; Hoeberichts, *Paradise*, 93–108, 206–214; Iriarte, *Vocazione*, 118–145; Kinsella, ""To Serve""; Linden, *Vater*, 237–246; Longpré, *François*, 99–116; Longpré, "Saint François", 1290–1291; Morant, *Unser Weg*, 115–126; Van Munster, *De mystiek*, 177–181; Nguyen-Van-Khanh, *Le Christ*, 131–139; Peters, *Aus Liebe*, 64–66; Short, *Poverty*, 37–57; Verhey, *Der Mensch*, 117–122; Veuthey, *Itinerarium*, 55–57.

[426] *Laud Dei* 4–6. *Tu es amor, caritas; tu es sapientia, tu es humilitas, tu es patientia* (Ps 70,5), *tu es pulchritudo, tu es mansuetudo, tu es securitas, tu es quietas, tu es gaudium, tu es spes nostra et laetitia, tu es iustitia, tu es temperantia, tu es omnia divitia nostra ad sufficientiam. Tu es pulchritudo, tu es mansuetudo; tu es protector* (Ps 30,5), *tu es custos et defensor noster; tu es fortitudo* (cfr. Ps 42,2), *tu es refrigerium. Tu es spes nostra, tu es fides nostra, tu es caritas nostra, tu es tota dulcedo nostra, tu es vita aeterna nostra: Magnus et admirabilis Dominus, Deus omnipotens, misericors Salvator.*

[427] *Cant Sol* 7. *Laudato si, mi signore, per sor aqua, la quale è multo utile et humile et pretiosa et casta.*

[428] Smit, "Gegrepen", 87.

[429] *Ep Ord* 27. *O admiranda altitudo et stupenda dignatio! O humilitas sublimis! O sublimitas humilis quod Dominus universitatis Deus et Dei Filius sic se humiliat ut pro nostra salute sub modica panis formula se abscondat!* (Armstrong, *Francis of Assisi*, 118).

In the form of this bread, the sacrament of the Eucharist, the servant who is the Son of God keeps humbling Himself day after day.[430] This is why the believers of Christ, the sheep for whom He has laid down his life, should be inspired with love, gratitude, humility, peace, sweetness, kindness, and desire.[431] Brothers in the Lord should follow the example of his humility and poverty,[432] serve Him with poverty and humility,[433] and humble themselves (*humiliamini et vos*) to be exalted by Him:

> Brothers, look at the humility of God,
> and pour out your hearts before Him!
> Humble yourselves,
> that you may be exalted by Him![434]

The Spirit of the Lord strives for humility and patience, the pure, simple, and true peace of the spirit.[435] The brothers should be loving and humble towards each other and towards others,[436] in particular when being tested

---

[430] *Adm* 1,16–18. *Ecce, quotidie humiliat se* (cfr. Phil 2,8), *sicut quando a regalibus sedibus* (Sap 18,15) *venit in uterum Virginis; quotidie venit ad nos ipse humilis apparens; quotidie descendit de sinu Patris* (cfr. Joa 1,18) *super altare in manibus sacerdotis.*

[431] *Ep Fid* 1,1,13; *Ep Fid* 2,56. *O quam sanctum et quam dilectum, beneplacitum, humilem, pacificum, dulcem, amabilem et super omnia desiderabilem habere talem fratrem et talem filium: Dominum nostrum Jesum Christum, qui posuit animam pro ovibus suis* (cfr. Joa 10,15) *et oravit patri dicens...; Ep Cust* 1,2. *Rogo vos plus quam de me ipso, quatenus, cum decet et videritis expedire, clericis humiliter supplicetis, quod sanctissimum corpus et sanguinem Domini nostri Jesu Christi et sancta nomina et verba eius scripta, quae sanctificant corpus, super omnia debeant venerari; RnB* 20,5. *Et sic contriti et confessi sumant corpus et sanguinem Domini nostri Jesu Christi cum magna humilitate et veneratione recordantes.*

[432] *RnB* 9,1. *Omnes fratres studeant sequi humilitatem et paupertatem Domini nostri Jesu Christi; Ep Fid* 2,87. *...et cum voluntate osculandi vestros pedes, quod haec verba et alia Domini nostri Jesu Christi cum humilitate et caritate debeatis recipere et operari et observare; RB* 12,4. *...ut semper subditi et subiecti pedibus eiusdem sanctae Ecclesiae stabiles in fide* (cfr. Col 1,23) *catholica paupertatem et humilitatem et sanctum evangelium Domini nostri Jesu Christi, quod firmiter promisimus, observemus.* Humility and poverty are sisters: *Domina sancta paupertas, Dominus te salvet cum tua sorore sancta humilitate* (*Sal Virt* 2).

[433] *RB* 6,2. *Et tanquam peregrini et advenae* (cfr. 1 Pet 2,11) *in hoc saeculo in paupertate et humilitate Domino famulantes....*

[434] *Ep Ord* 28. *Videte, fratres, humilitatem Dei et effundite coram illo corda vestra* (Ps 61,9); *humiliamini et vos ut exaltemini ab eo* (cfr. 1 Pet 5,6; Jac 4,10) (Armstrong, *Francis of Assisi*, 118).

[435] *RnB* 17,15. *Et studet ad humilitatem et patientiam et puram et simplicem et veram pacem spiritus.*

[436] *Ep Fid* 2,30. *Habeamus itaque caritatem et humilitatem; et faciamus eleemosynas, quia ipsa lavat animas a sordibus peccatorum* (cfr. Tob 4,11; 12,9); *Ep Fid* 2,44–45. *Nec ex delicto fratris irascatur in fratrem, sed cum omni patientia et humililate ipsum benigne moneat et sustineat. Non debemus secundum carnem esse sapientes et prudentes, sed magis debemus esse simplices, humiles et puri; RnB* 11,3. *Neque litigent inter se neque cum aliis, sed procurent humiliter respondere dicentes: Inutilis servus sum* (cfr. Luke 17,10); *RB* 3,11. *...sed sint mites, pacifici et modesti, mansueti et humiles, honeste loquentes omnibus, sicut decet.*

and corrected[437] or persecuted,[438] and especially when they are priests and ministers.[439] All lesser brothers, lay or cleric, should always preach, pray or work in a humble manner.[440] They should humbly ask all others to persevere in the true faith and in penance,[441] and, following the example of Francis, humbly beg the angels and the saints to give Him eternal thanks for all things.[442]

---

[437] *Adm* 13,2. *Cum autem venerit tempus, quod illi qui deberent sibi satisfacere, faciunt sibi contrarium, quantam ibi patientiam et humilitatem tantam habet et non plus; Adm* 22,2–3. *Beatus servus, qui reprehensus benigne acquiescit, verecunde obtemperat, humiliter confitetur et libenter satisfacit. Beatus servus, qui non est velox ad se excusandum et humiliter sustinet verecundiam et reprehensionem de peccato, ubi non commisit culpam; RnB* 5,5. *Si vero inter fratres ubicumque fuerit aliquis frater volens carnaliter et non spiritualiter ambulare, fratres, cum quibus est, moneant eum, instruant et corripiant humiliter et diligenter; RnB* 20,2. ...*absoluti erunt procul dubio ab illis peccatis, si poenitentiam sibi iniunctam procuraverint humiliter et fideliter observare; RB* 10,1. *Fratres, qui sunt ministri et servi aliorum fratrum, visitent et moneant fratres suos et humiliter et caritative corrigant eos, non praecipientes eis aliquid, quod sit contra animam suam et regulam nostram.*

[438] *RB* 10,9. ...*orare semper ad eum puro corde et habere humilitatem, patientiam in persecutione et infirmitate.* Patience and humility support each other: *Ubi est patientia et humilitas, ibi nec ira nec perturbatio* (*Adm* 27,2).

[439] *Adm* 23,1. *Beatus servus, qui ita inventus est humilis inter subditos suos, sicuti quando esset inter dominos suos; Ep Ord* 2. ...*et omnibus ministris et custodibus et sacerdotibus fraternitatis eiusdem in Christo humilibus*...

[440] *RnB* 17,5. *Unde deprecor in caritate, quae Deus est* (cfr. 1 Joa 4,16), *omnes fratres meos praedicatores, oratores, laboratores, tam clericos quam laicos, ut studeant se humiliare in omnibus; RB* 5,3–4. *De mercede vero laboris pro se et suis fratribus corporis necessaria recipiant praetere denarios vel pecuniam et hoc humiliter, sicut decet servos Dei et paupertatis sanctissimae sectatores; RnB* 23,11 ...*quotidie et continue credamus veraciter et humiliter et in corde teneamus et amemus, honoremus, adoremus, serviamus, laudemus et benedicamus, glorificemus et superexaltemus, magnificemus et gratias agamus altissimo et summo Deo aeterno*....

[441] *RnB* 23,7. *Et Domino Deo universos intra sanctam ecclesiam catholicam et apostolicam servire volentes et omnes sequentes ordines, sacerdotes, diaconos, subdiaconos, acolythos, exorcistas, lectores, ostiarios et omnes clericos, universos religiosos et religiosas, omnes conversos et parvulos, pauperes et egenos, reges et principes, laboratores et agricolas, servos et dominos, omnes virgines et continentes et maritatas, laicos, masculos et feminas, omnes infantes, adolescentes, iuvenes et senes, sanos et infirmos, omnes pusillos et magnos, et omnes populos, gentes, tribus et linguas* (cfr. Apoc 7,9), *omnes nationes et omnes homines ubicumque terrarum, qui sunt et erunt, humiliter rogamus et supplicamus nos omnes fratres minores, servi inutiles* (Luke 17,10), *ut omnes in vera fide et poenitentia perseveremus*....

[442] *RnB* 23,6. *Et gloriosam matrem beatissimam Mariam semper Virginem, beatum Michealem, Gabrielem et Raphaelem et omnes choros beatorum seraphim, cherubim, thronorum, dominationum, principatuum, potestatum* (cfr. Col 1,15), *virtutum, angelorum, archangelorum, beatum Joannem Baptistam, Joannem Evangelistam, Petrum, Paulum et beatos patriarchas, prophetas, innocentes, apostolos, evangelistas, discipulos, martyres, confessores, virgines, beatos Eliam et Enoch, et omnes sanctos, qui fuerunt et erunt et sunt, propter tuum amorem humiliter deprecamur, ut, sicut tibi placet, pro his tibi gratias referant summo vero Deo*....

God is both Humility and Sublimity. He descended from the highest height by becoming human, in order to exalt man to his sublimity. The fact that God is most sublime Humility in the incarnation of his Son can be acknowledged as well as seen: in the Eucharist. For Francis, God in the bread is Humility in substance. In this quality, Christ becoming human, the brothers have to follow Him so that by their humility and together with the Son they may be exalted to the Father.

Man

Humility is both a divine and a human *virtus*.[443] As a human virtue it is the humble recognition that all good things, including the virtues, come from God.[444] It is specifically connected to charity (*Ep Fid* 2,30; *Ep Fid* 2,87; *RB* 10,1), patience (*Adm* 13,2; *Adm* 27,2; *Ep Fid* 2,44; *RB* 10,9), and poverty (*RB* 6,2; *RB* 12,4; *RnB* 9,1; *Sal Virt* 2). Humility, which can be practiced by begging, is the true habit by which poverty and the other virtues can be developed.[445] It confounds pride and the things of the world.[446] It is also connected to self-abasement:[447] true and perfect joy lies in the utmost humiliation.[448]

Bonaventure

The root of all virtues

Humility is one of the most important virtues in the spiritual writings of Bonaventure, after charity and poverty.[449] According to Bonaventure, humility is "a great virtue" without which "virtue is worse than

---

[443] Its meaning is both "absteigend-sich-angleichend" and "ascetisch-aufsteigend" (Freyer, *Der demütige*, 222–226). Cf. Nguyen-Van-Khanh, *Le Christ*, 137: "L'humilité, selon François, n'est donc pas d'abord comme nous le croyons couramment, une attitude vertueuse et loin d'être encore une vertu humaine. Elle est d'abord un *acte*, et un acte de Dieu, un acte du Père par lequel il fait don de lui-même à l'homme dans l'incarnation de son Fils. L'humilité de l'homme sera le don de lui-même à Dieu en réponse à la démanche première de l'amour divin."

[444] *RnB* 17,17; *Sal Virt* 4. Cf. Hoeberichts, *Paradise*, 107. In negative terms it is *minoritas*: (in one of its definitions) the recognition that all bad things come from the self (Esser & Grau, *Antwort*, 247–259).

[445] Nolthenius, *Een man*, 237–238.

[446] *Sal Virt* 12.

[447] Cf. *Et ego frater Franciscus parvulus vester servus...* (*Test* 40).

[448] *Laet*. Cf. Veuthey, *Itinerarium*, 55–57.

[449] On Bonaventure and humility, see for instance: Bissen, "Les conditions", 399–400; Delio, *The Humility*; Gerken, *Theologie*, 315–334; Hayes, *The Hidden*, 26, 139–144; Martignetti, *Saint Bonaventure's*, 180–189; Schlosser, *Cognitio*, 228–236; Strack, *Christusleid*, 54–59, 107–113.

non-existent."⁴⁵⁰ Humility is "the virtue by which a man, knowing well what he is, deems himself worthless."⁴⁵¹ The truly humble man, therefore, wishes to be regarded as worthless, and not hailed as an example of humility.⁴⁵² The virtue of humility is the foundation of all other virtues, their root, their guardian, and their ornament.⁴⁵³ It is one of the great gifts of God to man.⁴⁵⁴ God sent to earth a humble Savior, Jesus Christ, who became a great Mirror and Teacher of humility on our path to eternal salvation:⁴⁵⁵

> You must call to mind that Christ was humbled (*humiliatus*) to the point of suffering a most infamous death; that He became so lowly (*humilis*) as to be compared to a leper. Thus speaks the prophet Isaias: We have thought Him as it were a leper, and as One struck by God and afflicted (*humiliatum*) – so much so (*humiliatus*) that, in His own time, no one was thought to be lowlier than He. Isaias also says: He was taken away from distress (*humilitate*) and from judgment, as if meaning: Such was his humiliation (*humilitas*), and so low did He Himself descend, that no one would take Him for what He was, no one would believe Him to be God. Our Lord and Master Himself

---

⁴⁵⁰ *Perf* 2,3. *...et ideo magna virtus est, sine cuius obtentu non solum virtus non est, sed etiam in superbiam erumpit* (*Doctoris* 8, 111; De Vinck, *The Works* 1, 218).

⁴⁵¹ *Perf* 2,1. *Humilitas enim est virtus, ut dicit beatus Bernardus, qua homo verissima sui cognitione sibi ipsi vilescit* (*Doctoris* 8, 110; De Vinck, *The Works* 1, 216). Cf. *Ex Reg* 3,12. *Humilitas est virtus, qua homo, vera cognitione sui sibi vilescens, appetit tractari vilius et non sublimius gubernari* (*Doctoris* 8, 410); *Ap Paup* 4,13. *...fugere ex humilitate mentis, qua homo infirmitatem propriam recognoscit...* (*Doctoris* 8, 255; De Vinck, *The Works* 4, 71).

⁴⁵² *Perf* 2,1. *Verum enim humilis, ut dicit beatus Bernardus, semper vult vilis reputari, non humilis praedicari* (*Doctoris* 8, 110; De Vinck, *The Works* 1, 216).

⁴⁵³ *Perf* 2,1. *...sic fundamentum omnium virtutum est humilitas* (*Doctoris* 8, 110; De Vinck, *The Works* 1, 216); *Lign Vit* 2,5. *...ab humilitate sumens initium, quae omnium est radix custosque virtutum* (*Doctoris* 8, 72; De Vinck, *The Works* 1, 107); *Leg Franc* 6,1. *Omnium virtutum custos et decor humilitas copiosa virum Dei ubertate repleverat* (*Doctoris* 8, 519; Cousins, *Bonaventure*, 228). Cf. *Reg Nov* 10,2. *...quia, sicut dicit Gregorius, qui ceteras virtutes sine humilitate congregat quasi pulverem ante ventum portat* (*Doctoris* 8, 485; Monti, *Works*, 167); *Ex Reg* 10,10. *Praemittit humilitatem patientiae, quia fundamentum eius est...* (*Doctoris* 8, 434).

⁴⁵⁴ *Ep Im* 6. *...et respondit, quod humilitas est magnum bonum et donum Dei* (*Doctoris* 8, 500).

⁴⁵⁵ *Ap Paup* 9,10. *...quem tamen acceptavit propter mysterium nostrae salutis et propter exemplum humilitatis...* (*Doctoris* 8, 297; De Vinck, *The Works* 4, 197); *Lign Vit* 2,5. *... remedium refugis salutis aeternae, ad quam pervenire nullatenus potes, nisi velis subsequi humilem Salvatorem* (*Doctoris* 8, 72; De Vinck, *The Works* 1, 107); *Lign Vit* 2,6. *...post vestigia humilis Christi revertaris in regionem tuam* (*Doctoris* 8, 72; De Vinck, *The Works* 1, 108); *Lign Vit* 7,25. *...qui post tam praeclarum humilitatis speculum superbia tolluntur in altum...* (*Doctoris* 8, 77; De Vinck, *The Works* 1, 123); *Perf* 2,7. *...quia magistrum habuistis humilem, scilicet Dominum nostrum Iesum Christum...* (*Doctoris* 8, 112; De Vinck, *The Works* 1, 220); *Leg Franc* 6,1. *...ut tam exemplo quam verbo Dominus et Magister humilitatem doceret* (*Doctoris* 8, 519; Cousins, *Bonaventure*, 228). Cf. *Lign Vit* 2,7. *Non suffecit magistro humilitatis perfectae...* (*Doctoris* 8, 72; De Vinck, *The Works* 1, 108).

chooses to say: "No servant is greater than his master, nor is one who is sent greater than he who sent him." If you are truly the handmaid of Christ, you must be lowly, contemptible, and humble (*humilis*).[456]

Christ not only began his life with an act of humility,[457] He also commended humility with all his words and deeds.[458] He became a great Example of humility and told his disciples to "learn from Me, for I am meek and humble of heart."[459] We can learn from Him, He who washed and wiped his disciples' feet and told them to "do as I have done to you," thereby exhibiting a bodily as well as spiritual humility (*humiliatio*), a humility of actions as well as of the heart.[460]

---

[456] *Perf* 2,4. *Rememorari debes, quod Christus humiliatus fuit usque ad vituperabilissimum genus mortis et in tantum factus est humilis, ut quasi leprosus reputaretur – unde dixit Isaias propheta: Reputavimus eum quasi leprosum et a Deo humiliatum* [cfr. Isa 53,4] – *immo in tantum fuit humiliatus, ut tempore ipsius nihil eo vilius reputaretur. Unde idem Isaias dicit: In humilitate iudicium eius sublatum est* [cfr. Isa 53,8]*; ac si diceret: tanta fuit eius humilitas, tantum se deiecerat, ut nullus de eo daret rectum iudicium, ut a nullo crederetur esse Deus. Si ergo ipse Dominus noster et magister inquit: Non est servus maior domino suo, et discipulus non est super magistrum* [cfr. John 13,16]*; si ancilla Christi es, si discipula Christi es, vilis et contemptibilis esse debes et humilis* (*Doctoris* 8, 111; De Vinck, *The Works* 1, 218).

[457] *Lign Vit* 2,5. *...ab humilitate sumens initium...* (*Doctoris* 8, 72; De Vinck, *The Works* 1, 107).

[458] *Lign Vit* 3,10. *...quatenus et hostilis pugnae humili perpessione nos humiles et victoriae faceret assecutione viriles* (*Doctoris* 8, 72; De Vinck, *The Works* 1, 110); *Leg Franc* 6,1. *...ut tam exemplo quam verbo Dominus et Magister humilitatem doceret* (*Doctoris* 8, 519; Cousins, *Bonaventure*, 228).

[459] *Perf* 2,1. *Hanc virtutem maxime a Filio Dei, mater Deo devota, discere debes, quia ipse dicit: Discite a me, quia mitis sum et humilis corde* [cfr. Matt 11,29] (*Doctoris* 8, 110; De Vinck, *The Works* 1, 216).

[460] *Ep Im* 4. *Primo igitur dico, quod Christus ambulavit per viam profundae humilitatis, quia tantum se humiliavit, ut lavaret pedes suis discipulis. Si ergo ipse Dei Filius, Rex Angelorum humiliavit se usque ad officium vilissimum in eo, quod inclinavit se ad pedes discipulorum suorum; considera, quantum nos oportet humiliare* (*Doctoris* 8, 500); *Ap Paup* 9,10. *Per hunc etiam modum, quando discipulorum pedes humiliter abluit, se magistrum et dominum esse et dici debere monstravit, ut per declarationem regiae celsitudinis discipulos induceret ad imitationem ostensae humilitatis* (*Doctoris* 8, 297; De Vinck, *The Works* 4, 197); *Ap Paup* 9,11. *...constat, quod humilitatis est haec refugere ad perfectam humilitatis Christi imitationem...* (*Doctoris* 8, 297; De Vinck, *The Works* 4, 198); *Ap Paup* 9,12. *...cum universorum Magister et Dominus non solum spiritualis, sed et corporalis humiliationis exempla praebuerit, quando discipulorum pedes lavit et tersit, ubi et dixit: Exemplum dedi vobis, ut, quemadmodum ego feci vobis, ita et vos faciatis* [cfr. John 13,15]*... Tanta quippe est humanae humilitatis utilitas, ut eam suo commendaret exemplo etiam divina sublimitas... Discamus, fratres, humilitatem ab Excelso, faciamus invicem humiles quod humiliter fecit Excelsus. Magna est haec commendatio humilitatis* (*Doctoris* 8, 298; De Vinck, *The Works* 4, 198–199); *Perf* 2,6. *Discite igitur, o virgines sacratae, humilem habere spiritum, humilem incessum, humiles sensus, humilem habitum...* (*Doctoris* 8, 111; De Vinck, *The Works* 1, 219); *Reg Nov* 10,2. *Et ut melius te conserves, stude semper in corde et opere humilitatem habere...* (*Doctoris* 8, 485; Monti, *Works*, 167).

Theological and social

The key to the essence of the virtue of humility lies in Christ's answer to the disciples: "Whoever (...) humbles himself as a little child, is the greatest in the kingdom of heaven."[461] The *theological* implication of this is that it is the firmest commitment to the virtue of humility and the deepest experience of humiliation that will ultimately lead one to heaven, just as the descent of Christ to earth and his utter humiliation became crucial for the return to his heavenly Father.[462] The *social* implication of Jesus's words and deeds might be thought even more important: to humiliate oneself in the footsteps of Christ and to consider oneself truly the servant of all, brings lasting peace and tranquillity with all.[463]

Spiritual

The suffering Christ is our Example of humility and Model of virtue in all circumstances:

> (...) consider how He is suffering, and put on Christ by endeavoring to resemble Him. He suffered most willingly as regards His brother, most severely as regards Himself, most obediently as regards His father, most providently as regards the enemy. Following His example, strive therefore to be kind to your neighbor, severe to yourself, humble before God, and shrewd against the devil's guile.[464]

Other great examples of humility are the Virgin Mary, Francis, and Clare.[465] These models show that perfect humility is always accompanied by

---

[461] *Ap Paup* 9,11. *Quicumque humiliaverit se sicut parvulus iste, hic maior est in regno caelorum* (*Doctoris* 8, 298; De Vinck, *The Works* 4, 198). Cf. *Reg Nov* 2,3. *Sed quia nemo ascendit ad Dei contemplationem, nisi prius descendat per sui humilitatem; ideo sequitur secundum, scilicet propriae parvitatis consideratio* (*Doctoris* 8, 477; Monti, *Works*, 153); *Perf* 2,6. *...sic qui toto corde humiliatus procedit magis propinquat ad Dominum, ut impetret gratiam* (*Doctoris* 8, 111; De Vinck, *The Works* 1, 220).

[462] Cf. Pansters, "De deemoed".

[463] *Ep Mem* 8. *...humiliando te ipsum, omnem hominem reputes tuum dominum et te verissime reputes servum omnium et in omnibus circa hominem te reputes sicut servum. Sic enim tranquillitatem et pacem cum omnibus perpetuam obtinens, scandalum penitus ignorabis* (*Doctoris* 8, 494; De Vinck, *The Works* 3, 255); *Reg Nov* 10,2. *Et ut melius te conserves, stude semper in corde et opere humilitatem habere...* (*Doctoris* 8, 485; Monti, *Works*, 167).

[464] *Trip Via* 3,3. *Quinto, quali forma patitur, et Christum induere per assimilationis studium. Passus est enim libentissime respectu proximi, severissime respectu sui, obedientissime respectu Dei, prudentissime respectu adversarii. Stude igitur ad habendum habitum benignitatis ad proximum, severitatis ad te ipsum, humilitatis ad Deum, perspicacitatis contra diabolum, secundum effigiem imitationis Christi* (*Doctoris* 8, 13; De Vinck, *The Works* 1, 83).

[465] *Perf* 2,7. *...et quia magistram habuistis humilem, scilicet Virginem Mariam, reginam omnium. Sitis humiles, quia patrem habuistis humilem, scilicet beatum Franciscum; sitis*

poverty, patience, and obedience.[466] The virtue of patience, in particular, is the proof of humility, and the vice of pride its opponent. The monastery, for example, is a "school of humility" where impatient and overbearing religious learn pride, and the meek ones learn forbearance.[467] Here, superiors should be models of humble behavior, humble accessibility, and humble use of temporal goods.[468] But everybody has the obligation to humiliate himself because God loves the humble, and only humility is pleasing to Him.[469] As a consequence, devotion humbles the heart;[470] spiritual progress on the path to God amounts to the humiliation of oneself;[471] and the path to perfect humility amounts to self-examination, remembrance of Christ, and contemplation of God.[472]

---

humiles, quia matrem habuistis humilem, scilicet beatam Claram, humilitatis exemplar (*Doctoris* 8, 112; De Vinck, *The Works* 1, 220). Cf. *Perf* 2,1. *Hac humilitate apud se ipsum viluit pater noster beatus Franciscus...* (*Doctoris* 8, 110; De Vinck, *The Works* 1, 216).

[466] *Lign Vit* 2,8. *Quoniam autem humilitatem perfectam trium specialiter adornari decet comitatu virtutum, scilicet paupertatis, in fugiendo divitias ut fomenta superbiae, patientiae vero in aequanimi perpessione contemptus, obedientiae quoque in alienis parendo mandatis...* (*Doctoris* 8, 72; De Vinck, *The Works* 1, 108–109).

[467] *Perf.* 2,7. *Sic tamen sitis humiles, ut testis humilitatis vestrae sit patientia. Virtus enim humilitatis per patientiam perficitur, neque est vera humilitas, cui non est adiuncta patientia... In humilitate tua patientiam habe* [cfr. *Sir* 2,4]... *Unde beatus Bernardus dicit: Video, quod multum doleo, post spretam saeculi pompam nonnullos in schola humilitatis superbiam magis addiscere ac sub alis mitis humilisque magistri gravius insolescere et impatientes amplius fieri in claustro, quam fuissent in saeculo...* (*Doctoris* 8, 112; De Vinck, *The Works* 1, 220). Cf. *Perf* 2,3. *O quot sunt hodie luciferiani, imitatores et imitatrices luciferi, filii et filiae superbiae, quos patienter tolerat Dominus...* (*Doctoris* 8, 110; De Vinck, *The Works* 1, 217).

[468] *Sex Alis* 5,3–5. *Sit etiam humilis moribus... Sit etiam humilis affabilitate... Sit etiam humilis in use rerum temporalium...* (*Doctoris* 8, 141; De Vinck, *The Works* 3, 166–167).

[469] *Ap Paup* 5,20. *Quis se non debet humiliare?* (*Doctoris* 8, 257; De Vinck, *The Works* 4, 76); *Ap Paup* 5,23. *...ex mentis humilitate suppleatur* (*Doctoris* 8, 264; De Vinck, *The Works* 4, 100); *Trip Via* 3,6,9. *...per amplexum humilium, humilitate* (*Doctoris* 8, 16; De Vinck, *The Works* 1, 90); *Leg Franc* 6,6. *...amator humilium Deus...* (*Doctoris* 8, 521; Cousins, *Bonaventure*, 234); *Perf* 2,3. *Humilitas enim sola placet Deo...* (*Doctoris* 8, 110; De Vinck, *The Works* 1, 217).

[470] *Sex Alis* 7,2. *Cor humiliat; Isaiae sexagesimo sexto: Super quem requiescet spiritus meus nisi super humilem etc.* [cfr. *Isa* 66,2] (*Doctoris* 8, 148; De Vinck, *The Works* 3, 188).

[471] *Ep Im* 6. *Item, fuit petitum a quodam sancto Patre, quid esset proficere in Deum; qui respondit, quod proficere erat humiliare se ipsum* (*Doctoris* 8, 501). Cf. *Reg Nov* 2,3. *Sed quia nemo ascendit ad Dei contemplationem, nisi prius descendat per sui humilitatem...* (*Doctoris* 8, 477; Monti, *Works*, 153).

[472] *Perf* 2,2–5. *Si igitur, mater dilectissima, ad perfectam humilitatem vis pervenire, oportet te per triplicem semitam incedere. Prima semita est consideratio Dei... Secunda semita est rememoratio Christi.... Tertia semita, per quam debes incedere, si vis ad perfectam humilitatem pervenire, est circumspectio tui* (*Doctoris* 8, 110; De Vinck, *The Works* 1, 217–219).

David

The virtue of humility

The virtue of humility adorns the manners of a good religious:

> Humility banishes any air of conceit, determines the quiet answer, gives grace to one's movements, aims at simplicity in dress, chooses the lower place, shuns ostentation, avoids singularity, is quick to see how others may be helped, closes the lips under reproach, maintains an unassuming manner, even when honours abound, is ever open to learn and slow to anger.[473]

Important as humble behavior may be and as much emulation it may arouse in this way,[474] the virtue is much more profound than this. While charity leads us towards the good, humility leads us towards the truth.[475] Humility is the acknowledgement of the truth about ourselves, that we are unworthy and sinful; humility is the expression of this acknowledgment in our manners and conversation.[476] It is the acknowledgement that others, be they equals, superiors, or subjects, are better and worthier than we are.[477] It is the acknowledgement that God is our Lord and our Judge,[478] to whom we should return all the goods and virtues that are not really ours but his.[479]

---

[473] *Prof* 3,18. *Humilitas morum deprimit cervicem, humile format responsum, gestus complanat, vestitum simplicem amat, sese inter novissimos locat, ostentationis notam declinat, singularitatem fugit, ad aliorum obsequia agilem facit, ad opprobria tacitum, ad honores oblatos verecundum, promptum ad discendum, difficilem ad indignandum* (David ab Augusta, 198; Devas, *Spiritual Life* 2, 38).

[474] *Prof* 3,18. *Humilitas reddit imitabilem...* (David ab Augusta, 198; Devas, *Spiritual Life* 2, 39).

[475] *Prof* 3,37. *Sicut ergo caritas ordinat nos ad bonitatem, ita humilitas habet nos ordinare ad veritatem* (David ab Augusta, 243; Devas, *Spiritual Life* 2, 80).

[476] *Prof* 3,37. *In nobis debemus esse humiles, nosmetipsos ex consideratione propriae vilitatis despiciendo, ut omnia, quae in nobis despicabilia agnoscimus... Secundo in nobis simus humiles, mores et gestus humiles habendo et verba humilia et responsa...* (David ab Augusta, 244–245; Devas, *Spiritual Life* 2, 81–82).

[477] *Prof* 3,37. *...primo, meliores et digniores nobis ipsos reputare...* (David ab Augusta, 245; Devas, *Spiritual Life* 2, 82); *Prof* 3,37. *Item, proximorum alii sunt aequales nobis, alii superiores, alii subditi* (David ab Augusta, 246; Devas, *Spiritual Life* 2, 83).

[478] *Prof* 3,37. *...primo, ut ipsum esse Deum ac Dominum et iudicem nostrum agnoscamus...* (David ab Augusta, 246; Devas, *Spiritual Life* 2, 83). Cf. *Prof* 3,38. *...sed totum refundit ei, a quo habet, unde gloriosus videtur; hic est humilis, non cogente necessitate, sed veritatis caritate* (David ab Augusta, 251; Devas, *Spiritual Life* 2, 87).

[479] *Prof* 3,38. *...totum illi refundens et integre restituens, a quo fluit omne bonum* (David ab Augusta, 249; Devas, *Spiritual Life* 2, 86). Cf. *Prof* 3,38. *...sed totum refundit ei, a quo habet...* (David ab Augusta, 251; Devas, *Spiritual Life* 2, 87).

To be humble means that we allow ourselves to be humbled and
that we humiliate ourselves in the light of this triple truth.[480] A perfect
example of self-humiliation can be found in the saints and in Jesus
Christ, who humbled Himself and who was meek and humble of heart.[481]
In self-humiliation as well as in humiliation by others, the virtues of
humility, joy (pleasure), and patience (endurance) prove to be closely
connected:

> He who is perfect in humility rejoices in the humiliations to which others
> expose him as much as in those which he imposes upon himself: and simi-
> larly he who is perfect in patience rejoices as much – other things being
> equal – in adversities occasioned by others as in those he deliberately sets
> out to meet.[482]

True humility, therefore, is the adornment of good manners, the acknowledgement of the truth about ourselves, others, and God, and pleasure and
patience in humiliation.

---

[480] *Prof* 1,37. ...*si minus bene, iterum lucraris meritum humiliationis tuae...* (*David ab
Augusta*, 50; Devas, *Spiritual Life* 1, 44); *Prof* 3,37. *Quod autem non sumus similiter monet nos
humiliari* (*David ab Augusta*, 244; Devas, *Spiritual Life* 2, 81); *Prof* 3,37. ...*ut ex eorum intuitu
apud nos humiliemur* (*David ab Augusta*, 245; Devas, *Spiritual Life* 2, 82); *Prof* 3,37. *Quasi
lugens et contristatus sic humiliabar* [cfr. Ps 34,14] (*David ab Augusta*, 245; Devas, *Spiritual
Life* 2, 82); *Prof* 3,42. *Quanto maior autem et purior et promptior fuerit humiliatio, tanto ple-
nior erit gratiae recuperatio et gloriae remuneratio. Magnitudo humiliationis attenditur in
difficultate iniuncti operis...* (*David ab Augusta*, 263; Devas, *Spiritual Life* 2, 98); *Prof* 3,58. ...
*aut est dispensativa permissio ad terrendum vel humiliandum et corrigendum vel purgan-
dum animum...* (*David ab Augusta*, 325; Devas, *Spiritual Life* 2, 158); *Prof* 3,69. *Una, humiliatio, quia magis humiliatur homo, cum non habet tunc devotionem, quam alio tempore...*
(*David ab Augusta*, 369; Devas, *Spiritual Life* 2, 201).

[481] *Prof* 3,37. *Haec est humilitas Sanctorum et magnorum, qui, quanto maiores se vident,
tanto magis humiliant se in omnibus* (*David ab Augusta*, 243–244; Devas, *Spiritual Life* 2,
80); *Prof* 3,38. *Talis est humilitas Christi... Humiliavit semet ipsum* [cfr. Eph 2,6] *etc.;
Matthaeus: Discite a me, quia mitis sum et humilis corde* [cfr. Matt 11,29] (*David ab Augusta*,
250; Devas, *Spiritual Life* 2, 86).

[482] *Prof* 3,41. *Vera enim humilitas sic gaudet ab alio humiliari sicut a se, et vera
patientia ita libenter sustinet adversa ab aliis illata sicut a se procurata, quantum spectat
ad se* (*David ab Augusta*, 261; Devas, *Spiritual Life* 2, 96). Cf. *Prof* 3,37. *Ad proximum
debemus esse humiles... Tertio modo, patienter eorum infirma tolerare et laesiones
sustinere...* (*David ab Augusta*, 245; Devas, *Spiritual Life* 2, 82); *Prof* 3,38. *Secundus gradus
potest dici, cum non solum se ipsum agnoscens homo spernit pro vilitate sua, sed etiam ab
aliis sperni se patienter accipit...* (*David ab Augusta*, 248; Devas, *Spiritual Life* 2, 85);
Prof 3,41. ...*cum ab alio infertur ei occasio patiendi, unde vel corpus affligitur, vel animus
humiliatur...* (*David ab Augusta*, 261; Devas, *Spiritual Life* 2, 96); *Prof* 3,58. ...*quia Deus per
hoc probat orantis constantiam et purgat humiliati conscientiam et remunerat afflicti
patientiam. Bernardus: Obsecrationibus insistendum est, sed in omni humilitate et patientia, quia non referunt fructum nisi in patientia* (*David ab Augusta*, 325; Devas, *Spiritual Life*
2, 157).

Degrees of humility

As is the case with the other key virtues, humility "influences us in three ways": it determines our attitude (*habere debemus*) towards ourselves, towards our neighbour, and towards God.[483] As regards content, humility has three degrees:

> In the first [degree] a man knows himself for what he is and recognizes that he is poor and weak, void of good, inclined to evil – a sinner. Whatever other defects there may be, these too he acknowledges, entertaining no delusions about himself, as greater than he really is, despite any high dignities he may reach (...).
>
> In the second degree of humility a man does more than recognize that lowness which determines his own estimate of himself, but bears patiently with contempt on the part of others. He goes further and, as a lover of truth devoid of self-love, is even anxious that others should have of him the same opinion he has of himself as one poor, ignoble and prone to vice (...).
>
> The third degree of humility belongs to those who, despite outstanding gifts of nature and grace, or high honours attained, are not one whit moved thereby or inclined to flatter themselves, but attribute all to God, referring all good to Him from whom it comes.[484]

Humility is the foundation of a true relationship with oneself, one's neighbour, and God, when a correct self-image leads to correct behavior.[485]

Humility and the other virtues

Humility is the solid foundation of the virtuous life.[486] It is the mother and custodian of virtues: when we hold ourselves aloof from it, we inevitably

---

[483] *Prof* 3,37. *Triplicem vero humilitatem habere debemus: humiles enim esse debemus in nobis, humiles ad proximum, humiles ad Deum* (*David ab Augusta*, 244; Devas, *Spiritual Life* 2, 81).

[484] *Prof* 3,38. *Primus est, ut homo se, quod est, vilem, infirmum, inopem boni, vitiosum, peccatorem, et si quos alios defectus habet, agnoscat et sciat et non mentiatur sibi, esse se maiorem, quacumque dignitate fulgeat... Secundus gradus potest dici, cum non solum se ipsum agnoscens homo spernit pro vilitate sua, sed etiam ab aliis sperni se patienter accipit, immo, quia veritatem amat et se privato amore non diligit contra veritatem, etiam desiderat ab aliis reputari talis, qualem se reputat, vilem scilicet et vitiosum et ignobilem... Tertius humilitatis gradus est, quando etiam in magnis virtutibus et donis et honoribus homo nihil extollitur, nihil sibi ex hoc blanditur, totum illi refundens et integre restituens, a quo fluit omne bonum* (*David ab Augusta*, 247–251; Devas, *Spiritual Life* 2, 84–87). Cf. *Prof* 3,37. *Humilitas est virtus, qua homo verissima cognitione sui sibimet ipsi vilescit* (*David ab Augusta*, 243; Devas, *Spiritual Life* 2, 80).

[485] Cf. Pansters, "De deemoed".

[486] *Prof* 3,38. *Qui ergo cito desiderat virtutis culmen attingere, studeat in humilitatis se profundo solidare...* (*David ab Augusta*, 249; Devas, *Spiritual Life* 2, 86). Cf. Bohl, *Geistlicher*, 413–414.

lack all the other virtues.[487] In David's explanation of the various functions
and names of charity, however, charity is the mother virtue and humility
is the virtue of one of her daughters: "Holding us back from self-assertion,
it [charity] is *humility*."[488] No matter how, humility is one of the virtues
(divine love, holy fear, the fervor of a good will, humility, alertness (piety),
joy born of hope, and devotion) that reign in the heart of God's servant[489]
and one of the qualities (gravity, humility, and kindliness) that adorn the
manners of a good religious.[490]

Consequently, humility is one of the virtues (humility, charity, obedience, meekness, and care in giving good example) in which a good religious should exercise himself constantly;[491] and, more importantly, one of
the seven key virtues of spiritual progress (charity, humility, patience,
obedience, poverty, sobriety, and chastity) in David's sixth stage of religious life. These virtues (viz., humility, patience, poverty, and obedience)
are to be developed in faithful imitation of Jesus Christ.[492] Humility is one
of the fruits of prayer (faith, hope, charity, humility, perseverance, and
desire to please God),[493] and it belongs to the "remedial" virtues (humility,
love of one's neighbour, meekness, love of God, contempt of riches, sobriety, and chastity) that oppose the capital vices[494] and that combat them

---

[487] *Prof* 3,38. *Unde non est mirum, si inopes sumus virtutum, cum matrem et custodem
virtutum, humilitatem, tam alienam a nobis sentiamus* (*David ab Augusta*, 249; Devas,
Spiritual Life 2, 85).

[488] *Prof* 3,32. ...*cum non extollitur inaniter supra se, humilitas est...* (*David ab Augusta*,
226; Devas, *Spiritual Life* 2, 65).

[489] *Prof* 3,59. *Affectus enim amoris Dei et sancti timoris cum fervore bonae voluntatis, in
spiritu humilitatis et motu pietatis et gaudio spei nunquam debet in corde servi Dei exstingui.
Ista namque sunt in quibus virtus devotionis maxime consistit* (*David ab Augusta*, 329;
Devas, *Spiritual Life* 2, 161–162).

[490] *Prof* 3,18. *Morum disciplina in Religiosi triplici colore decoratur: si sint maturi, humiles
et benigni* (*David ab Augusta*, 197; Devas, *Spiritual Life* 2, 38).

[491] *Prof*, Epist 2. *Tertius, opera exercitare virtutum, ut obsequia humilitatis, servitia caritatis, assiduitas obediendi, mansuete loquendi, variis exercitiis bonum exemplum dandi...*
(*David ab Augusta*, 60; Devas, *Spiritual Life* 1, 54). Cf. *Prof* 1,9. *Ad labores communes et ad
humilitatis officia esto paratus...* (*David ab Augusta*, 13; Devas, *Spiritual Life* 1, 13).

[492] *Prof* 2,28. *Pudet nos imitari Dominum in humilitate, patientia, paupertate, religione,
obedientia et despectione et contumeliis et confusione...* (*David ab Augusta*, 113; Devas,
Spiritual Life 1, 107). Cf. *Prof* 3,59. *Item, sublimia virtutum exercitia pauca videmus, ut eximiae obedientiae, perfectae patientiae et humilitatis praecipuae et paupertatis extremae*
(*David ab Augusta*, 331; Devas, *Spiritual Life* 2, 163).

[493] *Prof* 3,57. ...*item, per humilitatem, qua in supplicatione perseveramus...* (*David ab
Augusta*, 323; Devas, *Spiritual Life* 2, 156).

[494] *Prof* 3,30. *Huic per contrarium opponitur ordo virtutum, scilicet humilitas contra
superbiam, dilectio proximi contra invidiam, mititas contra iram, caritas Dei contra accidiam, contemptus divitiarum contra avaritiam, sobrietas contra gulam, castitas contra luxuriam* (*David ab Augusta*, 222; Devas, *Spiritual Life* 2, 61). In medieval theology, the list of

(humility, charity, self-control (benignity), zeal, generosity, temperance (sobriety), and chastity) in order to "set up the inward sanctuary of the soul."[495]

Humility and vice

Humbling oneself is one of the familiar means of practicing virtue and banishing vice.[496] As mentioned, not only does humility support other important virtues and religious practices,[497] it is also one of the remedial virtues, the virtues that fight the capital vices. While *all* vices (not only the capital vices, in particular anger, but also cowardice, fear, diffidence, and the like) contrast with true humility,[498] this virtue is particularly at odds with the leader of the capital vices, pride.[499] In order to acquire repute,

---

remedial virtues often consists of humility, patience, obedience, good works, penance, confession, and abstinence, but there are many variations. Cf. Newhauser, *The Treatise*, 58, 159; Pansters, *De kardinale*, 19, 103.

[495] *Prof* 2,3. *Hi sunt qui student interiorem hominem suum, in quo Christus inhabitat per fidem, componere et ad veras virtutes se exercere et vitia carnis et spiritus exstirpare, iram, invidiam, avaritiam, accidiam, superbiam, gulam, luxuriam, viriliter expugnare et his contrarias virtutes cordi inserere: humilitatem, caritatem, mansuetudinem, devotionem, largitatem, sobrietatem et castitatem. Istae enim virtutes sunt verum sanctuarium, et qui habet eas sanctus est* (*David ab Augusta*, 81; Devas, *Spiritual Life* 1, 76). Cf. *Prof* 2,48. *Instante vero iam tribulatione vel adversitate, consideranda est utilitas adversitatis, quomodo peccata purgat, cautos reddit a peccato et substrahit occasionem peccandi in multis, exercet ad virtutes: ad humilitatem et compassionem similia sustinentium, ad confugiendum sollicitius ad divinum adiutorium, ad experientiam divinae clementiae...* (*David ab Augusta*, 145; Devas, *Spiritual Life* 1, 137).

[496] *Prof* 3,29. *Quintum est studium familiare ad expugnanda vel mortificanda vitia et virtutes usitandas: ut semetipsum humiliare, irae motus reprimere, luxuriam domare, et ceteris vitiis impugnantibus resistere et operibus caritatis et obedientiae et aliarum virtutum insistere* (*David ab Augusta*, 219; Devas, *Spiritual Life* 2, 58).

[497] E.g., *Prof* 1,18. *Audi humiliter et pacifice bona, quae ab aliis dicuntur...* (*David ab Augusta*, 24; Devas, *Spiritual Life* 1, 21); *Prof* 3,61. *Ex his per contrarium potest adverti, quae valeant ad exauditionem orationis, scilicet culpae remotio, fervor et instantia et fidei confidentia, humilitas et aliorum suffragia et acceptae gratiae cum gratiarum actione studiosa conservatio...* (*David ab Augusta*, 337; Devas, *Spiritual Life* 2, 168); *Prof* 3,70. *Nimis etiam raro celebrare, quamvis ex reverentia soleat aliquando fieri et humilitate... Humilitas etiam non est usquequaque secura...* (*David ab Augusta*, 376–377; Devas, *Spiritual Life* 2, 210).

[498] E.g., *Prof* 2,39. *Ira etiam non habet misericordiam, nec humilitatem praetendit et excaecat intellectum...* (*David ab Augusta*, 129; Devas, *Spiritual Life* 1, 123); *Prof* 3,5. *...non ex humilitate, sed ex paviditate desperant...* (*David ab Augusta*, 175; Devas, *Spiritual Life* 2, 16); *Prof* 3,7. *Haec omnia illius tentationis anxietatem exprimunt, quae non valet melius superari, nisi patienter tolerando et humiliter exspectando...* (*David ab Augusta*, 178; Devas, *Spiritual Life* 2, 19); *Prof* 3,8. *...et cum indignanti humilitate cogitat se forte indignum tali gratia...* (*David ab Augusta*, 178; Devas, *Spiritual Life* 2, 20).

[499] *Prof* 1,22. *Virtus enim vitio non docetur, sic nec per impatientiam potes alios patientiam docere, nec humilitatem per superbiam* (*David ab Augusta*, 30; Devas, *Spiritual Life* 1, 27); *Prof* 2,35. *Haec et his similia cum in consuetudinem versa fuerint, mentem ad humilitatem*

pride disguises itself as humility[500] but, in reality, the habit of humility
wards off the vice.[501] Still, humility may become a vice itself when it no
longer holds the (Aristotelian) middle course but plunges, instead, into
over-anxiousness and exaggerated self-depreciation.[502]

7. JOY

Origin

In correlation with the experience of suffering, the experience of joy
informs moral conceptions and influences the doctrinal positions and
forms of activity that involve ethical values.[503] In Christianity, joy (*laetitia,
gaudium, iucunditas, hilaritas*) is, indeed, a powerful answer to suffering,
both liberational (rejecting its injustice) and soteriological (affirming its
Truth). Joy in this world is the fruit of redemption and, in connection with
peace and freedom, an essential element of the Birth of Christ.[504] It is
acknowledged in faith, a result of a clean conscience, and a sign of true
peace.[505] In the Bible, God's creation provides the people with joy in

---

*inclinant. Si autem vana gloria vel superbia pulsat mentem pro huiusmodi humiliatione, hoc
est ex novitate vel raritate huiusmodi humiliationis...* (*David ab Augusta*, 123–124; Devas,
Spiritual Life 1, 118); *Prof* 2,33. *...ita vitia contrariis exercitiorum remediis sanantur, ut superbia humiliatione...* (*David ab Augusta*, 122; Devas, *Spiritual Life* 1, 116); *Prof* 3,39. *Patientia
directe opponitur vitio irae, sicut caritas Dei opponitur accidiae, et caritas proximi invidiae,
et humilitas superbiae* (*David ab Augusta*, 253; Devas, *Spiritual Life* 2, 89–90).

[500] *Prof* 2,11. *Et saepe superbia assumit pallium humilitatis, aemulae suae, ut sub nomine
eius gloriam callide acquirat...* (*David ab Augusta*, 97; Devas, *Spiritual Life* 1, 92). Cf. *Prof*
3,49. *...torpor negligentiae vult humilitas videri altiora se non quaerendi...* (*David ab Augusta*,
285; Devas, *Spiritual Life* 2, 119).

[501] *Prof* 2,35. *Secundum* [*remedium superbiae*] *est exercere se in humilibus operibus, vilibus et despectis officiis et rusticanis laboribus, humili habitu incedere, humiles mores et verba
habere....* (*David ab Augusta*, 123; Devas, *Spiritual Life* 1, 118).

[502] *Prof* 3,48. *Humilitas, dum se nimis timet extollere ex indiscreta abiectione sui, perdit
confidentiam salutis vel profectus spiritualis* (*David ab Augusta*, 283; Devas, *Spiritual Life* 2,
117).

[503] Cf. Nossent, *Joie*.

[504] Volk, "Freude", 414: "Grund und Inhalt der christlichen Freude ist aber dies, daß der
Mensch, in der Gnade Christi aus der Verlorenheit der Sünde und des Todes errettet, im
Einklang und Frieden mit Gott steht, der sinnzerstörenden Übermacht des Ereignishaften
enthoben ist und damit nicht nur punkthaft und zufällig, sondern grundsätzlich und bis in
die Tiefe und Mitte seines Wesens in Hoffnung für sich und sein ganzes Leben eines erfül-
lenden Sinnes gewiß sein darf." Cf. "Joie"; Metz & Jossua, *Theology*; Moltmann, *Die ersten*;
Reggio, *Vergiß*; Schick & Auer, "Freude"; Thiede, *Das verheißene*.

[505] Psychologically speaking, in a scholastic sense, pleasure (joy) is "a movement of the
soul (...) establishing one in a condition which is in harmony with one's nature," the affective reflection of the development and fulfilment of humanity (Thomas Aquinas, *Summa*

things, in people, and in the Creator, who Himself is Joy.[506] Joy in God lies in existence ("we are in and for God"), election ("we are called by God"), confidence ("God will deliver us from evil"), knowledge ("we know that God is near"), activity ("we participate in God's work"), and hope ("we await the revelation of his glory").[507]

The people of the Old Testament pray that the Lord rejoice in his works.[508] Their joy comes from peace with God and justice, i.e., acceptance of the law: "But his delight is in the law of the Lord, and on his law he meditates day and night";[509] "a righteous one can sing and be glad."[510] In the New Testament (the "joyful message," *evangelium*), the incarnation is the joyful message to all people, as the angel said to the shepherds: "I bring you good news of great joy that will be for all the people."[511] Paul repeats this joyful message and recommends that all rejoice in the Lord always.[512] With love, peace, patience, kindness, goodness, faithfulness, gentleness, and self-control, joy is one of the fruits of the Holy Spirit.[513] It is the message of Christ who shares his joy with his people and promises them perfection of joy: "Rejoice and be glad, because great is your reward in heaven."[514]

Francis

The joy of God and the joy of faith

Francis's thought is greatly influenced by the (liturgical) psalms.[515] His words are laudations of God, for the Lord has brought joy to his heart. His joy is joy in the Lord because the Lord ís Joy:

---

theologiae 1a2ae,31,1; Busa, *S. Thomae Aquinatis*, 395; D'Arcy, *St. Thomas Aquinas*, 5); Schick & Auer, "Freude", 362.

[506] Volk, "Freude", 414.

[507] Schick & Auer, "Freude", 362. Cf. Perrin, *Die acht*, 19–50.

[508] Ps 103,31 (104,31).

[509] Ps 1,2. On "joy" in the Old Testament, see for instance: Ridder, *Vreugde*; Stendebach, *Glaube*; *Vreugde*; Wilms, *Freude*.

[510] Prov 29,6.

[511] Luke 2,10. On "joy" in the New Testament, see for instance: Backherms, *Religious*; Brosch, *Jesus*; Diniz, *Joy*; Lohse, *Freude*; Morrice, *Joy*; Schniewind, "Die Freude"; Sieron, Χαίρειν; Du Toit, *Der Aspekt*.

[512] E.g., Phil 4,4; Rom 15,13; 2 Cor 7,4; 1 Thess 5,16.

[513] Gal 5,22–23.

[514] John 15,11; Matt 5,12. Cf. Lotz, *Eure Freude*; Perrin, *Die acht*.

[515] Probably, it is also influenced by the courtly culture of his day, in which *hilaritas*/*iucunditas* is one of the sub-virtues of courtesy (*curialitas*) (cf. Paravicini, *Die*

You are love, charity; You are wisdom, You are humility,
You are patience, You are beauty, You are meekness,
You are security, You are rest,
You are gladness and joy, You are our hope, You are justice,
You are moderation, You are all our riches to sufficiency.
You are beauty, You are meekness,
You are the protector, You are our custodian and defender,
You are strength, You are refreshment. You are our hope,
You are our faith, You are our charity,
You are all our sweetness, You are our eternal life:
Great and wonderful Lord, Almighty God, Merciful Savior.[516]

Because God is our Joy, all the heavens and the earth should be joyful and glad: "Let the heavens rejoice and the earth exult; let the sea and all that is in it be moved; let the fields and all that is in them be glad."[517] God's creation provokes joy and exultation.[518] All penitents and just ones on earth might find an example of joy in heaven, where the blessed rejoice together.[519] In the beauty and strength of fire they can find an example of joy on earth; no other element complies so much with Francis's heartfelt appeal to pleasure in the Lord.[520]

---

ritterlich-höfische Kultur, 7). On Francis and joy, see for instance: Danneels, De vreugde; "Frères", 1332–1333; Geulen, Die Armut, 126–130; Gobry, St. François, 74–75; Van den Goorbergh & Zweerman, Was getekend, 70–71; Grau, "Die »vollkommene«"; Hardick, Die wahre; Jansen, "De echte vreugde"; Jansen, "The Story"; Lang, Ins Freie, 76–90; Linden, Vater, 132–135; Loeffen, De vreugde; Longpré, François, 99–116; Morant, Unser Weg, 56–63; Van Munster, De mystiek, 65–68; Rogers, "The Joy"; Rohr, Der Herr, 148–169; Thévenet, "La vera".

[516] Laud Dei 4–6. Tu es amor, caritas; tu es sapientia, tu es humilitas, tu es patientia (Ps 70,5), tu es pulchritudo, tu es mansuetudo, tu es securitas, tu es quietas, tu es gaudium, tu es spes nostra et laetitia, tu es iustitia, tu es temperantia, tu es omnia divitia nostra ad sufficientiam. Tu es pulchritudo, tu es mansuetudo; tu es protector (Ps 30,5), tu es custos et defensor noster; tu es fortitudo (cfr. Ps 42,2), tu es refrigerium. Tu es spes nostra, tu es fides nostra, tu es caritas nostra, tu es tota dulcedo nostra, tu es vita aeterna nostra: Magnus et admirabilis Dominus, Deus omnipotens, misericors Salvator (Armstrong, Francis of Assisi, 109).

[517] Of Pas 1,7,4; Of Pas 2,9,7; Of Pas 5,15,9. Laetentur caeli et exsultet terra, commoveatur mare et plenitudo eius, gaudebunt campi et omnia, quae in eis sunt (Ps 95,11–12a) (Armstrong, Francis of Assisi, 147).

[518] Laud Dei 8; Of Pas 2,9,5; Of Pas 5,15,6; RnB 16,16. Haec dies quam fecit Dominus, exsultemus et laetemur in ea (Ps 177,24-R). Alleluia, Alleluia, Alleluia! Rex Israel (Joa 12,13)! Joy has to do with the beauty of nature as a creation of God, for which He deserves praise. We are reminded here of Francis's Canticle of the Creatures.

[519] RnB 23,9. ...in quo (cfr. Rom 11,36) est omnis venia, omnis gratia, omnis gloria omnium poenitentium et iustorum, omnium beatorum in caelis congaudentium.

[520] Cant Sol 8. Laudato si, mi signore, per frate focu, per lo quale enn' allumini la nocte, ed ello è bello et iocundo et robustoso et forte.

Joyful brothers

Francis encourages his brothers to find only joy in the Lord: "Blessed are the religious who only find pleasure (*iucunditas*) and delight (*laetitia*) in the words and deeds of the Lord and, with these, lead people to the love of God with gladness (*gaudium*) and joy (*laetitia*)."[521] Joy is the expression of love of God and love of others when it is found in the good of others (which ultimately depends on their own love of God).[522] Francis prays that the poor may rejoice, and that his brothers may also rejoice when they go among them.[523] Joy is the expression of patience when it is found in times of physical and psychological trial for the sake of eternal life.[524] In the eradication of all greed and avarice, it is the fruit of poverty.[525] Joy is, indeed, a fundamental characteristic of the servant of God.[526]

True joy

Joy can also be false joy, for example, boastfulness or delight in oneself, or inward exaltation because of one's good words and deeds, or because of any good that God might say or do or work in and through a person.[527]

---

[521] *Adm* 20,1–2. *Beatus ille religiosus, qui non habet iucunditatem et laetitiam nisi in sanctissimis eloquiis et operibus Domini et cum his producit homines ad amorem Dei cum gaudio et laetitia* (cfr. Ps 50,10) (Armstrong, *Francis of Assisi*, 135); *Of Pas* 2,8,5. *Exsultent et laetentur in te omnes qui quaerunt te et dicant semper: Magnificetur Dominus: qui diligunt salutare tuum; RnB* 7,16. *Et caveant sibi, quod non se ostendant tristes extrinsecus et nubilosos hypocritas; sed ostendant se gaudentes in Domino* (cfr. Phil 4,4) *et hilares et convenienter gratiosos; RnB* 22,14. *Quod autem super petrosam cecidit* (cfr. Matt 13,20), *hi sunt, qui, cum audierint verbum, statim cum gaudio* (Mark 4,16) *suscipiunt* (Luke 8,13) *illud* (Mark 4,16); *RnB* 22,45. *Haec loquor in mundo, ut habeant gaudium in semetipsis.*

[522] *Ex Pat* 5. *...et proximos nostros amemus sicut et nosmetipsos omnes ad amorem tuum pro viribus trahendo, de bonis aliorum sicut de nostris gaudendo et in malis compatiendo et nemini ullam offensionem dando* (cfr. 2 Cor 6,3). *Of Pas* 3,11,5. *Laetabimur in salutari tuo et in nomine Domini nostri magnificabimur* (Ps 19,6; R).

[523] *Of Pas* 4,14,5. *Videant pauperes et laetentur; RnB* 9,2. *Et debent gaudere, quando conversantur inter viles et despectas personas, inter pauperes et debiles et infirmos et leprosos et iuxta viam mendicantes.*

[524] *RnB* 17,8. *Et magis debemus gaudere, cum in tentationes varias incideremus* (cfr. Jac 1,2) *et cum sustinueremus quascumque animae vel corporis angustias aut tribulationes in hoc mundo propter vitam aeternam.*

[525] *Adm* 27,3. *Ubi est paupertas cum laetitia, ibi nec cupiditas nec avaritia.*

[526] Armstrong, *Francis of Assisi*, 137.

[527] *RnB* 17,6. *...non gloriari nec in se gaudere nec interius se exaltare de bonis verbis et operibus, immo de nullo bono, quod Deus facit vel dicit et operatur in eis aliquando et per ipsos, secundum quod dicit Dominus: Veruntamen in hoc nolite gaudere, quia spiritus vobis subiciuntur* (Luke 10,20).

False joy can, furthermore, be found among blasphemers.[528] To the fourteenth-century biographical tradition belongs a "dictated writing" in which Francis tells Brother Leo about what true joy is.[529] Because of its illustrative value, I include this "true message of Francis" here:

> The same [Brother Leonard] related in the same place that one day at Saint Mary's, blessed Francis called Brother Leo and said: "Brother Leo, write." He responded: "Look, I'm ready!" "Write," he said, "what true joy is." "A messenger arrives and says all the Masters of Paris have entered the Order. Write: this isn't true joy! Or, that all the prelates, archbishops and bishops beyond the mountains, as well as the King of France and the King of England [have entered the Order]. Write: this isn't true joy! Again, that my brothers have gone to the non-believers and converted all of them to the faith; again, that I have so much grace from God that I heal the sick and perform many miracles. I tell you true joy doesn't consist in any of these things." "Then what is true joy?" "I return from Perugia and arrive here in the dead of night. It's winter time, muddy, and so cold that icicles have formed on the edges of my habit and keep striking my legs and blood flows from such wounds. Freezing, covered with mud and ice, I come to the gate and, after I've knocked and called for some time, a brother comes and asks: 'Who are you?' 'Brother Francis,' I answer. 'Go away!' he says. 'This is not a decent hour to be wandering about! You may not come in!' When I insist, he replies: 'Go away! You are simple and stupid! Don't come back to us again! There are many of us here like you—we don't need you!' I stand again at the door and say: 'For the love of God, take me in tonight!' And he replies: 'I will not! Go to the Crosiers' place and ask there!'" "I tell you this: If I had patience and did not become upset, true joy, as well as true virtue and the salvation of my soul, would consist in this."[530]

---

[528] *Of Pas* 1,5,10. *Et adversum me laetati sunt et convenerunt, congregata sunt super me flagella et ignoravi* (Ps 34,15).

[529] Armstrong, *Francis of Assisi*, 166; Grau, "Die »vollkommene«", 5.

[530] *Laet. Idem [fr. Leonardus] retulit ibidem quod una die beatus Franciscus apud Sanctam Mariam vocavit fratrem Leonem et dixit: Frater Leo, scribe. Qui respondit: Ecce paratus sum. Scribe - inquit - quae est vera laetitia. Venit nuntius et dicit quod omnes magistri de Parisius venerunt ad Ordinem, scribe, non vera laetitia. Item quod omnes praelati ultramontani, archiepiscopi et episcopi; item quod rex Franciae et rex Angliae: scribe, non vera laetitia. Item, quod fratres mei iverunt ad infideles et converterunt eos omnes ad fidem; item, quod tantam gratiam habeo a Deo quod sano infirmos et facio multa miracula: dico tibi quod in his omnibus non vera laetitia. Sed quae est vera laetitia? Redeo de Perusio et de nocte profunda venio huc et est tempus hiemis lutosum et adeo frigidum, quod dondoli aquae frigidae congelatae fiunt ad extremitates tunicae et percutiunt semper crura, et sanguis emanat ex vulneribus talibus. Et totus in luto et frigore et glacie venio ad ostium, et postquam diu pulsavi et vocavi, venit frater et quaerit: Quis est? Ego respondeo: Frater Franciscus. Et ipse dicit: Vade; non est hora decens eundi; non intrabis. Et iterum insistenti respondeat: Vade, tu es unus simplex et idiota; admodo non venis nobis; nos sumus tot et tales, quod non indigemus te. Et ego iterum sto ad ostium et dico: Amore Dei recolligatis me ista nocte. Et ille respondeat: Non faciam. Vade ad locum Cruciferorum et ibi pete. Dico tibi quod si patientiam*

With patience comes joy, accompanied by true virtue and the salvation of the soul. Here, the paradox of "joy in suffering" is dissolved in the closeness to Christ on the way of his suffering: true joy therefore comes with true faith in God.[531]

Bonaventure

Worldly, spiritual, heavenly

According to Bonaventure, joy is worldly, spiritual, or heavenly.[532] Worldly joy (*mundanum gaudium*) is "perfectly known only when perfectly despised."[533] It is worthy of nothing except scorn because it is vile in its object, impure in its subject, brief in itself, sad in its outcome, and wretched in its effects.[534] The stubborn heart, devoid of true life (i.e., the sweetness of Jesus), rejoices in his human misery.[535] Opposed to this false joy of worldly-minded men[536] is the true joy of spiritual lovers, i.e., inner joy (*interna laetitia*) or spiritual joy (*spiritualis iucunditas, spiritualis laetitia*), which roots in the purgation of the soul. The soul is prepared for the spiritual taste of inner joy by the process of meditation and the

---

habuero et non fuero motus, quod in hoc est vera laetitia et vera virtus et salus animae (Armstrong, *Francis of Assisi*, 166–167). It is important to notice the historical context and political content of this text: Francis shows that true joy lies in inner things, i.e., true spirituality, not in outer things, i.e., worldly issues and political successes of the Franciscan Order (cf. Jansen, "The Story", 281–282).

[531] Hardick, *Die wahre*, 29: "In dieser Nähe zu Christus auf dem Weg seines Leidens, der nicht im Leiden endet, sondern der in die sichere Herrlichkeit der Auferstehung führt, löst sich das Paradoxe der wahren und vollkommenen Freude des hl. Franziskus in der Harmonie des Erlösungswerkes Jesu Christi. Dies voll mit dem eigenen Leben zu bejahen, ist jedoch nur dem Glaubenden möglich. Franziskus war ein Glaubender, er war es gerade in seiner wahren und vollkommenen Freude." Cf. Linden, *Vater*, 132–135.

[532] On Bonaventure and joy, see: "Frères", 1332–1333.

[533] *Sol* 2,2,9. *O anima, aestimo, quod mundanum gaudium – si tamen potest dici gaudium et non potius flagellum incognitum – nunquam perfecte cognoscitur, nisi cum perfecte despicitur* (*Doctoris* 8, 47; De Vinck, *The Works* 3, 84).

[534] *Sol* 2,2,9. *Unde, sicut a perfectis mundi contemptoribus traditur, mundanum gaudium potissime propter quinque contemptibile est habendum: primo, quia habet vilitatem in obiecto... Secundo, habet impuritatem in subiecto... Tertio habet brevitatem in se ipso... Quarto habet tristitiam in termino... Quinto habet miseriam magnam in effectu proprio...* (*Doctoris* 8, 47–48; De Vinck, *The Works* 3, 84–85).

[535] *Lign Vit* 4,14. *O cor durum, vesanum et impium et tanquam vera privatum vita plangendum, cur more phrenetici, flente super te Sapientia Patris, in tantis miseriis laetaris et rides?* (*Doctoris* 8, 74; De Vinck, *The Works* 1, 113).

[536] *Sol* 2,2,10. *Iam mundum despicio, iam falsam laetitiam veramque tristitiam, falsam dulcedinem veramque mundi amaritudinem agnosco...* (*Doctoris* 8, 48; De Vinck, *The Works* 3, 86).

cleansing of conscience through benignity, the consideration of what is good, and the exclusion of all evil.[537] This cleansing meditation process terminates in a disposition (*affectus*) of spiritual joy:

> And this is the end of purgation by way of meditation, for every clean conscience is joyful and glad. Let anyone who wishes to be cleansed turn to the sting of conscience in the manner explained above – starting this meditation at will with any of the points suggested, then passing to another, dwelling upon each as long as may be necessary to arrive at tranquillity and peace. From this, in turn, proceeds an inner joy that makes our spirit ready to rise aloft. And so, this first way [the purgative way] originates in the sting of conscience, and terminates in a disposition of spiritual joy; it is pursued in pain, but consummated in love.[538]

Whereas spiritual joy begins in the spiritual stage of purgation (preceding illumination and perfection) by way of meditation, through which the soul leaves outer, worldly joys behind and becomes aware of inner, spiritual joys, it is perfected in gratefulness for the quality of the divine graces offered, in jubilation on account of the value of the gifts received, and in spiritual love, the transport of joy.[539]

Then, there is the "spectacle of all joy," joy "within and without, below and above, and all around," which is the joy of heaven (*futurum gaudium, gaudium Domini, caelestia gaudia, gaudia praeparata*):[540]

---

[537] *Trip Via* 1,1,8–9. *Post haec videndum est, quomodo vel qualiter stimulus conscientiae sit rectificandus in consideratione boni... Tertio sequitur benignitas, quae est quidam dulcor animae, excludens omnem nequitiam et habilitans ipsam animam ad benevolentiam, tolerantiam et internam laetitiam* (*Doctoris* 8, 5; De Vinck, *The Works* 1, 67–68).

[538] *Trip Via* 1,1,9. *Et hic est terminus purgationis secundum viam meditationis. Nam omnis conscientia munda laeta est et iucunda. Qui vult ergo purgari, vertat se modo praedicto ad stimulum conscientiae. In praedicta tamen exercitatione a quolibet praemissorum inchoari potest nostra meditatio. Transeundum autem est ab uno ad aliud et tamdiu immorandum, quousque tranquillitas et serenitas percipiatur, ex qua oritur spiritualis iucunditas, qua adepta, promptus est animus, ut sursum tendat. Incipit ergo via ista a stimulo conscientiae et terminatur ad affectum spiritualis laetitiae, et exercetur in dolore, sed consummatur in amore* (*Doctoris* 8, 5–6; De Vinck, *The Works* 1, 68).

[539] *Trip Via* 3,6,10. *Perfectio in gratitudine, in qua est vigilantia exsurgens ad canticum propter beneficiorum utilitatem; laetitia exsultans ad iubilum propter donorum pretiositatem...* (*Doctoris* 8, 16; De Vinck, *The Works* 1, 90); *Trip Via* 1,1,9. *...sed consummatur in amore* (*Doctoris* 8, 5–6; De Vinck, *The Works* 1, 68); *Trip Via* 3,4,6. *Gradus veniendi ad dulcorem caritatis per susceptionem Spiritus sancti sunt isti septem, scilicet... laetitia delectans...* (*Doctoris* 8, 14; De Vinck, *The Works* 1, 86); *Trip Via* 3,5,8. *...laetitia te inebriet propter amoris eius plenitudinem...* (*Doctoris* 8, 15; De Vinck, *The Works* 1, 88).

[540] *Trip Via* 3,3,4. *Quarto, paradisus desiderabilis manifestatus est per crucem, in quo est fastigium totius gloriae, spectaculum omnis laetitiae, promptuarium omnis opulentiae...* (*Doctoris* 8, 13; De Vinck, *The Works* 1, 85); *Sol* 4,4,2. *Cum futurum gaudium aspicio, iam pene prae admiratione deficio, quia gaudium erit intus et extra, subtus et supra, circumcirca*

How wonderful and great must be the joy whose object is so great and wonderful! Most certainly, O Lord Jesus, eye has not seen nor ear heard, nor has it entered into the heart of man in this present life what love belongs to Your elect in that blessed life. The more we love God here, the more we shall enjoy God there. Therefore, love God much in this life, and you shall enjoy Him much in the next; let the love of God increase in you now, so that you may have then the fullness of His joy. This is the truth to be pondered in your mind, proclaimed by your tongue, loved in your heart, expressed by your lips; your soul should hunger, your body thirst, your whole substance crave for nothing but this until you enter the joy of your God, until you are clasped in your Lover's arms, until you are led into the chamber of your beloved Spouse who, with the Father and the Holy Spirit, lives and reigns, one God, forever and ever. Amen.[541]

Increasing spiritual love here and now will lead us to the fullness of divine joy there and then.

David

Happy and blessed

Joy (*gaudium, laetitia, hilaritas*) is an essential virtue of religious life. It is one of the seven "movements of the will," with hope, fear, sorrow, love, hatred, and remorse;[542] and one of the seven "kinds of devotion,"

(*Doctoris* 8, 57; De Vinck, *The Works* 3, 108). Cf. *Sol* 4,4,1. *Erige rationem, dilata et expande affectionem et intra in gaudium Domini...* (*Doctoris* 8, 56; De Vinck, *The Works* 3, 107); *Sol* 4,4,3. *Haec gaudia debes tu, o anima, quotidie devota mente transcurrere...* (*Doctoris* 8, 57; De Vinck, *The Works* 3, 108); *Sol* 4,4,4. *Revera aestimo, o anima, si haec caelestia gaudia iugiter in mente teneres...* (*Doctoris* 8, 57; De Vinck, *The Works* 3, 109); *Sol* 4,5,24. *O anima, quantum, putas, gaudent et laetantur qui illud aeternitatis speculum iugiter contemplantur...* (*Doctoris* 8, 65; De Vinck, *The Works* 3, 124); *Sol* 4,5,27. *O anima, mente devota pertracta, quam sit plenum omni suavitate gaudium videre hominem hominis Conditorem...* (*Doctoris* 8, 66; De Vinck, *The Works* 3, 126); *Quin Fest* 4,4. *...thus devotionis propter gaudia praeparata...* (*Doctoris* 8, 94; De Vinck, *The Works* 3, 211).

[541] *Perf* 8,8. *Quale autem, vel quantum gaudium est, ubi tale ac tantum est bonum? Certe, Domine Iesu, nec oculus vidit, nec auris audivit, nec in cor hominis ascendit* [cfr. 1 Cor 2,9] *in hac vita, quantum tui Beati te amabunt et de te gaudebunt in illa beata vita. Quantum quisque hic Deum amat, tantum ibi de Deo gaudebit. Ergo hic Deum multum ama, ut ibi multum gaudeas; crescat hic in te amor Dei, ut ibi plene possideas gaudium Dei. Meditetur inde mens tua, loquatur inde lingua tua, amet illud cor tuum, sermocinetur os tuum, esuriat illud anima tua, sitiat illud caro tua, desideret tota substantia tua, donec intres in gaudium Dei tui, donec venias ad amplexus dilecti tui, donec introducat te in thalamum dilecti Sponsi tui, qui cum Patre et Spiritu sancto vivit et regnat unus Deus per omnia saecula saeculorum. Amen* (*Doctoris* 8, 126–127; De Vinck, *The Works* 1, 254–255).

[542] *Prof* 3,28. *Septem autem sunt affectiones mentis communiter: spes et timor, gaudium et moeror, amor et odium et pudor* (*David ab Augusta*, 215–216; Devas, *Spiritual Life* 2, 55).

with fear, sorrow, desire, love, compassion, and rapture of admiration.[543]
In devotion, joy can take the place of sorrow and embitterment.[544] But,
as real virtue lies between two extremes, spiritual joy may also degener-
ate into mere idle levity, and then sorrow is helpful.[545] Keeping the
mind fixed upon God "keeps the heart even, neither swayed by empty joy
on the one hand, nor foolish gloom on the other."[546] We have to bring
under the control of reason our thoughts, affections, and motives and
turn all God-wards (*in virtutes ordinare*), "so that love and hate, fear and
sorrow and joy (*gaudeat de gaudendis*) be not haphazard and indiscrimi-
nate, but wisely and quietly ordered under the calm guidance of right
reason."[547]

Cf. *Prof* 3,63. ...*ut iam non sit timor, non dolor, spes vel pudor, sed tantum suo gaudio fruens amor...* (*David ab Augusta*, 342; Devas, *Spiritual Life* 2, 175).

[543] *Prof* 3,65. *Aut enim surgit devotio ex timore, aut ex dolore, aut ex desiderio, aut ex amore, aut ex compassione, aut ex gaudio, aut ex admirationis stupore* (*David ab Augusta*, 352; Devas, *Spiritual Life* 2, 183); *Prof* 3,65. *Aliquando commixtum ex diversarum affectionum motibus devotio conflatur, ut timor cum dolore, amor cum gaudio et admira-tione, compassio cum desiderii ardore iungatur* (*David ab Augusta*, 354; Devas, *Spiritual Life* 2, 186). Cf. *Prof* 3,59. *Affectus enim amoris Dei et sancti timoris cum fervore bonae voluntatis, in spiritu humilitatis et motu pietatis et gaudio spei nunquam debet in corde servi Dei exstingui* (*David ab Augusta*, 329; Devas, *Spiritual Life* 2, 161–162); *Prof* 3,64. *Nec mirum, si hoc possunt affectiones divinae efficere, quarum virtus fortior est, cum etiam humanae affectiones hoc interdum valeant, ut subitus terror et subita et immoderata laetitia et subitus dolor et odium immensum et intemperatus amor* (*David ab Augusta*, 349; Devas, *Spiritual Life* 2, 181); *Prof* 3,65. *Ex gaudio surgit devotio...* (*David ab Augusta*, 353; Devas, *Spiritual Life* 2, 185).

[544] *Prof* 3,67. *Cor enim liberum et benevolentia iucundum aptius est ad devotionis gratiam recipiendam quam tristitia et amaritudine constrictum...* (*David ab Augusta*, 364; Devas, *Spiritual Life* 2, 196). Cf. *Prof* 1,39. ...*quia tunc non tristitiam, sed laetitiam inimico conferret* (*David ab Augusta*, 53; Devas, *Spiritual Life* 1, 46); *Prof* 2,48. ...*quia de quibus cor hominis non disponit sibi gaudium, si eveniant, de his etiam non tristatur, si non eveniant...* (*David ab Augusta*, 142; Devas, *Spiritual Life* 1, 134).

[545] *Prof* 3,48. *Spiritualis laetitia sic accidiam vel tristitiam declinat, ut quandoque in dis-solutionem incidat et vanam laetitiam* (*David ab Augusta*, 283; Devas, *Spiritual Life* 2, 117); *Prof* 2,20. ...*ut per maturitatem utilis luctus excludat levitatem vanae laetitiae, quae est nutrix dissolutionis* (*David ab Augusta*, 106; Devas, *Spiritual Life* 1, 101). Cf. *Prof* 3,64. ...*quod spiritualis laetitia, sicut caret amaritudine tristitiae saeculi et accidiae torpore, ita et dissolu-tionis levitate* (*David ab Augusta*, 350; Devas, *Spiritual Life* 2, 182).

[546] *Prof* 1,31. *Semper aliquid tecum defer in memoria, quod de Deo rumines cogitando et mentis tuae intuitum semper in eum defigere stude... hoc enim continet cor apud se, ne com-moveatur a se per vanam laetitiam vel irrationabilem tristitiam* (*David ab Augusta*, 41; Devas, *Spiritual Life* 1, 35–36).

[547] *Prof*, Epist 2. *Quintus, cogitationes et affectiones et intentiones mentis ad normam rationis componere et omnes affectus in virtutes ordinare, ut non amet nisi amanda, et prout sunt amanda, nec timeat nisi timenda, odiat odienda, doleat dolenda, gaudeat de gaudendis, et sic omnibus rationis ductu quasi naturali motu tranquille feratur...* (*David ab Augusta*, 60–61; Devas, *Spiritual Life* 1, 54–55). Cf. *Prof* 3,36. *Gaudere cum gaudentibus...* (*David ab Augusta*, 241; Devas, *Spiritual Life* 2, 78); *Prof* 3,54. *Interim in nobis operare tibi regnum in*

Furthermore,

> man is meant to be happy in God – the aptitude for joy is given him for this
> end – and in the hope of winning a joy that is eternal, and in the present
> relish of God's goodness to him. He is meant, too, to rejoice with his neigh-
> bour in the good that is his, and to find delight in praising God and working
> for God.[548]

Devotional joy grows in the acknowledgement of God's goodness, that
one, by his grace, has escaped many evils.[549] To know how to avoid more
sin makes the soul (conscience) equally happy and safe.[550] Sorrow and joy
over trivial things or things that never were nor will be, for example, is
foolish and empty.[551] False delight is idle and even harmful:

> If you have what you want, do not cling to it nor rest in the pleasure it brings
> you, but think how quickly the delight will pass, leaving no trace behind
> it – unless, perchance, a lingering sense of shame and sadness, and a debt of
> punishment.[552]

Real spiritual joy, on the other hand,

> is really of two kinds, according to its source. There is a very *special* grace or
> gift of joy infused by the Holy Ghost and based on the constant memory of
> God's goodness, His benefits and the blissful eternity in store for us. There is
> also a *general* spiritual joy, a cheerful habit of mind, arising from a happy
> spirit of confidence in God, and from the testimony of a good conscience.
> This is a fount of sympathy with others, and prompts a man to do and

---

iustitia et pace et gaudio Spiritus sancti [cfr. Rom 14,17] (*David ab Augusta*, 305; Devas,
Spiritual Life 2, 138).

[548] *Prof* 2,21. *Affectus gaudii datus fuit homini, ut gauderet in Deo et in spe aeterno-
rum bonorum et intuitu beneficiorum Dei, et congauderet proximo in bonis eius, et
delectaretur in laude Dei et in bonis operibus...* (*David ab Augusta*, 106–107; Devas, *Spiritual
Life* 1, 101).

[549] *Prof* 3,56. *Beatorum laetitiam, quod talia per Dei gratiam evaserunt* (*David ab
Augusta*, 316; Devas, *Spiritual Life* 2, 149).

[550] *Prof* 2,47. *...evitata vero facit securam et laetam* (*David ab Augusta*, 142; Devas,
Spiritual Life 1, 134).

[551] *Prof* 3,39. *...ut sublata aliqua laetitia vel consolatione minus utili vel nociva, verbi
gratia, ut cum propter pluviam vel aliam innoxiam causam non possumus spatiari vel alios
conceptus animi perficere pro libitu* (*David ab Augusta*, 252; Devas, *Spiritual Life* 2, 88); *Prof*
2,48. *...nonne stulta tristitia vel inanis gloria esset moveri de his, quae nunquam fuerunt nec
erunt? Tales enim vanas laetitias et tristitias semper habere possemus, imaginando nobis-
met...* (*David ab Augusta*, 144; Devas, *Spiritual Life* 1, 136).

[552] *Prof* 2,48. *Cum autem habes quod diligis, noli nimis inniti ei per delectationis
affectum, sed cogita, quod cito pertransiet ista laetitia et nihil post se relinquit, nisi vestigia
doloris et confusionis et debitum suppliciorum* (*David ab Augusta*, 144; Devas, *Spiritual Life*
1, 135).

endure much for God's sake, and to be keen on promoting God's interests in
every possible direction. Rejoice in the Lord always: again I say, rejoice.
Such was St. Paul's double greeting to the Philippians, urging them towards
this twofold joy.[553]

An example of both kinds of spiritual joy can be found in the saints who
suffered with patience and cheerfulness.[554] Their joy was also a special joy,
on account of the heavenly joys in store for them.[555] Sublime joy here on
earth, however, lies in the highest form of contemplation. It can only be
experienced when "all the affections of the will, linked in the single joy of
love, rest calmly in the sweet enjoyment of the Creator,"[556] the Joy of love
personified.[557]

---

[553] *Prof* 3,64. *Spiritualis enim laetitia dupliciter accipitur: specialiter et generaliter; specialiter, et tunc est motus specialis gaudii in Spiritu sancto ex intuitu beneficiorum Dei et
futurae gloriae et bonitatis divinae; generaliter, et tunc est quaedam mentis hilaritas ex bona
confidentia ad Deum et bonae conscientiae testimonio, reddens hominem benevolum et
devotum ad omnia agenda et sufferenda pro Deo et omnia, quae Dei sunt, diligenda et pro-
movenda. Ideo bis dicit Apostolus ad Philippenses: Gaudete in Domino semper, iterum dico,
gaudete* [cfr. Phil 4,4]; *primo generaliter, secundo specialiter* (David ab Augusta, 350–351;
Devas, *Spiritual Life* 2, 183).
[554] *Prof* 3,40. *Et haec est singularis laetitia Sanctorum in tribulatione patientium et gau-
dentium...* (David ab Augusta, 256; Devas, *Spiritual Life* 2, 91–92).
[555] *Prof* 3,56. *...qua pro parvo et brevi merito aeternam et ineffabilem Sanctis dat in
caelo gloriam et laetitiam et felicitatem... De malis propriis gaudent... gaudent de propria
felicitate... gaudent de omnium electorum gloria...* (David ab Augusta, 316; Devas, *Spiritual
Life* 2, 149). Cf. *Prof* 2,18. *...et quantum in ipsis est, spoliant ipsum caelum maiori gaudio, quod
ibi esset, si plures illuc venirent, cum singuli, qui ibi sunt, multam laetitiam faciant omnibus
civibus caeli...* (David ab Augusta, 105; Devas, *Spiritual Life* 1, 100); *Prof* 3,5. *...magna gaudia
caeli praedicant...* (David ab Augusta, 174; Devas, *Spiritual Life* 2, 16); *Prof* 3,28. *Sanctis etiam
in gloria augebit laetitiam damnatio reproborum, quod gaudent, se ab his salvatos, quae
poterant sicut et illi, nisi Deus eos liberasset, incidisse* (David ab Augusta, 217; Devas, *Spiritual
Life* 2, 56); *Prof* 3,29. *...maxime divini amoris et desiderii caelestis et gaudii spiritualis...*
(David ab Augusta, 217; Devas, *Spiritual Life* 2, 56); *Prof* 3,54. *...quasi non reputantes, sibi esse
plenum gaudium introduci ad epulas caelestes...* (David ab Augusta, 306; Devas, *Spiritual
Life* 2, 139).
[556] *Prof* 3,63. *...et omnes affectus, in amoris gaudio uniti, in sola Conditoris fruitione
suaviter quiescant* (David ab Augusta, 346; Devas, *Spiritual Life* 2, 178). Cf. *Prof* 3,64. *...quod
iubilus sit quoddam spirituale gaudium cordi repente ex aliqua devota cogitatione vel collatione infusum...* (David ab Augusta, 347; Devas, *Spiritual Life* 2, 179); *Prof* 3,64. *Ebrietas spiritus potest dici quaelibet magna amoris et gaudii devotio* (David ab Augusta, 348; Devas,
Spiritual Life 2, 180); *Prof* 3,64. *Quid etiam mirum, si ex magna spiritus hilaritate, quam sanctus Spiritus cordi infundit, aliquando erumpit in aliqua aperta hilaritatis indicia... Cor
namque divini amoris gaudio vel divinae fruitionis desiderio inflammatum in se dilatatur et
extenditur...* (David ab Augusta, 349–350; Devas, *Spiritual Life* 2, 181–182); *Prof* 3,64.
Spiritualis iucunditas dici potest gaudium quodlibet in Spiritu sancto... (David ab Augusta,
350; Devas, *Spiritual Life* 2, 182).
[557] *Prof* 3,67. *...quia Spiritus sanctus amor est et benevolentia et iucunditas Patris
et Filii...* (David ab Augusta, 364; Devas, *Spiritual Life* 2, 196).

8. Poverty

Origin

In the Christian tradition, the theme of poverty (*paupertas*) has always been of great importance.[558] As the Old Testament already shows, material needs raise social problems (and vice versa), for which people try to find explanations and solutions primarily of a religious kind. Analogously, answers to the ethical questions of social justice and the right distribution of wealth are often found in divine law. In fact, in a number of Bible books the actors are pre-eminently "wealthy" or "poor," and the wealthy and the poor play a predominantly religious role. Poverty may be God's punishment and wealth his reward. In some prophetical books (*Jeremiah, Ezekiel, Amos*), the poor, although perhaps not always very present, are a group of people as historically real as they are theologically stereotyped.[559] *Isaiah*, especially, pays a lot of attention to the poor as the "people of JHWH," nevertheless without a dominating reference to the concrete, social context of their poverty.[560]

In the New Testament, the poor are the ill, naked, or hungry.[561] They are beggars who have to fight for their lives (*ptōchos*) or people who possess little and have to live economically (*penēs*).[562] The New Testament thus raises the matter of the "rights" of the poor and the duty of charity.[563] It also gives poverty a metaphorical meaning, for example, when Jesus is called poor[564] or when He speaks about the "poor in spirit." This happens in the Sermon on the Mount, in which "spiritual" poverty is one of the beatitudes.[565] In this way, poverty in the New Testament is given

---

[558] "Armut"; "Armut und Armenfürsorge"; Böckmann, *Die Armut*; Bosl, *Armut*; Flood, *Poverty*; Geremek, *Poverty*; Henrici, *Die christliche*; Holman, *Wealth*; Kerber e.a., *Armut*; Légasse, *Les pauvres*; Little, *Religious Poverty*; Meggitt, *Paul*; Metz, *Armut*; Mollat, *Les pauvres*; Nissen, *Poverty*; "Pauvreté"; Schmitz, *Die Armut*; Stegemann, *Das Evangelium*; *Trekt de Kerk*; Trilling & Hardick, "Armut"; Wulf, *Evangelische*.

[559] Berges, "Die Armen", 155–156.

[560] Berges, "Die Armen", 161.

[561] Stegemann, *Das Evangelium*, 10–15.

[562] Stegemann, *Das Evangelium*, 8.

[563] Trilling & Hardick, "Armut", 103.

[564] 2 Cor 8,9.

[565] Matt 5,3; Luke 6,20–22. Cf. "Armut", 78: "Matthäus interpretierte die Seligpreisungen, um deutlich zu machen, daß nicht Armut, Hunger und Sorge als solche für das Reich qualifizieren. Was er genau unter den „geistlich Armen" verstand, bleibt etwas unklar; wahrscheinlich dachte er an jene, deren Geist niedergedrückt war (d.h. erniedrigt, bedingt durch aktuelle Verhältnisse), wie Worte wie „die Trauernden" und „die Bedrückten"

the religious meaning of "belonging to the kingdom of God"[566] (thereby following in the tradition of the Old Testament prophets) and, ultimately, comes to stand for the religious ideal and ideal existence of being totally propertyless.[567]

Francis

Christ

Although poverty can be said to be "the" Franciscan virtue and "the" Franciscan icon, Francis pays more attention to other virtues like charity, obedience, and humility.[568] These virtues are all closely related, but poverty seems to stand out as the virtue that especially shaped the history of Franciscan theology and legal discussion after Francis.[569] Francis himself uses the term in the first place to indicate the poverty of Christ, with humility the most characteristic virtue of his earthly life.[570] Christ was rich but chose to be poor.[571] That Christ was poor in his earthly life does not

---

(anawîm) zeigen. Es gibt keine Veranlassung anzunehmen, daß er damit meint: „Selig sind die, die freiwillig arm wurden" (...)."

[566] Luke 6,20.

[567] Luke 14,33. Cf. Trilling & Hardick, "Armut", 103.

[568] Cf. Lambert, *Franciscan*, 39.

[569] "Frères", 1325–1329; Lambert, *Franciscan*; Mäkinen, *Property*; Moorman, *A History*, 90, 307–319; Mueller, *The Privilege*. On Francis and poverty: Armstrong, *St. Francis of Assisi*, 152–165; "Armut"; Bisschops, *Franciscus*, 178–184; Bracaloni, "Le virtù", 160–166; Breton, "l'Exemple"; Da Campagnola, "La povertà"; Clasen, "Die Armut"; Van Corstanje, *Gottes Bund*, 41–80; Esser, *Anfänge*, 245–265; Esser, "Die Armutsauffassung"; Esser, "Mysterium"; Esser & Grau, *Antwort*, 141–164; Feld, *Franziskus*, 189–194; Garrido, *Die Lebensregel*, 174–193; Geulen, *Die Armut*; Gobry, *St. François*, 69–73; Hoeberichts, *Paradise*, 68–93, 196–206; Iriarte, *Vocazione*, 118–145; Kinsella, ""To Serve""; Lachance, "Mysticism", 68–71; Lambert, *Franciscan*, 33–72; Lang, *Ins Freie*, 35–42; Lapsanski, *Das Leben*, 81–106; *Leben*; Linden, *Vater*, 237–246; Longpré, *François*, 77–95; Longpré, "Saint François", 1286–1290; Manselli, "La povertà"; Matura, *François*, 249–251; Miccoli, *Le testament*, 51–69; Micó, "Franciscan"; Morant, *Unser Weg*, 105–115; Nolthenius, *Een man*, 233–239; Peters, *Aus Liebe*, 66–70; Roggen, *Die Lebensform*, 34–56; Rohr, *Der Herr*, 179–202; Rotzetter, *Franz von Assisi*, 80–100; Sevenhoven, *Verslag*, 77–130; Short, *Poverty*, 58–71; Strack, ""„Gib mir"", 32–36; Tils, *Der heilige*; Verhey, *Der Mensch*, 113–117; Veuthey, *Itinerarium*, 52–55; Wolf, *The Poverty*.

[570] *RB* 12,4. *...ut semper subditi et subiecti pedibus eiusdem sanctae Ecclesiae stabiles in fide* (cfr. Col 1,23) *catholica paupertatem et humilitatem et sanctum evangelium Domini nostri Jesu Christi, quod firmiter promisimus, observemus; RnB 9,1. Omnes fratres studeant sequi humilitatem et paupertatem Domini nostri Jesu Christi...* Cf. Micó, "Franciscan", 272: "The foundation and motivation of Francis's poverty must be sought in the Gospels as read and experienced from the radically poor point of view. The Christ whom Francis found in the Gospel was a poor Christ, not only poor in material things, but also aware of and accepting His own poverty as an instrument of liberation. His was a humble poverty."

[571] *Ep Fid* 2,5. *Qui, cum dives esset* (2 Cor 8,9) *super omnia, voluit ipse in mundo cum beatissima Virgine, matre sua, eligere paupertatem; RnB 9,5. Et fuit pauper et hospes et vixit*

imply that his most holy Body (the Eucharist) should now be reserved in a similar poor way. The symbol of his utmost poverty and humility should, by contrast, be placed and locked up in a precious place, carried about with great reverence, and administered to others with discernment.[572]

Man
Following Christ means, in particular, following his footprint and poverty,[573] following his humility and poverty:[574]

> Let the brothers not make anything of their own, neither house, nor place, nor anything at all. As pilgrims and strangers in this world, serving the Lord in poverty and humility, let them go seeking alms with confidence, and they should not be ashamed because, for our sakes, our Lord made Himself poor in this world. This is that sublime height of most exalted poverty which has made you, my most beloved brothers, heirs and kings of the Kingdom of Heaven, poor in temporal things but exalted in virtue. Let this be your portion which leads into the land of the living. Giving yourselves totally to this, beloved brothers, never seek anything else under heaven for the name of our Lord Jesus Christ.[575]

Poverty for the brothers in the first place refers to being "servants," living correctly "without anything of their own."[576] They should not make

---

de eleemosynis ipse et beata Virgo et discipuli eius. The poverty of Christ is Francis's main reason for wanting to be poor himself: "Franziskus will arm sein, *weil* [italics KP] Christus auf Erden arm war" (Esser, "Mysterium", 185).

[572] *Ep Cust* 1,4. *Et si in aliquo loco sanctissimum corpus Domini fuerit pauperrime collocatum, iuxta mandatum Ecclesiae in loco pretioso ab eis ponatur et consignetur et cum magna veneratione portetur et cum discretione aliis ministretur.*

[573] *Ep Leo* 3. *In quocumque modo melius videtur tibi placere Domino Deo et sequi vestigiam [!] et paupertatem suam, faciatis cum beneditione [!] Domini Dei et mea obedientia.*

[574] *RB* 12,4. *...ut semper subditi et subiecti pedibus eiusdem sanctae Ecclesiae stabiles in fide* (cfr. Col 1,23) *catholica paupertatem et humilitatem et sanctum evangelium Domini nostri Jesu Christi, quod firmiter promisimus, observemus; RnB* 9,1. *Omnes fratres studeant sequi humilitatem et paupertatem Domini nostri Jesu Christi....*

[575] *RB* 6,1–6. *Fratres nihil sibi approprient nec domum nec locum nec aliquam rem. Et tanquam peregrini et advenae* (cfr. 1 Pet 2,11) *in hoc saeculo in paupertate et humilitate Domino famulantes vadant pro eleemosyna confidenter, nec oportet eos verecundari, quia Dominus pro nobis se fecit pauperem in hoc mundo* (cfr. 2 Cor 8,9). *Haec est illa celsitudo altissimae paupertatis, quae vos, carissimos fratres meos, heredes et reges regni caelorum instituit, pauperes rebus fecit, virtutibus sublimavit* (cfr. Jac 2,5). *Haec sit portio vestra, quae perducit in terram viventium* (cfr. Ps 141,6). *Cui, dilectissimi fratres, totaliter inhaerentes nihil aliud pro nomine Domini nostri Jesu Christi in perpetuum sub caelo habere velitis* (Armstrong, *Francis of Assisi*, 103).

[576] *Adm* 11,3. *Ille servus Dei, qui non irascitur neque conturbat se pro aliquo recte vivit sine proprio; Test* 24. *Caveant sibi fratres, ut ecclesias, habitacula paupercula et omnia, quae pro ipsis construuntur, penitus non recipiant, nisi essent, sicut decet sanctam paupertatem, quam in regula promisimus, semper ibi hospitantes sicut advenae et peregrini* (cfr. 1 Pet 2,11).

anything their own (*sibi appropriare*), neither a house nor a settlement, nor anything at all.[577] They should accept payment for their work only as is necessary for bodily support, only humbly, and only as is becoming of servants of God and followers of most holy poverty.[578] This excludes money, which is at all times forbidden.[579] For the rest, they should give everything to the poor.[580] If necessary, they can seek alms like other poor people.[581] They should always regard themselves as beggars who receive everything from God.[582] Living in total poverty they will sing: "I am afflicted and poor; help me, O God,"[583] because the Lord has become the refuge of the poor.[584]

They follow the Gospel of Christ when they live "in obedience, without anything of their own and in chastity."[585] The brothers have to become poor not only in a material sense ("poor in temporal things"[586]), but also "poor in spirit" ("exalted in virtue"[587]): by hating themselves and loving those who strike them on the cheek.[588] "Hating yourself" here means giving up yourself completely, substituting your own interests for those of

---

[577] *RB* 6,1. *Fratres nihil sibi approprient nec domum nec locum nec aliquam rem*; *Ep Ord* 29. *Nihil ergo de vobis retineatis vobis.* Cf. Iriarte, *Vocazione*, 122–128.

[578] *RB* 5,3–4. *De mercede vero laboris pro se et suis fratribus corporis necessaria recipiant praetere denarios vel pecuniam et hoc humiliter, sicut decet servos Dei et paupertatis sanctissimae sectatores.* Cf. "Armut", 94: "Sie entschlossen sich zu einfacher Arbeit, um das Lebensnotwendige zu bestreiten, lehnten für sich jede Stelle ab, die Machtausübung in sich schließt, und verweigerten den Umgang mit Geld."

[579] Cf. *RnB* 8,6. *Et si in aliquo loco inveniremus denarios, de his non curemus tamquam de pulvere, quem pedibus calcamus....*

[580] *RB* 2,5; *RnB* 2,4. *...dicant illis verbum sancti Evangelii* (cfr. Matt 19,²¹par), *quod vadant et vendant omnia sua et ea studeant pauperibus erogare*; *RB* 2,8; *RnB* 2,7. *Si tamen consilium requiratur, licentiam habeant ministri mittendi eos ad aliquos Deum timentes, quorum consilio bona sua pauperibus erogentur*; *Test* 16. *Et illi qui veniebant ad recipiendam vitam, omnia quae habere poterant* (Tob 1,3), *dabant pauperibus; et erant contenti tunica una, intus et foris repeciata, cum cingulo et braccis.*

[581] *RnB* 7,8. *Et cum necesse fuerit, vadant pro eleemosynis sicut alii pauperes*; *RnB* 9,8. *Et eleemosyna est hereditas et iustitia, quae debetur pauperibus, quam nobis acquisivit Dominus noster Jesus Christus*; *Reg Er* 5. *Et, quando placuerit, possint petere ab eis eleemosynam sicut parvuli pauperes propter amorem Domini Dei.*

[582] Tils, *Der heilige*, 25.

[583] *Of Pas* 2,8,6. *Ego vero egenus et pauper sum. Deus, adiuva me* (Armstrong, *Francis of Assisi*, 148).

[584] *Of Pas* 3,11,7. *Et factus est Dominus refugium pauperum.*

[585] *RB* 1,1; *RnB* 1,1. *Regula et Vita Minorum Fratrum haec est, scilicet Domini nostri Jesu Christi sanctum Evangelium observare vivendo in obedientia, sine proprio et in castitate* (Armstrong, *Francis of Assisi*, 100). These are the three evangelical counsels (Hödl, "Evangelische"; Vicaire, "Evangelical").

[586] *RB* 6,4.

[587] *RB* 6,4.

[588] *Adm* 14,1–4. *Beati pauperes spiritu, quoniam ipsorum est regnum caelorum* (Matt 5,3)... *Hi non sunt pauperes spiritu; quia qui vere pauper est spiritu, se ipsum odit et eos*

God, and renouncing your own will.[589] Although, as a consequence, poverty is especially connected to humility,[590] it is also connected to other virtues like perseverance[591] and joy.[592] The brothers must rejoice when they live among poor and powerless people.[593] For Francis, poverty is opposed to wealth[594] but even more opposed to the desire for wealth, that is, to greed.[595] Poverty confounds the cares of this world[596] and therefore consists in "einer möglichst großen Ungesichertheit des ganzen äußeren Lebens."[597]

Kenosis

Only God is the rightful owner of all earthly things.[598] Consequently, Francis's "poverty" calls for disappropriation, begging, and the renunciation of money, but also amounts to a spiritual attitude: being prepared to follow the model of the "poor" Christ in a total and unqualified way, and observe the Gospel spiritually.[599] Real poverty encompasses the whole

---

diligit qui eum percutiunt in maxilla (cfr. Matt 5,39). Here, poverty is one of the beatitudes.

[589] Adm 2,3. Ille enim comedit de ligno scientiae boni, qui sibi suam voluntatem appropriat et se exaltat de bonis quae Dominus dicit et operatur in ipso....

[590] Sal Virt 2. Domina sancta paupertas, Dominus te salvet cum tua sorore sancta humilitate. Poverty is thus called the "exercise in humility" (Tils, Der heilige, 37, 67).

[591] RnB 23,7. ...pauperes et egenos... humiliter rogamus et supplicamus nos omnes fratres minores, servi inutiles (Luke 17,10), ut omnes in vera fide et poenitentia perseveremus, quia aliter nullus salvari potest.

[592] Adm 27,3. Ubi est paupertas cum laetitia, ibi nec cupiditas nec avaritia; Of Pas 4,14,5. Videant pauperes et laetentur.

[593] RnB 9,2. Et debent gaudere, quando conversantur inter viles et despectas personas, inter pauperes et debiles et infirmos et leprosos et iuxta viam mendicantes. The members of the order should be able to associate on equal terms with the poorest of men in the outside world (Lambert, Franciscan, 41).

[594] "Aus einem dialektischen Verhältnis zu den Privilegierten und den Benachteiligten in und um seine Heimatstadt entfaltet er die Grundideen der jungen franziskanischen Bewegung" ("Armut", 94).

[595] "What Francis wishes to condemn is the property-owning mind. The term "sibi appropriare" has a spiritual, as well as a purely economic, connotation" (Lambert, Franciscan, 55).

[596] Sal Virt 11. Sancta paupertas confundit cupiditatem et avaritiam et curas huius saeculi.

[597] Esser, "Mysterium", 178.

[598] "Um die Anerkennung der Eigentumsrechte Gottes am Besitz des Menschen geht es bei der Entäußerung des franziskanischen Menschen, wenn er auf allen irdischen Besitz verzichtet" (Esser & Grau, Antwort, 153). Cf. Bisschops, Franciscus, 179. Everything good should be given back to God, the rightful owner: Beatus servus, qui omnia bona reddit Domino Deo (Adm 18,2).

[599] Lambert, Franciscan, 59–60.

person and all areas of his life.[600] It has to be "external" as well as "internal."[601] It should not be regarded as an aim in itself but primarily serve *kenosis*: the renunciation of oneself for the sake of God's dwelling within.[602] In this way, the "spiritual" virtue of poverty becomes an "eschatological" one: "Das gottmenschliche Geheimnis Christi ist in der Armut des hl. Franziskus auf neue Weise zur Darstellung gekommen: Im Blick auf den menschgewordenen Gottessohn hat er die ganze „Entäußerung" menschlich nachvollzogen, um darin im Menschen vorbehaltlos für Gott Raum zu schaffen und „erfüllt zu werden mit der ganzen Fülle Gottes" (Eph 3,19). Wie die Armut des hl. Franziskus in diesem Menschendasein das Erdenleben Jesu nachbildet, so ist zugleich darin auch schon die künftige Vollendung des „Gott alles in allem" (1 Kor 15,28) vorgebildet."[603]

The poor
I conclude this reading with two alternative interpretations of Franciscan poverty. According to J. Hoeberichts, following D. Flood, Francis's brothers "cannot possibly be considered poor, nor do they have any intention of allowing Assisi to drive them the way of the poor, as is clear from the various measures they take."[604] Poverty is not an ideal, but a consequence of society's sins of oppression and exclusion. These sins can only be confounded by choosing a new economic system in solidarity with the poor, in which all people have access to the goods they need, and this is exactly what Francis does.[605] Next to this inherently "social" view of Franciscan poverty stands the iconoclastic view of K.B. Wolf. Wolf tries to reveal the irony of spiritual poverty by answering such questions as how Francis went about transforming himself from a rich to a poor man and how his self-imposed poverty compared to the involuntary poverty of the poor he met in Assisi. He finds that Francis's conception of poverty as a spiritual discipline may have opened the door to salvation for wealthy Christians like Francis himself, but it effectively precluded the idea that

---

[600] Esser, "Die Armutsauffassung", 69.
[601] "Er versteht die Armut als eine Gesamthaltung des ganzen Menschen, so daß die äußere, tatsächliche Armut der Ausdruck für eine viel tiefer greifende und weiter reichende innere Armut ist" (Esser, "Mysterium", 177). Cf. Bisschops, *Franciscus*, 178; Tils, *Der heilige*, 37.
[602] Esser, "Mysterium", 187; Bisschops, *Franciscus*, 179; Buirette, "A Short", 297; Tils, *Der heilige*, 27–28, 116.
[603] Esser, "Mysterium", 189. Cf. Morant, *Unser Weg*, 112.
[604] Hoeberichts, *Paradise*, 80.
[605] Hoeberichts, *Paradise*, 81.

the socio-economic poor could use their own involuntary poverty as a path to heaven.[606]

In my opinion, both interpretations bear the virtue of historical contextualization but lack the necessary acknowledgement of a "much deeper, interior poverty"[607] for which Francis ultimately stands: "Such a total embrace of poverty that moves ever more profoundly from material things to our inner selves and to what we cling to in our relations with one another leads us to consider its very roots, its most "radical" expression: a life in which we stand before God without anything of our own."[608]

Bonaventure

Christus pauper

"He taught by word and displayed by His example the perfection of holy poverty (*paupertas*), particularly when (...) by virtue of His own blood, He was suspended destitute (*pauper*) and naked (*nudus*) on the cross."[609] Jesus Christ, the Origin of all good, preached poverty by his word, advocated it by his example at his birth, during his life, and at the end of his life; He destroyed all evil and embraced the very opposite of covetousness.[610] He taught and displayed poverty *in extremis* by not having

---

[606] "In short, the poverty that Francis encountered in the world around him was not something that he chose to combat. Instead it was something he chose to emulate and even to exaggerate for the sake of the spiritual benefits that it offered to him and to other people who were not born poor" (Wolf, *The Poverty*, 25).

[607] Armstrong, *St. Francis of Assisi*, 154. Derived from Hoeberichts, *Paradise*, 81.

[608] Armstrong, *St. Francis of Assisi*, 164.

[609] *Ap Paup* 8,20. ...*dum sanctae paupertatis perfectionem et verbo docuit et exemplo monstravit, et tunc potissimum, quando, ut verus pontifex per sanguinem proprium ingressurus in Sancta, pauper et nudus in cruce pependit* (*Doctoris* 8, 292; De Vinck, *The Works* 4, 184–185). Cf. *Ap Paup* 7,9. *Quia vero magister et Dominus Christus non propter se, sed nostri causa paupertatem assumsit, ut perfectionem nobis exemplo monstraret...* (*Doctoris* 8, 275; De Vinck, *The Works* 4, 133); *Ex Reg* 6,18. ...*qui se exhibuit doctorem paupertatis verbo pariter et exemplo* (*Doctoris* 8, 423). On Bonaventure and poverty, see for instance: Carr, "Poverty"; Delio, *Simply Bonaventure*, 115–129; "Frères", 1328–1329; Hayes, *The Hidden*, 36–37; Hellmann, "Poverty"; Johnson, *Iste Pauper*, 27–75; Johnson, "Poverty"; Kölmel, "«Labor»"; Lambert, *Franciscan*, 126–140; Schalück, *Armut*; Scheuring, "Poverty"; Strack, *Christusleid*, 59–63, 128–133.

[610] *Ap Paup* 7,2. *Omnium itaque bonorum origo et novae civitatis Ierusalem fundamentum et fundator, Christus Iesus, qui in hoc apparuit, ut diaboli dissolveret opera* [cfr. 1 John 3,8], *huius cupiditatis oppositum summo debuit affectu complecti, exemplo ostendere et verbo praedicare* (*Doctoris* 8, 272; De Vinck, *The Works* 4, 126); *Ap Paup* 7,7. *Ex his colligitur, quod Christus pauper fuit in ortu, pauper in vitae progressu, pauper in termino* (*Doctoris* 8, 274; De Vinck, *The Works* 4, 131).

anything.[611] He was rich and became poor not for Himself but for us, to
atone for our greed and avidity so "that we might abound in plenty."[612]

Evangelical poverty
In the footsteps of Christ came the apostles who themselves lived in
extreme poverty, following his example.[613] They renounced all material
possessions and money and gave up all ownership, thereby fulfilling the
norm established by Christ Himself:

> Thus does the Lord impose upon the apostles and preachers of truth a form
> of extreme and rigorous poverty to be observed by renouncing not only
> material possessions, but even money and other things by which a commu-
> nity's life is generally sustained and held together. Being poor men estab-
> lished in a state of supreme renouncement to ownership, they could take
> with them no money or food, they had to wear simple clothing and walk
> without shoes. Hence, in their deeds and their manner of life they would lift
> before them holy poverty as a standard of perfection. Christ observed in
> Himself the same perfect norm of poverty as a special prerogative which He
> established for the apostles to observe, and which He counseled to those
> who wished to follow in their footsteps.[614]

---

[611] *Det Quaest* 4. *Dominus autem istam paupertatem docuit et tenuit, ut nil possessionis
in terra haberet...* (*Doctoris* 8, 340); *Ep Im* 7. *Secundo, fuit vita Domini nostri Iesu
Christi extremae paupertatis* (*Doctoris* 8, 501). Cf. *Ex Reg* 4,11. *...et pro ipsis in paupertate
informandis caruit loculis quasi semper nec habitos tenebat possessorie reconditos...*
(*Doctoris* 8, 416).

[612] Cf. *Ap Paup* 7,9. *Quia vero magister et Dominus Christus non propter se, sed nostri
causa paupertatem assumsit...* (*Doctoris* 8, 275; De Vinck, *The Works* 4, 133); *Ap Paup* 7,14. *...
quoniam propter vos egenus factus est, cum dives esset...* [cfr. 2 Cor 8,9] (*Doctoris* 8, 276; De
Vinck, *The Works* 4, 138); *Ap Paup* 12,28. *...qui, cum dives esset, amore nostrae salutis effici
voluit egenus et pauper...* (*Doctoris* 8, 326; De Vinck, *The Works* 4, 280); *Trip Via* 3,3,4. *...pro
cupiditate, qua nulla fuit avidior, per exquisitissimam paupertatem...* (*Doctoris* 8, 14; De
Vinck, *The Works* 1, 85); *Trip Via* 3,3,4. *...opulentissimus Dominus suscepit egestatem
extremam, ut locupletaremur in copia* (*Doctoris* 8, 13; De Vinck, *The Works* 1, 85).

[613] *Ap Paup* 8,19. *...ipsos Apostolos, qui, ut ex superioribus claret, in extrema paupertate
vixerunt...* (*Doctoris* 8, 292; De Vinck, *The Works* 4, 184). Cf. *Secundae autem paupertatis
exemplar et forma in vita praecessit Apostolorum, quam perfectionis magister Christus eisdem instituit...* (*Doctoris* 8, 273; De Vinck, *The Works* 4, 128); *Ap Paup* 7,9. *...ideo sacris
Apostolis tanquam suae sanctitatis imitatoribus perfectis hanc extremae paupertatis formam servandam instituit...* (*Doctoris* 8, 275; De Vinck, *The Works* 4, 133); *Ap Paup* 7,12. *Ex his
omnibus aperte colligitur, praescriptam paupertatis formam, qua nihil possidetur et in
summa rerum penuria vivitur, Apostolis fuisse praeceptam et ab eisdem servatam* (*Doctoris*
8, 276; De Vinck, *The Works* 4, 137); *Ap Paup* 7,20. *...de paupertatis forma mandatum datum
Apostolis dicit spiritualiter esse perscrutandum...* (*Doctoris* 8, 278; De Vinck, *The Works* 4,
143).

[614] *Ap Paup* 7,5. *In his igitur verbis Dominus Apostolis et praedicatoribus veritatis
extremae ac penuriosae paupertatis formam servandam imponit quantum ad carentiam
non solum possessionum, sed etiam pecuniarum et aliorum mobilium, quibus sustentari vel*

After the apostles came all people who wanted to live according to the Gospel and "be naked" as Christ was, i.e., practice evangelical poverty.[615] They followed the command given by Christ: "If you want to be perfect, go, sell your possessions and give to the poor, and you will have treasure in heaven. Then come, follow me."[616] Moreover, they abandoned the *right* to possess anything privately and they gave up their own *will*, and so adopted evangelical poverty or "nakedness of heart and body."[617] Next to the precepts, they now observed the evangelical counsel of poverty, which adds to the perfection of righteousness and consummates the law.[618] Their contempt for temporal goods gave perfection to them,[619] and mockery, penury, and humiliation could not discourage them from what was admired so greatly by men both spiritual and wise after Christ.[620]

---

communiri solet communis hominum vita, ut, tanquam veri pauperes in summa rerum constituti penuria, carerent pecuniis, alimenta non ferrent, simplici vestitu contenti essent et sine calceamentis incederent, ut sic paupertatem altissimam actu et habitu quasi quoddam perfectionis insigne praeferrent. Hanc paupertatis normam tanquam speciali praerogativa perfectam et Christus in se ipso servavit et Apostolis servandam instituit, et his qui eorum cupiunt imitari vestigia, consulendo suasit (Doctoris 8, 273; De Vinck, *The Works* 4, 129).

[615] *Ap Paup* 9,3. *...cuiusmodi fuerunt Apostoli et hi qui eorum exempla sequuntur* (Doctoris 8, 295; De Vinck, *The Works* 4, 190–191).

[616] *Ap Paup* 7,13. *Quod autem ipsorum, immo Christi vestigia sequi volentibus consulatur ab ipso, aperte clarescit ex consilio, quod dedit adolescenti, sicut legitur in Matthaeo: Si vis perfectus esse, vade, vende omnia, quae habes, et da pauperibus et veni, sequere me* [cfr. Matt 19,21] (Doctoris 8, 276; De Vinck, *The Works* 4, 137). Cf. *Ap Paup* 8,4. *...et evangelicae paupertatis perfectio novae legi proprie convenire docetur* (Doctoris 8, 287; De Vinck, *The Works* 4, 170).

[617] *Ap Paup* 7,22. *Nuditas autem cordis et corporis triplicem habet gradum. Nam quaedam est magna, quae attenditur in abiectione omnis superfluitatis et proprietariae possesionis... Est et alia nuditas maior, quae non solum consistit in his, verum etiam in abdicatione potestatis possidendi proprium et abnegatione propriae voluntatis... Est et tertia nuditas, quae consistit in his quae praedicta sunt et insuper in abdicatione omnis transitoriae facultatis cum penuria et indigentia opportunae sustentationis, et haec competit Apostolis et apostolicis viris...* (Doctoris 8, 279–280; De Vinck, *The Works* 4, 146).

[618] *Ap Paup* 3,20. *...in qua vovetur et paupertas altior et obedientia universalior et forma castitatis honestior* (Doctoris 8, 250; De Vinck, *The Works* 4, 53); *Ap Paup* 8,6. *...sic nec paupertatis consilium Legem destruit, sed consummat, quia nec in eadem evangelica lege consilia praeceptis contrariantur, sed potius addunt ad perfectionem iustitiae* (Doctoris 8, 288; De Vinck, *The Works* 4, 171).

[619] *Ap Paup* 8,21. *...quia perfectionem eis non contulit temporalium bonorum administratio, sed contemptus; non temporalis affluentia, sed spiritus paupertatis...* (Doctoris 8, 293; De Vinck, *The Works* 4, 186).

[620] *Ap Paup* 9,19. *Liquet autem, quod paupertas, pro qua quis deridetur et contemnitur, ea potissimum est, quae annexam habet exteriorum penuriam et vilificationem* (Doctoris 8, 300; De Vinck, *The Works* 4, 205); *Ap Paup* 8,1. *...post vero in tanta fuit admiratione spiritualium atque sapientium...* (Doctoris 8, 286; De Vinck, *The Works* 4, 165).

Poverty and property

There are many grades and shades of evangelical poverty,[621] but perfect evangelical poverty consists in the total renouncement of all temporal possessions.[622] This can be done in two ways (I quote here the full paragraph in order to illustrate the technicality of the discussion):

> Hence, the nature of evangelical perfection may be seen: it is the virtue which renounces temporal goods and by which a man lacking private property is sustained with things he does not own. Since the dominion over temporal goods may be given up in two ways, there are two ways of being sustained with what is not one's own. Correspondingly, there is a double mode and perfection in evangelical poverty. Since the dominion over things is twofold, that is, it may consist either in private or in common ownership, the one relating things to a person and the other to a group, and since it is possible to disclaim the former while retaining the latter, it is also possible to disclaim the latter together with the former. Hence, in parallel with this twofold mode of poverty, there will be two kinds of perfect possession of poverty. In the one, a man renounces all private and personal dominion over temporal goods and is sustained by things he does not own, things that are not his but are shared with a community. In the other, a man renounces all dominion over temporal goods, both private and common, and is sustained by things that are not his but someone else's: his sustenance is kindly and justly provided by an outsider.[623]

---

[621] Cf. *Ap Paup* 3,20. ...*et gradus habent et minus et maius recipiunt, ac per hoc tanto in maioris perfectionis statu constituunt...* (*Doctoris* 8, 250; De Vinck, *The Works* 4, 53); *Ap Paup* 7,21. *Est enim multiplex gradus et differentia nuditatis...* (*Doctoris* 8, 279; De Vinck, *The Works* 4, 145); *Ap Paup* 8,7. ...*pro eo quod varii sunt in ea modi perfectionis...* (*Doctoris* 8, 288; De Vinck, *The Works* 4, 172–173); *Ap Paup* 8,16. ...*omne, quod infra perfectionis apicem est, esse imperfectum* (*Doctoris* 8, 291; De Vinck, *The Works* 4, 180); *Ap Paup* 11,1. ...*sed et nos veraciter inficiari non possumus, quin inter perfectionis evangelicae professores perversi sint aliqui et imperfecti quamplurimi* (*Doctoris* 8, 311; De Vinck, *The Works* 4, 237); *Ap Paup* 11,4. ...*in quibus omnia confundit atque in tantum pervertit, ut in paupertate gradus non sit...* (*Doctoris* 8, 312; De Vinck, *The Works* 4, 240).

[622] *Ap Paup* 3,8. ...*invitat ad perfectam abdicationem temporalium possessionum* (*Doctoris* 8, 246; De Vinck, *The Works* 4, 42). Cf. *Ap Paup* 9,22. ...*quod in tanto sint perfectionis culmine cum amplitudine possessionis, sicut cum altitudine paupertatis* (*Doctoris* 8, 294; De Vinck, *The Works* 4, 187); *Ex Reg* 4,9. ...*quod nihil ex eis possessorie habeatur...* (*Doctoris* 8, 415).

[623] *Ap Paup* 7,4. *Ex his potest colligi paupertatis evangelicae ratio, videlicet, quod ipsa sit virtus temporalium abdicativa bonorum, qua quis, nil proprium habens, sustentatur de non suo. Et quoniam dupliciter contingit rerum temporalium abdicare dominium, dupliciter etiam sustentari de non suo; ideo paupertatis evangelicae duplex est modus duplexque perfectio. Cum enim duplex sit rerum dominium, privatum scilicet et commune, unum quidem spectans ad determinatam personam, alterum vero ad determinatum collegium; et primum abdicari possit, retento secundo, possit etiam abdicari secundum cum primo: duplex erit secundum hunc duplicem modum paupertatis perfecta professio, una videlicet, qua quis, temporalium omnium privato seu personali abdicato dominio, sustentatur de non suo, id est,*

As this elaboration shows, the virtue (*virtus*) of evangelical poverty is twofold: in the first form one has nothing for one's own, but is sustained by the goods shared in the community; in the second form one has nothing for one's own and nothing in common, but is sustained by outsiders. In any case, the preferred kind of evangelical poverty (wherein one "is sustained by what is not his") is the one in which, on the one hand, all ownership (*dominium*) and property (*proprietas*) of earthly things are renounced, but not necessarily their (limited) use (*usus*);[624] and, on the other hand, one in which one "treads upon all things and upon himself together with everything else" for the sake of freedom of spirit and the experience of real poverty, viz., begging.[625] True evangelical poverty is thus both of a material (*abdicatio mundi*) and of a spiritual (*abdicatio concupiscentiae eius, paupertas spiritus*) nature; it concerns the renouncement of all worldly things as well as of all worldly desires.[626]

---

non sibi proprio, communi tamen iure cum aliis participato et simul possesso; alia vero, qua quis, omni rerum abdicato dominio, tam in proprio quam in communi, sustentatur de non suo, id est non sibi proprio, sed alieno, pie tamen et iuste ab alio sibi pro sustentatione collato (*Doctoris* 8, 273; De Vinck, *The Works* 4, 127–128). Cf. *Ap Paup* 7,16. ...*quod Christum et Apostolos imitari non solum quoad abdicationem proprietatum, verum etiam quoad extremam temporalium rerum penuriam, quae consistit in carentia possessionum et pecuniarum, non solum est licitum, sed et laudabile et perfectum* (*Doctoris* 8, 277; De Vinck, *The Works* 4, 140). The fairly technical discussion in the *Apologia pauperum* about the true nature of evangelical poverty must be placed against the background of the political discussion raised in the Order at the time of writing. Cf. Lambert, *Franciscan*.

[624] *Ap Paup* 7,3. ...*evangelicae paupertatis est, possessiones terrenas quantum ad dominium et proprietatem relinquere, usum vero non omnino reiicere, sed arctare...* (*Doctoris* 8, 273; De Vinck, *The Works* 4, 127); *Ap Paup* 11,5. ...*nulla prorsus potest esse professio omnino temporalium rerum abdicans usum* (*Doctoris* 8, 312; De Vinck, *The Works* 4, 241). Cf. Lambert, *Franciscan*, 133–134.

[625] *Ap Paup* 12,28. ...*celsitudo paupertatis, qua quis omnia calcat et se ipsum cum omnibus, sursum agat in Deum, non solum propter spiritus libertatem, verum etiam propter experientiam incommodorum, quae pauperes comitantur...* (*Doctoris* 8, 326; De Vinck, *The Works* 4, 280); *Ap Paup* 12,33. ...*non solum in abdicatione proprietatum, verum etiam in acceptione necessariorum...* (*Doctoris* 8, 327; De Vinck, *The Works* 4, 285). Cf. *Ep Quaest* 3. ... *quin pauperibus, quantumcumque extremam voverint paupertatem, liceat recipere eleemosynam...* (*Doctoris* 8, 332).

[626] *Ap Paup* 7,3. *Si igitur gemina haec abdicatio, mundi scilicet et concupiscentiae eius, quae etiam paupertas spiritus dicitur, ipsa est, qua radix omnium malorum perfecte amputatur et Babylonis fundamentum evertitur; certa potest ratione concludi, quod perfectionis evangelicae, per quam Christo configuramur et complantamur et habitaculum eius efficimur, ipsa paupertas spiritus, secundum quandam analogiam et cohaerentiam ad praedicta, radix est et fundamentum* (*Doctoris* 8, 272; De Vinck, *The Works* 4, 126). Cf. *Ap Paup* 9,24. ...*quod voluntaria rerum inopia non solum est magnae pretiositatis, sed etiam mirae pulcritudinis* (*Doctoris* 8, 302; De Vinck, *The Works* 4, 211).

The virtue of poverty uproots vices and brings in virtues.[627] It needs virtues such as abstinence and austerity to be fruitful.[628] Unlike virtues that must be preserved without respite (mercy, kindness, humility, patience, modesty, chastity, faith, hope, love, etc.), poverty may be adapted with discretion to certain circumstances. In times of persecution, and in case of immediate danger of death, the carrying of money for food is permitted, for example.[629]

Poverty and perfection
Francis once told his brothers "that poverty is the special way to salvation, as the stimulus of humility and the root of perfection, whose fruit is manifold but hidden."[630] He saw in poverty the close companion of the Son of God and named it the queen of the virtues, after the pre-eminent poverty of Christ and his mother.[631] Voluntary poverty is the beginning and foundation of evangelical perfection, the foundation of Christian religion, and the primary foundation of the whole spiritual edifice.[632] Voluntary poverty

[627] *Ap Paup* 9,28. *Cum igitur contemnere divitias et amare pauperiem sit exstirpatio vitiorum et insertio virtutum...* (*Doctoris* 8, 303; De Vinck, *The Works* 4, 214); *Ap Paup* 9,14. *Valet primo ad exterminium iniquitatis, primum quidem propter expiationem perpetratarum culparum* (*Doctoris* 8, 298; De Vinck, *The Works* 4, 200); *Ap Paup* 9,16. *Valet etiam tertio propter abscissionem vitiosarum radicum* (*Doctoris* 8, 299; De Vinck, *The Works* 4, 202). Cf. *Ex Reg* 6,15. *...ut est possibile, parvitatem, vilitatem et asperitatem, quae tria paupertatem altissimam naturaliter consequuntur* (*Doctoris* 8, 422).
[628] *Ap Paup* 5,9. *Valet secundo ad custodiam paupertatis altissimae...* (*Doctoris* 8, 260; De Vinck, *The Works* 4, 86); *Trip Via* 1,1,9. *Deinde sequitur severitas, quae est quidam rigor mentis, restringens omnem concupiscentiam et habilitans ad amorem asperitatis, paupertatis et vilitatis* (*Doctoris* 8, 5; De Vinck, *The Works* 1, 68).
[629] *Ap Paup* 7,39. *Non eadem vivendi regula persecutionis, qua pacis tempore informat. Sunt namque virtutes, quae semper obnixeque tenendae sunt, et sunt quae tempore locoque provida sunt discretione mutandae. Quis enim nesciat, viscera misericordiae, benignitatem, humilitatem, patientiam, modestiam, castitatem, fidem, spem, caritatem et his similia sine ulla temporum intercapedine esse servanda?... Mortis vero instante periculo, et tota simul gente pastorem gregemque persequente, congruam tempori regulam decrevit, pecuniam scilicet victui necessariam, donec, sopita persecutorum insania, tempus evangelizandi redeat, tollere permittendo* (*Doctoris* 8, 285; De Vinck, *The Works* 4, 162).
[630] *Leg Franc* 7,1. *Paupertatem noveritis, Fratres, specialem viam esse salutis tanquam humilitatis fomentum perfectionisque radicem, cuius est fructus multiplex, sed occultus* (*Doctoris* 8, 523; Cousins, *Bonaventure*, 240). Cf. *Lign Vit* 2,8. *Quoniam autem humilitatem perfectam trium specialiter adornari decet comitatu virtutum, scilicet paupertatis in fugiendo divitias ut fomenta superbiae...* (*Doctoris* 8, 72; De Vinck, *The Works* 1, 108).
[631] *Leg Franc* 7,1. *...inde hanc virtutum asserens esse reginam...* (*Doctoris* 8, 523; Cousins, *Bonaventure*, 240).
[632] *Ap Paup* 7,3. *...certa potest ratione concludi, quod perfectionis evangelicae, per quam Christo configuramur et complantamur et habitaculum eius efficimur, ipsa paupertas spiritus, secundum quandam analogiam et cohaerentiam ad praedicta, radix est et*

forms the fastest way to perfection and it is needed for the fullness of perfection, as the perfect life cannot be attained without it.[633] Because of its
fundamental character, spiritual poverty, the first of the beatitudes, falls
under a vow.[634] Moreover, the vow of religion (of poverty, obedience, and
chastity) "is all the greater in merit as there is in it a promise of greater
poverty."[635]

David

Involuntary, voluntary, vowed
There is involuntary and voluntary poverty. Involuntary poverty (*paupertas saeculi, paupertas rebus*) is poverty that comes to a man forcibly and
against his will as something from which he cannot escape.[636] Voluntary
poverty, on the other hand, a virtue that combats vice, means having to do

---

fundamentum (Doctoris 8, 272; De Vinck, *The Works* 4, 126); *Ap Paup* 9,29. *...non minus
impugnat fundamentum christianae religionis quam evangelicae paupertatis (Doctoris* 8,
304; De Vinck, *The Works* 4, 215); *Con Narb* 1. *...paupertas sit totius spiritualis aedificii primarium fundamentum (Doctoris* 8, 450; Monti, *Works*, 76); *Reg Nov* 16,1. *Cum paupertas voluntaria sit totius spiritualis aedificii primarium fundamentum... (Doctoris* 8, 489; Monti,
Works, 174). Cf. *Ap Paup* 1,8. *...quod nullo modo potest stare cum evangelica perfectione, sicut
ducere uxorem, vel refugere paupertatem (Doctoris* 8, 238; De Vinck, *The Works* 4, 14); *Ap
Paup* 8,6. *...sed adversarius pauperum, super huiusmodi possessiones se fundans, perfectionis fundamenta non statuit, sed subvertit (Doctoris* 8, 288; De Vinck, *The Works* 4, 172); *Ap
Paup* 12,29. *...pro eo quod multo laudabilior est paupertas voluntaria quam coacta...
(Doctoris* 8, 326; De Vinck, *The Works* 4, 281).
[633] *Ep Im* 8. *Fuit quaesitum a beato Francisco, quod esset illud quod magis duceret
hominem ad perfectionem; et ipse respondit, quod erat paupertas (Doctoris* 8, 501); *Perf* 3,1.
*Est etiam paupertas virtus ad perfectionis integritatem necessaria in tantum, ut nullus
omnino sine ea possit esse perfectus... (Doctoris* 8, 112; De Vinck, *The Works* 1, 222).
[634] *Ap Paup* 3,10. *In cuius rei testimonium beatus pauperum patriarcha Franciscus in
principio regulae suae tria prima proponit ut vovenda tanquam fundamenta... (Doctoris* 8,
246–247; De Vinck, *The Works* 4, 43); *Ap Paup* 3,9. *Propter quod instar trium primorum
operum, quae sunt mundi fundamenta... tria prima ex his cadunt sub voto... (Doctoris* 8, 246;
De Vinck, *The Works* 4, 43).
[635] *Ap Paup* 3,20. *Similiter quantum ad votum Religionis illius est professio perfectior, in
qua vovetur et paupertas altior et obedientia universalior et forma castitatis honestior
(Doctoris* 8, 250; De Vinck, *The Works* 4, 53).
[636] *Prof* 2,30. *Necessitas autem alia est, cui se homo voluntarie subiicit, ut qui obligant se
voto ad obedientiam, castitatem, paupertatem et similia... Alia est coacta, quam homo invi-
tus tolerat, nec tamen potest effugere, ut paupertas saeculi... (David ab Augusta*, 117; Devas,
Spiritual Life 1, 112); *Prof* 3,44. *Quidam autem sunt pauperes rebus et non spiritu (David ab
Augusta*, 268; Devas, *Spiritual Life* 2, 103). Here, the basic solution lies in the virtue of generosity: giving liberally to the poor (*Prof* 3,32; *David ab Augusta*, 227; Devas, *Spiritual Life* 2, 65;
and *Prof* 3,44; *David ab Augusta*, 269; Devas, *Spiritual Life* 2, 104).

without as a consequence of free choice (viz., the personal vow of obedience, chastity, and poverty):

> Here are seven most effective remedies against vice in general. Firstly
> poverty: aim at the element of *having to do without* entering widely into
> your various purposes. I do not mean merely acquiescing in unsatisfied
> wants – after all, to have wants which outrun fulfilment is as much a char-
> acteristic of the wealthy as of others – but accepting a measure of lack even
> in such fundamental necessities as food, clothing, lodging, attendance, and
> so forth.[637]

Voluntary poverty is spiritual poverty (*paupertas spiritu, contemptus divitiarum*): the renunciation of wealth out of charity.[638]

Poverty as personal virtue
Spiritual poverty is the virtue that makes it possible to do without
what you want altogether.[639] It means to leave all for Christ,[640] who
"being rich became poor for your sakes, that through his poverty you
might become rich."[641] For it was the humble, patient, poor, and obedient

---

[637] *Prof* 2,33. *Efficaciora remedia contra omnia vitia sunt ista. Primum est paupertas, ut in
omnibus patiaris penuriam, non solum in his, quae desideras, quia illa est omnium, etiam
ditissimorum, qui plus cupiunt, quam habent: sed penuriam etiam in his, quibus necessario
indiges: in victu, vestitu, hospitio, ministris et similibus* (David ab Augusta, 120; Devas,
Spiritual Life 1, 114). The other remedies against vice are contempt, discipline, aloofness,
prayer, adversity, and the thought of death. Cf. *Prof* 2,2. *...et qui omnia relinquit propter
Christum et voluntariam paupertatem eligit minus infestatur a curis avaritiae...* (David ab
Augusta, 75; Devas, *Spiritual Life* 1, 70); *Prof* 2,45. *Secundum, considerare omnes perplexi-
tates divitiarum et laqueos avaritiae et paupertatis libertatem et utilitatem* (David ab
Augusta, 138; Devas, *Spiritual Life* 1, 130); *Prof* 2,47. *Unde quanto quis pauperior fuerit, tanto
minus in hac parte peccabit* (David ab Augusta, 141; Devas, *Spiritual Life* 1, 133); *Prof* 3,46. *...
paupertatis, pro necessitate penuriae...* (David ab Augusta, 276; Devas, *Spiritual Life* 2, 110).

[638] *Prof* 3,23. *Beati pauperes spiritu, id est voluntate, amore spiritualis profectus, quoniam
ipsorum est regnum caelorum* [cfr. Matt 5,3] (David ab Augusta, 210–211; Devas, *Spiritual
Life* 2, 50); *Prof* 3,44. *Contemptus divitiarum opponitur avaritiae rerum temporalium; haec
etiam quandoque paupertas spiritus appellatur* (David ab Augusta, 268; Devas, *Spiritual
Life* 2, 103); *Prof* 3,44. *Beati enim pauperes spiritu, quia ipsorum est regnum caelorum* [cfr.
Matt 5,3] (David ab Augusta, 270–271; Devas, *Spiritual Life* 2, 105). Cf. *Prof* 1,26. *Paupertatem
amato* (David ab Augusta, 36; Devas, *Spiritual Life* 1, 31); *Prof* 3,32. *...cum divitias abiicit,
paupertas spiritus est...* (David ab Augusta, 226–227; Devas, *Spiritual Life* 2, 65).

[639] *Prof* 3,47. *Et quamvis quoad paupertatem maior virtus sit non habere quod cupias...*
(David ab Augusta, 282; Devas, *Spiritual Life* 2, 116).

[640] Cf. *Prof* 2,2. *...et qui omnia relinquit propter Christum et voluntariam paupertatem
eligit...* (David ab Augusta, 75; Devas, *Spiritual Life* 1, 70); *Prof* 3,49. *...paupertas spiritus, id
est voluntaria pro Christo paupertas, magna et vera virtus est* (David ab Augusta, 284; Devas,
Spiritual Life 2, 118).

[641] *Prof* 1,34. *Collige etiam ex his, quae vides, passiones, labores, dolores et paupertates
Iesu Christi, qui, cum esset dives, pro nobis egenus factus est, ut illius inopia divites in*

Lord[642] who said: "If you want to be perfect, go, sell your possessions and give to the poor."[643] Like the other key virtues of spiritual progress in the sixth stage of religious life (charity, humility, patience, obedience, sobriety, chastity),[644] this virtue has three degrees. The first degree is grounded upon justice: "it excludes any unjust retention of goods personally acquired or left or given by others."[645] The second degree would rule out everything superfluous: "its aim is to be satisfied with what is necessary in all matters of food, clothing, housing, household utensils and service."[646] The third degree is "actually to desire to be without the goods of this world, and, in the very necessaries of life, to embrace penury for God's sake."[647] This last degree is true spiritual poverty.

Furthermore, spiritual poverty may also take the form of spiritual aridity, interior consolation withdrawn from a man:

> So a man abounding in many and varied spiritual consolations will pass over without thanks many a gift from God. He will omit to acknowledge what he should be most thankful for, he will think little of what in reality is great and many graces he will fail to recognize at all. But when all is withdrawn then will he be as a man seeing his poverty (Lam 3,1). He will recognize at last how much once was his which now is his no longer, and what opportunities he has lost (...). Similarly [as happens with a beggared man who now gathers up fragments] the withdrawal of grace and of consolation

---

caelestibus non essemus (*David ab Augusta*, 47; Devas, *Spiritual Life* 1, 41). Cf. *Prof* 1,7. *Paupertas Christi familiaris et amica placeat tibi in omnibus...* (*David ab Augusta*, 11; Devas, *Spiritual Life* 1, 10); Bohl, *Geistlicher*, 168.

[642] *Prof* 2,28. *Pudet nos imitari Dominum in humilitate, patientia, paupertate, religione, obedientia et despectione et contumeliis et confusione...* (*David ab Augusta*, 113; Devas, *Spiritual Life* 1, 107).

[643] *Prof* 2,45. *Si vis perfectus esse, vade et vende omnia, quae habes, et da pauperibus* [cfr. Matt 19,21] (*David ab Augusta*, 138; Devas, *Spiritual Life* 1, 130); *Prof* 3,44. *Si vis perfectus esse, vade et vende omnia, quae habes, et da pauperibus etc.* [cfr. Matt 19,21] (*David ab Augusta*, 269–270; Devas, *Spiritual Life* 2, 104).

[644] Cf. *Prof* 3,59. *Item, sublimia virtutum exercitia pauca videmus, ut eximiae obedientiae, perfectae patientiae et humilitatis praecipuae et paupertatis extremae* (*David ab Augusta*, 331; Devas, *Spiritual Life* 2, 163).

[645] *Prof* 3,45. *Primus autem gradus in contemptu divitiarum est nihil habere velle iniusti lucri, nec per se acquisitum nec ab aliis datum vel relictum...* (*David ab Augusta*, 272–273; Devas, *Spiritual Life* 2, 107).

[646] *Prof* 3,45. *Secundus gradus est nihil velle superfluum habere, sed solis necessariis esse contentum in victu et vestitu, hospitio, utensilibus et obsequentium famulatu...* (*David ab Augusta*, 273; Devas, *Spiritual Life* 2, 108).

[647] *Prof* 3,45. *Tertius gradus est nihil velle possidere in mundo et in omnibus necessariis multiplicem pati penuriam propter Deum* (*David ab Augusta*, 274; Devas, *Spiritual Life* 2, 109). Cf. *Prof* 3,47. *Secundus gradus abstinentiae est velle carere pro Deo etiam illis, quae possent haberi, amore sobrietatis et paupertatis et boni exempli* (*David ab Augusta*, 281; Devas, *Spiritual Life* 2, 115).

profits a man, for it makes him appreciate even the least little good thought
or devout aspiration, with which God may inspire him (...).[648]

Here, spiritual poverty brings about a conversion experience and a new
sense of gratefulness for even "the least little" of spiritual experiences.

9. PENANCE

Origin

Penance (penitence, *poenitentia*) in the Christian tradition is a complex
phenomenon bearing several meanings: it can be called a virtue, a spiritual state, an exercise, a purification process, a sanction, a remedy, and a
sacrament.[649] In general, a distinction should be made between *poenitentia* as a spiritual habit (viz., virtue, spiritual state, exercise) and *poenitentia* as an act to redeem sin (viz., sanction, remedy, sacrament). Penance
has an outer as well as an inner dimension: outer penance should last only
for a fixed time according to the measure of a sin one has committed;
inner penance, on the other hand, should last until the end of life.[650]

In the Old Testament, in primitive times, grave sinning against the law
called for stoning and banishment,[651] while in later times sinning against
the honor of God, the tradition of learning, or fellow men could be pun-
ished by milder forms of exclusion, which always included the possibility
of returning into the community upon conversion from evil.[652] The
excluded or "banned" found themselves in a state of penance: they were
the "mourners," the "expelled," for whom the community was obliged

---

[648] *Prof* 3,11. *Sic homo abundans diversis consolationum donis plurima beneficia Dei
sine debita gratiarum actione praeterit, plurimas gratias negligit opere exercere, plurima
parva reputat, quae magna sunt, plurima nec agnoscit. Sed his omnibus subtractis, sicut vir
videns paupertatem suam* [cfr. Lam 3,1]*, recolit, quanta prius habuit et potuit, quae iam non
habet... Subtractio gratiae et consolationis proficit homini, ut gratus fiat postmodum etiam
ad parva beneficia, cum ei Dominus reddiderit...* (*David ab Augusta*, 182–183; Devas, *Spiritual
Life* 2, 23).

[649] Merle, *La pénitence*, 17. On Christianity and penance, see further: Anciaux, *Le sacre-
ment*; "Buße"; "Convertissez-vous"; *Dienst*; Finkenzeller & Griesl, *Entspricht*; Firey, *A New
History*; Galtier, *Aux origines*; Greshake, "Zur Erneuerung"; Hausammann, *Buße*; Jean-
Nesmy, *La joie*; Lendi, *Die Wandelbarkeit*; "Pénitence"; Poschmann, *Paenitentia*; Rahner,
Sämtliche; De Vaux, *Revenir*; Vogel, *Le pécheur*; Vogel, *Le pécheur et la pénitence dans
l'église ancienne*; Vorgrimler, "Buss-Sakrament".

[650] Thomas Aquinas, *Summa theologiae* 3a,84,8 (Busa, *S. Thomae Aquinatis*, 918;
Masterson & O'Brien, *St. Thomas Aquinas*, 35–37).

[651] Deut 13.

[652] Joel 2,12; Jon 3,8.

to pray.[653] In the same vein, the early Christian community retaliated with expulsion from the community but forgave and re-admitted converted sinners; the community's aversion was aimed at the sinner's conversion.[654] In the New Testament, penance is conversion (*metanoia*).[655]

Francis

Inner penance

In the early scholastic period (from the early twelfth century) there is a definite shift towards the sacramental understanding of penance as inner conversion, or repentance of the heart (*contritio*).[656] Penance is now a sacrament but also a moral act of goodness out of a virtuous habit (*habitus*).[657] This habit joins the inner act of repentance with an ascetic penitential practice[658] and is connected to virtues such as humility, faith, and prudence.[659] Francis, although not a scholastic theologian, proves himself a witness of his time when he makes a distinction between "inner" and "outer" penance:[660]

---

[653] Vorgrimler, "Buss-Sakrament", 205. More personal forms of "penance" (confession and atonement of sin) can be found in fasting and circumcision regulations (cf. Lev 23,27–32; Isa 58,1–14; Jer 4,4).

[654] Vorgrimler, "Buss-Sakrament", 207. Cf. 1 Tim 1,20; Mark 1,14–15; John 20,23; 2 Cor 2,5–11; Jac 5,16.

[655] Dukker, *Umkehr*, 25–72; "Buße", 1124: "Buße bedeutet nach dem NT Umkehr. Als innerliches Bekehrungsgeschehen ist sie die Abwendung von der sündhaften Vergangenheit; sichtbar wird sie in einem öffentlichen Zeichen der Lossprechung und Lösung von dieser Schuld." Cf. Matt 3,8; Matt 4,17; Luke 3,8; Luke 5,32; Luke 10,13; Luke 11,32; Luke 13,3; Apoc 2; Apoc 3,3; Apoc 3,19. On Christian conversion, see: Conn, *Christian*.

[656] "Buße", 1138. Repentance is an "Akt der inwendigen, gnadenhaften Bekehrung, wie sie David im AT (2 Sam 12,13) und Petrus im NT (Lk 22,62) bezeugen" ("Buße", 1139). Subsequently, repentance should be accompanied by the outer sign of confession and followed by atonement.

[657] "Pénitence", 978. Cf. Esser & Grau, *Antwort*, 13–25; Pohier, "La pénitence"; Senftle, *Menschenbildung*, 27–36; De Vaux, *Revenir*, 181–234.

[658] Cf. "Pénitence", 979: "La vertu de pénitence constitue la vertu du repentir qui offre satisfaction. Elle entraîne naturellement à la pratique d'actes non seulement intérieurs, mais extérieurs d'ascèse (...)."

[659] RnB 20,2. ...*absoluti erunt procul dubio ab illis peccatis, si poenitentiam sibi iniunctam procuraverint humiliter et fideliter observare*; RnB 23,7. ...*ut omnes in vera fide et poenitentia perseveremus, quia aliter nullus salvari potest*; *Fidelis et prudens servus est* (cfr. Matt 24,45), *qui in omnibus suis offensis non tardat interius punire per contritionem et exterius per confessionem et operis satisfactionem.* Cf. Goorbergh & Zweerman, *Was getekend*, 23–26.

[660] Esser & Grau, *Antwort*, 117. On Francis and penance, see for instance: Armstrong, ""If My Words", 69–72; Dukker, *De evangelische*; Dukker, *Umkehr*; Esser, *Anfänge*, 210–216;

Blessed is the servant who has been found as humble among his subjects as he was among his masters. Blessed is the servant who always remains under the rod of correction. Faithful and prudent is the servant who does not delay in punishing himself for all his offenses, inwardly through contrition and outwardly through confession and penance for what he did.[661]

The first form of penance is the inner one, here called "contrition." It is sincere repentance (*poenitet*).[662] It is the way of living the life of the blessed. It refers to "those who do penance" and persevere in it,[663] who "love the Lord with their whole heart, with their whole soul and mind, with their whole strength and love their neighbours as themselves, who hate their bodies with their vices and sins, who receive the Body of Blood of our Lord Jesus Christ, and who produce worthy fruits of penance."[664] Penitential life is living according to the Gospel: Francis here provides a basic program for living by summing up the essential ingredients of "doing penance." Although he does not further explicate the "worthy fruits of penance" (which therefore seems to be tautological), the "fruits" of penitential, evangelical life, are indeed the dwelling of the Spirit and kinship to Christ.[665]

Esser & Grau, *Antwort*, 13–139, 261–278; Van den Goorbergh & Zweerman, *Was getekend*, 20–30; Iriarte, *Vocazione*, 27–38; Linden, *Vater*, 31–40; Longpré, *François*, 108–111; Longpré, "Saint François", 1292; Matura, *François*, 232–236; Morant, *Unser Weg*, 30–48; Rotzetter, *Die Funktion*, 115–117; Senftle, *Menschenbildung*; Verhey, "Das Leben"; Verhey, *Der Mensch*, 35–40, 68–80.

[661] *Adm* 23. *Beatus servus, qui ita inventus est humilis inter subditos suos, sicuti quando esset inter dominos suos. Beatus servus, qui semper permanet sub virga correctionis. Fidelis et prudens servus est* (cfr. Matt 24,45), *qui in omnibus suis offensis non tardat interius punire per contritionem et exterius per confessionem et operis satisfactionem* (Armstrong, *Francis of Assisi*, 136).

[662] *RnB* 8,7. *Et si forte, quod absit, aliquem fratrem contigerit pecuniam vel denarios colligere vel habere, excepta solummodo praedicta infirmorum necessitate, omnes fratres teneamus eum pro falso fratre et apostata et fure et latrone et loculos habente* (cfr. Joa 12,6), *nisi vere poenituerit.*

[663] *Ep Fid* 1,1,5. [*De illis qui faciunt poenitentiam*]. ...*O quam beati et benedicti sunt illi et illae, dum talia faciunt et in talibus perseverant...*

[664] *Ep Fid* 1,1,1–4. *Omnes qui Dominum diligunt ex toto corde, ex tota anima et mente, ex tota virtute* (cfr. Mark 12,30) *et diligunt proximos suos sicut se ipsos* (cfr. Matt 22,39), *et odio habent corpora eorum cum vitiis et peccatis, et recipiunt corpus et sanguinem Domini nostri Jesu Christi, et faciunt fructus dignos poenitentiae* [Luke 3,8]... (Armstrong, *Francis of Assisi*, 41). Cf. *Ep Fid* 2,18–25; *RnB* 21,3. The fulfilment of penance thus lies in self-abnegation and total surrender to God (Esser & Grau, *Antwort*, 19–25; Verhey, *Der Mensch*, 36–37).

[665] *Ep Fid* 1,1,6–7. ...*quia requiescet super eos spiritus Domini* (cfr. Isa 11,2) *et faciet apud eos habitaculum et mansionem* (cfr. Joa 14,23), *et sunt filii patris caelestis* (cfr. Matt 5,45), *cuius opera faciunt et sunt sponsi, fratres et matres Domini nostri Jesu Christi* (cfr. Matt 12,50). The fruit of penance is heaven: *RnB* 21,7–8. *Beati qui moriuntur in poenitentia, quia erunt in regno caelorum; RnB* 23,9. ...*omnis gloria omnium poenitentium et iustorum, omnium beatorum in caelis congaudentium.*

Conversely, Francis cautionarily sums up the vices and negligences of those who "do not do penance":

> All those men and women who are not living in penance, who do not receive the Body and Blood of our Lord Jesus Christ, who practice vice and sin and walk after the evil concupiscence and the evil desires of their flesh, who do not observe what they promised to the Lord, and who in their body serve the world through the desires of the flesh, the concerns of the world and the cares of this life: They are held captive by the devil, whose children they are, and whose works they do. They are blind because they do not see the true light, our Lord Jesus Christ. They do not possess spiritual wisdom because they do not have the Son of God, the true wisdom of the Father. It is said of them: *Their wisdom has been swallowed up* and *Cursed are those who turn away from your commands.* They see and acknowledge, know and do evil, and knowingly lose their souls.[666]

As is shown here, both doing penance and *not* doing penance manifest themselves inwardly and outwardly.

Outer penance

The second form of penance is the outer one, here called "confession and penance for what one did." This is an important issue for Francis.[667] First of all, he instructs priests to "remind people about penance and that no one can be saved unless he receives the most holy Body and Blood of the Lord" in every sermon they give.[668] The sacraments are absolutely necessary for Christians to be saved, especially Holy Communion and Penance.[669] People should go to Communion and confession on a regular basis. But, so the brothers are told, only when their repentance is sincere

---

[666] *Ep Fid* 1,2,1–10; *Ep Fid* 2,63–68. *Omnes autem illi et illae, qui non sunt in poenitentia, et non recipiunt corpus et sanguinem Domini nostri Jesu Christi, et operantur vitia et peccata et qui ambulant post malam concupiscentiam et mala desideria carnis suae, et non observant, quae promiserunt Domino, et serviunt corporaliter mundo carnalibus desideriis et sollicitudinibus saeculi et curis huius vitae: detenti a diabolo, cuius sunt filii et eius opera faciunt* (cfr. Joa 8,41), *caeci sunt, quia verum lumen non vident Dominum nostrum Jesum Christum. Sapientiam non habent spiritualem, quia non habent Filium Dei, qui est vera sapientia Patris, de quibus dicitur: Sapientia eorum deglutita est* (Ps 106,27) *et: Maledicti qui declinant a mandatis tuis* (Ps 118,21). *Vident et agnoscunt, sciunt et faciunt mala et ipsi scienter perdunt animas* (Armstrong, *Francis of Assisi*, 43).

[667] Cf. Esser & Grau, *Antwort*, 107–123; Verhey, "Das Leben", 171–172; Verhey, *Der Mensch*, 75–77.

[668] *Ep Cust* 6. *Et in omni praedicatione, quam facitis, de poenitentia populum moneatis, et quod nemo potest salvari, nisi qui recipit sanctissimum corpus et sanguinem Domini* (cfr. Joa 6,54) (Armstrong, *Francis of Assisi*, 57). As mentioned, receiving Holy Communion is an important part of "living in penance" in general (*Ep Fid* 1,1,1; *Ep Fid* 2,63).

[669] Cf. Esser & Grau, *Antwort*, 132, 90–105.

(*poenitet*) can they be forgiven for their sins.[670] Secondly, in some instances where Francis speaks about "giving penance" (*iniungere/dare poenitentiam*) and "receiving penance" (*recipere poenitentiam*), he uses the term for priestly absolution and the satisfaction of sins, *after* confession.[671]

Fraternity

The difference between "outer" and "inner" penance should not be exaggerated. In the writings of Francis, outward and inward are closely connected: penance (acknowledging sin and making up for it) can be the start of a life "in penance" while "living in penance" needs the sacrament of penance to be fruitful.[672] For example, Francis speaks of "the guilt of sin without penance and satisfaction" (i.e., the sacrament) in the context of "not doing penance" (i.e., not living the penitential life).[673] In the same way confession needs remorse ("sincere repentance") and remorse prompts confession to a priest. Thus, outer and inner penance are complementary.[674]

---

[670] RnB 8,7. *Et si forte, quod absit, aliquem fratrem contigerit pecuniam vel denarios colligere vel habere, excepta solummodo praedicta infirmorum necessitate, omnes fratres teneamus eum pro falso fratre et apostata et fure et latrone et loculos habente* (cfr. Joa 12,6), *nisi vere poenituerit.*

[671] Ep Fid 2,77. *Et statim faciunt venire sacerdotem; dicit ei sacerdos: «Vis recipere poenitentiam de omnibus peccatis tuis»?; Ep Min* 19–20. *Et si non fuerit ibi sacerdos, confiteatur fratri suo, donec habebit sacerdotem, qui eum absolvat canonice, sicut dictum est. Et isti penitus non habeant potestatem iniungendi aliam poenitentiam nisi istam: Vade et noli amplius peccare* (cfr. Joa 8,11); *RB* 7,2. *Ipsi vero ministri, si presbyteri sunt, cum misericordia iniungant illis poenitentiam; RnB* 12,3. *Sacerdotes honeste loquantur cum eis dando poenitentiam vel aliud spirituale consilium; RnB* 20,2. *Et si non potuerint, confiteantur aliis discretis et catholicis sacerdotibus scientes firmiter et attendentes, quia a quibuscumque sacerdotibus catholicis acceperint poenitentiam et absolutionem, absoluti erunt procul dubio ab illis peccatis, si poenitentiam sibi iniunctam procuraverint humiliter et fideliter observare.*

[672] Penance can therefore be regarded as a day-to-day renewal of conversion (Dukker, *Umkehr*, 146). Cf. Verhey, *Der Mensch*, 74–75.

[673] Ep Fid 1,2,15. *Et ubicumque, quandocumque, qualitercumque moritur homo in criminali peccato sine poenitentia et satisfactione, si potest satisfacere et non satisfacit, diabolus rapit animam suam de corpore eius cum tanta angustia et tribulatione, quod nemo potest scire, nisi qui recipit.*

[674] Cf. Verhey, "Das Leben", 173: "Die Selbstverleugnung und Abtötung, die primär in der Bekehrung von der Sündhaftigkeit und in der Überwindung der Neigung zum Bösen besteht und die als Bußakt auch die Sühnung der Schuld und das Erleiden der Strafe impliziert, bewirkt so, daß des erlöste Mensch, von jeglichem Hindernis befreit, sich ganz der Führung und dem Willem Gottes hingibt in einem Gehorsam, der nach dem Beispiel Christi auch das eigene Leben riskiert."

In his *Testament*, Francis tells us of his conversion and the beginning of his *poenitentia*: he used to be in sin (*cum essem in peccatis*) but the Lord called him to begin doing penance (*Dominus ita dedit mihi fratri Francisco incipere faciendi poenitentiam*).[675] Formulations such as "to do penance" (*facere poenitentiam/agere poenitentiam*),[676] "to be in penance" (*esse in poenitentia*),[677] "to serve in penance" (*servire in poenitentia*),[678] "to persevere in penance" (*perseverare in poenitentia*),[679] and "to die in penance" (*mori in poenitentia*)[680] refer to a spiritual way of life that extends until death and that is eventually rewarded with heaven.[681] Ideally, it is a way of life out of a virtuous habit, beyond vice and sin, in which the will of God is followed in everything and the sacraments are celebrated as prescribed by church officials.[682] It is the evangelical life of the brothers of Francis, their answer to God's call.[683]

---

[675] *Test* 1,3. This conversion "from sin to penance" can be regarded as the beginning of the Franciscan Order (Esser, *Anfänge*, 210). Cf. Dukker, *Umkehr*, 75–84; Morant, *Unser Weg*, 30–35; Verhey, *Der Mensch*, 72–75.

[676] *Ep Fid* 1. *De illis qui faciunt poenitentiam; De illis qui non agunt poenitentiam; Ep Ord* 44. *Quicumque autem fratrum haec observare noluerint, non teneo eos catholicos nec fratres meos; nolo etiam ipsos videre nec loqui, donec poenitentiam egerint; RnB* 12,4. *Et nulla penitus mulier ab aliquo fratre recipiatur ad obedientiam, sed dato sibi consilio spirituali, ubi voluerit agat poenitentiam; RnB* 13,2. *Et postea poenitentiam faciat de peccatis* (cfr. 1 Cor 5,4–5); *RnB* 21,3. *Agite poenitentiam* (cfr. Matt 3,2)...; *RnB* 23,4. ...*qui poenitentiam non egerunt...; Test* 1. *Dominus ita dedit mihi fratri Francisco incipere faciendi poenitentiam...; Test* 26. ...*sed ubicumque non fuerint recepti, fugiant in aliam terram ad faciendam poenitentiam cum benedictione Dei.*

[677] *Ep Fid* 1,2,1; *Ep Fid* 2,63. *Omnes autem illi et illae, qui non sunt in poenitentia....*

[678] *RnB* 23,4. ...*omnibus, qui te cognoverunt et adoraverunt et tibi servierunt in poenitentia....*

[679] *RnB* 23,7. ...*ut omnes in vera fide et poenitentia perseveremus, quia aliter nullus salvari potest.*

[680] *RnB* 21,8. *Vae illis qui non moriuntur in poenitentia....*

[681] *RnB* 21,7. *Beati qui moriuntur in poenitentia, quia erunt in regno caelorum.* Cf. Verhey, "Das Leben", 169–171.

[682] Cf. Esser, *Anfänge*, 211: "„Buße" ist ihm also die Umkehr des Menschen von einem Leben, das auf das eigene Ich bezogen ist, zu einem Leben, das ganz unter dem Willen, unter der Herrschaft Gottes steht (...) Buße ist also „Metanoia" im biblischen Sinne (vlg. Mk 1,15) und muß nach Auffassung des Heiligen die Grundhaltung im Leben aller seiner Nachfolger sein."

[683] Cf. Verhey, "Das Leben", 162–165; Van den Goorbergh & Zweerman, *Was getekend*, 21: "De versterving en inperking die moesten helpen om goed te maken wat in het verleden verkeerd gegaan was, vormden één kant van de boete. 'Boete doen' hield ook in, dat mensen zich met Gods genade voorgoed wilden toewenden naar de levenswijze die zij in het spoor van Jezus Christus als verlosten wilden leiden. Met andere woorden: de dubbele betekenis die "bekeert u" in Jezus' mond had, namelijk die van afwending van een vroegere levenswijze en bevrijdende toewending naar God, klonk na zoveel eeuwen nog door in het woord 'boete'."

Bonaventure

The Order of Penance

The "Order of the Brothers of Penance," the Franciscan Order, was instituted by Saint Francis, who invited all to his way of living in penance:[684]

> Set on fire by the fervor of his preaching, a great number of people bound themselves by new laws of penance according to the rule which they received from the man of God. Christ's servant decided to name his way of life the Order of the Brothers of Penance. As the road of penance is common to all who are striving toward heaven, so this way of life admits clerics and laity, single and married of both sexes. How meritorious it is before God is clear from the numerous miracles performed by some of its members. Young women, too, were drawn to perpetual celibacy (...). Many people also, not only stirred by devotion but inflamed by a desire for the perfection of Christ, despised the emptiness of worldly things and followed in the footsteps of Francis. Their numbers increased daily and quickly reached to the ends of the earth.[685]

"To despise the emptiness of worldly things and follow in the footsteps of Christ" (as done by Francis) may be a good definition of the Franciscan penitential life. The road of penance (*poenitentiae via*) is characterized by devotion, a "striving toward heaven," and a "desire for the perfection of Christ," with additional elements like a rule, miracles, and chosen celibacy.

Spiritual and sacramental penance

The "order" of penance is the organizational reflection of the shared "inner habit" (or "virtue") of spiritual penance. It was God who in his mercy, by his promise to send a Savior, put sinners upon the path of

---

[684] *Leg Franc* 3,2. *Coepit ex hoc vir Dei divino instinctu evangelicae perfectionis aemulator existere et ad poenitentiam ceteros invitare* (*Doctoris* 8, 510; Cousins, *Bonaventure*, 200). Cf. *Det Quaest* 2,16 ...*cur Ordinem illum, qui dicitur Poenitentium...* (*Doctoris* 8, 368).

[685] *Leg Franc* 4,6–7. *Nam praedicationis ipsius fervore succensi, quam plurimi secundum formam a Dei viro acceptam novis se poenitentiae legibus vinciebant, quorum vivendi modum idem Christi famulus Ordinem Fratrum de poenitentia nominari decrevit. Nimirum, sicut in caelum tendentibus poenitentiae viam omnibus constat esse communem, sic et hic status clericos et laicos, virgines et coniugatos in utroque sexu admittens, quanti sit apud Deum meriti, ex pluribus per aliquos ipsorum patratis miraculis innotescit. Convertebantur etiam virgines ad perpetuum coelibatum... Multi etiam non solum devotione compuncti, sed et perfectionis Christi desiderio inflammati, omni mundanorum vanitate contempta, Francisci vestigia sequebantur, qui quotidianis succrescentes profectibus, usque ad fines orbis terrae celeriter pervenerunt* (*Doctoris* 8, 514; Cousins, *Bonaventure*, 210–211).

penance and gave them hope.[686] Christ the Good Shepherd thereupon "displayed a paternal affection for the repentant, showing them the open arms of divine mercy."[687] Bonaventure calls doing penance ("the desire to leave worldly things behind and follow in the footsteps of Christ") a divine precept, according to the words of the Gospel: "Repent, for the kingdom of heaven is near."[688] Man is a sinner who has "offended his beloved Christ without restraint."[689] He should now "recall whether he has failed to guard his heart, make good use of his time, or act with the right purpose," and "remember any negligence in doing penance, in resisting evil, or in making spiritual progress."[690] One has the choice to do penance and repent, or "condemn himself to hell."[691] The penitent is moved by his conscience to choose the suffering of penance in order to "have recourse to the laver of penance" and cleanse his soul with the tears of contrition.[692] Apart from

---

[686] *Lign Vit* 1,2. *...superna misericordia non distulit hominem errabundum revocare ad poenitentiae viam, spem veniae dando per repromissum Salvatoris adventum* (*Doctoris* 8, 71; De Vinck, *The Works* 1, 104). Cf. *Lign Vit* 5,20. *...cum et ille impiissimus Iudas, poenitentia ductus, tanta postmodum fuerit ex hoc amaritudine repletus, ut maluerit mori quam vivere? Vae tamen homini illi, qui nec sic ad fontem misericordiae per spem veniae rediit, sed proprii sceleris immanitate perterritus desperavit!* (*Doctoris* 8, 76; De Vinck, *The Works* 1, 118–119); *Trip Via* 1,2,12. *Secundo, quod dedit gratiam poenitentialem quantum ad temporis opportunitatem, animi voluntatem, religionis sublimitatem* (*Doctoris* 8, 6; De Vinck, *The Works* 1, 69–70).

[687] *Lign Vit* 4,13. *Ad poenitentes quoque paternum praetendebat affectum, apertum ostendens eis divinae misericordiae sinum* (*Doctoris* 8, 74; De Vinck, *The Works* 1, 112).

[688] *Quare* 18. *Praeceptum Dei est poenitentiam agere; nam dicitur: Poenitentiam agite, Matthaei quarto* [Matt 4,17]... (*Doctoris* 8, 380).

[689] *Perf* 5,2. *...quia sine modo tuum dilectum Iesum offendisti* (*Doctoris* 8, 118; De Vinck, *The Works* 1, 233).

[690] *Trip Via* 1,1,4. *Circa negligentiam autem attendendum est, quod primo debet recogitare homo, si in se fuerit negligentia cordis custodiendi, temporis expendendi et finis intendendi... Tertio debet recogitare, si negligens fuerit ad poenitendum, ad resistendum, ad proficiendum* (*Doctoris* 8, 4; De Vinck, *The Works* 1, 64–65). Cf. *Det Quaest* 1,27. *...cum multi lapsi per poenitentiam surgentes...* (*Doctoris* 8, 348); *Ex Reg* 2,26. *Qui ergo sunt poenitentiae perpetuae professores ab eis tritis et integris omni tempore debent abstinere, quantum patitur fragilitas humana* (*Doctoris* 8, 406).

[691] *Trip Via* 1,4,19. *...conscientia assumit: Tu es ille: ergo vel oportet te damnari, vel poenitentiae stimulis affligi...* (*Doctoris* 8, 7; De Vinck, *The Works* 1, 72).

[692] *Ep Mem* 24. *...ideo necessarium est, ut ad poenitentiae lavacrum recurrens...* (*Doctoris* 8, 497; De Vinck, *The Works* 3 260); *Trip Via* 1,4,19. *...aut lamentis poenitentiae purgari... assumit voluntarie poenitentiae lamenta* (*Doctoris* 8, 7; De Vinck, *The Works* 1, 72). Cf. *Perf* 5,2. *Et statim pro his omnibus debes cum publicano pectus tuum percutere, cum propheta David debes rugire a gemitu cordis tui* [Luke 18,13], *et cum Maria Magdalena debes lacrymis rigare pedes* [Luke 7,38] *Domini Iesu; nec debes aliquem modum habere in lacrymis...* (*Doctoris* 8, 117–118; De Vinck, *The Works* 1, 233); *Reg Nov* 3,2. *Et sit confessio tua frequens, aperta et integra, verecunda et lacrymosa et cum contritione et sine excusatione* (*Doctoris* 8, 480; Monti, *Works*, 158).

contrition, however, penance also needs confession and satisfaction to be true and effective penance.[693] Penance is, indeed, a sacrament (next to a way of life, a virtue, and a divine precept), in which confession to and absolution by a priest are added to real tears.[694]

David

Penance and punishment

For David, penance is a way of life and a virtue. The penitential life (*carceri poenitentiae*) replaces wealth, honor, comfort, and love of friends and of oneself with a holy form of life (*via Dei*), a religious life lived totally for God's sake (*propter Deum*).[695] The goal of this life (*religio*) is, among other things, to acquire virtue and tread down vice, to do penance, to edify one's neighbour, to keep the mind alert, to attain wisdom, and to secure the glory of heaven.[696] The works of penance (*opera poenitentiae*) such as fasts, vigils, and discipline, bring the body into the service of the soul.[697] The *virtue* of penance, on the other hand, is grief over past sin.[698] Sin leads

---

[693] *Reg Nov* 3,1. *Quia ad remissionem peccatorum requiritur contritio amara, confessio pura et satisfactio condigna... (Doctoris 8, 479;* Monti, *Works,* 157).

[694] *Quare* 18. *Praeceptum Dei est poenitentiam agere; nam dicitur: Poenitentiam agite, Matthaei quarto* [Matt 4,17], *cuius pars est confessio facta sacerdoti, primae Ioannis primo: Si confiteamur etc.* [1 John 1,9] *Cum ergo poenitens confitetur nobis, et absolvimus eum per auctoritate domini Papae vel episcopi, non tenetur iterum a plebano suo de eisdem absolvi, cum sit absolutus (Doctoris 8, 380); Reg Nov* 3,2. *Et sit confessio tua frequens, aperta et integra, verecunda et lacrymosa et cum contritione et sine excusatione (Doctoris 8, 480;* Monti, *Works,* 158). Cf. "Buße", 1141.

[695] *Prof* 1,29. *...nec pro divitiis, honoribus vel deliciis, nec pro amore amicorum vel proprii corporis dubitavit se tradere carceri poenitentiae propter Deum, non debet modo vilior esse, quam tunc fuit, ut pro verbis hominum deserat modo viam Dei, a cuius ingressu nec terroribus nec blanditiis potuit averti (David ab Augusta,* 39; Devas, *Spiritual Life* 1, 34).

[696] *Prof* 3,46. *...religionis, pro virtute obtinenda, pro vitio calcando, pro poenitentia agenda, pro aedificatione proximorum, pro gloria promerenda, pro acuendo intellectu et sapientia inquirenda (David ab Augusta,* 276; Devas, *Spiritual Life* 2, 110–111).

[697] *Prof,* Epist 2. *Primus, opera poenitentiae, quibus corpus spiritui servire cogitur, ut abstinentiae, vigiliae, disciplinae et similia (David ab Augusta,* 59–60; Devas, *Spiritual Life* 1, 54). Cf. *Prof* 2,1. *...quapropter poenitentiam age et prima opera fac* [cfr. Apoc 2,5] *(David ab Augusta,* 66; Devas, *Spiritual Life* 1, 61); *Prof* 3,29. *Quartum sunt opera poenitentiae, ut ieiunia, vigiliae, flagella et aliae corporales exercitationes et castigationes... (David ab Augusta,* 219; Devas, *Spiritual Life* 2, 58).

[698] *Prof* 3,39. *Pro se enim quilibet contristari debet pro praeteritis defectibus iustitiae, et tunc est virtus poenitentiae... (David ab Augusta,* 253; Devas, *Spiritual Life* 2, 89). Cf. *Prof* 1,13. *Primus annus est vera poenitentia de peccatis praeteritis... (David ab Augusta,* 18; Devas, *Spiritual Life* 1, 16). Our ignorance, concupiscence, malice, and weakness are the penalty (*poena*) of original sin (*Prof* 2,16; *David ab Augusta,* 102; Devas, *Spiritual Life* 1, 97).

to vengeance in the form of pain (*poena*) or punishment (*poenitentia*),[699] and only sinners who truly repent (*poenitentes*) will flee eternal punishment (*poenae aeternae*).[700]

10. PEACE

Origin

Although peace (*pax*) is a "universal value" and a highly secularised political concept in modern society, its western guise is deeply rooted in biblical, patristic, and medieval theology.[701] In the Old Testament, the word peace (*shalom*) has several meanings: it is used as a greeting, on epitaphs, and to describe the state of well-being or the state opposed to war.[702] In a theological and Messianic sense, it is the blessing and salvation of God, e.g., "He will proclaim peace to the nations."[703] Peace (*eirene*) in the New Testament is, in the Messianic sense of *shalom*, the salvation in Jesus Christ. It might be regarded as Jesus's main message: peace is reconciliation with oneself, peace of heart by the grace of God, eternal salvation, and the peace of heaven.[704] In Christ the peace of God has come to this

---

[699] *Prof* 2,28. *Sed cuncta, quae ad usum pravitatis infleximus, ad usum nobis vertentur ultionis, sive per poenam, sive per poenitentiam...* (*David ab Augusta*, 114; Devas, *Spiritual Life* 1, 108).

[700] *Prof* 2,20. *...quomodo poenitentes clementer suscepit...* (*David ab Augusta*, 26; Devas, *Spiritual Life* 1, 22); *Prof* 2,26. *...et impropitius amicis suis iustis et poenitentibus et convertentibus se ad ipsum...* (*David ab Augusta*, 112; Devas, *Spiritual Life* 1, 106); *Prof* 3,47. *...ut Religiosi et devoti et poenitentes...* (*David ab Augusta*, 280; Devas, *Spiritual Life* 2, 114); *Prof* 2,45. *Poenas aeternas amatoribus suis lucrantur* (*David ab Augusta*, 138; Devas, *Spiritual Life* 1, 131). Cf. *Prof* 3,19. *...ne velut poenitens boni inchoati quaerat diverticula declinandi de via perfectionis, in quo voverat ambulare* (*David ab Augusta*, 201; Devas, *Spiritual Life* 2, 42); *Prof* 3,37. *...ut cito et digne poeniteamus et satisfaciamus et emendemus* (*David ab Augusta*, 247; Devas, *Spiritual Life* 2, 83); *Prof* 3,56. *...et qui in Deum infinitum peccaverunt in infinitum quoad durationem poenarum crucientur* (*David ab Augusta*, 315; Devas, *Spiritual Life* 2, 148).

[701] Baarlink, *Vrede*; Becker & Hödl, "Friede"; Biser, "Friede"; De Blois & Bredero, *Kerk*; Brandenburger, *Frieden*; Comblin, *Théologie*; "Frieden und Gerechtigkeit"; Gross, *Die Idee*; Jüngel, *Zum Wesen*; Klassen, *Love*; *La paix*; Macquarrie, *The Concept*; Musto, *The Catholic*; "Paix"; Portolano, *L'etica*; Renna, "The idea"; Schmid, *Salôm*; Schmidt, *Frieden*; Vögtle, *Was ist Frieden?*.

[702] De Blois & Bredero, *Kerk*, 12. Cf. Biser, "Friede", 420–422; Comblin, *Théologie*; Gross, *Die Idee*, 61–63; "Paix", 40–42; Schmid, *Salôm*, 45–90.

[703] Zech 9,10. Cf. De Blois & Bredero, *Kerk*, 12.

[704] De Blois & Bredero, *Kerk*, 24. Cf. Biser, "Friede", 420–422; Comblin, *Théologie*; Klassen, *Love*; "Paix", 42–45; Vögtle, *Was ist Frieden?*. In Ef 6,15 the gospel of the revelation of God and the salvation in Jesus Christ is called "the gospel of peace."

earth; in the words of the angels who appeared to the shepherds: "Glory to God in the highest, and on earth peace to men on whom his favor rests."[705] Christ Himself is our peace.[706]

In Christian doctrine peace is a gift from God as well as a human task; it is built on the basic values and virtues of Christian anthropology.[707] Peace may indeed be called a virtue itself: with other virtues like charity, humility, and patience, for example, it is part of the Pauline virtue catalogues.[708] Within these catalogues, it fulfils a central role as the keeper of spiritual unity: "Be completely humble and gentle; be patient, bearing with one another in love. Make every effort to keep the unity of the Spirit through the bond of peace."[709] Peace is one of the fruits of the Holy Spirit: "But the fruit of the Spirit is love, joy, peace, patience, kindness, goodness, faithfulness, gentleness, and self-control."[710] Likewise, it is one of the beatitudes: "Blessed are the peacemakers, for they will be called sons of God."[711]

Francis

God and his gift

The early monastic authors concentrate on peace as "the interior repose of the holy soul in God" and "the inner rest (*tranquillitas*) as a foretaste of the heavenly *requies*."[712] In medieval theology, distinctions are made such as those between peace with God, with fellow man, and in spirit; between peace in time, in the inner self, and in eternity; and between peace with God, with oneself, and with others.[713] For Francis, peace is, first of all, heavenly peace (*pacem veram de caelo*)[714] and, as such, a gift from

---

[705] Luke 2,14; Rom 5,1.

[706] Eph 2,14.

[707] Cf. *Peace with Justice*, 17, 123.

[708] Wibbing, *Die Tugend- und Lasterkataloge*, 77–127. Cf. Thomas Aquinas, *Summa theologiae* 2a2ae,29,4 (Busa, *S. Thomae Aquinatis*, 566–567; Batten, *St. Thomas Aquinas*, 204–207).

[709] Eph 4,2–3. Other examples of these catalogues are: 2 Cor 6,6; Gal 5,22–23; 1 Tim 6,11; 2 Tim 2,22; 1 Pet 3,8.

[710] Gal 5,22–23.

[711] Matt 5,9; Luke 10,5. Cf. Lotz, *Eure Freude*; Perrin, *Die acht*.

[712] Renna, "The idea", 146.

[713] Becker & Hödl, "Friede", 920.

[714] *Ep Fid* 2,1. *...frater Franciscus, eorum servus et subditus, obsequium cum reverentia, pacem veram de caelo et sinceram in Domino caritatem.*

God: "May the Lord give you peace."[715] In this quality, it is also a salutation. The Peacegiver himself has revealed it to Francis as a greeting that the brothers should say to everybody, in whatever house they enter: "Let them first say: "Peace be to this house!""[716] This salutation of peace is as it were the Lord's "second gift," by which the brothers can convey his "first gift" (peace) to humanity.

The Lord's gift of peace to humanity brings "peace in the Lord." This is what Francis sends to the readers of his letter: "greetings and holy peace in the Lord."[717] In another instance, Francis sends esteem and reverence, true peace from heaven and sincere love in the Lord to all Christian religious people.[718] A true greeting brings true peace and true peace is holy peace, peace from heaven. This truth is implied in every greeting, even the simplest one from one simple brother to another.[719]

The human task

Like many of his predecessors, Francis is deeply influenced by the Augustinian idea that peace of heart in man will bring social peace in the world.[720] Peace, always a gift from God, will manifest itself in the world both individually ("in spirit and body") and collectively ("on earth").[721] His Spirit strives for true peace of spirit and for the (personal) virtues that

---

[715] Test 23. Salutationem mihi Dominus revelavit, ut diceremus: Dominus det tibi pacem (Armstrong, Francis of Assisi, 126); Ben Leo 2. Convertat vultum suum ad te et det tibi pacem (Num 6,24–26). Cf. RnB 11,2. ...immo studeant retinere silentium, quandocumque eis Deus gratiam largietur. On Francis and peace, see for instance: Bisschops, Franciscus, 379–382; Feld, Franziskus, 209–211; Flood, Francis, 76–78; Freeman, "Franciscus' vrede"; "Frieden"; Geulen, Die Armut, 121–126; Haskamp, "Franziskus"; Iriarte, Vocazione, 207–208; Jansen, "Vrede"; Karris, The Admonitions, 132–148; Kinsella, ""To Serve""; Lachance, "Mysticism", 71–75; Miccoli, "Francesco"; Rotzetter, Franz von Assisi, 109–110; Verhey, Der Mensch, 93–94; Zweerman, "Jezus' woord".

[716] RB 3,13; RnB 14,2. In quamcumque domum intraverint, primum dicant: Pax huic domui (cfr. Luke 10,5) (Armstrong, Francis of Assisi, 102).

[717] Ep Cust 2,1. Universis custodibus Fratrum Minorum, ad quos istae litterae pervenerint, frater Franciscus, minimus servorum Dei salutem et sanctam pacem in Domino (Armstrong, Francis of Assisi, 60).

[718] Ep Fid 2,1. ...frater Franciscus, eorum servus et subditus, obsequium cum reverentia, pacem veram de caelo et sinceram in Domino caritatem.

[719] Ep Leo 1. Frater Leo, frater Francisco tuo salutem et pacem. Cf. Ep Rec 1. ...frater Franciscus, vester in Domino Deo servus parvulus ac despectus, salutem et pacem omnibus vobis optans.

[720] Cf. Renna, "The idea", 147.

[721] Cf. Feld, Franziskus, 209. Man, the peacemaker, is an instrument in the hands of God, the Peacegiver. Peace has a "metaphysical, ethical, and organizational" dimension (Jansen, "Vrede").

make "pure and simple" peace possible, such as humility and patience.[722] Those preserving "peace of spirit and body" out of love of the Lord Jesus Christ, regardless of what they suffer in the world, are truly peacemakers:

> Blessed are the peacemakers, for they will be called children of God. Those people are truly peacemakers who, regardless of what they suffer in this world, preserve peace of spirit and body out of love of our Lord Jesus Christ.[723]

Blessed, children of God, will be those who keep their peace inwardly and outwardly out of love for Jesus Christ.[724] In fact, to have such a Brother and such a Son is peace-giving itself.[725] Peace originates in reverence and honor to the Body and Blood of the Lord Jesus Christ because in Him "that which is in heaven and on earth has been brought to peace" and reconciled to almighty God.[726] From this follows that those of good will (i.e., the virtuous and faithful) will enjoy peace on earth,[727] while peacemakers on earth will be blessed with peace in heaven.[728]

---

[722] RnB 17,15. Et studet ad humilitatem et patientiam et puram et simplicem et veram pacem spiritus; Adm 13,1–2. Beati pacifici, quoniam filii Dei vocabuntur (Matt 5,9). Non potest cognoscere servus Dei, quantam habeat patientiam et humilitatem in se, dum satisfactum est sibi; RB 3,11. ...sed sint mites, pacifici et modesti, mansueti et humiles, honeste loquentes omnibus, sicut decet. The combination of humility and patience can further be found in Adm 27,2; Ep Fid 2,44; RB 10,9.

[723] Adm 15,1–2. Beati pacifici, quoniam filii Dei vocabuntur (Matt 5,9). Illi sunt vere pacifici, qui de omnibus, quae in hoc saeculo patiuntur, propter amorem Domini nostri Jesu Christi in animo et corpore pacem servant (Armstrong, Francis of Assisi, 134). Here, peace is one of the beatitudes. It is also connected to suffering (cf. Freeman, "Vrede", 39–40; Zweerman, "Jezus' woord", 7–12).

[724] Cf. Ep Fid 1,1,10. Matres, quando portamus eum in corde et corpore nostro (cfr. 1 Cor 6,20)... Zweerman's (correct) interpretation of in animo et corpore pacem (Adm 15,2) is "peace of heart and peaceful behavior," peace "having to do with the actual harmony between inner disposition and outer conduct" (Zweerman, "Jezus' woord", 24–27). R.J. Karris speaks about "internal and external" peacemaking: "After religious have taken care of the war that rages internally between their mind (animus) and their vices, then they can engage in external peacemaking through their bodies (corpore)" (Karris, The Admonitions, 148).

[725] Ep Fid 2,56. O quam sanctum et quam dilectum, beneplacitum, humilem, pacificum, dulcem et amabilem et super omnia desiderabilem habere talem fratrem et filium, qui posuit animam suam pro ovibus suis (cfr. Joa 10,15) et oravit Patrem pro nobis dicens: Pater sancte, serva eos in nomine tuo, quos dedisti mihi (Joa 17,11).

[726] Ep Ord 12–13. Deprecor itaque omnes vos fratres cum osculo pedum et ea caritate, qua possum, ut omnem reverentiam et omnem honorem, quantumcumque poteritis, exhibeatis sanctissimo corpori et sanguini Domini nostri Jesu Christi, in quo quae in caelis et quae in terris sunt, pacificata sunt et reconciliata omnipotenti Deo (cfr. Col 1,20).

[727] Of Pas 5,15,8. Gloria in altissimis Domino Deo et in terra pax hominibus bonae voluntatis (cfr. Luke 2,14).

[728] Cant Sol 11. Beati quelli ke 'l sosterrano in pace, ka da te, altissimo, sirano incoronati.

Bonaventure

Outer, inner, eternal

Peace (*pax*) is threefold: inner, outer, and eternal.[729] Outer peace is directed at one's neighbour.[730] Being a true evangelical virtue – in particular, one of the beatitudes[731] – it delivers men from evil and promotes the good among them.[732] It makes them meek, pacifying (*pacificus*), modest, mild, humble, and honest.[733] Peace implies concordance (*concordia*) between men,[734] a bond (*nexus, connexio*) between two alike elements, such as there exists in the Godhead, where the First Principle, its Image, and the Bond between the two are present.[735] Whereas God is Uncontained Peace,[736] Christ is the King of Peace, born "in the quiet silence of universal peace," under the reign of Caesar Augustus.[737]

Peace among neighbours is fostered and guarded by silence, a "virtue" that preserves the peace of heart and body.[738] Inner peace (*pax pectoris*,

---

[729] *Serm Reg* 10. ...*pax pectoris, pax temporis, pax aeternitatis...* (*Doctoris* 8, 441). On Bonaventure and peace, see: Delio, *Simply Bonaventure*, 145–157.

[730] *Serm Reg* 9. *Item, virtus ordinans in proximum est pax* (*Doctoris* 8, 440).

[731] *Ap Paup* 3,8. ...*et: Beati pacifici...* (*Doctoris* 8, 246; De Vinck, *The Works* 4, 42).

[732] *Ex Reg* 3,15. ...*primum dicant: Pax huic domui, secundum doctrinam Christi, Matthaei decimo. Optando autem pacem optamus omnem liberationem a malo et promotionem in bono* (*Doctoris* 8, 411).

[733] *Serm Reg* 9. *Sint mites quoad animum, pacifici quoad verbum, modesti quoad factum, mansueti quoad proximum, humiles quoad Deum, honeste loquentes omnibus, sicut decet, quoad exemplum* (*Doctoris* 8, 440); *Ex Reg* 3,12. *Sed sint mites, cedendo improbitatibus; pacifici, minoritatis suae servando ordinem; et modesti, per disciplinam sensuum, operum et verborum; mansueti, moribus non impetuosi; et humiles, nullum honorem appetendo et omnem gloriam fugiendo* (*Doctoris* 8, 410).

[734] *Serm Reg* 9. *Pax est hominum ordinata concordia* (*Doctoris* 8, 410). Cf. *Serm Reg* 39. *Sed duplex est pax, scilicet quoad praelatum corrigentem et quoad Fratrem peccantem* (*Doctoris* 8, 447).

[735] *Trip Via* 3,7,11. *Pax etiam includit nexum plurium... necesse est ergo, quod si in divinis est vera pax, quod ibi sit prima origo, eius imago, utriusque connexio* (*Doctoris* 8, 17; De Vinck, *The Works* 1, 92).

[736] *Trip Via* 3,7,11. *Deus est lux inaccessibilis, mens invariabilis, pax incomprehensibilis...* (*Doctoris* 8, 17; De Vinck, *The Works* 1, 91).

[737] *Lign Vit* 1,4. *Sane, cum quietum silentium universalis pacis sub Caesaris Augusti imperio perturbata prius saecula serenasset in tantum... Et iam a conceptu excursis mensibus novem, Rex ille pacificus...* (*Doctoris* 8, 71; De Vinck, *The Works* 1, 106).

[738] *Perf* 4,1. ...*sic ex silentio nutritur iustitia, ex qua velut ex quadam arbore colligitur fructus pacis. Unde cum claustralibus pax sit summe necessaria, valde necessarium est eis silentium, per quod pax eis tam cordis quam corporis conservatur... tantae virtutis est silentium, quod in homine conservat Dei iustitiam et inter proximos pacem nutrit et custodit* (*Doctoris* 8, 115; De Vinck, *The Works* 1, 228).

pax animae, pax mentis), the second form of peace, consists in the avoidance of anything spiritually useless; in not being concerned or entangled in any way with things external or internal in which you find no profit for the soul; and in not letting anyone involve you in such things.[739] Internal peace and joy are restored in man if the flesh obeys the spirit, and if good work comes to fruit.[740] Purgation leads the soul to peace, as illumination leads it to truth and perfective union to love.[741] Through meditation, prayer, worship, and gradual ascension in love, great peace (*multitudo pacis*) and the consummation of inner rest (*finis quietis*) can be reached, consisting of perfect tranquillity (*perfectio tranquillitatis*).[742] Tranquillity, therefore, is the sixth and highest degree of the virtue of love (after sensitivity, avidity, satiety, ebriety, and security), wherein there "is such quiet (*requies*) and peace (*pax*) that the soul is, in a way, established in silence and is asleep, as if in Noah's Ark where tempests cannot reach." In this final degree, the soul "is at the goal, in peace and quiet," and here "the true Solomon finds its rest, for his place is in peace."[743] Seven further virtuous steps may lead the soul to the tranquillity of peace (*sopor pacis*), namely, shame, fear, sorrow, insistence, resoluteness, ardor, and quiet, the last step of which consists in "reposing in the shade of Christ, in a state (*status*) of happiness and rest (*requies*)."[744]

---

[739] *Ep Mem* 9. *Nonum, ut nihil eorum tangas, quae te spirituali utilitate non tangunt, hoc est, de nulla re cures vel implices te in aliquo exterius vel interius quoquo modo, ubi non invenis animae tuae lucrum, neque etiam in huiusmodi te ab aliquo implicari permittas...* (*Doctoris* 8, 494; De Vinck, *The Works* 3, 255); *Ep Mem*, Con. *...ingredi non poteris ad pacem mentis...* (*Doctoris* 8, 497; De Vinck, *The Works* 3, 262).

[740] *Quin Fest* 2,1. *...quia, dum quod diu mente conceptum est ad effectum boni operis perducitur, pax interioris hominis reformatur... Econtra, quando caro spiritui subiugatur, postquam bonum opus, quod diu per carnem est impeditum, perducitur ad effectum, pax et exsultatio interior reformatur* (*Doctoris* 8, 91; De Vinck, *The Works* 3, 206).

[741] *Trip Via* Prol,1. *Purgatio autem ad pacem ducit, illuminatio ad veritatem, perfectio ad caritatem* (*Doctoris* 8, 3; De Vinck, *The Works* 1, 63). Cf. *Trip Via* 3,1,1. *...ut scilicet habeat soporem pacis, splendorem veritatis, dulcorem caritatis* (*Doctoris* 8, 12; De Vinck, *The Works* 1, 80).

[742] *Trip Via* 2,5,12. *...debet per meditationem... Et sic per orationem... Tertio exhibeat latriam... Qui autem sic excitaverit se continue et intente, proficiet in caritate secundum sex gradus praedictos, quibus pervenitur ad perfectionem tranquillitatis, ubi est multitudo pacis et quasi quidam finis quietis...* (*Doctoris* 8, 11; De Vinck, *The Works* 1, 79).

[743] *Trip Via* 2,4,9. *Sextus gradus est vera et plena tranquillitas, in qua est tanta pax et requies, ut anima quodam modo sit in silentio et in somno et quasi in arca Noe collocata, ubi nullo modo perturbatur... In tali mente pax est et status ultimus et quies, et ibi requiescit verus Salomon, quoniam in pace factus est locus eius* (*Doctoris* 8, 10; De Vinck, *The Works* 1, 78).

[744] *Trip Via* 3,2,2. *Gradus autem perveniendi ad soporem pacis sunt isti septem... Nam primo occurrit pudor... Secundo, timor... Tertio dolor... Quarto, clamor... Quinto, rigor...*

The third form of peace, eternal peace, is the heavenly continuation of perfect outer and perfect inner peace. By "a tranquil and peaceful lifting of the heart" the souls of the just are made to conform to the heavenly Jerusalem, which is interpreted as "a vision of peace."[745] The "eternal possession of supreme peace" is one of the gifts of the glory of heaven constituting the full reward, together with the "clear vision of supreme truth" and the "full enjoyment of supreme goodness or love."[746] The just will find that heavenly peace is beautiful, of a wealthy rest, and undisturbed, i.e., without end.[747]

David

In and at peace

The good religious is at peace with himself, with others, and with God. First, he keeps his peace (*habere pacem secum*) and tranquillity in the face of malice from others.[748] Without inner peace he cannot be peaceful toward others:

> Do not wrangle (*esto pacificus*) on the road nor dispute with your companions, though you may be better informed and of steadier judgement than they. Asquiesce readily, cherish a kindly silence (*tace in tranquillitate animae*): seldom is anyone the better for argument. If you do not enjoy interior peace (*in te pacificus non es*) you will not be able to spread around you the spirit of peace (*pacificare*) or to lead others to it.[749]

Sexto, ardor... Septimo loco sequitur sopor in obumbratione Christi, ubi status est et requies... (*Doctoris* 8, 12; De Vinck, *The Works* 1, 81).

[745] *Ap Paup* 3,8. *...et: Beati pacifici, allicit ad sursumactionem limpidam in intellectu et tranquillam sive pacificam in affectu, quibus anima perfecti viri Ierusalem conformis efficitur, quae visio pacis interpretatur* (*Doctoris* 8, 246; De Vinck, *The Works* 4, 42).

[746] *Trip Via* 3,1,1. *In gloria autem triplex est dos, in qua consistit perfectio praemii, scilicet summae pacis aeternalis tentio, summae veritatis manifesta visio, summae bonitatis vel caritatis plena fruitio* (*Doctoris* 8, 11–12; De Vinck, *The Works* 1, 80).

[747] *Sol* 4,3,10. *...quia ibi est requies sine labore, vita sine morte, iuventus sine senectute, lux sine tenebris, pax imperturbabilis. Sedebit enim populus meus, dicit Dominus, in pulchritudine pacis, in tabernaculis fiduciae et in requie opulenta* (*Doctoris* 8, 59; De Vinck, *The Works* 3, 113).

[748] *Prof* 1,39. *...unde tu habeto pacem tecum...* (*David ab Augusta*, 53; Devas, *Spiritual Life* 1, 46). Cf. *Prof* 3,41. *...tu esto in pace apud te* (*David ab Augusta*, 259; Devas, *Spiritual Life* 2, 94).

[749] *Prof* 1,22. *Per terram autem vadens, esto pacificus; cum socio nunquam contendas de aliquo, etiamsi tu melius vel plus sentis quam ipse vel iustius noveris; sed cito cede et tace in*

Thus, second, the good religious strives to be mild and peaceably inclined (*habere cor pacificum, esse pacificus*) towards all.[750] Lastly, he shows himself a righteous man when he is at peace with God.[751]

Heavenly peace indeed begins here on earth, and the measure of the joys of heaven is determined by our charity now.[752] If it is truly spiritual love, it is quiet (*pacificus*), reasonable, and very tolerant of mistakes and shortcomings.[753] Peace, implying freedom from every trouble, is the fruit of patience born out of charity and humility.[754] Like these virtues it is a human (inner) quality,[755] an inducement to spiritual progress removing sin and subduing carnal instincts and unruly desires.[756] To men

---

tranquillitate animae, quia in contentionibus raro aliquis emendatur. Cogita, quod, si tu in te pacificus non es, vix vel nunquam poteris alium pacificare sive placare (David ab Augusta, 30; Devas, Spiritual Life 1, 26).

[750] *Prof 1,39. ...ad omnes cor mite et pacificum habere stude... (David ab Augusta, 52; Devas, Spiritual Life 1, 45); Prof 2,3. ...sicut quidam, qui ideo desiderant esse cum pacificis... (David ab Augusta, 82; Devas, Spiritual Life 1, 77); Prof 2,38. ...studemus in nobis esse pacifici... (David ab Augusta, 127; Devas, Spiritual Life 1, 121); Prof 3,22. Tertium est, ut semper cor pacificum cum omnibus habere studeamus... (David ab Augusta, 207; Devas, Spiritual Life 2, 47). Cf. Prof 1,3. Habe pacem semper cum praelatis... (David ab Augusta, 5; Devas, Spiritual Life 1, 5); Prof 1,18. Audi humiliter et pacifice bona... (David ab Augusta, 24; Devas, Spiritual Life 1, 21); Prof 2,16. ...ne filii Israel in ea pacifice habitarent... (David ab Augusta, 102; Devas, Spiritual Life 1, 97).*

[751] *Prof 1,24. ...si vis habere pacem cordis cum Deo (David ab Augusta, 34; Devas, Spiritual Life 1, 29); Prof 3,14. Sapiens corde est et fortis robore, quis restitit ei et pacem habuit? [cfr. Job 9,4] (David ab Augusta, 190; Devas, Spiritual Life 2, 31).*

[752] *Prof 2,38. Futuri enim domestici in domo Patris caelestis hic debent aeternae pacis foedus inchoare, quia, quanto hic ferventior dilectio, tanto illic iucundior fruitio aeternae pacis (David ab Augusta, 127; Devas, Spiritual Life 1, 121). Cf. Prof 3,57. Item, temporalia subsidia, ut pacem et aëris temperiem... (David ab Augusta, 323; Devas, Spiritual Life 2, 155).*

[753] *Prof 3,35. Spiritualis vero amor pacificus est, tractabilis, ignoscens errori et infirmitati proximi... (David ab Augusta, 238; Devas, Spiritual Life 2, 76).*

[754] *Prof 3,39. Ex caritate et humilitate nascitur virtus patientiae; haec ordinat nos ad fruitionem summae pacis. Nihil enim pati molestiae est pacem habere... (David ab Augusta, 251; Devas, Spiritual Life 2, 87). Cf. Prof 3,22. Semper ergo muniti incedamus contra iacula verborum et ictus factorum adversorum, ut pacem, quam exterius non possumus in hac vita sperare durabilem, saltem intus per patientiam conservemus... (David ab Augusta, 208; Devas, Spiritual Life 2, 48).*

[755] Cf. *Prof 3,54. Interim in nobis operare tibi regnum in iustitia et pace et gaudio Spiritus sancti [cfr. Rom 14,17] (David ab Augusta, 305; Devas, Spiritual Life 2, 138).*

[756] *Prof 3,51. ...et cito reliquos duos inimicos eius convertet ad pacem, ut subiiciat ei exactores suos, carnis libidinosum pruritum et affectionis illecebrosum appetitum (David ab Augusta, 290; Devas, Spiritual Life 2, 123).* Anger, for example, destroys peace of soul: *Et multa huiusmodi ira operatur et pacem cordis turbat... (Prof 2,39; David ab Augusta, 128; Devas, Spiritual Life 1, 122).*

of goodwill it is a gift of God, who crushes the assaults of temptation and vice.[757] In contemplation, finally, wherein "He seeks to settle His place in peace,"[758] the soul rests in the security of a peace all wholly divine.[759]

---

[757] *Prof* 3,51. *...quoniam ipse est Deus, qui tam potenter potuit et tam pie voluit impetus tentationum et vitiorum opprimere et pacem, quam per Scripturas saepe promittit, hominibus bonae voluntatis donare; Levitici, vigesimo sexto: Dabo pacem in finibus vestris* [cfr. Lev 26,6]... (*David ab Augusta*, 293; Devas, *Spiritual Life* 2, 126).

[758] *Prof* 2,39. *In pace factus est locus eius* [cfr. Ps 75,2] (*David ab Augusta*, 129; Devas, *Spiritual Life* 1, 123).

[759] *Prof* 3,63. *Ibi vere quiescit anima, ibi deliciatur in splendore lucis, in amoenitate divinae dulcedinis, in securitate pacis* (*David ab Augusta*, 347; Devas, *Spiritual Life* 2, 179).

CHAPTER THREE

THE VIRTUE OF VIRTUE

The early Franciscan writings concerned with the spirituality and organization of the fraternity, are central to the thirteenth-century formation process of the Franciscan Order, while the Franciscan notion of virtue in them is central to the early development of Franciscan thought. Francis, Bonaventure and David of Augsburg, among others, each offer a spiritual program for virtuous living. The virtues (charity, obedience, goodness, truth, faith, humility, joy, poverty, penance, peace, etc.) are central, organizing elements in the lives of the brothers and sisters who follow in the footsteps of their model, Jesus Christ.

1. CONFIGURATION

Franciscan virtues are essential building blocks of the Franciscan program of moral spirituality, in which virtuous living is the means (e.g., "to follow the teaching and footprints of our Lord Jesus Christ"[1]) to spiritual perfection (e.g., "their contempt for temporal goods gave perfection to them"[2]).[3] Within this program all virtues are co-virtues:[4] they frequently appear in the context of other virtues and rarely march alone. And although the program is built on many (more) biblical,[5] theological,[6] legal,[7] and spiritual[8] elements, the virtues participate in certain

---

[1] *RnB* 1,1. *...et Domini nostri Jesu Christi doctrinam et vestigia sequi...* (Armstrong, *Francis of Assisi*, 63–64).

[2] *Ap Paup* 8,21. *...quia perfectionem eis non contulit temporalium bonorum administratio, sed contemptus; non temporalis affluentia, sed spiritus paupertatis...* (*Doctoris* 8, 293; De Vinck, *The Works* 4, 186).

[3] See below, 3.8.

[4] The virtues are connected: *Sal Virt* 6. *Qui unam habet et alias non offendit, omnes habet* (Armstrong, *Francis of Assisi*, 164). Cf. Cessario, *The Moral*, 138–146.

[5] E.g., *RnB* 4,4. *...Quaecumque vultis, ut faciant vobis homines et vos facite illis* (Matt 7,12)... (Armstrong, *Francis of Assisi*, 66).

[6] E.g., *RnB* 4,5. *...Quod non vis tibi fieri, non facias alteri* (*Regula Benedicti* 61,14; 70,7; Armstrong, *Francis of Assisi*, 66).

[7] E.g., *RnB* 4,1. *In nomine Domini!* (A traditional formula used at the beginning of legal documents; Armstrong, *Francis of Assisi*, 66).

[8] E.g., *RnB* 4,3. *...quae spectant ad salutem animae...* (Armstrong, *Francis of Assisi*, 66).

well-known (e.g., *sunt communiter*)[9] sequences and schemes of biblical and/or theological origin,[10] that stand out to configure Franciscan spiritual life and structure Franciscan spiritual progress.[11] Francis mentions the theological virtues (*faith*, hope, *charity*);[12] the evangelical counsels or monastic vows (*obedience*, chastity, *poverty*);[13] the beatitudes (viz., *peace*, *poverty of spirit*, purity of heart);[14] and (what might be called) remedial virtues (*charity*, wisdom, patience, *humility*, *poverty*, *joy*, rest, fear, mercy, discernment).[15] He adds his own schemes of divine virtues (*goodness*, mercy, gentleness, delight, sweetness, holiness, justice, *truth*, holiness [*sic*], uprightness, kindness, innocence, cleanness;[16] and strength, greatness, highness, *goodness*, *truth*, *love* (charity), wisdom, *humility*, patience, beauty, meekness, security, rest, *gladness* (joy), hope, justice, moderation, richness, refreshment, *faith*, sweetness);[17] virtues of Christ (*humility*, *poverty*);[18] virtues of the Spirit (*humility*, patience, (purity, simplicity, *truth*), *peace*, fear, wisdom, *love*);[19] devotional virtues (*love*, gratitude, *humility*,

---

[9] *Prof* 3,28 (*David ab Augusta*, 215; Devas, *Spiritual Life* 2, 55).

[10] E.g., the evangelical counsels of *obedience*, chastity, and *poverty* (Matt 19; Mark 10; Luke 18), the beatitudes of *poverty of spirit*, sorrow, meekness, justice, mercy, purity of heart, and *peace* (Matt 5,3; Luke 6,20–22), and the Pauline catalogues of being *humble*, gentle, patient, bearing, *loving*, and *peaceful* (Eph 4,2–3); of purity, understanding, patience, kindness, and *love* (2 Cor 6,6); of *love*, *joy*, *peace*, patience, kindness, *goodness*, *faithfulness*, gentleness, and self-control (Gal 5,22–23); of *goodness*, justice, and *truth* (Eph 5,9); of patience, kindness, justice, *joy*, *truthfulness*, *faith*, hope, and perseverance (1 Cor 13); of *love*, *faith*, and purity (1 Tim 4,12); of justice, godliness, faith, *love*, endurance, and gentleness (1 Tim 6,11); of justice, *faith*, *love*, *peace*, and purity (2 Tim 2,22); of *faith*, patience, *love*, and endurance (2 Tim 3,10); and of *faith*, *goodness*, knowledge, self-control, perseverance, godliness, kindness, and *love* (2 Pet 1,5–7). Cf. Wibbing, *Die Tugend- und Lasterkataloge*, 77–127. Virtues from my selection are in italics.

[11] See below, 3.7. Behind the need for schematization and structuring of spiritual programs lies the general medieval need for order and orientation, and the growing tendency of medieval moral and spiritual thought to express itself in methodologies, systems, structures, degrees and lists (Pansters, *De kardinale*, 215–216); cf. Forster, "Über Reihen"; Hamm, "Von der spätmittelalterlichen", 76–77; Hellmann, *Ordo*; Krings, "Das Sein"; Krings, *Ordo*; Meier, "Organisation"; Müller, "Gradualismus"; Troelstra, *Stof*; Weber, "Richtungen"; Wildiers, *Kosmologie*, p. 95–97.

[12] *RnB* 23,11 (Armstrong, *Francis of Assisi*, 86); *Or Cruc* (Armstrong, *Francis of Assisi*, 40); *Laud Dei* 6 (Armstrong, *Francis of Assisi*, 109). Virtues from my selection are in italics.

[13] *RB* 1,1 (Armstrong, *Francis of Assisi*, 100); *RnB* 1,1 (Armstrong, *Francis of Assisi*, 63).

[14] *Adm* 13–16 (Armstrong, *Francis of Assisi*, 133–134).

[15] *Adm* 27 (Armstrong, *Francis of Assisi*, 136–137).

[16] *RnB* 23,9 (Armstrong, *Francis of Assisi*, 85).

[17] *Laud Dei* (Armstrong, *Francis of Assisi*, 109).

[18] *RnB* 9,1 (Armstrong, *Francis of Assisi*, 70); *RB* 6,2 (Armstrong, *Francis of Assisi*, 103); *RB* 12,4 (Armstrong, *Francis of Assisi*, 106); *Sal Virt* 2 (Armstrong, *Francis of Assisi*, 164).

[19] *RnB* 17,15–16 (Armstrong, *Francis of Assisi*, 76).

peace, sweetness, kindness, desire);[20] salutational virtues (wisdom, simplicity, *poverty*, *humility*, *charity*, *obedience*), which are also remedial
virtues;[21] and social (Pauline) virtues (meekness, *peace*, modesty, gentleness, *humility*, courtesy).[22]

Bonaventure mentions the theological virtues (*faith*, hope, *charity*);[23] the evangelical counsels or monastic vows (*obedience*, chastity,
poverty);[24] the beatitudes (*poverty of spirit*, meekness, sorrow, justice,
mercy, purity of heart, *peace*);[25] and Francis's social virtues (meekness,
peace, modesty, gentleness, *humility*, courtesy).[26] He adds his own
schemes of virtues of Mother and Child (*humility*, *poverty*, patience, *obedience*);[27] virtues of the perfect life (self-knowledge, *humility*, *poverty*,
silence, assiduity, remembrance, *love*, perseverance;[28] and mercy, kindness, *humility*, patience, modesty, chastity, *faith*, hope, *love*);[29] and virtues
of the imitation of Christ (*humility*, *poverty*, *charity*, patience,
obedience).[30]

David mentions the theological virtues (*faith*, hope, *charity*);[31] the cardinal virtues;[32] the evangelical counsels or monastic vows (*obedience*,
chastity, *poverty*);[33] the affections or movements of the will (hope, fear,
joy, sorrow, *love*, hatred, remorse);[34] the kinds of devotion (fear, sorrow,

---

[20] *Ep Fid* 1,1,13 (Armstrong, *Francis of Assisi*, 42); *Ep Fid* 2,56 (Armstrong, *Francis of Assisi*, 49).
[21] *Sal Virt* (Armstrong, *Francis of Assisi*, 164–165).
[22] *RB* 3,11 (Armstrong, *Francis of Assisi*, 102).
[23] *Vit Myst* 24,1 (*Doctoris* 8, 187; De Vinck, *The Works* 1, 202); *Ap Paup* 7,1 (*Doctoris* 8, 272; De Vinck, *The Works* 4, 125); *Ap Paup* 7,39 (*Doctoris* 8, 285; De Vinck, *The Works* 4, 162).
[24] *Ex Reg* 1,4 (*Doctoris* 8, 394); *Ap Paup* 3,10 (*Doctoris* 8, 247; De Vinck, *The Works* 4, 43).
[25] *Ap Paup* 3,8 (*Doctoris* 8, 246; De Vinck, *The Works* 4, 42).
[26] *Serm Reg* 9 (*Doctoris* 8, 440); *Ex Reg* 3,12 (*Doctoris* 8, 410); according to *RB* 3,11 (Armstrong, *Francis of Assisi*, 102).
[27] *Lign Vit* 2,8 (*Doctoris* 8, 72; De Vinck, *The Works* 1, 108–109).
[28] *Perf* (*Doctoris* 8, 107–127; De Vinck, *The Works* 1, 207–255).
[29] *Ap Paup* 7,39 (*Doctoris* 8, 285; De Vinck, *The Works* 4, 162).
[30] *Ep Im* 3 (Doctoris 8, 499).
[31] *Prof* 3,2 (*David ab Augusta*, 166; Devas, *Spiritual Life* 2, 8); *Prof* 3,28 (*David ab Augusta*, 217; Devas, *Spiritual Life* 2, 56); *Prof* 3,57 (*David ab Augusta*, 323; Devas, *Spiritual Life* 2, 156).
[32] *Prof* 3,28 (*David ab Augusta*, 217; Devas, *Spiritual Life* 2, 56).
[33] *Prof* 3,16 (*David ab Augusta*, 193; Devas, *Spiritual Life* 2, 34); *Prof* 2,30 (*David ab Augusta*, 117; Devas, *Spiritual Life* 1, 111).
[34] *Prof* 3,28 (*David ab Augusta*, 215–216; Devas, *Spiritual Life* 2, 55); *Prof*, Epist 2 (*David ab Augusta*, 60–61; Devas, *Spiritual Life* 1, 54–55); *Prof* 3,63 (*David ab Augusta*, 342; Devas, *Spiritual Life* 2, 174–175). Elsewhere these are fervor of *faith*, steadfastness of hope, sweet-ness of *charity*, alacrity in well doing, confidence about the forgiveness of past sin, and devotion to the person of Christ (*Prof* 3,2; *David ab Augusta*, 165; Devas, *Spiritual Life* 2, 7).

desire, *love*, compassion, *joy*, rapture of admiration);[35] and remedial virtues (*humility, charity*, self-control (benignity), zeal, generosity, temperance (sobriety), chastity).[36] He adds his own schemes of virtues of spiritual progress (*charity, humility*, patience, *obedience, poverty*, temperance, chastity);[37] virtues of the good religious (*humility, charity, obedience*, meekness, care in giving good example);[38] virtues of the imitation of Christ (*humility*, patience, *poverty, faith, obedience*, (service, contumeliousness, contempt));[39] virtues of God's servant (*love*, fear, fervor, *goodness, humility*, alertness, *joy*, hope, devotion);[40] novices' virtues (*goodness, peace*, silence, *charity, obedience, humility, poverty*, zeal, purity, wisdom, fear, diffidence, mercy, benignity, discernment, patience, chastity, devotion, justice), which are not listed as such;[41] virtues of humiliation (*humility, joy, patience*);[42] fruits of edification by patience (chastity, frugality, *poverty, humility*, generosity, devotion, wisdom, constancy, *faith*);[43] virtues for effective prayer (fervor, perseverance, *faith*, trust, *humility*);[44] and fruits of prayer (*faith*, hope, *charity, humility*, perseverance, desire).[45]

In spite of their differences of perspective and approach, the three authors show that many theological and spiritual schemes consist of virtues, while most virtues (and all the virtues of my selection except for penance) are part of one or more, traditional or new, schemes. In general, these schemes point out the ingredients necessary for a vigorous mental constitution, a good spiritual inclination, and an inspired life of devotion and prayer, all in the context of a healthy religious community. There are also dynamic schemes indicating trajectories of the soul moving towards God, or steps in the formation process of a

[35] *Prof* 3,65 (*David ab Augusta*, 352; Devas, *Spiritual Life* 2, 183).
[36] *Prof* 2,3 (*David ab Augusta*, 81; Devas, *Spiritual Life* 1, 76). Elsewhere, these are *humility, love of one's neighbour*, meekness, *love of God, contempt of riches*, sobriety, and chastity (*Prof* 3,30; *David ab Augusta*, 222; Devas, *Spiritual Life* 2, 61).
[37] *Prof* 3,27–51 (*David ab Augusta*, 214–294; Devas, *Spiritual Life* 2, 54–127).
[38] *Prof*, Epist 2 (*David ab Augusta*, 60; Devas, *Spiritual Life* 1, 54). Elsewhere, these are *faith, charity*, justice, *truth*, chastity, *obedience*, and *contempt for worldly interests* (*Prof* 2,12; *David ab Augusta*, 97; Devas, *Spiritual Life* 1, 93); and gravity, *humility*, and kindliness (*Prof* 3,18; *David ab Augusta*, 197; Devas, *Spiritual Life* 2, 38).
[39] *Prof* 2,28 (*David ab Augusta*, 113; Devas, *Spiritual Life* 1, 107); *Prof* 3,59 (*David ab Augusta*, 331; Devas, *Spiritual Life* 2, 163).
[40] *Prof* 3,59 (*David ab Augusta*, 329; Devas, *Spiritual Life* 2, 161–162).
[41] *Prof* 1 (*David ab Augusta*, 3–57; Devas, *Spiritual Life* 1, 1–49).
[42] *Prof* 3,41 (*David ab Augusta*, 261; Devas, *Spiritual Life* 2, 96).
[43] *Prof* 3,40 (*David ab Augusta*, 255; Devas, *Spiritual Life* 2, 91).
[44] *Prof* 3,61 (*David ab Augusta*, 337; Devas, *Spiritual Life* 2, 168).
[45] *Prof* 3,57 (*David ab Augusta*, 323; Devas, *Spiritual Life* 2, 156).

bonum spiritual community. All schemes consist of structuring elements, viz., virtues, that are crucial for spiritual life and progress. Furthermore, there is also a formal side to the structuring application of virtues, concerned with the organization of spiritual discourse and its mnemotechnical functionality. Configurations of virtues not only represent an intrinsic norm for moral and spiritual life, they also function as key compositional elements of texts (i.e., instruments in the hands of the composer) that aid the reader's memorization practices.[46] Whether in accordance with the overall plan of the work in which they appear (e.g., Bonaventure's eight "virtues" as the eight chapters of *De perfectione*) or not (e.g., David's seven virtues of spiritual progress as the nucleus of the sixth *processus*), all Franciscan configurations, structures, and sequences of virtues may be regarded as concrete literary manifestations of *ordo*-consciousness.[47]

2. Conceptualization

Regarding Franciscan virtues, a distinction must be made between (what I call) *divine qualities* (characteristics, substantials) and *spiritual* (divine-human) *virtues*. Franciscan *divine qualities* are properties of God that represent his perfect state of being, such as his immutability (*immutabilitas*), invisibility (*invisibilitas*), indescribability (*inenarrabilitas*), ineffability (*ineffabilitas*), sublimity (*sublimitas*), delightfulness (*delectabilitas*), and desirability (*desiderabilitas*).[48] These (non-human) "virtues" are here

---

[46] Cf. D'Avray, *The Preaching*, 249: "Formulae like *intellectus-affectus-effectus* and *fides-proles-sacramentum* belong to the history of the association of ideas. In the right context one knows that when one sees the first concept of the cluster the others will almost surely follow. The clusters are like molecules in which the individual concepts are held together by some mutual attraction."

[47] Cf. Pansters, *De kardinale*, 215–216.

[48] E.g., RnB 23,11. *...eum, qui sine initio et sine fine immutabilis, invisibilis, inenarrabilis, ineffabilis, incomprehensibilis, investigabilis* (cfr. Rom 11,33), *benedictus, laudabilis, gloriosus, superexaltatus (cfr. Dan 3,52), sublimis, excelsus, suavis, amabilis, delectabilis et totus super omnia desiderabilis in saecula.* Related to these is the species of angels called "virtues;" e.g., *Of Pas* 1,1 (Ant 3) *...ora pro nobis cum S. Michaele archangelo et omnibus virtutibus caelorum et omnibus sanctis apud tuum sanctissimum dilectum Filium, Dominum et magistrum* (Armstrong, *Francis of Assisi*, 141); RnB 23,6. *...et omnes choros beatorum seraphim, cherubim, thronorum, dominationum, principatuum, potestatum* (cfr. Col 1,15), *virtutum, angelorum, archangelorum...* (Armstrong, *Francis of Assisi*, 83); *Test* 40. *Et quicumque haec observaverit, incaelo repleatur benedictione altissimi Patris et in terra repleatur benedictione dilecti Filii sui cum sanctissimo Spiritu Paraclito et omnibus virtutibus caelorum et omnibus sanctis* (Armstrong, *Francis of Assisi*, 127).

called divine qualities, as the Franciscan authors attribute them only to God. The fact that they rarely appear in the Franciscan writings selected here makes clear that the authors did not want to write philosophical and theological treatises on the nature of God, but spiritual and pastoral treatises on the imitation of Christ and the soul's journey to God.

Much more frequent is the application of Franciscan *spiritual virtues*, which are "possessions" (*habere*) that have been "given from above" (*datum desuper*) by the Lord to all "who have died first" (i.e., who have died to the world and laid their lives in God's hands) and "who love the Lord with their whole heart, with their whole soul and mind, with their whole strength (*virtus*)."[49] Spiritual virtues are "fundamental characteristics" of the servant of God;[50] "right reasons" attaining their final end, followed by beatific life;[51] or "habits" (*habitus*) of the trained religious person.[52] These virtues may be called *human* (non-divine) virtues when they are only attributed to man and nowhere to God, as is the case with virtues such as zeal (*studium, diligentia, fervor, zelus*), fear (*timor*),[53] diffidence (*verecundia*), gratitude (*gratitudo*), solicitude (*sollicitudo*), reverence (*reverentia*), and sincerity (*sinceritas*). They may be called *divine* virtues when they are also (or primarily) attributed to God.[54] They may be called *biblical* virtues when they are taken from the Gospel where they are

---

[49] Cf. *Sal Virt* 5. *Nullus homo est penitus in toto mundo, qui unam ex vobis possit habere, nisi prius moriatur* (Armstrong, *Francis of Assisi*, 164); *Sal Virt* 18. *...ut possint facere de eo, quicquid voluerint, quantum fuerit eis datum desuper a Domino* (cfr. Joa 19,11) (Armstrong, *Francis of Assisi*, 165); *Ep Fid* 1,1,1. *Omnes qui Dominum diligunt ex toto corde, ex tota anima et mente, ex tota virtute* (cfr. Mark 12,30)... (Armstrong, *Francis of Assisi*, 41); *RnB* 23,8. *Omnes diligamus ex toto corde, ex tota anima, ex tota mente, ex tota virtute* (cfr. Mark 12,30)... (Armstrong, *Francis of Assisi*, 84). It is unclear if this *datum desuper* here refers to obedience (*Sal Virt* 14) only or to all the virtues in the *Salutation*, but in my opinion it can be applied to all spiritual virtues in Francis's conception.

[50] Armstrong, *Francis of Assisi*, 137.

[51] *Ap Paup* 2,3. *Denique, cum virtus omnis, ut ait Augustinus, sit ratio recta...* (*Doctoris* 8, 240; De Vinck, *The Works* 4, 21); *Ap Paup* 3,2. *Vere, perfecta virtus est ratio perveniens usque ad finem, quem beata vita consequitur* (*Doctoris* 8, 245; De Vinck, *The Works* 4, 38).

[52] *Prof* 2,5. *...ita virtus per corporalia exercitia addiscitur et in habitum vertitur* (*David ab Augusta* 87; Devas, *Spiritual Life* 1, 83). David's conception of *habitus* might be influenced by such influential scholastic definitions as Aquinas's "habits perfecting man" and Lombard's "good qualities of the mind." See also 1.9.

[53] I do not agree with the highly projective (anthropomorphic) view that *timor Domini* should be interpreted as a divine virtue (*timor Domini* as *genetivus subjectivus*) (Zweerman, "„Timor Domini'", 214).

[54] Cf. Ps 45,8 (46,7); Ps 45,12 (46,11); Ps 47,9 (48,8); Ps 58,6 (59,5).

displayed by Jesus, the Model of all virtue. They may be called *material virtues* when they are (sporadically and allegorically) attributed to material elements (or animals) in God's creation.[55] They may be attributed to other virtues.[56] Their *object* may be fellow man, the self, or God. But they are all *divine in origin*,[57] as everything good is, and essentially concerned with the human *Grundhaltung* that springs from the zeal (or "attention of love") for God.[58] Spiritual virtues are immediately concerned with the *whole* field of spirituality, here defined as a divine-human relational process:[59]

Table 3.1. Franciscan virtue: divine-human

Spiritual virtue		
Divine	*Relational process*	*Human*
Gift from God		*Human habit*

---

[55] E.g., *RnB* 16,2. *Estote ergo prudentes sicut serpentes et simplices sicut columbae* (Matt 10,16) (Armstrong, *Francis of Assisi*, 74); *Cant Sol* 7. *Laudato si, mi signore, per sor aqua, la quale è multo utile et humile et pretiosa et casta* (Armstrong, *Francis of Assisi*, 114); *Cant Sol* 8. *Laudato si, mi signore, per frate focu, per lo quale enn' allumini la nocte, ed ello è bello et iocundo et robustoso et forte* (Armstrong, *Francis of Assisi*, 114).

[56] E.g., *Adm* 3,6. *Nam haec est caritativa obedientia* (cfr. 1 Petr 1,22)... (Armstrong, *Francis of Assisi*, 130); *Adm* 9,2. *Ille enim veraciter diligit inimicum suum...* (Armstrong, *Francis of Assisi*, 132); *RnB* 4,3. *Et omnes alii fratres mei benedicti diligenter obediant eis in his...* (Armstrong, *Francis of Assisi*, 66).

[57] Spiritual virtue "responds to God's virtuous presence in the life of every Christian" (Armstrong, *Francis of Assisi*, 163). Cf. Nguyen-Van-Khanh, *Le Christ*, 137: "L'humilité, selon François, n'est donc pas d'abord comme nous le croyons couramment, une attitude vertueuse et loin d'être encore une vertu humaine. Elle est d'abord un *acte*, et un acte de Dieu, un acte du Père par lequel il fait don de lui-même à l'homme dans l'incarnation de son Fils. L'humilité de l'homme sera le don de lui-même à Dieu en réponse à la démanche première de l'amour divin;" Cessario, *The Moral*, 102–109.

[58] Cf. Esser & Grau, *Antwort*, 254–255: "Hier ist nun zunächst die überraschende Feststellung zu machen, daß sich Franziskus über einzelne Werke oder Übungen der Selbstverleugnung nur sehr spärlich äußert. Offensichtlich kommt es ihm viel mehr auf die G r u n d h a l t u n g an als auf bestimmte Anweisungen und Vorschriften. Daß sich der Mensch um Gottes willen und um des Reiches Gottes willen selbst verleugnen und alles ungeordnete Begehren seines eigenen Ich abtöten muß, darüber läßt Franziskus keinen Zweifel. Wie das aber im einzelnen zu geschehen hat, das anzuregen und durchzuführen überläßt er der „göttlichen Eingebung""; Cessario, *The Moral*, 34–44, 109–125. See also 1.9.

[59] Waaijman, *Spirituality*, 6, 312. See also 1.8.

Both aspects (given and inhabited) are equally important for the understanding of Franciscan virtues as *supernatural* virtues, as "habits received
through the Spirit from God" (*habitus a Deo dati*).[60] Franciscan spiritual
virtues are always both gifts from God (*datum desuper, bona gratiae, dona*,
etc.) *and* spiritual qualities of character (*habitus, possideas, ratio recta*,
etc.) to be acquired, developed, put into practice, and applied by a person
who wishes to follow in the footsteps of Jesus Christ and become perfect.[61]
As *moral* strengths,[62] they are the means and outcome of *spiritual* growth.
They are "gifts of grace" to religiously inspired people who "make God's
will their own"[63] and practice "good works," religious exercises like preaching and fasting.[64] They set people of good intention and great faith to good
behavior (*se habere; actu et habitu, mores et gestus et verba habere*) as an
expression of interior habit, virtuous behavior when aimed at higher
things. They are not, therefore, "natural" gifts (like nobility of birth, good
looks, physical health, mental ability)[65] nor manifestations of prowess,
but shares in God's virtue, Who *is* goodness, truth, charity, humility, joy,
faith, etc.

Apart from the distinction between divine qualities and spiritual virtues, one further distinction needs attention here: that between "fundamental characteristics of the servant of God" and "more specific
characteristics involving and flowing from prayer."[66] Whereas "normal"
spiritual virtues must be practiced in order to be had, or had in order to be
practiced,[67] the authors' definitions are broad enough to include spiritual
"virtues" that can only be had and not practiced, such as self-knowledge,

---

[60] See Appendix 3 for instances of (what I call) *"habitus datus"* in the writings of Francis,
Bonaventure, and David. Cf. *Sent* 2,9,1. *Vocatur autem hic gratia non aliquis habitus gratis
datus, sed gratia dicitur gratuita Dei influentia* (*Doctoris* 2, 239).

[61] Cf. Thomas Aquinas, *Summa theologiae* 1a2ae,55,1: "Virtue denotes a determinate perfection of a power (...) A power is said to be perfect, therefore, in so far as it is determined
to its act" (Busa, *S. Thomae Aquinatis*, 423; Hughes, *St. Thomas Aquinas*, 5).

[62] Matanic, *Francesco d'Assisi*, 57; Freyer, *Der demütige*, 197.

[63] *Adm* 2,3. *Ille enim comedit de ligno scientiae boni, qui sibi suam voluntatem appropriat et se exaltat de bonis quae Dominus dicit et operatur in ipso...* (Armstrong, *Francis of
Assisi*, 129).

[64] *Prof* 2,12. *Bona gratiae sunt virtutes, scientia et opera de genere bonorum, ut praedicare, ieiunare et similia* (*David ab Augusta*, 96; Devas, *Spiritual Life* 1, 92).

[65] *Prof* 2,12. *Bona naturae sunt quae natura contulit, ut nobilitas, pulchritudo, fortitudo,
ingenium et similia* (*David ab Augusta*, 96; Devas, *Spiritual Life* 1, 92).

[66] Armstrong, *Francis of Assisi*, 137.

[67] Cf. Thomas Aquinas, *Summa theologiae* 1a2ae,55,1: "A power is said to be perfect,
therefore, in so far as it is determined to its act" (Busa, *S. Thomae Aquinatis*, 423; Hughes,
St. Thomas Aquinas, 5).

or can only be practiced (viz., held) and not had, such as silence.[68] In other instances, these virtues would more likely be defined as the prerequisites, or products, of virtue.

3. SYSTEMATIZATION

The works selected here are not scholastic works, but many of them contain one or more scholastic schemes, concepts, classifications, distinctions, arrangements, correspondences, or indexes. Francis seems to have some (indirect) knowledge of early scholastic concepts and themes, such as the *connexio virtutum* and the function of remedial virtues, and he "structures" some of his texts according to enumerations, pairs, or oppositions.[69] Some of these do not seem to follow much logic and are therefore surprising, e.g., "where there is charity and wisdom, there is neither fear nor ignorance,"[70] instead of "there is no fear in love" (1 John 4,18). The question remains why Francis uses *pairs* at all here,[71] although he is used to thinking in pairs (the humility and poverty of Christ;[72] to humbly and faithfully fulfil;[73] to be simple and infirm;[74] etc.). Other "structuring elements" in his writings are more understandable, although they also seem to do no more than *list* the virtues in question by way of parataxis or chiasmus: the three theological virtues,[75] the virtues of the Spirit,[76] the wonderful loftiness and stupendous dignity and sublime humility and humble sublimity of Christ,[77] etc. Further, although Francis sometimes

---

[68] E.g., *Perf* 1 and 4.

[69] This is what I call the "external" (macro-level) configuration of virtues (see 3.1). Apart from this, there is a "defining" (meso-level) conceptualization, or classification, of virtues (see 3.2), and an "internal" (micro-level) subdivision or gradation of virtues. Cf. Pansters, *De kardinale*, 210.

[70] *Adm* 27,1. *Ubi caritas est et sapientia, ibi nec timor nec ignorantia* (Armstrong, *Francis of Assisi*, 136).

[71] Zweerman, "„Timor Domini"", 203.

[72] E.g., *RnB* 9,1. *Omnes fratres studeant sequi humilitatem et paupertatem Domini nostri Jesu Christi...* (Armstrong, *Francis of Assisi*, 70).

[73] *RnB* 20,2. *...si poenitentiam sibi iniunctam procuraverint humiliter et fideliter observare* (Armstrong, *Francis of Assisi*, 77).

[74] *Test* 29. *Et quamvis sim simplex et infirmus...* (Armstrong, *Francis of Assisi*, 126).

[75] E.g., *Laud Dei* 6. *Tu es spes nostra, tu es fides nostra, tu es caritas nostra...* (Armstrong, *Francis of Assisi*, 109).

[76] *RnB* 17,15. *Et studet ad humilitatem et patientiam et puram et simplicem et veram pacem spiritus* (Armstrong, *Francis of Assisi*, 75–76).

[77] *Ep Ord* 27. *O admiranda altitudo et stupenda dignatio! O humilitas sublimis! O sublimitas humilis...* (Armstrong, *Francis of Assisi*, 118).

subordinates virtues to have one virtue serve another,[78] or *quantifies* virtue in terms of "how much" one has of it,[79] he adds no *gradations* of virtue, which would have been convenient, for example, to emphasize that spiritual life is a process towards perfection consisting of successive (elements of) virtues. Nor does he *subdivide* single virtues into sub-virtues, degrees, effects, or stages, as do Bonaventure and David so often in their writings.

Unlike Francis, Bonaventure has a scholastic background, which not only shows itself in the structure and contents of his theological works, but is also evident from the structure and contents of his pastoral and spiritual works. He adds many lists and distinctions to clarify his argument and, most likely, support the memorization of the contents. Virtues are not only defined and described, but also listed, gradated, and subdivided.[80] They function as stages in a spiritual process, for example, as virtuous steps to peace (shame, fear, sorrow, insistence, resoluteness, ardor, quiet).[81] An Augustinian hierarchy (*ordo*) of virtue connects the main virtues and appoints them to their respective functions: humility is the foundation (*fundamentum*) of virtue and charity the purpose (*finis*) and fulfilment (*complementum*) of perfection.[82] But charity is also the source of virtue (*fecunditas*) and root (*radix*) of perfection,[83] whereas poverty is the foundation of perfection.[84] In whatever role, the

---

[78] E.g., *Adm* 3,3. *Nam haec est caritativa obedientia* (cfr. 1 Petr 1,22)... (Armstrong, *Francis of Assisi*, 130).

[79] E.g., *Adm* 13,1–2. *Non potest cognoscere servus Dei, quantam habeat patientiam et humilitatem in se, dum satisfactum est sibi. Cum autem venerit tempus, quod illi qui deberent sibi satisfacere, faciunt sibi contrarium, quantam ibi patientiam et humilitatem tantam habet et non plus* (Armstrong, *Francis of Assisi*, 133).

[80] Viz., on a meso-, macro-, and micro-level.

[81] *Trip Via* 3,2,2. *Gradus autem perveniendi ad soporem pacis sunt isti septem... Nam primo occurrit pudor... Secundo, timor... Tertio dolor... Quarto, clamor... Quinto, rigor... Sexto, ardor... Septimo loco sequitur sopor in obumbratione Christi, ubi status est et requies...* (*Doctoris* 8, 12; De Vinck, *The Works* 1, 81).

[82] E.g., *Perf* 2,1. *...sic fundamentum omnium virtutum est humilitas* (*Doctoris* 8, 110; De Vinck, *The Works* 1, 216); *Ap Paup* 3,2. *Sciendum est igitur, quod radix, forma, finis, complementum et vinculum perfectionis caritas est...* (*Doctoris* 8, 244; De Vinck, *The Works* 4, 37). Cf. Schaffner, *Christliche*, 287–293.

[83] *Sol* 1,4,45. *O felix amor, ex quo oritur strenuitas morum, puritas affectuum, subtilitas intellectuum, sanctitas desideriorum, claritas operum, fecunditas virtutum, dignitas meritorum, sublimitas praemiorum et honorum* (*Doctoris* 8, 43; De Vinck, *The Works* 3, 73); *Ap Paup* 3,2. *Sciendum est igitur, quod radix, forma, finis, complementum et vinculum perfectionis caritas est...* (*Doctoris* 8, 244; De Vinck, *The Works* 4, 37).

[84] E.g., *Ap Paup* 7,3. *...certa potest ratione concludi, quod perfectionis evangelicae, per quam Christo configuramur et complantamur et habitaculum eius efficimur, ipsa paupertas spiritus, secundum quandam analogiam et cohaerentiam ad praedicta, radix est et*

virtues have plural acts (*actus*)[85] and consist of various states (*status*), steps, and levels or degrees (*gradus*), from imperfect to perfect.[86]

Like Bonaventure, David is a much more systematic thinker than Francis. He sums up many virtues and vices, defines and describes their nature, and explains the function of many of them by analyzing their different steps, levels, and operations.[87] He subdivides religious life into three kinds and stages[88] and spiritual life into seven stages (*processus*), the sixth of which is the acquisition of seven key virtues.[89] Virtue is "well-ordered love" (*amor ordinatus*) arranging the human affections, while charity (the "well-ordered will to serve God"[90]) consists of eighteen sub-virtues, a list including the double commandment, the theological virtues, the cardinal virtues, and the virtue that is elsewhere called the "mother of the virtues," humility.[91] Charity has three principles and three degrees

---

fundamentum (*Doctoris* 8, 272; De Vinck, *The Works* 4, 126). Poverty is also the queen of the virtues, e.g., *Leg Franc* 7,1. *...inde hanc virtutum asserens esse reginam...* (*Doctoris* 8, 523; Cousins, *Bonaventure*, 240).

[85] E.g., *Ap Paup* 3,3. *...insinuans triplicem actum caritatis, videlicet declinare mala, prosequi bona et patienter ferre adversa. Nam propter declinationem malorum dicitur de corde puro; propter prosecutionem bonorum, de conscientia bona; propter tolerantiam adversorum, de fide non ficta...* (*Doctoris* 8, 245; De Vinck, *The Works* 4, 38–39).

[86] E.g., *Trip Via* 2,3,8. *Et hic est status et gradus perfectae caritatis, ante cuius assecutionem nemo debet se aestimare perfectum* (*Doctoris* 8, 9; De Vinck, *The Works* 1, 76); *Trip Via* 2,4,9–11 *...quod sex sunt gradus, quibus paulatim et ordinate proceditur, ut ad perfectum perveniatur* (*Doctoris* 8, 10–11; De Vinck, *The Works* 1, 77–79); *Trip Via* 3,4,6. *Gradus veniendi ad dulcorem caritatis per susceptionem Spiritus sancti sunt isti septem, scilicet vigilantia sollicitans, confidentia confortans, concupiscentia inflammans, excedentia elevans, complacentia quietans, laetitia delectans, adhaerentia conglutinans; in quibus hoc ordine progredi debes, qui vis ad perfectionem caritatis pertingere et ad amorem Spiritus sancti* (*Doctoris* 8, 14; De Vinck, *The Works* 1, 86); *Ap Paup* 3,2. *Ipsa vero caritas triplicem habet statum: unum quidem infimum, in observantia mandatorum legalium; secundum vero medium, qui constat in adimpletione spiritualium consiliorum; tertium autem supremum, in perfruitione sempiternalium iucunditatum* (*Doctoris* 8, 244; De Vinck, *The Works* 4, 37); *Ap Paup* 2,3. *Cum ergo aliqua caritas sit imperfecta...* (*Doctoris* 8, 240; De Vinck, *The Works* 4, 21); *Ex Reg* 1,6. *Obedientia tamen, secundum quod dicit statum eminentem virtutis obedientiae, plures habet gradus* (*Doctoris* 8, 394).

[87] Viz., on a macro-, meso-, and micro-level.

[88] *Prof* 2,3 (*David ab Augusta*, 77–83; Devas, *Spiritual Life* 1, 73–79); *Prof* 2,4 (*David ab Augusta*, 84–85; Devas, *Spiritual Life* 1, 79–80).

[89] There are alternative *ordines virtutum*, e.g., that of remedial virtues (*Prof* 3,30. *Huic per contrarium opponitur ordo virtutum, scilicet humilitas contra superbiam, dilectio proximi contra invidiam, mititas contra iram, caritas Dei contra accidiam, contemptus divitiarum contra avaritiam, sobrietas contra gulam, castitas contra luxuriam* (*David ab Augusta*, 222; Devas, *Spiritual Life* 2, 61)).

[90] *Prof* 3.31. *Caritas est ordinata et magna voluntas serviendi Deo...* (*David ab Augusta*, 223; Devas, *Spiritual Life* 2, 62).

[91] *Prof* 3,32. *Ita caritas est una virtus in se omnem habens virtutem, sed propter diversos effectus eius ex diversis extrinsecis occasionibus vel causis illatis, quibus se vel contra malum*

marked by three stages,[92] as do the other virtues.[93] In this way, many more distinctions and degrees clarify the nature of virtuous living in a static (e.g., *ordo virtutum*) or dynamic (e.g., *paulatim et ordinate proceditur*) way.

All in all, the above-mentioned examples of systematization (enumeration, categorization, subordination, gradation, etc.) show that the development of the formal side of Franciscan virtue discourse, concerned with the *structure* of spiritual texts as with the *structure* of spiritual lives,[94] may be considered to be a most important part of Franciscan moral spirituality.[95] It finds its great parallel in the historical development from a primitive fraternity to a highly organized spiritual order,[96] much of which Francis is the spiritual father, Bonaventure the architect, and David a key project manager.

4. ELABORATION

In the spiritual writings of Francis, Bonaventure, and David, many theological key themes are closely connected to the theme of virtue. In order to further explain the theological contents and contexts of *virtus*, I will now have a look at some of these themes (vice, precept, will, zeal, and fruit) in relation to the acquisition and realization of virtue. First, vice (*vitium*) and sin (*peccatum*) are related to worldly and bodily, as opposed

---

opponit, vel ad bonum extendit, diversa officia vel nomina sortitur. Virtus enim, sicut definit Augustinus, 'est amor ordinatus'... (David ab Augusta, 226–227; Devas, *Spiritual Life* 2, 65–66); *Prof*, Epist 2. *...et omnes affectus in virtutes ordinare...* (David ab Augusta, 61–62; Devas, *Spiritual Life* 1, 54–55); *Prof* 3,38. *Unde non est mirum, si inopes sumus virtutum, cum matrem et custodem virtutum, humilitatem, tam alienam a nobis sentiamus* (David ab Augusta, 249; Devas, *Spiritual Life* 2, 85).

[92] E.g., *Prof* 3,31. *Dilectio nostra in tribus consistit: in voluntate, in opere, in affectu* (David ab Augusta, 224; Devas, *Spiritual Life* 2, 62–63); *Prof* 3,33. *...et quibus profectuum gradibus distinguantur. Unaquaeque enim virtus, teste beato Gregorio, habet initium suum et profectum et perfectionem...* (David ab Augusta, 227; Devas, *Spiritual Life* 2, 66); *Prof* 3,33. *Caritas Dei, mater et nutrix omnium virtutum, tres habet gradus...* (David ab Augusta, 228; Devas, *Spiritual Life* 2, 66).

[93] E.g., *Prof* 3,42. *Ratio obedientiae triplex est...* (David ab Augusta, 262; Devas, *Spiritual Life* 2, 97).

[94] Cf. Bertaud & Rayez, "Échelle"; Blommestijn, "Progrès", 2384; Rahner, "Über das Problem"; Saudreau, *Les degrés*; Solignac, "Voies".

[95] Cf. Hellmann, *Ordo*; Speer, *Triplex*; Bohl, *Geistlicher*, 228; Pansters, "Gerechtigkeit"; Zweerman, ",,Timor Domini''", 223.

[96] See below, 3.7.

to holy and spiritual, things.[97] They go against the soul and the rule.[98] They are the opposite of virtue, and virtue is their remedy (*curatio, remedium*[99]): virtue "confounds vice and sin."[100] In opposition to his list of "remedial" virtues, Francis mentions fear, ignorance, anger, disturbance, greed and avarice, anxiety, restlessness, excess, and hardness of heart.[101] Two of these belong to the seven capital vices, or cardinal sins, of medieval morality: pride (*superbia*), envy (*invidia*), anger (*ira*), sloth (*accidia*), avarice (*avaritia*), gluttony (*gula*), and lust (*luxuria*).[102] Certain vices pose as virtues but are in reality, and in an Aristotelian sense, the harmful extremes of a healthy middle (virtue).[103] The capital and many other vices hamper inner reform and the virtuous ascension to perfection, and must therefore be earnestly hated and deplored.[104]

Second, the precept (*praeceptum*) of virtue is one of the main instructive elements of Franciscan spiritual (pastoral, educational,

---

[97] E.g., *Ep Fid* 1,1,1–4. *Omnes qui Dominum diligunt ex toto corde, ex tota anima et mente, ex tota virtute* (cfr. Mark 12,30) *et diligunt proximos suos sicut se ipsos* (cfr. Matt 22,39), *et odio habent corpora eorum cum vitiis et peccatis, et recipiunt corpus et sanguinem Domini nostri Jesu Christi, et faciunt fructus dignos poenitentiae...* (Armstrong, *Francis of Assisi*, 41); *Test* 1. ...*cum essem in peccatis...* (Armstrong, *Francis of Assisi*, 41). David's view is different: he sees vice not so much as a bodily threat to spiritual health, but as disease threatening the health of both body and soul (*vitia carnis et spiritus*), the last of which is much more precious: *Prof* 3,15. *In quantum vero plus de corporis sanitate sumus quam de animae salute solliciti, in tantum convincimur illud plus diligere et eius sanitatem amplius desiderare* (David ab Augusta, 192; Devas, *Spiritual Life* 2, 33). In any case, the sinful man thinks of nothing other than what is material and corporal, e.g., *Prof* 2, Praef 1. ...*et quia iam non intelligit nisi corporalia...* (David ab Augusta, 65; Devas, *Spiritual Life* 1, 59).

[98] *RB* 10,1. ...*quod sit contra animam suam et regulam nostram* (Armstrong, *Francis of Assisi*, 105).

[99] E.g., *Prof* 3,15. *Hic potest status curationis vel remediorum spiritualium dici...* (David ab Augusta, 192; Devas, *Spiritual Life* 2, 33).

[100] *Sal Virt* 8. *Et unaquaque confundit vitia et peccata* (Armstrong, *Francis of Assisi*, 164). Here, Francis mentions wisdom of this world, wisdom of the body, desire for riches, greed, cares of this world, pride, carnal temptation, and carnal fear as the vices confounded by virtue.

[101] *Adm* 27 (Armstrong, *Francis of Assisi*, 126).

[102] In the order of David's second book. Cf. *Prof* 3,30. *Huic per contrarium opponitur ordo virtutum, scilicet humilitas contra superbiam, dilectio proximi contra invidiam, mititas contra iram, caritas Dei contra accidiam, contemptus divitiarum contra avaritiam, sobrietas contra gulam, castitas contra luxuriam* (David ab Augusta, 222; Devas, *Spiritual Life* 2, 61). On the capital vices in the Middle Ages, see Newhauser, *In the Garden*.

[103] *Prof* 3,48 (David ab Augusta, 282–284; Devas, *Spiritual Life* 2, 116–117). Cf. *Prof* 3,48. *Spiritualis laetitia sic accidiam vel tristitiam declinat, ut quandoque in dissolutionem incidat et vanam laetitiam* (David ab Augusta, 283; Devas, *Spiritual Life* 2, 117).

[104] E.g., *Prof* 2,16. ...*et quae ex peccato in vitium mutatae sunt, studeamus reformare et in virtutes mutare, expulsis corruptionibus vitiorum* (David ab Augusta, 103; Devas,

edifying) literature. Francis and his learned brothers preach the Gospel above all, and they do this for "those who desire to become perfect."[105] Divine law is their source and inspiration;[106] they follow and elaborate on biblical imperatives like the ten commandments (Exod 20,2–17; Deut 5,6–21), the beatitudes (Matt 5,3–11; Luke 6,20–26), and the three evangelical counsels (cf. Matt 19,10–12, Matt 19,20–21, Mark 10, 20–21; Luke 18,21–22; 1 Cor 7).[107] They repeat the Lord's *hoc est praeceptum meum*,[108] summon their brothers to live in obedience, chastity, and poverty,[109] and proclaim

---

Spiritual Life 1, 98); *Prof* 3,2. *...quae afficiunt hominem ad Deum et ad amorem virtutum et ad odium vitiorum...* (*David ab Augusta*, 165; Devas, *Spiritual Life* 2, 7); *Perf* 1,2. *Item debes recogitare, quam negligens sis vel fueris ad poenitendum, quam negligens ad resistendum et quam negligens ad proficiendum. Debes enim cum summa diligentia deflere mala commissa, repellere diabolica tentamenta et proficere de una virtute in aliam* [cfr. Ps. 83,8], *ut possis pervenire ad terram promissam* (*Doctoris* 8, 108); De Vinck, *The Works* 1, 212–213); *Sol* 1,4,45. *...in iniquitate gemens...* (*Doctoris* 8, 43; De Vinck, *The Works* 3, 73); *Adm* 9,3. *...sed de peccato animae suae uritur propter amorem Dei* (Armstrong, *Francis of Assisi*, 132).

[105] Cf. Matt 19,21.

[106] E.g., *Ap Paup*, Prol,1. *Summi legislatoris inviolabili constat definitione sancitum, sic maiestati aeternae cultum debitum esse reddendum, quod idolorum cultura vitetur; sic redigendum intellectum creatum in summae veritatis obsequium, quod nullus falsitati praebeatur assensus; sic vacandum sanctificationi spirituum, quod ferietur a servitute carnalium voluptatum; sic denique virtutum deiformium approbandam esse rectitudinem, quod deformantium vitiorum pravitas reprobetur* (*Doctoris* 8, 233; De Vinck, *The Works* 4, 1).

[107] E.g., *Ep Fid* 2,39. *Debemus observare praecepta et consilia Domini nostri Jesu Christi* (Armstrong, *Francis of Assisi*, 48); *Ep Fid* 2,16. *...nolentes adimplere mandata Dei...* (Armstrong, *Francis of Assisi*, 46); *Ap Paup* 3,2. *Ipsa vero caritas triplicem habet statum: unum quidem infimum, in observantia mandatorum legalium; secundum vero medium, qui constat in adimpletione spiritualium consiliorum; tertium autem supremum, in perfruitione sempiternalium iucunditatum. Ideo triplex est perfectionis differentia in Scriptura sacra descripta...* (*Doctoris* 8, 244; De Vinck, *The Works* 4, 37); *Ap Paup* 3,3. *Omnia vero, tam praecepta quam consilia, referuntur ad caritatis illius impletionem et observantiam, quam sic describit Apostolus ad Timotheum: Caritas est finis praecepti de corde puro, conscientia bona et fide non ficta, insinuans triplicem actum caritatis, videlicet declinare mala, prosequi bona et patienter ferre adversa* (*Doctoris* 8, 245; De Vinck, *The Works* 4, 38); *Prof* 3,43. *Profectus vel gradus obedientiae, quantum ad illa, in quibus obediendum est, colligi possunt ex praedictis, id est obedire ad praecepta communia, obedire ad aliqua etiam consilia, obedire ad omnia bona et possibilia* (*David ab Augusta*, 265; Devas, *Spiritual Life* 2, 100).

[108] E.g., *RnB* 11,5. *Et diligant se ad invicem, sicut dicit Dominus: Hoc est praeceptum meum ut diligatis invicem sicut dilexi vos* (Joa 15,12) (Armstrong, *Francis of Assisi*, 72); *Quare* 18. *Praeceptum Dei est poenitentiam agere; nam dicitur: Poenitentiam agite, Matthaei quarto* [Matt 4,17]*...* (*Doctoris* 8, 380); *Prof* 3,34. *...propter Deum, quia ipse mandavit...* (*David ab Augusta*, 232; Devas, *Spiritual Life* 2, 70).

[109] E.g., *RnB* 1,1. *Regula et vita istorum fratrum haec est, scilicet vivere in obedientia, in castitate et sine proprio...* (Armstrong, *Francis of Assisi*, 63); *Prof* 3,16. *...voti proprii sponsionem discretam, ut est votum continentiae, obedientiae et abdicationis proprietatis...* (*David ab Augusta*, 193; Devas, *Spiritual Life* 2, 34).

that pure virtues "proceed from the eternal law."[110] In this way, principle of precept and pedagogical zeal are starting-points for their development of an evangelical program of virtuous living.

Third, the human will (voluntas) on its own expresses itself in sinful wishes,[111] but in three ways it is possible to bend it and aim it back at the good.[112] First of all, when by voluntary obedience[113] and for the sake of God[114] one's own will is sacrificed[115] and renounced for that of a superior,[116] corporal and carnal wishes are confounded.[117] Then, when all desires and wishes are rightly set upon loving God[118] in order to do the will of the

---

[110] E.g., Sex Alis 2,7. Horum quaedam procedunt a lege aeterna, ut purae virtutes: humilitas, castitas, caritas, misericordia et similes, sine quibus nullus quocumque tempore poterit salvari... (Doctoris 8, 134; De Vinck, The Works 3, 144); Prof 2,12. Bona nostra, ad quae tenemur ex praecepto Dei vel Ecclesiae, vel ad quae ex manifesto voto adstringimur, debemus hominibus ostendere, ut fidem, caritatem, iustitiam, veritatem, castitatem, obedientiam et contemptum mundanorum (David ab Augusta, 97; Devas, Spiritual Life 1, 93).

[111] E.g., RnB 22,6. ...quia nos per culpam nostram sumus foetidi, miseri et bono contrarii, ad mala autem prompti et voluntarii... (Armstrong, Francis of Assisi, 79); Prof 3,48. Obedientia indiscreta sic fugit propriae voluntatis vitium, ut obediat superiori etiam ad peccatum... (David ab Augusta, 283–284; Devas, Spiritual Life 2, 117).

[112] E.g., Of Pas 5,15,8. ...et in terra pax hominibus bonae voluntatis (cfr. Luke 2,14) (Armstrong, Francis of Assisi, 156).

[113] E.g., RnB 5,14. ...immo magis per caritatem spiritus voluntarie serviant et obediant invicem (cfr. Gal 5,13) (Armstrong, Francis of Assisi, 67–68); Test 8. Et ipsos et omnes alios volo timere, amare et honorare, sicut meos dominos (Armstrong, Francis of Assisi, 125); Prof 1,12. Nam tam voluntarius debes esse ad obedientiam... (David ab Augusta, 16; Devas, Spiritual Life 1, 14).

[114] E.g., Ap Paup 3,15. ...et omnino se alienae propter Deum voluntati subiicere (Doctoris 8, 248; De Vinck, The Works 4, 49).

[115] Ep Im 13. Sacrificium obedientiae est maius sacrificium omnium aliorum, quia dat propriam voluntatem ad sacrificium (Doctoris 8, 502).

[116] E.g., Adm 3,3–4. Ille homo relinquit omnia, quae possidet, et perdit corpus suum, qui se ipsum totum praebet ad obedientiam in manibus sui praelati. Et quidquid facit et dicit, quod ipse sciat, quod non sit contra voluntatem eius, dum bonum sit quod facit, vera obedientia est (Armstrong, Francis of Assisi, 130); Test 28. Et ita volo esse captus in manibus suis, ut non possim ire vel facere ultra obedientiam et voluntatem suam, quia dominus meus est (Armstrong, Francis of Assisi, 125); Ep Mem 20. In bonis et indifferentibus semper alterius studeas facere voluntatem... (Doctoris 8, 495; De Vinck, The Works 3, 258); Reg Nov 14,3. ... non ut faciam voluntatem meam, sed aliorum (Doctoris 8, 488; Monti, Works 5, 172); Prof 3,42. Obedientia est propriae voluntatis subiectio arbitrio superioris ad licita et honesta (David ab Augusta, 261; Devas, Spiritual Life 2, 97).

[117] Sal Virt 14. Sancta obedientia confundit omnes corporales et carnales voluntates (Armstrong, Francis of Assisi, 165).

[118] E.g., RnB 23,8. Omnes diligamus ex toto corde, ex tota anima, ex tota mente, ex tota virtute (cfr. Mark 12,30) et fortitudine, ex toto intellectu (cfr. Mark 12,33), ex omnibus viribus (cfr. Luke 10,27), toto nisu, toto affectu, totis visceribus, totis desideriis et voluntatibus Dominum Deum (Mark 12,30par.) (Armstrong, Francis of Assisi, 84); Prof 3,31. Caritas est ordinata et magna voluntas serviendi Deo, placendi Deo, fruendi Deo (David ab Augusta, 223; Devas, Spiritual Life 2, 62).

Father,[119] one's own will is "substituted" for his will[120] and thereby set upon the good.[121] Finally, by developing good intentions (*fervor bonae voluntatis*) on the level of *personal* virtue,[122] one's own will is ordered to "move in accord with a legitimate judgement."[123]

Fourth, zeal (*studium, diligentia, fervor, zelus*) is the product of both precept (external incentive) and will (internal incentive), itself producing both external (*in opere*) and internal (*in corde*) effects.[124] Externally, it expresses itself in good behavior (*habitus exterior, mores exteriores compositi, mores et verba habere*) and doing good things like spiritual exercises (*opera poenitentiae, bona opera, spiritualia exercitia*) and religious duties (*exteriores caerimoniales observantia, labor, praecepta servare*).[125]

---

[119] E.g., *Ep Fid* 1,1,9; *Ep Fid* 2,52. *Fratres ei sumus, quando facimus voluntatem patris qui in caelis est* (Matt 12,50) (Armstrong, *Francis of Assisi*, 42); *Ex Pat* 5–6. *Fiat voluntas tua sicut in caelo et in terra...* (Armstrong, *Francis of Assisi*, 158); *Prof* 3,43. *...sicut Christus non venit facere voluntatem suam, sed Patris* (*David ab Augusta*, 268; Devas, *Spiritual Life* 2, 103).

[120] E.g., *Ep Fid* 2,10. *Posuit tamen voluntatem suam in voluntate Patris dicens: Pater, fiat voluntas tua* (Matt 26,42) (Armstrong, *Francis of Assisi*, 46); *RB* 10,2. *...quod propter Deum abnegaverunt proprias voluntates* (Armstrong, *Francis of Assisi*, 105); *Reg Nov* 14,3. *...non ut faciam voluntatem meam, sed eius qui misit me Patris* [John 6,38] (*Doctoris* 8, 488; Monti, *Works* 5, 172).

[121] E.g., *Prof* 2,5. *...per voluntatem potens est capere bonitatem Dei* (*David ab Augusta*, 85; Devas, *Spiritual Life* 1, 81); Cf. *Trip Via* 3,7,12. *Ubi est summa bonitas iuncta cum voluntate...* (*Doctoris* 8, 17; De Vinck, *The Works* 1, 92).

[122] E.g., *Prof* 3,59. *Affectus enim amoris Dei et sancti timoris cum fervore bonae voluntatis, in spiritu humilitatis et motu pietatis et gaudio spei nunquam debet in corde servi Dei exstingui. Ista namque sunt in quibus virtus devotionis maxime consistit* (*David ab Augusta*, 329; Devas, *Spiritual Life* 2, 161–162).

[123] Cf. *Prof* 3,27. *Virtus est ordinatus secundum veritatis iudicium mentis affectus* (*David ab Augusta*, 215; Devas, *Spiritual Life* 2, 54); *Prof* 3,2. *Ornatus voluntatis sunt sanctae affectiones et devotio ad Deum, fervor fidei, fiducia spei, dulcedo caritatis et bonae voluntatis alacritas, spes de remissione peccatorum, devotio circa Christi humanitatem et passionem nec non circa eius divinitatem...* (*David ab Augusta*, 165; Devas, *Spiritual Life* 2, 7).

[124] E.g., *Reg Nov* 10,2. *Et ut melius te conserves, stude semper in corde et opere humilitatem habere...* (*Doctoris* 8, 485; Monti, *Works*, 167).

[125] E.g., *Prof* 3,29. *Primus est habitus exterior... Secundum sunt exteriores caerimoniales observantiae... Tertium sunt mores exteriores compositi... Quartum sunt opera poenitentiae...* (*David ab Augusta*, 218–219; Devas, *Spiritual Life* 2, 57–58); *RnB* 7,10. *Omnes fratres studeant bonis operibus insudare...* (Armstrong, *Francis of Assisi*, 69). *RnB* 9,9. *Et fratres, qui eam acquirendo laborant...* (Armstrong, *Francis of Assisi*, 71); *RB* 2,2. *Ministri vero diligenter examinent eos de fide catholica et ecclesiasticis sacramentis* (Armstrong, *Francis of Assisi*, 100); *RB* 5,1. *Fratres illi, quibus gratiam dedit Dominus laborandi, laborent fideliter et devote...* (Armstrong, *Francis of Assisi*, 102); *Sol* 2,3,16. *...quia quos amor veritatis afficit bonorum operum exercitatio et malorum perpessio nunquam frangit* (*Doctoris* 8, 50; De Vinck, *The Works* 3, 89–90); *Reg An* 9. *Exerce te quoque ad iustitiam...*

These are "outward signs of a reality that should lie beneath."[126] Internally, zeal shapes the inner habit (*habitus*)[127] by the banishment of vice and the practice of virtue (*familiare ad expugnanda vel mortificanda vitia et virtutes usitandas*), and the establishment in God of all the movements of the will (*nucleus affectualis virtutis, bona voluntas, devotio*).[128] Thus, religious zeal is moved by the desire for Christ, forming the endeavor to resemble Him.[129]

(*Doctoris* 8, 130; De Vinck, *The Works* 3, 245); *Prof* 1,9. *Ad labores communes et ad humilitatis officia esto paratus...* (*David ab Augusta*, 13; Devas, *Spiritual Life* 1, 13); *Prof* 2,35. *Secundum est exercere se in humilibus operibus, vilibus et despectis officiis et rusticanis laboribus, humili habitu incedere, humiles mores et verba habere....* (*David ab Augusta*, 123; Devas, *Spiritual Life* 1, 118); *Prof* 3,20. *...sit promptus ad quaeque spiritualia exercitia, quae vel obedientia iusserit, vel caritas fraterna requirit, vel devotionis studio apta sint, vel cuiuslibet alterius virtutis* (*David ab Augusta*, 205; Devas, *Spiritual Life* 2, 45); *Prof* 3,33. *Secundus gradus potest esse, cum homo voluntate pleniori et affectu ferventiori non solum communia contentus est praecepta servare, sine quibus non est salus, sed etiam ad omnia, quae Dei sunt, studiosus est et voluntarius, tam faciendo in se quam in aliis promovendo et desiderando...* (*David ab Augusta*, 229; Devas, *Spiritual Life* 2, 67–69).

[126] *Prof* 3,29. *Sed haec sunt tantum signa interiorum...* (*David ab Augusta*, 218; Devas, *Spiritual Life* 2, 57). Here, zeal manifests itself in the "outward covering to adorn and shield holiness [virtue]."

[127] E.g., *Trip Via* 3,3. *Stude igitur ad habendum habitum benignitatis ad proximum, severitatis ad te ipsum, humilitatis ad Deum, perspicacitatis contra diabolum, secundum effigiem imitationis Christi* (*Doctoris* 8, 13; De Vinck, *The Works* 1, 83); *Prof* 2,5. *...ita virtus per corporalia exercitia addiscitur et in habitum vertitur* (*David ab Augusta* 87; Devas, *Spiritual Life* 1, 83). External and internal zeal supplement each other.

[128] E.g., *Prof* 3,29. *Quintum est studium familiare ad expugnanda vel mortificanda vitia et virtutes usitandas... Sextum est ipse nucleus affectualis virtutis...* (*David ab Augusta*, 219–220; Devas, *Spiritual Life* 2, 58–60); *Trip Via* 2,4,11. *Studendum est igitur ad proficiendum in caritate...* (*Doctoris* 8, 11; De Vinck, *The Works* 1, 78–79); *Prof* 3,2. *Ornatus voluntatis sunt sanctae affectiones et devotio ad Deum, fervor fidei, fiducia spei, dulcedo caritatis et bonae voluntatis alacritas, spes de remissione peccatorum, devotio circa Christi humanitatem et passionem nec non circa eius divinitatem... quae afficiunt hominem ad Deum et ad amorem virtutum et ad odium vitiorum et dilectionem proximorum et ad studia bonorum operum...* (*David ab Augusta*, 165; Devas, *Spiritual Life* 2, 7); *Prof* 3,30. *Quid prodest altiora profiteri et exterius in habitu perfectiora praetendere, si in studio virtutum et exercitio operis non distamus ab infimis...* (*David ab Augusta*, 222; Devas, *Spiritual Life* 2, 62). *Prof* 3,59. *Affectus enim amoris Dei et sancti timoris cum fervore bonae voluntatis, in spiritu humilitatis et motu pietatis et gaudio spei nunquam debet in corde servi Dei exstingui. Ista namque sunt in quibus virtus devotionis maxime consistit* (*David ab Augusta*, 329; Devas, *Spiritual Life* 2, 161–162).

[129] E.g., *Ex Pat* 5. *...ut amemus te ex toto corde* (cfr. Luke 10,27) *te semper cogitando, ex tota anima te semper desiderando, ex tota mente omnes intentiones nostras ad te dirigendo, honorem tuum in omnibus quaerendo et ex omnibus viribus nostris omnes vires nostras et sensus animae et corporis in obsequium tui amoris et non in alio expendendo...* (Armstrong, *Francis of Assisi*, 158–159); *Trip Via* 3,3. *Quinto, quali forma patitur, et Christum induere per assimilationis studium* (*Doctoris* 8, 13; De Vinck, *The Works* 1, 83).

Finally, spiritual fruit (*fructus*) is the product of zeal[130] and the reward of virtuous merit (*meritum*).[131] It starts with a clean conscience (*conscientium*)[132] and ends with spiritual joy.[133] *Bona nostra* such as penance, keeping the Word of God, silence, fraternal edification, poverty, serving Mass, patience, prayer, and the right comportment amid spiritual consolations, all bear manifold spiritual fruit.[134] To the sweetest fruits of virtuous accomplishment belong such things as the dwelling of the Spirit, kinship with Christ, conformity to God, exaltation, salvation, and heaven.[135]

---

[130] E.g., *Prof* 2,38. ...*quanto hic ferventior dilectio, tanto illic iucundior fruitio aeternae pacis* (*David ab Augusta*, 127; Devas, *Spiritual Life* 1, 121).

[131] E.g., *Ex Pat* 7. ...*et per beatissimae Virginis et omnium electorum tuorum merita intercessionem* (Armstrong, *Francis of Assisi*, 159); *Sol* 1,4,45. *O felix amor, ex quo oritur strenuitas morum, puritas affectuum, subtilitas intellectuum, sanctitas desideriorum, claritas operum, fecunditas virtutum, dignitas meritorum, sublimitas praemiorum et honorum* (*Doctoris* 8, 43; De Vinck, *The Works* 3, 73); *Prof* 2,5. ...*relicto debito studio virtutum, in quo est maximum meritum...* (*David ab Augusta*, 87; Devas, *Spiritual Life* 1, 82–83).

[132] E.g., *Ep Fid* 1,1,10; *Ep Fid* 2,52. ...*per divinum amorem et puram et sinceram conscientiam...* (Armstrong, *Francis of Assisi*, 42); *Trip Via* 1,1,9. *Nam omnis conscientia munda laeta est et iucunda* (*Doctoris* 8, 5–6; De Vinck, *The Works* 1, 68); *Prof* 1,14. *Qui autem magis veretur hominum aspectus quam Dei et Angelorum et propriae conscientiae non est castus amator boni...* (*David ab Augusta*, 19; Devas, *Spiritual Life* 1, 17).

[133] E.g., *Ap Paup* 3,2. ...*tertium autem supremum, in perfruitione sempiternalium iucunditatum* (*Doctoris* 8, 244; De Vinck, *The Works* 4, 37); *Prof* 3,63. *Nec mirum: spiritualis enim iucunditas... fructuosa caritas et meritoria sublimium praemiorum* (*David ab Augusta*, 344; Devas, *Spiritual Life* 2, 176).

[134] *Ep Fid* 1,1,4. ...*et faciunt fructus dignos poenitentiae...* (Armstrong, *Francis of Assisi*, 41); *RnB* 22,17. ...*qui in corde bono et optimo audientes verbum* (Luke 8,15) *intelligunt et* (cfr. Matt 13,23) *retinent et fructum afferunt in patientia* (Luke 8,15) (Armstrong, *Francis of Assisi*, 80); *Perf* 4,1. ...*sic ex silentio nutritur iustitia, ex qua velut ex quadam arbore colligitur fructus pacis* (*Doctoris* 8, 115; De Vinck, *The Works* 1, 228); *Ap Paup* 3,19. ...*in qua radix caritatis est pinguior et sublimitas operationis excelsior et fraternae aedificationis fructus uberior* (*Doctoris* 8, 249; De Vinck, *The Works* 4, 52); *Leg Franc* 7,1. *Paupertatem noveritis, Fratres, specialem viam esse salutis tanquam humilitatis fomentum perfectionisque radicem, cuius est fructus multiplex, sed occultus* (*Doctoris* 8, 523; Cousins, *Bonaventure*, 240); *Prof* 1,10. *In hoc enim ministerio multiplex fructus est...* (*David ab Augusta*, 14; Devas, *Spiritual Life* 1, 13); *Prof* 3,58. ...*quia non referunt fructum nisi in patientia* (*David ab Augusta*, 325; Devas, *Spiritual Life* 2, 157); *Prof* 3,62. *Omnis igitur orationis fructus et finis est Deo adhaerere et unus cum eo spiritus* [cfr. 1 Cor 6,17] *fieri per liquefactionem purissimi amoris...* (*David ab Augusta*, 338; Devas, *Spiritual Life* 2, 169–170); Cf. *Prof* 3,68. ...*in quibus maior vis est et certior veritas et fructuosior profectus et purior perfectio...* (*David ab Augusta*, 365–366; Devas, *Spiritual Life* 2, 197–198).

[135] E.g., *Ep Fid* 1,1,6–7. ...*et faciet apud eos habitaculum et mansionem* (cfr. Joa 14,23), *et sunt filii patris caelestis* (cfr. Matt 5,45), *cuius opera faciunt et sunt sponsi, fratres et matres Domini nostri Jesu Christi* (cfr. Matt 12,50) (Armstrong, *Francis of Assisi*, 41); *Ap Paup*, Prol,1. ...*sic denique virtutum deiformium approbandam esse rectitudinem...* (*Doctoris* 8, 233; De Vinck, *The Works* 4, 1); *Ep Ord* 28. ...*humiliamini et vos ut exaltemini ab eo* (cfr. 1 Petr 5,6; Jac 4,10) (Armstrong, *Francis of Assisi*, 118); *Laet* 15. ...*quod in hoc est vera*

5. PROGRESSION

One theme that should be further investigated is Franciscan spiritual *pro-gress* and, specifically, progress in the virtues (*profectus virtutum*).[136] Here, I can only provide some first steps toward a more detailed analysis. The Franciscan *ordo virtutum* is one of many *ordines* within the worldly order of things (*ordo in universitate rerum*).[137] As such, it is a hierarchy of virtues that connect and cooperate by virtue of their respective places and functions.[138] Moreover, when man follows in the footsteps of Christ (*Domini nostri Jesu Christi doctrinam et vestigia sequi*),[139] (His) virtues, functioning as core orientation marks, become milestones on the spiritual path (*via*).[140] For Francis, Christ is the way (*via*), and the virtuous would be the one who, instead of walking after his own evil desires, loves and serves and follows Him (*sequi vestigiam et paupertatem suam*).[141] Without question, all of Francis's virtues are spiritual virtues: they have their well-defined places and functions in the world (in nature, in the fraternity,

---

laetitia et vera virtus et salus animae (Armstrong, *Francis of Assisi*, 167); RnB 21,7. *Beati qui moriuntur in poenitentia, quia erunt in regno caelorum* (Armstrong, *Francis of Assisi*, 78).

[136] On the Christian conceptualization of spiritual progress, see Pansters, "Didactiek"; Pansters, "*Profectus virtutum*. From Psalm".

[137] Cf. Hellmann, *Ordo*, 93. David, for example, sees the grouping (*ordo*) of virtues on earth as a reflection of the heavenly hierarchy of virtues, e.g., *Prof* 3,33. *...cur non etiam spirituales virtutum hierarchiae eundem ordinem in terris imitentur...* (*David ab Augusta*, 228; Devas, *Spiritual Life* 2, 66).

[138] "The life of the christian in the state of grace is explained in terms of a kind of hier-archization of powers and virtues" (Fehlner, *The Role*, 151). Cf. Bohl, *Geistlicher*, 426–429; Schlosser, *Cognitio*, 117–123.

[139] RnB 1,1 (Armstrong, *Francis of Assisi*, 63–64). Cf. Ps 118,59 (119,59); Matt 19,21; John 1,43; 1 Pet 2,21.

[140] Cf. Zweerman, *Wondbaar*, 100–105, 200–201; Benz, "Der (neu)platonische", 101; Bohl, *Geistlicher*, 358–360; Cargnoni, "l'Itineranza"; Delio, *Simply Bonaventure*, 115–129; Dukker, *Umkehr*, 134–145; Hayes, *The Hidden*, 25–52; Lapsanski, *Perfectio*, 45–59; Milchner, *Nachfolge*, 306–320; Morant, *Unser Weg*, 97–206; Strack, *Christusleid*, 107–136; Verhey, *Der Mensch*, 81–88; Verheij, "De leer"; Veuthey, *Itinerarium*. Cf. *Sent* 1,3,3. *Item, vestigium sive creatura est sicut scala ad ascendendum vel sicut via ad perveniendum ad Deum...* (*Doctoris* 1, 74); *Itin* 1,2. *...oportet nos transire per vestigium, quod est corporale et temporale et extra nos, et hoc est deduci in via Dei...* (*Doctoris* 5, 297).

[141] E.g., Adm 1,1. *Dicit Dominus Jesus discipulis suis: Ego sum via...* (Armstrong, *Francis of Assisi*, 128); Ep Fid 1,2,3. *...et qui ambulant post malam concupiscentiam et mala desideria carnis suae...* (Armstrong, *Francis of Assisi*, 43); Ep Fid 1,1,1. *Omnes qui Dominum diligunt ex toto corde, ex tota anima et mente, ex tota virtute* (cfr. Mark 12,30)... (Armstrong, *Francis of Assisi*, 41); Cant Sol 14. *Laudate et benedicete mi signore, et rengratiate et serviateli cun grande humilitate* (Armstrong, *Francis of Assisi*, 114); Ep Leo 3. *In quocumque modo melius videtur tibi placere Domino Deo et sequi vestigiam et paupertatem suam...* (Armstrong, *Francis of Assisi*, 122).

in the soul) while stemming from a higher spiritual *order*, and at the same time they operate within the compass of a "divine-human relational *process*"[142] in order to "exalt" us.[143] But his conception of them remains fairly *static*: there seems to be no real movement and development between virtues, nor within each and every one of them.

For Bonaventure, the human soul is transformed and reformed (or repaired) *in via*,[144] and virtues are coordinates on its way back to God (*reductio, ascensus*).[145] They (as opposed to the virtues mentioned by Francis) become efficacious in multiple *dynamic* ways, when the soul advances from one virtue to another (*de virtute in virtutem*)[146] and traverses the different levels of each of them.[147] The soul is cleansed by doing penance, resisting evil, and making spiritual progress,[148] i.e., progress on the path to God by becoming humble, etc.[149] One must exercise oneself constantly and intensely in every virtue[150] and "proceed from virtue to virtue" (Psalm 83,3) so as to finally reach the promised land.[151] Dedication to the development (*profectus*) of virtues, in other words, makes all that pertains to perfection easy.[152]

---

[142] See 1.8.

[143] *RB* 6,4. ...*virtutibus sublimavit* (cfr. Jac 2,5) (Armstrong, *Francis of Assisi*, 103).

[144] Cf. Gerken, *Theologie*, 225–234; Schlosser, *Cognitio*, 99.

[145] Cf. Benz, "Der (neu)platonische", 100; Cuttini, *Ritorno*; Fisher, *De Deo*; Gerken, *Theologie*, 139–144; Guardini, *Systembildende*, 166–173; Hülsbusch, "Die Theologie"; Ménard, "Le "Transitus""; Speer, *Triplex*, 197; Zweerman, ""Danken". In the *Itinerarium*, Bonaventure describes God as *virtus superior nos elevans* (*Itin* 1,1; *Doctoris* 5, 296).

[146] E.g., *Perf* 7,1. ...*ut quasi gradatim ascendere possis et de virtute in virtutem proficere* (*Doctoris* 8, 124; De Vinck, *The Works* 1, 248).

[147] E.g., *Trip Via* 2,3,7. *Benevolentiam autem simili modo debemus Deo tripliciter exhibere, scilicet magnam, maiorem, maximam...* (*Doctoris* 8, 9; De Vinck, *The Works* 1, 75). See also the dubious *Summa de gradibus virtutum* (*Doctoris* 8, 646–654).

[148] E.g., *Trip Via* 1,1,4. *Tertio debet recogitare, si negligens fuerit ad poenitendum, ad resistendum, ad proficiendum* (*Doctoris* 8, 4; De Vinck, *The Works* 1, 65). According to the three stages of purification, illumination, and perfection (cf. Coughlin, *Works*, 41–68; Epping, "Seraphische", 240–244; Schlosser, *Bonaventura*, 32–34).

[149] E.g., *Ep Im* 6. *Item, fuit petitum a quodam sancto Patre, quid esset proficere in Deum; qui respondit, quod proficere erat humiliare se ipsum* (*Doctoris* 8, 501).

[150] E.g., *Trip Via* 2,4,12. *Qui autem sic excitaverit se continue et intente, proficiet in caritate...* (*Doctoris* 8, 11; De Vinck, *The Works* 1, 79).

[151] E.g., *Perf* 1,2. ...*proficere de una virtute in aliam, ut possis pervenire ad terram promissam* (*Doctoris* 8, 108; De Vinck, *The Works* 1, 212–213).

[152] E.g., *Trip Via* 2,4,11. *Studendum est igitur ad proficiendum in caritate, cum profectus eius inducat perfectionem omnium bonorum...* (*Doctoris* 8, 11; De Vinck, *The Works* 1, 78–79). Cf. *Prof* 3,46. *Tota autem intentio debet esse circa optimum occupata, circa profectum animae in Dei notitia et amore et in his, quae ad hunc profectum promovent et conducunt...* (*David ab Augusta*, 277; Devas, *Spiritual Life* 2, 111).

David's conception of virtue is at least as dynamic as that of Bonaventure. Spiritual life (viz., *profectus religiosorum*) consists first and foremost of acquiring, developing, and maintaining virtues (*profectus virtutum*).[153] In order to reach a higher degree of sanctity (than an ordinary person),[154] spiritual man must progress from virtue to virtue and go through several stages of each and every virtue.[155] Virtue's three successive degrees (beginning, progress, perfection; or lowest, middle, highest)[156] coincide with the three stages of spiritual life (*incipientes, proficientes, perfecti*),[157] in which the rational soul learns to avoid and combat vices, and be disciplined in the exercises of virtue and devotion. Whereas one with ardent zeal in each of the three stages (in David's three books) undergoes a continuous transformation process,[158] the life of virtue is situated in the dynamics of spiritual development as a continuous discovery and interiorization of the good (*in bonis*) that is God. Inextricably bound up with the other (six) stages of the spiritual transformation process,[159] which in itself consists of a continuous *proficere* (*progredi, promovere, procedere, ascendere*), progress in the virtues relates to this whole process (*processus*) from beginning (*incipere*) to end (*perfectio*).

6. PERFECTION

Franciscan spiritual *perfection* is another theme needing further investigation, and a first step might be to view it as the realization of virtue and

---

[153] E.g., *Prof* 3,50. *Ad castitatis autem acquisitionem et profectum et conservationem valent ea...* (*David ab Augusta*, 288; Devas, *Spiritual Life* 2, 122). Cf. Pansters, "*Profectus virtutum*. The Roots".

[154] *Prof* 3,30. *Profectus ad Religiosos magis congrue pertinent, qui meliores esse studere debent...* (*David ab Augusta*, 222; Devas, *Spiritual Life* 2, 62).

[155] E.g., *Prof* 3,33. *Laboremus tantum hic fideliter de virtute in virtutem eundo proficere...* (*David ab Augusta*, 228; Devas, *Spiritual Life* 2, 67); *Prof* 3,30. *...quantum in singulis virtutibus profecerint...* (*David ab Augusta*, 221; Devas, *Spiritual Life* 2, 61).

[156] E.g., *Prof* 3,33. *Unaquaeque enim virtus, teste beato Gregorio, habet initium suum et profectum et perfectionem... Caritas Dei, mater et nutrix omnium virtutum, tres habet gradus: infimum, medium et summum...* (*David ab Augusta*, 227–228; Devas, *Spiritual Life* 2, 66).

[157] And the corresponding stages *animalis, rationalis, spiritualis*; derived from the prevalent *Epistola ad fratres de Monte Dei* of William of St. Thierry. Cf. Bohl, *Geistlicher*, 132–134.

[158] Cf. Blommestijn, "Progrès", 2397.

[159] In David's third book: fervor, austerity, consolation, temptation, self-mastery, and wisdom.

the fruit of spiritual zeal and merit.[160] It is, in any case, the state of the blessed servant, to which the evangelical beatitudes call.[161] Servants of God observe his commands with their whole heart and fulfil his counsels with a perfect mind.[162] They have true faith, certain hope, and perfect charity.[163] They do the works of the heavenly Father, and theirs is the kingdom of heaven.[164] Because man is "placed in great excellence," as he was created in the image and likeness of Christ,[165] perfection is a promise to those who persevere *in bono*.[166] Francis thus calls for evangelical perfection: "If you wish to be perfect, go, sell everything you have and give it to the poor, and you will have treasure in heaven; and come, follow me."[167]

Bonaventure sees in Christ the Model of all virtue whose example is perfect because his virtues and deeds proceed from the most perfect love.[168] Perfection is indeed impossible without love because only love, the "root, form, purpose, fulfillment, and bond of perfection," leads man to it.[169] Both Bonaventure and David see love as the mark of the

---

[160] E.g., *Leg Franc* 7,1. *Paupertatem noveritis, Fratres, specialem viam esse salutis tanquam humilitatis fomentum perfectionisque radicem, cuius est fructus multiplex, sed occultus* (*Doctoris* 8, 523; Cousins, *Bonaventure*, 240). See also 3.4. On the Christian conceptualization of spiritual perfection, see for instance: Burgess, *Reaching*; Frank, "Perfection"; Lapsanski, *Perfectio*; Murdoch, *The Sovereignty*, 1–45. On Franciscan perfection, see for instance: Bougerol, "La perfection"; Carr, "Poverty"; Lapsanski, *Perfectio*; Phillips, "The Way".

[161] E.g., *Adm* 10–26, 28 (Armstrong, *Francis of Assisi*, 132–137).

[162] *Ep Ord* 7. *Servate in toto corde vestro mandata eius et consilia eius perfecta mente implete* (Armstrong, *Francis of Assisi*, 117).

[163] *Or Cruc. ...et da mihi fidem rectam, spem certam et caritatem perfectam...* (Armstrong, *Francis of Assisi*, 40).

[164] E.g., *Ep Fid* 1,1,7. *...et sunt filii patris caelestis* (cfr. Matt 5,45), *cuius opera faciunt...* (Armstrong, *Francis of Assisi*, 41–42); *Adm* 14,1. *Beati pauperes spiritu, quoniam ipsorum est regnum caelorum* (Matt 5,3) (Armstrong, *Francis of Assisi*, 133).

[165] *Adm* 5,1. *Attende, o homo, in quanta excellentia posuerit te Dominus Deus, quia creavit et formavit te ad imaginem dilecti Filii sui secundum corpus et similitudinem* (cfr. Gen 1,26) *secundum spiritum* (Armstrong, *Francis of Assisi*, 131).

[166] *RnB* 21,9. *...et perseverate usque in finem in bono* (Armstrong, *Francis of Assisi*, 78).

[167] *RnB* 1,2. *Si vis perfectus esse, vade* (Matt 19,21) *et vende omnia* (cfr. Luke 18,22) *quae habes, et da pauperibus et habebis thesaurum in caelo; et veni, sequere me* (Matt 19,21) (Armstrong, *Francis of Assisi*, 64). Cf. *Benedictio fr. Bernardo* 2. *...qui primo incepit et complevit perfectissime perfectionem sancti evangelii distribuendo bona sua omnia pauperibus.*

[168] *Ap Paup* 6,2. *...utrumque tamen perfectum in Christo, quia ex perfectissima caritate processit* (*Doctoris* 8, 267; De Vinck, *The Works* 4, 108); *Ap Paup* 7,9. *...ut perfectionem nobis exemplo monstraret...* (*Doctoris* 8, 275; De Vinck, *The Works* 4, 133). Cf. *Prof* 3,44. *Unde Filius Dei dans nobis exemplum perfectionis...* (*David ab Augusta*, 271; Devas, *Spiritual Life* 2, 105).

[169] E.g., *Ap Paup* 3,2. *Sciendum est igitur, quod radix, forma, finis, complementum et vinculum perfectionis caritas est...* (*Doctoris* 8, 244; De Vinck, *The Works* 4, 37); *Perf* 7,1.

perfect,[170] who outshine those who are beginners or advanced on the spiritual path.[171] Every virtue has three (corresponding) degrees: beginning, progress, and perfection;[172] and virtue is perfect when "reason attains its final end, which is followed by beatic life."[173] In David's conception, perfection is reached in seven steps, whereby the right-ordered quest of virtue brings great merit, joyous security, and perfect holiness and wisdom.[174]

7. Contextualization

A lot has been said about the place, function, and operation of Franciscan virtue in the human soul, in the intellect, in the Franciscan fraternity, in God, and in spiritual texts. But how does it work in a wider intellectual context? What is its further history, its broader morality, its deeper spirituality? In order to initiate further scholarly contextualization of Franciscan *virtus/virtutes*, I will now deal with these areas briefly and in a preliminary way.

Nunc septimo loco restat dicendum de forma virtutum, scilicet caritate, quae sola ducit hominem ad perfectionem (Doctoris 8, 124; De Vinck, *The Works* 1, 248). Likewise, poverty is the root and foundation of evangelical perfection: *Ap Paup* 7,3. *...certa potest ratione concludi, quod perfectionis evangelicae, per quam Christo configuramur et complantamur et habitaculum eius efficimur, ipsa paupertas spiritus, secundum quandam analogiam et cohaerentiam ad praedicta, radix est et fundamentum (Doctoris* 8, 272; De Vinck, *The Works* 4, 126).

[170] E.g., *Trip Via* Prol,1. *Purgatio autem ad pacem ducit, illuminatio ad veritatem, perfectio ad caritatem... (Doctoris* 8, 3; De Vinck, *The Works* 1, 63); *Prof* 3,42. *...quam affectus amoris Dei includitur, quorum primum est incipientium, secundum proficientium, tertium perfectorum (David ab Augusta,* 263; Devas, *Spiritual Life* 2, 98–99).

[171] E.g., *Prof* 2,4. *...scilicet incipientium, proficientium, perfectorum (David ab Augusta,* 84; Devas, *Spiritual Life* 1, 79). Cf. *Ap Paup* 3,20. *...et gradus habent et minus et maius recipiunt, ac per hoc tanto in maioris perfectionis statu constituunt... (Doctoris* 8, 250; De Vinck, *The Works* 4, 53).

[172] E.g., *Ap Paup* 3,2. *Ipsa vero caritas triplicem habet statum: unum quidem infimum... secundum vero medium... tertium autem supremum... (Doctoris* 8, 244; De Vinck, *The Works* 4, 37); *Prof* 3,33. *Unaquaeque enim virtus, teste beato Gregorio, habet initium suum et profectum et perfectionem... (David ab Augusta,* 227; Devas, *Spiritual Life* 2, 66).

[173] *Ap Paup* 3,2. *Vere, perfecta virtus est ratio perveniens usque ad finem, quem beata vita consequitur (Doctoris* 8, 245; De Vinck, *The Works* 4, 38). Cf. *Prof* 3,29. *Sextum est ipse nucleus affectualis virtutis, quae est perfectio vitae activae et ingressus ordinatus contemplativae... (David ab Augusta,* 220; Devas, *Spiritual Life* 2, 59).

[174] E.g., *Prof* 2,5. *Ita est de homine, maxime Religioso, magna imprudentia, si, relicto debito studio virtutum, in quo est maximum meritum, maxima perfectio sanctitatis et sapientiae, maxima etiam delectatio et securitas... (David ab Augusta,* 87; Devas, *Spiritual Life* 1, 82–83).

History

Many more sources would have to be studied in order to determine the exact historical role of Franciscan virtue, i.e., the effects of the Franciscan program of virtuous living on the history of the Order and late medieval society, the origin and reception of its main concepts, and the intellectual context of Franciscan virtue theology. There are still many questions to be answered: How does moral spirituality generally influence and shape the political, economic, social, and intellectual course of history? Against what historical background did the intellectual (ideological, social, spiritual) concepts in question come into being? Under what circumstances were they developed? What was their effect on people? How did they transfer to the milieus of later generations? Were early Franciscan authors successful in delivering their message, and what did later authors do with it? I propose three strategies for answering these and similar questions: a *begriffsgeschichtliche,* a thematic, and an exemplary one.

The first way to contextualize the Franciscan virtues historically is to research their place and function in early Franciscan discourse. A good example of how to set about this systematically is Duane V. Lapsanski's *begriffsgeschichtliche Untersuchung* on evangelical perfection *im früh-franziskanischen Schrifttum.*[175] In order to situate the concept of *vita evangelica* in the pre-Franciscan period, Lapsanski studies the works of theologians such as Peter Damiani and Hugh of St. Victor, and the *vitae* of preachers such as Robert of Arbrissel and Norbert of Gennep. Then, in order to shed light on the role of *perfectio evangelica* in the pre-Bonaventurian period, and in order to trace its *development* in the early Franciscan period, he studies dozens of early documents: the writings of Francis, the letters of brother Elias, the *Sacrum commercium*, the Lives and Miracles of Saint Francis by Thomas of Celano, the Legend and Divine Office of Saint Francis by Julian of Speyer, the *Legend of the Three Companions*, some early liturgical texts, the writings of Clare, the Commentary on the Rule by the four masters, the Commentary on the Rule by Hugh of Digne, the Chronicle by Jordan of Giano, the Chronicle by Thomas of Eccleston, the Chronicle by Salimbene de Adam, the papal documents, and some other contemporary sources dealing with the Franciscan Order. Now, the same kind of discourse analysis would greatly benefit the understanding of the place, function, and development of Franciscan humility, or penance,

---

[175] Lapsanski, *Perfectio*. Another good historical example is Wesjohann, "*Simplicitas*."

or peace, in the thirteenth century. It must even be possible to start from hagiography (biography, legend) and work from these sources toward the historical, moral, or spiritual essence of Franciscan virtues, provided that new research questions are developed and better research criteria applied.[176]

Secondly, a thematic approach to early Franciscanism would certainly allow for an in-depth study of the many historical circumstances of Franciscan virtue. By looking at certain areas of Franciscan activity and accomplishment, such as those of education and preaching, the role of the virtues would be further mapped out. In many catechistic texts, for example, a lot of chapters are devoted to such religious instructions as the articles of faith, the commandments, the sacraments, the gifts, the vices, and the virtues.[177] What do these texts, many of which were hugely popular, then say about the religious needs, and capacities, of the readers? How did they help people on the road to spiritual perfection, e.g., to internalize the virtues?[178] In another genre, that of novice treatises, the virtues are part of the central teachings on the Franciscan way of life. But how did they contribute to the basic religious formation of postulants? In what way were they instruments to coach and monitor them, and in how far did they actually "transform" them?[179] Regarding Franciscan preaching, the earliest sources already tell us that the brothers should "announce to them vices and virtues, punishment and glory, with brevity."[180] The brothers indeed preached many virtues and about many vices, but how much repentence and real practice did their exhortations generate? Were the virtues preached and called for real inspirations to a better, a truly Christian life?[181]

A third way to historical contextualization of the virtues is to look first at the virtue for which many of the historical questions have already been answered more or less adequately: that of poverty.[182] The origin and

---

[176] Cf. Dalarun, *The Misadventure*. In the older franciscanological literature, the many hagiographical elements in these texts were not clearly defined and "facts" were not clearly distinguished from "fiction"; therefore, a priori spiritual assumptions ("Nachfolge") strongly facilitated (see 1.6–1.7).

[177] Roest, *Franciscan*, 230–249.

[178] Cf. Roest, *Franciscan*, 232, 247–248.

[179] Cf. Roest, *Franciscan*, 206–209.

[180] *RB* 9,4. *...annuntiando eis vitia et virtutes, poenam et gloriam cum brevitate sermonis...* (cfr. Rom 9,28) (Armstrong, *Francis of Assisi*, 105). Cf. D'Avray, *The Preaching*, 72, 140.

[181] Cf. Roest, *Franciscan*, 1–2.

[182] On the role of poverty in Franciscan history, see for instance: "Armut"; Bailey, "Religious"; Da Campagnola, "La povertà"; Esser, *Anfänge*, 245–265; Esser, "Mysterium";

essence of Franciscan poverty is evangelical (apostolic, voluntary) or spiritual poverty (*paupertas spiritu*): "Blessed are the poor in spirit, for theirs is the kingdom of heaven."[183] Evangelical poverty means to live without anything of one's own (*sine proprio*), to make nothing one's own (*sibi appropriare*), and to hold back (*retinere*) nothing of oneself for oneself.[184] It means to follow in the footsteps of Christ who lived in extreme poverty,[185] sell all one's possessions and give to the poor,[186] and desire to be, as well as actually be, without the goods of this world.[187] Franciscan poverty, from a *historical* perspective, is much more than this. It is, above all things, a paradoxal poverty:

> But this ideal of sanctified destitution, which was realisable by the small flock of disciples at Rivo Torto, posed insuperable problems when the fraternity expanded into a world-wide missionary order. How could preachers and priests be educated for their task if they had no books or writing materials or rooms in which to study? How could the friars preach and administer the sacraments if they had no churches? And how could any of these essentials be acquired without funds?[188]

The major historical role of this paradox of poverty is uncontested. Franciscan poverty brought great political, ideological, and intellectual discussion, and occasioned many vicissitudes in the thirteenth century: the question of what constituted perfect poverty was fiercely debated; a *nuntius* or trustee was appointed to receive and hold money on behalf of

---

Feld, *Franziskus*; Garrido, *Die Lebensregel*, 174–193; Hoeberichts, *Paradise*, 68–93, 196–206, 257–269; Iriarte, *Vocazione*, 118–145; Lambert, *Franciscan*; Lapsanski, *Das Leben*, 81–106; Lawrence, *The Friars*, 26–64; Mäkinen, *Property*; Micó, "Franciscan"; Moorman, *A History*; Nolthenius, *Een man*, 233–239; Paton, *Preaching*, 197–205; Roggen, *Die Lebensform*; Wolf, *The Poverty*.

[183] *Adm* 14,1. *Beati pauperes spiritu, quoniam ipsorum est regnum caelorum* (Matt 5,3) (Armstrong, *Francis of Assisi*, 133).

[184] *RnB* 1,1. *...vivendo in obedientia, sine proprio et in castitate* (Armstrong, *Francis of Assisi*, 63); *RB* 6,1. *Fratres nihil sibi approprient nec domum nec locum nec aliquam rem* (Armstrong, *Francis of Assisi*, 103); *Ep Ord* 29. *Nihil ergo de vobis retineatis vobis..* (Armstrong, *Francis of Assisi*, 118). See 2.8.

[185] E.g., *Ap Paup* 7,5. *Hanc paupertatis normam tanquam speciali praerogativa perfectam et Christus in se ipso servavit et Apostolis servandam instituit, et his qui eorum cupiunt imitari vestigia, consulendo suasit* (*Doctoris* 8, 273; De Vinck, *The Works* 4, 129).

[186] E.g., *Ap Paup* 7,13. *Si vis perfectus esse, vade, vende omnia, quae habes, et da pauperibus et veni, sequere me* [cfr. Matt 19,21] (*Doctoris* 8, 276; De Vinck, *The Works* 4, 137).

[187] E.g., *Prof* 3,45. *Secundus gradus est nihil velle superfluum habere, sed solis necessariis esse contentum in victu et vestitu, hospitio, utensilibus et obsequentium famulatu... Tertius gradus est nihil velle possidere in mundo et in omnibus necessariis multiplicem pati penuriam propter Deum* (*David ab Augusta*, 273–274; Devas, *Spiritual Life* 2, 108–109).

[188] Lawrence, *The Friars*, 39.

the brothers so that gifts could be accepted and houses and books used "without ownership"; concessions to absolute poverty were authorised and legal devices sponsored by the pope; churches were built, pastoral tasks taken on, and studies begun; constitutions were written; and property rights, use, loans, and rents were painfully re-examined by general chapters and *magistri*. Total dependence upon divine providence without some corporate property soon appeared impossible, however contradictory the accumulation of houses, offices and the like might be to the wishes and commands of Francis.[189] Franciscan poverty became burdened with inner contradictions and tensions as an original ideal, that of absolute poverty in imitation of Christ, met with the many problematic realities of a developing order.[190] It must, however, be stated that the discussion about poverty has exaggerated the historical significance of this virtue at the expense of the virtues that are at least as important in a moral and spiritual sense. It is now their turn to be studied in the context of late medieval order and society, in much the same way as has been done with poverty, so that a more complete historical picture of Franciscan virtue may be drawn.

A treatment of the wider context of Franciscan texts on the virtues makes clear that discourses comprising the building blocks of moral spirituality were not only brought to bear on the wider socio-religious and intellectual world the friars were living in, but were also products of a living experience. Three cases may illustrate the pre-, syn-, or post-practice *Sitz im Leben* of early Franciscan virtue discourse. First, there is the communal practice of prayer.[191] In the *Dicta* of Giles of Assisi, one of the original companions of Francis, prayer is described as the beginning and the end of everything worth pursuing.[192] Perseverance in prayer results in fourteen graces and virtues, which together bring love, happiness, and peace of mind. The normative texts such as rules and admonitions are thus not the only early sources to support the thesis that the cultivation of the virtues is one of the core tenets of the regulated and prayerful existence of the fraternity.[193] From the *Legend of the Three Companions*, in which Francis compares himself to a mother hen with many sons and a simple dove "flying up to heaven with the winged affects of the virtues,"

---

[189] Lawrence, *The Friars*, 34, 40–50.
[190] Cf. Lawrence, *The Friars*, 26, 29, 39.
[191] Cf. Johnson, *Franciscans*.
[192] Roest, "The Discipline", 417.
[193] Cf. Roest, "The Discipline", 417.

the conclusion may not only be drawn that "in the Franciscan fraternity, relationship is a matter of love and care,"[194] but also that the affective practice of the virtues plays a central role in it. Furthermore, when Peter Olivi's text *Informatio ad virtutum opera* (on spiritual self-improvement through the contemplation of such matters as the wisdom of God and the nobility of virtue) appears in translation in a manuscript of Beguin origin (Todi Bibliotheca Comunale Ms. 128), we are likely to know "what those mysterious Beguins of 1299 – and the Beguins who came after – were actually doing when they got together in those weekly meetings to "talk about God"."[195]

Second, there are the social translations and transformations of early virtue focal points. The main example here is the new role that the "classic" Franciscan virtues of poverty and obedience adopted in the clash of the Franciscans with Pope John XXII on the issues of *usus* and *dominium*: while some (spiritual) Franciscans took up a stance that "displayed a massively individualist interpretative thrust in the living of a Christian life of virtue," John XXII maintained that "no religious Rule was identical with the Gospel" and that "it was up to superiors to define how practices were to be measured in the circumstances."[196] Next, in the works of John of Parma, Salimbene de Adam, and others, communal virtues such as courtesy and humility are cultivated *ad status*: the same virtues "can express themselves in diverse ways according to the particular circumstances of the individual," whereas "an individual's particular status constitutes a unique path" to a common set of virtues.[197] This may well be the development of a general tenor already present in the *Rules* and *Admonitions* of Francis, and implicit in fraternal warnings such as this one: "I admonish and exhort them not to look down upon or judge those whom they see dressed in soft and fine clothes and enjoying the choicest food and drink, but rather let everyone judge and look down upon himself."[198] Finally, later Franciscan narratives of holiness tend to move away from the mendicancy and the love of poverty that is so central in Francis's hagiography. In the *Vita prima* of Anthony of Padua, for example, little to nothing can be found on these matters. Instead, the *vita* focuses on Anthony's preaching and intellectual work. Only in the virtue of humility does he resemble

---

194 Godet-Calogeras, "*Illi qui volunt*", 323.
195 Burnham, "Just Talking", 259–260.
196 Coleman, "Using", 73.
197 Foote, "Mendicants", 213, 216.
198 *RB* 2,17 (Armstrong, *Francis of Assisi*, 101); Foote, "Mendicants", 213.

Francis, and this virtue indeed "comes to be the common element used to characterize the Franciscan saints when considered collectively."[199] The *vitae* of female saints such as Elizabeth of Hungary, who never experienced material poverty or mendicancy, illustrate the new ways in which Franciscan virtues were construed broadly for those (women) not living mendicant lives.[200]

Third, there is the historical origin and functioning of David's *Profectus religiosorum*. C. Bohl, who deals extensively with the contents and structure of this work, also places the author and text in their historical context. While using text-internal arguments to define the primary target group, namely, Franciscan novices and other *religiosi*,[201] he compares the text to other primary documents (Celano's *Vita secunda*, Bonaventure's *Epistola officialis*, the *Statuta Generalia*, and Jordan of Giano's *Chronica*) in order to describe Franciscan daily life around 1250.[202] He then places the text in its "Rezeptions- und Wirkungsgeschichte" by looking at how the work spread in male and female communities, how it was applied there in practice, and how it inspired later authors in the field of the Devotio Moderna and the Observant Movement.[203] In addition, he presents the "relation between the text and its historical impact" theoretically as an hermeneutical event in which a "common cause" connects the instances of text and recipient,[204] and in which the historical success of the text (=*Schlüssel*) proves (=*Deutung*) the significance (=*Bedeutung*) of its spiritual contents and methodical perspectives.[205] Lastly, he shows how the text itself continually focuses on actual experience, practice, exercise, custom, and imitation,[206] which are all concrete and psychologically refined "Spuren tatsächlich durchlebter Erfahrung"[207] that reveal the author's pragmatic intention while writing "from experience."[208]

---

[199] Prudlo, "Mendicancy", 98.

[200] Prudlo, "Mendicancy", 98–99.

[201] Bohl, *Geistlicher*, 101–103.

[202] Bohl, *Geistlicher*, 170–183. The *Profectus religiosorum* is thus "Ausdruck eines weitgehend monastisierten und institutionalisierten Alltags der Minderbrüder um 1250" (Bohl, *Geistlicher*, 184).

[203] Bohl, *Geistlicher*, 188–215.

[204] Bohl, *Geistlicher*, 222.

[205] Bohl, *Geistlicher*, 227–228.

[206] Bohl, *Geistlicher*, 233–254.

[207] Bohl, *Geistlicher*, 254.

[208] Bohl, *Geistlicher*, 254, 265, 269.

Morality

There are at least three areas in which the study of Franciscan virtues needs further moral contextualization. First of all, there are many more important Franciscan virtues than the ten I have selected for this study, for example zeal, mercy, purity, wisdom, fear, justice, simplicity, diffidence, benignity, perseverance, patience, discernment, chastity, quietude, devotion, silence, and sobriety.[209] Their relation to each other, to my selected ten virtues, and to the academic, intellectual, and classical virtues such as the cardinal virtues, has to be further elucidated. Moral and ethical debate focuses a lot on these classical virtues,[210] but could be seriously enriched by the "softer" Franciscan virtues of charity, obedience, goodness, truth, faith, humility, joy, poverty, penance, and peace. Franciscan morality, on the other hand, would benefit greatly from the focus on "harder" intellectual and moral virtues such as understanding, prudence, and fortitude, which are indeed authentically Franciscan.[211]

Second, the relation between Franciscan virtues, values, and practices has to be clarified, and their cultural role better understood. What *is* authentically Franciscan and really virtuous, for example, about creating a caring community; showing compassion; reverencing all of creation; respecting each person's dignity; offering hospitality, courtesy, kindness, and friendship; fostering loving relationships; fostering a simple lifestyle and responsible stewardship; preserving the environment; respecting all creatures; forgiving others; healing and reconciling, resolving conflicts; promoting non-violence; investigating and wondering; and searching for truth, understanding, and excellence?[212] To be able to answer this important question, Franciscan sources have to be studied further, moral concepts defined more precisely, and existing practices reassessed and attuned to the main moral and spiritual principles of Franciscan virtue.

---

[209] See 1.4.

[210] See 1.1.

[211] E.g., *Adm* 23,3. *Fidelis et prudens servus est* (cfr. Matt 24,45), *qui in omnibus suis offensis non tardat interius punire per contritionem et exterius per confessionem et operis satisfactionem* (Armstrong, *Francis of Assisi*, 136); *RnB* 23,8. *Omnes diligamus ex toto corde, ex tota anima, ex tota mente, ex tota virtute* (cfr. Mark 12,30) *et fortitudine, ex toto intellectu* (cfr. Mark 12,33), *ex omnibus viribus* (cfr. Luke 10,27), *toto nisu, toto affectu, totis visceribus, totis desideriis et voluntatibus Dominum Deum* (Mark 12,30par.)... (Armstrong, *Francis of Assisi*, 84).

[212] Cf. http://www.stritch.edu/about/franciscanvalues.aspx; http://www.sbu.edu/about_sbu.aspx?id=1858; http://www.lourdes.edu/AboutLourdes/MissionMinistry/FranciscanValues.aspx (1 October 2010).

Third, how does the application of Franciscan virtues bring forth
good behavior in the field of spirituality, politics, society, economy, and
ecology? Here, again, Francis may be the main inspiration for many
actions and convictions, which nevertheless have to be critically examined in the light of real Franciscan virtues, and vices. Where people aim to
be "poor" in the Franciscan spirit, for example, it should be made clear
to what extent they actually desire, neglect, struggle, fail, resist, or succeed to realize it,[213] and what poverty they have in mind: spiritual poverty
(e.g., no self-will),[214] ascetic poverty (e.g., no goods),[215] intellectual poverty
(e.g., no books),[216] organizational poverty (e.g., no "priors"),[217] economic
poverty (e.g., no money),[218] political poverty (e.g., no offices),[219] or any
other kind of poverty? It is, furthermore, necessary to know what definition, source, function, object, act, class, level, or opposite of virtue the
spiritual (political, economic, ecological) practioner of virtue is dealing
with, and if he respects such fundamental Franciscan truths as the fact
that "some virtues must be kept always and steadfastly, while others
must be adapted with discretion to the circumstances."[220] Knowledge of
the true nature of virtue, not moral judgment, then decides if spiritual

---

[213] Cf. *Ap Paup* 3,2. *Vere, perfecta virtus est ratio perveniens usque ad finem, quem
beata vita consequitur* (*Doctoris* 8, 245; De Vinck, *The Works* 4, 38); *Prof* 3,27. *Virtus est ordinatus secundum veritatis iudicium mentis affectus* (*David ab Augusta*, 215; Devas, *Spiritual
Life* 2, 54).

[214] E.g., *Ep Fid* 2,10. *Posuit tamen voluntatem suam in voluntate Patris dicens: Pater, fiat
voluntas tua* (Matt 26,42); *non sicut ego volo, sed sicut tu* (Matt 26,39) (Armstrong, *Francis
of Assisi*, 46).

[215] E.g., *RB* 6,1. *Fratres nihil sibi approprient nec domum nec locum nec aliquam rem*
(Armstrong, *Francis of Assisi*, 103).

[216] E.g., *RnB* 3,7. *Et libros tantum necessarios ad implendum eorum officium possint
habere* (Armstrong, *Francis of Assisi*, 65).

[217] E.g., *RnB* 6,3. *Et nullus vocetur prior, sed generaliter omnes vocentur fratres minores*
(Armstrong, *Francis of Assisi*, 68).

[218] E,g, *RnB* 8,3. *Unde nullus fratrum, ubicumque sit et quocumque vadit, aliquo modo
tollat nec recipiat nec recipi faciat pecuniam aut denarius...* (Armstrong, *Francis of
Assisi*, 69).

[219] E.g., *RnB* 7,1. *Omnes fratres, in quibuscumque locis steterint apud alios ad serviendum
vel laborandum, non sint camerarii neque cancellarii neque praesint in domibus in quibus
serviunt; nec recipiant aliquod officium, quod scandalum generet vel animae suae faciat
detrimentum* (cfr. Mark 8,36)... (Armstrong, *Francis of Assisi*, 68).

[220] *Ap Paup* 7,39. *Sunt namque virtutes, quae semper obnixeque tenendae sunt, et sunt
quae tempore locoque provida sunt discretione mutandae* (*Doctoris* 8, 285; De Vinck, *The
Works* 4, 162).

(political, economic, ecological) behavior in a certain circumstance, is truly virtuous.

Spirituality

Spiritual contextualization of the virtues concerns the analysis of their deeper meaning in spiritual processes, their effects in the "other" (than moral) fields of spirituality, and their spiritual operation in "non-spiritual" ("sinful," threatening, secularized, etc.) environments. The Franciscan authors see spiritual processes as inextricably bound up with the workings of divine grace and human virtue. Virtues are important witnesses to the experience of vocation, conversion, or spiritual transformation. When a person is called to follow Christ, he will find that he must walk his path of "profound humility, extreme poverty, perfect charity, immense patience, and admirable obedience."[221] When Francis was called by God to the life of penance, he found himself in a state of mercy and sweetness, and when he "left the world," he received great faith and simplicity.[222] When religious advance on the spiritual path, they "go from virtue to virtue" and strengthen each virtue as they go along. With this, the power of virtue seeks ever new territory in the field of moral spirituality, and beyond. Virtues call for asceticism, prompt action, lead to contemplation, accompany mystical experiences, and answer all imperatives of grace. Finally, they especially thrive in "non-spiritual" environments. The Franciscan authors say strikingly little about the effects of the cultivation of virtue on the outside world: their absolute priority lies with the spiritual fate and the *interior* life of the vicious or virtuous person.[223] But given

---

[221] *Ep Im* 3. *...inveniemus, quod ipse primo ambulavit per viam profundae humilitatis. Secundo, per viam extremae paupertatis. Tertio, per viam perfectae caritatis. Quarto, per viam immensae patientiae. Quinto, per viam admirabilis obedientiae. Per istam viam oportet nos ambulare, si volumus Christum sequi et invenire* (*Doctoris* 8, 499–500).

[222] *Test* 1–4. *Dominus ita dedit mihi fratri Francisco incipere faciendi poenitentiam: quia cum essem in peccatis nimis mihi videbatur amarum videre leprosos. Et ipse Dominus conduxit me inter illos et feci misericordiam cum illis. Et recedente me ab ipsis, id quod videbatur mihi amarum, conversum fuit mihi in dulcedinem animi et corporis; et postea parum steti et exivi de saeculo. Et Dominus dedit mihi talem fidem in ecclesiis, ut ita simpliciter orarem et dicerem...* (Armstrong, *Francis of Assisi*, 124).

[223] E.g., *Adm* 13,1. *Beati pacifici, quoniam filii Dei vocabuntur* (Matt 5,9) (Armstrong, *Francis of Assisi*, 133); *Prof* 1,13. *...prius volentes facere fructum in aliis, quam in se fixerint radices virtutis* (*David ab Augusta*, 17; Devas, *Spiritual Life* 1, 15).

that all Franciscan virtues are essentially remedial, i.e., aimed at the subversion of vice and sin, and essentially spiritual, i.e., aimed at the full realization of the Good that is God,[224] their application must also have
transformative effects on other people and on outside, foreign, "non-
spiritual," non-Christian, or "non-virtuous" situations. This *external* spiritual operation should be further examined as an original facet of
Franciscan virtue.

8. Conclusion

Our investigation into the meaning and function of Franciscan virtue in
the thirteenth century brings us to the following conclusions.

1. Virtue is a *basso continuo* of Franciscan moral and spiritual instruction. For Francis, Bonaventure, and David of Augsburg, virtue constitutes
the moral space in which the brothers (and sisters) "have died first," "have
been given to begin doing penance by the Lord," and now follow "the
teaching and footprints of our Lord Jesus Christ." When they pursue evangelical life with devotion, dedication, and "a seriousness of the right kind,"
virtue gradually fills their hearts and minds and (mainly by implication)
all areas of their communal life, with the Love, Goodness, and Truth that
is God. When they "truly repent" and open up to the gifts of heaven, inter-
nalizing them as a habit as well as passing them on in good behavior, virtues (viz., charity, obedience, goodness, truth, faith, humility, joy, poverty,
penance, peace) become steps on the way to eternal salvation. Evangelical
and apostolic virtue can thus be called the root, form, purpose, fulfilment,
and bond of Franciscan moral spirituality.[225]

2. Franciscan virtue is *spiritual* virtue: morality *propter Deum*. While
some virtues (like faith and joy) are typically human virtues in that they
are "fundamental characteristics" of the servant of God, and other virtues
(like love and humility) are "subjective" divine virtues that can also be had
and given back to Him "objectively," in the end, all virtues are human
"possessions" that have been "given from above."

---

[224] E.g., *Sal Virt* 8. *Et unaquaque confundit vitia et peccata* (Armstrong, *Francis of
Assisi*, 164); *Adm* 21,2. *Vae illi religioso, qui bona, quae Dominus sibi ostendit, non retinet
in corde suo* (cfr. Luke 2,19.51) *et aliis non ostendit per operationem...* (Armstrong, *Francis of
Assisi*, 135).

[225] Cf. *Ap Paup* 3,2. *Sciendum est igitur, quod radix, forma, finis, complementum et vinculum perfectionis caritas est...* (*Doctoris* 8, 244; De Vinck, *The Works* 4, 37).

3. Franciscan virtue is *formal* virtue: as an essential part of the pattern (*forma*) of evangelical life according to which the brothers (and sisters) should live, it gives form to their spiritual orientation and communal practice. Virtue is thus an expression (reflection, imitation) of the given form (the *forma* of the bread, which is Christ; the *forma* (rite) of the Church, according to which one lives uprightly; the *forma* (image) of God to which humans are created in his likeness; the *forma* of creation, which is an example for virtue), but it also *formalizes* "spiritual life and progress." The Franciscan "code of conduct" defines Franciscan virtuous culture by shaping it according to certain points of departure, states, stages, degrees, and processes of progress towards spiritual perfection.

4. Franciscan virtue is *historical* virtue: it transforms people during the various stages of their lives as much as it undergoes transformation itself throughout the decades of early Franciscan spiritual teaching. Single virtues are developed continuously according to certain rules or principles and with the help of certain mental or corporal techniques, while individual (and communal) lives are improved by moving "from virtue to virtue." But virtue also moves from generation to generation, and is being transformed along the way. The main change in thirteenth-century Franciscan virtue is not so much a configurational or conceptual one, as the origin (God, Spirit, will, etc.) and essence (*habitus datus*) of virtue remain the same, but has much more to do with the levels of theological explication and spiritual structuralization for the sake of intellectual clarity: under the growing influence of academic thought, organizational imperative, pastoral rationale, and monastic practice (with Bonaventure on the left side of this scale and David on the right), virtue is being dealt with more, more explicitly (e.g., new definitions), and more systematically. Historically viewed, a fairly simple and practical concept becomes girded with theory, "burdened" with ideology, and leavened with the order of schemes, steps, and other spiritually most profitable distinctions.

5. Franciscan virtue is *holistic* virtue: it is concerned with the whole field of moral spirituality. It lovingly responds to all graces of God, actuates all the powers of mind, heart, body, and soul, and involves all human wishes, desires, feelings, affections, and powers. It is the divine gift of human realization, as complex and total as Francis manages to express from gracious experience in his prayer:

With our whole heart,
our whole soul,
our whole mind,
with our whole strength and fortitude
with our whole understanding
with all our powers
with every effort,
every affection,
every feeling,
every desire and wish
let us all love the Lord God
Who has given and gives to each one of us
our whole body, our whole soul and our whole life[226]

Franciscan moral spirituality reveals the true *virtue* of Franciscan virtue: that it realizes integral personal virtuousness in the footsteps of Jesus Christ and, by doing so, "virtualizes" spiritual communities.

---

[226] *RnB* 23,8. *Omnes diligamus ex toto corde, ex tota anima, ex tota mente, ex tota virtute* (cfr. Mark 12,30) *et fortitudine, ex toto intellectu* (cfr. Mark 12,33), *ex omnibus viribus* (cfr. Luke 10,27), *toto nisu, toto affectu, totis visceribus, totis desideriis et voluntatibus Dominum Deum* (Mark 12,30par.), *qui totum corpus, totam animam et totam vitam dedit...* (Armstrong, *Francis of Assisi*, 64). The prayer continues as follows: *...et dat omnibus nobis, qui nos creavit, redemit et sua sola misericordia salvabit* (cfr. Tob 13,5), *qui nobis miserabilibus et miseris, putridis et foetidis, ingratis et malis omnia bona fecit et facit.*

APPENDICES

THE VIRTUES IN THE *OPUSCULA SANCTI FRANCISCI ASSISIENSIS*

Admonitiones:[1]

[Cap. I: De corpore Domini]: **veritas, fides, humilitas, firmitas**

[1] Dicit Dominus Jesus discipulis suis: Ego sum via, **veritas** et vita; nemo venit ad Patrem nisi per me. [2] Si cognosceretis me, et Patrem meum utique cognosceretis; et amodo cognoscetis eum et vidistis eum. [3] Dicit ei Philippus: Domine, ostende nobis Patrem, et sufficit nobis. [4] Dicit ei Jesus: Tanto tempore vobiscum sum et non cognovistis me? Philippe, qui videt me, videt et Patrem (Joa 14,6–9) meum. [5] Pater lucem habitat inaccessibilem (cfr. 1 Tim 6,16), et spiritus est Deus (Joa 4,24), et Deum nemo vidit umquam (Joa 1,18). [6] Ideo nonnisi in spiritu videri potest, quia spiritus est qui vivificat; caro non prodest quidquam (Joa 6,64). [7] Sed nec Filius in eo, quod aequalis est Patri, videtur ab aliquo aliter quam Pater, aliter quam Spiritus Sanctus. [8] Unde omnes qui viderunt Dominum Jesum secundum humanitatem et non viderunt et **crediderunt** secundum spiritum et divinitatem, ipsum esse **verum** Filium Dei, damnati sunt; [9] ita et modo omnes qui vident sacramentum, quod sanctificatur per verba Domini super altare per manum sacerdotis in forma panis et vini, et non vident et **credunt** secundum spiritum et divinitatem, quod sit **veraciter** sanctissimum corpus et sanguis Domini nostri Jesu Christi, damnati sunt, [10] ipso altissimo attestante, qui ait: Hoc est corpus meum et sanguis mei novi testamenti [qui pro multis effundetur] (cfr. Mark 14,22.24); [11] et: Qui manducat carnem meam et bibit sanguinem meum, habet vitam aeternam (cfr. Joa 6,55). [12] Unde spiritus Domini, qui habitat in **fidelibus** suis, ille est qui recipit sanctissimum corpus et sanguinem Domini. [13] Omnes alii, qui non habent de eodem spiritu et praesumunt recipere eum, iudicium sibi manducant et bibunt (cfr. 1 Cor 11,29).
[14] Unde: Filii hominum, usquequo gravi corde? (Ps 4,3). [15] Ut quid non cognoscitis **veritatem** et **creditis** in Filium Dei (cfr. Joa 9,35)? [16] Ecce, quotidie **humiliat** se (cfr. Phil 2,8), sicut quando a regalibus sedibus (Sap 18,15) venit in uterum Virginis; [17] quotidie venit ad nos ipse **humilis** apparens; [18] quotidie descendit de sinu Patris (cfr. Joa 1,18) super altare in manibus sacerdotis. [19] Et sicut sanctis apostolis in **vera** carne, ita et modo se nobis ostendit in sacro pane. [20] Et sicut ipsi intuitu

---

[1] This appendix is based on Menestò & Brufani, *Fontes*/Esser & Grau, *Die Opuscula*. In quotations from the Bible, I have adjusted u (v) to v. Virtues are in **bold**.

carnis suae tantum eius carnem videbant, sed ipsum Deum esse **credebant** oculis spiritualibus contemplantes, [21] sic et nos videntes panem et vinum oculis corporeis videamus et **credamus firmiter**, eius sanctissimum corpus et sanguinem vivum esse et **verum**. [22] Et tali modo semper est Dominus cum **fidelibus** suis, sicut ipse dicit: Ecce ego vobiscum sum usque ad consummationem saeculi (cfr. Matt 28,20).

[Cap. II: De malo propriae voluntatis]: **bonitas, obedientia**

[1] Dixit Dominus ad Adam: De omni ligno comede, de ligno autem scientiae **boni** et mali non comedas (cfr. Gen 2,16.17). [2] De omni ligno paradisi poterat comedere, quia, dum non venit contra **obedientiam**, non peccavit. [3] Ille enim comedit de ligno scientiae **boni**, qui sibi suam voluntatem appropriat et se exaltat de **bonis** quae Dominus dicit et operatur in ipso; [4] et sic per suggestionem diaboli et transgressionem mandati factum est pomum scientiae mali. [5] Unde oportet, quod sustineat poenam.

[Cap. III: De perfecta obedientia]: **obedientia, bonitas, veritas, utilitas, studium, caritas/dilectio**

[1] Dicit Dominus in Evangelio: Qui non renuntiaverit omnibus, quae possidet, non potest meus esse discipulus (Luke 14,33); [2] et: Qui voluerit animam suam salvam facere perdet illam (Luke 9,24). [3] Ille homo relinquit omnia, quae possidet, et perdit corpus suum, qui se ipsum totum praebet ad **obedientiam** in manibus sui praelati. [4] Et quidquid facit et dicit, quod ipse sciat, quod non sit contra voluntatem eius, dum **bonum** sit quod facit, **vera obedientia** est. [5] Et si quando subditus videat meliora et **utiliora** animae suae quam ea, quae sibi praelatus praecipiat, sua voluntarie Deo sacrificet; quae autem sunt praelati, opere **studeat** adimplere. [6] Nam haec est **caritativa obedientia** (cfr. 1 Pet 1,22), quia Deo et proximo satisfacit.
[7] Si vero praelatus aliquid contra animam suam praecipiat, licet ei non **obediat**, tamen ipsum non dimittat. [8] Et si ab aliquibus persecutionem inde sustinuerit, magis eos **diligat** propter Deum. [9] Nam qui prius persecutionem sustinet, quam velit a suis fratribus separari, vere permanet in **perfecta obedientia**, quia ponit animam suam (cfr. Joa 15,13) pro fratribus suis. [10] Sunt enim multi religiosi, qui sub specie meliora videndi quam quae sui praelati praecipiunt, retro aspiciunt (cfr. Luke 9,62) et ad vomitum propriae voluntatis redeunt (cfr. Prov 26,11; 2 Pet 2,22); [11] hi homicidae sunt et propter mala sua exempla multas animas perdere faciunt.

[Cap. IV: Ut nemo appropriet sibi praelationem]:

[1] Non veni ministrari, sed ministrare (cfr. Matt 20,28), dicit Dominus. [2] Illi qui sunt super alios constituti, tantum de illa praelatione glorientur, quantum si essent in

abluendi fratrum pedes officio deputati. ³ Et quanto magis turbantur de ablata sibi praelatione quam de pedum officio, tanto magis sibi loculos ad periculum animae componunt (cfr. Joa 12,6).

[Cap. V: Ut nemo superbiat, sed glorietur in cruce Domini]: **obedientia, sapientia, pulchritudo, infirmitas**

¹ Attende, o homo, in quanta excellentia posuerit te Dominus Deus, quia creavit et formavit te ad imaginem dilecti Filii sui secundum corpus et similitudinem (cfr. Gen 1,26) secundum spiritum. ² Et omnes creaturae, quae sub caelo sunt, secundum se serviunt, cognoscunt et **obediunt** Creatori suo melius quam tu. ³ Et etiam daemones non crucifixerunt eum, sed tu cum ipsis crucifixisti eum et adhuc crucifigis delectando in vitiis et peccatis. ⁴ Unde ergo potes gloriari? ⁵ Nam si tantum esses subtilis et **sapiens** quod omnem scientiam (cfr. 1 Cor 13,2) haberes et scires interpretari omnia genera linguarum (cfr. 1 Cor 12,28) et subtiliter de caelestibus rebus perscrutari, in omnibus his non potes gloriari; ⁶ quia unus daemon scivit de caelestibus et modo scit de terrenis plus quam omnes homines, licet aliquis fuerit, qui summae **sapientiae** cognitionem a Domino receperit specialem. ⁷ Similiter et si esses **pulchrior** et ditior omnibus et etiam si faceres mirabilia, ut daemones fugares, omnia ista tibi sunt contraria et nihil ad te pertinet et in his nil potes gloriari; ⁸ sed in hoc possumus gloriari in **infirmitatibus** nostris (cfr. 2 Cor 12,5) et baiulare quotidie sanctam crucem Domini nostri Jesu Christi (cfr. Luke 14,27).

[Cap. VI: De imitatione Domini]: **bonitas, verecundia, infirmitas, magnitudo, honor**

¹ Attendamus, omnes fratres, **bonum** pastorem, qui pro ovibus suis salvandis crucis sustinuit passionem. ² Oves Domini secutae fuerunt eum in tribulatione et persecutione, **verecundia** et fame, in **infirmitate** et tentatione et ceteris aliis; et de his receperunt a Domino vitam sempiternam. ³ Unde **magna verecundia** est nobis servis Dei, quod sancti fecerunt opera et nos recitando ea volumus recipere gloriam et **honorem**.

[Cap. VII: Ut bona operatio sequatur scientiam]: **sapientia, bonitas**

¹ Dicit apostolus: Littera occidit, spiritus autem vivificat (2 Cor 3,6). ² Illi sunt mortui a littera qui tantum sola verba cupiunt scire, ut **sapientiores** teneantur inter alios et possint acquirere **magnas** divitias dantes consanguineis et amicis. ³ Et illi religiosi sunt mortui a littera, qui spiritum divinae litterae nolunt sequi, sed solum verba magis cupiunt scire et aliis interpretari. ⁴ Et illi sunt vivificati a spiritu divinae litterae, qui omnem litteram, quam sciunt et cupiunt scire, non attribuunt corpori, sed verbo et exemplo reddunt ea altissimo Domino Deo cuius est omne **bonum**.

[Cap. VIII: De peccato invidiae vitando]: **bonitas**

[1] Ait apostolus: Nemo potest dicere: Dominus Jesus, nisi in Spiritu Sancto (1 Cor 12,3); [2] et: Non est qui faciat **bonum**, non est usque ad unum (Rom 3,12). [3] Quicumque ergo invidet fratri suo de **bono**, quod Dominus dicit et facit in ipso, pertinet ad peccatum blasphemiae, quia ipsi Altissimo invidet (cfr. Matt 20,15), qui dicit et facit omne **bonum**.

[Cap. IX: De dilectione]: **dilectio/amor, veritas, dolor**

[1] Dicit Dominus: **Diligite** inimicos vestros [benefacite his qui oderunt vos, et orate pro persequentibus et calumniantibus vos] (Matt 5,44). [2] Ille enim **veraciter diligit** inimicum suum, qui non **dolet** de iniuria, quam sibi facit, [3] sed de peccato animae suae uritur propter **amorem** Dei. [4] Et ostendat ei ex operibus **dilectionem**.

[Cap. X: De castigatione corporis]: **sapientia**

[1] Multi sunt, qui dum peccant vel iniuriam recipiunt, saepe inculpant inimicum vel proximum. [2] Sed non est ita: quia unusquisque in sua potestate habet inimicum, videlicet corpus, per quod peccat. [3] Unde beatus ille servus (Matt 24,46), qui talem inimicum traditum in sua potestate semper captum tenuerit et **sapienter** se ab ipso custodierit; [4] quia dum hoc fecerit, nullus alius inimicus visibilis vel invisibilis ei nocere poterit.

[Cap. XI: Ut nemo corrumpatur malo alterius]: **caritas, rectitudo, sine proprio**

[1] Servo Dei nulla res displicere debet praeter peccatum. [2] Et quocumque modo aliqua persona peccaret, et propter hoc servus Dei non ex **caritate** turbaretur et irasceretur, thesaurizat sibi culpam (cfr. Rom 2,5). [3] Ille servus Dei, qui non irascitur neque conturbat se pro aliquo **recte** vivit **sine proprio**. [4] Et beatus est, qui non remanet sibi aliquid reddens quae sunt caesaris caesari, et quae sunt Dei Deo (Matt 22,21).

[Cap. XII: De cognoscendo spiritu Domini]: **bonitas, vilitas, parvitas**

[1] Sic potest cognosci servus Dei, si habet de spiritu Domini: [2] cum Dominus operaretur per ipsum aliquod **bonum**, si caro eius non inde se exaltaret, quia semper est contraria omni **bono**, [3] sed si magis ante oculos se haberet **viliorem** et omnibus aliis hominibus **minorem** se existimaret.

[Cap. XIII: De patientia]: '**pacificus**', **patientia, humilitas**

[1] Beati **pacifici**, quoniam filii Dei vocabuntur (Matt 5,9). Non potest cognoscere servus Dei, quantam habeat **patientiam** et **humilitatem** in se, dum satisfactum est sibi. [2] Cum autem venerit tempus, quod illi qui deberent sibi satisfacere,

faciunt sibi contrarium, quantam ibi **patientiam** et **humilitatem** tantam habet et non plus.

[Cap. XIV: De paupertate spiritus]: **paupertas, abstinentia, dilectio**

¹ Beati **pauperes** spiritu, quoniam ipsorum est regnum caelorum (Matt 5,3). ² Multi sunt, qui orationibus et officiis insistentes multas **abstinentias** et afflictiones in suis corporibus faciunt, ³ sed de solo verbo, quod videtur esse iniuria suorum corporum vel de aliqua re, quae sibi auferretur, scandalizati continuo perturbantur. ⁴ Hi non sunt **pauperes** spiritu; quia qui vere **pauper** est spiritu, se ipsum odit et eos **diligit** qui eum percutiunt in maxilla (cfr. Matt 5,39).

[Cap. XV: De pace]: **'pacificus', amor**

¹ Beati **pacifici**, quoniam filii Dei vocabuntur (Matt 5,9). ² Illi sunt vere **pacifici**, qui de omnibus, quae in hoc saeculo patiuntur, propter **amorem** Domini nostri Jesu Christi in animo et corpore **pacem** servant.

[Cap. XVI: De munditia cordis]: **munditia, veritas**

¹ Beati **mundo** corde, quoniam ipsi Deum videbunt (Matt 5,8). ² Vere **mundo** corde sunt qui terrena despiciunt, caelestia quaerunt et semper adorare et videre Dominum Deum vivum et **verum mundo** corde et animo non desistunt.

[Cap. XVII: De humili servo Dei]: **bonitas**

¹ Beatus ille servus (Matt 24,46), qui non magis se exaltat de **bono**, quod Dominus dicit et operatur per ipsum, quam quod dicit et operatur per alium. ² Peccat homo, qui magis vult recipere a proximo suo, quam non vult dare de se Domino Deo.

[Cap. XVIII: De compassione proximi]: **fragilitas, bonitas**

¹ Beatus homo, qui sustinet proximum suum secundum suam **fragilitatem** in eo, quod vellet sustineri ab ipso, si in consimili casu esset (cfr. Gal 6,2; Matt 7, 12). ² Beatus servus, qui omnia **bona** reddit Domino Deo, quia qui sibi aliquid retinuerit abscondit in se pecuniam Domini Dei sui (Matt 25,18) et quod putabat habere, auferetur ab eo (Luke 8,18).

[Cap. XIX: De humili servo Dei]: **vilitas, simplicitas, 'despectus'**

¹ Beatus servus, qui non tenet se meliorem, quando magnificatur et exaltatur ab hominibus, sicuti quando tenetur **vilis**, **simplex** et **despectus**, ² quia quantum est homo coram Deo, tantum est et non plus. ³ Vae illi religioso, qui ab aliis positus est in alto et per suam voluntatem non vult descendere. ⁴ Et beatus ille servus (Matt 24,46), qui non per suam voluntatem ponitur in alto et semper desiderat esse sub pedibus aliorum.

[Cap. XX: De bono et vano religioso]: **iucunditas/laetitia/gaudium, amor**

[1] Beatus ille religiosus, qui non habet **iucunditatem** et **laetitiam** nisi in sanctissi-mis eloquiis et operibus Domini [2] et cum his producit homines ad **amorem** Dei cum **gaudio** et **laetitia** (cfr. Ps 50,10). [3] Vae illi religioso, qui delectat se in verbis otiosis et vanis et cum his producit homines ad risum.

[Cap. XXI: De inani et loquaci religioso]: **sapientia, bonitas**

[1] Beatus servus, qui quando loquitur, sub specie mercedis omnia sua non mani-festat et non est velox ad loquendum (cfr. Prov 29,20), sed **sapienter** providet, quae debet loqui et respondere. [2] Vae illi religioso, qui **bona**, quae Dominus sibi ostendit, non retinet in corde suo (cfr. Luke 2,19.51) et aliis non ostendit per ope-rationem, sed sub specie mercedis magis hominibus verbis cupit ostendere. [3] Ipse recipit mercedem suam (cfr. Matt. 6,2.16) et audientes parum fructum reportant.

[Cap. XXII: De correctione]: **patientia, benignitas, verecundia, humilitas, libentia**

[1] Beatus servus, qui disciplinam, accusationem et reprehensionem ita **patienter** ab aliquo sustineret sicut a semetipso. [2] Beatus servus, qui reprehensus **benigne** acquiescit, **verecunde** obtemperat, **humiliter** confitetur et **libenter** satisfacit. [3] Beatus servus, qui non est velox ad se excusandum et **humiliter** sustinet **vere-cundiam** et reprehensionem de peccato, ubi non commisit culpam.

[Cap. XXIII: De humilitate]: **humilitas, fides, prudentia**

[1] Beatus servus, qui ita inventus est **humilis** inter subditos suos, sicuti quando esset inter dominos suos. [2] Beatus servus, qui semper permanet sub virga correc-tionis. [3] **Fidelis** et **prudens** servus est (cfr. Matt 24,45), qui in omnibus suis offen-sis non tardat interius punire per contritionem et exterius per confessionem et operis satisfactionem.

[Cap. XXIV: De vera dilectione]: **dilectio, infirmitas**

Beatus servus, qui tantum **diligeret** fratrem suum, quando est **infirmus**, quod non potest ei satisfacere, quantum quando est sanus, qui potest ei satisfacere.

[Cap. XXV: Item de eodem]: **dilectio/caritas, timor**

Beatus servus, qui tantum **diligeret** et **timeret** fratrem suum, cum esset longe ab ipso, sicuti quando esset cum eo, et non diceret aliquid post ipsum, quod cum **caritate** non posset dicere coram ipso.

[Cap. XXVI: Ut servi Dei honorent clericos]: **fides, rectitudo**

[1] Beatus servus, qui portat **fidem** in clericis, qui vivunt **recte** secundum formam Ecclesiae Romanae. [2] Et vae illis qui ipsos despiciunt; licet enim sint peccatores, tamen nullus debet eos iudicare, quia ipse solus Dominus reservat sibi ipsos ad iudicandum. [3] Nam quantum est maior administratio eorum, quam habent de sanctissimo corpore et sanguine Domini nostri Jesu Christi, quod ipsi recipiunt et ipsi soli aliis ministrant, [4] tantum plus peccatum habent, qui peccant in ipsis, quam in omnibus aliis hominibus istius mundi.

[Cap. XXVII: De virtute effugante vitio]: **caritas, sapientia, timor, patientia, humilitas, paupertas, laetitia, quies, sollicitudo, misericordia, discretio**

[1] Ubi **caritas** est et **sapientia**, ibi nec **timor** nec ignorantia.
[2] Ubi est **patientia** et **humilitas**, ibi nec ira nec perturbatio.
[3] Ubi est **paupertas** cum **laetitia**, ibi nec cupiditas nec avaritia.
[4] Ubi est **quies** et meditatio, ibi neque **sollicitudo** neque vagatio.
[5] Ubi est **timor Domini** ad atrium suum custodiendum (cfr. Luke 11,21),
ibi inimicus non potest habere locum ad ingrediendum.
[6] Ubi est **misericordia** et **discretio**, ibi nec superfluitas nec induratio.

[Cap. XXVIII: De abscondendo bono ne perdatur]: **bonitas**

[1] Beatus servus, qui thesaurizat in caelo (cfr. Matt 6,20) **bona**, quae Dominus sibi ostendit et sub specie mercedis non cupit manifestare hominibus, [2] quia ipse altissimus manifestabit opera eius quibuscumque placuerit. [3] Beatus servus qui secreta Domini observat in corde suo (cfr. Luke 2,19.51).

Canticum fratris solis vel Laudes creaturarum: bonitas, dignitas, claritas, pretiositas, serenitas, utilitas, humilitas, castitas, iucunditas, robur, fortitudo, amor, infirmitas, pax

[1] Altissimu onnipotente **bon** signore,
tue so le laude la gloria e l'onore et onne benedictione.
[2] Ad te solo, altissimo, se konfano,
et nullu homo ene **dignu** te mentovare.
[3] Laudato si, mi signore, cun tucte le tue creature,
spetialmente messor lo frate sole,
lo qual'è iorno, et allumini noi per loi.
[4] Et ellu è **bellu** e radiante cun grande splendore,
de te, altissimo, porta significatione.
[5] Laudato si, mi signore, per sora luna e le stelle,
in celu l'ài formate **clarite** et **pretiose** et **belle**.

[6] Laudato si, mi signore, per frate vento,
et per aere et nubilo et **sereno** et onne tempo,
per lo quale a le tue creature dai sustentamento.
[7] Laudato si, mi signore, per sor aqua,
la quale è multo **utile** et **humile** et **pretiosa** et **casta**.
[8] Laudato si, mi signore, per frate focu,
per lo quale enn' allumini la nocte,
ed ello è **bello** et **iocundo** et **robustoso** et **forte**.
[9] Laudato si, mi signore, per sora nostra matre terra,
la quale ne sustenta et governa,
et produce diversi fructi con coloriti flori et herba.
[10] Laudato si, mi signore, per quelli ke perdonano per lo tuo **amore**,
et sostengo **infirmitate** et tribulatione.
[11] Beati quelli ke 'l sosterrano in **pace**,
ka da te, altissimo, sirano incoronati.
[12] Laudato si, mi signore, per sora nostra morte corporale,
da la quale nullu homo vivente pò skappare.
[13] Guai a quelli, ke morrano ne le peccata mortali:
beati quelli ke trovarà ne le tue sanctissime voluntati,
ka la morte secunda nol farrà male.
[14] Laudate et benedicete mi signore,
et rengratiate et serviateli cun grande **humilitate**.

Chartula fr. Leoni data

A. **Laudes Dei altissimi** [LaudDei]: **fortitudo, magnitudo, bonitas, veritas, amor/caritas, sapientia, humilitas, patientia, pulchritudo, mansuetudo, securitas, quietas, gaudium, spes, laetitia, iustitia, temperantia, fides, dulcedo, admirabilitas, misericordia**

[1] Tu es sanctus Dominus Deus solus, qui facis mirabilia (Ps 76,15). [2] Tu es **fortis**, tu es **magnus** (cfr. Ps 85,10), tu es altissimus, tu es rex omnipotens, tu pater sancte (Joa 17,11), rex caeli et terrae (cfr. Matt 11,25). [3] Tu es trinus et unus Dominus Deus deorum (cfr. Ps 135,2); tu es **bonum**, omne **bonum**, summum **bonum**, Dominus Deus vivus et **verus** (cfr. 1 Thess 1,9). [4] Tu es **amor, caritas**; tu es **sapientia**, tu es **humilitas**, tu es **patientia** (Ps 70,5), tu es **pulchritudo**, tu es **mansuetudo**, tu es **securitas**, tu es **quietas**, tu es **gaudium**, tu es **spes** nostra et **laetitia**, tu es **iustitia**, tu es **temperantia**, tu es omnia divitia nostra ad sufficientiam. [5] Tu es **pulchritudo**, tu es **mansuetudo**; tu es protector (Ps 30,5), tu es custos et defensor noster; tu es **fortitudo** (cfr. Ps 42,2), tu es refrigerium. [6] Tu es **spes** nostra, tu es **fides** nostra, tu es **caritas** nostra, tu es tota **dulcedo** nostra, tu es vita aeterna nostra: **Magnus** et **admirabilis** Dominus, Deus omnipotens, **misericors** Salvator.

B. Benedictio fr. Leoni data: (pax), gratitudo

Beatus Franciscus duobus annis ante mortem suam fecit quadragesimam in loco Alvernae ad honorem beatae Virginis, matris Dei, et beati Michaelis archangeli a festo assumptionis sanctae Mariae virginis usque ad festum sancti Michaelis septembris; et facta est super eum manus Domini; post visionem et allocutionem Seraphim et impressionem stigmatum Christi in corpore suo fecit has laudes ex alio latere chartulae scriptas et manu sua scripsit gratias agens Deo de beneficio sibi collata.

¹ Benedicat tibi Dominus et custodiat te; ostendat faciem suam tibi et misereatur tui. ² Convertat vultum suum ad te et det tibi **pacem** (Num 6,24–26).
Beatus Franciscus scripsit manu sua istam benedictionem mihi fratri Leoni.
³ Dominus benedicat, frater Leo, te (cfr. Num 6,27b).
Simili modo fecit istum signum thau [!] cum capite manu sua.

Epistola ad sanctum Antonium: studium, devotio

¹ Fratri Antonio episcopo meo frater Franciscus salutem. ² Placet mihi quod sacram theologiam legas fratribus, dummodo inter huius **studium** orationis et **devotionis** spiritum non exstinguas, sicut in regula continetur.

Epistola ad clericos I (recensio prior): magnitudo, vilitas, pietas, firmitas, pretiositas

¹ Attendamus, omnes clerici, **magnum** peccatum et ignorantiam, quam quidam habent super sanctissimum corpus et sanguinem Domini nostri Jesu Christi et sacratissima nomina et verba eius scripta, quae sanctificant corpus. ² Scimus, quia non potest esse corpus, nisi prius sanctificetur a verbo. ³ Nihil enim habemus et videmus corporaliter in hoc saeculo de ipso Altissimo nisi corpus et sanguinem, nomina et verba, per quae facti sumus et redempti de morte ad vitam (1 Joa 3,14). ⁴ Omnes autem illi qui ministrant tam sanctissima mysteria, considerent intra se, maxime hi qui illicite ministrant, quam **viles** sint calices, corporales et linteamina, ubi sacrificatur corpus et sanguis eiusdem. ⁵ Et a multis in locis **vilibus** collocatur et relinquitur, miserabiliter portatur et indigne sumitur et indiscrete aliis ministratur. ⁶ Nomina etiam et verba eius scripta aliquando pedibus conculcantur; ⁷ quia animalis homo non percipit ea quae Dei sunt (1 Cor 2,14). ⁸ Non movemur de his omnibus **pietate**, cum ipse **pius** Dominus in manibus nostris se praebeat et eum tractemus et sumamus quotidie per os nostrum? ⁹ An ignoramus, quia venire debemus in manus eius? ¹⁰ Igitur de his omnibus et aliis cito et **firmiter** emendemus; ¹¹ et ubicumque fuerit sanctissimum corpus Domini nostri Jesu Christi illicite collocatum et relictum, removeatur de loco illo et in loco **pretioso** ponatur et consignetur. ¹² Similiter nomina et verba Domini scripta, ubicumque inveniantur in locis immundis, colligantur et in loco honesto debeant collocari. ¹³ Haec omnia usque in finem universi clerici tenentur super omnia observare. ¹⁴ Et qui hoc non fecerint, sciant se debere coram Domino nostro Jesu Christo in die iudicii reddere rationem (cfr. Matt 12,36). ¹⁵ Hoc scriptum, ut melius

debeat observari, sciant se benedictos a Domino Deo, qui illud fecerint exemplari.

Epistola ad clericos II (recensio posterior): vilitas, pietas, firmitas, pretiositas

[1] Attendamus, omnes clerici, magmum peccatum et ignorantiam, quam quidam habent super sanctissimum corpus et sanguinem Domini nostri Jesu Christi et sacratissima nomina et verba eius scripta, quae sanctificant corpus. [2] Scimus, quia non potest esse corpus, nisi prius sanctificetur a verbo. [3] Nihil enim habemus et videmus corporaliter in hoc saeculo de ipso Altissimo, nisi corpus et sanguinem, nomina et verba, per quae facti sumus et redempti de morte ad vitam (1 Joa 3,14). [4] Omnes autem illi qui ministrant tam sanctissima ministeria, considerent intra se, maxime hi qui indiscrete ministrant, quam **viles** sint calices, corporalia et linteamina, ubi sacrificatur corpus et sanguis Domini nostri. [5] Et a multis in locis **vilibus** relinquitur, miserabiliter portatur et indigne sumitur et indiscrete aliis ministratur. [6] Nomina etiam et verba eius scripta aliquando pedibus conculcantur; [7] quia animalis homo non percipit ea quae Dei sunt (1 Cor 2,14). [8] Non movemur de his omnibus **pietate**, cum ipse **pius** Dominus in manibus nostris se praebeat et eum tractemus et sumamus quotidie per os nostrum? [9] An ignoramus, quia debemus venire in manus eius? [10] Igitur de his omnibus et aliis cito et **firmiter** emendemus; [11] et ubicumque fuerit sanctissimum corpus Domini nostri Jesu Christi illicite collocatum et relictum, removeatur de loco illo et in loco **pretioso** ponatur et consignetur. [12] Similiter nomina et verba Domini scripta, ubicumque inveniantur in locis immundis, colligantur et in loco honesto debeant collocari. [13] Et scimus, quia haec omnia tenemur super omnia observare secundum praecepta Domini et constitutiones sanctae matris Ecclesiae. [14] Et qui hoc non fecerit, sciat, se coram Domino nostro Jesu Christo in die iudicii reddere rationem (cfr. Matt 12,36). [15] Hoc scriptum, ut melius debeat observari, sciant se benedictos a Domino Deo, qui ipsum fecerint exemplari.

Epistola ad custodes I: parvitas, magnitudo, humilitas, veneratio, pretiositas, paupertas, discretio, poenitentia, honor, veritas, obedientia, gratitudo

[1] Universis custodibus Fratrum Minorum, ad quos litterae istae pervenerint, frater Franciscus in Domino Deo vester servus et **parvulus**, salutem cum novis signis caeli et terrae, quae **magna** et excellentissima sunt apud Deum et a multis religiosis et aliis hominibus minima reputantur.

[2] Rogo vos plus quam de me ipso, quatenus, cum decet et videritis expedire, clericis **humiliter** supplicetis, quod sanctissimum corpus et sanguinem Domini nostri Jesu Christi et sancta nomina et verba eius scripta, quae sanctificant corpus, super omnia debeant **venerari**. [3] Calices, corporalia, ornamenta altaris et omnia, quae pertinent ad sacrificium, **pretiosa** habere debeant. [4] Et si in aliquo loco sanctissimum corpus Domini fuerit **pauperrime** collocatum, iuxta mandatum Ecclesiae in loco **pretioso** ab eis ponatur et consignetur et cum **magna veneratione** portetur et cum **discretione** aliis ministretur. [5] Nomina etiam et verba Domini scripta, ubicumque inveniantur in locis immundis, colligantur et in loco honesto debeant collocari. [6] Et in omni praedicatione, quam facitis, de

poenitentia populum moneatis, et quod nemo potest salvari, nisi qui recipit sanctissimum corpus et sanguinem Domini (cfr. Joa 6,54); [7] et quando a sacerdote sacrificatur super altare et in aliqua parte portatur, omnes gentes flexis genibus reddant laudes, gloriam et **honorem** Domino Deo vivo et **vero**. [8] Et de laude eius ita omnibus gentibus annuntietis et praedicetis, ut omni hora et quando pulsantur campanae semper ab universo populo omnipotenti Deo laudes et **gratiae** referantur per totam terram.
[9] Et, ad quoscumque fratres meos custodes pervenerit hoc scriptum et exemplaverint et apud se habuerint et pro fratribus, qui habent officium praedicationis et custodiam fratrum, fecerint exemplari et omnia, quae continentur in hoc scripto, praedicaverint usque in finem, sciant se habere benedictionem Domini Dei et meam. [10] Et ista sint eis per **veram** et sanctam **obedientiam**. Amen.

Epistola ad custodes II: pax, sublimitas, vilitas, magnitudo, diligentia

[1] Universis custodibus Fratrum Minorum, ad quos istae litterae pervenerint, frater Franciscus, minimus servorum Dei salutem et sanctam **pacem** in Domino. [2] Scitote, quod in conspectu Dei sunt quaedam res nimis altae et **sublimes**, quae aliquando reputantur inter homines pro **vilibus** et abiectis; [3] et aliae sunt carae et spectabiles inter homines, quae coram Deo tenentur pro **vilissimis** et abiectis. [4] Rogo vos coram Domino Deo nostro, quantum possum, quod litteras illas, quae tractant de sanctissimo corpore et sanguine Domini nostri, detis episcopis et aliis clericis; [5] et memoria retineatis, quae super his vobis commendavimus. [6] Aliarum litterarum, quas vobis mitto, ut eas detis potestatibus, consulibus et rectoribus, et in quibus continetur, ut publicentur per populos et plateas Dei laudes, facite statim multa exemplaria, [7] et cum **magna diligentia** eas porrigite illis, quibus debeant dari.

Epistola ad fideles (recensio prior) (Exhortatio ad fratres et sorores de Poenitentia): dilectio/amor/caritas, virtus, dignitas, poenitentia, perseverantia, requies, fides, puritas, sinceritas, magnitudo, pulchritudo, admirabilitas, 'beneplacitus', humilitas, 'pacificus', dulcedo, amabilitas, desiderabilitas, claritas, sollicitudo, veritas, sapientia, infirmitas, benignitas

Haec sunt verba vitae et salutis quae si quis legeret et fecerit inveniet vitam, et hauriet salutem a domino.

[Cap. I] De illis qui faciunt poenitentiam.
In nomine Domini!
[1] Omnes qui Dominum **diligunt** ex toto corde, ex tota anima et mente, ex **tota virtute** (cfr. Mark 12,30) et **diligunt** proximos suos sicut se ipsos (cfr. Matt 22,39), [2] et odio habent corpora eorum cum vitiis et peccatis, [3] et recipiunt corpus et sanguinem Domini nostri Jesu Christi, [4] et faciunt fructus **dignos poenitentiae**: [5] O quam beati et benedicti sunt illi et illae, dum talia faciunt et in talibus **perseverant**, [6] quia **requiescet** super eos spiritus Domini (cfr. Isa 11,2) et faciet apud eos habitaculum et mansionem (cfr. Joa 14,23), [7] et sunt filii patris caelestis

(cfr. Matt 5,45), cuius opera faciunt et sunt sponsi, fratres et matres Domini nostri Jesu Christi (cfr. Matt 12,50). [8] Sponsi sumus, quando Spiritu Sancto coniungitur **fidelis** anima Domino nostro Jesu Christo. [9] Fratres ei sumus, quando facimus voluntatem patris qui in caelis est (Matt 12,50). [10] Matres, quando portamus eum in corde et corpore nostro (cfr. 1 Cor 6,20) per divinum **amorem** et **puram** et **sinceram** conscientiam; parturimus eum per sanctam operationem, quae lucere debet aliis in exemplum (cfr. Matt 5,16). [11] O quam gloriosum est, sanctum et **magnum** in caelis habere patrem! [12] O quam sanctum, praeclarum, **pulchrum** et **admirabilem** talem habere sponsum! [13] O quam sanctum et quam **dilectum, beneplacitum, humilem, pacificum, dulcem, amabilem** et super omnia **desiderabilem** habere talem fratrem et talem filium: Dominum nostrum Jesum Christum, qui posuit animam pro ovibus suis (cfr. Joa 10,15) et oravit patri dicens: [14] Pater sancte, serva eos in nomine tuo (Joa 17,11), quos dedisti mihi in mundo; tui erant et mihi dedisti eos (Joa 17,6). [15] Et verba, quae mihi dedisti, dedi eis, et ipsi acceperunt et **crediderunt** vere, quia a te exivi et cognoverunt, quia tu me misisti (Joa 17,8). [16] Rogo pro eis et non pro mundo (cfr. Joa 17,9). [17] Benedic et sanctifica (Joa 17,17) et pro eis sanctifico me ipsum (Joa 17,19). [18] Non pro eis rogo tantum, sed pro eis qui **credituri** sunt per verbum illorum in me (Joa 17,20), ut sint sanctificati in unum (cfr. Joa 17,23) sicut et nos (Joa 17,11). [19] Et volo, pater, ut ubi ego sum et illi sint mecum, ut videant **claritatem** meam (Joa 17,24) in regno tuo (Matt 20,21). Amen.

[Cap. II] De illis qui non agunt poenitentiam.
[1] Omnes autem illi et illae, qui non sunt in **poenitentia**, [2] et non recipiunt corpus et sanguinem Domini nostri Jesu Christi, [3] et operantur vitia et peccata et qui ambulant post malam concupiscentiam et mala desideria carnis suae, [4] et non observant, quae promiserunt Domino, [5] et serviunt corporaliter mundo carnalibus desideriis et **sollicitudinibus** saeculi et curis huius vitae: [6] detenti a diabolo, cuius sunt filii et eius opera faciunt (cfr. Joa 8,41), [7] caeci sunt, quia **verum** lumen non vident Dominum nostrum Jesum Christum. [8] **Sapientiam** non habent spiritualem, quia non habent Filium Dei, qui est **vera sapientia** Patris, [9] de quibus dicitur: **Sapientia** eorum deglutita est (Ps 106,27) et: Maledicti qui declinant a mandatis tuis (Ps 118,21). [10] Vident et agnoscunt, sciunt et faciunt mala et ipsi scienter perdunt animas. [11] Videte, caeci, decepti ab inimicis vestris: a carne, mundo et diabolo; quia corpori **dulce** est facere peccatum et amarum est facere servire Deo; [12] quia omnia vitia et peccata de corde hominum exeunt et procedunt, sicut dicit Dominus in Evangelio (cfr. Mark 7,21). [13] Et nihil habetis in hoc saeculo neque in futuro. [14] Et putatis diu possidere vanitates huius saeculi, sed decepti estis, quia veniet dies et hora, de quibus non cogitatis, nescitis et ignoratis; **infirmatur** corpus, mors appropinquat et sic moritur amara morte. [15] Et ubicumque, quandocumque, qualitercumque moritur homo in criminali peccato sine **poenitentia** et satisfactione, si potest satisfacere et non satisfacit, diabolus rapit animam suam de corpore eius cum tanta angustia et tribulatione, quod nemo potest scire, nisi qui recipit. [16] Et omnia talenta et potestas et scientia et **sapientia** (2 Par 1,12), quae putabant habere, auferetur ab eis (cfr. Luke 8,18; Mark 4,25). [17] Et propinquis et amicis relinquunt et ipsi tulerunt et diviserunt substantiam

eius et dixerunt postea: Maledicta sit anima sua, quia potuit plus dare nobis et acquirere quam non acquisivit. [18] Corpus comedunt vermes, et ita perdiderunt corpus et animam in isto brevi saeculo et ibunt in inferno, ubi cruciabuntur sine fine.

[19] Omnes illos quibus litterae istae pervenerint, rogamus in **caritate** quae Deus est (cfr. 1 Joa 4,16), ut ista supradicta odorifera verba Domini nostri Jesu Christi cum divino **amore benigne** recipiant. [20] Et qui nesciunt legere, saepe legere faciant; [21] et apud se retineant cum sancta operatione usque in finem, quia spiritus et vita sunt (Joa 6,64). [22] Et qui hoc non fecerint, tenebuntur reddere rationem in die iudicii (cfr. Matt 12,36) ante tribunal Domini nostri Jesu Christi (cfr. Rom 14,10).

Epistola ad fideles (recensio posterior): reverentia, pax, veritas, sinceritas, caritas/dilectio/amor, infirmitas, dignitas, fragilitas, paupertas, gratitudo, puritas, castitas, suavitas, discretio, poenitentia, bonitas, misericordia, humilitas, veneratio, abstinentia, firmitas, obedientia, parvitas, patientia, benignitas, sapientia, prudentia, simplicitas, 'despectus', perseverantia, requies, fides, magnitudo, pulchritudo, admirabilitas, 'beneplacitus', 'pacificus', dulcedo, amabilitas, desiderabilitas, claritas, honor, virtus, fortitudo, laudabilitas, sollicitudo, confidentia

[1] In nomine Domini Patris et Filii et Spiritus Sancti. Amen.
Universis christianis religiosis, clericis et laicis, masculis et feminis, omnibus qui habitant in universo mundo, frater Franciscus, eorum servus et subditus, obsequium cum **reverentia, pacem veram** de caelo et **sinceram** in Domino **caritatem.**
[2] Cum sim servus omnium, omnibus servire teneor et administrare odorifera verba Domini mei. [3] Unde in mente considerans, quod cum personaliter propter **infirmitatem** et debilitatem mei corporis non possim singulos visitare, proposui litteris praesentibus et nuntiis verba Domini nostri Jesu Christi, qui est Verbum Patris, vobis referre et verba Spiritus Sancti, quae spiritus et vita sunt (Joa 6,64).
[4] Istud Verbum Patris tam **dignum**, tam sanctum et gloriosum nuntiavit altissimus Pater de caelo per sanctum Gabrielem angelum suum in uterum sanctae et gloriosae virginis Mariae, ex cuius utero **veram** recepit carnem humanitatis et **fragilitatis** nostrae. [5] Qui, cum dives esset (2 Cor 8,9) super omnia, voluit ipse in mundo cum beatissima Virgine, matre sua, eligere **paupertatem.** [6] Et prope passionem celebravit pascha cum discipulis suis et accipiens panem **gratias** egit et benedixit et fregit dicens: Accipite et comedite, hoc est corpus meum (Matt 26,26). [7] Et accipiens calicem dixit: Hic est sanguis meus novi testamenti, qui pro vobis et pro multis effundetur in remissionem peccatorum (Matt 26,27). [8] Deinde oravit Patrem dicens: Pater, si fieri potest, transeat a me calix iste (Matt 26,39).
[9] Et factus est sudor eius sicut guttae sanguinis decurrentis in terram (Luke 22,44).
[10] Posuit tamen voluntatem suam in voluntate Patris dicens: Pater, fiat voluntas tua (Matt 26,42); non sicut ego volo, sed sicut tu (Matt 26,39). [11] Cuius Patris talis

fuit voluntas, ut filius eius benedictus et gloriosus, quem dedit nobis et natus fuit pro nobis, se ipsum per proprium sanguinem suum sacrificium et hostiam in ara crucis offerret; [12] non propter se, per quem facta sunt omnia (cfr. Joa 1,3), sed pro peccatis nostris, [13] relinquens nobis exemplum, ut sequamur vestigia eius (cfr. 1 Pet 2,21). [14] Et vult ut omnes salvemur per eum et recipiamus ipsum **puro** corde et **casto** corpore nostro. [15] Sed pauci sunt, qui velint eum recipere et salvi esse per eum, licet eius iugum **suave** sit et onus ipsius leve (cfr. Matt 11,30).

[16] Qui nolunt gustare, quam **suavis** sit Dominus (cfr. Ps 33,9) et **diligunt** tenebras magis quam lucem (Joa 3,19) nolentes adimplere mandata Dei, maledicti sunt; [17] de quibus dicitur per prophetam: Maledicti qui declinant a mandatis tuis (Ps 118,21). [18] Sed, o quam beati et benedicti sunt illi, qui Deum **diligunt** et faciunt, sicut dicit ipse Dominus in evangelio: Diliges Dominum Deum tuum ex toto corde et ex tota mente, et proximum tuum sicut te ipsum (Matt 22,37.39).

[19] **Diligamus** igitur Deum et adoremus eum **puro** corde et **pura** mente, quia ipse super omnia quaerens dixit: **Veri** adoratores adorabunt Patrem in spiritu et **veritate** (Joa 4,23). [20] Omnes enim, qui adorant eum, in spiritu **veritatis** oportet eum adorare (cfr. Joa 4,24). [21] Et dicamus ei laudes et orationes die ac nocte (Ps 31,4) dicendo: Pater noster, qui es in caelis (Matt 6,9), quia oportet nos semper orare et non deficere (Luke 18,1).

[22] Debemus siquidem confiteri sacerdoti omnia peccata nostra; et recipiamus corpus et sanguinem Domini nostri Jesu Christi ab eo. [23] Qui non manducat carnem suam et non bibit sanguinem suum (cfr. Joa 6,55.57), non potest introire in regnum Dei (Joa 3,5). [24] **Digne** tamen manducet et bibat, quia qui indigne recipit, iudicium sibi manducat et bibit, non diiudicans corpus Domini (1 Cor 11,29), id est non **discernit**. [25] Faciamus insuper fructus **dignos poenitentiae** (Luke 3,8). [26] Et **diligamus** proximos sicut nos ipsos (cfr. Matt 22,39). [27] Et si quis non vult eos **amare** sicut se ipsum, saltim non inferat eis mala, sed faciat **bona**.

[28] Qui autem potestatem iudicandi alios receperunt iudicium cum **misericordia** exerceant, sicut ipsi volunt a Domino **misericordiam** obtinere. [29] Iudicium enim sine **misericordia** erit illis qui non fecerint **misericordiam** (Jac 2,13). [30] Habeamus itaque **caritatem** et **humilitatem**; et faciamus eleemosynas, quia ipsa lavat animas a sordibus peccatorum (cfr. Tob 4,11; 12, 9). [31] Homines enim omnia perdunt, quae in hoc saeculo relinquunt; secum tamen portant **caritatis** mercedem et eleemosynas, quas fecerunt, de quibus habebunt a Domino praemium et **dignam** remunerationem.

[32] Debemus etiam ieiunare et **abstinere** a vitiis et peccatis (cfr. Sir 3,32) et a superfluitate ciborum et potus et esse catholici. [33] Debemus etiam ecclesias visitare frequenter et **venerari** clericos et **revereri**, non tantum propter eos, si sint peccatores, sed propter officium et administrationem sanctissimi corporis et sanguinis Christi, quod sacrificant in altari et recipiunt et aliis administrant. [34] Et **firmiter** sciamus omnes, quia nemo salvari potest, nisi per sancta verba et sanguinem Domini nostri Jesu Christi, quae clerici dicunt, annuntiant et ministrant. [35] Et ipsi soli ministrare debent et non alii. [36] Specialiter autem religiosi, qui

renuntiaverunt saeculo, tenentur, plura et maiora facere, sed ista non dimittere (cfr. Luke 11,42). [37] Debemus odio habere corpora nostra cum vitiis et peccatis, quia Dominus dicit in evangelio: Omnia mala, vitia et peccata a corde exeunt (Matt 15,18–19; Mark 7,23). [38] Debemus **diligere** inimicos nostros et benefacere his, qui nos odio habent (cfr. Matt 5,44; Luke 6,27). [39] Debemus observare praecepta et consilia Domini nostri Jesu Christi. [40] Debemus etiam nosmetipsos abnegare (cfr. Matt 16,24) et ponere corpora nostra sub iugo servitutis et sanctae **obedientiae**, sicut unusquisque promisit Domino. [41] Et nullus homo teneatur ex **obedientia obedire** alicui in eo, ubi committitur delictum vel peccatum.

[42] Cui autem **obedientia** commissa est et qui habetur maior, sit sicut **minor** (Luke 22,26) et aliorum fratrum servus. [43] Et in singulos fratres suos **misericordiam** faciat et habeat, quam vellet sibi fieri, si in consimili casu esset (cfr. Matt 7,12). [44] Nec ex delicto fratris irascatur in fratrem, sed cum omni **patientia** et **humililate** ipsum **benigne** moneat et sustineat. [45] Non debemus secundum carnem esse **sapientes** et **prudentes**, sed magis debemus esse **simplices**, **humiles** et **puri**. [46] Et habeamus corpora nostra in opprobrium et **despectum**, quia omnes per culpam nostram sumus miseri et putridi, foetidi et vermes, sicut dicit Dominus per prophetam: Ego sum vermis et non homo, opprobrium hominum et abiectio plebis (Ps 21,7). [47] Numquam debemus desiderare esse super alios, sed magis debemus esse servi et subditi omni humanae creaturae propter Deum (1 Pet 2,13).

[48] Et omnes illi et illae, dum talia fecerint et **perseveraverint** usque in finem, **requiescet** super eos spiritus Domini (Isa 11,2) et faciet in eis habitaculum et mansionem (cfr. Joa 14,23). [49] Et erunt filii Patris caelestis (cfr. Matt 5,45), cuius opera faciunt. [50] Et sunt sponsi, fratres et matres Domini nostri Jesu Christi (cfr. Matt 12,50). [51] Sponsi sumus, quando Spiritu Sancto coniungitur **fidelis** anima Jesu Christo. [52] Fratres enim sumus, quando facimus voluntatem patris eius, qui est in caelo (cfr. Matt 12,50); [53] matres, quando portamus eum in corde et corpore nostro (cfr. 1 Cor 6,20) per **amorem** et **puram** et **sinceram** conscientiam; parturimus eum per sanctam operationem, quae lucere debet aliis in exemplum (cfr. Matt 5,16).

[54] O quam gloriosum et sanctum et **magnum** habere in caelis Patrem! [55] O quam sanctum, praeclarum, **pulchrum** et **admirabilem** habere sponsum! [56] O quam sanctum et quam **dilectum**, **beneplacitum**, **humilem**, **pacificum**, **dulcem** et **amabilem** et super omnia **desiderabilem** habere talem fratrem et filium, qui posuit animam suam pro ovibus suis (cfr. Joa 10,15) et oravit Patrem pro nobis dicens: Pater sancte, serva eos in nomine tuo, quos dedisti mihi (Joa 17,11). [57] Pater, omnes, quos dedisti mihi in mundo, tui erant et mihi eos dedisti (Joa 17,6). [58] Et verba, quae dedisti mihi, dedi eis; et ipsi acceperunt et cognoverunt vere, quia a te exivi, et **crediderunt**, quia tu me misisti (Joa 17,8); rogo pro eis et non pro mundo (cfr. Joa 17,9); benedic et sanctifica eos (Joa 17,17). [59] Et pro eis sanctifico me ipsum, ut sint sanctificati in (Joa 17,19) unum sicut et nos (Joa 17,11) sumus. [60] Et volo, Pater, ut ubi ego sum et illi sint mecum, ut videant **claritatem** meam (Joa 17,24) in regno tuo (Matt 20,21).

⁶¹ Ei autem qui tanta sustinuit pro nobis, tot **bona** contulit et conferet in futurum, omnis creatura, quae est in caelis, in terra, in mari et in abyssis reddat laudem Deo, gloriam, **honorem** et benedictionem (cfr. Apoc 5,13), ⁶² quia ipse est **virtus** et **fortitudo** nostra, qui est solus **bonus**, solus altissimus, solus omnipotens, **admirabilis**, gloriosus et solus sanctus, **laudabilis** et benedictus per infinita saecula saeculorum. Amen.

⁶³ Omnes autem illi, qui non sunt in **poenitentia** et non recipiunt corpus et sanguinem Domini nostri Jesu Christi, ⁶⁴ et operantur vitia et peccata, et qui ambulant post malam concupiscentiam et mala desideria, et non observant, quae promiserunt, ⁶⁵ et serviunt corporaliter mundo carnalibus desideriis, curis et **sollicitudinibus** huius saeculi et curis huius vitae, ⁶⁶ decepti a diabolo, cuius filii sunt et eius opera faciunt (cfr. Joa 8,41), caeci sunt, quia **verum** lumen non vident Dominum nostrum Jesum Christum. ⁶⁷ **Sapientiam** non habent spiritualem, quia non habent Filium Dei in se, qui est **vera sapientia** Patris; de quibus dicitur: **Sapientia** eorum devorata est (Ps 106,27). ⁶⁸ Vident, agnoscunt, sciunt et faciunt mala; et scienter perdunt animas. ⁶⁹ Videte, caeci, decepti ab inimicis nostris scilicet a carne, a mundo et a diabolo, quia corpori **dulce** est facere peccatum et amarum servire Deo, quia omnia mala, vitia et peccata de corde hominum exeunt et procedunt (cfr. Mark 7,21.23), sicut dicit Dominus in evangelio. ⁷⁰ Et nihil habetis in hoc saeculo neque in futuro. ⁷¹ Putatis diu possidere vanitates huius saeculi, sed decepti estis, quia veniet dies et hora, de quibus non cogitatis et nescitis et ignoratis.

⁷² **Infirmatur** corpus, mors appropinquat, veniunt propinqui et amici dicentes: Dispone tua. ⁷³ Ecce uxor eius et filii eius et propinqui et amici fingunt flere. ⁷⁴ Et respiciens videt eos flentes, movetur malo motu; cogitando intra se dicit: Ecce animam et corpus meum et omnia mea pono in manibus vestris. ⁷⁵ Vere, iste homo est maledictus, qui **confidit** et exponit animam suam et corpus et omnia sua in talibus manibus; ⁷⁶ unde Dominus per prophetam: Maledictus homo, qui **confidit** in homine (Jer 17,5). ⁷⁷ Et statim faciunt venire sacerdotem; dicit ei sacerdos: «Vis recipere **poenitentiam** de omnibus peccatis tuis?» ⁷⁸ Respondet: «Volo». «Vis satisfacere de commissis et his quae fraudasti et decepisti homines sicut potes de tua substantia?» ⁷⁹ Respondet: «Non». Et sacerdos dicit: «Quare non?» ⁸⁰ «Quia omnia disposui in manibus propinquorum et amicorum». ⁸¹ Et incipit perdere loquelam et sic moritur ille miser.

⁸² Sed sciant omnes, quod ubicumque et qualitercumque homo moriatur in criminali peccato sine satisfactione et potest satisfacere et non satisfecit, diabolus rapit animam eius de corpore suo cum tanta angustia et tribulatione, quantam nullus scire potest, nisi qui recipit. ⁸³ Et omnia talenta et potestas et scientia, quam putabat habere (cfr. Luke 8,18), auferetur ab eo (Mark 4,25). ⁸⁴ Et propinquis et amicis relinquit, et ipsi tollent et dividant substantiam eius et dicent postea: «Maledicta sit anima eius, quia potuit plus dare nobis et acquirere quam non acquisivit». ⁸⁵ Corpus comedunt vermes; et ita perdit corpus et animam in isto brevi saeculo et ibit in inferno, ubi cruciabitur sine fine.

⁸⁶ In nomine Patris et Filii et Spiritus Sancti. Amen. ⁸⁷ Ego frater Franciscus, **minor** servus vester, rogo et obsecro vos in **caritate**, quae Deus est (cfr. 1 Joa 4,16), et cum

voluntate osculandi vestros pedes, quod haec verba et alia Domini nostri Jesu Christi cum **humilitate** et **caritate** debeatis recipere et operari et observare. [88] Et omnes illi et illae, qui ea **benigne** recipient, intelligent et mittent aliis in exemplum, et si in ea **perseveraverint** usque in finem (Matt 24,13), benedicat eis Pater et Filius et Spiritus Sanctus. Amen.

Epistola ad fratrem Leonem: pax, paupertas, obedientia, consolatio

Edition by Esser (1978)
[1] Frater Leo, frater Francisco tuo salutem et **pacem**. [2] Ita dico tibi, fili mei, sicut mater: quia omnia verba quae diximus in via, breviter in hoc verba [!] dispono et consilio, et si dopo [tibi?] oportet propter consilium venire ad me, quia ita consilio tibi: [3] In quocumque modo melius videtur tibi placere Domino Deo et sequi vestigiam [!] et **paupertatem** suam, faciatis cum beneditione [!] Domini Dei et mea **obedientia**. [4] Et si tibi est necessarium animam tuam propter aliam **consolationem** tuam, et vis, Leo, venire ad me, veni.

Epistola ad ministrum: amor/dilectio, veritas, firmitas, obedientia, verecundia, magnitudo, misericordia, poenitentia

[1] Fratri N. ministro: Dominus te benedicat (cfr. Num 6,24a). [2] Dico tibi, sicut possum, de facto animae tuae, quod ea quae te impediunt **amare** Dominum Deum, et quicumque tibi impedimentum fecerit sive fratres sive alii, etiam si te verberarent, omnia debes habere pro gratia. [3] Et ita velis et non aliud. [4] Et hoc sit tibi per **veram obedientiam** Domini Dei et meam, quia **firmiter** scio, quod ista est **vera obedientia**. [5] Et **dilige** eos qui ista faciunt tibi. [6] Et non velis aliud de eis, nisi quantum Dominus dederit tibi. [7] Et in hoc **dilige** eos; et non velis quod sint meliores christiani. [8] Et istud sit tibi plus quam eremitorium. [9] Et in hoc volo cognoscere, si tu **diligis** Dominum et me servum suum et tuum, si feceris istud, scilicet quod non sit aliquis frater in mundo, qui peccaverit, quantumcumque potuerit peccare, quod, postquam viderit oculos tuos, numquam recedat sine **misericordia** tua, si quaerit **misericordiam**. [10] Et si non quaereret **misericordiam**, tu quaeras ab eo, si vult **misericordiam**. [11] Et si millies postea coram oculis tuis peccaret, **dilige** eum plus quam me ad hoc, ut trahas eum ad Dominum; et semper **misereraris** talibus. [12] Et istud denunties guardianis, quando poteris, quod per te ita **firmus** es facere.
[13] De omnibus autem capitulis, quae sunt in regula, quae loquuntur de mortalibus peccatis, Domino adiuvante in capitulo Pentecostes cum consilio fratrum faciemus istud tale capitulum: [14] Si quis fratrum instigante inimico mortaliter peccaverit, per **obedientiam** teneatur recurrere ad guardianum suum. [15] Et omnes fratres, qui scirent eum peccasse, non faciant ei **verecundiam** neque detractionem, sed **magnam misericordiam** habeant circa ipsum et teneant multum privatum peccatum fratris sui; quia non est opus sanis medicus, sed male habentibus (Matt 9,12). [16] Similiter per **obedientiam** teneantur eum mittere

custodi suo cum socio. [17] Et ipse custos **misericorditer** provideat ei, sicut ipse vellet provideri sibi, si in consimili casu esset (cfr. Matt 7,12). [18] Et si in alio peccato
veniali ceciderit, confiteatur fratri suo sacerdoti. [19] Et si non fuerit ibi sacerdos,
confiteatur fratri suo, donec habebit sacerdotem, qui eum absolvat canonice,
sicut dictum est. [20] Et isti penitus non habeant potestatem iniungendi aliam
poenitentiam nisi istam: Vade et noli amplius peccare (cfr. Joa 8,11).
[21] Hoc scriptum, ut melius debeat observari, habeas tecum usque ad Pentecosten;
ibi eris cum fratribus tuis. [22] Et ista et omnia alia, quae minus sunt in regula,
Domino Deo adiuvante, procurabitis adimplere.

**Epistola toti ordini missa: reverentia, dilectio/caritas/amor, humilitas, sim-
plicitas, obedientia, vilitas, parvitas, pretiositas, timor, 'percipitus', bonitas,
perseverantia, firmitas, honor, 'pacificatus', puritas/munditia, veritas, discretio, dignitas, veneratio, iustitia, magnitudo, infirmitas, altitudo, sublimitas,
'contentus', virtus, venerabilitas, devotio, poenitentia, inutilitas, studium, sollicitudo, 'beneplacitus', diligentia, misericordia**

[1] In nomine summae Trinitatis et sanctae Unitatis Patris et Filii et Spiritus Sancti.
Amen.
[2] **Reverendis** et multum **diligendis** fratribus universis, fratri A., generali ministro
religionis minorum fratrum, domino suo, et ceteris ministris generalibus, qui
post eum erunt, et omnibus ministris et custodibus et sacerdotibus fraternitatis
eiusdem in Christo **humilibus** et omnibus fratribus **simplicibus** et **obedientibus**,
primis et novissimis, [3] frater Franciscus, homo **vilis** et caducus, vester **parvulus**
servulus, salutem in eo qui redemit et lavit nos in **pretiosissimo** sanguine suo
(cfr. Apoc 1,5), [4] cuius nomen audientes adorate eum cum **timore** et **reverentia**
proni in terra (cfr. Esdr 8,6), Dominus Jesus Christus, Altissimi Filius nomen illi
(cfr. Luke 1,32), qui est benedictus in saecula (Rom 1,25).
[5] Audite, domini filii et fratres mei, et auribus **percipite** verba mea (Act 2,14).
[6] Inclinate aurem (Isa 55,3) cordis vestri et **obedite** voci Filii Dei. [7] Servate in toto
corde vestro mandata eius et consilia eius perfecta mente implete. [8] Confitemini
ei quoniam **bonus** (Ps 135,1) et exaltate eum in operibus vestris (Tob 13,6); [9] quoniam ideo misit vos (cfr. Tob 13,4) in universo mundo, ut verbo et opere detis
testimonium voci eius et faciatis scire omnes, quoniam non est omnipotens
praeter eum (Tob 13,4). [10] In disciplina et **obedientia** sancta **perseverate** (Hebr
12,7) et quae promisistis ei **bono** et **firmo** proposito adimplete. [11] Tamquam filiis
offert se nobis Dominus Deus (Hebr 12,7).
[12] Deprecor itaque omnes vos fratres cum osculo pedum et ea **caritate**, qua possum, ut omnem **reverentiam** et omnem **honorem**, quantumcumque poteritis,
exhibeatis sanctissimo corpori et sanguini Domini nostri Jesu Christi, [13] in quo
quae in caelis et quae in terris sunt, **pacificata** sunt et reconciliata omnipotenti
Deo (cfr. Col 1,20).
[14] Rogo etiam in Domino omnes fratres meos sacerdotes, qui sunt et erunt et esse
cupiunt sacerdotes Altissimi, quod quandocumque missam celebrare voluerint,
puri pure faciant cum **reverentia verum** sacrificium sanctissimi corporis et sanguinis Domini nostri Jesu Christi sancta intentione et **munda** non pro ulla

terrena re neque **timore** vel **amore** alicuius hominis, quasi placentes hominibus (cfr. Eph 6,6; Col 3,22); [15] sed omnis voluntas, quantum adiuvat gratia ad Deum dirigatur soli ipsi summo Domino inde placere desiderans, quia ipse ibi solus operatur sicut sibi placet; [16] quoniam sicut ipse dicit: Hoc facite in meam commemorationem (Luke 22,19; 1 Cor 11,24), si quis aliter fecerit, Judas traditor efficitur et reus fit corporis et sanguinis Domini (cfr. 1 Cor 11,27).

[17] Recordamini, fratres mei sacerdotes, quod scriptum est de lege Moysi, quam transgrediens etiam in corporalibus sine ulla miseratione per sententiam Domini moriebatur (cfr. Hebr 10,28). [18] Quanto maiora et deteriora meretur pati supplicia, qui Filium Dei conculcaverit et sanguinem testamenti pollutum duxerit, in quo sanctificatus est, et Spiritui gratiae contumeliam fecerit (Hebr 10,29)? [19] Despicit enim homo, polluit et conculcat Agnum Dei, quando, sicut dicit apostolus, non diiudicans (1 Cor 11,29) et **discernens** sanctum panem Christi ab aliis cibariis vel operibus vel indignus manducat vel etiam, si esset **dignus**, vane et indigne manducat, cum Dominus per prophetam dicat: Maledictus homo qui opus Dei facit fraudulenter (cfr. Jer 48,10). [20] Et sacerdotes, qui nolunt hoc ponere super cor in **veritate** condemnat dicens: Maledicam benedictionibus vestris (Mal 2,2).

[21] Audite, fratres mei: Si beata Virgo sic **honoratur**, ut **dignum** est, quia ipsum portavit in sanctissimo utero; si Baptista beatus contremuit et non audet tangere sanctum Dei verticem; si sepulcrum, in quo per aliquod tempus iacuit, **veneratur**, [22] quantum debet esse sanctus, **iustus** et **dignus**, qui non iam moriturum, sed in aeternum victurum et glorificatum, in quo desiderant angeli prospicere (1 Pet 1,12), contractat manibus, corde et ore sumit et aliis ad sumendum praebet!

[23] Videte **dignitatem** vestram, fratres (cfr. 1 Cor 1,26) sacerdotes, et estote sancti, quia ipse sanctus est (cfr. Lev 19,2). [24] Et sicut super omnes propter hoc ministerium **honoravit** vos Dominus Deus, ita et vos super omnes ipsum **diligite, reveremini** et **honorate**. [25] **Magna** miseria et miseranda **infirmitas**, quando ipsum sic praesentem habetis et vos aliquid aliud in toto mundo curatis. [26] Totus homo paveat, totus mundus contremiscat, et caelum exsultet, quando super altare in manu sacerdotis est Christus, Filius Dei vivi (Joa 11,27)! [27] O admiranda **altitudo** et stupenda **dignatio**! O **humilitas sublimis**! O **sublimitas humilis**, quod Dominus universitatis, Deus et Dei Filius, sic se **humiliat**, ut pro nostra salute sub modica panis formula se abscondat! [28] Videte, fratres, **humilitatem** Dei et effundite coram illo corda vestra (Ps 61,9); **humiliamini** et vos, ut exaltemini ab eo (cfr. 1 Pet 5,6; Jac 4,10). [29] Nihil ergo de vobis retineatis vobis, ut totos vos recipiat, qui se vobis exhibet totum.

[30] Moneo propterea et exhortor in Domino, ut in locis, in quibus fratres morantur, una tantum missa celebretur in die secundum formam sanctae ecclesiae. [31] Si vero plures in loco fuerint sacerdotes, sit per **amorem caritatis** alter **contentus** auditu celebrationis alterius sacerdotis; [32] quia praesentes et absentes replet, qui eo **digni** sunt, Dominus Jesus Christus. [33] Qui, licet in pluribus locis esse videatur, tamen indivisibilis manet et aliqua detrimenta non novit, sed unus ubique, sicut ei placet, operatur cum Domino Deo Patre et Spiritu Sancto Paraclito in saecula saeculorum. Amen.

[34] Et, quia qui est ex Deo verba Dei audit (cfr. Joa 8,47), debemus proinde nos, qui specialius divinis sumus officiis deputati, non solum audire et facere, quae dicit Deus, **verum** etiam ad insinuandam in nobis **altitudinem** Creatoris nostri et in ipso subiectionem nostram vasa et officialia cetera custodire, quae continent verba sua sancta. [35] Propterea moneo fratres meos omnes et in Christo conforto, quatinus, ubicumque invenerint divina verba scripta, sicut possunt, **venerentur;** [36] et, quantum ad eos spectat, si non sunt reposita bene vel inhoneste iacent in loco aliquo dispersa, recolligant et reponant **honorantes** in sermonibus Dominum, quos locutus est (3 Reg 2,4). [37] Multa enim sanctificantur per verba Dei (cfr. 1 Tim 4,5), et in **virtute** verborum Christi altaris conficitur sacramentum.

[38] Confiteor praeterea Domino Deo Patri et Filio et Spiritui Sancto, beatae Mariae perpetuae Virgini et omnibus sanctis in caelo et in terra, fratri .H. ministro religionis nostrae sicut **venerabili** domino meo et sacerdotibus ordinis nostri et omnibus aliis fratribus meis benedictis omnia peccata mea. [39] In multis offendi mea gravi culpa, specialiter quod regulam, quam Domino, promisi, non servavi, nec officium, sicut regula praecipit, dixi sive negligentia sive **infirmitatis** meae ocasione sive quia ignorans sum et idiota. [40] Ideoque per omnia oro sicut possum fratrem .H. generalem dominum meum ministrum, ut faciat regulam ab omnibus inviolabiliter observari; [41] et quod clerici dicant officium cum **devotione** coram Deo non attendentes melodiam vocis, sed consonantiam mentis, ut vox concordet menti, mens vero concordet cum Deo, [42] ut possint per **puritatem** cordis placare Deum et non cum lascivitate vocis aures populi demulcere. [43] Ego enim promitto haec **firmiter** custodire, sicut dederit mihi gratiam Deus; et haec fratribus, qui mecum sunt, observanda tradam in officio et ceteris regularibus constitutis.

[44] Quicumque autem fratrum haec observare noluerint, non teneo eos catholicos nec fratres meos; nolo etiam ipsos videre nec loqui, donec **poenitentiam** egerint. [45] Hoc etiam dico de omnibus aliis, qui vagando vadunt, postposita regulae disciplina; [46] quoniam Dominus noster Jesus Christus dedit vitam suam, ne perderet sanctissimi Patris **obedientiam** (cfr. Phil 2,8).

[47] Ego frater Franciscus, homo **inutilis** et indigna creatura Domini Dei, dico per Dominum Jesum Christum fratri H. ministro totius religionis nostrae et omnibus generalibus ministris, qui post eum erunt, et ceteris custodibus et guardianis fratrum, qui sunt et erunt, ut hoc scriptum apud se habeant, operentur et **studiose** reponant. [48] Et exoro ipsos, ut, quae scripta sunt in eo, **sollicite** custodire ac facere **diligentius** observari secundum **beneplacitum** omnipotentis Dei, nunc et semper, donec fuerit mundus iste.

[49] Benedicti vos a Domino (Ps 113,23), qui feceritis ista et in aeternum Dominus sit vobiscum. Amen.

[Oratio]

[50] Omnipotens, aeterne, **iuste** et **misericors** Deus, da nobis miseris propter temetipsum facere, quod scimus te velle, et semper velle, quod tibi placet, [51] ut interius **mundati**, interius illuminati et igne sancti Spiritus accensi sequi possimus vestigia (cfr. 1 Pet 2,21) dilecti Filii tui, Domini nostri Jesu Christi, [52] et ad te,

Altissime, sola tua gratia pervenire, qui in Trinitate perfecta et Unitate **simplici** vivis et regnas et gloriaris Deus omnipotens per omnia saecula saeculorum. Amen.

Epistola ad populorum rectores: parvitas, 'despectus', pax, reverentia, sollicitudo, sapientia, firmitas, benignitas, honor, gratitudo

[1] Universis potestatibus et consulibus, iudicibus atque rectoribus ubique terrarum et omnibus aliis, ad quos litterae istae pervenerint, frater Franciscus, vester in Domino Deo servus **parvulus** ac **despectus**, salutem et **pacem** omnibus vobis optans.
[2] Considerate et videte, quoniam dies mortis appropinquat (cfr. Gen 47,29).
[3] Rogo ergo vos cum **reverentia**, sicut possum, ne propter curas et **sollicitudines** huius saeculi, quas habetis, Dominum oblivioni tradatis et a mandatis eius declinetis, quia omnes illi, qui eum oblivioni tradunt et a mandatis eius declinant, maledicti sunt (cfr. Ps 118,21) et ab eo oblivioni tradentur (Ezech 33,13). [4] Et, cum venerit dies mortis, omnia, quae putabant habere, auferentur ab eis (cfr. Luke 8,18). [5] Et, quanto **sapientiores** et potentiores fuerint in hoc saeculo, tanto maiora tormenta sustinebunt in inferno (cfr. Sap 6,7). [6] Unde **firmiter** consulo vobis, dominis meis, ut omni cura et **sollicitudine** posthabitis et sanctissimum corpus et sanctissimum sanguinem Domini nostri Jesu Christi in eius sancta commemoratione **benigne** recipiatis. [7] Et tantum **honorem** in populo vobis commisso Domino conferatis, ut quolibet sero annuntietur per nuntium vel per aliud signum, quo omnipotenti Domino Deo ab universo populo laudes et **gratiae** referantur. [8] Et, si hoc non feceritis, sciatis vos debere coram Domino Deo vestro Jesu Christo in die iudicii reddere rationem (cfr. Matt 12,36).
[9] Hoc scriptum qui apud se retinuerint et observaverint illud, a Domino Deo se noverint benedictos.

Exhortatio ad laudem Dei: timor, honor, dignitas, laetitia, bonitas

[1] **Timete** Dominum et date illi **honorem** (Apoc 14,7). [2] **Dignus** est Dominus accipere laudem et **honorem** (cfr. Apoc 4,11). [3] Omnes, qui **timete** Dominum, laudate eum (cfr. Ps 21,24). [4] Ave Maria, gratia plena, Dominus tecum (Luke 1,28). [5] Laudate eum caelum et terra (cfr. Ps 68,35-R). [6] Laudate omnia flumina Dominum (cfr. Dan 3,87). [7] Benedicite filii Dei Dominum (cfr. Dan 3,82). [8] Haec dies quam fecit Dominus, exsultemus et **laetemur** in ea (Ps 177,24-R). Alleluia, Alleluia, Alleluia! Rex Israel (Joa 12,13)! [9] Omnis spiritus laudet Dominum (Ps 150,6). [10] Laudate Dominum, quoniam **bonus** est (Ps 146,1); omnes qui legitis haec, benedicite Dominum (Ps 102,21-R). [11] Omnes creaturae benedicite Dominum (cfr. Ps 102,22). [12] Omnes volucres caeli laudate Dominum (cfr. Dan 3,80; Ps 148,7–10). [13] Omnes pueri laudate Dominum (cfr. Ps 112,1). [14] Iuvenes et virgines laudate Dominum (cfr. Ps 148,12). [15] **Dignus** est agnus, qui occisus est, recipere laudem, gloriam et **honorem** (cfr. Apoc 5,12). [16] Benedicta sit sancta Trinitas atque indivisa Unitas. [17] Sancte Michael Archangele, defende nos in proelio.

Expositio in Pater Noster: amor/dilectio, bonitas, claritas, latitudo, longitudo, sublimitas, profunditas, honor, gaudium, reverentia, misericordia, virtus, veritas, devotio, studium

¹ O sanctissime Pater noster: creator, redemptor, consolator et salvator noster.

² Qui es in caelis: in angelis et in sanctis; illuminans eos ad cognitionem, quia tu, Domine, lux es; inflammans ad **amorem**, quia tu, Domine, **amor** es; inhabitans et implens eos ad beatitudinem, quia tu, Domine, summum **bonum** es, aeternum, a quo omne **bonum**, sine quo nullum **bonum**.

³ Sanctificetur nomen tuum: **clarificetur** in nobis notitia tua, ut cognoscamus, quae sit **latitudo** (cfr. Eph 3,18) beneficiorum tuorum, **longitudo** promissorum tuorum, **sublimitas** maiestatis et **profundum** iudiciorum.

⁴ Adveniat regnum tuum: ut tu regnes in nobis per gratiam et facias nos venire ad regnum tuum, ubi est tui visio manifesta, tui **dilectio** perfecta, tui societas beata, tui fruitio sempiterna.

⁵ Fiat voluntas tua sicut in caelo et in terra: ut **amemus** te ex toto corde (cfr. Luke 10,27) te semper cogitando, ex tota anima te semper desiderando, ex tota mente omnes intentiones nostras ad te dirigendo, **honorem** tuum in omnibus quaerendo et ex omnibus viribus nostris omnes vires nostras et sensus animae et corporis in obsequium tui **amoris** et non in alio expendendo; et proximos nostros **amemus** sicut et nosmetipsos omnes ad **amorem** tuum pro viribus trahendo, de **bonis** aliorum sicut de nostris **gaudendo** et in malis compatiendo et nemini ullam offensionem dando (cfr. 2 Cor 6,3).

⁶ Panem nostrum quotidianum: dilectum Filium tuum, Dominum nostrum Jesum Christum, da nobis hodie: in memoriam et intelligentiam et **reverentiam amoris**, quem ad nos habuit, et eorum, quae pro nobis dixit, fecit et sustulit.

⁷ Et dimitte nobis debita nostra: per tuam **misericordiam** ineffabilem, per passionis dilecti Filii tui **virtutem** et per beatissimae Virginis et omnium electorum tuorum merita et intercessionem.

⁸ Sicut et nos dimittimus debitoribus nostris: et quod non plene dimittimus, tu, Domine, fac nos plene dimittere, ut inimicos propter te **veraciter diligamus** et pro eis apud te **devote** intercedamus, nulli malum pro malo reddentes (cfr. 1 Thess 5,15) et in omnibus in te prodesse **studeamus**.

⁹ Et ne nos inducas in tentationem: occultam vel manifestam, subitam vel importunam.

¹⁰ Sed libera nos a malo: praeterito, praesenti et futuro. Gloria Patri etc.

Forma vivendi S. Clarae: dilectio, sollicitudo

¹ Quia divina inspiratione fecistis vos filias et ancillas altissimi summi Regis Patris caelestis, et Spiritui Sancto vos desponsastis eligendo vivere secundum perfectionem sancti Evangelii: ² volo et promitto per me et Fratres meos semper habere de vobis tamquam de ipsis curam **diligentem** et **sollicitudinem** specialem.

Laudes ad omnes horas dicendae: dignitas, honor, virtus, sapientia, fortitudo, timor, magnitudo, bonitas, gratitudo

[1] Sanctus, sanctus, sanctus Dominus Deus omnipotens,
  qui est et qui erat et qui venturus est (cfr. Apoc 4,8):
  Et laudemus et superexaltemus eum in saecula.
[2] **Dignus** es, Domine Deus noster,
  accipere laudem, gloriam et **honorem** et benedictionem (cfr. Apoc 4,11):
  Et laudemus et superexaltemus eum in saecula.
[3] **Dignus** est agnus, qui occisus est
  accipere **virtutem** et divinitatem et **sapientiam** et **fortitudinem** et honorem et gloriam et benedictionem (Apoc 5,12):
  Et laudemus et superexaltemus eum in saecula.
[4] Benedicamus Patrem et Filium cum Sancto Spiritu:
  Et laudemus et superexaltemus eum in saecula.
[5] Benedicite omnia opera Domini Domino (Dan 3,57):
  Et laudemus et superexaltemus eum in saecula.
[6] Laudem dicite Deo nostro
  omnes servi eius et qui **timetis** Deum, pusilli et **magni** (cfr. Apoc 19,5):
  Et laudemus et superexaltemus eum in saecula.
[7] Laudent eum gloriosum caeli et terra (cfr. Ps 68,35-R):
  Et laudemus et superexaltemus eum in saecula.
[8] Et omnis creatura, quae in caelo est et super terram
  et quae subtus terram et mare et quae in eo sunt (cfr. Apoc 5,13):
  Et laudemus et superexaltemus eum in saecula.
[9] Gloria Patri et Filio et Spiritui Sancto:
  Et laudemus et superexaltemus eum in saecula.
[10] Sicut erat in principio et nunc et semper et in saecula saeculorum. Amen.
  Et laudemus et superexaltemus eum in saecula.
[11] Oratio: Omnipotens sanctissime, altissime et summe Deus,
  omne **bonum**, summum **bonum**, totum **bonum**,
  qui solus es **bonus** (cfr. Luke 18,19),
  tibi reddamus omnem laudem, omnem gloriam, omnem **gratiam**,
  omnem **honorem**, omnem benedictionem et omnia **bona**.
  Fiat. Fiat. Amen.

Officium passionis Domini:

[Introductio]

Incipiunt psalmi, quos ordinavit beatissimus pater noster Franciscus ad reverentiam et memoriam et laudem passionis Domini. Qui dicendi sunt per quaslibet horas diei et noctis unum. Et incipiunt a completorio feriae sextae Parasceve, eo quod in illa nocte traditus fuit et captus Dominus noster Jesus Christus. Et nota, quod sic dicebat istud officium beatus Franciscus: Primo dicebat orationem, quam

nos docuit Dominus et Magister: Sanctissime pater noster etc. cum laudibus,
scilicet: Sanctus, sanctus, sanctus sicut superius continetur. Finitis laudibus cum
oratione incipiebat hanc antiphonam, scilicet: Sancta Maria. Psalmos dicebat
primo de sancta Maria; postea dicebat alios psalmos quos elegerat, et in fine
omnium psalmorum, quos dicebat, dicebat psalmos passionis. Finito psalmo dice-
bat hanc antiphonam, scilicet: Sancta Maria virgo. Finita antiphona expletum
erat officium.

[Pars I: Pro sacro triduo hebdomadae maioris et feriis per annum]:
bonitas, dilectio, reverentia, veritas, honor, spes, confidentia, misericordia,
fortitudo, timor, zelus, laetitia/gaudium, dolor, virtus, iustitia, magnitudo,
laudabilitas

Ad Completorium
Antiphona: Sancta Maria Virgo
Psalmus [I]

[1] Deus vitam meam annuntiavi tibi
 * posuisti lacrimas meas in conspectu tuo (Ps 55,8b-9).
[2] Omnes inimici mei adversum me cogitabant mala mihi (Ps 40,8a; R)
 * et consilium fecerunt in unum (cfr. Ps 70,10c; G).
[3] Et posuerunt adversum me mala pro vobis·
 * et odium pro **dilectione** mea (cfr. Ps 108,5).
[4] Pro eo, ut me **diligerent**, detrahebant mihi
 * ego autem orabam (Ps 108,4).
[5] Mi pater sancte (Joa 17,11), rex caeli et terrae, ne discesseris a me
 * quoniam tribulatio proxima est et non est qui adiuvet (Ps 21,12; R).
[6] Convertantur (R) inimici mei retrorsum
 * in quacumque die invocavero te, ecce cognovi, quoniam Deus meus es
(Ps 55,10; cfr. R).
[7] Amici mei et proximi mei adversum me appropinquaverunt et steterunt
 * et proximi mei a longe steterunt (Ps 37,12; R).
[8] Longe fecisti notos meos a me
 * posuerunt me abominationem sibi, traditus sum et non egrediebar (Ps
87,9; cfr. R).
[9] Pater sancte (Joa 17,11), ne elongaveris auxilium tuum a me (Ps 21,20)
 * Deus meus ad auxilium meum respice (cfr. Ps 70,12).
[10] Intende in adiutorium meum
 * Domine Deus salutis meae (Ps 37,23).
Gloria Patri et Filio et Spiritui Sancto: Sicut erat in principio et nunc et semper et
in saecula saeculorum. Amen.

Antiphona: [1] Sancta Maria virgo, non est tibi similis nata in mundo in mulieribus,
[2] filia et ancilla altissimi summi Regis Patris caelestis, mater sanctissimi Domini
nostri Jesu Christi, sponsa Spiritus Sancti: [3] ora pro nobis cum S. Michaele archangelo et omnibus virtutibus caelorum et omnibus sanctis apud tuum sanctissimum dilectum Filium, Dominum et magistrum.- Gloria Patri. Sicut erat.

Nota, quod haec antiphona supradicta dicitur ad omnes horas; et dicitur pro
antiphona, capitulo, hymno, versiculo et oratione; et ad matutinum et ad omnes
horas similiter. Nihil aliud in ipsis dicebat nisi hanc antiphonam cum suis psalmis.
Ad absolutionem officii semper dicebat beatus Franciscus:

Benedicamus Domino Deo vivo et **vero**: laudem, gloriam, **honorem**, benedictionem et omnia **bona** referamus ei semper. Amen. Amen. Fiat. Fiat.

Ad Matutinum
Antiphona: Sancta Maria Virgo
Psalmus [II]

¹ Domine Deus salutis meae
     * in die clamavi et nocte coram te (Ps 87,2).
² Intret in conspectu tuo oratio mea
     * inclina aurem tuam ad precem meam (Ps 87,3).
³ Intende animae meae et libera eam
     * propter inimicos meos eripe me (Ps 68,19).
⁴ Quoniam tu es, qui abstraxisti (R) me de ventre '
   spes mea ab uberibus matris meae
     * in te proiectus sum ex utero (Ps 21,10).
⁵ De ventre matris meae Deus meus es tu
     * ne discesseris a me (Ps 21,11).
⁶ Tu scis improperium meum et confusionem meam
     * et **reverentiam** meam (Ps 68,20).
⁷ In conspectu tuo sunt omnes, qui tribulant me
     * improperium exspectavit cor meum et miseriam (Ps 68,21a-b).
⁸ Et sustinui, qui simul contristaretur et non fuit
     * et qui consolaretur et non inveni (Ps 68,21c-d).
⁹ Deus, iniqui insurrexerunt in me
     * et synagoga potentium quaesierunt animam meam
   et non proposuerunt te in conspectu suo (Ps 85,14).
¹⁰ Aestimatus sum cum descendentibus in lacum
     * factus sum sicut homo sine adiutorio inter mortuos liber (Ps 87,5–6a).
¹¹ Tu es sanctissimus pater meus
     * Rex meus et Deus meus (cfr. Ps 43,5a).
¹² Intende in adiutorium meum * Domine Deus salutis meae (Ps 37,23).

Ad Primam
Antiphona: Sancta Maria Virgo
Psalmus [III]

¹ Miserere mei, Deus, miserere mei
     * quoniam in te **confidit** anima mea (Ps 56,2a).
² Et in umbra alarum tuarum **sperabo**
     * donec transeat iniquitas (Ps 56,2b).
³ Clamabo ad sanctissimum patrem meum altissimum
     * Dominum, qui benefecit mihi (cfr. Ps 56,3).

⁴ Misit de caelo et liberavit me
    * dedit in opprobrium conculcantes me (Ps 56,4a-b).
⁵ Misit Deus **misericordiam** suam et **veritatem** suam
    * animam meam eripuit (Ps 56,4c-5a; R) de inimicis meis **fortissimis**
    et ab his, qui oderunt me, quoniam confortati sunt super me (Ps 17,18).
⁶ Laqueum paraverunt pedibus meis
    * et incurvaverunt animam meam (Ps 56,7a-b).
⁷ Foderunt ante faciem meam foveam
    * et inciderunt in eam (Ps 56,7c-d).
⁸ Paratum cor meum, Deus, paratum cor meum
    * cantabo et psalmum dicam (Ps 56,8).
⁹ Exsurge, gloria mea, exsurge psalterium et cithara
    * exsurgam diluculo (Ps 56,9).
¹⁰ Confitebor tibi in populis, Domine
    * et psalmum dicam tibi in gentibus (Ps 56,10).
¹¹ Quoniam magnificata est usque ad caelos **misericordia** tua
    * et usque ad nubes **veritas** tua (Ps 56,11).
¹² Exaltare super caelos Deus
    * et super omnem terram gloria tua (Ps 56,12).

Nota, quod praedictus psalmus semper dicitur ad primam.

Ad Tertiam
Antiphona: Sancta Maria Virgo
Psalmus [IV]

¹ **Miserere** mei, Deus, quoniam conculcavit me homo
    * tota die impugnans tribulavit me (Ps 55,2).
² Conculcaverunt me inimici mei tota die
    * quoniam multi bellantes adversum me (Ps 55,3).
³ Omnes inimici mei adversum me cogitabant mala mihi
    * verbum iniquum constituerunt adversum me (Ps 40,8b-9a; cfr. R).
⁴ Qui custodiebant animam meam
    * consilium fecerunt in unum (Ps 70,10b).
⁵ Egrediebantur foras
    * et loquebantur (Ps 40,7; R) in idipsum (Ps 40,8a; G).
⁶ Omnes videntes me deriserunt me
    * locuti sunt labiis et moverunt caput (Ps 21,8).
⁷ Ego autem sum vermis et non homo
    * opprobrium hominum et abiectio plebis (Ps 21,7).
⁸ Super omnes inimicos meos factus sum opprobrium vicinis meis valde
    * et **timor** notis meis (Ps 30,12a-b).
⁹ Pater sancte (Joa 17,11) ne elongaveris auxilium tuum a me
    * ad defensionem meam conspice (Ps 21,20).
¹⁰ Intende in adiutorium meum
    * Domine Deus salutis meae (Ps 37,23).

Ad Sextam
Antiphona: Sancta Maria Virgo
Psalmus [V]

[1] Voce mea ad Dominum clamavi
    * voce mea ad Dominum deprecatus sum (Ps 141,2).
[2] Effundo in conspectu eius orationem meam
    * et tribulationem meam ante ipsum pronuntio (Ps 141,3).
[3] In deficiendo ex me spiritum meum
    * et tu cognovisti semitas meas (Ps 141,4a-b).
[4] In via hac qua ambulabam
    * absconderunt superbi laqueum mihi (Ps 141,4c-d; cfr. R).
[5] Considerabam ad dexteram et videbam
    * et non erat qui cognosceret me (Ps 141,5a-b).
[6] Periit fuga a me
    * et non est, qui requirat animam meam (Ps 141,5c-d).
[7] Quoniam propter te sustinui opprobrium
    * operuit confusio faciem meam (Ps 68,8).
[8] Extraneus factus sum fratribus meis
    * et peregrinus filiis matris meae (Ps 68,9).
[9] Pater sancte (Joa 17,11), **zelus** domus tuae comedit me
    * et opprobria exprobrantium tibi ceciderunt super me (Ps 68,10).
[10] Et adversum me **laetati** sunt et convenerunt
    * congregata sunt super me flagella et ignoravi (Ps 34,15).
[11] Multiplicati sunt super capillos capitis mei
    * qui oderunt me gratis (Ps 68,5a-b).
[12] Confortati sunt, qui persecuti sunt me inimici mei iniuste
    * quae non rapui tunc exsolvebam (Ps 68,5c-d).
[13] Surgentes testes iniqui
    * quae ignorabant interrogabant me (Ps 34,11).
[14] Retribuebant mihi mala pro **bonis** (Ps 34,12a) et detrahebant mihi
    * quoniam sequebar **bonitatem** (Ps 37,21).
[15] Tu es sanctissimus pater meus
    * Rex meus et Deus meus (Ps 43,5).
[16] Intende in adiutorium meum
    * Domine Deus salutis meae (Ps 37,23).

Ad Nonam
Antiphona: Sancta Maria Virgo
Psalmus [VI]

[1] O vos omnes, qui transitis per viam
    * attendite et videte, si est **dolor** sicut **dolor** meus (Lam 1,12a-b).
[2] Quoniam circumdederunt me canes multi
    * concilium malignantium obsedit me (Ps 21,17).
[3] Ipsi vero consideraverunt et inspexerunt me

* diviserunt sibi vestimenta mea et super vestem meam miserunt sortem (Ps 21,18b-19).
⁴ Foderunt manus meas et pedes meos
      * et dinumeraverunt omnia ossa mea (Ps 21,17c-18a; R).
⁵ Aperuerunt super me os suum
      * sicut leo rapiens et rugiens (Ps 21,14).
⁶ Sicut aqua effusus sum
      * et dispersa sunt omnia ossa mea (Ps 21,15a-b).
⁷ Et factum est cor meum tamquam cera liquescens
      * in medio ventris mei (Ps 21,15c; R).
⁸ Aruit tamquam testa **virtus** mea
      * et lingua mea adhaesit faucibus meis (Ps 21,16a-b).
⁹ Et dederunt in escam meam fel
      * et in siti mea potaverunt me aceto (Ps 68,22).
¹⁰ Et in pulverem mortis deduxerunt me (cfr. Ps 21,16c)
      * et super **dolorem** vulnerum meorum addiderunt (Ps 68,27b).
¹¹ Ego dormivi et resurrexi (Ps 3,6; R)
      * et pater meus sanctissimus cum gloria suscepit me (cfr. Ps 72,24c).
¹² Pater sancte (Joa 17,11) tenuisti manum dexteram meam '
      et in voluntate tua deduxisti me
      * et cum gloria assumpsisti me (Ps 72,24; R).
¹³ Quid enim mihi est in caelo
      * et a te quid volui super terram (Ps 72,25)?
¹⁴ Videte, videte, quoniam ego sum Deus, dicit Dominus
      * exaltabor in gentibus et exaltabor in terra (cfr. Ps 45,11).
¹⁵ Benedictus Dominus Deus Israel (Luke 1,68a), qui redemit animas servorum suorum de proprio sanctissimo sanguine suo
      * et non derelinquet omnes qui **sperant** in eo (Ps 33,23; R).
¹⁶ Et scimus, quoniam venit
      * quoniam veniet **iustitiam** iudicare (cfr. Ps 95,13b; R!).

Ad Vesperam
Antiphona: Sancta Maria Virgo
Psalmus [VII]

¹ Omnes gentes plaudite manibus
      * iubilate Deo in voce exsultationis (Ps 46,2).
² Quoniam Dominus excelsus
      * terribilis Rex **magnus** super omnem terram (Ps 46,3).
³ Quia sanctissimus Pater de caelo, Rex noster ante saecula
      * misit dilectum Filium suum de alto et operatus est salutem in medio terrae (Ps 73,12).
⁴ **Laetentur** caeli et exsultet terra,
      commoveatur mare et plenitudo eius
      * **gaudebunt** campi et omnia, quae in eis sunt (Ps 95,11–12a).
⁵ Cantate ei canticum novum
      * cantate Domino omnis terra (cfr. Ps 95,1).

⁶ Quoniam **magnus** Dominus et **laudabilis** nimis
  * terribilis est super omnes deos (Ps 95,4).
⁷ Afferte Domino patriae gentium,
    afferte Domino gloriam et **honorem**
      * afferte Domino gloriam nomini eius (Ps 95,7–8a).
⁸ Tollite corpora vestra
    et baiulate sanctam crucem eius
      * et sequimini usque in finem sanctissima praecepta eius (cfr. Luke 14,27; 1 Petr 2,21).
⁹ Commoveatur a facie eius universa terra
      * dicite in gentibus, quia Dominus regnavit a ligno (Ps 95,9b-10a; G/R).

Usque huc dicitur a feria sexta Parasceven usque ad festum Ascensionis quotidie. In festo vero Ascensionis superadduntur isti versiculi:

¹⁰ Et ascendit ad caelos et sedet ad dexteram sanctissimi Patris in caelis exaltare super caelos Deus
      * et super omnem terram gloria tua (Ps 56,12).
¹¹ Et scimus quoniam venit
      * quoniam veniet **iustitiam** iudicare.

Et nota, quod ab Ascensione usque ad Adventum Domini dicitur eodem modo quotidie iste psalmus, scilicet: Omnes gentes cum supradictis versiculis dicendo ibi Gloria Patri, ubi finitur psalmus, scilicet: quoniam veniet iustitiam iudicare.

Nota quod hi psalmi supradicti dicuntur a feria sexta Parasceven usque ad dominicam Resurrectionis. Eo modo dicuntur ab octava Pentecostes usque ad Adventum Domini et ab octava Epiphaniae usque ad dominicam Resurrectionis exceptis dominicis diebus et festis principalibus, in quibus non dicuntur; aliis vero diebus quotidie dicuntur.

[Pars II: Pro tempore paschali]: reverentia, laetitia/gaudium, dilectio, paupertas, iustitia, misericordia, honor, magnificentia, virtus, fortitudo

In sabbato sancto, scilicet expleto die sabbati:
Ad Completorium
Antiphona: Sancta Maria Virgo
Psalmus [VIII]

¹ Deus in adiutorium meum intende
      * Domine ad adiuvandum me festina.
² Confundantur et **revereantur**
      * qui quaerunt animam meam.
³ Avertantur retrorsum et erubescant
      * qui volunt mihi mala.
⁴ Avertantur statim erubescentes
      * qui dicunt mihi: Euge, euge.

⁵ Exsultent et **laetentur** in te omnes qui quaerunt te
    * et dicant semper: Magnificetur Dominus: qui **diligunt** salutare tuum.
⁶ Ego vero egenus et **pauper** sum
    * Deus, adiuva me.
⁷ Adiutor et liberator meus es tu
    * Domine ne moreris (Ps 69,2–6).

Ad Matutinum Dominicae Resurrectionis
Antiphona: Sancta Maria Virgo
Psalmus [IX]

¹ Cantate Domino canticum novum
    * quia mirabilia fecit (Ps 97,1a-b).
² Sacrificavit dilectum Filium suum dextera eius
    * et brachium sanctum suum (cfr. Ps 97,1c-d).
³ Notum fecit Dominus salutare suum
    * in conspectu gentium revelavit **iustitiam** suam (Ps 97,2).
⁴ In illa die mandavit Dominus **misericordiam** suam
    * et nocte canticum eius (cfr. Ps 41,9a-b).
⁵ Haec est dies, quam fecit Dominus
    * exsultemus et **laetemur** in ea (Ps 117,24).
⁶ Benedictus qui venit in nomine Domini
    * Deus Dominus, et illuxit nobis (Ps 117,26a.27a).
⁷ **Laetentur** caeli et exsultet terra,
    commoveatur mare et plenitudo eius
        * **gaudebunt** campi et omnia quae in eis sunt (Ps 95,11–12a).
⁸ Afferte Domino patriae gentium,
    afferte Domino gloriam et **honorem**
        * afferte Domino gloriam nomini eius (Ps 95,7–8a).

Usque huc dicitur a dominica Resurrectionis usque ad festum Ascensionis quotidie ad omnes horas praeter ad vesperam et ad completorium et primam. Nocte vero Ascensionis superadduntur isti versiculi:

⁹ Regna terrae cantate Deo
    * psallite Domino (Ps 67,33a).
¹⁰ Psallite Deo, qui ascendit super caelum caeli
    * ad orientem (Ps 67,33b-34a).
¹¹ Ecce dabit voci suae vocem **virtutis**,
    date gloriam Deo super Israel
        * **magnificentia** eius et **virtus** eius in nubibus (Ps 67,34b-35).
¹² Mirabilis Deus in sanctis suis
    * Deus Israel ipse dabit **virtutem** et **fortitudinem** plebi suae, benedictus Deus (Ps 67,36). Gloria.

Et nota, quod iste psalmus ab Ascensione Domini usque ad octavam Pentecostes dicitur quotidie cum supradictis versiculis ad matutinum, et tertiam et sextam et nonam, dicendo ibi Gloria Patri ubi dicitur: benedictus Deus, et non alibi.

Item nota, quod eodem modo dicitur solummodo ad matutinum in dominicis diebus et principalibus festis ab octava Pentecostes usque ad adventum Domini, et ab octava Epiphaniae usque ad feriam quintam Coenae Domini, quia in ipsa die cum discipulis suis Dominus pascha manducavit; vel alius psalmus potest dici ad matutinum vel ad vesperam, quando vult, scilicet: Exaltabo te Domine etc. [Ps 29], sicut in psalterio habetur; et hoc a dominica Resurrectionis usque ad festum Ascensionis, et non plus.

Ad Primam
Antiphona: Sancta Maria Virgo.
Psalmus: Miserere mei, Deus, miserere mei
ut supra [Ps III]

Ad Tertiam, Sextam et Nonam
dicitur Psalmus: Cantate ut supra [Ps IX]

Ad Vesperam
Psalmus: Deus in adiutorium sicut habetur in psalterio [Ps VIII]

[Pars III: Pro dominicis et principalibus festivitatibus]: virtus, timor, magnitudo, laetitia, iustitia, paupertas, spes, misericordia, patientia, benignitas, miseratio

Incipiunt alii psalmi, quos similiter ordinavit beatissimus pater noster Franciscus, qui dicendi sunt loco psalmorum supradictorum passionis Domini in dominicis diebus et principalibus festivitatibus ab octava Pentecostes usque ad Adventum et ab octava Epiphaniae usque ad feriam quintam Coenae Domimi; sane intelligas, ut dicantur in ipsa die, quia pascha Domini est.

Ad Completorium
Antiphona: Sancta Maria Virgo.
Psalmus: Deus in adiutorium
sicut habetur in psalterio [Ps VIII]

Ad Matutinum
Antiphona: Sancta Maria Virgo.
Psalmus: Cantate ut supra [Ps IX]

Ad Primam
Antiphona: Sancta Maria Virgo.
Psalmus: Miserere mei, Deus, miserere mei
ut supra [Ps III]

Ad Tertiam
Antiphona: Sancta Maria Virgo.
Psalmus [X]

¹ Jubilate Domino omnis terra,
    psalmum dicite nomini eius
        * date gloriam laudi eius (cfr. Ps 65,1–2).
² Dicite Deo, quam terribilia sunt opera tua, Domine
        * in multitudine **virtutis** tuae mentientur tibi inimici tui (Ps 65,3).
³ Omnis terra adoret te et psallat tibi
        * psalmum dicat nomini tuo (Ps 65,4).
⁴ Venite, audite et narrabo, omnes qui **timetis** Deum
        * quanta fecit animae meae (Ps 65,16).
⁵ Ad ipsum ore meo clamavi
        * et exsultavi sub lingua mea (Ps 65,17; R).
⁶ Et exaudivit de templo sancto suo vocem meam
        * et clamor meus in conspectu eius (Ps 17,7c-d).
⁷ Benedicite gentes Dominum nostrum
        * et auditam facite vocem laudi eius (cfr. 65,8).
⁸ Et benedicentur in ipso omnes tribus terrae
        * omnes gentes magnificabunt eum (Ps 71,17c-d).
⁹ Benedictus Dominus Deus Israel
        * qui facit mirabilia **magna** solus (Ps 71,18; R).
¹⁰ Et benedictum nomen maiestatis eius in aeternum
        * et replebitur maiestate eius omnis terra, fiat, fiat (Ps 71,19).

Ad Sextam
Antiphona: Sancta Maria Virgo.
Psalmus [XI]

¹ Exaudiat te Dominus in die tribulationis
        * protegat te nomen Dei Jacob (Ps 19,2).
² Mittat tibi auxilium de sancto
        * et de Sion tueatur te (Ps 19,3).
³ Memor sit omnis sacrificii tui
        * et holocaustum tuum pingue fiat (Ps 19,4).
⁴ Tribuat tibi secundum cor tuum
        * et omne consilium tuum confirmet (Ps 19,5).
⁵ **Laetabimur** in salutari tuo
        * et in nomine Domini Dei nostri magnificabimur (Ps 19,6; R).
⁶ Impleat Dominus omnes petitiones tuas,
    nunc cognovi, quoniam (Ps 19,7a-b) misit Dominus Jesum Christum Filium
suum
        * et iudicabit populos in **iustitia** (Ps 9,9b).
⁷ Et factus est Dominus refugium **pauperum**,
    adiutor in opportunitatibus in tribulatione
        * et **sperent** in te qui noverunt nomen tuum (Ps 9,10–11a; R).
⁸ Benedictus Dominus Deus meus (Ps 143,1b),
    quia factus est susceptor meus et refugium meum
        * in die tribulationis meae (cfr. Ps 58,17c-d).
⁹ Adiutor meus, tibi psallam
    quia Deus susceptor meus
        * Deus meus, **misericordia** mea (Ps 58,18).

Ad Nonam
Antiphona: Sancta Maria Virgo.
Psalmus [XII]

¹ In te, Domine, **speravi**, non confundar in aeternum
     * in **iustitia** tua libera me et eripe me (Ps 70,1b-2a).
² Inclina ad me aurem tuam
     * et salva me (Ps 70,2b).
³ Esto mihi in Deum protectorem
    et in locum munitum
     * ut salvum me facias (Ps 70,3a-b).
⁴ Quoniam tu es **patientia** mea Domine
     * Domine, **spes** mea a iuventute mea (Ps 70,5).
⁵ In te confirmatus sum ex utero,
    de ventre matris meae tu es protector meus
     * in te cantatio mea semper (Ps 70,6).
⁶ Repleatur os meum laude
    ut cantem gloriam tuam
     * tota die **magnitudinem** tuam (Ps 70,8).
⁷ Exaudi me, Domine, quoniam **benigna** est **misericordia** tua
     * secundum multitudinem **miserationum** tuarum respice in me
(Ps 68,17).
⁸ Et ne avertas faciem tuam a puero tuo
     * quoniam tribulor, velociter exaudi me (Ps 68,18).
⁹ Benedictus Dominus Deus meus (Ps 143,1b),
    quia factus est susceptor meus et refugium meum
     * in die tribulationis meae.
¹⁰ Adiutor meus tibi psallam,
    quia Deus susceptor meus
     * Deus meus, **misericordia** mea (Ps 58,18).

Ad Vesperam
Antiphona: Sancta Maria Virgo.
Psalmus: Omnes gentes ut supra [Ps VII]

[Pars IV: Pro tempore Adventus Domini]: dolor, misericordia, spes, fiducia, timor, fortitudo, paupertas, laetitia, dilectio, bonitas

Incipiunt alii psalmi, quos simililer ordinavit beatissimus pater noster Franciscus, qui dicendi sunt loco psalmorum supradictorum passionis Domimi ab Adventu Domini usque ad vigiliam Nativitatis et non plus.

Ad Completorium
Antiphona: Sancta Maria Virgo.
Psalmus [XIII]

¹ Usquequo, Domine oblivisceris me in finem?
     * Usquequo avertis faciem tuam a me?

² Quamdiu ponam consilia in anima mea
          * **dolorem** in corde meo per diem?
³ Usquequo exaltabitur inimicus meus super me?
          * Respice, et exaudi me, Domine, Deus meus.
⁴ Illumina oculos meos, ne unquam obdormiam in morte
          * nequando dicat inimicus meus: Praevalui adversus eum.
⁵ Qui tribulant me, exsultabunt si motus fuero
          * ego autem in **misericordia** tua **speravi**.
⁶ Exsultabit cor meum in salutari tuo; cantabo Domino, qui **bona** tribuit mihi
          * et psallam nomini Domini altissimi (Ps 12,1–6).

Ad Matutinum
Antiphona: Sancta Maria Virgo.
Psalmus [XIV]

¹ Confitebor tibi, Domine, sanctissime Pater, Rex caeli et terrae
          * quoniam consolatus es me (cfr. Isa 12,1).
² Tu es Deus salvator meus
          * **fiducialiter** agam et non **timebo** (cfr. Isa 12,2a-b).
³ **Fortitudo** mea et laus mea, Dominus
          * et factus est mihi in salutem (Isa 12,2c-d).
⁴ Dextera tua, Domine, magnificata est in **fortitudine**,
      dextera tua, Domine, percussit inimicum
          * et in multitudine gloriae tuae deposuisti adversarios meos (Exod 15,6–7a).
⁵ Videant **pauperes** et **laetentur**
          * quaerite Deum et vivet anima vestra (Ps 68,33)
⁶ Laudent illum caeli et terra
          * mare et omnia reptilia in eis (Ps 68,35).
⁷ Quoniam Deus salvam faciet Sion
          * et aedificabuntur civitates Iudae (Ps 68,36a-b; R).
⁸ Et inhabitabunt ibi
          * et hereditate acquirent eam (Ps 68,36c).
⁹ Et semen servorum eius possidebit eam
          * et qui **diligunt** nomen eius habitabunt in ea (Ps 68,37).

Ad Primam
Antiphona: Sancta Maria Virgo.
Psalmus: Miserere mei, Deus, miserere mei
ut supra [Ps III]

Ad Tertiam
Antiphona: Sancta Maria Virgo.
Psalmus: Jubilate Deo ut supra [Ps X]

Ad Sextam
Antiphona: Sancta Maria Virgo.
Psalmus: Exaudiat te ut supra [Ps XI]

Ad Nonam
Antiphona: Sancta Maria Virgo.
Psalmus: In te, Domine, **speravi** ut supra [Ps XII]

Ad Vesperam
Antiphona: Sancta Maria Virgo.
Psalmus: Omnes gentes ut supra [Ps VII]

Nota etiam, quod non dicitur totus psalmus, sed usque ad versum scilicet: Commoveatur a facie eius universa terra; sane intelligas, ut dicatur totus versus: Tollite corpora vestra. Finito isto versu dicitur ibi: Gloria Patri et sic dicitur ad vesperam quotidie ab Adventu usque ad vigiliam Nativitatis.

[Pars V: Pro tempore Nativitatis Domini usque ad octavam Epiphaniae]: veritas, magnitudo, misericordia, laetitia/gaudium, pax, bonitas, laudabilitas, honor

Ad Vesperam in Nativitate Domini
Antiphona: Sancta Maria Virgo.
Psalmus [XV]

¹ Exsultate Deo adiutori nostro (Ps 80,2a)
    * iubilate Domino Deo vivo et **vero** in voce exsultationis (cfr. Ps 46,2b).
² Quoniam Dominus excelsus
    * terribilis Rex **magnus** super omnem terram (Ps 46,3).
³ Quia sanctissimus pater de caelo, Rex noster ante saecula (Ps 73,12a),
    misit dilectum Filium suum de alto
    * et natus fuit de beata virgine sancta Maria.
⁴ Ipse invocavit ipsum: Pater meus es tu (Ps 88,27a)
    * et ego primogenitum ponam illum, excelsum prae regibus terrae (Ps 88,27a-28).
⁵ In illa die mandavit Dominus **misericordiam** suam
    * et nocte canticum eius (cfr. Ps 41,9a-b).
⁶ Haec est dies, quam fecit Dominus
    * exsultemus et **laetemur** in ea (Ps 117,24).
⁷ Quia sanctissimus puer dilectus datus est nobis
    et natus fuit pro nobis (cfr. Isa 9,6) in via et positus in praesepio
    * quia non habebat locum in diversorio (cfr. Luke 2,7).
⁸ Gloria in altissimis Domino Deo
    * et in terra **pax** hominibus **bonae** voluntatis (cfr. Luke 2,14).
⁹ **Laetentur** caeli et exsultet terra,
    commoveatur mare et plenitudo eius
    * **gaudebunt** campi et omnia, quae in eis sunt (Ps 95,11–12a).
¹⁰ Cantate ei canticum novum
    * cantate Domino omnis terra (cfr. Ps 95,1).
¹¹ Quoniam **magnus** Dominus et **laudabilis** nimis
    * terribilis est super omnes deos (Ps 95,4).

¹² Afferte Domino patriae gentium,
   afferte Domino gloriam et **honorem**
      * afferte Domino gloriam nomini eius (Ps 95,7–8a).
¹³ Tollite corpora vestra '
   et baiulate sanctam crucem eius
      * et sequimini usque in finem sanctissima praecepta eius (cfr. Luke 14,27; 1
Pet 2,21).

*Nota, quod iste psalmus dicitur a Nativitate Domini usque ad octavam Epiphaniae
ad omnes horas. Si quis voluerit dicere hoc officium beati Francisci, ita dicat illud:
primo dicat Pater noster cum laudibus, scilicet: Sanctus, sanctus, sanctus. Finitis·
laudibus cum oratione ut supra incipiatur antiphona: Sancta Maria cum psalmo,
qui constitutus est unicuique horae diei et noctis. Et cum magna reverentia
dicatur.*

Oratio ante crucifixum dicta: fides, rectitudo, spes, certitudo, caritas

Summe, gloriose Deus, illumina tenebras cordis mei et da mihi **fidem rectam**,
spem certam et **caritatem** perfectam, sensum et cognitionem, Domine, ut faciam
tuum sanctum et verax mandatum.

Regula bullata:

[Honorius, episcopus, servus servorum Dei, dilectis filiis, fratri Francisco et aliis
fratribus de ordine Fratrum Minorum, salutem et apostolicam benedictionem.
Solet annuere Sedes Apostolica piis votis et honestis petentium desideriis
favorem benivolum impertiri. Eapropter, dilecti in Domino filii, vestris piis
precibus inclinati, ordinis vestri regulam, a bonae memoriae Innocentio papa,
praedecessore nostro, approbatam, annotatam praesentibus, autorictate vobis
apostolica confirmamus et praesentis scripti patrocinio communimus. Quae
talis est:]

[CAPUT I]: **obedientia, sine proprio, castitas, reverentia**

In nomine Domini!
Incipit vita Minorum Fratrum:
¹ Regula et Vita Minorum Fratrum haec est, scilicet Domini nostri Jesu Christi
sanctum Evangelium observare vivendo in **obedientia, sine proprio** et in **castitate.** ² Frater Franciscus promittit **obedientiam** et **reverentiam** domino papae
Honorio ac successoribus eius canonice intrantibus et Ecclesiae Romanae. ³ Et
alii fratres teneantur fratri Francisco et eius successoribus **obedire.**

[CAPUT II]: **diligentia, fides, firmitas, continentia, studium, bonitas, sollicitudo, timor, obedientia, vilitas, 'despectus'**

De his qui volunt vitam istam accipere, et qualiter recipi debeant.
¹ Si qui voluerint hanc vitam accipere et venerint ad fratres nostros, mittant eos
ad suos ministros provinciales, quibus solummodo et non aliis recipiendi fratres

licentia concedatur. ² Ministri vero **diligenter** examinent eos de **fide** catholica et ecclesiasticis sacramentis. ³ Et si haec omnia **credant** et velint ea **fideliter** confiteri et usque in finem **firmiter** observare, ⁴ et uxores non habent vel, si habent, et iam monasterium intraverint uxores vel, licentiam eis dederint auctoritate dioecesani episcopi, voto **continentiae** iam emisso, et illius sint aetatis uxores, quod non possit de eis oriri suspicio, ⁵ dicant illis verbum sancti Evangelii (cfr. Matt 19,21par), quod vadant et vendant omnia sua et ea **studeant** pauperibus erogare. ⁶ Quod si facere non potuerint, sufficit eis **bona** voluntas. ⁷ Et caveant fratres et eorum ministri, ne **solliciti** sint de rebus suis temporalibus, ut libere faciant de rebus suis, quidquid Dominus inspiraverit eis. ⁸ Si tamen consilium requiratur, licentiam habeant ministri mittendi eos ad aliquos Deum **timentes**, quorum consilio **bona** sua pauperibus erogentur. ⁹ Postea concedant eis pannos probationis, videlicet duas tunicas sine caputio et cingulum, et braccas et caparonem usque ad cingulum, ¹⁰ nisi eisdem ministris aliud secundum Deum aliquando videatur. ¹¹ Finito vero anno probationis, recipiantur ad **obedientiam** promittentes vitam istam semper et regulam observare. ¹² Et nullo modo licebit eis de ista religione exire iuxta mandatum domini papae, ¹³ quia secundum sanctum Evangelium nemo mittens manum ad aratrum et aspiciens retro aptus est regno Dei (Luke 9,62). ¹⁴ Et illi qui iam promiserunt **obedientiam** habeant unam tunicam cum caputio et aliam sine caputio qui voluerint habere. ¹⁵ Et qui necessitate coguntur possint portare calciamenta. ¹⁶ Et fratres omnes vestimentis **vilibus** induantur et possint ea repeciare de saccis et aliis peciis cum benedictione Dei. ¹⁷ Quos moneo et exhortor, ne despiciant neque iudicent homines, quos vident mollibus vestimentis et coloratis indutos, uti cibis et potibus delicatis, sed magis unusquisque iudicet et **despiciat** semetipsum.

[CAPUT III]: **mititas, 'pacificus'/pax, modestia, mansuetudo, humilitas, honestas, infirmitas**

De divino officio et ieiunio, et quomodo fratres debeant ire per mundum.
¹ Clerici faciant divinum officium secundum ordinem sanctae Romanae Ecclesiae excepto psalterio, ² ex quo habere poterunt breviaria. ³ Laici vero dicant viginti quattuor Pater noster pro matutino, pro laude quinque, pro prima, tertia, sexta, nona, pro qualibet istarum septem, pro vesperis autem duodecim, pro completorio septem; ⁴ et orent pro defunctis. ⁵ Et ieiunent a festo Omnium Sanctorum usque ad Nativitatem Domini. ⁶ Sanctam vero quadragesimam, quae incipit ab Epiphania usque ad continuos quadraginta dies, quam Dominus suo sancto ieiunio consecravit (cfr. Matt 4,2), qui voluntarie eam ieiunant benedicti sint a Domino, et qui nolunt non sint astricti. ⁷ Sed aliam usque ad Resurrectionem Domini ieiunent. ⁸ Aliis autem temporibus non teneantur nisi sexta feria ieiunare. ⁹ Tempore vero manifestae necessitatis non teneantur fratres ieiunio corporali. ¹⁰ Consulo vero, moneo et exhortor fratres meos in Domino Jesu Christo, ut, quando vadunt per mundum, non litigent neque contendant verbis (cfr. 2 Tim 2,14), nec alios iudicent; ¹¹ sed sint **mites, pacifici** et **modesti, mansueti** et **humiles, honeste** loquentes omnibus, sicut decet. ¹² Et non debeant equitare, nisi manifesta necessitate vel **infirmitate** cogantur. ¹³ In quamcumque domum intraverint, primum dicant: **Pax** huic domui (cfr. Luke 10,5). ¹⁴ Et secundum sanctum Evangelium de omnibus cibis, qui apponuntur eis, liceat manducare (cfr. Luke 10,8).

[CAPUT IV]: **firmitas, infirmitas, sollicitudo**

Quod fratres non recipiant pecuniam.
[1] Praecipio **firmiter** fratribus universis, ut nullo modo denarios vel pecuniam recipiant per se vel per interpositam personam. [2] Tamen pro necessitatibus **infirmorum** et aliis fratribus induendis per amicos spirituales ministri tantum et custodes **sollicitam** curam gerant secundum loca et tempora et frigidas regiones, sicut necessitati viderint expedire; [3] eo semper salvo, ut, sicut dictum est, denarios vel pecuniam non recipiant.

[CAPUT V]: **fides, devotio, humilitas, paupertas**

De modo laborandi.
[1] Fratres illi, quibus gratiam dedit Dominus laborandi, laborent **fideliter** et **devote**, [2] ita quod, excluso otio animae inimico, sanctae orationis et **devotionis** spiritum non exstinguant, cui debent cetera temporalia deservire. [3] De mercede vero laboris pro se et suis fratribus corporis necessaria recipiant praeter denarios vel pecuniam [4] et hoc **humiliter**, sicut decet servos Dei et **paupertatis** sanctissimae sectatores.

[CAPUT VI]: **infirmitas, paupertas, humilitas, confidentia, verecundia, celsitudo, virtus, sublimitas, dilectio**

Quod nihil approprient sibi fratres, et de eleemosyna petenda et de fratribus **infirmis.**
[1] Fratres nihil sibi approprient nec domum nec locum nec aliquam rem. [2] Et tanquam peregrini et advenae (cfr. 1 Pet 2,11) in hoc saeculo in **paupertate** et **humilitate** Domino famulantes vadant pro eleemosyna **confidenter,** [3] nec oportet eos **verecundari**, quia Dominus pro nobis se fecit **pauperem** in hoc mundo (cfr. 2 Cor 8,9). [4] Haec est illa **celsitudo** altissimae **paupertatis**, quae vos, carissimos fratres meos, heredes et reges regni caelorum instituit, **pauperes** rebus fecit, **virtutibus sublimavit** (cfr. Jac 2,5). [5] Haec sit portio vestra, quae perducit in terram viventium (cfr. Ps 141,6). [6] Cui, dilectissimi fratres, totaliter inhaerentes nihil aliud pro nomine Domini nostri Jesu Christi in perpetuum sub caelo habere velitis. [7] Et, ubicumque sunt et se invenerint fratres, ostendant se domesticos invicem inter se. [8] Et secure manifestet unus alteri necessitatem suam, quia, si mater nutrit et **diligit** filium suum (cfr. 1 Thess 2,7) carnalem, quanto **diligentius** debet quis **diligere** et nutrire fratrem suum spiritualem? [9] Et, si quis eorum in **infirmitate** ceciderit, alii fratres debent ei servire, sicut vellent sibi serviri (cfr. Matt 7,12).

[CAPUT VII]: **misericordia, poenitentia, caritas**

De poenitentia fratribus peccantibus imponenda.
[1] Si qui fratrum, instigante inimico, mortaliter peccaverint, pro illis peccatis, de quibus ordinatum fuerit inter fratres, ut recurratur ad solos ministros provinciales, teneantur praedicti fratres ad eos recurrere quam citius poterint, sine mora. [2] Ipsi vero ministri, si presbyteri sunt, cum **misericordia** iniungant illis **poenitentiam**; si vero presbyteri non sunt, iniungi faciant per alios sacerdotes ordinis, sicut eis secundum Deum melius videbitur expedire. [3] Et cavere debent,

ne irascantur et conturbentur propter peccatum alicuius, quia ira et conturbatio in se et in aliis impediunt **caritatem**.

[CAPUT VIII]: **firmitas, obedientia**

De electione generalis ministri huius fraternitatis et de capitulo Pentecostes.
[1] Universi fratres unum de fratribus istius religionis teneantur semper habere generalem ministrum et servum totius fraternitatis et ei teneantur **firmiter obedire**. [2] Quo decedente, electio successoris fiat a ministris provincialibus et custodibus in capitulo Pentecostes, in quo provinciales ministri teneantur semper insimul convenire, ubicumque a generali ministro fuerit constitutum; [3] et hoc semel in tribus annis vel ad alium terminum maiorem vel minorem, sicut a praedicto ministro fuerit ordinatum. [4] Et si aliquo tempore appareret universitati ministrorum provincialium et custodum, praedictum ministrum non esse sufficientem ad servitium et communem utilitatem fratrum, teneantur praedicti fratres, quibus electio data est, in nomine Domini alium sibi eligere in custodem. [5] Post capitulum vero Pentecostes ministri et custodes possint singuli, si voluerint et eis expedire videbitur, eodem anno in suis custodiis semel fratres suos ad capitulum convocare.

[CAPUT IX]: **castitas, utilitas, virtus**

De praedicatoribus.
[1] Fratres non praedicent in episcopatu alicuius episcopi, cum ab eo illis fuerit contradictum. [2] Et nullus fratrum populo penitus audeat praedicare, nisi a ministro generali huius fraternitatis fuerit examinatus et approbatus, et ab eo officium sibi praedicationis concessum. [3] Moneo quoque et exhortor eosdem fratres, ut in praedicatione, quam faciunt, sint examinata et **casta** eorum eloquia (cfr. Ps 11,7; 17,31), ad **utilitatem** et aedificationem populi, [4] annuntiando eis vitia et **virtutes**, poenam et gloriam cum brevitate sermonis; quia verbum abbreviatum fecit Dominus super terram (cfr. Rom 9,28).

[CAPUT X]: **humilitas, caritas, firmitas, obedientia, benignitas, familiaritas, sollicitudo, patientia, infirmitas, dilectio, iustitia, perseverantia**

De admonitione et correctione fratrum.
[1] Fratres, qui sunt ministri et servi aliorum fratrum, visitent et moneant fratres suos et **humiliter** et **caritative** corrigant eos, non praecipientes eis aliquid, quod sit contra animam suam et regulam nostram. [2] Fratres vero, qui sunt subditi, recordentur, quod propter Deum abnegaverunt proprias voluntates. [3] Unde **firmiter** praecipio eis, ut **obediant** suis ministris in omnibus quae promiserunt Domino observare et non sunt contraria animae et regulae nostrae. [4] Et ubicumque sunt fratres, qui scirent et cognoscerent, se non posse regulam spiritualiter observare, ad suos ministros debeant et possint recurrere. [5] Ministri vero **caritative** et **benigne** eos recipiant et tantam **familiaritatem** habeant circa ipsos, ut dicere possint eis et facere sicut domini servis suis; [6] nam ita debet esse, quod ministri sint servi omnium fratrum. [7] Moneo vero et exhortor in Domino Jesu

Christo, ut caveant fratres ab omni superbia, vana gloria, invidia, avaritia (cfr. Luke 12,15), cura et **sollicitudine** huius saeculi (cfr. Matt 13,22), detractione et murmuratione, et non curent nescientes litteras litteras discere; [8] sed attendant, quod super omnia desiderare debent habere Spiritum Domini et sanctam eius operationem, [9] orare semper ad eum **puro** corde et habere **humilitatem, patientiam** in persecutione et **infirmitate,** [10] et **diligere** eos qui nos persequuntur et reprehendunt et arguunt, quia dicit Dominus: **Diligite** inimicos vestros et orate pro persequentibus et calumniantibus vos (cfr. Matt 5,44). [11] Beati qui persecutionem patiuntur propter **iustitiam,** quoniam ipsorum est regnum caelorum (Matt 5,10). [12] Qui autem **perseveraverit** usque in finem hic salvus erit (Matt 10,22).

[CAPUT XI]: **firmitas**

Quod fratres non ingrediantur monasteria monacharum.
[1] Praecipio **firmiter** fratribus universis, ne habeant suspecta consortia vel consilia mulierum, [2] et ne ingrediantur monasteria monacharum praeter illos, quibus a sede apostolica concessa est licentia specialis; [3] nec fiant compatres virorum vel mulierum nec hac occasione inter fratres vel de fratribus scandalum oriatur.

[CAPUT XII]: **obedientia, stabilitas, fides, paupertas, humilitas, firmitas**

De euntibus inter saracenos et alios infideles.
[1] Quicumque fratrum divina inspiratione voluerint ire inter saracenos et alios infideles petant inde licentiam a suis ministris provincialibus. [2] Ministri vero nullis eundi licentiam tribuant, nisi eis quos viderint esse idoneos ad mittendum. [3] Ad haec per **obedientiam** iniungo ministris, ut petant a domino papa unum de sanctae Romanae Ecclesiae cardinalibus, qui sit gubernator, protector et corrector istius fraternitatis, [4] ut semper subditi et subiecti pedibus eiusdem sanctae Ecclesiae **stabiles** in **fide** (cfr. Col 1,23) catholica **paupertatem** et **humilitatem** et sanctum evangelium Domini nostri Jesu Christi, quod **firmiter** promisimus, observemus.

[Nulli ergo omnino hominum liceat hanc paginam nostrae confirmationis infringere vel ei ausu temerario contraire. Si quis autem hoc attentare praesumpserit, indignationem omnipotentis Dei et beatorum Petri et Pauli apostolorum eius se noverit incursurum. Datum Laterani tertio kalendas decembris, Pontificatus nostri anno octavo.]

Regula non bullata:

[Prologus]: **obedientia, reverentia**

[1] In nomine Patris et Filii et Spiritus Sancti! [2] Haec est vita evangelii Jesu Christi, quam frater Franciscus petiit a domino papa concedi et confirmari sibi; et ille concessit et confirmavit sibi et suis fratribus habitis et futuris. [3] Frater Franciscus

et quicumque erit caput istius religionis promittat **obedientiam** domino Innocentio papae et **reverentiam** et suis successoribus. ⁴ Et omnes alii fratres teneantur **obedire** fratri Francisco et eius successoribus.

[Cap. I: Quod fratres debent vivere sine proprio et in castitate et obedientia]: **obedientia, castitas, sine proprio**

¹ Regula et vita istorum fratrum haec est, scilicet vivere in **obedientia**, in **castitate** et **sine proprio**, et Domini nostri Jesu Christi doctrinam et vestigia sequi, qui dicit: ² Si vis perfectus esse, vade (Matt 19,21) et vende omnia (cfr. Luke 18,22) quae habes, et da pauperibus et habebis thesaurum in caelo; et veni, sequere me (Matt 19,21). ³ Et: Si quis vult post me venire, abneget semetipsum et tollat crucem suam et sequatur me (Matt 16,24). ⁴ Item: Si quis vult venire ad me et non odit patrem et matrem et uxorem et filios et fratres et sorores, adhuc autem et animam suam, non potest meus esse discipulus (Luke 14,26). ⁵ Et: Omnis, qui reliquerit patrem aut matrem, fratres aut sorores, uxorem aut filios, domos aut agros propter me, centuplum accipiet et vitam aeternam possidebit (cfr. Matt 19,29; Mark 10,29; Luke 18,29).

[Cap. II: De receptione et vestimentis fratrum]: **benignitas, firmitas, diligentia/ studium, obedientia, vilitas, pretiositas**

¹ Si quis divina inspiratione volens accipere hanc vitam venerit ad nostros fratres, **benigne** recipiatur ab eis. ² Quodsi fuerit **firmus** accipere vitam nostram, multum caveant sibi fratres, ne de suis temporalibus negotiis se intromittant, sed ad suum ministrum, quam citius possunt, eum repraesentent. ³ Minister vero **benigne** ipsum recipiat et confortet et vitae nostrae tenorem sibi **diligenter** exponat. ⁴ Quo facto, praedictus, si vult et potest spiritualiter sine impedimento, omnia sua vendat et ea omnia pauperibus **studeat** erogare. ⁵ Caveant sibi fratres et minister fratrum, quod de negotiis suis nullo modo intromittant se ⁶ neque recipiant aliquam pecuniam neque per se neque per interpositam personam. ⁷ Si tamen indigent, alia necessaria corporis praeter pecuniam recipere possunt fratres causa necessitatis sicut alii pauperes. ⁸ Et cum reversus fuerit, minister concedat ei pannos probationis usque ad annum, scilicet duas tunicas sine caputio et cingulum et braccas et caparonem usque ad cingulum. ⁹ Finito vero anno et termino probationis recipiatur ad **obedientiam**. ¹⁰ Postea non licebit ei ad aliam religionem accedere neque extra **obedientiam** evagari iuxta mandatum domini papae et secundum evangelium; quia nemo mittens manum ad aratrum et aspiciens retro aptus est regno Dei (Luke 9,62). ¹¹ Si autem aliquis venerit, qui sua dare non potest sine impedimento et habet spiritualem voluntatem, relinquat illa, et sufficit sibi. ¹² Nullus recipiatur contra formam et institutionem sanctae Ecclesiae. ¹³ Alii vero fratres qui promiserunt **obedientiam** habeant unam tunicam cum caputio et aliam sine caputio, si necesse fuerit, et cingulum et braccas. ¹⁴ Et omnes fratres **vilibus** vestibus induantur, et possint eas repeciare de saccis et aliis peciis cum benedictione Dei; quia dicit Dominus in evangelio: Qui in veste **pretiosa** sunt et in deliciis (Luke 7,25) et qui mollibus vestiuntur, in domibus regum sunt (Matt 11,8). ¹⁵ Et licet dicantur hypocritae, non tamen cessent bene facere nec

quaerant caras vestes in hoc saeculo, ut possint habere vestimentum in regno caelorum.

[Cap. III: De divino officio et ieiunio]:

[1] Dicit Dominus: Hoc genus daemoniorum non potest exire nisi in ieiunio et oratione (cfr. Mark 9,28); [2] et iterum: Cum ieiunatis nolite fieri sicut hypocritae tristes (Matt 6,16). [3] Propter hoc omnes fratres sive clerici sive laici faciant divinum officium, laudes et orationes, secundum quod debent facere. [4] Clerici faciant officium et dicant pro vivis et pro mortuis secundum consuetudinem clericorum. [5] Et pro defectu et negligentia fratrum dicant omni die Miserere mei Deus (Ps 50) cum Pater noster; [6] et pro fratribus defunctis dicant De profundis (Ps 129) cum Pater noster. [7] Et libros tantum necessarios ad implendum eorum officium possint habere. [8] Et laicis etiam scientibus legere psalterium liceat eis habere illud. [9] Aliis vero nescientibus litteras librum habere non liceat. [10] Laici dicant Credo in Deum et viginti quattuor Pater noster cum Gloria Patri pro matutino; pro laudibus vero quinque; pro prima Credo in Deum et septem Pater noster cum Gloria Patri; pro tertia, sexta et nona et unaquaque hora septem; pro vesperis duodecim; pro completorio Credo in Deum et septem Pater noster cum Gloria Patri; pro mortuis septem Pater noster cum Requiem aeternam; et pro defectu et negligentia fratrum tria Pater noster omni die.
[11] Et similiter omnes fratres ieiunent a festo Omnium Sanctorum usque ad Natale et ab Epiphania, quando Dominus noster Jesus Christus incepit ieiunare usque ad Pascha. [12] Aliis autem temporibus non teneantur secundum hanc vitam nisi sexta feria ieiunare. [13] Et liceat eis manducare de omnibus cibis, qui apponuntur eis, secundum evangelium (cfr. Luke 10,8).

[Cap. IV: De ministris et aliis fratribus qualiter ordinentur]: **diligentia, obedientia**

[1] In nomine Domini! [2] Omnes fratres, qui constituuntur ministri et servi aliorum fratrum, in provinciis et in locis, in quibus fuerint, collocent suos fratres, quos saepe visitent et spiritualiter moneant et confortent. [3] Et omnes alii fratres mei benedicti **diligenter obediant** eis in his quae spectant ad salutem animae et non sunt contraria vitae nostrae. [4] Et faciant inter se sicut dicit Dominus: Quaecumque vultis, ut faciant vobis homines et vos facite illis (Matt 7,12); [5] et: Quod non vis tibi fieri, non facias alteri. [6] Et recordentur ministri et servi, quod dicit Dominus: Non veni ministrari, sed ministrare (Matt 20,28) et quia commissa est eis cura animarum fratrum, de quibus, si aliquid perderetur propter eorum culpam et malum exemplum, in die iudicii oportebit eos reddere rationem (cfr. Matt 12,36) coram Domino Jesu Christo.

[Cap. V: De correctione fratrum in offensione]: **obedientia, rationabilitas, diligentia, rectitudo, humilitas, parvitas, caritas, veritas, perseverantia**

[1] Ideoque animas vestras et fratrum vestrorum custodite; quia horrendum est incidere in manus Dei viventis (Hebr 10,31). [2] Si quis autem ministrorum alicui

fratrum aliquid contra vitam nostram praeciperet vel contra animam suam, non teneatur ei **obedire**; quia illa **obedientia** non est, in qua delictum vel peccatum committitur. [3] Verumtamen omnes fratres, qui sunt sub ministris et servis, facta ministrorum et servorum considerent **rationabiliter** et **diligenter**. [4] Et si viderint aliquem illorum carnaliter et non spiritualiter ambulare pro **rectitudine** vitae nostrae, post tertiam admonitionem, si non se emendaverit, in capitulo Pentecostes renuntient ministro et servo totius fraternitatis nulla contradictione impediente. [5] Si vero inter fratres ubicumque fuerit aliquis frater volens carnaliter et non spiritualiter ambulare, fratres, cum quibus est, moneant eum, instruant et corripiant **humiliter** et **diligenter**. [6] Quod si ille post tertiam admonitionem noluerit se emendare, quam citius possunt, mittant eum vel significent suo ministro et servo, qui minister et servus de eo faciat sicut sibi secundum Deum melius videbitur expedire.

[7] Et caveant omnes fratres, tam ministri et servi quam alii, quod propter peccatum alterius vel malum non turbentur vel irascantur, quia diabolus propter delictum unius multos vult corrumpere; [8] sed spiritualiter, sicut melius possunt, adiuvent illum qui peccavit, quia non est sanis opus medicus, sed male habentibus (cfr. Matt 9,12 cum Mark 2,17).

[9] Similiter omnes fratres non habeant in hoc potestatem vel dominationem maxime inter se. [10] Sicut enim dicit Dominus in evangelio: Principes gentium dominantur eorum, et qui maiores sunt potestatem exercent in eos (Matt 20,25), non sic erit inter fratres (cfr. Matt 20,26a); [11] et quicumque voluerit inter eos maior fieri sit eorum minister (cfr. Matt 20,26b) et servus; [12] et qui maior est inter eos fiat sicut **minor** (cfr. Luke 22,26).

[13] Nec aliquis frater malum faciat vel malum dicat alteri; [14] immo magis per **caritatem** spiritus voluntarie serviant et **obediant** invicem (cfr. Gal 5,13). [15] Et haec est **vera** et sancta **obedientia** Domini nostri Jesu Christi. [16] Et omnes fratres, quoties declinaverint a mandatis Domini et extra **obedientiam** evagaverint, sicut dicit propheta (Ps 118,21), sciant se esse maledictos extra **obedientiam** quousque steterint in tali peccato scienter. [17] Et quando **perseveraverint** in mandatis Domini, quae promiserunt per sanctum evangelium et vitam ipsorum, sciant se in **vera obedientia** stare, et benedicti sint a Domino.

[Cap. VI: De recursu fratrum ad ministros et quod aliquis frater non vocetur prior]: **studium**

[1] Fratres, in quibuscumque locis sunt, si non possunt vitam nostram observare, quam citius possunt, recurrant ad suum ministrum hoc sibi significantes. [2] Minister vero taliter eis **studeat** providere, sicut ipse vellet sibi fieri, si in consimili casu esset (cfr. Matt 7,12). [3] Et nullus vocetur prior, sed generaliter omnes vocentur fratres minores. [4] Et alter alterius lavet pedes (cfr. Joa 13,14).

[Cap. VII: De modo serviendi et laborandi]: **parvitas, studium, bonitas, benignitas, diligentia, honor, gaudium/hilaritas, gratiositas**

[1] Omnes fratres, in quibuscumque locis steterint apud alios ad serviendum vel laborandum, non sint camerarii neque cancellarii neque praesint in domibus in

quibus serviunt; nec recipiant aliquod officium, quod scandalum generet vel animae suae faciat detrimentum (cfr. Mark 8,36); [2] sed sint **minores** et subditi omnibus, qui in eadem domo sunt. [3] Et fratres, qui sciunt laborare, laborent et eandem artem exerceant, quam noverint, si non fuerit contra salutem animae et honeste poterit operari. [4] Nam propheta ait: Labores fructuum tuorum manducabis; beatus es et bene tibi erit (Ps 127,2;-R); [5] et apostolus: Qui non vult operari non manducet (cfr. 2 Thess 3,10); [6] et: Unusquisque in ea arte et officio, in quo vocatus est, permaneat (cfr. 1 Cor 7,24). [7] Et pro labore possint recipere omnia necessaria praeter pecuniam. [8] Et cum necesse fuerit, vadant pro eleemosynis sicut alii pauperes. [9] Et liceat eis habere ferramenta et instrumenta suis artibus opportuna.

[10] Omnes fratres **studeant bonis** operibus insudare, quia scriptum est: Semper facito aliquid **boni**, ut te diabolus inveniat occupatum. [11] Et iterum: Otiositas inimica est animae. [12] Ideo servi Dei semper orationi vel alicui **bonae** operationi insistere debent.

[13] Caveant sibi fratres, ubicumque fuerint, in eremis vel in aliis locis, quod nullum locum sibi approprient nec alicui defendant. [14] Et quicumque ad eos venerit amicus vel adversarius, fur vel latro **benigne** recipiatur. [15] Et ubicumque sunt fratres et in quocumque loco se invenerint, spiritualiter et **diligenter** debeant se revidere et **honorare** ad invicem sine murmuratione (1 Pet 4,9). [16] Et caveant sibi, quod non se ostendant tristes extrinsecus et nubilosos hypocritas; sed ostendant **se gaudentes** in Domino (cfr. Phil 4,4) et **hilares** et convenienter **gratiosos.**

[Cap. VIII: Quod fratres non recipiant pecuniam]: **sollicitudo, infirmitas, utilitas, poenitentia**

[1] Dominus praecipit in evangelio: Videte, cavete ab omni malitia et avaritia (cfr. Luke 12,15); [2] et: Attendite vobis a **sollicitudine** huius saeculi et a curis huius vitae (cfr. Luke 21,34).

[3] Unde nullus fratrum, ubicumque sit et quocumque vadit, aliquo modo tollat nec recipiat nec recipi faciat pecuniam aut denarios neque occasione vestimentorum nec librorum nec pro pretio alicuius laboris, immo nulla occasione, nisi propter manifestam necessitatem **infirmorum** fratrum; quia non debemus maiorem **utilitatem** habere et reputare in pecunia et denariis quam in lapidibus. [4] Et illos vult diabolus excaecare, qui eam appetunt vel reputant lapidibus meliorem. [5] Caveamus ergo nos, qui omnia relinquimus (cfr. Matt 19,27), ne pro tam modico regnum caelorum perdamus. [6] Et si in aliquo loco inveniremus denarios, de his non curemus tamquam de pulvere, quem pedibus calcamus, quia vanitas vanitatum et omnia vanitas (Eccle 1,2). [7] Et si forte, quod absit, aliquem fratrem contigerit pecuniam vel denarios colligere vel habere, excepta solummodo praedicta **infirmorum** necessitate, omnes fratres teneamus eum pro falso fratre et apostata et fure et latrone et loculos habente (cfr. Joa 12,6), nisi vere **poenituerit.** [8] Et nullo modo fratres recipiant nec recipi faciant nec quaerant nec quaeri faciant pecuniam pro eleemosyna neque denarios pro aliquibus domibus vel locis; neque cum persona pro talibus locis pecunias vel denarios quaerente vadant. [9] Alia autem servitia, quae non sunt contraria vitae nostrae, possunt fratres locis facere

cum benedictione Dei. ¹⁰ Fratres tamen in manifesta necessitate leprosorum possunt pro eis quaerere eleemosynam. ¹¹ Caveant tamen multum a pecunia. ¹² Similiter caveant omnes fratres, ut pro nullo turpi lucro terras circueant.

[Cap. IX: De petenda eleemosyna]: **studium, humilitas, paupertas, 'contentus', gaudium, vilitas, 'despectus', infirmitas, verecundia, gratitudo, magnitudo, honor, patientia, iustitia, caritas/dilectio**

¹ Omnes fratres **studeant** sequi **humilitatem** et **paupertatem** Domini nostri Jesu Christi et recordentur, quod nihil aliud oportet nos habere de toto mundo, nisi, sicut dicit apostolus, habentes alimenta et quibus tegamur, his **contenti** sumus (cfr. 1 Tim 6,8). ² Et debent **gaudere**, quando conversantur inter **viles** et **despectas** personas, inter **pauperes** et debiles et **infirmos** et leprosos et iuxta viam mendicantes. ³ Et cum necesse fuerit, vadant pro eleemosynis. ⁴ Et non **verecundentur** et magis recordentur, quia Dominus noster Jesus Christus, Filius Dei vivi (Joa 11,27) omnipotentis, posuit faciem suam ut petram durissimam (Isa 50,7), nec **verecundatus** fuit. ⁵ Et fuit **pauper** et hospes et vixit de eleemosynis ipse et beata Virgo et discipuli eius. ⁶ Et quando facerent eis homines **verecundiam** et nollent eis dare eleemosynam, referant inde **gratias** Deo; quia de **verecundiis** recipient **magnum honorem** ante tribunal Domini nostri Jesu Christi. ⁷ Et sciant, quod **verecundia** non **patientibus**, sed inferentibus imputatur. ⁸ Et eleemosyna est hereditas et **iustitia**, quae debetur **pauperibus**, quam nobis acquisivit Dominus noster Jesus Christus. ⁹ Et fratres, qui eam acquirendo laborant, **magnam** mercedem habebunt et faciunt lucrari et acquirere tribuentes; quia omnia quae relinquent homines in mundo peribunt, sed de **caritate** et de eleemosynis, quas fecerunt, habebunt praemium a Domino.
¹⁰ Et secure manifestet unus alteri necessitatem suam, ut sibi necessaria inveniat et ministret. ¹¹ Et quilibet **diligat** et nutriat fratrem suum, sicut mater **diligit** et nutrit filium suum (cfr. 1 Thess 2,7), in quibus ei Deus gratiam largietur. ¹² Et qui non manducat, manducantem non iudicet (Rom 14,3b).
¹³ Et quandocumque necessitas supervenerit, liceat universis fratribus, ubicumque fuerint, uti omnibus cibis, quos possunt homines manducare, sicut Dominus dicit de David, qui comedit panes propositionis (cfr. Matt 12,4), quos non licebat manducare nisi sacerdotibus (Mark 2,26). ¹⁴ Et recordentur, quod dicit Dominus: Attendite autem vobis ne forte graventur corda vestra in crapula et ebrietate et curis huius vitae et superveniat in vobis repentina dies illa; ¹⁵ tanquam enim laqueus superveniet in omnes, qui sedent super faciem orbis terrae (cfr. Luke 21,34–35). ¹⁶ Similiter etiam tempore manifestae necessitatis faciant omnes fratres de eorum necessariis, sicut eis Dominus gratiam largietur, quia necessitas non habet legem.

[Cap. X: De infirmis fratribus]: **infirmitas, gratitudo, sollicitudo, dilectio**

¹ Si quis fratrum in **infirmitate** ceciderit, ubicumque fuerit, alii fratres non dimittant eum, nisi constituatur unus de fratribus vel plures, si necesse fuerit, qui serviant ei, sicut vellent sibi serviri (cfr. Matt 7,12); ² sed in maxima necessitate

possunt ipsum dimittere alicui personae quae suae debeat satisfacere **infirmitati.** [3] Et rogo fratrem **infirmum,** ut referat de omnibus **gratias** Creatori; et quod qualem vult eum Dominus talem se esse desideret sive sanum sive **infirmum,** quia omnes, quos Deus ad vitam praeordinavit aeternam (cfr. Act 13,48), flagellorum atque **infirmitatum** stimulis et compunctionis spiritu erudit, sicut Dominus dicit: Ego quos amo corrigo et castigo (Apoc 3,19). [4] Et si quis turbabitur vel irascetur sive contra Deum sive contra fratres, vel si forte **sollicite** postulaverit medicinas nimis desiderans liberare carnem cito morituram, quae est animae inimica, a malo sibi evenit et carnalis est, et non videtur esse de fratribus, quia plus **diligit** corpus quam animam.

[Cap. XI: Quod fratres non blasphement nec detrahant, sed diligant se ad invicem]: **studium, silentium, humilitas, inutilitas, dilectio, veritas, modestia, mansuetudo**

[1] Et omnes fratres caveant sibi, ut non calumnientur neque contendant verbis (cfr. 2 Tim 2,14); [2] immo **studeant** retinere **silentium,** quandocumque eis Deus gratiam largietur. [3] Neque litigent inter se neque cum aliis, sed procurent **humiliter** respondere dicentes: **Inutilis** servus sum (cfr. Luke 17,10). [4] Et non irascantur, quia omnis qui irascitur fratri suo, reus erit iudicio; qui dixerit fratri suo raca, reus erit concilio; qui dixerit fatue, reus erit gehennae ignis (Matt 5,22). [5] Et **diligant** se ad invicem sicut dicit Dominus: Hoc est praeceptum meum ut **diligatis** invicem sicut **dilexi** vos (Joa 15,12). [6] Et ostendant ex operibus (cfr. Jac 2,18) **dilectionem,** quam habent ad invicem sicut dicit apostolus: Non **diligamus** verbo neque lingua, sed opere et **veritate** (1 Joa 3,18). [7] Et neminem blasphement (cfr. Tit 3,2); [8] non murmurent, non detrahant aliis, quia scriptum est: Susurrones et detractores Deo sunt odibiles (cfr. Rom 1,29). [9] Et sint **modesti** omnem ostendentes **mansuetudinem** ad omnes homines (cfr. Tit 3,2); [10] non iudicent, non condemnent. [11] Et, sicut dicit Dominus, non considerent minima peccata aliorum (cfr. Matt 7,3; Luke 6,41), [12] immo magis sua recogitent in amaritudine animae suae (Isa 38,15). [13] Et contendant intrare per angustam portam (Luke 13,24), quia dicit Dominus: Angusta porta et arcta via est, quae ducit ad vitam; et pauci sunt, qui inveniunt eam (Matt 7,14).

[Cap. XII: De malo visu et frequentia mulierum]: **honestas, poenitentia, obedientia, munditia**

[1] Omnes fratres, ubicumque sunt vel vadunt, caveant sibi a malo visu et frequentia mulierum. [2] Et nullus cum eis consilietur aut per viam vadat solus aut ad mensam in una paropside comedat. [3] Sacerdotes **honeste** loquantur cum eis dando **poenitentiam** vel aliud spirituale consilium. [4] Et nulla penitus mulier ab aliquo fratre recipiatur ad **obedientiam,** sed dato sibi consilio spirituali, ubi voluerit agat **poenitentiam.** [5] Et multum omnes nos custodiamus et omnia membra nostra **munda** teneamus, quia dicit Dominus: Qui viderit mulierem ad concupiscendam eam, iam moechatus est eam in corde suo (Matt 5,28). [6] Et apostolus: An ignoratis, quia membra vestra templum sunt Spiritus Sancti? (cfr. 1 Cor 6,19); itaque qui templum Dei violaverit, disperdet illum Deus (1 Cor 3,17).

[Cap. XIII: De vitanda fornicatione]: **poenitentia**

¹ Si quis fratrum diabolo instigante fornicaretur, habitu exuatur, quem pro sua turpi iniquitate amisit, et ex toto deponat et a nostra religione penitus repellatur. ² Et postea **poenitentiam** faciat de peccatis (cfr. 1 Cor 5,4–5).

[Cap. XIV: Quomodo fratres debeant ire per mundum]: **pax**

¹ Quando fratres vadunt per mundum, nihil portent per viam neque (cfr. Luke 9,3) sacculum (cfr. Luke 10,4) neque peram neque panem neque pecuniam (cfr. Luke 9,3) neque virgam (cfr. Matt 10,10). ² Et in quamcumque domum intraverint, dicant primum: **Pax** huic domui (cfr. Luke 10,5). ³ Et in eadem domo manentes edant et bibant quae apud illos sunt (cfr. Luke 10,7). ⁴ Non resistant malo (cfr. Matt 5,39), sed qui eos percusserit in una maxilla, praebeant et alteram (cfr. Matt 5,39 et Luke 6,29). ⁵ Et qui aufert eis vestimentum, et tunicam non prohibeant (cfr. Luke 6,29). ⁶ Omni petenti se tribuant; et qui aufert quae sua sunt, ea non repetant (cfr. Luke 6,30).

[Cap. XV: Quod fratres non equitent]: **infirmitas, magnitudo**

¹ Iniungo omnibus fratribus meis tam clericis quam laicis euntibus per mundum vel morantibus in locis, quod nullo modo apud se nec apud alium nec alio aliquo modo bestiam aliquam habeant. ² Nec eis liceat equitare, nisi **infirmitate** vel **magna** necessitate cogantur.

[Cap. XVI: De euntibus inter saracenos et alios infideles]: **prudentia, simplicitas, fides, amor, iustitia, gaudium, timor, patientia, perseverantia**

¹ Dicit Dominus: Ecce ego mitto vos sicut oves in medio luporum. ² Estote ergo **prudentes** sicut serpentes et **simplices** sicut columbae (Matt 10,16). ³ Unde quicumque frater voluerit ire inter saracenos et alios infideles, vadat de licentia sui ministri et servi. ⁴ Et minister det eis licentiam et non contradicat, si viderit eos idoneos ad mittendum; nam tenebitur Domino reddere rationem (cfr. Luke 16,2), si in hoc vel in aliis processerit indiscrete. ⁵ Fratres vero, qui vadunt, duobus modis inter eos possunt spiritualiter conversari. ⁶ Unus modus est, quod non faciant lites neque contentiones, sed sint subditi omni humanae creaturae propter Deum (1 Pet 2,13) et confiteantur se esse christianos. ⁷ Alius modus est, quod, cum viderint placere Domino, annuntient verbum Dei, ut **credant** Deum omnipotentem, Patrem et Filium et Spiritum Sanctum, creatorem omnium, redemptorem et salvatorem Filium, et ut baptizentur et efficiantur christiani, quia quis renatus non fuerit ex aqua et Spiritu Sancto, non potest intrare in regnum Dei (cfr. Joa 3,5). ⁸ Haec et alia, quae placuerint Domino, ipsis et aliis dicere possunt, quia dicit Dominus in evangelio: Omnis, qui confitebitur me coram hominibus, confitebor et ego eum coram Patre meo, qui in caelis est (Matt 10,32). ⁹ Et: Qui erubuerit me et sermones meos, et Filius hominis erubescet eum, cum venerit in maiestate sua et Patris et angelorum (cfr. Luke 9,26).

[10] Et omnes fratres, ubicumque sunt, recordentur, quod dederunt se et reliquerunt corpora sua Domino Jesu Christo. [11] Et pro eius **amore** debent se exponere inimicis tam visibilibus quam invisibilibus; quia dicit Dominus: Qui perdiderit animam suam propter me, salvam faciet eam (cfr. Luke 9,24) in vitam aeternam (Matt 25,46). [12] Beati qui persecutionem patiuntur propter **iustitiam**, quoniam ipsorum est regnum caelorum (Matt 5,10). [13] Si me persecuti sunt, et vos persequentur (Joa 15,20). [14] Et: Si persequuntur vos in una civitate, fugite in aliam (cfr. Matt 10,23). [15] Beati estis (Matt 5,11), cum vos oderint homines (Luke 6,22) et maledixerint vobis (Matt 5,11) et persequentur vos (cfr. l.c.) et separaverint vos et exprobraverint et eiecerint nomen vestrum tamquam malum (Luke 6,22) et cum dixerint omne malum adversum vos mentientes propter me (Matt 5,11). [16] **Gaudete** in illa die et exsultate (Luke 6,23), quoniam merces vestra multa est in caelis (cfr. Matt 5,12). [17] Et ego dico vobis amicis meis, non terreamini ab his (cfr. Luke 12,4), [18] et nolite **timere** eos qui occidunt corpus (Matt 10,28) et post hoc non habent amplius quid faciant (Luke 12,4). [19] Videte, ne turbemini (Matt 24,6). [20] In **patientia** enim vestra possidebitis animas vestras (Luke 21,19); [21] et qui **perseveraverit** usque in finem, hic salvus erit (Matt 10,22; 24,13).

[Cap. XVII: De praedicatoribus]: **caritas/amor, studium, humilitas, gaudium, bonitas, firmitas, sapientia, prudentia, 'despectus', vilitas, patientia, puritas, simplicitas, veritas, pax, timor, gratitudo, honor, reverentia**

[1] Nullus frater praedicet contra formam et institutionem sanctae Ecclesiae et nisi concessum sibi fuerit a ministro suo. [2] Et caveat sibi minister, ne alicui indiscrete concedat. [3] Omnes tamen fratres operibus praedicent. [4] Et nullus minister vel praedicator approopriet sibi ministerium fratrum vel officium praedicationis, sed quacumque hora ei iniunctum fuerit, sine omni contradictione dimittat suum officium.

[5] Unde deprecor in **caritate**, quae Deus est (cfr. 1 Joa 4,16), omnes fratres meos praedicatores, oratores, laboratores, tam clericos quam laicos, ut **studeant** se **humiliare** in omnibus, [6] non gloriari nec in se **gaudere** nec interius se exaltare de **bonis** verbis et operibus, immo de nullo **bono**, quod Deus facit vel dicit et operatur in eis aliquando et per ipsos, secundum quod dicit Dominus: Veruntamen in hoc nolite **gaudere**, quia spiritus vobis subiciuntur (Luke 10,20). [7] Et **firmiter** sciamus, quia non pertinent ad nos nisi vitia et peccata. [8] Et magis debemus **gaudere**, cum in tentationes varias incideremus (cfr. Jac 1,2) et cum sustinueremus quascumque animae vel corporis angustias aut tribulationes in hoc mundo propter vitam aeternam.

[9] Omnes ergo fratres caveamus ab omni superbia et vana gloria; [10] et custodiamus nos a **sapientia** huius mundi et a **prudentia** carnis (Rom 8,6) [11] spiritus enim carnis vult et **studet** multum ad verba habenda, sed parum ad operationem, [12] et quaerit non religionem et sanctitatem in interiori spiritu, sed vult et desiderat habere religionem et sanctitatem foris apparentem hominibus. [13] Et isti sunt, de quibus dicit Dominus: Amen dico vobis, receperunt mercedem suam (Matt 6,2). [14] Spiritus autem Domini vult mortificatam et **despectam, vilem** et abiectam esse carnem. [15] Et **studet** ad **humilitatem** et **patientiam** et **puram** et **simplicem** et

veram pacem spiritus. [16] Et semper super omnia desiderat divinum **timorem** et divinam **sapientiam** et divinum **amorem** Patris et Filii et Spiritus Sancti.
[17] Et omnia **bona** Domino Deo altissimo et summo reddamus et omnia **bona** ipsius esse cognoscamus et de omnibus ei **gratias** referamus, a quo **bona** cuncta procedunt. [18] Et ipse altissimus et summus, solus **verus** Deus habeat et ei reddantur et ipse recipiat omnes **honores** et **reverentias**, omnes laudes et benedictiones, omnes **gratias** et gloriam, cuius est omne **bonum**, qui solus est **bonus** (cfr. Luke 18,19).
[19] Et quando nos videmus vel audimus malum dicere vel facere vel blasphemare Deum, nos **bene** dicamus et **bene** faciamus et laudemus Deum (cfr. Rom 12,21), qui est benedictus in saecula (Rom 1,25).

[Cap. XVIII: Qualiter ministri conveniant ad invicem]:

[1] Quolibet anno unusquisque minister cum fratribus suis possit convenire, ubicumque placuerit eis, in festo sancti Michaelis archangeli de his quae ad Deum pertinent, tractaturus. [2] Omnes enim ministri, qui sunt in ultramarinis et ultramontanis partibus, semel in tribus annis, et alii ministri semel in anno veniant ad capitulum Pentecostes apud ecclesiam sanctae Mariae de Portiuncula, nisi a ministro et servo totius fraternitatis aliter fuerit ordinatum.

[Cap. XIX: Quod fratres vivant catholice]: **fides, veneratio**

[1] Omnes fratres sint catholici, vivant et loquantur catholice. [2] Si quis vero erraverit a **fide** et vita catholica in dicto vel in facto et non se emendaverit, a nostra fraternitate penitus expellatur. [3] Et omnes clericos et omnes religiosos habeamus pro dominis in his quae spectant ad salutem animae et a nostra religione non deviaverint; et ordinem et officium eorum et administrationem in Domino **veneremur.**

[Cap. XX: De poenitentia et receptione corporis et sanguinis Domini nostri Jesu Christi]: **discretio, firmitas, poenitentia, humilitas, magnitudo, fides, veneratio**

[1] Et fratres mei benedicti tam clerici quam laici confiteantur peccata sua sacerdotibus nostrae religionis. [2] Et si non potuerint, confiteantur aliis **discretis** et catholicis sacerdotibus scientes **firmiter** et attendentes, quia a quibuscumque sacerdotibus catholicis acceperint **poenitentiam** et absolutionem, absoluti erunt procul dubio ab illis peccatis, si **poenitentiam** sibi iniunctam procuraverint **humiliter** et **fideliter** observare. [3] Si vero tunc non potuerint habere sacerdotem, confiteantur fratri suo, sicut dicit apostolus Jacobus: Confitemini alterutrum peccata vestra (Jac 5,16). [4] Non tamen propter hoc dimittant recurrere ad sacerdotem, quia potestas ligandi et solvendi solis sacerdotibus est concessa. [5] Et sic contriti et confessi sumant corpus et sanguinem Domini nostri Jesu Christi cum **magna humilitate** et **veneratione** recordantes, quod Dominus dicit: Qui manducat carnem meam et bibit sanguinem meum

habet vitam aeternam (cfr. Joa 6,55); [6] et: Hoc facite in meam commemorationem (Luke 22,19).

[Cap. XXI: De laude et exhortatione, quam possunt omnes fratres facere]: **timor, honor, gratitudo, poenitentia, dignitas, abstinentia, perseverantia, bonitas**

[1] Et hanc vel talem exhortationem et laudem omnes fratres mei, quandocumque placuerit eis, annuntiare possunt inter quoscumque homines cum benedictione Dei: [2] **Timete** et **honorate**, laudate et benedicite, **gratias** agite (1 Thess 5,18) et adorate Dominum Deum omnipotentem in trinitate et unitate, Patrem et Filium et Spiritum Sanctum, creatorem omnium. [3] Agite **poenitentiam** (cfr. Matt 3,2), facite **dignos** fructus **poenitentiae** (cfr. Luke 3,8), quia cito moriemur. [4] Date et dabitur vobis (Luke 6,38). [5] Dimittite et dimittetur vobis (cfr. Luke 6,37). [6] Et si non dimiseritis hominibus peccata eorum (Matt 6,14), Dominus non dimittet vobis peccata vestra (Mark 11,25); confitemini omnia peccata vestra (cfr. Jac 5,16). [7] Beati qui moriuntur in **poenitentia**, quia erunt in regno caelorum. [8] Vae illis qui non moriuntur in **poenitentia**, quia erunt filii diaboli (1 Joa 3,10), cuius opera faciunt (cfr. Joa 8,41) et ibunt in ignem aeternum (Matt 18,8; 25,41). [9] Cavete et **abstinete** ab omni malo et **perseverate** usque in finem in **bono**.

[Cap. XXII: De admonitione fratrum]: **dilectio/amor/caritas, verecundia, dolor, bonitas, fides, gaudium, sollicitudo, patientia, requies, munditia/puritas, honor, vigilantia, dignitas, veritas, claritas**

[1] Attendamus, omnes fratres, quod dicit Dominus: **Diligite** inimicos vestros et benefacite his qui oderunt vos (cfr. Matt 5,44par.), [2] quia Dominus noster Jesus Christus, cuius sequi vestigia debemus (cfr. 1 Pet 2,21), traditorem suum vocavit amicum (cfr. Matt 26,50) et crucifixoribus suis sponte se obtulit. [3] Amici igitur nostri sunt omnes illi qui nobis iniuste inferunt tribulationes et angustias, **verecundias** et iniurias, **dolores** et tormenta, martyrium et mortem; [4] quos multum **diligere** debemus, quia ex hoc quod nobis inferunt, habemus vitam aeternam.

[5] Et odio habeamus corpus nostrum cum vitiis et peccatis suis; quia carnaliter vivendo vult diabolus a nobis auferre **amorem** Jesu Christi et vitam aeternam et se ipsum cum omnibus perdere in infernum; [6] quia nos per culpam nostram sumus foetidi, miseri et **bono** contrarii, ad mala autem prompti et voluntarii, quia, sicut Dominus dicit in evangelio: [7] De corde procedunt et exeunt cogitationes malae, adulteria, fornicationes, homicidia, furta, avaritia, nequitia, dolus, impudicitia, oculus malus, falsa testimonia, blasphemia, stultitia (cfr. Mark 7,21–22; Matt 15,19). [8] Haec omnia mala ab intus de corde hominis procedunt (cfr. Mark 7,23) et haec sunt, quae coinquinant hominem (Matt 15,20).

[9] Nunc autem, postquam dimisimus mundum, nihil aliud habemus facere, nisi sequi voluntatem Domini et placere sibi ipsi. [10] Multum caveamus, ne simus terra secus viam vel petrosa vel spinosa, secundum quod dicit Dominus in evangelio: [11] Semen est verbum Dei (Luke 8,11). [12] Quod autem secus viam cecidit et conculcatum est (cfr. Luke 8,5), hi sunt qui audiunt (Luke 8,12) verbum et non intelligunt (cfr. Matt 13,19); [13] et confestim (Mark 4,15) venit diabolus (Luke 8,12) et rapit (Matt 13,19), quod seminatum est in cordibus eorum (Mark 4,15) et tollit verbum

de cordibus eorum, ne **credentes** salvi fiant (Luke 8,12). ¹⁴ Quod autem super petrosam cecidit (cfr. Matt 13,20), hi sunt, qui, cum audierint verbum, statim cum **gaudio** (Mark 4,16) suscipiunt (Luke 8,13) illud (Mark 4,16). ¹⁵ Facta autem tribulatione et persecutione propter verbum, continuo scandalizantur (Matt 13,21) et hi radicem in se non habent, sed temporales sunt (cfr. Mark 4,17), quia ad tempus **credunt** et in tempore tentationis recedunt (Luke 8,13). ¹⁶ Quod autem in spinis cecidit, hi sunt (Luke 8,14), qui verbum Dei audiunt (cfr. Mark 4,18), et **sollicitudo** (Matt 13,22) et aerumnae (Mark 4,19) istius saeculi et fallacia divitiarum (Matt 13,22) et circa reliqua concupiscentiae introeuntes suffocant verbum et sine fructu efficiuntur (cfr. Mark 4,19). ¹⁷ Quod autem in terram **bonam** (Luke 8,15) seminatum est (Matt 13,23), hi sunt, qui in corde **bono** et optimo audientes verbum (Luke 8,15) intelligunt et (cfr. Matt 13,23) retinent et fructum afferunt in **patientia** (Luke 8,15). ¹⁸ Et propterea nos fratres, sicut dicit Dominus, dimittamus mortuos sepelire mortuos suos (Matt 8,22).

¹⁹ Et multum caveamus a malitia et subtilitate satanae, qui vult, quod homo mentem suam et cor non habeat ad Deum. ²⁰ Et circuiens desiderat cor hominis sub specie alicuius mercedis vel adiutorii tollere et suffocare verbum et praecepta Domini a memoria et volens cor hominis per saecularia negotia et curam excaecare et ibi habitare, sicut dicit Dominus: ²¹ Cum immundus spiritus exierit ab homine, ambulat per loca arida (Matt 12,43) et inaquosa quaerens **requiem**; ²² et non inveniens dicit: Revertar in domum meam, unde exivi (Luke 11,24). ²³ Et veniens invenit eam vacantem scopis **mundatam** et ornatam (Matt 12,44). ²⁴ Et vadit et assumit alios septem spiritus nequiores se, et ingressi habitant ibi, et sunt novissima hominis illius peiora prioribus (cfr. Luke 11,26).

²⁵ Unde, omnes fratres, custodiamus nos multum, ne sub specie alicuius mercedis vel operis vel adiutorii perdamus vel tollamus nostram mentem et cor a Domino. ²⁶ Sed in sancta **caritate**, quae Deus est (cfr. 1 Joa 4,16), rogo omnes fratres tam ministros quam alios, ut omni impedimento remoto et omni cura et **sollicitudine** postposita, quocumque modo melius possunt, servire, **amare, honorare** et adorare Dominum Deum **mundo** corde et **pura** mente faciant, quod ipse super omnia quaerit ²⁷ et semper faciamus ibi habitaculum et mansionem (cfr. Joa 14,23) ipsi, qui est Dominus Deus omnipotens, Pater et Filius et Spiritus Sanctus, qui dicit: **Vigilate** itaque omni tempore orantes, ut **digni** habeamini fugere omnia mala, quae ventura sunt et stare ante Filium hominis (Luke 21,36). ²⁸ Et cum stabitis ad orandum (Mark 11,25) dicite (Luke 11,2): Pater noster qui es in caelis (Matt 6,9). ²⁹ Et adoremus eum **puro** corde, quoniam oportet semper orare et non deficere (Luke 18,1); ³⁰ nam Pater tales quaerit adoratores. ³¹ Spiritus est Deus et eos qui adorant eum, in spiritu et **veritate** oportet eum adorare (cfr. Joa 4,23–24). ³² Et ad ipsum recurramus tamquam ad pastorem et episcopum animarum nostrarum (1 Pet 2,25), qui dicit: Ego sum pastor **bonus**, qui pasco oves meas et pro ovibus meis pono animam meam. ³³ Omnes vos fratres estis; ³⁴ et patrem nolite vobis vocare super terram, unus est enim Pater vester, qui in caelis est. ³⁵ Nec vocemini magistri; unus est enim magister vester, qui in caelis est (cfr. Matt 23,8–10). ³⁶ Si manseritis in me, et verba mea in vobis manserint, quodcumque volueritis, petetis et fiet vobis (Joa 15,7). ³⁷ Ubicumque sunt duo vel tres congregati in nomine meo, ibi sum in medio eorum (Matt 18,20). ³⁸ Ecce ego sum vobiscum usque ad consummationem saeculi (Matt 28,20). ³⁹ Verba, quae locutus sum vobis, spiritus et vita sunt (Joa 6,64). ⁴⁰ Ego sum via, **veritas** et vita (Joa 14,6).

⁴¹ Teneamus ergo verba, vitam et doctrinam et sanctum eius evangelium, qui **dignatus** est pro nobis rogare Patrem suum et nobis eius nomen manifestare dicens: Pater **clarifica** nomen tuum (Joa 12,28a) et **clarifica** Filium tuum, ut Filius tuus **clarificet** te (Joa 17,1b). ⁴² Pater, manifestavi nomen tuum hominibus, quos dedisti mihi (Joa 17,6); quia verba quae dedisti mihi, dedi eis; et ipsi acceperunt et cognoverunt, quia a te exivi et **crediderunt** quia tu me misisti. ⁴³ Ego pro eis rogo, non pro mundo, ⁴⁴ sed pro his quos dedisti mihi, quia tui sunt et omnia mea tua sunt (Joa 17,8-10). ⁴⁵ Pater sancte, serva eos in nomine tuo, quos dedisti mihi, ut ipsi sint unum sicut et nos (Joa 17,11b). ⁴⁶ Haec loquor in mundo, ut habeant **gaudium** in semetipsis. ⁴⁷ Ego dedi eis sermonem tuum; et mundus eos odio habuit, quia non sunt de mundo, sicut et ego non sum de mundo. ⁴⁸ Non rogo ut tollas eos de mundo, sed ut serves eos a malo (Joa 17,13b-15). ⁴⁹ Mirifica eos in **veritate**. ⁵⁰ Sermo tuus **veritas** est. ⁵¹ Sicut tu me misisti in mundum, et ego misi eos in mundum. ⁵² Et pro eis sanctifico meipsum, ut sint ipsi sanctificati in **veritate**. ⁵³ Non pro eis rogo tantum, sed pro eis, qui **credituri** sunt propter verbum eorum in me (cfr. Joa 17,17–20), ut sint consummati in unum, et cognoscat mundus, quia tu me misisti et **dilexisti** eos, sicut me **dilexisti** (Joa 17,23). ⁵⁴ Et notum faciam eis nomen tuum, ut **dilectio**, qua **dilexisti** me, sit in ipsis et ego in ipsis (cfr. Joa 17,26). ⁵⁵ Pater, quos dedisti mihi, volo, ut ubi ego sum, et illi sint mecum, ut videant **claritatem** tuam (cfr. Joa 17,24) in regno tuo (Matt 20,21). Amen.

[Cap. XXIII: Oratio et gratiarum actio]: **iustitia, gratitudo, dilectio/amor, veritas, poenitentia, dignitas, humilitas, continentia, infirmitas, magnitudo, inutilitas, fides, perseverantia, virtus, fortitudo, misericordia, bonitas, pietas, mititas, suavitas, dulcedo, rectitudo, benignitas, innocentia, munditia, gaudium, honor, spes, laudabilitas, sublimitas, amabilitas, delectabilitas, desiderabilitas**

¹ Omnipotens, sanctissime, altissime et summe Deus, Pater sancte (Joa 17,11) et **iuste**, Domine rex caeli et terrae (cfr. Matt 11,25), propter temetipsum **gratias** agimus tibi, quod per sanctam voluntatem tuam et per unicum Filium tuum cum Spiritu Sancto creasti omnia spiritualia et corporalia et nos ad imaginem tuam et similitudinem factos in paradiso posuisti (cfr. Gen 1,26; 2,15). ² Et nos per culpam nostram cecidimus. ³ Et **gratias** agimus tibi, quia sicut per Filium tuum nos creasti, sic per sanctam **dilectionem** tuam, qua **dilexisti** nos (cfr. Joa 17,26), ipsum **verum** Deum et **verum** hominem ex gloriosa semper Virgine beatissima sancta Maria nasci fecisti et per crucem et sanguinem et mortem ipsius nos captivos redimi voluisti. ⁴ Et **gratias** agimus tibi, quia ipse Filius tuus venturus est in gloria maiestatis suae mittere maledictos, qui **poenitentiam** non egerunt et te non cognoverunt, in ignem aeternum, et dicere omnibus, qui te cognoverunt et adoraverunt et tibi servierunt in **poenitentia**: Venite, benedicti Patris mei, percipite regnum, quod vobis paratum est ab origine mundi (cfr. Matt 25,34).
⁵ Et quia nos omnes miseri et peccatores non sumus **digni** nominare te, suppliciter exoramus, ut Dominus noster Jesus Christus Filius tuus dilectus, in quo tibi bene complacuit (cfr. Matt 17,5), una cum Spiritu Sancto Paraclito **gratias** agat tibi, sicut tibi et ipsi placet, pro omnibus, qui tibi semper sufficit ad omnia, per quem nobis tanta fecisti. Alleluia.

⁶ Et gloriosam matrem beatissimam Mariam semper Virginem, beatum Michaelem, Gabrielem et Raphaelem et omnes choros beatorum seraphim, cherubim, thronorum, dominationum, principatuum, potestatum (cfr. Col 1,15), virtutum, angelorum, archangelorum, beatum Joannem Baptistam, Joannem Evangelistam, Petrum, Paulum et beatos patriarchas, prophetas, innocentes, apostolos, evangelistas, discipulos, martyres, confessores, virgines, beatos Eliam et Enoch, et omnes sanctos, qui fuerunt et erunt et sunt, propter tuum **amorem humiliter** deprecamur, ut, sicut tibi placet, pro his tibi **gratias** referant summo **vero** Deo, aeterno et vivo, cum Filio tuo carissimo Domino nostro Jesu Christo et Spiritu Sancto Paraclito in saecula saeculorum (Apoc 19,3). Amen. Alleluia (Apoc 19,4).

⁷ Et Domino Deo universos intra sanctam ecclesiam catholicam et apostolicam servire volentes et omnes sequentes ordines, sacerdotes, diaconos, subdiaconos, acolythos, exorcistas, lectores, ostiarios et omnes clericos, universos religiosos et religiosas, omnes conversos et parvulos, pauperes et egenos, reges et principes, laboratores et agricolas, servos et dominos, omnes virgines et **continentes** et maritatas, laicos, masculos et feminas, omnes infantes, adolescentes, iuvenes et senes, sanos et **infirmos**, omnes pusillos et **magnos**, et omnes populos, gentes, tribus et linguas (cfr. Apoc 7,9), omnes nationes et omnes homines ubicumque terrarum, qui sunt et erunt, **humiliter** rogamus et supplicamus nos omnes fratres minores, servi **inutiles** (Luke 17,10), ut omnes in vera **fide** et **poenitentia perseveremus**, quia aliter nullus salvari potest.

⁸ Omnes **diligamus** ex toto corde, ex tota anima, ex tota mente, ex tota **virtute** (cfr. Mark 12,30) et **fortitudine**, ex toto intellectu (cfr. Mark 12,33), ex omnibus viribus (cfr. Luke 10,27), toto nisu, toto affectu, totis visceribus, totis desideriis et voluntatibus Dominum Deum (Mark 12,30par.), qui totum corpus, totam animam et totam vitam dedit et dat omnibus nobis, qui nos creavit, redemit et sua sola **misericordia** salvabit (cfr. Tob 13,5), qui nobis miserabilibus et miseris, putridis et foetidis, ingratis et malis omnia **bona** fecit et facit.

⁹ Nihil ergo aliquid aliud desideremus, nihil aliud velimus, nihil aliud placeat et delectet nos nisi Creator et Redemptor et Salvator noster, solus **verus** Deus, qui est plenum **bonum**, omne **bonum**, totum **bonum**, verum et summum **bonum**, qui solus est **bonus** (cfr. Luke 18,19), **pius, mitis, suavis** et **dulcis**, qui solus est sanctus, **iustus, verus**, sanctus et **rectus**, qui solus est **benignus, innocens, mundus**, a quo et per quem et in quo (cfr. Rom 11,36) est omnis venia, omnis gratia, omnis gloria omnium **poenitentium** et **iustorum**, omnium beatorum in caelis **congaudentium**. ¹⁰ Nihil ergo impediat, nihil separet, nihil interpolet; ¹¹ ubique nos omnes omni loco, omni hora et omni tempore, quotidie et continue **credamus veraciter** et **humiliter** et in corde teneamus et **amemus, honoremus**, adoremus, serviamus, laudemus et benedicamus, glorificemus et superexaltemus, magnificemus et **gratias** agamus altissimo et summo Deo aeterno, trinitati et unitati, Patri et Filio et Spiritui Sancto, creatori omnium et salvatori omnium in se **credentium** et **sperantium** et **diligentium** eum, qui sine initio et sine fine immutabilis, invisibilis, inenarrabilis, ineffabilis, incomprehensibilis, investigabilis (cfr. Rom 11,33), benedictus, **laudabilis**, gloriosus, superexaltatus (cfr. Dan 3,52), **sublimis**, excelsus, **suavis, amabilis, delectabilis** et totus super omnia **desiderabilis** in saecula. Amen.

[Cap. XXIV: Conclusio]: **dilectio, obedientia, firmitas**

[1] In nomine Domini! Rogo omnes fratres, ut addiscant tenorem et sensum eorum quae in ista vita ad salvationem animae nostrae scripta sunt et ista frequenter ad memoriam reducant. [2] Et exoro Deum, ut ipse, qui est omnipotens, trinus et unus, benedicat omnes docentes, discentes, habentes, recordantes et operantes ista quoties repetunt et faciunt quae ibi ad salutem animae nostrae scripta sunt, [3] et deprecor omnes cum osculo pedum, ut multum **diligant**, custodiant et reponant. [4] Et ex parte Dei omnipotentis et domini papae et per **obedientiam** ego frater Franciscus **firmiter** praecipio et iniungo, ut ex his, quae in ista vita scripta sunt, nullus minuat vel in ipsa scriptum aliquod desuper addat (cfr. Deut 4,2; 12,32), nec aliam regulam fratres habeant.
[5] Gloria Patri et Filio et Spiritui Sancto, sicut erat in principio et nunc et semper et in saecula saeculorum. Amen.

Regula pro eremitoriis data: studium, silentium, iustitia, parvitas, amor, obedientia, sollicitudo, studium

[1] Illi, qui volunt religiose stare in eremis sint tres fratres vel quattuor ad plus; duo ex ipsis sint matres et habeant duos filios vel unum ad minus. [2] Isti duo qui sunt matres, teneant vitam Marthae et duo filii teneant vitam Mariae (cfr. Luke 10,38-42) et habeant unum claustrum, in quo unusquisque habeat cellulam suam, in qua oret et dormiat. [3] Et semper dicant completorium de die statim post occasum solis; et **studeant** retinere **silentium**; et dicant horas suas; et in matutinis surgant et primum quaerant regnum Dei et **iustitiam** eius (Matt 6,33). [4] Et dicant primam hora qua convenit et post tertiam absolvant **silentium**; et possint loqui et ire ad matres suas. [5] Et, quando placuerit, possint petere ab eis eleemosynam sicut **parvuli pauperes** propter **amorem** Domini Dei. [6] Et postea dicant sextam et nonam; et vesperas dicant hora qua convenit. [7] Et in claustro, ubi morantur non permittant aliquam personam introire et neque ibi comedant. [8] Isti fratres, qui sunt matres, **studeant** manere remote ab omni persona; et per **obedientiam** sui ministri custodiant filios suos ab omni persona, ut nemo possit loqui cum eis. [9] Et isti filii non loquantur cum aliqua persona nisi cum matribus suis et cum ministro et custode suo, quando placuerit eos visitare cum benedictione Domini Dei. [10] Filii vero quandoque officium matrum assumant, sicut vicissitudinaliter eis pro tempore visum fuerit disponendum; quod omnia supradicta **sollicite** et **studiose studeant** observare.

Salutatio beatae Mariae virginis: bonitas, fides

[1] Ave Domina, sancta Regina, sancta Dei genetrix Maria, quae es virgo Ecclesia facta [2] et electa a sanctissimo Patre de caelo, quam consecravit cum sanctissimo dilecto Filio suo et Spiritu sancto Paraclito, [3] in qua fuit et est omnis plenitudo gratiae et omne **bonum**. [4] Ave palatium eius; ave tabernaculum eius; ave domus eius. [5] Ave vestimentum eius; ave ancilla eius; ave mater eius [6] et vos

omnes sanctae virtutes, quae per gratiam et illuminationem Spiritus sancti infundimini in corda **fidelium**, ut de infidelibus **fideles** Deo faciatis.

Salutatio virtutum: sapientia, puritas, simplicitas, paupertas, humilitas, caritas, obedientia, timor

[1] Ave, regina **sapientia**, Dominus te salvet cum tua sorore sancta **pura simplicitate**. [2] Domina sancta **paupertas**, Dominus te salvet cum tua sorore sancta **humilitate**. [3] Domina sancta **caritas**, Dominus te salvet cum tua sorore sancta **obedientia**. [4] Sanctissimae **virtutes**, omnes vos salvet Dominus, a quo venitis et proceditis.
[5] Nullus homo est penitus in toto mundo, qui unam ex vobis possit habere, nisi prius moriatur. [6] Qui unam habet et alias non offendit, omnes habet. [7] Et qui unam offendit, nullam habet et omnes offendit (cfr. Jac 2,10). [8] Et unaquaque confundit vitia et peccata.
[9] Sancta **sapientia** confundit satan et omnes malitias eius. [10] **Pura** sancta **simplicitas** confundit omnem **sapientiam** huius mundi (cfr. 1 Cor 2,6) et **sapientiam** corporis. [11] Sancta **paupertas** confundit cupiditatem et avaritiam et curas huius saeculi. [12] Sancta **humilitas** confundit superbiam et omnes homines, qui sunt in mundo, similiter et omnia, quae in mundo sunt. [13] Sancta **caritas** confundit omnes diabolicas et carnales tentationes et omnes carnales **timores** (cfr. 1 Joa 4,18). [14] Sancta **obedientia** confundit omnes corporales et carnales voluntates [15] et habet mortificatum corpus suum ad **obedientiam** spiritus et ad **obedientiam** fratris sui [16] et est subditus et suppositus omnibus hominibus, qui sunt in mundo [17] et non tantum solis hominibus, sed etiam omnibus bestiis et feris, [18] ut possint facere de eo, quicquid voluerint, quantum fuerit eis datum desuper a Domino (cfr. Joa 19,11).

Testamentum: poenitentia, misericordia, dulcedo, fides, simplicitas, sapientia, paupertas, timor, amor, honor, discretio, veneratio, pretiositas, honestas, 'contentus', libentia, firmitas, obedientia, infirmitas, fortitudo, parvitas, puritas

[1] Dominus ita dedit mihi fratri Francisco incipere faciendi **poenitentiam**: quia cum essem in peccatis nimis mihi videbatur amarum videre leprosos. [2] Et ipse Dominus conduxit me inter illos et feci **misericordiam** cum illis. [3] Et recedente me ab ipsis, id quod videbatur mihi amarum, conversum fuit mihi in **dulcedinem** animi et corporis; et postea parum steti et exivi de saeculo. [4] Et Dominus dedit mihi talem **fidem** in ecclesiis, ut ita **simpliciter** orarem et dicerem: [5] Adoramus te, Domine Jesu Christe, et ad omnes ecclesias tuas, quae sunt in toto mundo, et benedicimus tibi, quia per sanctam crucem tuam redimisti mundum. [6] Postea Dominus dedit mihi et dat tantam **fidem** in sacerdotibus, qui vivunt secundum formam sanctae Ecclesiae Romanae propter ordinem ipsorum, quod si facerent mihi persecutionem, volo recurrere ad ipsos. [7] Et si haberem tantam **sapientiam**, quantam Salomon habuit, et invenirem **pauperculos** sacerdotes huius saeculi, in parochiis, quibus morantur, nolo praedicare ultra voluntatem ipsorum. [8] Et ipsos

et omnes alios volo **timere, amare** et **honorare**, sicut meos dominos. [9] Et nolo in ipsis considerare peccatum, quia Filium Dei **discerno** in ipsis, et domini mei sunt. [10] Et propter hoc facio, quia nihil video corporaliter in hoc saeculo de ipso altissimo Filio Dei, nisi sanctissimum corpus et sanctissimum sanguinem suum, quod ipsi recipiunt et ipsi soli aliis ministrant. [11] Et haec sanctissima mysteria super omnia volo **honorari, venerari** et in locis **pretiosis** collocari. [12] Sanctissima nomina et verba eius scripta, ubicumque invenero in locis illicitis, volo colligere et rogo, quod colligantur et in loco **honesto** collocentur. [13] Et omnes theologos, et qui ministrant sanctissima verba divina, debemus **honorare** et **venerari**, sicut qui ministrant nobis spiritum et vitam (cfr. Joa 6,64).

[14] Et postquam Dominus dedit mihi de fratribus, nemo ostendebat mihi, quid deberem facere, sed ipse Altissimus revelavit mihi, quod deberem vivere secundum formam sancti Evangelii. [15] Et ego paucis verbis et **simpliciter** feci scribi et dominus Papa confirmavit mihi. [16] Et illi qui veniebant ad recipiendam vitam, omnia quae habere poterant (Tob 1,3), dabant pauperibus; et erant **contenti** tunica una, intus et foris repeciata, cum cingulo et braccis. [17] Et nolebamus plus habere. [18] Officium dicebamus clerici secundum alios clericos, laici dicebant: Pater noster; et satis **libenter** manebamus in ecclesiis. [19] Et eramus idiotae et subditi omnibus. [20] Et ego manibus meis laborabam, et volo laborare; et omnes alii fratres **firmiter** volo, quod laborent de laboritio, quod pertinet ad **honestatem**. [21] Qui nesciunt, discant, non propter cupiditatem recipiendi pretium laboris, sed propter exemplum et ad repellendam otiositatem. [22] Et quando non daretur nobis pretium laboris, recurramus ad mensam Domini, petendo eleemosynam ostiatim. [23] Salutationem mihi Dominus revelavit, ut diceremus: Dominus det tibi **pacem**. [24] Caveant sibi fratres, ut ecclesias, habitacula **paupercula** et omnia, quae pro ipsis construuntur, penitus non recipiant, nisi essent, sicut decet sanctam **paupertatem**, quam in regula promisimus, semper ibi hospitantes sicut advenae et peregrini (cfr. 1 Pet 2,11). [25] Praecipio **firmiter** per **obedientiam** fratribus universis, quod ubicumque sunt, non audeant petere aliquam litteram in curia Romana, per se neque per interpositam personam, neque pro ecclesia neque pro alio loco neque sub specie praedicationis neque pro persecutione suorum corporum; [26] sed ubicumque non fuerint recepti, fugiant in aliam terram ad faciendam **poenitentiam** cum benedictione Dei.

[27] Et **firmiter** volo **obedire** ministro generali huius fraternitatis et alio guardiano, quem sibi placuerit mihi dare. [28] Et ita volo esse captus in manibus suis, ut non possim ire vel facere ultra **obedientiam** et voluntatem suam, quia dominus meus est. [29] Et quamvis sim **simplex** et **infirmus**, tamen semper volo habere clericum, qui mihi faciat officium, sicut in regula continetur. [30] Et omnes alii fratres teneantur ita **obedire** guardianis suis et facere officium secundum regulam. [31] Et qui inventi essent, quod non facerent officium secundum regulam, et vellent alio modo variare, aut non essent catholici, omnes fratres, ubicumque sunt, per **obedientiam** teneantur, quod ubicumque invenerint aliquem ipsorum, proximiori custodi illius loci, ubi ipsum invenerint, debeant repraesentare. [32] Et custos **firmiter** teneatur per **obedientiam** ipsum **fortiter** custodire, sicuti hominem in vinculis die noctuque, ita quod non possit eripi de manibus suis, donec propria sua persona ipsum repraesentet in manibus sui ministri. [33] Et minister **firmiter**

teneatur per **obedientiam** mittendi ipsum per tales fratres, quod die noctuque custodiant ipsum sicuti hominem in vinculis, donec repraesentent ipsum coram domino Ostiensi, qui est dominus, protector et corrector totius fraternitatis. [34] Et non dicant fratres: Haec est alia regula; quia haec est recordatio, admonitio, exhortatio et meum testamentum, quod ego frater Franciscus **parvulus** facio vobis fratribus meis benedictis propter hoc, ut regulam, quam Domino promisimus, melius catholice observemus.

[35] Et generalis minister et omnes alii ministri et custodes per **obedientiam** teneantur, in istis verbis non addere vel minuere. [36] Et semper hoc scriptum habeant secum iuxta regulam. [37] Et in omnibus capitulis quae faciunt, quando legunt regulam, legant et ista verba. [38] Et omnibus fratribus meis clericis et laicis praecipio **firmiter** per **obedientiam**, ut non mittant glossas in regula neque in istis verbis dicendo: Ita volunt intelligi. [39] Sed sicut dedit mihi Dominus **simpliciter** et **pure** dicere et scribere regulam et ista verba, ita **simpliciter** et sine glossa intelligatis et cum sancta operatione observetis usque in finem.

[40] Et quicumque haec observaverit, in caelo repleatur benedictione altissimi Patris et in terra repleatur benedictione dilecti Filii sui cum sanctissimo Spiritu Paraclito et omnibus virtutibus caelorum et omnibus sanctis. [41] Et ego frater Franciscus **parvulus** vester servus quantumcumque possum, confirmo vobis intus et foris istam sanctissimam benedictionem.

Ultima voluntas s. Clarae scripta: parvitas, paupertas, perseverantia

[1] Ego frater Franciscus **parvulus** volo sequi vitam et **paupertatem** altissimi Domini nostri Jesu Christi et eius sanctissimae matris et **perseverare** in ea usque in finem; [2] et rogo vos, dominas meas, et consilium do vobis, ut in ista sanctissima vita et **paupertate** semper vivatis. [3] Et custodite vos multum, ne doctrina vel consilio alicuius ab ipsa in perpetuum ullatenus recedatis.

Opuscula dictata

Benedictio fr. Bernardo data: bonitas, dilectio, honor

[1] Scribe, sicut dico tibi: [2] Primus frater, quem dedit mihi Dominus, fuit frater Bernardus, et: qui primo incepit et complevit perfectissime perfectionem sancti evangelii distribuendo **bona** sua omnia pauperibus; [3] propter quod et propter multas alias praerogativas teneor ipsum magis **diligere** quam aliquem fratrem totius religionis. [4] Unde volo et praecipio, sicut possum, quod, quicumque fuerit generalis minister, ipsum **diligat** et **honoret** tamquam me ipsum, [5] et etiam alii ministri provinciales et fratres totius religionis ipsum teneant vice mea.

Benedictio s. Clarae et eius sororibus in scriptis missa:

... ad consolandum ipsam scripsit ei per litteram [2] suam benedictionem ac etiam absolvit ipsam ab omni defectu, si quem habuisset, in eius mandatis et voluntatibus et mandatis et voluntatibus Filii Dei.

De epistola civibus Bononiensibus scripta:

Dixit etiam [scl. fr. Martinus de Bartona] quod frater quidam, qui stetit in oratione Brixiae in die Natali Domini, in terrae motu, quem praedixerat sanctus Franciscus et per omnes scholas Bononiae per fratres praedicari fecerat, per litteram, in qua fuit falsum Latinum, et ecclesia corruit, sub ruina lapidum illaesus inventus est.

Epistola s. Clarae de ieiunio scripta: caritas, prudentia, (infirmitas), discretio

[1] Super his autem, quae me iam tibi reserare mandasti, quae scilicet essent festa, quae forte ut te opinor aliquatenus aestimasse in varietate ciborum gloriosissimus pater noster sanctus Franciscus nos celebrare specialiter monuisset, **caritati** tuae duxi respondendum: [2] Noverit quidem tua **prudentia**, quod praeter debiles et **infirmas**, quibus de quibuscumque cibariis omnem **discretionem** quam possemus facere nos monuit et mandavit, nulla nostrum sana et valida nisi cibaria quadragesimalia tantum, tam in diebus ferialibus quam festivis, manducare deberet, die quolibet ieiunando exceptis diebus dominicis et Natalis Domini, in quibus bis in die comedere deberemus. [3] Et in diebus quoque Jovis solitis temporibus pro voluntate cuiuslibet, ut quae scilicet nollet, ieiunare non teneretur. [4] Nos tamen sanae ieiunamus cotidie praeter dies dominicos et Natalis. [5] In omni vero Pascha, ut scriptum beati Francisci dicit, et festivitatibus sanctae Mariae ac Sanctorum Apostolorum ieiunare etiam non tenemur, nisi haec festa in sexta feria evenirent; [6] et sicut praedictum est, semper, quae sanae sumus et validae, cibaria quadragesimalia manducamus.

De epistola dominae Jacobae scripta:

(... invenitur mulier sancta portasse quidquid ad patris portandum exsequias facta prius littera continebat): Nam cinerei coloris pannum, quo recedentis corpusculum tegeretur, cereos quoque plurimos, sindonem pro facie, pulvillum pro capite et ferculum quoddam, quod sanctus appetierat detulit.

Epistola fratribus Franciae missa:

[1] ... scripsit beatus Franciscus propria manu litteram ... ministro et fratribus Franciae, [2] ut visis litteris iubilarent, laudes Deo Trinitati dicentes: [3] Benedicamus Patrem et Filium cum Spiritu Sancto.

Testamentum Senis factum: dolor, infirmitas, dilectio, paupertas, fides

[1] Scribe qualiter benedico cunctis fratribus meis, qui sunt in religione et qui venturi erunt usque ad finem saeculi... [2] Quoniam propter debilitatem et **dolorem infirmitatis** loqui non valeo, breviter in istis tribus verbis patefacio fratribus meis voluntatem meam, videlicet: [3] ut in signum memoriae meae benedictionis et mei testamenti semper **diligant** se ad invicem, [4] semper **diligant** et observent domi-

nam nostram sanctam **paupertatem**, [5] et ut semper praelatis et omnibus clericis sanctae Matris Ecclesiae **fideles** et subiecti exsistant.

De vera et perfecta laetitia: laetitia, fides, infirmitas, simplicitas, amor, patientia, veritas

[1] Idem [fr. Leonardus] retulit ibidem quod una die beatus Franciscus apud Sanctam Mariam vocavit fratrem Leonem et dixit: Frater Leo, scribe. [2] Qui respondit: Ecce paratus sum. [3] Scribe - inquit - quae est **vera laetitia**. [4] Venit nuntius et dicit quod omnes magistri de Parisius venerunt ad Ordinem, scribe, non **vera laetitia**. [5] Item quod omnes praelati ultramontani, archiepiscopi et episcopi; item quod rex Franciae et rex Angliae: scribe, non **vera laetitia**. [6] Item, quod fratres mei iverunt ad infideles et converterunt eos omnes ad **fidem**; item, quod tantam gratiam habeo a Deo quod sano **infirmos** et facio multa miracula: dico tibi quod in his omnibus non **vera laetitia**. [7] Sed quae est **vera laetitia**? [8] Redeo de Perusio et de nocte profunda venio huc et est tempus hiemis lutosum et adeo frigidum, quod dondoli aquae frigidae congelatae fiunt ad extremitates tunicae et percutiunt semper crura, et sanguis emanat ex vulneribus talibus. [9] Et totus in luto et frigore et glacie venio ad ostium, et postquam diu pulsavi et vocavi, venit frater et quaerit: Quis est? Ego respondeo: Frater Franciscus. [10] Et ipse dicit: Vade; non est hora decens eundi; non intrabis. [11] Et iterum insistenti respondeat: Vade, tu es unus **simplex** et idiota; admodo non venis nobis; nos sumus tot et tales, quod non indigemus te. [12] Et ego iterum sto ad ostium et dico: **Amore** Dei recolligatis me ista nocte. [13] Et ille respondeat: Non faciam. [14] Vade ad locum Cruciferorum et ibi pete. [15] Dico tibi quod si **patientiam** habuero et non fuero motus, quod in hoc est **vera laetitia** et **vera virtus** et salus animae.

BIBLIOGRAPHICAL OVERVIEW

Franciscan studies dealing with virtue:
L. Bracaloni, "Le virtù religiose fondamentali secondo la spiritualità francescana" (1933); A. Ghinato, "La vita virtuosa" in his *Profilo spirituale di san Francesco. Tratto dai suoi scritti e dalle primitive biografie* (1961); L. Iriarte, *Vocazione francescana. Sintesi degli ideali di san Francesco e di santa Chiara* (1987²); A. Matanic, "Virtù e devozioni francescane" in his *Francesco d'Assisi. Fattori causali della sua spiritualità* (1984).

Franciscan studies dealing with virtues incidentally:
H. Bisschops, *Franciscus van Assisi. Mysticus en mystagoog* (2008; in particular, obedience, chastity, poverty, humility, obedience); K. Esser & E. Grau, *Antwort der Liebe* (1958/1960; in particular, penance, poverty, chastity, obedience); H. Feld, *Franziskus von Assisi und seine Bewegung* (1994; in particular, poverty, simplicity, humility, peace, chastity); M. Geulen, *Die Armut des heiligen Franz von Assisi im Lichte der Wertethik* (1947/2005; in particular, poverty, humility, freedom, peace, joy); E. van den Goorbergh & T. Zweerman, *Was getekend: Franciscus van Assisi. Aspecten van zijn schrijverschap en brandpunten van zijn spiritualiteit* (1998/2002; in particular, penance, faith, patience, wisdom, obedience, humility, mercy, diffidence); P. Morant, *Unser Weg zu Gott. Das Vollkommenheitsstreben im Geiste des hl. Franziskus* (1965; in particular, penance, obedience, simplicity, poverty, humility, chastity, charity); H. van Munster, *De mystiek van Franciscus. De macht van barmhartigheid* (2002/2003; in particular, mercy, humility, charity, patience, justice, joy, peace); F. Peters, *Aus Liebe zur Liebe. Der Glaubensweg des Menschen als Nachfolge Christi in der Spiritualität des hl. Franziskus von Assisi* (1995; humility, charity, poverty, patience, obedience).

Franciscan studies treating individual Franciscan works or chapters on virtues:
* The *Salutation of the Virtues*: J. Hoeberichts, *Paradise Restored. The Social Ethics of Francis of Assisi. A Commentary on Francis' "Salutation of the Virtues"* (2004); A. Jansen, "Lofzang op de deugden" (1982); L. Lehmann, *Tiefe und Weite. Der universale Grundzug in den Gebeten des Franziskus von Assisi* (1984); S. Verhey, *Der Mensch unter der Herrschaft Gottes. Versuch einer Theologie des Menschen nach dem hl. Franziskus von Assisi* (1960).
* *Admonition* 27: A. Jansen, "Words of Salvation of Saint Francis. A Commentary on Admonition 27" (1994); R.J. Karris, *The Admonitions of St. Francis. Sources and Meanings* (1999).

Franciscan studies focussing on a (small) selection of virtues:
A. Engemann, *Das neue Lied. Glaube, Hoffnung und Liebe aus franziskanischer Geistigkeit* (1959; faith, hope, charity); "Frères mineurs" (1964; poverty, charity, joy); J.-B. Freyer, *Der demütige und geduldige Gott. Franziskus und sein Gottesbild –*

ein Vergleich mit der Tradition (1991; humility, patience); J. Garrido, *Die Lebensregel des Franz von Assisi. Inspiration für heute* (2001; poverty, obedience, humility, faith); A. Gerken, "Die theologische Intuition des heiligen Franziskus von Assisi" (1982; charity, humility); I. Gobry, *St. François d'Assise et l'esprit franciscain* (1957; charity, humility, poverty, joy); J. Lang, *Ins Freie geführt. Aspekte der franziskanischen Spiritualität* (1986; simplicity, charity, fortitude, joy); E. Longpré, *François d'Assise et son expérience spirituelle* (1966; poverty, humility, obedience, penance, charity); T. Matura, *François d'Assise, «auteur spirituel». Le message de ses écrits* (1996; charity, penance, poverty); N. Nguyen-Van-Khanh, *Le Christ dans la pensée de saint François d'Assise d'après ses écrits* (1989; humility, faith, charity, wisdom, truth); H. Nolthenius, *Een man uit het dal van Spoleto. Franciscus tussen zijn tijdgenoten* (1988; obedience, poverty, chastity, humility); E. Rohr, *Der Herr und Franziskus* (1966; charity, obedience, joy, poverty, chastity, penance, peace); A. Rotzetter e.a., *Franz von Assisi. Ein Anfang und was davon bleibt* (1981; obedience, poverty); H. Sevenhoven, "How Obedience Turns Into Love" (1997; obedience, charity); L. Veuthey, *Itinerarium animae franciscanum. Commentarium theologico-ascetico-mysticum* (1938; humility, poverty).

Franciscan studies focussing on one particular virtue:
"Armut" (1982; poverty); S. da Campagnola, "La povertà nelle «Regulae» di Francesco d'Assisi" (1975; poverty); S. Clasen, "Die Armut als Beruf: Franziskus von Assisi" (1964; poverty); A. van Corstanje, *Gottes Bund mit den Armen. Biblische Grundgedanken bei Franziskus von Assisi* (1964; poverty); C. Dukker, *Umkehr des Herzen. Der Bußgedanke des heiligen Franziskus von Assisi* (1956; penance); K. Esser, "Die Armutsauffassung des hl. Franziskus" (1975; poverty); K. Esser, "Gehorsam und Autorität in der frühfranziskanischen Gemeinschaft (1971; obedience); K. Esser, "Mysterium paupertatis. Die Armutsauffassung des hl. Franziskus v. Assisi" (1951; poverty); G.P. Freeman, "Franciscus' vrede: een goed verhaal" (1990; peace); G.P. Freeman, "Wat een boetvaardige doen moet" (1998; penance); "Frieden" (1982; peace); E. Grau, "Die »vollkommene Freude« des hl. Franziskus" (1974; joy); L. Hardick, *Die wahre und vollkommene Freude des heiligen Franziskus* (1981; joy); L. Hardick, "„Schenke mir vollendete Liebe"" (1985; charity); R. Haskamp, "„Du bist unsere Liebe"" (1985; charity); R. Haskamp, "Franziskus auf dem Weg zum Frieden mit sich selbst" (1983; peace); W. Hellmann, "Poverty: the Franciscan Way to God" (1974; poverty); A. Jansen, "De echte vreugde" (1982; joy); A. Jansen, "The Story of the True Joy. An Autobiographical Reading" (1981; joy); A. Jansen, "Vrede, een zaak met vele dimensies" (1990; peace); R. Koper, *Das Weltverständnis des hl. Franziskus von Assisi. Eine Untersuchung über das „Exivi de Saeculo"* (1959; faith); M.D. Lambert, *Franciscan Poverty. The Doctrine of the Absolute Poverty of Christ and the Apostles in the Franciscan Order 1210–1323* (1998²; poverty); D.V. Lapsanski, *Das Leben nach dem Evangelium am Anfang des Minderbrüderordens* (1974; poverty); B. van Leeuwen, "Gehoorzaamheid in vrijmoedigheid" (1983; obedience); R. Manselli, "La povertà nella vita di Francesco d'Assisi" (1975; poverty); G. Miccoli, "Francesco e la pace" (2006; peace); J. Micó, "Franciscan Poverty" (1997; poverty); J. Micó, "Obedience" (1995; obedience); K. Pansters, "Deemoed. Een cruciale deugd" (2011; humility); R. Reijsbergen, "Bevrijdende gehoorzaamheid. Het mysterie van de gehoorzaamheid bij Franciscus van Assisi" (1991; obedience); C.M. Rogers, "The Joy of St. Francis"

(1976; joy); H. Roggen, *Die Lebensform des heiligen Franziskus von Assisi in ihrem Verhältnis zur feudalen und bürgerlichen Gesellschaft Italiens* (1965; poverty); A. Rotzetter, "„Aus Liebe zur Liebe". Zu einem Wort des hl. Franziskus von Assisi" (1981; charity); L.M.F. Scheuring, "Poverty in Relationship to Francis of Assisi and John of the Cross" (1991; poverty); A. Senftle, *Menschenbildung in franziskanischer Geistigkeit. Die Bedeutung der franziskanischen Poenitentialehre* (1959; penance); K. Synowczyk, "l'Obbedienza universale di San Francesco d'Assisi" (1991; obedience); D.-M. Thévenet, "La vera e perfetta letizia negli scritti di Francesco d'Assisi. Aspetti cristologici" (1991; joy); A.A. Tils, *Der heilige Franziskus von Assisi und die Armut. Eine genetische Darstellung seiner religiösen Anschauung von der Armut im Lichte der Quellen des 13. Jahrhunderts* (1961; poverty); S. Verhey, "Das Leben in der Buße nach Franziskus von Assisi" (1959; penance); S. Verhey, "Gehoorzaamheid als levensweg volgens Franciscus van Assisi" (1975; obedience); K.B. Wolf, *The Poverty of Riches. St. Francis of Assisi Reconsidered* (2003; poverty); T. Zweerman, "Jezus' woord: "zalig de vredestichters..." in de interpretatie van Franciscus van Assisi" (1990; peace).

INSTANCES OF *HABITUS DATUS*

In the scheme of instances of *"habitus datus"* (see 3.2) in the writings of Francis, Bonaventure, and David, I follow the order of the writings in the main editions. The list is based on the passages dealt with in Chapter 2, and is not exhaustive.

Francis		
Habitus datus		
Divine	*Relational process*	*Human*
(divine virtues)[1]		
You are You are You are You are		our hope our faith our charity all our sweetness
peace[2]		
and give you		
charity, virtue, penance, perseverance[3]		
The Spirit of the Lord will rest upon them and make Its home (*habitaculum*) and dwelling place		with their whole strength (*virtute*)

---

[1] *Laud Dei* 6. *Tu es spes nostra, tu es fides nostra, tu es caritas nostra, tu es tota dulcedo nostra...* (Armstrong, *Francis of Assisi*, 109).

[2] *Ben Leo* 2. *Convertat vultum suum ad te et det tibi pacem* (Num 6,24–26) (Armstrong, *Francis of Assisi*, 112).

[3] *Ep Fid* 1,1,1–7. *Omnes qui Dominum diligunt ex toto corde, ex tota anima et mente, ex tota virtute* (cfr. Mark 12,30) *et diligunt proximos suos sicut se ipsos* (cfr. Matt 22,39), *et odio habent corpora eorum cum vitiis et peccatis, et recipiunt corpus et sanguinem Domini nostri Jesu Christi, et faciunt fructus dignos poenitentiae: O quam beati et benedicti sunt illi et illae, dum talia faciunt et in talibus perseverant, quia requiescet super eos spiritus Domini* (cfr. Is 11,2) *et faciet apud eos habitaculum et mansionem* (cfr. Joa 14,23), *et sunt filii patris caelestis* (cfr. Matt 5,45), *cuius opera faciunt et sunt sponsi, fratres et matres Domini nostri Jesu Christi* (cfr. Matt 12,50) (Armstrong, *Francis of Assisi*, 41–42).

among them they are children of the heavenly Father they are spouses, brothers, and mothers of our Lord Jesus Christ	who produce worthy fruits of penance while they do such things and persevere in doing them Whose works they do	
peace, love[4]		
from heaven in the Lord		
charity, humility[5]		
	it washes the stains of our sins from our souls	let us have (*habemus*)
power (virtue), strength[6]		
He is		our power (*virtus*) and strength
power (virtue)[7]		
many things are made holy by the words of God in the power (*virtute*) of the words of Christ		
mercy, love, power (virtue)[8]		

---

[4] *Ep Fid* 2,1. *...frater Franciscus, eorum servus et subditus, obsequium cum reverentia, pacem veram de caelo et sinceram in Domino caritatem* (Armstrong, *Francis of Assisi*, 45).

[5] *Ep Fid* 2,30. *Habeamus itaque caritatem et humilitatem; et faciamus eleemosynas, quia ipsa lavat animas a sordibus peccatorum* (cfr. Tob 4,11; 12, 9) (Armstrong, *Francis of Assisi*, 47).

[6] *Ep Fid* 2,62. *...quia ipse est virtus et fortitudo nostra....* (Armstrong, *Francis of Assisi*, 49).

[7] *Ep Ord* 37. *Multa enim sanctificantur per verba Dei* (cfr. 1 Tim 4,5), *et in virtute verborum Christi altaris conficitur sacramentum* (Armstrong, *Francis of Assisi*, 119).

[8] *Ex Pat* 7. *Et dimitte nobis debita nostra: per tuam misericordiam ineffabilem, per passionis dilecti Filii tui virtutem et per beatissimae Virginis et omnium electorum tuorum merita et intercessionem* (Armstrong, *Francis of Assisi*, 159).

through the power (*virtutem*) of the passion of Your beloved Son	through the merits and intercession of all Your elect	
humility, patience[9]		
	in persecution and infirmity	to have (*habere*)
wisdom[10]		
the true wisdom of the father	have the Son of God	possess (*habent*)
divine virtues[11]		
the only true God, Who is the fullness of good, all good, every good, the true and supreme good, Who alone is good, merciful, gentle, delightful, and sweet, Who alone is holy, just, true, holy, and upright, Who alone is kind, innocent, clean	let us desire nothing else, let us want nothing else	
holy virtues[12]		
poured in (*infundimini*) through the grace and enlightenment of the Holy Spirit	make them faithful to God	into the hearts of the faithful

---

[9] *RB* 10,9. ...*et habere humilitatem, patientiam in persecutione et infirmitate* (Armstrong, *Francis of Assisi*, 105).

[10] *Ep Fid* 1,2,8; *Ep Fid* 2,67. *Sapientiam non habent spiritualem, quia non habent Filium Dei, qui est vera sapientia Patris* (Armstrong, *Francis of Assisi*, 43, 50).

[11] *RnB* 23,9 *Nihil ergo aliquid aliud desideremus, nihil aliud velimus, nihil aliud placeat et delectet nos nisi Creator et Redemptor et Salvator noster, solus verus Deus, qui est plenum bonum, omne bonum, totum bonum, verum et summum bonum, qui solus est bonus* (cfr. Luke 18,19), *pius, mitis, suavis et dulcis, qui solus est sanctus, iustus, verus, sanctus et rectus, qui solus est benignus, innocens, mundus...* (Armstrong, *Francis of Assisi*, 85).

[12] *Sal Mar* 6. ...*et vos omnes sanctae virtutes, quae per gratiam et illuminationem Spiritus sancti infundimini in corda fidelium, ut de infidelibus fideles Deo faciatis* (Armstrong, *Francis of Assisi*, 163).

	holy virtues[13]	
from Whom you come and proceed		
(*holy virtues*)[14]		
	dying first	who can possess (*habere*) any one
(*holy virtues*)[15]		
		whoever possesses (*habet*) one possesses (*habet*) all
(*holy virtues*)[16]		
given from above (*datum desuper*) by the Lord		
*peace*[17]		
may the Lord give		

Bonaventure		
Habitus datus		
Divine	*Relational process*	*Human*

[13] *Sal Virt* 4. *Sanctissimae virtutes, omnes vos salvet Dominus, a quo venitis et proceditis* (Armstrong, *Francis of Assisi*, 164).

[14] *Sal Virt* 5. *Nullus homo est penitus in toto mundo, qui unam ex vobis possit habere, nisi prius moriatur* (Armstrong, *Francis of Assisi*, 164).

[15] *Sal Virt* 6. *Qui unam habet et alias non offendit, omnes habet* (Armstrong, *Francis of Assisi*, 164).

[16] *Sal Virt* 18. *...ut possint facere de eo, quicquid voluerint, quantum fuerit eis datum desuper a Domino* (cfr. Joa 19,11) (Armstrong, *Francis of Assisi*, 165).

[17] *Test* 23. *Salutationem mihi Dominus revelavit, ut diceremus: Dominus det tibi pacem* (Armstrong, *Francis of Assisi*, 126).

	love, poverty[18]	
	prepares (*habilitans*) the soul for	
joy[19]		
	prepares (*habilitans*) the soul for	internal (*internam*) joy
joy, love[20]		
consummated in love	this first way / pursued in pain	terminates in a disposition (*affectus*)
peace, truth, love[21]		
to attain beatitude	through his merits	to obtain (*habeat*)
kindness, severity, humility[22]		
before God	following His example / strive	to be (*habendum habitum*)
love, joy[23]		
then the fullness of His joy	let the love of God increase in you now	so that you may have (*possideas*)

[18] *Trip Via* 1,1,9. *Deinde sequitur severitas, quae est quidam rigor mentis, restringens omnem concupiscentiam et habilitans ad amorem asperitatis, paupertatis et vilitatis* (*Doctoris* 8, 5; De Vinck, *The Works* 1, 68).

[19] *Trip Via* 1,1,9. *Tertio sequitur benignitas, quae est quidam dulcor animae, excludens omnem nequitiam et habilitans ipsam animam ad benevolentiam, tolerantiam et internam laetitiam* (*Doctoris* 8, 5; De Vinck, *The Works* 1, 68).

[20] *Trip Via* 1,1,9. *Incipit ergo via ista a stimulo conscientiae et terminatur ad affectum spiritualis laetitiae, et exercetur in dolore, sed consummatur in amore* (*Doctoris* 8, 5–6; De Vinck, *The Works* 1, 68).

[21] *Trip Via* 3,1,1. *Necesse est ergo, ut qui vult ad illam beatitudinem per merita pervenire, istorum trium similitudinem, secundum quod possible est, in via sibi comparet, ut scilicet habeat soporem pacis, splendorem veritatis, dulcorem caritatis* (*Doctoris* 8, 12; De Vinck, *The Works* 1, 80).

[22] *Trip Via* 3,3. *Stude igitur ad habendum habitum benignitatis ad proximum, severitatis ad te ipsum, humilitatis ad Deum, perspicacitatis contra diabolum, secundum effigiem imitationis Christi* (*Doctoris* 8, 13; De Vinck, *The Works* 1, 83).

[23] *Perf* 8,8. *...crescat hic in te amor Dei, ut ibi plene possideas gaudium Dei* (*Doctoris* 8, 127; De Vinck, *The Works* 1, 255).

pure virtues[24]		
proceeding (*procedunt*) from eternal law	man may be saved	
religious virtues[25]		
the binding force of divine law		proceed from a personal vow
truth, God-conforming virtue[26]		
plainly established by the inviolable law of the supreme Legislator	serve he must consent to the righteousness God-conforming	
every virtue[27]		
		right reason
perfect virtue[28]		
beatific life	attaining its final end	Reason
love[29]		

---

[24] *Sex Alis* 2,7. *Horum quaedam procedunt a lege aeterna, ut purae virtutes: humilitas, castitas, caritas, misericordia et similes, sine quibus nullus quocumque tempore poterit salvari...* (*Doctoris* 8, 134; De Vinck, *The Works* 3, 144).

[25] *Sex Alis* 2,7. *Quaedam ex voto proprio proveniunt, ut ea, ad quae nemo cogitur, sed qui ea sponte voverit iam velut ex praecepto Dei compellitur observare, ut continentia religiosorum et obedientia et abdicatio proprii in monasterio et alia, quae per regulam vel cuiusque ordinis definitiones eius professoribus imponuntur...* (*Doctoris* 8, 134; De Vinck, *The Works* 3, 144).

[26] *Ap Paup,* Prol,1. *Summi legislatoris inviolabili constat definitione sancitum, sic maiestati aeternae cultum debitum esse reddendum, quod idolorum cultura vitetur; sic redigendum intellectum creatum in summae veritatis obsequium, quod nullus falsitati praebeatur assensus; sic vacandum sanctificationi spirituum, quod ferietur a servitute carnalium voluptatum; sic denique virtutum deiformium approbandam esse rectitudinem, quod deformantium vitiorum pravitas reprobetur* (*Doctoris* 8, 233; De Vinck, *The Works* 4, 1).

[27] *Ap Paup* 2,3. *Denique, cum virtus omnis, ut ait Augustinus, sit ratio recta...* (*Doctoris* 8, 240; De Vinck, *The Works* 4, 21).

[28] *Ap Paup* 3,2. *Vere, perfecta virtus est ratio perveniens usque ad finem, quem beata vita consequitur* (*Doctoris* 8, 245; De Vinck, *The Works* 4, 38).

[29] *Ap Paup* 3,22. *...perfectio vero meriti obtineri non possit sine caritate, quae est donum Spiritus sancti...* (*Doctoris* 8, 250; De Vinck, *The Works* 4, 55).

perfection	of merit	
a gift of the Holy Spirit	obtained	
holy poverty[30]		
as a standard of perfection	in their deeds they would lift before them	and their manner of life (*habitu*)
virtues[31]		
in precepts	acts (of virtue)	
well-ordered virtue, love, discretion[32]		
	becoming conduct is the mark of well-ordered virtue so let your every word and deed manifest	
humility[33]		
	strive always and in your actions	to have (*habere*) in your heart

David		
Habitus datus		
Divine	*Relational process*	*Human*

---

[30] *Ap Paup* 7,5. ...*ut sic paupertatem altissimam actu et habitu quasi quoddam perfectionis insigne praeferrent* (*Doctoris* 8, 273; De Vinck, *The Works* 4, 129).

[31] *Ex Reg* 1,3. *Licet enim virtutum actus sint in praecepto...* (*Doctoris* 8, 394).

[32] *Reg Nov* 10,1. *Cum honestas sensuum exteriorum sit ornativa virtutum, ideo in omni verbo et actu tuo semper honestatem cum dilectione et discretione praetendas* (*Doctoris* 8, 485; Monti, *Works*, 166).

[33] *Reg Nov* 10,2. *Et ut melius te conserves, stude semper in corde et opere humilitatem habere...* (*Doctoris* 8, 485; Monti, *Works*, 167).

peace[34]		
with God	wish	to be at (*habere*)
faith, real virtues[35]		
Christ may dwell (*inhabitat*)	who endeavour to build up they set themselves to the acquisition of	in the soul an inward sanctuary wherein
real virtues[36]		
that set up a real sanctuary holy is he		who possesses (*habet*) them
goodness[37]		
the highest good of such good, viz., of God	it is capable of reaching its supreme achievement	the possession (*in se habere*)
sanctity (virtue)[38]		
	is learnt and developed by the use of bodily, i.e., exterior observances	into a habit (*habitum*)

---

[34] *Prof* 1,24. ...*si vis habere pacem cordis cum Deo* (*David ab Augusta*, 34; Devas, *Spiritual Life* 1, 29).

[35] *Prof* 2,3. *Hi sunt qui student interiorem hominem suum, in quo Christus inhabitat per fidem, componere et ad veras virtutes se exercere...* (*David ab Augusta*, 81; Devas, *Spiritual Life* 1, 76).

[36] *Prof* 2,3. *Istae enim virtutes sunt verum sanctuarium, et qui habet eas sanctus est* (*David ab Augusta*, 81; Devas, *Spiritual Life* 1, 76).

[37] *Prof* 2,5. *Cum ergo summa dignitas animae sit, quod est capax summi boni, et summa utilitas eius sit Deum in se habere et cum ipso omne bonum* (*David ab Augusta*, 85; Devas, *Spiritual Life* 1, 81).

[38] *Prof* 2,5. ...*ita virtus per corporalia exercitia addiscitur et in habitum vertitur* (*David ab Augusta* 87; Devas, *Spiritual Life* 1, 83).

virtues[39]		
are gifts of grace		(habits)
poverty[40]		
spiritual consolations (*donis*) many a gift from God many graces (*gratias*)		his poverty how much once was his (*habuit*) which now is his (*habet*) no longer
love[41]		
all the gifts of God (*beneficia Dei dantis*) the affection of generous love which prompts them		
virtue[42]		
		a movement of the will acting in accord with a legitimate judgement formed by the intellect
love, goodness[43]		
	its diversity of action tending towards good	embracing (*in se habens*) all the rest

---

[39] *Prof* 2,12. *Bona gratiae sunt virtutes, scientia et opera de genere bonorum, ut praedicare, ieiunare et similia* (*David ab Augusta*, 96; Devas, *Spiritual Life* 1, 92).

[40] *Prof* 3,11. *Sic homo abundans diversis consolationum donis plurima beneficia Dei sine debita gratiarum actione praeterit, plurimas gratias negligit opere exercere, plurima parva reputat, quae magna sunt, plurima nec agnoscit. Sed his omnibus subtractis, sicut vir videns paupertatem suam* [cfr. Lam 3,1], *recolit, quanta prius habuit et potuit, quae iam non habet...* (*David ab Augusta*, 182–183; Devas, *Spiritual Life* 2, 23).

[41] *Prof* 3,11. *Beneficia Dei nobilia et pretiosa sunt ex dignitate dantis, ex affectu liberalitatis et caritatis...* (*David ab Augusta*, 183; Devas, *Spiritual Life* 2, 24).

[42] *Prof* 3,27. *Virtus est ordinatus secundum veritatis iudicium mentis affectus* (*David ab Augusta*, 215; Devas, *Spiritual Life* 2, 54).

[43] *Prof* 3,32. *...ita caritas est una virtus in se omnem habens virtutem, sed propter diversos effectus eius ex diversis extrinsecis occasionibus vel causis illatis, quibus se vel contra malum*

virtue, love[44]		
that only being loved which is deserving	well-ordered love in the right manner and measure	
love[45]		
for it flows from Him it is infused (*mandatur*) into us from God Himself	it is able to render meritorious both natural and social love	
humility[46]		
	our whole demeanour and especially our conversation	should show itself in our manners (*in nobis*) should be marked by (*habendo*)
humility, goodness[47]		
and grace (*donis*) from whom it comes	attribute all to God, referring all good to Him	despite outstanding gifts of nature (*virtutibus*)
peace, goodness[48]		

---

opponit, vel ad bonum extendit, diversa officia vel nomina sortitur (David ab Augusta, 226; Devas, *Spiritual Life* 2, 65).

[44] *Prof* 3,32. *Virtus enim, sicut definit Augustinus, est amor ordinatus, videlicet, ut amet solum quod debet et sicut debet et quantum debet* (David ab Augusta, 226; Devas, *Spiritual Life* 2, 65).

[45] *Prof* 3,34. *Spiritualis dilectio a Spiritu sancto denominata, a quo fluit, qui amor Patris et Filii dicitur, est illa, quae mandatur nobis a Domino, et meritoria est per se sola et duas priores efficit meritorias...* (David ab Augusta, 234; Devas, *Spiritual Life* 2, 72).

[46] *Prof* 3,37. *Secundo in nobis simus humiles, mores et gestus humiles habendo et verba humilia et responsa...* (David ab Augusta, 245; Devas, *Spiritual Life* 2, 82).

[47] *Prof* 3,38. *Tertius humilitatis gradus est, quando etiam in magnis virtutibus et donis et honoribus homo nihil extollitur, nihil sibi ex hoc blanditur, totum illi refundens et integre restituens, a quo fluit omne bonum* (David ab Augusta, 249; Devas, *Spiritual Life* 2, 86).

[48] *Prof* 3,51. *...quoniam ipse est Deus, qui tam potenter potuit et tam pie voluit impetus tentationum et vitiorum opprimere et pacem, quam per Scripturas saepe promittit, hominibus bonae voluntatis donare; Levitici, vigesimo sexto: Dabo pacem in finibus vestris* [cfr. Lev 26,6]... (David ab Augusta, 293; Devas, *Spiritual Life* 2, 126).

bestowing (*donare*) on men I will give (*dabo*)	of goodwill	
peace, joy[49]		
in the Holy Ghost	build up	a kingdom for thyself within thy own soul
love[50]		
His benevolence (*dat beneficia*) towards us		no human mind can measure it
love, obedience[51]		
His love and benefits (*beneficiis*) (His commands)		
fervor, faith, humility[52]		
of the graces (*gratiae*) granted to us on God's will and time	upon fervent and persevering faith and trust due acknowledgment and careful safeguarding	the frame of mind which prompts us to condition our prayers

---

[49] Cf. *Prof* 3,54. *Interim in nobis operare tibi regnum in iustitia et pace et gaudio Spiritus sancti* [cfr. Rom 14,17] (*David ab Augusta*, 305; Devas, *Spiritual Life* 2, 138).

[50] *Prof* 3,55. *Tanto etiam affectu et benevolentia dat beneficia sua homini, quod, si etiam modica daret, gratanter essent recipienda; caritas enim eius supereminet omni scientiae* [cfr. Eph 3,19], *ita quod a nullo sensu potest aestimari...* (*David ab Augusta*, 309; Devas, *Spiritual Life* 2, 141).

[51] *Prof* 3,55. *...et pro dilectione et beneficiis reddimus ei contumelias et contemptum, inobedientes, negligentes, ingrati et elati* (*David ab Augusta*, 310; Devas, *Spiritual Life* 2, 142).

[52] *Prof* 3,61. *...quae valeant ad exauditionem orationis, scilicet culpae remotio, fervor et instantia et fidei confidentia, humilitas et aliorum suffragia et acceptae gratiae cum gratiarum actione studiosa conservatio, et ut ea tantum petantur a Domino, quae ipse novit magis expedire et quando* (*David ab Augusta*, 337; Devas, *Spiritual Life* 2, 168).

joy[53]		
with infusion (*infusum*) of grace	coming upon the soul	as the result of some devout thought

joy[54]		
which the Holy Spirit infuses (*infundit*) into them	breaking out into open manifestations of delight	

love, joy[55]		
is kindled with the joys of a divine delight and aflame	with desires	the human heart

joy[56]		
infused (*infunditur*) by that same divine spirit		

---

[53] *Prof* 3,64. ...*quod iubilus sit quoddam spirituale gaudium cordi repente ex aliqua devota cogitatione vel collatione infusum...* (*David ab Augusta*, 347; Devas, *Spiritual Life* 2, 179).

[54] *Prof* 3,64. *Quid etiam mirum, si ex magna spiritus hilaritate, quam sanctus Spiritus cordi infundit, aliquando erumpit in aliqua aperta hilaritatis indicia...* (*David ab Augusta*, 349; Devas, *Spiritual Life* 2, 181).

[55] *Prof* 3,64. *Cor namque divini amoris gaudio vel divinae fruitionis desiderio inflammatum in se dilatatur et extenditur...* (*David ab Augusta*, 349–350; Devas, *Spiritual Life* 2, 182).

[56] *Prof* 3,64. *Spiritualis iucunditas dici potest gaudium quodlibet in Spiritu sancto, quod a Spiritu sancto infunditur...* (*David ab Augusta*, 350; Devas, *Spiritual Life* 2, 182).

BIBLIOGRAPHY

1. SOURCES AND EDITIONS; REFERENCE TOOLS

Aristoteles latinus 26, 1–3 (Leiden & Bruxelles 1972).

Aristotle, The Nicomachean Ethics. The Loeb Classical Library 73 (London & Cambridge 1962).

Bohl, C., "Bibliografie zur Regel des Minderbrüderordens", in: *Regel und Leben. Materialien zur Franziskusregel.* Werkstatt Franziskanische Forschung 1 (Münster 2007).

Bougerol, J.-G., *Lexique Saint Bonaventure* (Paris 1969).

Busa, R. (ed.), *S. Thomae Aquinatis opera omnia* 2 (Stuttgart 1980).

Cicero, De inventione. De optimo genere oratorum. Topica. The Loeb Classical Library 386 (London & Cambridge 1960).

David ab Augusta, De exterioris et interioris hominis compositione secundum triplicem statum incipientium, proficientium et perfectorum libri tres (Quaracchi 1899).

Doctoris irrefragabilis Alexandri de Hales Ordinis Minorum Summa theologica 1 (Quaracchi 1924).

Doctoris seraphici S. Bonaventurae S.R.E. episcopi cardinalis opera omnia 1 (Quaracchi 1882).

Doctoris seraphici S. Bonaventurae S.R.E. episcopi cardinalis opera omnia 3 (Quaracchi 1887).

Doctoris seraphici S. Bonaventurae S.R.E. episcopi cardinalis opera omnia 5 (Quaracchi 1891).

Doctoris seraphici S. Bonaventurae S.R.E. episcopi cardinalis opera omnia 8 (Quaracchi 1898).

Doctoris seraphici S. Bonaventurae S.R.E. episcopi cardinalis opera omnia 9 (Quaracchi 1901).

Esser, C. (ed.), *Opuscula sancti patris Francisci Assisiensis.* Bibliotheca franciscana ascetica Medii Aevi 12 (Grottaferrata 1978).

Esser, K. & Grau, E. (ed.), *Die Opuscula des hl. Franziskus von Assisi. Neue textkritische Edition.* Spicilegium bonaventurianum 13 (Grottaferrata 1989[2]).

Denzinger, H. & Hünermann, P. (ed.), *Kompendium der Glaubensbekentnisse und kirchlichen Lehrentscheidungen/Enchiridion symbolorum definitionum et declarationum de rebus fidei et morum* (Freiburg etc. 2005[40]).

Guillelmi a Sancto Theodorico opera omnia 3. Corpus christianorum, continuatio mediaevalis 88 (Turnhout 2003).

Guillelmi de Militona, Quaestiones de sacramentis 1–2 (Quaracchi 1961).

Jean de la Rochelle, Tractatus de divisione multiplici potentiarum animae. Textes philosophiques du Moyen Age 11 (Paris 1964).

Magistri Alexandri de Hales, Glossa in quatuor libros Sententiarum Petri Lombardi 2 (Quaracchi 1952).

Magistri Alexandri de Hales, Glossa in quatuor libros Sententiarum Petri Lombardi 3 (Quaracchi 1954).

Magistri Alexandri de Hales, Quaestiones disputatae 'Antequam esset frater' 1-3 (Quaracchi 1960).

Magistri Petri Lombardi, Sententiae in IV libris distinctae. Editio tertia 1,2. Spicilegium bonaventurianum 4 (Grottaferrata 1971).

Menestò, E. & Brufani, S. (ed.), *Fontes Franciscani* (Assisi 1995).

Paolazzi, C. (ed.), "La *Regula non bullata* dei frati minori (1221), dallo "Stemma codicum" al testo critico", in: *Archivum fratrum minorum* 100 (2007), 5–148.

Platonis opera 4 (Oxford [1905]).
Stanford Encyclopedia of Philosophy (http://plato.stanford.edu/)

2. TRANSLATIONS

Armstrong, R.J. e.a. (transl.), *Francis of Assisi. Early Documents* 1–3 (New York etc. 1999–2001).
Batten, R.J. (transl.), *St. Thomas Aquinas. Summa theologiae Volume 34. Charity. Latin text, English translation, Notes, Appendices & Glossary* (London & New York 1975).
Bougerol, J.G. (transl.), *Saint Bonaventure. La triple voie. De triplici via. Traduction française. Commentaires et Notes* (Paris 1998).
Coughlin, F.E. (transl.), *Works of St. Bonaventure 10. Writings on the Spiritual Life* (Saint Bonaventure 2006).
Cousins, E. (transl.), *Bonaventure. The Soul's Journey into God. The Tree of Life. The Life of St. Francis* (New York etc. 1978).
D'Arcy, E. (transl.), *St. Thomas Aquinas. Summa theologiae Volume 20. Pleasure. Latin text, English translation, Introduction, Notes and Glossary* (London & New York 1975).
De Zes Vleugelen van den Seraf of Noodzakelijke Deugden en Eigenschappen van een goed Overste (Mechelen 1947).
Devas, D. (transl.), *Spiritual Life and Progress. Being a Translation of His* De Exterioris et Interioris Hominis Compositione 1–2 (London 1937).
Freeman, G.P. e.a. (transl.), *Franciscus van Assisi. De geschriften* (Haarlem 2006²).
Hayes, Z. (transl.), *Works of St. Bonaventure 2. Itinerarium Mentis in Deum* (Saint Bonaventure 2002).
Hughes, W.D. (transl.), *St. Thomas Aquinas. Summa theologiae Volume 23. Virtue. Latin text. English translation, Introduction, Notes, Appendices & Glossary* (London & New York 1969).
Kenny, A. (transl.), *St. Thomas Aquinas. Summa theologiae Volume 22. Dispositions for Human Acts. Latin text. English translation, Introduction, Notes, Appendices & Glossary* (London & New York 1964).
Masterson, R. & O'Brien, T.C. (transl.), *St. Thomas Aquinas. Summa theologiae Volume 60. Penance. Latin text. English translation, Introduction, Notes, Appendices & Glossary* (London & New York 1963).
Monti, D. (transl.), *Works of Saint Bonaventure 5. St. Bonaventure's Writings Concerning The Franciscan Order* (St. Bonaventure 1994).
O'Connor, E.D. (transl.), *St. Thomas Aquinas. Summa theologiae Volume 24. The Gifts of the Spirit. Latin text. English translation, Introduction, Notes, Appendices & Glossary* (London & New York 1974).
Schlosser, M. (transl.), "Bonaventura. De perfectione vitae", in: *Wissenschaft und Weisheit* 57 (1994), 21–75.
Schlosser, M. (transl.), *Bonaventura. De triplici via. Über den dreifachen Weg.* Fontes christiani 14 (Freiburg etc. 1993).
Stump, E. (transl.), *Boethius's* De topicis differentiis. *Translated, with Notes and Essays on the Text* (Ithaca & London 1978).
The Works of Bernard of Clairvaux 2. Cistercian Fathers Series 13 (Spencer, Mass. 1974).
Vinck, J. de (transl.), *The Works of Bonaventure* (Paterson 1960–1970).

3. LITERATURE

Accrocca, F. & Ciceri, A., *Francesco e i suoi frati. La Regola non bollata: una regola in cammino.* Tau 7 (Milano 1998).
Adams, R.M., *A Theory of Virtue. Excellence in Being for the Good* (Oxford 2006).

Alencherry, F., *The Truth of Holy Scripture According to Vatican II and in Catholic Theology, 1965–92* (diss. Roma 1994).

Allen, J.L., "The Standard of Covenant Love", in: J.L. Allen, *Love & Conflict. A Covenantal Model of Christian Ethics* (Nashville 1984), 49–81.

Alszeghy, Z., *Grundformen der Liebe. Die Theorie der Gottesliebe bei dem hl. Bonaventura.* Analecta Gregoriana 38 (Roma 1946).

Anciaux, P., *Le sacrement de la pénitence* (Louvain & Paris 1957).

Armstrong, R.J., ""If My Words Remain in You...". Foundations of the Evangelical Life", in: J.M. Hammond, *Francis of Assisi. History, Hagiography and Hermeneutics in the Early Documents* (New York & London 2004), 64–89.

Armstrong, R.J., *St. Francis of Assisi. Writings for a Gospel Life* (New York 1994).

"Armut", in: A. Müller e.a. (ed.), *Franziskus von Assisi 1182–1982. Das Evangelium Leben. Armut, Brüderlichkeit, Kirche, Friede, Umwelt* (Bonn 1982), 6–29.

"Armut", in: *Theologische Realenzyklopädie* 4 (1979), 69–121.

"Armut und Armenfürsorge", in: *Lexikon des Mittelalters* 1 (1980), 984–992.

Aubert, J.-M., "Vertus", in: *Dictionnaire de spiritualité* 16 (1994), 486–497.

Auer, J., "Demut", in: *Lexikon des Mittelalters* 3 (1986), 693–694.

Baarlink, H., *Vrede op aarde. De messiaanse vrede in bijbels perspectief.* Serie exegetische studies 2 (Kampen 1985).

Backherms, R.E., *Religious Joy in General in the New Testament and Its Sources in Particular* (diss. Fribourg 1963).

Bailey, M.D., "Religious Poverty, Mendicancy, and Reform in the Late Middle Ages", in: *Church History* 72 (2003), 457–483.

Balthasar, H.U. von, "Gehorsam im Licht des Evangeliums", in: *Zur Pastoral der geistlichen Berufe* 16 (1978), 17–27.

Balthasar, H.U. von, *Herrlichkeit. Eine theologische Ästhetik* (Einsiedeln 1961–1969).

Balthasar, H.U. von, *Theologik* (Einsiedeln 1985–1987).

Bars, H., *Trois vertus-clefs: foi, espérance, charité.* Je sais-je crois 27 (Paris 1960).

Bautz, M., *Virtutes. Studien zu Funktion und Ikonographie der Tugenden im Mittelalter und im 16. Jahrhundert* (diss. Berlin 1999).

Becker, H.-J. & Hödl, L., "Friede", in: *Lexikon des Mittelalters* 4 (1989), 919–921.

Beemer, T., "Over de deugden. Van menselijke ontplooiing tot de navolging van Christus; of omgekeerd?", in: *Franciscaans leven* 64 (1981), 193–201.

Bejczy, I. (ed.), *Virtue Ethics in the Middle Ages. Commentaries on Aristotle's Nicomachean Ethics, 1200–1500.* Brill's Studies in Intellectual History 160 (Leiden 2008).

Beld, A. van den, "Is geloof een deugd?", in: A. van den Beld, *Is geloof een deugd? Studies over God, deugd en het eeuwige leven* (Baarn 1990), 9–24.

Bell, D.N., "The Tripartite Soul and the Image of God in the Latin Tradition", in: *Recherches de théologie ancienne et médiévale* 47 (1980), 16–52.

Benz, H., "Der (neu)platonische Aufstiegsgedanke bei Bonaventura und Nikolaus von Kues", in: *Wissenschaft und Weisheit* 64 (2001), 95–128.

Berges, U., "Die Armen im Buch Jesaja. Ein Beitrag zur Literaturgeschichte des AT", in: *Biblica* 80 (1999), 153–177.

Berkhof, H., "Christian Faith", in: H. Berkhof, *Christian Faith. An Introduction to the Study of the Faith* (Grand Rapids 1990²), 19–26.

Bertaud, É. & Rayez, A., "Échelle spirituelle", in: *Dictionnaire de spiritualité* 4 (1960), 62–86.

Bertocci, P.A., *The Goodness of God* (Washington 1981).

Bertocci, P.A. & Millard, R.M., "A Scheme of Virtues", in: P.A. Bertocci & R.M. Millard, *Personality and the Good. Psychological and Ethical Perspectives* (New York 1963), 381–408.

Bertocci, P.A. & Millard, R.M., "Traits, Virtues, and Personality", in: P.A. Bertocci & R.M. Millard, *Personality and the Good. Psychological and Ethical Perspectives* (New York 1963), 361–380.

Biser, E., "Friede", in: H. Fries (ed.), *Handbuch theologischer Grundbegriffe* 1 (München 1962), 419–424.

Bishop, J., *Believing by Faith. An Essay in the Epistomology and Ethics of Religious Belief* (Oxford 2007).

Bisschops, H.J., *Franciscus van Assisi. Mysticus en mystagoog.* Scripta Franciscana 11 (Assen 2008).

Bissen, J.-M., "Les conditions de la contemplation selon Saint Bonaventure", in: *La France Franciscaine* 17 (1934), 387–404.

Blank, J. & Hasenhüttl, G. (ed.), *Glaube an Jesus Christus* (Düsseldorf 1980).

Blanshard, B., *Reason and Goodness* (London 1961).

Blois, L. de & Bredero, A.H. (ed.), *Kerk en Vrede in oudheid en middeleeuwen* (Kampen 1980).

Blommestijn, H., "Progrès-progressants", in: *Dictionnaire de spiritualité* 12 (1986), 2383–2405.

Böckmann, A., *Die Armut in der innerkirchlichen Diskussion heute. Ein Beitrag zu einem Neuverständnis der Ordensarmut.* Münsterschwarzacher Studien 25 (Münsterschwarzach 1973).

Boesak, A., *Walking on Thorns. The Call to Christian Obedience* (Geneva 1984).

Bohl, C., *Geistlicher Raum. Räumliche Sprachbilder als Träger spiritueller Erfahrung, dargestellt am Werk* De compositione *des David von Augsburg.* Franziskanische Forschungen 42 (Werl 2000).

Böhm, T., "Das Wahrheitsverständnis in Bibel und Früher Kirche", in: M. Enders & J. Szaif (ed.), *Die Geschichte des philosophischen Begriffs der Wahrheit* (Berlin & New York 2006), 49–64.

Böhm, T. e.a., "Wahrheit", in: J. Ritter e.a. (ed.), *Historisches Wörterbuch der Philosophie* 12 (Darmstadt 2004), 48–123.

Bonnefoy, F., "The Triple Way: A Bonaventurian Summa of Mystical Theology", in: *Greyfriars Review* 16 Supplement (2002), 1–129/ *Une somme bonaventurienne de théologie mystique: le "De triplici via"* (Paris 1934).

"Bonté", in: *Dictionnaire de spiritualité* 1 (1937), 1860–1868.

Borak, A., "Le beatitudini come espressione della muturita' della vita cristiana", in: A. Pompei (ed.), *San Bonaventura. Maestro di vita francescana e di sapienza cristiana. Atti del Congresso Internazionale per il VII centenario di San Bonaventura da Bagnoregio. Roma, 19–26 settembre 1974* 3 (Roma 1976), 281–292.

Borok, H., *Der Tugendbegriff des Wilhelm von Auvergne (1180–1249). Eine moralhistorische Untersuchung zur ideengeschichtlichen Rezeption der aristotelischen Ethik.* Moraltheologische Studien 5 (Düsseldorf 1979).

Bosl, K., *Armut Christi. Ideal der Mönche und Ketzer, Ideologie der aufsteigenden Gesellschaftsschichten vom 11. bis zum 13. Jahrhundert* (München 1981).

Bougerol, J.G., *Introduction a l'étude de S. Bonaventure.* Bibliothèque de théologie. Série 1. Théologie dogmatique 2 (Paris etc. 1961)/ *Introduction à Saint Bonaventure* (Paris 1988)/ *Introduction to the Works of Bonaventure* (Rockport 1993).

Bougerol, J.G., "La perfection chrétienne et la structuration des trois voies de la vie spirituelle dans la pensée de saint Bonaventure", in: *Études franciscaines* 19 (1969), 397–409.

Bracaloni, L., "Le virtù religiose fondamentali secondo la spiritualità francescana", in: *Studi Francescani* 30 (1933), 145–170.

Brandenburger, E., *Frieden im Neuen Testament. Grundlinien urchristlichen Friedensverständnisses* (Gütersloh 1973).

Brechtken, J., *Augustinus Doctor Caritatis. Sein Liebesbegriff im Widerspruch von Eigennutz und selbstloser Güte im Rahmen der antiken Glückseligkeits-Ethik.* Monographien zur philosophischen Forschung 136 (Meisenheim am Glan 1975).

Breton, V.-M., "l'Exemple de Saint François", in: V.-M. Breton, *La pauvreté* (Paris 1959²).

Brosch, J., *Jesus und die Freude* (Mönchengladbach 1946).

Brümmer, V., *The Model of Love. A Study in Philosophical Theology* (Cambridge 1993).

Buirette, J.-J., "A Short Glossary of Terms Used by Francis of Assisi", in: *Greyfriars Review* 18 (2004), 293–299.

Burgess, S.M. (ed.), *Reaching Beyond. Chapters in the History of Perfectionism* (Peabody 1986).

Burnham, L.A., "Just Talking about God: Orthodox Prayer, among the Heretical Beguins", in: T.J. Johnson (ed.), *Franciscans at Prayer*. The Medieval Franciscans 4 (Leiden & Boston 2007), 249–270.

"Buße", in: *Lexikon des Mittelalters* 2 (1983), 1123–1151.

Campagnola, S. da, "La povertà nelle «Regulae» di Francesco d'Assisi", in: Società Internazionale di Studi Francescani, *La povertà del secolo XII e Francesco d'Assisi. Atti del II Convegno Internazionale. Assisi, 17–19 ottobre 1974* (Assisi 1975), 217–253.

Canning, R., *The Unity of Love for God and Neighbour in St. Augustine* (Heverlee-Leuven 1993).

Cargnoni, C., "l'Itineranza francescana: significati e rapporti", in: *Laurentianum* 45 (2004), 143–177.

Carr, A., "Poverty in Perfection According to St. Bonaventure", in: *Franciscan Studies* 7 (1947), 313–323, 415–425.

Casey, M., *A Guide to Living in the Truth. Saint Benedict's Teaching on Humility* (Liguori 2001).

Casutt, L., *Die älteste franziskanische Lebensform. Untersuchungen zur* Regula prima sine bulla (Graz etc. 1955).

Cessario, R., *The Moral Virtues and Theological Ethics* (Notre Dame 2009²).

"Charité", in: *Dictionnaire de spiritualité* 2 (1953), 507–691.

Châtillon, J., "Le primat de la vertu de charité dans la théologie de Saint Bonaventure", in: A. Pompei (ed.), *San Bonaventura. Maestro di vita francescana e di sapienza cristiana. Atti del Congresso Internazionale per il VII centenario di San Bonaventura da Bagnoregio. Roma, 19–26 settembre 1974* 3 (Roma 1976), 217–238.

"Christelijke gehoorzaamheid"; *Concilium* 16 (1980).

Chydenius, J., *The Symbolism of Love in Medieval Thought*. Commentationes humanarum litterarum 44 (Helsinki 1970).

Clasen, S., "Die Armut als Beruf: Franziskus von Assisi", in: P. Wilpert (ed.), *Miscellanea mediaevalia* 3 (Berlin 1964), 73–85.

Coleman, J., "Using, Not Owning – Duties, Not Rights: The Consequences of Some Franciscan Perspectives on Politics", in: M.F. Cusato & G. Geltner (ed.), *Defenders and Critics of Franciscan Life. Essays in Honor of John V. Fleming*. The Medieval Franciscans 6 (Leiden & Boston 2009), 65–84.

Comblin, J., *Théologie de la paix* 1–2 (Paris 1960–1963).

Conn, W., *Christian Conversion. A Developmental Interpretation of Autonomy and Surrender* (Mahwah 1986).

"Convertissez-vous et faites pénitence", in: *Christus. Cahiers spirituels* 39 (1963).

Corselis, M.-A., "Les ordres apostoliques au XIIIe siècle", in: *l'Obéissance* (Paris 1951⁴), 37–50.

Corstanje, A. van, *Gottes Bund mit den Armen. Biblische Grundgedanken bei Franziskus von Assisi*. Bücher franziskanischer Geistigkeit 10 (Werl 1964).

Coventry, J., *Christian Truth* (London 1975).

Crisp, R. & Slote, M. (ed.), *Virtue Ethics* (Oxford 1997).

Cullen, C.M., *Bonaventure* (Oxford 2006).

Cuttini, E., *Ritorno a Dio. Filosofia, teologia, etica della mens nel pensiero di Bonaventura da Bagnoregio* (Soveria Manelli 2002).

Dalarun, J., *The Misadventure of Francis of Assisi* (Saint Bonaventure 2002).

D'Andrea, T.D., *Tradition, Rationality, and Virtue. The Thought of Alasdair MacIntyre* (Aldershot 2006).

Daniel, E.R., "St. Bonaventure a Faithful Disciple of St. Francis? A Reexamination of the Question", in: *S. Bonaventura, 1274–1974* 2 (Roma 1973).

Danneels, G., *De vreugde van de Poverello. Achtste eeuwfeest van Franciscus' geboorte (1181–1981)* (Mechelen 1982).

D'Avray, D.L., *The Preaching of the Friars. Sermons diffused from Paris before 1300* (Oxford 1985).

Deden, D., *De bijbel over de liefde* (Roermond & Maaseik 1964).

Delhaye, P., "La charité, «premier commandment» chrétien chez S. Bonaventure", in: *S. Bonaventura, 1274–1974* 4 (Roma 1974).

Delhaye, P., "Les conditions generales de l'agir chrétien selon Saint Bonaventure", in: A. Pompei (ed.), *San Bonaventura. Maestro di vita francescana e di sapienza cristiana. Atti del Congresso Internazionale per il VII centenario di San Bonaventura da Bagnoregio. Roma, 19–26 settembre 1974* 3 (Roma 1976), 183–215.

Delio, I, *Simply Bonaventure. An Introduction to His Life, Thought, and Writings* (New York 2001).

Delio, I., *The Humility of God. A Franciscan Perspective* (Cincinnati 2005).

Dent, N.J.H., *The Moral Psychology of the Virtues* (Cambridge etc. 1984).

Desbonnets, T., *De l'intuition à l'institution. Les franciscains* (Paris 1983).

Dettloff, W., "Franziskanertheologie", in: H. Fries (ed.), *Handbuch theologischer Grundbegriffe* 1 (München 1962), 387–392.

Deus caritas est. Encyclical Letter of the Supreme Pontiff Benedict XVI to the Bishops Priests and Deacons Men and Women Religious and All the Lay Faithful on Christian Love (Vatican City [2005]).

Dienst der Versöhnung. Umkehr, Buße und Beichte- Beiträge zu ihrer Theologie und Praxis. Trierer theologische Studien 31 (Trier 1974).

Dillenberger, J., "Faith", in: D.W. Musser & J.L. Price (ed.), *A New Handbook of Christian Theology* (Nashville 1992), 182–185.

Diniz, E.A.A., *Joy in the Presence of Jesus Christ According to the Synoptics.* Studia theologica- Teresianum 8 (Roma 1991).

Dominian, J., *The Capacity to Love* (London 1985).

Doyle, E. & McElrath, D., "St. Francis of Assisi and the Christocentric Character of Franciscan Life and Doctrine", in: D. McElrath (ed.), *Franciscan Christology. Selected Texts, Translations and Introductory Essays.* Franciscan Sources 1 (St. Bonaventure 1980), 1–13.

Drewermann, E., *Ein Mensch braucht mehr als nur Moral. Über Tugenden und Laster* (Düsseldorf & Zürich 2001).

Dukker, C., *De evangelische en franciscaanse zin der boetvaardigheid* (Brummen [1955]).

Dukker, C., *Umkehr des Herzens. Der Bußgedanke des heiligen Franziskus von Assisi.* Bücher franziskanischer Geistigkeit 1 (Werl 1956).

Dulles, A., *The Assurance of Things Hoped For. A Theology of Christian Faith* (New York & Oxford 1994).

Ebeling, G., *Die Wahrheit des Evangeliums. Eine Lesehilfe zum Galaterbrief* (Tübingen 1981).

Eilers, E., "Der biblische Ansatz des religiösen Gehorsams", in: *Gehorsam und Autorität. Werkwoche der Franziskanischen Arbeitsgemeinschaft 1970. Wandlung in Treue* 12 (Werl 1971), 58–78.

Einhorn, W.J., "Der Begriff der 'Innerlichkeit' bei David von Augsburg und Grundzüge der Franziskanermystik", in: *Franziskanische Studien* 48 (1966), 336–376.

Eley, G., "Is all the World a Text? From Social History to the History of Society Two Decades Later", in: G.M. Spiegel (ed.), *Practicing History. New Directions in Historical Writing after the Linguistic Turn* (New York & London 2005), 35–61.

Elsässer, A., *Christus der Lehrer des Sittlichen. Die christologischen Grundlagen für die Erkenntnis des Sittlichen nach der Lehre Bonaventuras.* Münchener Universitäts-Schriften/Veröffentlichungen des Grabmann-Institutes. Neue Folge 6 (München etc. 1968).

Emery Jr., K., "Reading the World Rightly and Squarely: Bonaventure's Doctrine of the Cardinal Virtues", in: *Traditio* 39 (1983), 184–218.

Engemann, A., *Das neue Lied. Glaube, Hoffnung und Liebe aus franziskanischer Geistigkeit.* Bücher franziskanischer Geistigkeit 5 (Werl 1959).

Ennis, H.J., "The Place of Love in the Theological System of St. Bonaventure in General", in: *S. Bonaventura, 1274–1974* 4 (Roma 1974).

Ennis, H., "The Primacy of the Virtue of Charity in Morality According to Saint Bonaventure", in: *Antonianum* 50 (1975), 418–456.

Epping, A., "Seraphische Weisheit", in: *Franziskanische Studien* 56 (1974), 221–248.

Ernst, S., "Glaube", in: *Lexikon des Mittelalters* 4 (1989), 1492–1494.

Esser, K., *Anfänge und ursprüngliche Zielsetzungen des Ordens der Minderbrüder.* Studia et documenta franciscana 4 (Leiden 1966).

Esser, K., *Das Testament des hl. Franziskus. Eine Untersuchung über seine Echtheit and seine Bedeutung.* Vorreformationsgeschichtliche Forschungen 15 (Münster 1949).

Esser, K., "Die Armutsauffassung des hl. Franziskus", in: D. Flood (ed.), *Poverty in the Middle Ages.* Franziskanische Forschungen 27 (Werl 1975), 60–70.

Esser, K., *Die endgültige Regel der Minderen Brüder im Lichte der neuesten Forschung* (Werl 1965).

Esser, K., "Gehorsam und Autorität in der frühfranziskanischen Gemeinschaft", in: *Wissenschaft und Weisheit* 34 (1971), 1–18.

Esser, K., "Gehorsam und Autorität in Franziskanischer Sicht", in: *Gehorsam und Autorität. Werkwoche der Franziskanischen Arbeitsgemeinschaft 1970.* Wandlung in Treue 12 (Werl 1971), 113–132.

Esser, C., "Meditations on *The Admonitions* of St. Francis of Assisi", in: *Greyfriars Review* 6 Supplement (1992)/ *Le Ammonizioni di San Francesco* (unpublished).

Esser, K., "Mysterium paupertatis. Die Armutsauffassung des hl. Franziskus v. Assisi", in: *Wissenschaft und Weisheit* 14 (1951), 177–189.

Esser, K., *Textkritische Untersuchungen zur Regula non bullata der Minderbrüder.* Spicilegium bonaventurianum 9 (Grottaferrata 1974).

Esser, K. & Grau, E., *Antwort der Liebe. Der Weg des franziskanischen Menschen zu Gott.* Bücher franziskanischer Geistigkeit 3 (Werl 1967³).

Fehlner, P.D., *The Role of Charity in the Ecclesiology of St. Bonaventure.* Selecta seraphica 2 (Rome 1965).

Feld, H., *Franziskus von Assisi und seine Bewegung* (Darmstadt 1994).

Finkenzeller, J. & Griesl, G., *Entspricht die Beichtpraxis der Kirche der Forderung Jesu zur Umkehr? Eine Orientierungshilfe* (München 1971).

Firey, A., (ed.), *A New History of Penance.* Brill's Companions to the Christian Tradition 14 (Leiden & Boston 2008).

Fischediek, T.K., *Der Gehorsamsverständnis der «Regula Benedicti». Der Gehorsam als Grundlage für ein exemplarisch christliches Gemeinschaftsleben.* Regulae Benedicti studia. Supplementa 13 (St. Ottilien 1993).

Fisher, K., *De Deo trino et uno. Das Verhältnis von productio und reductio in seiner Bedeutung für die Gotteslehre Bonaventuras.* Forschungen zur systematischen und ökumenischen Theologie 38 (Göttingen 1978).

Flood, D., "Die Regelerklärung des David von Augsburg", in: *Franziskanische Studien* 75 (1993), 201–242.

Flood, D.E., *Die Regula non bullata der Minderbrüder.* Franziskanische Forschungen 19 (Werl 1967).

Flood, D., *Francis of Assisi and the Franciscan Movement* (Quezon City 1989).

Flood, D. (ed.), *Poverty in the Middle Ages.* Franziskanische Forschungen 27 (Werl 1975).

"Foi", in: *Dictionnaire de spiritualité* 5 (1964), 529–630.

Foote, D., "Mendicants and the Italian Communes in Salimbene's *Cronaca*", in: D.S. Prudlo (ed.), *The Origin, Development, and Refinement of Medieval Religious Mendicancies.* Brill's Companions to the Christian Tradition 24 (Leiden & Boston 2011), 197–238.

Ford, J.E., *Love, Marriage, and Sex in the Christian Tradition From Antiquity To Today* (San Francisco etc. 1999).

Forster, L., "Über Reihen und Gliedern vornehmlich in mittlerer deutscher Literatur", in: J.P. Strelka & J. Jungmayr (ed.), *Virtus et fortuna. Zur deutschen Literatur zwischen 1400 und 1720. Festschrift für Hans-Gert Roloff zu seinem 50. Geburtstag* (Bern etc. 1983), 15–36.

Fowler, J.W., *Stages of Faith. The Psychology of Human Development and the Quest for Meaning* (New York 1995).

Frank, K.S., "Perfection III: Moyen Age", in: *Dictionnaire de spiritualité* 12 (1984), 1118–1131.

Freeman, G.P., "De zieke die zich niet bekeert", in: *Franciscaans leven* 81 (1998), 3–11.

Freeman, G.P., "Franciscus' vrede: een goed verhaal", in: T. Zweerman e.a., *De Heer geve u vrede. Drie beschouwingen over Franciscus' vredespiritualiteit*. Franciscaanse studies 6 (Utrecht 1990), 29–63.

Freeman, G.P., "Het woord van de Vader", in: *Franciscaans leven* 81 (1998), 99–106.

Freeman, G.P., "Kinderen van de hemelse Vader. Bij 2BrGel 48–56", in: *Franciscaans leven* 81 (1998), 251–259.

Freeman, G.P., "Wat een boetvaardige doen moet", in: *Franciscaans leven* 81 (1998), 147–154.

Freeman, G.P. & Sevenhoven, H., *De nalatenschap van een arme. Commentaar op het Testament van Franciscus van Assisi*. Reeks commentaren op de Franciscaanse bronnen 1 (Utrecht 1989²).

"Frères mineurs", in: *Dictionnaire de spiritualité* 5 (1964), 1268–1422.

Freyer, J.-B., *Der demütige und geduldige Gott. Franziskus und sein Gottesbild – ein Vergleich mit der Tradition*. Veröffentlichungen der Johannes-Duns-Skotus-Akademie für franziskanische Geistesgeschichte und Spiritualität 1/Pontificium Athenaeum Antonianum. Theses 318 (Mönchengladbach 1991).

"Frieden", in: A. Müller e.a. (ed.), *Franziskus von Assisi 1182–1982. Das Evangelium Leben. Armut, Brüderlichkeit, Kirche, Friede, Umwelt* (Bonn 1982), 79–100.

"Frieden und Gerechtigkeit. Der Friedensbegriff der Kirche," in: F.-M. Schmölz (ed.), *Christlicher Friedensbegriff und europäische Friedensordnung*. Entwicklung und Frieden. Wissenschaftliche Reihe 12 (München & Mainz 1977), 15–46.

Furnish, V.P., *The Love Command in the New Testament* (Nashville & New York 1972).

Galtier, P., *Aux origines du sacrement du pénitence*. Analecta Gregoriana 54 (Roma 1951).

Gardiner, S.M. (ed.), *Virtue Ethics, Old and New* (Ithaca & London 2005).

Garlington, D.B., *Faith, Obedience and Perseverance. Aspects of Paul's Letter to the Romans*. Wissenschaftliche Untersuchungen zum Neuen Testament 79 (Tübingen 1994).

Garrido, J., *Die Lebensregel des Franz von Assisi. Inspiration für heute* (Freiburg im Breisgau 2001).

Geremek, B., *Poverty. A History* (Oxford & Cambridge, Mass. 1994).

Gerken, A., "Die theologische Intuition des heiligen Franziskus von Assisi", in: *Wissenschaft und Weisheit* 45 (1982), 2–25.

Gerken, A., *Theologie des Wortes. Das Verhältnis von Schöpfung und Inkarnation bei Bonaventura* (Düsseldorf 1963).

Geulen, M., *Die Armut des heiligen Franz von Assisi im Lichte der Wertethik* (diss. Bonn 1947; Köln 2005).

Ghinato, A., *Profilo spirituale di san Francesco. Tratto dai suoi scritti e dalle primitive biografie* (Roma 1961).

Gill, C., *Virtue, Norms, and Objectivity. Issues in Ancient and Modern Ethics* (Oxford 2005).

Gilman, J., *Faith, Reason, and Compassion. A Philosophy of the Christian Faith* (Lanham etc. 2007).

Gilson, É., *La philosophie de Saint Bonaventure*. Études de philosophie médiévale 4 (Paris 1924).

Glazier, M., *Gospel Love. A Narrative Theology*. Good News Studies 12 (Wilmington 1984).

Gobry, I., *St. François d'Assise et l'esprit franciscain*. Maîtres spirituels 10 (Paris 1957).

Godet-Calogeras, J.-F., *Illi qui volunt religiose stare in eremis*: Eremitical Practice in the Life of the Early Franciscans", in: T.J. Johnson (ed.), *Franciscans at Prayer*. The Medieval Franciscans 4 (Leiden & Boston 2007), 307–331.

Goorbergh, E. van den & Zweerman, T., *Was getekend: Franciscus van Assisi. Aspecten van zijn schrijverschap en brandpunten van zijn spiritualiteit*. Scripta Franciscana 5 (Assen 2002²).

Graham, G., *The Idea of Christian Charity. A Critique of Some Contemporary Conceptions*. Library of Religious Philosophy 3 (Notre Dame & London 1990).

Grau, E., "Der heilige Franziskus von Assisi und die Gründung seines Ordens", in: G. Atanassiu e.a., *Franz von Assisi* (Stuttgart etc. 1990), 45–90.

Grau, E., "Die »vollkommene Freude« des hl. Franziskus", in: *Dienender Glaube* 50 (1974), 39–46.

Greshake, G., *Gottes Willen tun. Gehorsam und geistliche Unterscheidung* (Freiburg etc. 1984).

Greshake, G., "Zur Erneuerung des kirchlichen Busswesens. Überlegungen aus dogmenge- schichtlicher und systematischer Sicht", in: A. Exeler e.a., *Zum Thema Busse und Bussfeier* (Stuttgart 1971), 61–121.

Griffith Thomas, W.H., *The Principles of Theology. An Introduction to the Thirty-nine Articles* (Grand Rapids 1979).

Gross, H., *Die Idee des ewigen and allgemeinen Weltfriedens im Alten Orient und im Alten Testament*. Trierer theologische Studien 7 (Trier 1956).

Gründel, J., "Tugend", in: *Lexikon für Theologie und Kirche* 10 (1965), 395–399.

Guardini, R., *Systembildende Elemente in der Theologie Bonaventuras. Die Lehren vom lumen mentis, von der gradatio entium und der influentia sensus et motus*. Studia et documenta franciscana 3 (Leiden 1964).

"Gut, das Gute", in: *Lexikon für Theologie und Kirche* 4 (1995), 1113–1116.

"Gut, das Gute, das Gut", in: J. Ritter (ed.), *Historisches Wörterbuch der Philosophie* 3 (Darmstadt 1974), 937–972.

Hallett, G.L., *Christian Neighbor-Love. An Assessment of Six Rival Versions* (Washington D.C. 1989).

Hamm, B., "Von der spätmittelalterlichen reformatio zur Reformation: der Prozeß norma- tiver Zentrierung von Religion und Gesellschaft in Deutschland", in: *Archiv für Reformationsgeschichte* 84 (1993), p. 7–82.

Hardick, L., *Die wahre und vollkommene Freude des heiligen Franziskus*. Bücher franziska- nischer Geistigkeit 23 (Werl 1981).

Hardick, L., ""Schenke mir vollendete Liebe"", in: *Glaube Hoffnung Liebe. Studientage der Franziskanischen Arbeitsgemeinschaft 1985*. Wandlung in Treue 28 (Werl 1985), 63–72.

Haskamp, R., ""Du bist unsere Liebe"", in: *Glaube Hoffnung Liebe. Studientage der Franziskanischen Arbeitsgemeinschaft 1985*. Wandlung in Treue 28 (Werl 1985), 73–86.

Haskamp, R., "Franziskus auf dem Weg zum Frieden mit sich selbst", in: *Pax et bonum. Studientage der Franziskanischen Arbeitsgemeinschaft 1983*. Wandlung in Treue 26 (Werl 1983), 18–32.

Hauerwas, S. & Pinches, C., *Christians among the Virtues. Theological Conversations with Ancient and Modern Ethics* (Notre Dame 1997).

Hausammann, S., *Buße als Umkehr und Erneuerung von Mensch und Gesellschaft. Eine the- ologiegeschichtliche Studie zu einer Theologie der Buße*. Studien zur Dogmengeschichte und systematischen Theologie 33 (Zürich [1972]).

Hayes, Z., "Bonaventure: Mystery of the Triune God", in: K.B. Osborne (ed.), *The History of Franciscan Theology* (St. Bonaventure 2007²), 39–125.

Hayes, Z., *The Hidden Center. Spirituality and Speculative Christology in St. Bonaventure* (St. Bonaventure 1992).

Hebblethwaite, B., *The Essence of Christianity. A Fresh Look at the Nicene Creed* (London 1996).

Hellmann, J.A.W., *Ordo. Untersuchung eines Grundgedankens in der Theologie Bonaventuras*. Münchener Universitätsschriften. Neue Folge 18 (München etc. 1974).

Hellmann, W., "Poverty: the Franciscan Way to God", in: *Theology Digest* 22 (1974), 339–345.

Hemmerle, K., *Theologie als Nachfolge. Bonaventura - ein Weg für heute* (Freiburg etc. 1975).

Henrici, P., *Die christliche Armut. Aus der Zeitschrift „Christus", Paris, übertragen und herausgegeben* (Frankfurt am Main 1966).

Hertling, L., "Die professio der Kleriker und die Entstehung der drei Gelübde", in: *Zeitschrift für katholische Theologie* 56 (1932), 148–174.

Hillmann, W., "Perfectio evangelica. Der klösterliche Gehorsam in biblisch-theologischer Sicht", in: *Wissenschaft und Weisheit* 25 (1962), 163–168.

Hochschild, J.P., "Porphyry, Bonaventure and Thomas Aquinas. A Neoplatonic Hierarchy of Virtues and Two Christian Appropriations", in: J. Inglis (ed.), *Medieval Philosophy and the Classical Tradition. In Islam, Judaism and Christianity* (London & New York 2002), 245–259.

Hödl, L., "Evangelische Räte", in: *Lexikon des Mittelalters* 4 (1989), 133–134.

Hödl, L. & Dinzelbacher, P., "Liebe", in: *Lexikon des Mittelalters* 5 (1991), 1963–1968.

Hoeberichts, J., "Franciscus' Lofzang op de deugden", in: *Tijdschrift voor verkondiging* 75 (2003), 299–302.

Hoeberichts, J., *Paradise Restored. The Social Ethics of Francis of Assisi. A Commentary on Francis' "Salutation of the Virtues"* (Quincy 2004).

Hoeberichts, J., "The Authenticity of Admonition 27 of Francis of Assisi. A Discussion with Carlo Paolazzi and Beyond", in: *Collectanea Franciscana* 75 (2005), 499–523.

Hoefs, K.-H., *Erfahrung Gottes bei Bonaventura. Untersuchungen zum Begriff "Erfahrung" in seinem Bezug zum Göttlichen*. Erfurter theologische Studien 57 (Leipzig 1989).

Hollencamp, C.H., *«Nemo bonus nisi unus Deus»: The Divine Attribute of Goodness Studied According to St. Thomas* (diss. Roma 1987).

Holman, S.R. (ed.), *Wealth and Poverty in Early Church and Society* (Grand Rapids 2008).

Hooft, S. van, *Understanding Virtue Ethics* (Chesham 2006).

Houdijk, R., "Deugt de deugd? Voorzichtig!", in: *Speling* 2 (1996), 4–11.

House, A., *Francis of Assisi* (London 2000).

Houser, R.E., *The Cardinal Virtues. Aquinas, Albert, and Philip the Chancellor*. Mediaeval Sources in Translation 39/Studies in Medieval Moral Teaching 4 (Toronto 2004).

Hülsbusch, W., "Die Theologie des transitus bei Bonaventura", in: *S. Bonaventura, 1274–1974* 4 (Roma 1974).

Hülsbusch, W., *Elemente einer Kreuzestheologie in den Spätschriften Bonaventuras* (Düsseldorf 1968).

"Humilité", in: *Dictionnaire de spiritualité* 7 (1961), 1136–1187.

Ibuki, Y., *Die Wahrheit im Johannesevangelium*. Bonner biblische Beiträge 39 (Bonn 1972).

Iriarte, L., *Vocazione francescana. Sintesi degli ideali di san Francesco e di santa Chiara*. Collana Laurentianum 3 (Casale Monferrato 1987²).

Israël, G., *Die Tugendlehre Bonaventuras* (diss. Berlin 1914).

Jackson, T.P., *The Priority of Love. Christian Charity and Social Justice* (Princeton & Oxford 2003).

Jansen, A., "De echte vreugde", in: *Franciscaans leven* 65 (1982), 179–188.

Jansen, A., "Lofzang op de deugden I", in: *Franciscaans leven* 75 (1992), 60–74.

Jansen, A., "Lofzang op de deugden II", in: *Franciscaans leven* 75 (1992), 167–182.

Jansen, A., "The Story of the True Joy. An Autobiographical Reading", in: *Franziskanische Studien* 63 (1981), 271–288.

Jansen, A., "Vrede, een zaak met vele dimensies", in: T. Zweerman e.a., *De Heer geve u vrede. Drie beschouwingen over Franciscus' vredespiritualiteit*. Franciscaanse studies 6 (Utrecht 1990), 65–76.

Jansen, A., "Woorden van heil van Franciscus. Vertaling en uitleg van zijn „Vermaningen"", in: *Franciscaans leven* 64 (1981), 163–186.

Jansen, A., "Words of Salvation of Saint Francis. A Commentary on Admonition 27", in: *Franciscan Digest* 4 (1994), 1–24.

Jean-Nesmy, C., *La joie de la pénitence. L'esprit liturgique* 29 (Paris 1968).

Johnson, O.A., *Rightness and Goodness. A Study in Contemporary Ethical Theory*. International Scholars Forum 13 (The Hague 1959).

Johnson, T.J. (ed.), *Franciscans at Prayer*. The Medieval Franciscans 4 (Leiden & Boston 2007).

Johnson, T., *Iste Pauper Clamavit. Saint Bonaventure's Mendicant Theology of Prayer*. European University Studies 32- 390 (Frankfurt am Main etc. 1990).

Johnson, T., "Poverty and Prayer in the Theology of Saint Bonaventure", in: *Miscellanea Francescana* 90 (1990), 19–60.

"Joie", in: *Dictionnaire de spiritualité* 8 (1974), 1236–1256.

Jones, S.L. (ed.), *Psychology and the Christian Faith. An Introductory Reader* (Grand Rapids 1986).

Jüngel, E., *Zum Wesen des Friedens. Frieden als Kategorie theologischer Anthropologie* (München 1983).

Kaiser, O., *In der Wahrheit leben. Perspectiven des Johannesevangeliums. Kritisch-theologisch-meditativ*. Der Christ in der Welt. Eine Enzyklopädie 6–9a/b (Aschaffenburg 1975).

Karris, R.J., *The Admonitions of St. Francis. Sources and Meanings* (St. Bonaventure 1999).

Kaup, J., *Die theologische Tugend der Liebe nach der Lehre des hl. Bonaventura* (Münster 1927).

Kemp, K.W., "The Virtue of Faith in Theology, Natural Science, and Philosophy", in: *Faith and Philosophy* 15 (1998), 462–477.

Kerber, W. e.a., *Armut und Reichtum*. Christlicher Glaube in moderner Gesellschaft 17 (Freiburg etc. 1981).

Kieffer, R., *Le primat de l'amour. Commentaire épistémologique de 1 Corinthiens 13*. Lectio divina 85 (Paris 1975).

Kiilunen, J., *Das Doppelgebot der Liebe in synoptischer Sicht. Ein redaktionskritischer Versuch über Mk 12,28–34 und die Parallelen*. Annales academiae scientiarum Fennicae. Sarja-ser. B 250 (Helsinki 1989).

Kinsella, S.E., ""To Serve the Lord with Poverty and Humility": the Witness to Peace in the Life and Works of Saint Francis of Assisi", in: *Laurentianum* 45 (2004), 377–429.

Kittredge, C.B., *Community and Authority. The Rhetoric of Obedience in the Pauline Tradition*. Harvard Theological Studies 45 (Harrisburg 1998).

Klassen, W., *Love of Enemies. The Way to Peace*. Overtures to Biblical Theology 15 (Philadelphia 1984).

Kölmel, W., "«Labor» und «paupertas» bei Bonaventura", in: A. Pompei (ed.), *San Bonaventura. Maestro di vita francescana e di sapienza cristiana*. Atti del Congresso Internazionale per il VII centenario di San Bonaventura da Bagnoregio. Roma, 19–26 settembre 1974 2 (Roma 1976), 569–582/ *Miscellanea Francescana* 75 (1975), 569–582.

Koper, R., *Das Weltverständnis des hl. Franziskus von Assisi. Eine Untersuchung über das „Exivi de Saeculo"*. Franziskanische Forschungen 14 (Werl 1959).

Krings, H., "Das Sein und die Ordnung. Eine Skizze zur Ontologie des Mittelalters", in: *Deutsche Vierteljahrsschrift für Literaturwissenschaft und Geistesgeschichte* 18 (1940), 233–249.

Krings, H., *Ordo. Philosophisch-historische Grundlegung einer abendländischen Idee* (Hamburg 1982²).

Krings, O. & Gnilka, J., "Wahrheit", in: H. Fries (ed.), *Handbuch theologischer Grundbegriffe* 2 (München 1963), 786–800.

Kuhn, H., *"Liebe". Geschichte eines Begriffs* (München 1975).

La paix. Recueils de la Société Jean Bodin pour l'Histoire Comparative des Institutions 14–15 (Bruxelles 1961–1962).

Lachance, P., "Mysticism and Social Transformation According to the Franciscan Way", in: J.K. Ruffing (ed.), *Mysticism & Social Transformation* (Syracuse 2001).

Lambert, M.D., *Franciscan Poverty. The Doctrine of the Absolute Poverty of Christ and the Apostles in the Franciscan Order 1210–1323* (St. Bonaventure 1998²).

Lambrecht, J. (ed.), *The Truth of the Gospel* (*Galatians 1:1–4:11*). Monographic Series of «Benedictina». Biblical-Ecumenical Section 12 (Rome 1993).

Lamparter, H., *Der Aufruf zum Gehorsam. Das fünfte Buch Mose*. Die Botschaft des Alten Testaments 9 (Stuttgart 1977).

Lang, J., *Ins Freie geführt. Aspekte der franziskanischen Spiritualität*. Bücher franziskanischer Geistigkeit 28 (Werl 1986).

Lapsanski, D.V., *Das Leben nach dem Evangelium am Anfang des Minderbrüderordens*. Bücher franziskanischer Geistigkeit 17 (Werl 1974).

Lapsanski, D.V., *Perfectio evangelica. Eine begriffsgeschichtliche Untersuchung im frühfranziskanischen Schrifttum* (München etc. 1974)

Laudien, K., "Wahrheit, ewige", in: J. Ritter e.a. (ed.), *Historisches Wörterbuch der Philosophie* 12 (Darmstadt 2004), 141–146.

Lawrence, C.H., *The Friars. The Impact of the Early Mendicant Movement on Western Society* (London & New York 1994).

Leben in Armut. Werkwochen der Franziskanischen Arbeitsgemeinschaft 1972. Wandlung in Treue 14 (Werl 1972).

Leclercq, J., "Gehorsam", in: *Lexikon des Mittelalters* 4 (1989), 1174.

Leeuwen, B. van, "Gehoorzaamheid in vrijmoedigheid", in: T. Zweerman e.a., *Franciscus: wegwijzer naar de ware vrijheid* (Haarlem 1983), 97–123.

Leeuwen, B. van, "Het geloof volgens de heilige Bonaventura", in: *Doctor seraphicus. Vier studies over de h. Bonaventura*. Collectanea Franciscana Neerlandica 7–3 ('s Hertogenbosch 1950), 33–62.

Leeuwen, P. van & Verheij, S., *Woorden van heil van een kleine mens. Commentaar op de Vermaningen van Franciscus van Assisi*. Reeks commentaren op de Franciscaanse bronnen 2 (Utrecht 1986).

Légasse, S., *Les pauvres en esprit. Evangile et non-violence*. Lectio divina 78 (Paris 1974).

Lehmann, L., *Franz von Assisi. Wenn Leben Beten wird*. Bücher franziskanischer Geistigkeit 34 (Werl 1998).

Lehmann, L., *Tiefe und Weite. Der universale Grundzug in den Gebeten des Franziskus von Assisi*. Franziskanische Forschungen 29 (Werl 1984).

Lendi, R., *Die Wandelbarkeit der Buße. Hermeneutische Prinzipien und Kriterien für eine heutige Theorie und Praxis der Buße und der Sakramente allgemein erhellt am Beispiel der Bußgeschichte*. Europäische Hochschulschriften. Reihe 23 218 (Bern etc. 1983).

Linden, R., *Vater und Vorbild. Franziskus- Forma Minorum*. Bücher franziskanischer Geistigkeit 6 (Werl 1960).

Little, L.K., *Religious Poverty and the Profit Economy in Medieval Europe* (Ithaca 1978).

Loeffen, H.J., *De vreugde bij Franciscus van Assisi* (master's thesis; Nijmegen 1976).

Lohse, E., *Freude des Glaubens. Die Freude im Neuen Testament* (Göttingen 2007).

Long, D.S., *The Goodness of God. Theology, Church, and the Social Order* (Grand Rapids 2001).

Longpré, E., *François d'Assise et son expérience spirituelle* (Paris 1966).

Longpré, E., "Saint François d'Assise (1182–1226)", in: *Dictionnaire de spiritualité* 5 (1964), 1271–1303.

Lottin, O., *Psychologie et morale aux XIIe et XIIIe siècles* 3 (Louvain 1949).

Lotz, J.B., *Eure Freude wird groß sein. Die acht Seligpreisungen als Weg in die Tiefe* (Freiburg etc. 1977).

Lüdke, F., "Christus die Wahrheit", in: C. Herrmann (ed.), *Wahrheit und Erfahrung-Themenbuch zur systematischen Theologie* 2 (Wuppertal 2005), 36–46.

MacDonald, S. (ed.), *Being and Goodness. The Concept of the Good in Metaphysics and Philosophical Theology* (Ithaca & London 1991).

MacIntyre, A., *After Virtue. A Study in Moral Theory* (Notre Dame 1984²).

MacNamara, V., "The Truth in Love", in: V. MacNamara, *The Truth of Love. Reflections on Christian Morality* (Dublin 1989), 62–85.

Macquarrie, J., *The Concept of Peace. The Firth Lectures, 1972* (London 1973).

Macquarrie, J., *The Humility of God. Christian Meditations* (London 1978).

Mähl, S., *Quadriga virtutum. Die Kardinaltugenden in der Geistesgeschichte der Karolingerzeit*. Beihefte zum Archiv für Kulturgeschichte 9 (Köln & Wien 1969).

Mäkinen, V., *Property Rights in the Late Medieval Discussion on Franciscan Poverty*. Recherches de Théologie et Philosophie médiévales. Bibliotheca 3 (Leuven 2001).

Manselli, R., "La povertà nella vita di Francesco d'Assisi", in: Società Internazionale di Studi Francescani, *La povertà del secolo XII e Francesco d'Assisi. Atti del II Convegno Internazionale. Assisi, 17–19 ottobre 1974* (Assisi 1975), 255–282.

Manselli, R., *San Francesco d'Assisi* (Roma 1980)/ *Franziskus. Der solidarische Bruder* (Zürich etc. 1984)/ *St. Francis of Assisi* (Quincy 1984).

Maranesi, P., *Facere misericordiam. La conversione di Francesco d'Assisi: confronto critico tra il Testamento a le Biografie* (Assisi 2007).

Marcucci, B., "La virtù dell'obbedienza nella perfezione secondo la dottrina di S. Bonaventura", in: *Studi Francescani* 25 (1953), 3–30.

Martignetti, R.S., *Saint Bonaventure's Tree of Life*. Theology of the Mystical Journey. Pensiero Francescano 2 (Grottaferrata 2004).

März, F., *Hören, Gehorchen und personale Existenz. Zur Phänomenologie des Gehorsams* (München 1962).

Matanic, A., *Francesco d'Assisi. Fattori causali della sua spiritualità*. Pubblicazioni dell'Istituto Apostolico Pontificio Ateneo Antonianum 10 (Roma 1984).

Matanic, A., "Virtù", in: E. Caroli (ed.), *Dizionario Francescano* (Padova 1983), 1979–1988, 2354–2356.

Matanic, A., *Virtù francescane. Aspetti ascetici della spiritualità francescana* (Roma 1964).

Matura, T., *François d'Assise, «auteur spirituel». Le message de ses écrits* (Paris 1996).

McEvoy, J., *Robert Grosseteste. Exegete and Philosopher*. Variorum Collected Studies 446 (Aldershot 1994).

Meggitt, J.J., *Paul, Poverty, and Survival* (Edinburgh 1998).

Meier, C., "Organisation of Knowledge and Encyclopaedic *ordo*: Functions and Purposes of a Universal Literary Genre", in: P. Binkley (ed.), *Pre-modern Encyclopaedic Texts. Proceedings of the Second COMERS Congress, Groningen, 1–4 july 1996* (Leiden etc. 1997), 103–126.

Ménard, A., "Le "Transitus" dans l'œuvre de Bonaventure. Un itinéraire de conversion biblique et de conformation progressive au Christ pascal", in: *Laurentianum* 41 (2000), 379–412.

Menestò, E., "A Re-reading of Francis of Assisi's Letter to the Faithful", in: *Greyfriars* 14 (2000), 97–110/ "Per una rilettura della *Epistola ad fideles* di San Francesco d'Assisi", in: *Analecta TOR* 29 (1998), 9–23.

Merle, R., *La pénitence et la peine. Théologie, droit canonique, droit pénal* (Paris 1985).

Metz, J.B., *Armut im Geiste* (München 1962).

Metz, J.B. & Jossua, J.-P. (ed.), *Theology of Joy*. Concilium 95 (New York 1974).

Miccoli, G., "Francesco e la pace", in: *Franciscan Studies* 64 (2006), 33–52.

Miccoli, G., *Le testament de Saint François* (Paris 1996).

Micó, J., "Franciscan Poverty", in: *Greyfriars Review* 11 (1997), 257–300.

Micó, J., "Obedience", in: *Greyfriars Review* 9 (1995), 223–245.

Mieth, D., *Die neuen Tugenden. Ein ethischer Entwurf* (Düsseldorf 1984).

Milchner, H.J., *Nachfolge Jesu und Imitatio Christi. Die theologische Entfaltung der Nachfolgethematik seit den Anfängen der Christenheit bis in die Zeit der devotio moderna – unter besonderer Berücksichtigung religionspädagogischer Ansätze. Religionspädagogische Kontexte und Konzepte* 11 (Münster 2004).

Miller, J.C., *The Obedience of Faith, the Eschatological People of God, and the Purpose of Romans. SBL Dissertation Series* 177 (Atlanta 2000).

Mockler, A, *Francis of Assisi. The Wandering Years* (Oxford 1976).

Mollat, M., *Les pauvres au Moyen Age. Étude sociale* (Paris 1978).

Moltmann, J., *Die ersten Freigelassenen der Schöpfung. Versuche über die Freude an der Freiheit und das Wohlgefallen am Spiel. Kaiser Traktate* 2 (München 1971).

Moorman, J., *A History of the Franciscan Order. From Its Origins to the Year 1517* (Chicago 1968).

Moorman, J.R.H., *Saint Francis of Assisi* (London 1963).

Morant, P., *Unser Weg zu Gott. Das Vollkommenheitsstreben im Geiste des hl. Franziskus. Franziskanische Lebenswerte* 6 (Zürich etc. 1965).

Morrice, W.G., *Joy in the New Testament* (Exeter 1984).

Mörschel, U., "Gut", in: *Lexikon des Mittelalters* 4 (1989), 1797–1800.

Mueller, J., *The Privilege of Poverty. Clare of Assisi, Agnes of Prague, and the Struggle for a Franciscan Rule for Women* (Pennsylvania 1994).

Müller, D., *Gesellschaft und Individuum um 1300 in volkssprachlicher franziskanischer Prosa* (diss. Köln 2003).

Müller, G., "Gradualismus. Eine Vorstudie zur altdeutschen Literaturgeschichte", in: *Deutsche Vierteljahrsschrift* 2 (1924), 681–720.

Munster, H. van, *De mystiek van Franciscus. De macht van barmhartigheid* (Haarlem 2003²).

Murdoch, I., *The Sovereignty of Good* (London 1970).

Murphy, N. e.a. (ed.), *Virtues & Practices in the Christian Tradition. Christian Ethics after MacIntyre* (Harrisburg 1997).

Murray, A., *Humility. The Journey toward Holiness* (Bloomington 2001).

Musto, R.G., *The Catholic Peace Tradition* (New York 1986).

Newbigin, L., *Proper Confidence. Faith, Doubt, and Certainty in Christian Discipleship* (Grand Rapids 1995).

Newbigin, L., *Truth to Tell. The Gospel as Public Truth* (Grand Rapids 1991).

Newhauser, R. (ed.), *In the Garden of Evil. The Vices and Culture in the Middle Ages. Papers in Mediaeval Studies* 18 (Toronto 2005).

Newhauser, R., *The Treatise on Vices and Virtues in Latin and the Vernacular. Typologie des sources du Moyen Age occidental* 68 (Turnhout 1993).

Newlands, G.M., *Theology of the Love of God* (London 1980).

Nguyen-Van-Khanh, N., *Le Christ dans la pensée de saint François d'Assise d'après ses écrits* (Paris 1989).

Nickl, P., *Ordnung der Gefühle. Studien zum Begriff des habitus. Paradeigmata* 24 (Hamburg 2001).

Nissen, J., *Poverty and Mission. New Testament Perspectives on a Contemporary Theme. IIMO Research Pamphlet* 10 (Leiden & Utrecht 1984).

Nolthenius, H., *Een man uit het dal van Spoleto. Franciscus tussen zijn tijdgenoten* (Amsterdam 1988).

Nossent, G., *Joie, Souffrance et Vie morale. Museum Lessianum. Section Philosophique* 55 (s.l. 1968).

Nouwen, H., *The Selfless Way to Christ. Downward Mobility and the Spiritual Life* (New York 2007).

"Obéissance", in: *Dictionnaire de spiritualité* 11 (1982), 535–563.

l'Obéissance (Paris 1951⁴).

Oliger, L., "Servasanto da Faenza o.f.m. e il suo «Liber de virtutibus et vitiis»", in: *Miscellanea Francesco Ehrle. Scritti di storia e paleografia* 1. Studi e testi 37 (Roma 1924), 148–189.

Omme, A.N. van, *"Virtus", een semantiese studie* (diss. Utrecht [1947]).

O'Neill, H.C., *Biblical Truth and the Morality of herem* (diss. Providence 1984).

"Paix", in: *Dictionnaire de spiritualité* 12,1 (1984), 40–73.

Pansters, K., *De kardinale deugden in de Lage Landen, 1200–1500.* Middeleeuwse studies en bronnen 108 (Hilversum 2007).

Pansters, K., "Deemoed. Een cruciale deugd", in: K. Pansters & W.M. Speelman (ed.), *De deemoed Gods. Verkenningen in het licht van Franciscus van Assisi* (Nijmegen 2011).

Pansters, K.,"Didactiek en dynamiek: 'voortgaan in deugden' in de geschriften van de Moderne devoten", in: *Trajecta* 16 (2007), 311–334.

Pansters, K., "Gerechtigkeit als Strukturelement katechetischer Texten des 15. Jahrhunderts", in: G. Annas & P. Schulte (ed.), *Gerechtigkeit im gesellschaftlichen Diskurs des späteren Mittelalters.* Zeitschrift für historische Forschung. Beihefte (Berlin), forthcoming.

Pansters, K., *"Profectus virtutum.* From Psalm 83,8 to David of Augsburg's *Profectus religiosorum"*, in: *Studies in spirituality* 18 (2008), 185–194.

Pansters, K., *"Profectus virtutum.* The Roots of Devout Moral Praxis", in: H. Blommestijn e.a. (ed.), *Seeing the Seeker. Explorations in the Discipline of Spirituality. A Festschrift for Kees Waaijman on the Occasion of his 65th Birthday.* Studies in Spirituality. Supplement 19 (Louvain 2008), 231–249.

Paolazzi, C., "Per l'autenticità della *Admonitio* XXVII e il lessico di frate Francesco: una risposta a Jan Hoeberichts", in: *Collectanea Franciscana* 76 (2006), 475–505.

Paravicini, W., *Die ritterlich-höfische Kultur des Mittelalters.* Enzyklopädie Deutscher Geschichte 32 (München 1994).

Partoens, G. e.a. (ed.), *Virtutis imago. Studies on the Conceptualisation and Transformation of an Ancient Ideal.* Collection d'études classiques 19 (Louvain 2004).

Paton, B., *Preaching Friars and the Civic Ethos: Siena, 1380–1480.* Westfield Publications in Medieval Studies 7 (London 1992).

"Pauvreté", in: *Dictionnaire de spiritualité* 12,1 (1984), 614–697.

Pelikan, J., *Credo. Historical and Theological Guide to Creeds and Confessions of Faith in the Christian Tradition* (New Haven & London 2003).

"Pénitence", in: *Dictionnaire de spiritualité* 12,1 (1984), 943–1010.

Perkins, P., *Love Commands in the New Testament* (Ramsey 1982).

Perrin, J.M., *Die acht Seligkeiten als Botschaft der Freude* (Basel etc. 1959).

Peters, F., *Aus Liebe zur Liebe. Der Glaubensweg des Menschen als Nachfolge Christi in der Spiritualität des hl. Franziskus von Assisi.* Veröffentlichungen der Johannes-Duns-Skotus-Akademie für franziskanische Geistesgeschichte und Spiritualität 6 (Kevelaer 1995).

Peterson, C. & Seligman, M.E.P., "Humility and Modesty", in: C. Peterson & M.E.P. Seligman, *Character, Strengths and Virtues. A Handbook and Classification* (Oxford 2004), 461–475.

Pezzini, D., "La tradizione manoscritta inglese del De exterioris et interioris hominis compositione di David de Augusta", in: A. Cacciotti & B. Faes de Mottoni (ed.), *Editori de Quaracchi 100 anni dopo. Bilancio e prospettive* (Roma 1997), 251–259.

Phillips, D., "The Way to Religious Perfection according to St. Bonaventure's *De Triplici Via*", in: J. Mundy e.a. (ed.), *Essays in Medieval Life and Thought* (New York 1955), 31–58.

Pieper, J., *Das Viergespann. Klugheit, Gerechtigkeit, Tapferkeit, Maß*. Herder-Bücherei 361 (Freiburg 1964).

Pieper, J., *Lieben hoffen glauben* (München 1986).

Pieper, J., "Tugend", in: H. Fries (ed.), *Handbuch theologischer Grundbegriffe* 2 (München 1963), 714–718.

Pohier, J.-M., "La pénitence, vertu de la culpabilité chrétienne", in: J.-M. Pohier, *Psychologie et théologie* (Paris 1967), 283–332.

Popkes, E.E., *Die Theologie der Liebe Gottes in den johanneischen Schriften*. Wissenschaftliche Untersuchungen zum Neuen Testament. 2. Reihe 197 (Tübingen 2005).

Portolano, A., *L'etica della pace nei primi secoli del Cristianesimo* (Napoli 1974).

Poschmann, B., *Paenitentia secunda. Die kirchliche Buße im ältesten Christentum bis Cyprian und Origenes. Eine dogmengeschichtliche Untersuchung*. Theophaneia 1 (Bonn 1940/1964).

Post, S.G., *A Theory of Agape. On the Meaning of Christian Love* (London & Toronto 1990).

Pourrat, P., "Commençants", in: *Dictionnaire de spiritualité* 2 (1953), 1143–1156.

Prentice, R.P., *The Psychology of Love According to St. Bonaventure*. Franciscan Institute Publications. Philosophy Series 6 (St. Bonaventure & Louvain 1951).

Preußner, A., *Die Komplexität der Tugend. Eine historisch-systematische Untersuchung*. Epistemata. Reihe Philosophie 199 (Würzburg 1997).

Prudlo, D.S., "Mendicancy among the Early Saints of the Begging Orders", in: D.S. Prudlo (ed.), *The Origin, Development, and Refinement of Medieval Religious Mendicancies*. Brill's Companions to the Christian Tradition 24 (Leiden & Boston 2011), 85–116.

Pybus, E., *Human Goodness. Generosity and Courage* (New York etc. 1991).

Quinten, E., *Die Liebe als Angelpunkt theologischen Denkens. Das paulinische Modell einer Theologie der Liebe* (diss. Saarbrücken 1983).

Rahner, K., *Sämtliche Werke 11. Mensch und Sünde. Schriften zur Geschichte und Theologie der Buße* (Freiburg etc. 2005).

Rahner, K., "Über das Problem des Stufenweges zur christlichen Vollendung", in: *Schriften zur Theologie* 3 (Einsiedeln etc. 1961), 11–34.

Ratzinger, J., *Auf Christus schauen. Einübung in Glaube, Hoffnung, Liebe* (Freiburg etc. 1989).

Reggio, P.-A., *Vergiß die Freude nicht* (Freiburg 1957).

Reijsbergen, R., "Bevrijdende gehoorzaamheid. Het mysterie van de gehoorzaamheid bij Franciscus van Assisi", in: *Franciscaans leven* 74 (1991), 60–71.

Renna, T., "The Idea of Peace in the West, 500–1150", in: *Journal of Medieval History* 6 (1980), 143–167.

Reynolds, T. (ed.), *The Phenomenon of Religious Faith* (New Jersey 2005).

Rice, H., *God and Goodness* (Oxford 2000).

Ridder, A.W., *Vreugde als aanzet tot geloof. Over geloofservaring, vreugde en angst, toegespitst op het Oude Testament* (Zoetermeer 2002).

Robinson, E.A., *These Three. The Theological Virtues of Faith, Hope, and Love* (Cleveland 2004).

Robson, M., *St. Francis of Assisi. The Legend and the Life* (London & New York 1999).

Roest, B., *Franciscan Literature of Religious Instruction before the Council of Trent*. Studies in the History of Christian Traditions 117 (Leiden & Boston 2004).

Roest, B., "The Discipline of the Heart: Pedagogies of Prayer in Medieval Franciscan Works of Religious Instruction", in: T.J. Johnson (ed.), *Franciscans at Prayer*. The Medieval Franciscans 4 (Leiden & Boston 2007), 413–448.

Rogers, C.M., "The Joy of St. Francis", in: *Francesco d'Assisi nel 750ᵐᵒ della morte (1226–1976)* (Jerusalem 1976), 233–250.

Roggen, H., *Die Lebensform des heiligen Franziskus von Assisi in ihrem Verhältnis zur feudalen und bürgerlichen Gesellschaft Italiens* (Mechelen 1965).

Rohr, E., *Der Herr und Franziskus*. Bücher franziskanischer Geistigkeit 11 (Werl 1966).
Romaniuk, K., *L'amour du Père et du Fils dans la sotériologie de St.-Paul* (Rome 1961).
Rondholz, P., *Die Demut*. Christliches Tugendleben 1 (Leutesdorf 1960²).
Rotzetter, A., "„Aus Liebe zur Liebe". Zu einem Wort des hl. Franziskus von Assisi", in: *Wissenschaft und Weisheit* 44 (1981), 154–167.
Rotzetter, A., *Die Funktion der franziskanischen Bewegung in der Kirche. Eine pastoraltheologische Interpretation der grundlegenden franziskanischen Texte* (Schwyz 1977).
Rotzetter, A. e.a., *Franz von Assisi. Ein Anfang und was davon bleibt* (Zürich etc. 1981).
Rüegg, C., *David von Augsburg. Historische, theologische und philosophische Schwierigkeiten zu Beginn des Franziskanerordens in Deutschland*. Deutsche Literatur von den Anfängen bis 1700 4 (Bern etc. 1989).
Ruh, K., "David von Augsburg", in: *Geschichte der abendländischen Mystik* 2 (München 1993), 524–537.

S. Bonaventura, 1274–1974 1–5 (Roma 1973–1974).
Sabatier, P., *Vie de S. François d'Assise* (Paris 1894).
Sakaguchi, F., *Der Begriff der Weisheit in den Hauptwerken Bonaventuras*. Epimeleia. Beiträge zur Philosophie 12 (München & Salzburg 1968).
Saudreau, A., *Les degrés de la vie spirituelle* (Paris 1896).
Schaffner, O., *Christliche Demut. Des Hl. Augustinus Lehre von der humilitas*. Cassiciacum 17 (Würzburg 1959).
Schaffner, O., "Demut", in: H. Fries (ed.), *Handbuch theologischer Grundbegriffe* 1 (München 1962), 217–225.
Schalück, H.F., *Armut und Heil. Eine Untersuchung über den Armutsgedanken in der Theologie Bonaventuras*. Münchener Universitäts-Schriften/Veröffentlichungen des Grabmann-Institutes. Neue Folge 14 (München etc. 1971).
Scheuring, L.M.F., "Poverty in Relationship to Francis of Assisi and John of the Cross", in: *Laurentianum* 32 (1991), 409–428.
Schick, E. & Auer, A., "Freude", in: *Lexikon für Theologie und Kirche* 4 (1960), 361–363.
Schillebeeckx, E., *On Christian Faith. The Spiritual, Ethical and Political Dimensions* (New York 1987).
Schlosser, M., *Cognitio et amor. Zum kognitiven und voluntativen Grund der Gotteserfahrung nach Bonaventura*. Veröffentlichungen des Grabmann-Institutes zur Erforschung der mittelalterlichen Theologie und Philosophie 35 (Paderborn 1990).
Schlosser, M., "Wahrheitsverständnis bei Bonaventura", in: M. Enders & J. Szaif (ed.), *Die Geschichte des philosophischen Begriffs der Wahrheit* (Berlin & New York 2006), 181–190.
Schmaus, M., *Der Glaube der Kirche. Handbuch katholischer Dogmatik* 1 (München 1969).
Schmid, H.H., *Salôm. »Frieden« im Alten Orient und im Alten Testament*. Stuttgarter Bibelstudien 51 (Stuttgart 1971).
Schmidt, H., *Frieden*. Themen der Theologie 3 (Stuttgart & Berlin 1969).
Schmitz, P., *Die Armut in der Welt als Frage an die christliche Sozialethik* (Frankfurt am Main 1973).
Schniewind, J., "Die Freude im Neuen Testament", in: J. Schniewind, *Die Freude der Buße. Zur Grundfrage der Bibel* (Göttingen 1958), 9–18.
Schuster, J., *Moralisches Können. Studien zur Tugendethik* (Würzburg 1997).
Seckler, M., "Glaube", in: H. Fries (ed.), *Handbuch theologischer Grundbegriffe* 1 (München 1962), 528–548.
Senftle, A., *Menschenbildung in franziskanischer Geistigkeit. Die Bedeutung der franziskanischen Poenitentialehre*. Grundfragen der Pädagogik 8 (Freiburg im Breisgau 1959).
Sequeira, R., "The Act of Faith According to St. Bonaventure", in: *Laurentianum* 12 (1971), 129–168.
Sequeira, R., "The Concept of Faith According to St. Bonaventure", in: *Laurentianum* 12 (1971), 3–23.

Sevenhoven, H., "How Obedience Turns Into Love", in: *Franciscan Digest* 7 (1997), 1–11.
Sevenhoven, H., *Verslag van een ontdekkingsreis naar Franciscus. Enkele patronen uit het denkweefsel van een geestelijk leider* (Haarlem 1979).
Short, W.J., *Poverty and Joy. The Franciscan Tradition* (London 1999).
Sieron, R.B., *Χαίρειν e i suoi derivati nel Corpus Paulinum. Studio linguistico-teologico* (diss. Roma 2003).
Singer, I., *The Nature of Love* 1. *Plato to Luther* (Chicago & London 1984²).
Smit, J., "Gegrepen door Christus. Paulus als navolger van Christus in Filippenzen 2 en 3", in: K. Pansters & W.M. Speelman (ed.), *De deemoed Gods. Verkenningen in het licht van Franciscus van Assisi* (Nijmegen 2011), 87–101.
Smith, G., *The Truth That Frees*. The Aquinas Lecture, 1956 (Milwaukee 1956).
Smith, J.E., *The Analogy of Experience. An Approach to Understanding Religious Truth* (New York etc. 1973).
Smits, C.S., "David van Augsburg en de invloed van zijn Profectus op de Moderne Devotie", in: *Collectanea Franciscana Neerlandica* (1927), 171–203.
Söding, T., *Die Trias Glaube, Hoffnung, Liebe bei Paulus. Eine exegetische Studie*. Stuttgarter Bibelstudien 150 (Stuttgart 1992).
Solignac, A., "Voies", in: *Dictionnaire de spiritualité* 16 (Paris 1994), 1200–1215.
Sparshott, F.E., *An Enquiry Into Goodness and Related Concepts; With Some Remarks on the Nature and Scope of Such Enquiries* (Toronto 1958).
Speelman, W.M. e.a., *Om de hele wereld. Inleiding in de franciscaanse spiritualiteit* (Nijmegen 2010).
Speer, A., *Triplex veritas. Wahrheitsverständnis und philosophische Denkform Bonaventuras*. Franziskanische Forschungen 32 (Werl 1986).
Splett, J., "Wahrheit Gottes", in: *Lexikon für Theologie und Kirche* 10 (2001), 939–940.
Springsted, E.O., *The Act of Faith. Christian Faith and the Moral Self* (Grand Rapids & Cambridge 2002).
Stegemann, W., *Das Evangelium und die Armen. Über den Ursprung der Theologie der Armen im Neuen Testament* (München 1981).
Stendebach, F.J., *Glaube bringt Freude. Das Alte Testament und die Freude an Mensch und Welt* (Würzburg 1983).
Stoellger, P., "Ordnung der Gefühle: Studien zum Begriff des habitus. By Peter Nickl", in: http://www.arsdisputandi.org.
Stöger, A. & Scholz, F., "Gehorsam", in: H. Fries (ed.), *Handbuch theologischer Grundbegriffe* 1 (München 1962), 452–461.
Stolzenburg, R., *Gehoorzaamheid* (s.l. 2008).
Stooker, K. & Verbeij, T., "'Uut Profectus'. Over de verspreiding van Middelnederlandse kloosterliteratuur aan de hand van de 'Profectus religiosorum' van David van Augsburg", in: T. Mertens (ed.), *Boeken voor de eeuwigheid. Middelnederlands geestelijk proza*. Nederlandse literatuur en cultuur in de middeleeuwen 8 (Amsterdam 1993), 318–340.
Strack, B., *Christusleid im Christusleben. Ein Beitrag zur Theologie des christlichen Lebens nach dem heiligen Bonaventura*. Franziskanische Forschungen 13 (Werl 1960).
Strack, B., "Das bonum Gottes", in: *Pax et bonum. Studientage der Franziskanischen Arbeitsgemeinschaft 1983*. Wandlung in Treue 26 (Werl 1983).
Strack, B., "„Gib mir rechten Glauben, o Herr"", in: *Glaube Hoffnung Liebe. Studientage der Franziskanischen Arbeitsgemeinschaft 1985*. Wandlung in Treue 28 (Werl 1985), 18–37.
Streithofen, H.B., *Macht, Moneten und Moral. Die Kardinaltugenden als Normen für Politik und Wirtschaft* (Aachen 2005).
Synan, E.A., "Cardinal Virtues in the Cosmos of Saint Bonaventure", in: *S. Bonaventura 1274–1974* 3 (Roma 1974), 21–38.
Synowczyk, K., "l'Obbedienza universale di San Francesco d'Assisi", in: *Miscellanea Francescana* 91 (1991), 89–103.

Tantiono, P.T., *Speaking the Truth in Christ. An Exegetico-Theological Study of Galatians 4,12–20 and Ephesians 4,12–16*. Tesi Gregoriana. Serie Teologia 164 (Roma 2008).

"The Definition of Morality", in: *Stanford Encyclopedia* (http://plato.stanford.edu/entries/morality-definition).

Thévenet, D.-M., "La vera e perfetta letizia negli scritti di Francesco d'Assisi. Aspetti cristologici", in: *Miscellanea Francescana* 91 (1991), 281–336.

Thiede, W., *Das verheißene Lachen. Humor in theologischer Perspektive* (Göttingen 1986).

Tils, A.A., *Der heilige Franziskus von Assisi und die Armut. Eine genetische Darstellung seiner religiösen Anschauung von der Armut im Lichte der Quellen des 13. Jahrhunderts* (diss. Brixen 1961).

Toit, A.B. du, *Der Aspekt der Freude im urchristlichen Abendmahl* (diss. Winterthur 1965).

Tongeren, P. van, *Deugdelijk leven. Een inleiding in de deugdethiek* (Amsterdam 2003).

Trappe, T., "Wahrheit (christlich-theologisch)", in: J. Ritter e.a. (ed.), *Historisches Wörterbuch der Philosophie* 12 (Darmstadt 2004), 123–133.

Trekt de Kerk zich de armoede in de wereld aan? (Amersfoort 1977).

Trilling, W. & Hardick, L., "Armut", in: H. Fries (ed.), *Handbuch theologischer Grundbegriffe* 1 (München 1962), 101–111.

Troelstra, A., *Stof en methode der catechese in Nederland vóór de Reformatie* (Groningen 1903).

"Tugend", in: J. Ritter & K. Gründer (ed.), *Historisches Wörterbuch der Philosophie* 10 (Darmstadt 1998), 1532–1570.

"Tugenden und Laster, Tugend- und Lasterkataloge", in: *Lexikon des Mittelalters* 8 (1997), 1085–1089.

Ulrichs, K.F., *Christusglaube. Studien zum Syntagma πίστις Χριστου und zum paulinischen Verständnis von Glaube und Rechtfertigung*. Wissenschaftliche Untersuchungen zum Neuen Testament. 2. Reihe 227 (Tübingen 2007).

Vanstone, W.H., *Love's Endeavour, Love's Expense. The Response of Being to the Love of God* (London 1977).

Varghese, J., *The Imagery of Love in the Gospel of John* (Roma 2009).

Varillon, F., *L'humilité de Dieu* (Paris 2000).

Vaux, B. de, *Revenir à Dieu. Pénitence, conversion, confession* (Paris 1967).

Vennix, A.C.M., *Wat is waarheid? De virtus quaestionis in het licht van Thomas van Aquino* (diss. Nijmegen 1998).

Verheij, S., "De leer en de voetstappen van Jezus Christus volgen. Het model van het evangelie volgens Franciscus", in: *Franciscaans leven* 66 (1983), 24–34.

Verheij, S., *Naar het land van de levenden. Regel van Franciscus van Assisi voor de minderbroeders* (Utrecht 2007).

Verhey, S., "Das Leben in der Buße nach Franziskus von Assisi", in: *Wissenschaft und Weisheit* 22 (1959), 161–174.

Verhey, S., *Der Mensch unter der Herrschaft Gottes. Versuch einer Theologie des Menschen nach dem hl. Franziskus von Assisi* (Düsseldorf 1960).

Verhey, S., "Gehoorzaamheid als levensweg volgens Franciscus van Assisi", in: *Franciscaans leven* 58 (1975), 194–209.

"Verité", in: *Dictionnaire de spiritualité* 16 (1994), 413–453.

Veuthey, L., *Itinerarium animae franciscanum. Commentarium theologico-ascetico-mysticum* (Romae 1938).

Veuthey, L., *Kleine reisgids van de franciscaanse ziel. Ascetisch mystieke leidraad voor het inwendige leven volgens de geest van de h. Franciscus van Assisië* (Roermond 1949).

Vicaire, M.-H., "Evangelical Counsels", in: A. Vauchez e.a. (ed.), *Encyclopedia of the Middle Ages* (Cambridge etc. 2000), 508–509.

Viller, M., "Le Speculum monachorum et la Dévotion moderna", in: *Revue d'ascétique et de mystique* 3 (1922), 45–56.

"Virtus, virtutis", in: O. Weijers & M. Gumbert-Hepp, *Lexikon latinitatis Nederlandicae medii aevi. Woordenboek van het middeleeuws latijn van de noordelijke Nederlanden* (Leiden & Boston 2005), 5358–5362.

"Virtus", in: J.F. Niermeyer, *Mediae latinitatis lexikon minus* (Leiden 1976), 1111–1112.

Vogel, C., *Le pécheur et la pénitence au Moyen Age. Textes choisis, traduits et présentés* (Paris 1969).

Vogel, C., *Le pécheur et la pénitence dans l'église ancienne. Textes choisis, traduits et présentés* (Paris 1965).

Vögtle, A., *Was ist Frieden? Orientierungshilfen aus dem Neuen Testament* (Freiburg etc. 1983).

Volk, H., "Freude", in: H. Fries (ed.), *Handbuch theologischer Grundbegriffe* 1 (München 1962), 415–419.

Vorgrimler, H., "Buss-Sakrament", in: H. Fries (ed.), *Handbuch theologischer Grundbegriffe* 1 (München 1962), 204–217.

Vorgrimler, H., "Wahrheit als Kategorie der katholischen Kirche und Theologie", in: H.-P. Müller (ed.), *Was ist Wahrheit?* (Stuttgart etc. 1989), 40–52.

Vreugde om de Tora. OJEC-serie 2 (Kampen 1984).

Vroom, H.M., "Waarheid in de christelijke traditie", in: H.M. Vroom, *Religies en de waarheid* (Kampen 1988), 167–197.

Waaijman, K., *Spirituality. Forms, Foundations, Methods* (Leuven 2002).

"Wahrheit", in: *Lexikon für Theologie und Kirche* 10 (2001), 926–939.

Wallis, I.G., *The Faith of Jesus Christ in Early Christian Traditions* (Cambridge 1995).

Walter, E., *Glaube Hoffnung und Liebe im Neuen Testament* (Freiburg im Breisgau 1940).

Walzel, O.F., *Gehalt und Gestalt im Kunstwerk des Dichters* (Berlin-Neubabelsberg 1923).

Ward, K., *The Rule of Love. Reflections on the Sermon on the Mount* (London 1989).

Warnach, V., *Agape. Die Liebe als Grundmotiv der neutestamentlichen Theologie* (Düsseldorf 1951).

Warnach, V., "Liebe", in: H. Fries (ed.), *Handbuch theologischer Grundbegriffe* 2 (München 1963), 54–75.

Weber, M., "Richtungen und Stufen religiöser Weltablehnung", in: *Soziologie. Universalgeschichtliche Analysen. Politik* (Stuttgart 1973), 441–483.

Welchman, J. (ed.), *The Practice of Virtue. Classic and Contemporary Readings in Virtue Ethics* (Indianapolis 2006).

Welte, B., *Dialektik der Liebe. Gedanken zur Phänomenologie der Liebe und zur christlichen Nächstenliebe im technologischen Zeitalter* (Frankfurt am Main 1973).

Welzen, H., "Weest onverdeeld goed. Deugdzaam leven in bijbelse benadering", in: *Franciscaans leven* 64 (1981), 187–192.

Wengst, K., *Demut- Solidarität der Gedemütigten. Wandlungen eines Begriffes und seines sozialen Bezugs in griechisch-römischer, alttestamentlich-jüdischer und urchristlicher Tradition* (München 1987).

Wenham, J.W., *The Goodness of God* (London 1974).

Wesjohann, A., "*Simplicitas* als franziskanisches Ideal und der Prozess der Institutionalisierung des Minoritenordens", in: G. Melville & J. Oberste (ed.), *Die Bettelorden im Aufbau. Beiträge zu Institutionalisierungsprozessen im mittelalterlichen Religiosentum.* Vita regularis 11 (Münster etc. 1999), 107–167.

White, H.V., *Truth and the Person in Christian Theology. A Theological Essay in Terms of the Spiritual Person* (New York 1963).

Wibbing, S., *Die Tugend- und Lasterkataloge im Neuen Testament und ihre Traditionsgeschichte unter besonderer Berücksichtigung der Qumran-Texte.* Beihefte zur Zeitschrift für die neutestamentliche Wissenschaft und die Kunde der älteren Kirche 25 (Berlin 1959).

Wiener, C., *Récherches sur l'amour pour Dieu dans l'Ancien Testament* (Paris 1957).

Wildiers, M., *Kosmologie in de westerse cultuur* (Kapellen & Kampen 1988).

Wilms, F.-E., *Freude vor Gott. Kult und Fest in Israel* (Regensburg 1981).
Wingren, G., *Credo. The Christian View of Faith and Life* (Minneapolis 1981).
Wolf, K.B., *The Poverty of Riches. St. Francis of Assisi Reconsidered* (New York 2003).
Wright, G.H. von, *The Varieties of Goodness* (New York 1963).
Wulf, F., *Evangelische Armut. Sinn und Verwirklichung heute* (Freising 1973).

Young, F. & Ford, D.F., *Meaning and Truth in 2 Corinthians* (Grand Rapids 1987).

Zagzebski, L., "The Virtues of God and the Foundation of Ethics", in: *Faith and Philosophy* 15 (1998), 538–553.
Zemmrich, E., *Demut. Zum Verständnis eines theologischen Schlüsselbegriffs.* Ethik im theologischen Diskurs 4 (Berlin etc. 2006).
Zimmermann, A., "Wahrheit", in: *Lexikon des Mittelalters* 8 (1997), 1918–1920.
Zweerman, T., "'Danken' en 'dragen'"; in: T. Zweerman, *Om de eer van de mens. Verkenningen op het grensvlak van filosofie en spiritualiteit* (Delft 1993²), 105–144.
Zweerman, T., "Jezus' woord: "zalig de vredestichters..." in de interpretatie van Franciscus van Assisi", in: T. Zweerman e.a., *De Heer geve u vrede. Drie beschouwingen over Franciscus' vredespiritualiteit.* Franciscaanse studies 6 (Utrecht 1990), 5–28.
Zweerman, T., ""Timor Domini"". Versuch einer Deutung der 27. Ermahnung des hl. Franziskus von Assisi", in: *Franziskanische Studien* 60 (1978), 202–223.
Zweerman, T., *Wondbaar en vrijmoedig. Verkenningen in het licht van de spiritualiteit van Franciscus van Assisi.* Annalen van het Thijmgenootschap 89–2 (Nijmegen 2001).

INDEX